THE DRAMATIC WORKS IN THE BEAUMONT AND FLETCHER CANON

THE
DRAMATIC WORKS IN
THE BEAUMONT AND
FLETCHER CANON

GENERAL EDITOR
FREDSON BOWERS

Linden Kent Professor Emeritus of English Literature
University of Virginia

VOLUME VI

WIT WITHOUT MONEY   THE PILGRIM

THE WILD-GOOSE CHASE   A WIFE FOR A MONTH

RULE A WIFE AND HAVE A WIFE

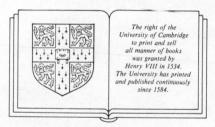

The right of the
University of Cambridge
to print and sell
all manner of books
was granted by
Henry VIII in 1534.
The University has printed
and published continuously
since 1584.

CAMBRIDGE UNIVERSITY PRESS

CAMBRIDGE

LONDON   NEW YORK   NEW ROCHELLE

MELBOURNE   SYDNEY

Published by the Press Syndicate of the University of Cambridge
The Pitt Building, Trumpington Street, Cambridge CB2 1RP
32 East 57th Street, New York, NY 10022, USA
10 Stamford Road, Oakleigh, Melbourne 3166, Australia

© Cambridge University Press 1985

First published 1985

Printed in Great Britain by
the University Press, Cambridge

Library of Congress catalogue card number: 66–74421

British Library cataloguing in publication data
Beaumont, Francis
The dramatic works in the Beaumont and Fletcher canon.
Vol. 6
I. Title   II. Fletcher, John   III. Bowers, Fredson
822'.3   PR2420
ISBN 0 521 25941 X

U P

CONTENTS

v

FOREWORD

These volumes contain the text and apparatus for the plays conventionally assigned to the Beaumont and Fletcher canon, although in fact Fletcher collaborated with dramatists other than Beaumont in numerous plays of the canon and some of the preserved texts also represent revision at a later date by various hands. The plays have been grouped chiefly by authors; this arrangement makes for an order that conveniently approximates the probable date of composition for most of the works.

The texts of the several plays have been edited by a group of scholars according to editorial procedures set by the general editor, who closely supervised in matters of substance as well as of detail the initially contrived form of the texts. Otherwise the individual editors have been left free to develop their concepts of the plays according to their own views. We hope that the intimate connection of one individual, in this manner, with all the different editorial processes will lend to the results some uniformity not ordinarily found when diverse editors approach texts of such complexity. At the same time, the peculiar abilities of the several editors have had sufficient free play to ensure individuality of point of view in its proper role; and thus, we hope, the deadness of compromise that may fasten on collaborative effort has been avoided, even at the risk of occasional internal disagreement.

The principles on which each text has been edited have been set forth in detail in 'The Text of this Edition' prefixed to volume I, pp. ix–xxv, followed by an account on pp. xxvii–xxxv of the Folio of 1647. Necessary acknowledgements will be found in the present volume in each Textual Introduction.

F. B.

Charlottesville, Virginia
1985

vii

WIT WITHOUT MONEY

edited by

HANS WALTER GABLER

TEXTUAL INTRODUCTION

Wit Without Money (Greg, *Bibliography*, no. 563) was entered in the Stationers' Register on 25 April 1639. Q1 appeared the same year, printed by Thomas Cotes for Andrew Crooke and William Cooke. The commendation subtitle advertises it as having been 'Presented with good Applause at the private house in *Drurie Lane*, by her Majesties Servants.' The theatre is the Cockpit, house of the King and Queen's Young Company and Queen Henrietta's Company. The play is claimed as the Young Company's property in a list of plays drawn up by William Beeston, their manager. The list forms the substance of the Lord Chamberlain's edict of 10 August 1639 against apparent attempts of rival companies to perform their plays.

Wit Without Money is known to have been performed between 1637 and 1639 by both 'Beeston's Boys' and Queen Henrietta's Men. Though Beeston's list claims the play for the boys, it seems yet less than convincing, in view of the long and close links in fortune and management of the two companies, to assume that the Lord Chamberlain's edict was issued to guard against practices of Queen Henrietta's Company.[1] If Queen Henrietta's men had rival claims to the play, rather than perhaps merely complementary ones to those of the boys, these had, by August 1639, already been very effectively put forth. For it can easily be shown that the play as it survives descends from Queen Henrietta's Company. In publication, *Wit Without Money* is conspicuously linked to four other of their plays, among them John Fletcher's *The Night-Walker*, which was revised for the company by James Shirley in 1633. The licensing entry in the Stationer's Register joins the two Fletcher plays to three plays of Shirley's sole authorship. All five, while all claimed by Beeston for the Young Company in August 1639, were printed after 25 April of that year as having been played 'by her Majesties Servants', i.e. Queen Henrietta's Company.

---

[1] On the issue, cf. G. E. Bentley, *The Jacobean and Caroline Stage*, I (Oxford, 1941), 331; and the 'Textual Introduction' to *Monsieur Thomas*, vol. IV of this edition.

3

The property rights and claims of 1639 are the best clues available to the origin and descent of *Wit Without Money*. John Fletcher is believed to be the play's original sole author, despite the titlepage statement of collaboration: 'Written by Francis Beamount and John Flecher'; and revision has not until recently been considered. The obvious descent of the property in plays of the King and Queen's Young Company and Queen Henrietta's Company is from the Queen's Revels Children or the Lady Elizabeth's Men. The traditional assignation of *Wit Without Money* to 'around 1614' would date the composition within the period when John Fletcher – preceding, or overlapping with, the beginnings of his attachment to the King's Men – is assumed to have written other plays (e.g., *Monsieur Thomas* and, indeed, *The Night-Walker*) for the Queen's Revels Children. Chambers suggests that *Wit Without Money* was written for the Lady Elizabeth's Men.[1] But there is too little of substance in the surviving evidence to determine beyond doubt whether it was originally a play for the children or the men.

The date of 1614 has been disputed by Baldwin Maxwell on the grounds mainly of assumed topical allusions.[2] Although declaring himself unable to retrieve textual indications for revision, Maxwell would advocate at least revision, if not composition, around 1620. Cyrus Hoy, on the basis of the linguistic minutiae that have enabled him to establish the patterns of collaboration in the Beaumont and Fletcher cánon, has remarked on the virtual absence of the distinctive Fletcherian *ye* in the extant text. Hoy's linguistic tests are sufficiently strong to affirm that 'the final form of the extant substantive edition...is the work of a non-Fletcherian hand', but not strong enough to identify the reviser beyond doubt. However, from the printed play's whole provenance, and its surprisingly constant association therein specifically with *The Night-Walker*, which in 1639 was published in the version revised by Shirley, Hoy tentatively suggests a Shirleyan revision also for *Wit Without Money*.[3]

If only from a desire for an economy of hypotheses, one may feel

[1] *The Elizabethan Stage* (Oxford, 1923), III, 229.
[2] *Studies in Beaumont, Fletcher and Massinger* (Chapel Hill, 1939), pp. 194–209.
[3] Cf. *Studies in Bibliography*, XII (1959), 110–12.

tempted to combine speculatively Maxwell's and Hoy's findings and suggestions. A lost original, wholly Fletcherian, version of around 1614 would then have been worked over by James Shirley to result in the manuscript behind Q1. If so, Maxwell's suggested revision date of 1620 would seem too early. But a date around 1625 would not be irreconcilable with Shirley's biography. He resigned the position as master of St Albans Grammar School probably in mid-1624. In London, he immediately entered upon a continuous association with the company, or companies, playing at the Cockpit. The manager of the Lady Elizabeth's Men there (subsequently Queen Henrietta's Company) was Christopher Beeston, whose son William was to succeed him in 1638. Shirley's first play on record, *Love Trials*, was licensed on 11 February 1624/5. This rapid establishment of himself as a playwright with a company may imply earlier private or professional connections with the London theatre world. Our speculative hypothesis would at least have to posit that revisions of existing company repertoire were assigned to Shirley from the outset of his association with the Cockpit. The lack of distinctive traces of his hand in *Wit Without Money* would seem explicable on the assumption that specifically Shirleyan characteristics of style and language had not yet become established when he undertook the revision. Beyond, one might merely remark that the repeated reference to St Albans in the play could be more than a coincidence.

Following Hoy, we must assume that the extant substantive text of the play constitutes an undistinctive, but pervasive revision of a lost pure Fletcherian original. Though it was from Queen Henrietta's Company that the play was available for publication in the spring of 1639, the manuscript behind Q1 is unlikely to have been a theatre prompt-book. It appears admittedly to have had some theatrical notation. There is a repeated call for torches in Act V; and, more interestingly, exits are often given before the last words spoken to those leaving, or entries marked in advance of the dialogue and action involving those entering. On the other hand, exits are at times negligently provided, and no attention is given to props.

Q1's most consistent, and disconcerting, feature is its virtually complete lack of versification. As the eighteenth-century editors were the first to discover, *Wit Without Money* is a verse play throughout. Yet the Quarto is set entirely in prose and prints verse only on I3ᵛ, the very last page. To a significant degree, no doubt, this is a measure of printing economy. While short lines of dialogue are often printed two to a type-line and every possible white space on the pages is filled, the type-setting sometimes reveals that more of the versification was discernible in the copy than is reproduced. Thus, half a dozen of verse lines or half-lines scattered over the play are set as new lines in type and capitalized; and the editorial re-versification uncovers some incidence of capitalization in midline of the Quarto's prose which moves into initial positions in verse.

Nevertheless, it is hard to believe that the printer's copy itself did not lend itself to faulty prose setting. One may consider a format and a lay-out of the manuscript that obscured the distinction of prose and verse. Whereas early extant dramatic manuscripts tend to be inscribed in folio to a width of column that renders verse-lines distinguishable even without initial capitalization (which is a printing but not a manuscript convention), later dramatic manuscripts survive from at least the 1620s onwards inscribed in quarto, where lines of verse often run to the whole width of the page. Such manuscripts tend to have an origin or to have served a purpose outside the professional ambience of the theatre. It would appear not inconceivable that Shirley as the putative reviser of *Wit Without Money*, whose scribal conventions would have been formed at Cambridge and St Albans Grammar School, copied his revision into the lesser format, and that this copy served the printers.

All editors from Seward to McKerrow have verse-lined the play. Only Weber retains prose for two scenic units (II.iii.1–58, and II.iv.80–118) and a few occasional speeches. Reflecting the classicistic concern for prosody, the verse realization for *Wit Without Money* was controversial among the eighteenth-century editors. McKerrow in 1905 was content to retain the versification of Dyce, who refined on Weber. The present edition was relined independently, directly from the prose of Q1, without initial reference to Dyce or McKerrow. A high degree of coincidence with McKerrow's lineation, however, was discovered in the result.

Following McKerrow's example, this edition refrains from swelling its apparatus by a notation of the differences in lineation between the play's successive previous editions. The considered departures in the present edition from the versification of its predecessors ultimately take their measure from the verse preserved on the last page of Q1. For example, of the group

> O I know them, come boy sing the song I taught you,
> And sing it lustily, come forward Gentlemen, you're welcome,
> Welcome, now we are all friends, goe get the Priest ready,
> And let him not be long, we have much businesse:
>
> (V.v.38–42)

every line is considered a legitimate line of dramatic blank verse. The resulting tautness and irregularity of rhythm suggests non-syllabic conventions of prosody that do not essentially rely on latinate elision but on a variation of speech tempo between stresses in the prosodic traditions of the Germanic languages. Such conventions, it is true, if they can be more widely established for early seventeenth-century drama, as yet await systematic recovery by modern scholarship.

Q1 is divided into acts, and the act divisions indicate first scenes, but no subsequent scene divisions are given. Scenes were first marked by Weber, whose divisions, but for those for Act III (where Weber's first scene divides in two), remain valid by the clear-stage criterion. The play's textual problems are few, and the text is not discernibly influenced or affected by the mechanics of printing. Q1 was machined by at least two, but probably three, skeleton formes. To all appearances, Skeleton I prints B(i), D(o), F(i), G(i) and I(i), Skeleton II prints C(i), D(i), F(o), H(i) and I(o), although a constant set of four running-titles per forme cannot safely be identified throughout in either forme. Single recognizable running-titles recur in B(o), E(i) and G(o), others in C(o) and F(o), which suggests a probable third forme at least, and at the same time repeats the pattern of fluidity in individual running-titles found in the identifiable formes. The machining implies a setting by more than one compositor, but no clear patterns of orthography or typography emerge to distinguish compositors or to establish a mode of composition *seriatim* or by formes.

Q1 is the only substantive edition and thus provides the copy-text for the present edition. The press-variants discovered in copies of Q1 reveal mainly typographical concerns and do not inevitably suggest reference to copy (see Textual Note to I.ii.34–5). Q2 of 1661 is a page-by-page and largely line-by-line reprint of Q1. Thereby clearly of no independent authority, it yet introduces one compelling phrase absent from Q1 (see I.i.96). The text in the Second Folio of 1679 is a modernized, somewhat re-punctuated and mildly sophisticated reprint of Q2.

Wit Without Money was regularly staged in the 1660s and 1670s. Dryden wrote a Prologue for the production at the Duke's old theatre in Lincoln's Inn Fields, 26 February 1671/2. A Third Quarto of 1718, a reprint of Langbaine's edition of 1711, as well as the adapted version (undated; 1708?) '(With Alterations and Amendments, by some Persons of Quality.) As it is now Acted at the Queen's Theatre in the Hay-Market, By Her Majesty's Company of Comedians', testify to the play's continued popularity in the Restoration period. Thereafter its fortunes on the stage lapsed permanently, though perhaps undeservedly. The entertainment value of its dramatic pacing and comic character reversals yet stands to be rediscovered in the theatre.

The Actors names.

Vallentine, *a Gallant that will not bee perswaded to keepe his estate.*
Franscisco, *his younger brother.*
Master Lovegood *their Uncle.*
A Merchant, *friend to Master* Lovegood.
Fountaine, ⎫
Bellamore, ⎬ *companions of* Vallentine, *and sutors to the* Widdow.
Harebraine, ⎭
Lance *a Faulkoner, and an ancient servant to* Vallentines *Father.*
Shorthose *the clowne, and servant to the* Widdow.
Roger, Ralph, *and* Humphrey, *three servants to the* Widdow.
Three Servants.
[Tennants.]
Musitians.

Lady Hartwell *a Widdow.*
Isabell *her Sister.*
Luce *a waiting Gentlewoman to the Widdow.*

WIT WITHOUT MONEY

Enter Uncle *and* Merchant.

Merchant. When saw you *Vallentine?*
Uncle.   Not since the Horserace,
He's taken up with those that wooe the Widdow.
Merchant. How can he live by snatches from such people?
He bore a worthy minde.
Uncle.   Alas, he's sunke,
His meanes are gone, he wants, and which is worse,
Takes a delight in doing so.
Merchant.   That's strange.
Uncle. Runs Lunaticke, if you but talk of states,
He cannot be brought now he has spent his owne,
To thinke theres inheritance, or meanes,
But all a common riches, all men bound   10
To be his Bailiffes.
Merchant.   This is something dangerous.
Uncle. No Gentleman that has estate to use it
In keeping house, or followers, for those wayes
He cries against, for eating sins, dull surfets,
Cramming of serving men, mustering of beggers,
Maintaining hospitals for Kites, and curs,
Grounding their fat faithes upon old Countrey proverbs,
God blesse the founders; these he would have vented
Into more manly uses, Wit and carriage,
And never thinkes of state, or meanes, the ground workes: 20
Holding it monstrous, men should feed their bodies,
And starve their understandings.
Merchant.   Thats more certaine.
Uncle. Yes, if he could stay there.

I.i] *Actus* 1. *Scæna* 1. Q 1–2, F 2   12 Gentleman,] F 2; Gent, Q 1–2
16 Maintaining] F 2; maintaine Q 1–2   *18 vented] *stet* Q 1

Merchant.   Why let him marry,
And that way rise againe.
Uncle.   Its most impossible,
He will not looke with any hansomenesse
Upon a woman.
Merchant.   Is he so strange to women?
Uncle.   I know not what it is, a foolish glory
He has got, I know not where, to balke those benefits,
And yet he will converse and flatter um,
Make um, or faire, or foule, rugged, or smooth,   30
As his impression serves, for he affirmes,
They are onely lumps, and undigested peeces,
Lickt over to a forme, by our affections,
And then they show. The lovers: let um passe.

Enter Fountaine, Bellamore, Harebraine.

Merchant.   He might be one, he carries as much promise;
They are wondrous merry.
Uncle.   O their hopes are high sir.
Fountaine.   Is *Vallentine* come to Towne?
Bellamore.   Last night I heard.
Fountaine.   We misse him monstrously in our directions,
For this Widdow is as stately, and as crafty,
And stands I warrant you——
Harebraine.   Let her stand sure,   40
She falls before us else, come lets goe seeke *Vallentine.*
                [*Exeunt* Fountaine, Bellamore, Harebraine.]
Merchant.   This Widdow seemes a gallant.
Uncle.   A goodly woman,
And to her hansomnesse she beares her state,
Reserved, a great Fortune has made her Mistresse
Of a full meanes, and well she knowes to use it.
Merchant.   I would *Vallentine* had her.
Uncle.   Theres no hope of that Sir.
Merchant.   A that condition, he had his morgage in againe.
Uncle.   I would he had.

44 a] and Q 1–2, F 2

12

Merchant.   Seeke meanes, and see what Ile doe,
However let the money be paid in,
I never sought a Gentlemans undoing,   50
Nor eate the bread of other mens vexations,
The morgage shall be rendred backe, take time fort;
You told me of another brother.
Uncle.   Yes sir,
More miserable then he, for he has eate him,
And drunke him up, a handsome Gentleman,
And a fine Scholler.

        Enter [Lance *and two other*] tennants.

Merchant.   What are these?
Uncle.   The tennants,
Th'le doe what they can.
Merchant.   It is well prepared,
Be earnest honest friends and loud upon him,
He is deafe to his owne good.
Lance.   We meane to tell him
Part of our mindes ant please you.
Merchant.   Doe, and doe it home,   60
And in what my care may helpe, or my perswasions
When we meete next——
Uncle.   Doe but perswade him fairely;
And for your money, mine, and these mens thankes too,
And what we can be able——
Merchant.   Yare most honest,
You shall finde me no lesse, and so I leave you,
Prosper your businesse my friends.   *Exit* Merchant.
Uncle.   Pray heaven it may sir.
Lance.   Nay if hee will be mad, Ile be mad
With him, and tell him that Ile not spare him,
His Father kept good meate, good drinke, good fellowes,
Good hawkes, good hounds, and bid his neighbours welcome;   70
Kept him too, and supplyed his prodigality,
Yet kept his state still; must wee turne Tennants now,

        56 [Lance *and two other*] tennants] V; *three tennants* Q 1–2, F 2

13

After we have lived under the race of Gentry,
And maintaind good yeomantry, to some of the City,
To a great shoulder of Mutton, and a Custard,
And have our state turned into Cabbidge Gardens,
Must it be so?
Uncle.   You must be milder to him.
Lance.   Thats as he makes his game.
Uncle.   Intreate him lovingly,
And make him feele.
Lance.   Ile pinch him to the bones else.
Vallentine (within).   And tell the Gentleman, Ile be with him
     presently,   80
Say I want money too, I must not faile boy.
Lance.   Youle want clothes, I hope.

                   Enter Vallentine.

Vallentine.   Bid the young Courtier
Repaire to me anon, Ile reade to him.
Uncle.   He comes, be diligent, but not too rugged,
Start him, but afright him not.
Vallentine.   Phew, are you there?
Uncle.   We come to see you Nephew, be not angry.
Vallentine.   Why doe you dogge me thus, with these strange
     people?
Why, all the world shall never make me rich more,
Nor master of these troubles.
Tennants.   We beseech you
For our poore childrens sake.
Vallentine.   Who bid you get um?   90
Have you not thrashing worke enough, but children
Must be bangd out oth' sheafe too? other men
With all their delicates, and healthfull diets,
Can get but winde egges: you with a clove of garlicke,
A peece of cheese would breake a saw, and sowre milke,
Can mount like Stallions, and I must maintaine these tumblers.
Lance.   You ought to maintaine us, wee have maintained

                96 Can mount like Stallions,] Q2; *omit* Q1

                            14

You, and when you slept provided for you;
Who bought the silke you weare? I thinke our labours;
Reckon, youle find it so: who found your horses　　　　　100
Perpetuall pots of ale, maintain'd your Tavernes,
And who extold you in the halfe crowne boxes,
Where you might sit and muster all the beauties?
Wee had no hand in these, no, we are puppies:
Your tennants base vexations.
Vallentine.　　　　　　　　　Very well sir.
Lance.　Had you Land, and honest men to serve your purposes,
Honest, and faithfull, and will you run away from um,
Betray your selfe, and your poore tribe to misery;
Morgage all us, like old cloakes; where will you hunt next?
You had a thousand acres, faire and open:　　　　　110
The Kings bench is enclosed, thers no good riding,
The Counter is full of thornes and brakes, take heed sir,
And bogges, youle quickly finde what broth they're made of.
Vallentine.　Yare short and pithie.
Lance.　　　　　　　　　They say yare a fine Gentleman,
And of excellent judgment, they report you have a wit;
Keepe your selfe out oth raine and take your Cloake with you,
Which by interpretation is your state, sir,
Or I shall thinke your fame belyed you, you have money
And may have meanes.
Vallentine.　　　　　　　I prethee leave prating,
Does my good lye within thy braine to further,　　　　　120
Or my undoing in thy pitty? goe,
Goe, get you home, there whistle to your horses,
And let them edifie; away, sow hempe,
And hang your selves withall: what am I to you,
Or you to me; am I your Landlord, puppies?
Uncle.　This is uncivill.
Vallentine.　　　　　　　Morc unmercifull you,
To vex me with these bacon broth and puddings,
They are the walking shapes of all my sorrowes.
Tennants.　Your Fathers Worship, would have used us better.

115 of] F2; *omit* Q 1-2　　　129 Tennants.] 3. *Tennants.* Q 1-2, F 2

Vallentine.   My Fathers worship, was a foole.

Lance.   Hey, hey boyes,   130
  Old *Vallentine* ifaith, the old boy still.

Uncle.   Fie Cosen.

Vallentine.   I meane besotted to his state,
  He had never left mee the misery of so much meanes else,
  Which till I sold was a meere meagrome to me:
  If you will talke, turne out these tennants,
  They are as killing to my nature Uncle,
  As water to a feaver.

Lance.   We will goe,
  But it is like Rammes to come againe the stronger,
  And you shall keepe your state.

Vallentine.   Thou lyest, I will not.

Lance.   Sweete sir, thou lyest, thou shalt, and so good morrow.   140

                    Exeunt [Lance *and*] Tennants.

Vallentine.   This was my man, and of a noble breeding:
  Now to your businesse Uncle.

Uncle.   To your state then.

Vallentine.   Tis gone, and I am glad on't, name it no more,
  Tis that I pray against, and heaven has heard mee,
  I tell you sir, I am more fearefull of it,
  I meane of thinking of more lands, or livings,
  Then sickely men are travelling a Sundaies,
  For being queld with Carryers; out upont,
  Caveat emptor, let the foole out sweat it
  That thinkes he has got a catch ont.

Uncle.   This is madnesse   150
  To be a willfull begger.

Vallentine.   I am mad then
  And so I meane to be, will that content you?
  How bravely now I live, how jocund, how neare
  The first inheritance, without feares, how free
  From title troubles.

Uncle.   And from meanes too.

Vallentine.   Meanes,

135 tennants] Q2; tenements Q1

16

Why all good men's my meanes, my wits my plow,
The Townes my stock, Tavernes my standing house,
And all the world knowes theres no want; all Gentlemen
That love society, love me; all purses
That wit and pleasure opens, are my Tennants;   160
Every mans clothes fit me, the next faire lodging
Is but my next remoove, and when I please
To be more eminent, and take the aire,
A peece is levied, and a Coach prepared,
And I goe I care not whether, what neede state here?
Uncle.   But say these meanes were honest, will they last, sir?
Vallentine.   Far longer then your jerkin, and weare fairer,
Should I take ought of you, tis true, I begd now,
Or which is worse then that, I stole a kindnesse,
And which is worst of all, I lost my way int;   170
Your mindes enclosed, nothing lies open nobly,
Your very thoughts are hindes that worke on nothing
But daily sweate, and trouble: were my way
So full of dirt as this, tis true I'd shift it;
Are my acquaintance Grasiers? but sir, know
No man that I am allyed too, in my living,
But makes it equal, whether his owne use,
Or my necessity pull first, nor is this forc'd,
But the meere quallity and poysure of goodnesse,
And doe you thinke I venter nothing equall?   180
Uncle.   You pose me Cosen.
Vallentine.   Whats my knowledge Uncle,
Ist not worth money? whats my understanding, .
My travell, reading, wit, all these digested,
My daily making men, some to speake,
That too much flegme had frozen up, some other
That spoke too much to hold their peace, and put
Their tongues to pensions, some to weare their clothes,
And some to keepe um, these are nothing Uncle;
Besides these wayes, to teach the way of nature,
A manly love, community to all   190

172 hindes] Q2; hid Q1   174 I'd shift it] F2; I shifted Q1-2

17

That are deservers, not examining
How much, or whats done for them, tis wicked,
And such a one like you, chewes his thoughts double,
Making um onely food for his repentance.

Enter two Servants.

First Servant.   This cloake and hat sir, and my Masters love.
Vallentine.   Commend's to thy Master, and take that,
   And leave um at my lodging.
First Servant.   I shall doe it sir.
Vallentine.   I doe not thinke of these things.
Second Servant.   Please you sir,
   I have gold here for you.
Vallentine.   Give it me, drinke that
   And commend me to thy Master; [*Exeunt* Servants.]
                    looke you Uncle,   200
   Doe I begge these?
Uncle.   No sure tis your worth sir.
Vallentine.   Tis like enough, but pray satisfie me,
   Are not these wayes as honest as persecuting
   The starved inheritance, with musty Corne,
   The very rats were faine to run away from,
   Or selling rotten wood by the pound, like spices,
   Which Gentlemen doe after burne byth ounces?
   Doe not I know your way of feeding beasts,
   With graines, and windy stuffe, to blow up butchers?
   Your racking pastures, that have eaten up   210
   As many singing Shepherds, and their issues,
   As *Andeluria* breedes? these are authentique,
   I tell you sir, I would not change wayes with you,
   Unlesse it were to sell your state, that houre,
   And if it were possible to spend it then too,
   For all your beanes in *Rumnillo*, now you know me.
Uncle.   I would you knew your selfe, but since you are growne
   Such a strange enemy, to all that fits you,
   Give mee leave to make your brothers fortune.
Vallentine.   How?

18

Uncle.   From your morgage, which yet you may recover,   220
 Ile finde the meanes.
Vallentine.   Pray save your labour sir,
 My brother and my selfe, will runne one fortune,
 And I thinke what I hold a meere vexation,
 Cannot be safe for him, I love him better,
 He has wit at will, the world has meanes, hee shall live
 Without this tricke of state, we are heires both,
 And all the world before us.
Uncle.   My last offer,
 And then I am gone.
Vallentine.   What ist, and then Ile answer.
Uncle.   What thinke you of a Wife yet to restore you,
 And tell me seriously without these trifles.   230
Vallentine.   And you can finde one, that can please my fancy,
 You shall not finde me stubborne.
Uncle.   Speake your woman.
Vallentine.   One without eyes, that is, selfe commendations,
 For when they finde they are hansome, they are unholsome;
 One without eares, not giving time to flatterers,
 For shee that heares her selfe commended, wavers,
 And points men out a way to make um wicked;
 One without substance of her selfe; that woman
 Without the pleasure of her life, thats wanton;
 Though she be young, forgetting it, though faire,   240
 Making her glasse the eyes of honest men,
 Not her owne admiration, all her ends
 Obedience, all her houres new blessings:
 If there may be such a woman——
Uncle.   Yes there may be.
Vallentine.   And without state too.
Uncle.   You are disposed to trifle,
 Well, fare you well sir, when you want me next,
 Youle seeke me out a better sence.
Vallentine.   Farewell Uncle,
 And as you love your estate, let not me heare on't.   [*Exit.*]

224 for] Q2; from Q1

Uncle. It shall not trouble you: Ile watch him still,
And when his friends fall of, then bend his will. 250

Exit.

Enter Isabella, *and* Luce. [I. ii]

Luce. I know the cause of all this sadnesse now,
Your sister has ingrost all the brave lovers.
Isabella. Shee has wherewithall, much good may doe her,
Prethee speake softly, we are open to mens eares.
Luce. Feare not, we are safe, we may see all that passe,
Heare all, and make our selves merry with their language,
And yet stand undiscovered, bee not melancholly,
You are as faire as shee.
Isabella.   Who I? I thanke you,
I am as haste ordain'd mee, a thing slubberd,
My sister is a goodly portly Lady, 10
A woman of a presence, she spreads satten,
As the Kings ships doe canvas, every where,
She may spare me her misen, and her bonnets,
Strike her maine petticoate, and yet outsaile me,
I am a Carvell to her.
Luce.   But a tight one.
Isabella. She is excellent, well built too.
Luce.   And yet shees old.
Isabella. Shee never saw above one voyage *Luce*,
And credit me after another, her hull
Will serve againe, and a right good Merchant:
Shee plaies and sings too, dances and discourses, 20
Comes very neere essaies a pretty poet,
Begins to piddle with Phylosophie,
A subtill Chimicke wench, and can extract
The spirit of mens estates, she has the light
Before her, and cannot misse her choice, for me

---

250 of] *i.e.,* off. *Interchangeable* of *and* off *will not be further noted.*
[I.ii]] W; *no scene division* Q 1–2, F 2
3 may doe her] *stet* Q 1; *cf.* III.i.43; IV.ii.5

Tis reason, I waite my meane fortune.

Luce.   You are so bashfull.

Isabella.   It is not at first word up and ride, thou art cosend,
  That would shew mad I faith: besides, wee lose
  The meane part of our polliticke government,
  If we become provokers; then wee are faire,   30
  And fit for mens imbraces, when like townes,
  They lie before us ages, yet not carried,
  Hold out their strongest batteries, then compound too
  Without the losse of honour, and march oft
  With our faire wedding Colours flying. Who are these?

Enter Franscisco *and* Lance.

Luce.   I know not, nor I care not.

Isabella.   Prethee peace then,
  A well built Gentleman.

Luce.   But poorely thatcht.

Lance.   Has he devoured you to?

Franscisco.   Has gulped me downe *Lance.*

Lance.   Left you no meanes to study?

Franscisco.   Not a farthing:
  Dispatcht my poore annuity I thanke him,   40
  Heres all the hope I have left, one bare ten shillings.

Lance.   You are fit for great mens services.

Franscisco.   I am fit,
  But who'le take me thus? mens miseries are now
  Accounted staines in their natures. I have travelled,
  And I have studdied long, observed all kingdomes,
  Know all the promises of Art and manners,
  Yet that I am not bold, nor cannot flatter,
  I shall not thrive, all these are but vaine Studdies,
  Art thou so rich as to get me a lodging *Lance?*

Lance.   Ile sell the titles of my house else, my Horse, my Hawke, 50

---

34 Without] Q2; with Q1
*34–35 oft...Colours] C; oft with our faire wedding: Colours Q1(c)
35 wedding Colours] S; ~ : ~ Q1–2, F2, L
38 to] Q(u); too Q(c). *Interchangeable* to *and* too *will not be further noted.*

Nay death Ile pawne my wife: Oh Mr. *Francis*,
That I should see your Fathers house fall thus.
Isabella.   An honest fellow.
Lance.   Your Fathers house, that fed me,
That bred up all my name.
Isabella.   A gratefull fellow.
Lance.   And fall by——
Franscisco.   Peace, I know you are angry *Lance*,
But I must not heare with whom, he is my brother——
And though he hold him slight, my most deare brother——
A gentleman, excepting some few rubbes,
He were too excellent to live here else,
Fraughted as deepe with noble and brave parts,   60
The issues of a noble and manly spirit
As any he alive, I must not heare you;
Though I am miserable, and he made me so,
Yet still he is my brother, still I love him,
And to that tye of blood linke my affections.
Isabella.   A noble nature, dost thou know him *Luce?*
Luce.   No Mistresse.
Isabella.   Thou shouldest ever know such good men,
What a faire body and mind are married there together;
Did he not say he wanted?
Luce.   Whats that to you?
Isabella.   Tis true, but tis great pitty.
Luce.   How she changes!   70
Ten thousand more than he, as hansome men too.
Isabella.   Tis like enough, but as I live, this Gentleman
Among ten thousand thousand! is there no knowing him;
Why should he want? fellowes of no merit,
Slight and puft soules, that walke like shadowes by,
Leaving no print of what they are, or poise,
Let them complaine.
Luce.   Her colour changes strangely.
Isabella.   This man was made, to mark his wants to waken us,
Alas poore Gentleman, but will that fledge him,

*57 he] stet Q1(u)   61 The] Q2; *omit* Q1   68 mind] F2; a ~ Q1–2

22

Keepe him from cold, beleeve me he is well bred,   80
And cannot be but of a noble linnage,
Mark him, and marke him well.
Luce.   'Is a hansome man.
Isabella.   The sweetnesse of his suffrance sets him off,
  O *Luce*, but whether goe I?
Luce.   You cannot hide it.
Isabella.   I would he had what I can spare.
Luce.   Tis charitable.
Lance.   Come sir, Ile see you lodged, you have tied my tongue fast,
  Ile steale before you want, tis but a hanging.
                              Exeunt Lance *and* Franscisco.
Isabella.   Thats a good fellow too, an honest fellow,
  Why, this would move a stone, I must needes know;
  But that some other time.
Luce.   Is the winde there?   90
  That makes for me.
Isabella.   Come, I forgot a businesse.
                                              [*Exeunt.*]

                      Enter Widdow *and* Luce.   II. i

Widdow.   My sister, and a woman of so base a pitty!
  What was the fellow?
Luce.   Why an ordinary man Madam.
Widdow.   Poore?
Luce.   Poore enough, and no man knowes from whence
      neither.
Widdow.   What could she see?
Luce.   Onely his misery,
  For else she might behold a hundred handsumer.
Widdow.   Did she change much?
Luce.   Extreamely, when he spoke,
  And then her pitty like an Orator,

87.1 *Exeunt* Lance *and* Franscisco.] '*Exit Lance. and Fran.*' *after line* 90 *time.*
Q1–2, F2
  II.i] *Actus* 2. *Scæna* 1. Q1–2; *Actus Quartus. Scena Prima.* F2

I feare her love framed such a commendation,
And followed it so farre, as made me wonder.
Widdow. Is she so hot, or such a want of lovers,   10
That shee must doate upon afflictions?
Why do's shee not goe romage all the Prisons,
And there bestow her youth, bewray her wantonnesse,
And flie her honour, common both to beggery;
Did she speake to him?
Luce.   No, hee saw us not,
But ever since, she hath beene mainely troubled.
Widdow. Was he young?
Luce.   Yes, young enough.
Widdow.   And looked he like
A gentleman?
Luce.   Like such a Gentleman, would pawne
Ten oathes for twelve pence.
Widdow.   My sister, and sinke basely;
This must not be, do's she use meanes to know him?   20
Luce. Yes Madam, and has employed a Squire called *Shorthose.*
Widdow. O thats a precious Knave: keepe all this private,
But still be neere her lodging; *Luce* what you can gather
By any meanes, let me understand: Ile stoppe her heate,
And turne her charitie another way,
To blesse her selfe first; be still close to her Councells;
A begger and a stranger, theres a blessednesse,
Ile none of that; I have a toy yet sister,
Shall tell you this is foule, and make you find it;
And for your paines take you the last gowne I wore;   30
This makes me mad, but I shall force a remedy.
                                                    [*Exeunt.*]

Enter Fountaine, Bellamore, Harebraine, Vallentine.   [II. ii]

Fountaine. Sirra, we have so lookt thee, and long'd for thee,
This Widdow is the strangest thing, the stateliest,
And stands so much upon her excellencies.

    [II.ii]] W; *no scene division* Q 1–2, F 2, L–C   *1 lookt thee] *stet* Q 1

24

Bellamore.   She has put us off this moneth now, for an answer.
Harebraine.   No man must visit her, nor looke upon her,
   Not say good morrow nor good even, till thats past.
Vallentine.   She has found what dough you are made of, and so
      kneads you:
   Are you good at nothing, but these aftergames?
   I have told you often enough what things they are,
   What precious things, these widdowes.
Harebraine.   If we had um.   10
Vallentine.   Why the devill has not craft enough to woe um,
   There be three kindes of fooles, marke this note gentlemen,
   Marke it, and understand it.
Fountaine.   Well, goe forward.
Vallentine.   An Innocent, a Knave foole, a foole politicke:
   The last of which are lovers, widdow lovers.
Bellamore.   Will you allow no Fortune?
Vallentine.   No such blind one.
Fountaine.   We gave you reasons, why twas needfull for us.
Vallentine.   As you are those fooles, I did allow those reasons,
   But as my Schollers and companions damn'd um:
   Doe you know what it is to wooe a widdow?   20
   Answer me coolely now, and understandingly.
Harebraine.   Why to lie with her, and to enjoy her wealth.
Vallentine.   Why there you are fooles still, craftie to catch your
      selves,
   Pure polliticke fooles, I lookt for such an answer;
   Once more heare me,
   It is to wed a widdow, to be doubted mainely,
   Whether the state you have be yours or no,
   Or those old bootes you ride in. Marke me, widdowes
   Are long extents in Law upon mens livings,
   Upon their bodies winding-sheetes, they that enjoy um,   30
   Lie but with dead mens monuments, and beget
   Onely their owne ill Epitaphs: Is not this plaine now?
Bellamore.   Plaine spoken.

11 woe] *i.e.*, woo (*cf. O.E.D., s.v.* woe)   28 Or] Q2; are Q1
29 mens‸ livings,] S; newes, livings‸ Q1-2, F2, L

Vallentine.　　　　　　　　And plaine truth; but if you'le needes
　　Doe things of danger, doe but loose your selves,
　　Not any part concernes your understandings,
　　For then you are Meacockes, fooles, and miserable,
　　March of a maine, within an inch of a Furcug,
　　Turne me oth' toe like a Weathercocke,
　　Kill every day a Sergeant for a twelve moneth,
　　Robbe the Exchequor, and burne all the roules,　　　　40
　　And these will make a shew.
Harebraine.　　　　　　　　And these are trifles.
Vallentine.　　Considered to a Widdow, emptie nothing,
　　For here you venture but your persons, there
　　The varnish of your persons, your discretions;
　　Why tis a monstrous thing to marry at all,
　　Especially as now tis made; me thinkes a man,
　　An understanding man, is more wife to me,
　　And of a nobler tie, than all these trinkets;
　　What doe we get by women, but our senses,
　　Which is the rankest part about us, satisfied,　　　　50
　　And when thats done what are we? Crest falne cowards.
　　What benefite can children be, but charges
　　And disobedience? whats the love they render
　　At one and twentie yeares? I pray die father:
　　When they are young, they are like bells rung backwards,
　　Nothing but noise, and giddinesse, and come to yeares once,
　　There droppes a sonne, byth' sword in's Mistresses quarrell,
　　A great joy to his parents: a daughter ripe too,
　　Growes high and lustie in her blood, must have
　　A heating, runnes away with a supple ham'd Servingman:　　60
　　His twentie nobles spent, takes to a trade,
　　And learnes to spinne mens haire off; theres another,
　　And most are of this nature. Will you marry?
Fountaine.　　For my part yes, for any doubt I feele yet.
Vallentine.　　And this same Widdow?
Fountaine.　　　　　　　　If I may, and me thinkes,
　　How ever you are pleased to dispute these dangers,

　　　　47 wife] S; wise Q1-2, F2, L　　60 ham'd] Q2; hand Q1

26

Such a warme match, and for you sir, were not hurtfull.
Vallentine.   Not halfe so killing as for you, for mee shee cannot
  With all the Art shee has, make mee more miserable,
  Or much more fortunate, I have no state left,   70
  A benefit that none of you can bragge of,
  And theres the Antidote against a Widdow,
  Nothing to lose, but that my soule inherits,
  Which shee can neither law nor claw away;
  To that, but little flesh, it were too much else;
  And that unholsome too, it were too rich else;
  And to all this contempt of what shee do's
  I can laugh at her teares, neglect her angers,
  Heare her without a faith, so pitty her
  As if shee were a traytor, moane her person,   80
  But deadly hate her pride; if you could doe these,
  And had but this discretion and like fortune,
  It were but an equall venture.
Fountaine.   This is mallice.
Vallentine.   When shee lies with your land, and not with you,
  Growes great with joyntures, and is brought to bed
  With all the state you have, you'le finde this certaine;
  But is it come to passe you must marry,
  Is there no buffe wil hold you?
Bellamore.   Grant it be so.
Vallentine.   Then chuse the tamer evill, take a maide,
  A maide not worth a penny; make her yours,   90
  Knead her, and mould her yours, a maide worth nothing,
  Theres a vertuous spell, in that word nothing;
  A maide makes conscience
  Of halfe a crowne a weeke for pinnes and puppits,
  A maide content with one Coach and two horses,
  Not falling out because they are not matches;
  With one man satisfied, with one raine guided,
  With one faith, one content, one bed agreed,
  Shee makes the wife, preserves the fame and issue;
  A Widdow is a Christmas box that sweepes all.   100

  98 bed∧ agreed,] D; bed, aged∧ Q1–2, F2, L, C–W; ~ , one Good. S

27

Fountaine.   Yet all this cannot sinke us.
Vallentine.   You are my friends,
  And all my loving friends, I spend your money,
  Yet I deserve it too, you are my friendes still,
  I ride your horses, when I want I sell um;
  I eate your meate, helpe to weare your linnen,
  Sometimes I make you drunke, and then you seale,
  For which Ile do you this commoditie,
  Be ruled, and let me try her, I will discover her,
  The truth is, I will never leave to trouble her,
  Till I see through her, then if I finde her worthy——   110
Harebraine.   This was our meaning *Valentine.*
Vallentine.   Tis done then,
  I must want nothing.
Harebraine.   Nothing but the woman.
Vallentine.   No jealousie, for when I marry,
  The devill must be wiser than I take him;
  And the flesh foolisher: come lets to dinner,
  And when I am well whetted with wine, have at her.
                                        Exeunt.

                  Enter Isabella *and* Luce.   [II. ii

Isabella.   But art thou sure?
Luce.   No surer then I heard.
Isabella.   That it was that flouting fellowes brother?
Luce.   Yes,
  Shorthose told me so.
Isabella.   He did search out the truth?
Luce.   It seemes he did.
Isabella.   Prethee *Luce,* call him hether,
  If he be no worse, I never repent my pitty.
  Now sirra, what was he wee sent you after,
  The Gentleman ith blacke?

105 your] L; her Q 1–2, F 2   115 come] Q 2; comes Q 1
[II.iii]] W; *no scene division* Q 1–2, F 2, L–C   1 surer] Q 2; suerer Q 1
2, 4 *Isabella.*] L; *Har.* Q 1–2, F 2   3 *Isabella.*] L; *omit* Q 2; *Har.* Q 1, F 2

28

Enter Shorthose.

Shorthose.   Ith torne blacke?
Isabella.   Yes, the same sir.
Shorthose.   What would your Worship with him?
Isabella.   Why my worship would know his name, and what he is.
Shorthose.   'Is nothing, he is a man, and yet he is no man.   10
Isabella.   You must needes play the foole.
Shorthose.   Tis my profession.
Isabella.   How is he a man, and no man?
Shorthose.   Hees a begger,
    Onely the signe of a man, the bush puld downe,
    Which showes the house stands emptie.
Isabella.   Whats his calling?
Shorthose.   They call him begger.
Isabella.   Whats his kindred?
Shorthose.   Beggers.
Isabella.   His worth?
Shorthose.   A learned begger, a poore Scholler.
Isabella.   How does he live?
Shorthose.   Like wormes, he eates old Bookes.
Isabella.   Is *Vallentine* his brother?
Shorthose.   His begging brother.
Isabella.   What may his name be?
Shorthose.   *Orson.*
Isabella.   Leave your fooling.
Shorthose.   You had as good say, leave your living.
Isabella.   Once more 20
    Tell me his name directly.
Shorthose.   Ile be hangd first,
    Unlesse I heare him Christned, but I can tell
    What foolish people call him.
Isabella.   What?
Shorthose.   *Franscisco.*
Isabella.   Where lies this learning sir?
Shorthose.   In *Paules* Church yard forsooth.

22 heare] Q 1(u); heard Q 1(c), Q 2, F 2

29

Isabella.   I meane that Gentleman, foole.

Shorthose.   O that foole,
Hee lies in loose sheetes every where, thats no where.

Luce.   You have gleand since you came to *London*: in the Countrey
   Shorthose,
You were an arrant foole, a dull cold coxcombe,
Here every Taverne teaches you, the pint pot
Has so belaboured you with wit, your brave acquaintance   30
That gives you ale, so fortified your mazard,
That now theres no talking to you.

Isabella.   'Is much improved, a fellow, a fine discourser.

Shorthose.   I hope so, I have not waited at the taile of wit
So long to be an asse.

Luce.   But say now *Shorthose,*
My Lady should remoove into the Countrie.

Shorthose.   I had as leeve she should remoove to heaven,
And as soone I would undertake to follow her.

Luce.   Where no old Charnico is, nor no Anchoves,
Nor Master such a one, to meete at the Rose,   40
And bring my Lady such a ones chiefe Chambermaide.

Isabella.   No bouncing health to this brave Lad, deare *Shorthose,*
Nor downe oth knees to that illustrious Lady.

Luce.   No fidles, nor no lusty noyse of drawer,
Carry this pottle to my father *Shorthose.*

Isabella.   No playes, nor gally foistes, no strange Embassadors
To runne and wonder at, till thou beest oyle,
And then come home againe, and lye bith Legend.

Luce.   Say she should goe.

Shorthose.   If I say so, Ile bee hangd first,
Or if I thought shee would goe——

Luce.   What?

Shorthose.   I would goe with her. 50

Luce.   But *Shorthose,* where thy heart is——

Isabella.   Doe not fright him.

Luce.   By this hand Mistris tis a noyse, a loud one too,
And from her owne mouth, presently to be gone too,

33 'Is] F2; Is Q1-2   45 father] F2; ~ , Q1-2

But why, or to what end?

Shorthose.   May not a man dye first,
Sheele give him so much time.

Isabella.   Gone oth' sudden?
Thou dost but jest, shee must not mocke the Gentlemen.

Luce.   She has put them off a moneth, they dare not see her,
Beleeve me Mistris, what I heare I tell you.

Isabella.   Is this true wench? gone on so short a warning,
What tricke is this, she never told me of it,   60
It must not be: sirra, attend me presently,
You know I have beene a carefull friend unto you,
Attend me in the hall, and next be faithfull,
Cry not, we shall not goe.

Shorthose.   Her Coach may cracke.

Exeunt.

Enter Vallentine, Franscisco, *and* Lance.   [II. iv]

Vallentine.   Which way to live! how darest thou come to towne,
To aske such an idle question?

Franscisco.   Me thinkes tis necessary,
Unlesse you could restore that annuity
You have tippled up in Tavernes.

Vallentine.   Where hast thou beene,
And how brought up *Franscisco*, that thou talkest
Thus out of *France*? thou wert a pretty fellow,
And of a hansome knowledge; who has spoyld thee?

Lance.   He that has spoyld himselfe, to make himselfe sport,
And by his Coppie, will spoile all comes neere him,
Buy but a glasse, if you be yet so wealthy,   10
And looke there who?

Vallentine.   Well said old Coppihold.

Lance.   My hearts good freehold sir, and so youle finde it,
This Gentlemans your brother, your hopefull brother,
For there is no hope of you, use him thereafter.

[II.iv]] W; *no scene division* Q1-2, F2, L-C
13 Gentlemans] Q2; Gentleman Q1

31

Vallentine.   Ene aswell as I use my selfe, what wouldst thou have
   Francke?
Franscisco.   Can you procure me a hundred pound?
Lance.   Harke what he saies to you, O try your wits,
   They say you are excellent at it, for your land
   Has laine long bed rid, and unsensible.
Franscisco.   And Ile forget all wrongs, you see my state,   20
   And to what wretchednesse your will has brought me;
   But what it may be, by this benefit,
   If timely done, and like a noble brother,
   Both you and I may feele, and to our comforts.
Vallentine.   (A hundred pound!) dost thou know what thou hast
   said boy?
Franscisco.   I said a hundred pound.
Vallentine.   Thou hast said more
   Then any man can justifie, beleeve it:
   Procure a hundred pounds, I say to thee,
   Theres no such summe in nature, fortie shillings
   There may be now ith Mint, and thats a treasure,   30
   I have seene five pound, but let me tell it,
   And tis as wonderfull, as Calves with five legges,
   Heeres five shillings *Francke*, the harvest of five weekes,
   And a good crop too, take it, and pay thy first fruites,
   Ile come downe and eate it out.
Franscisco.   Tis patience
   Must meete with you sir, not love.
Lance.   Deale roundly,
   And leave these fiddle faddles.
Vallentine.   Leave thy prating,
   Thou thinkest thou art a notable wise fellow,
   Thou and thy rotten Sparrow hawke; two of the reverent.
Lance.   I thinke you are mad, or if you be not will be,   40
   With the next moone, what would you have him doe?
Vallentine.   How?
Lance.   To get money first, thats to live,
   You have shewed him how to want.
Vallentine.   Slife, how doe I live?

Why, what dull foole would aske that question?
Three hundred three pilds more, I and live bravely,
The better halfe oth towne, and live most gloriously,
Aske them what states they have, or what annuities,
Or when they pray for seasonable harvests:
Thou hast a hansome wit, stirre into the world, *Francke,*
Stirre, stirre, for shame, thou art a pretty Scholler: 50
Aske how to live? write, write, write any thing,
The worlds a fine beleeving world, write newes.
Lance.   Dragons in *Sussex* sir, or fierie battles
Seene in the aire at *Aspurge.*
Vallentine.   Theres the way *Francke,*
And in the taile of these, fright me the Kingdome
With a sharpe Prognostication, that shal scowre them,
Dearth upon dearth, like leven taffaties,
Predictions of Sea breaches, warres, and want
Of herrings on our coast, with bloody noses.
Lance.   Whirle windes, that shall take of the toppe   60
Of *Grantam* steeple, and clap it on *Poules,* and after these,
A Lenvoy to the Citty for their sinnes.
Vallentine.   *Probatum est,* thou canst not want a pension,
Go switch me up a Covey of young Schollers,
Theres twenty nobles, and two loades of coales,
Are not these ready wayes? Cosmography
Thou art deeply read in, draw me a mappe from the Mermaide,
I meane a midnight mappe to scape the watches,
And such long sencelesse examinations,
And Gentlemen shall feede thee, right good Gentlemen,   70
I cannot stay long.
Lance.   You have read learnedly,
And would you have him follow these *Megeras,*
Did you beginne with ballads?
Franscisco.   Well, I will leave you,
I see my wants are growne ridiculous,
Yours may be so, I will not curse you neither;
You may thinke, when these wanton fits are over,

68 midnight] Q2; midnighe Q1   *72 *Megeras*] megeras Q1; megera's Q2, F2

33

Who bred me, and who ruined me,
Looke to your selfe sir, a providence I waite on.
Vallentine. Thou art passionate, hast thou beene brought up with
girles?

Enter Shorthose *with a bagge.*

Shorthose. Rest you merry Gentlemen.
Vallentine. Not so merry as you suppose sir. 80
Shorthose. Pray stay a while, and let mee take a view of you,
I may put my spoone into the wrong pottage pot else.
Vallentine. Why wilt thou muster us?
Shorthose. No you are not he,
You are a thought too hansome.
Lance. Who wouldst thou speake withall,
Why doest thou peepe so?
Shorthose. I am looking birds nests,
I can finde none in your bush beard, I would speake with you
Blacke Gentleman.
Franscisco. With me my friend?
Shorthose. Yes sure,
And the best friend sir, it seemes you spake withall
This twelve moneths. Gentleman, theres money for you.
Vallentine. How?
Shorthose. Theres none for you sir, be not so briefe, 90
Not a penny; law how he itches at it, stand of,
You stirre my colour.
Lance. Take it, tis money.
Shorthose. You are too quicke too, first be sure you have it,
You seeme to be a Faulckoner, but a foolish one.
Lance. Take it, and say nothing.
Shorthose. You are cosend too,
Tis take it, and spend it.
Franscisco. From whom came it sir?
Shorthose. Such another word, and you shall have none ont.
Franscisco. I thanke you sir, I doubly thanke you.
Shorthose. Well sir,

92 colour] *i.e.,* choler   96 spend] Q2; spent Q1

34

Then buy you better clothes, and get your hat drest,
And your Laundresse to wash your bootes white.
Franscisco.   Pray stay sir,   100
May you not be mistaken.
Shorthose.   I thinke I am,
Give me the money again, come quick, quicke, quicke.
Franscisco.   I would be loath to render, till I am sure it be so.
Shorthose.   Harke in your eare, is not your name *Franscisco?*
Franscisco.   Yes.
Shorthose.   Be quiet then, it may thunder a hundred times,
Before such stones fall; doe not you neede it?
Franscisco.   Yes.
Shorthose.   And tis thought you have it.
Franscisco.   I thinke I have.
Shorthose.   Then hold it fast, tis not flyblowne, you may
Pay for the poundage, you forget your selfe,
I have not seene a Gentleman so backward,   110
A wanting Gentleman.
Franscisco.   Your mercy sir.
Shorthose.   Freind you have mercy, a whole bagge full of mercy,
Be merry with it, and be wise.
Franscisco.   I would faine
If it please you, but know——
Shorthose.   It does not please me,
Tell over your money and be not mad boy.
Vallentine.   You have no more such bagges?
Shorthose.   More such there are sir,
But few I feare for you, I have cast your water,
You have wit, you need no money.   *Exit.*
Lance.   Be not amazed sir, tis good gold, good old gold,
This is restorative, and in good time,   120
It comes to doe you good, keepe it and use it,
Let honest fingers feele it, yours be too quicke sir.
Franscisco.   He named me, and he gave it me, but from whom?
Lance.   Let um send more, and then examine it,
This can be but a preface.
Franscisco.   Being a stranger,

Of whom can I deserve this?
Lance.   Sir, of any man
That has but eyes, and manly understanding
To finde mens wants, good men are bound to doe so.
Vallentine.   Now you see *Francke*, there are more waies then
   certainties,
Now you beleeve: What plow brought you this harvest,   130
What sale of timber, coales, or what annuities,
These feede no hindes, nor waite the expectation
Of quarter dayes, you see it showers into you,
You are an asse, lie plodding, and lie fooleing,
About this blazing starre, and that bopeepe,
Whyneing, and fasting, to finde the naturall reason
Why a dogge turnes twice about before he lie downe,
What use of these, or what joy in annuities,
Where every mans thy studdy, and thy tennant,
I am ashamed on thee.
Lance.   Yes I have seene   140
This fellow, theres a wealthy Widdow hard by.
Vallentine.   Yes marry is there.
Lance.   I think hees her servant,
I am cosend if after her, I am sure ont.
Franscisco.   I am glad ont.
Lance.   Shees a good woman.
Franscisco.   I am gladder.
Lance.   And young enough beleeve.
Franscisco.   I am gladder of all sir.
Vallentine.   *Franck*, you shall lye with me soone.
Franscisco.   I thanke my money.
Lance.   His money shall lie with mee, three in a bed sir
Will be too much this weather.
Vallentine.   Meete me at the Mermaide,
And thou shalt see what things——
Lance.   Trust to your selfe sir.
                        Exeunt Franscisco *and* Lance.

*143 I...her] *stet* Q1   149.1 Lance] L; *Val.* Q1–2, F2

Enter Fountaine, Bellamore *and* Harebraine.

Fountaine.   O *Vallentine*!
Vallentine.   How now, why doe you looke so?   150
Bellamore.   The Widdowes going man.
Vallentine.   Why let her goe man.
Harebraine.   Shees going out oth Towne.
Vallentine.   The Townes the happier,
   I would they were all gone.
Fountaine.   We cannot come
   To speake with her.
Vallentine.   Not to speake to her?
Bellamore.   She will
   Be gone within this houre, either now *Vallentine*——
Fountaine, Harebraine.   Now, now, now, good *Vallentine*.
Vallentine.   I had rather
   March ith mouth oth Cannon, but adiew,
   If she be above ground, goe, away to your praiers,
   Away I say, away, she shall be spoken withall.

                                                  Exeunt.

                Enter Shorthose *with one boote on,*   [II. v]
                      Roger *and* Humphrey.

Roger.   She will goe *Shorthose*.
Shorthose.   Who can helpe it *Roger*?
Ralph (*within*).   *Roger* helpe downe with the hangings.
Roger.   By and by *Raph*,
   I am making up oth trunckes here.
Ralph.   *Shorthose*.
Shorthose.   Well.
Ralph.   Who lookes to my Ladies Wardrobe? *Humphrey*.
Humphrey.   Heere.
Ralph.   Downe with the boxes in the gallery,
   And bring away the Coach Cushions.

          149.2 Harebraine] S; *Vallentine* Q 1–2, F 2; *omit* L
          [II.v]] W; *no scene division* Q 1–2, F 2, L–C

                            37

Shorthose.   Will it not raine,
No conjuring abroad, nor no devises
To stop this journey?
Roger.   Why goe now, why now,
Why oth sudden, now? what preparation,
What horses have we ready, what provision   10
Laid in ith Country?
Humphrey.   Not an egge I hope.
Roger.   No nor one drop of good drink boyes, ther's the devil.
Shorthose.   I heartily pray the malt be musty, and then
We must come up againe.
Humphrey.   What saies the Steward?
Roger.   Hees at's wits end, for some foure houres since,
Out of his haste and providence, he mistooke
The Millers maunjey mare, for his owne nagge.
Shorthose.   And she may breake his necke, and save the journey,
Oh *London* how I love thee.
Humphrey.   I have no bootes,
Nor none Ile buy (or if I had) refuse me   20
If I would venture my abillity,
Before a cloake bagge, men are men.
Shorthose.   For my part,
If I be brought, as I know it will be aimed at,
To carry any durty dairy creame pot,
Or any gentle Lady of the Laundry,
Chambring, or wantonnesse behinde my gelding,
With all her streamers, knapsackes, glasses, gugawes,
As if I were a running flippery,
Ile give um leave to cut my girts and flay me.
Ile not be troubled with their distillations,   30
At every halfe miles end, I understand my selfe,
And am resolved.
Humphrey.   To morrow night at *Olivers,*
Who shalbe there boyes, who shall meete the wenches?
Roger.   The well brued stand of Ale, we should have met at.

9 now?] F2; now‸ Q1–2
30 distillations] S; distibations Q1–2, F2, L

Shorthose.   These griefes like to another tale of *Troy*,
Would mollifie the hearts of barbarous people,
And Tom Butcher weepe *Eneas enters*,
And now the townes lost.

[*Enter* Ralph.]

Ralph.   Why whether run you,
My Lady is mad.
Shorthose.   I would she were in Bedlam.
Ralph.   The carts are come, no hands to helpe to load um?   40
The stuffe lies in the hall, the plate——
Widdow (*within*).   Why knaves there,
Where be these idle fellowes?
Shorthose.   Shall I ride with one boote?
Widdow [*within*].   Why where I say?
Ralph.   Away, away, it must be so.
Shorthose.   O for a tickling storme, to last but ten dayes.

                                        Exeunt.

Enter Isabella *and* Luce.   III. i

Luce.   By my troth Mistris I did it for the best.
Isabella.   It may be so, but *Luce*, you have a tongue,
A dish of meate in your mouth, which if it were minced *Luce*,
Would doe a great deale better.
Luce.   I protest Mistresse.
Isabella.   It will be your owne one time or other: *Walter*.
Walter (*within*).   Anon forsooth.
Isabella.   Lay my hat ready, my fanne and cloake,
You are so full of providence; and *Walter*,
Tucke up my little box behinde the Coach,
And bid my maide make ready, my sweete service
To your good Lady Mistresse; and my dog,   10
Good let the Coachman carry him.
Luce.   But heare me.
Isabella.   I am in love sweete *Luce*, and you are so skillfull,

III.i] *Actus* 3. *Scæn*, 1. Q 1–2, F 2

39

That I must needes undoe my selfe; and heare me,
Let *Oliver* packe up my glasse discreetly,
And see my Curles well carried. O sweete *Luce*,
You have a tongue, and open tongues have open
You know what *Luce*.

Luce.   Pray you be satisfied.

Isabella.   Yes and contented too, before I leave you:
Theres a *Roger*, which some call a Butcher,
I speake of certainties, I doe not fish *Luce*,   20
Nay doe not stare, I have a tongue can talke too:
And a greene Chamber *Luce*, a backe doore opens
To a long gallery; there was a night *Luce*,
Doe you perceive, doe you perceive me yet:
O doe you blush *Luce*: a Friday night
I saw your Saint *Luce*; for tother box of Marmaladde,
Alls thine sweete *Roger*, this I heard and kept too.

Luce.   Ene as you are a woman Mistresse——

Isabella.   This I allow
As good and physicall sometimes these meetings,
And for the cheering of the heart; but *Luce*,   30
To have your owne turne served, and to your friend
To be a dogbolt.

Luce.   I confesse it Mistresse.

Isabella.   As you have made my sister jealous of me,
And foolishly, and childishly pursued it,
I have found out your haunt, and traced your purposes,
For which mine honour suffers, your best wayes
Must be applied to bring her backe againe,
And seriously and suddenly, that so
I may have a meanes to cleare my selfe, and she
A faire opinion of me, else you peevish——   40

Luce.   My power and prayers Mistresse.

Isabella.   Whats the matter?

Enter Shorthose *and* Widdow.

Shorthose.   I have beene with the Gentleman, he has it,
Much good may doe him with it.

Widdow.　　　　　　　　　　　Come are you ready,
　You love so to delay time, the day growes on.
Isabella.　I have sent for a few triffles, when those are come;
　And now I know your reason.
Widdow.　Know your owne honour then, about your businesse,
　See the Coach ready presently, Ile tell you more then.
　　　　　　　　　　　　　　Exeunt Luce *and* Shorthose.
　And understand it well, you must not thinke me sister,
　So tender eyed as not to see your follies,　　　　　　　　　　50
　Alas I know your heart, and must imagine,
　And truely too; tis not your charitie
　Can coyne such sums to give away as you have done,
　In that you have no wisedome *Isabel*, no nor modestie
　Where nobler uses are at home; I tell you,
　I am ashamed to finde this in your yeares,
　Farre more in your discretion, none to chuse
　But things for pittie, none to seale your thoughts on,
　But one of no abiding, of no name;
　Nothing to bring you but this, cold and hunger:　　　　　　　60
　A jolly Joynture sister, you are happy,
　No mony, no not tenne shillings.
Isabella.　　　　　　　　　You search nearely.
Widdow.　I know it as I know your folly, one that knows not
　Where he shall eate his next meale, take his rest,
　Unlesse it be ith stockes; what kindred has he,
　But a more wanting brother, or what vertues.
Isabella.　You have had rare intelligence, 1 see sister.
Widdow.　Or say the man had vertue,
　Is vertue in this age a full inheritance:
　What Joynture can he make you, *Plutarchs Moralls*,　　　　70
　Or so much penny rent in the small poets,
　This is not well, tis weake, and I grive to know it.
Isabella.　And this you quit the towne for?
Widdow.　　　　　　　　　　　Ist not time?

49 me] W; my Q1; your Q2, F2, L–C　　　63 knows] F2; know Q1–2
65 ith] in th Q1　　　　　　　　　　　　71 poets] Q2; pots Q1
72 grive] *i.e.*, grieve　　　　　　　　　　73 Ist] Q2; Its Q1

Isabella.   You are better read in my affaires than I am,
  Thats all I have to answer, Ile goe with you,
  And willingly, and what you thinke most dangerous,
  Ile sit and laugh at. For sister tis not folly
  But good discretion governes our maine fortunes.
Widdow.   I am glad to heare you say so.
Isabella.   I am for you.

                                    [*Exeunt.*]

        Enter Shorthose *and* Humphrey *with riding rods.*   [III. ii]

Humphrey.   The devill cannot stay her, she'le ont,
  Eate an egge now, and then we must away.
Shorthose.   I am gaulled already,
  Yet I will pray: may *London* wayes from henceforth
  Be full of holes, and Coaches cracke their wheeles,
  May zealous Smithes so housell all our Hackneyes,
  That they may feele compunction in their feete,
  And tire at *Highgate*, may it raine above all Almanackes
  Till carriers saile, and the Kings Fishmonger ride
  Like *Bike Arion* upon a Trout to *London*.   10
Humphrey.   At S. *Albones*, let all the Innes be drunke,
  Not an Host sober to bid her worship welcome.
Shorthose.   Not a Fiddle, but all preacht downe with Puritans;
  No meate but legges of beefe.
Humphrey.   No beds but Woollpackes.
Shorthose.   And those so crammed
  With warrens of sterved Fleas that bite like bandogges;
  Let *Mims* be angry at their S. *Bellswagger*,
  And we passe in the heate ont and be beaten,
  Beaten abominably, beaten horse
  And man, and all my Ladies linnen sprinkled   20
  With suddes and dishwater.
Humphrey.   Not a wheele but out of joynt.

          [III.ii]] *no scene division* Q 1–2, F 2, L–V
          22 *Humphrey.*] C; *Short.* Q 1–2, F 2, L–S

Enter Roger *laughing*.

Why dost thou laugh?

Roger.   Theres a Gentleman, and the rarest Gentleman,
And makes the rarest sport.

Shorthose.   Where, where?

Roger.   Within here,
Has made the gayest sport with *Tom* the Coachman,
So tewed him up with sacke that hee lies lashing
A butt of Malmsie for his Mares.

Shorthose.   Tis very good.

Roger.   And talkes and laughes, and singes the rarest songs,
And *Shorthose*, he has so mauld the red Deere pies,
Made such an almes ith butterie.

Shorthose.   Better still.   30

Enter Vallentine [*and*] Widdow.

Humphrey.   My Lady in a rage with the Gentleman?

Shorthose.   May he anger her into a feather.

Exeunt [*Servants*].

Widdow.   I pray tell me, who sent you hether?
For I imagine it is not your condition,
You looke so temperately, and like a Gentleman,
To aske me these milde questions.

Vallentine.   Doe you thinke
I use to walke of errands gentle Lady,
Or deale with women out of dreames from others?

Widdow.   You have not knowne me sure?

Vallentine.   Not much.

Widdow.   What reason
Have you then to be so tender of my credit,   40
You are no kinsman.

Vallentine.   If you take it so,
The honest office that I came to doe you,
Is not so heavy but I can returne it:

22 Why] C; *Hum.* ~ Q1-2, F2, L-S   36 milde] *stet* Q1

Now I perceive you are too proud, not worth
My visit.
Widdow.   Pray stay, a little: proud.
Vallentine.   Monstrous proud,
    I grieve to heare a woman of your value,
    And your abundant parts stung by the people,
    But now I see tis true, you looke upon mee
    As if I were a rude and sawcie fellow
    That borrowed all my breeding from a dunghill,   50
    Or such a one, as should now fall and worship you
    In hope of pardon: you are cosen'd Lady,
    I came to prove opinion a loud lier,
    To see a woman onely great in goodnesse,
    And Mistresse of a greater fame than fortune,
    But——
Widdow.   You are a strange Gentleman,
    If I were proud now, I should be monstrous angry,
    Which I am not, and shew the effects of pride;
    I should dispise you, but you are welcome sir:
    To thinke well of our selves, if we deserve it,   60
    Is a luster in us, and every good we have,
    Strives to show gracious, what use is it else?
    Old age like Seer trees, is seldome seene affected,
    Stirs sometimes at rehearsall of such acts
    His daring youth endeavour'd.
Vallentine.   This is well,
    And now you speake to the purpose, you please me,
    But to be place proud——
Widdow.   If it be our owne,
    Why are we set here with distinction else,
    Degrees, and orders given us? in you men,
    Tis held a coolenesse if you lose your right,   70
    Affronts and losse of honour: streetes, and walls,
    And upper ends of tables, had they tongues
    Could tell what blood has followed, and what fude
    About your rankes; are we so much below you,
    That till you have us, are the toppes of nature,

To be accounted drones, without a difference?
You will make us beasts indeed.
Vallentine.   Nay worse then this too,
Proud of your cloathes, they sweare a Mercers Lucifer,
A tumer tackt together by a Taylor,
Nay yet worse, proud of red and white, a varnish   80
That buttermilke can better.
Widdow.   Lord how little
Will vex these poore blinde people! if my cloathes
Be sometimes gay and glorious, does it follow
My minde must be my Mercers too, or say my beauty
Please some weake eyes, must it please them to thinke
That blowes mee up, that every houre blowes of?
This is an Infants anger.
Vallentine.   Thus they say too,
What though you have a Coach lined through with velvet
And foure faire Flaunders Mares, why should the streets be
     troubled
Continually with you, till Carmen curse you?   90
Can there be ought in this but pride of shew Lady,
And pride of bum-beating, till the learned lawyers
With their fat bagges are thrust against the bulkes
Till all their Cases cracke? why should this Lady,
And tother Lady, and the third sweete Ladie,
And Madam at *Mile End*, be dailie visited,
And your poorer neighbours, with course nappes neglected,
Fashions conferd about, pouncings, and paintings,
And young mens bodies read on like Anotamies.
Widdow.   You are very credulous,   100
And somewhat desperate to deliver this sir,
To her you know not, but you shall confesse me,
And finde I will not start; in us all meetings
Lie open to these leud reports, and our thoughts at Church,
Our very meditations some will sweare,
Which all should feare to judge, at least uncharitably,
Are mingled with your memories, cannot sleepe,

But this sweet Gentleman swimmes in our fancies,
That scarlet man of warre, and that smooth Senior;
Not dresse our heads without new ambushes,   110
How to surprise that greatnesse or that glory;
Our very smiles are subject to constructions;
Nay sir, its come to this, we cannot pish,
But tis a favour for some foole or other:
Should we examine you thus, wert not possible
To take you without Prospectives?
Vallentine.   It may be,
But these excuse not.
Widdow.   Nor yours force no truth sir,
What deadly tongues you have, and to those tongues
What hearts, and what inventions; ah my conscience,
And 'twere not for sharpe justice, you would venture   120
To aime at your owne mothers, and account it glory
To say you had done so; all you thinke are Counsells
And cannot erre, tis we still that shew double,
Giddie, or gorg'd with passion; we that build
Babells for mens confusions, we that scatter
As day do's his warme light, our killing curses
Over Gods creatures, next to the devills malice:
Lets intreate your good words.
Vallentine.   Well, this woman
Has a brave soule.
Widdow.   Are not we gaily blest then,
And much beholding to you for your substance?   130
You may doe what you list, we what beseemes us,
And narrowly doe that too, and precisely,
Our names are served in else at Ordinaries,
And belcht a broad in Tavernes.
Vallentine.   O most brave Wench,
And able to redeeme an age of women.
Widdow. You are no Whoremasters; alas no Gentlemen,
It were an impudencie to thinke you vicious;
You are so holy, handsome Ladies fright you,
You are the coole things of the time, the temperance,

46

Meere emblems of the Law, and vales of Vertue,   140
You are not daily mending like Dutch Watches,
And plastering like old walls; they are not Gentlemen,
That with their secret sinnes encrease our Surgeons,
And lie in forraine Countries, for new sores;
Women are all these vices; you are not envious,
False, covetous, vaineglorious, irreligious,
Drunken, revengefull, giddie-eyed, like Parrats,
Eaters of others honours.
Vallentine.   You are angry.
Widdow.   No by my troth, and yet I could say more too,
For when men make me angry, I am miserable.   150
Vallentine.   Sure tis a man, she could not beare it thus bravely
     else——
It may be I am tedious.
Widdow.   Not at all sir,
I am content at this time you should trouble me.
Vallentine.   You are distrustfull.
Widdow.   Where I finde no truth sir.
Vallentine.   Come, come, you are full of passion.
Widdow.   Some I have,
I were too neere the nature a god else.
Vallentine.   You are monstrous peevish.
Widdow.   Because they are monstrous foolish,
And know not how to use that should trie me.
Vallentine.   I was never answered thus, was you never drunke
     Lady?
Widdow.   No sure, not drunke sir; yet I love good wine   160
As I love health and joy of heart, but temperately,
Why doe you aske that question?
Vallentine.   For that sinne
That they most charge you with, is this sinnes servant,
They say you are monstrous——
Widdow.   What sir, what?
Vallentine.   Most strangely——
Widdow.   It has a name sure?

140 vales] *i.e.,* veils

47

Vallentine.　　　　　　　　Infinitly lustfull,
Without all bounds, they sweare you kild your husband.
Widdow.　　Lets have it all for heavens sake, tis good mirth sir.
Vallentine.　　They say you will have foure now, and those foure
Stucke in foure quarters like foure windes to coole you;
Will she not cry nor curse?
Widdow.　　　　　　　　On with your Story.　　　　　170
Vallentine.　　And that you are forcing out of dispensations
With summes of money to that purpose.
Widdow.　　　　　　　　Foure husbands!
Should not I be blest sir, for example? Lord
What should I doe with them, turne a Malt mill,
Or tyth them out like towne Bulls to my tennants,
You come to make me angry, but you cannot.
Vallentine.　　Ile make you merry then, you are a brave woman,
And in dispite of envie a right one,
Goe thy wayes, truth thou art as good a woman,
As any Lord of them all can lay his legge over,　　　180
I doe not often commend your sexe.
Widdow.　　　　　　　　It seemes so,
Your commendations are so studied for.
Vallentine.　　I came to see you, and sift you into a flower,
To know your purenesse, and I have found you
Excellent, I thanke you; continue so, and shew
Men how to tread, and women how to follow;
Get an husband, an honest man, you are a good woman,
And live hedg'd in from scandall, let him be too
An understanding man, and to that steedfast;
Tis pittie your faire Figure should miscarrie,　　　190
And then you are fixt, farewell.
Widdow.　　　　　　　Pray stay a little,
I love your company now you are so pleasant,
And to my disposition set so even.
Vallentine.　　I can no longer.　　　　　　　　*Exit.*
Widdow.　　　　　　As I live a fine fellow,
This manly handsome bluntnesse, shewes him honest;
What is he, or from whence? blesse me, foure husbands!

48

How prettily he fooled me into vices,
To stirre my jealousie and finde my nature,
A proper Gentleman: I am not well oth' sudden,
Such a companion I could live and die with,   200
His angers are meere mirth.

Enter Isabella.

Isabella.   Come, come, I am ready.
Widdow.   Are you so?
Isabella.   What ailes she? the Coach staies, and the people,
The day goes on, I am as ready now
As you desire sister: fie, who stayes now,
Why doe you sit and poute thus?
Widdow.   Prethee be quiet,
I am not well.
Isabella.   For heavens sake lets not ride
Staggering in the night, come, pray you take
Some sweetemeates in your pocket, if your stomacke——
Widdow.   I have a little businesse.
Isabella.   To abuse me,
You shall not finde new dreames, and new suspitions,   210
To horse withall.
Widdow.   Lord who made you a Commander:
Hay ho, my heart.
Isabella.   Is the winde come thether,
And coward like doe you lose your colours to um?
Are you sicke ath *Valentine?* sweete sister,
Come lets away, the countrey will so quicken you,
And we shall live so sweetely: *Luce,* my Ladies cloake;
Nay, you have put me into such a gogge of going
I would not stay for all the world; if I live here,
You have so knocked this love into my head,
That I shall love any body, and I finde my body,   220
I know not how, so apt; pray lets be gone sister,
I stand on thornes.
Widdow.   I prethee *Isabella,*
I faith I have some businesse that concernes me,

49

I will suspect no more, here, weare that for me,
And Ile pay the hundred pound you owe your tayler.

Enter Shorthose, Roger, Humphrey, Ralph.

Isabella.   I had rather goe, but——
Widdow.   Come walke in with me,
Weele goe to Cardes, unsadle the horses.
Shorthose.   A Jubile, a jubile, we stay boyes.

Exeunt.

Enter Uncle, Lance; Fountaine, Bellamore,   [III. iii]
Harebraine *following*.

Uncle.   Are they behinde us?
Lance.   Close, close, speake aloud sir.
Uncle.   I am glad my nephew has so much discretion
At length to finde his wants: did she entertaine him?
Lance.   Most bravely, nobly, and gave him such a welcome.
Uncle.   For his owne sake doe you thinke?
Lance.   Most certaine sir,
And in his owne cause bestir'd himselfe too,
And wan such liking from her, she dotes on him,
Has the command of all the house already.
Uncle.   He deales not well with his friends.
Lance.   Let him deale on,
And be his owne friend, hee has most neede of her.   10
Uncle.   I wonder they would put him——
Lance.   You are in the right ont,
A man that must raise himselfe, I knew he would cosen um,
And glad I am he has, he watched occasion,
And found it ith' nicke.
Uncle.   He has deceived me.
Lance.   I told you howsoever he wheel'd about,
Hee would charge home at length, how I could laugh now,
To thinke of these tame fooles.

226 in with] Q 2; within Q 1
[III.iii]] *no scene division* Q 1–2, F 2, L–C; Scene ii. W–V
15 wheel'd] Q 2; weel'd Q 1   16 home] Q 2; whom Q 1

Uncle.　　　　　　　　　　　Twas not well done,
　Because they trusted him, yet——
Bellamore.　　　　　　　　　Harke you Gentlemen.
Uncle.　We are upon a businesse, pray excuse us——
　They have it home.
Lance.　　　　　Come let it worke.——Good e'n Gentlemen.　20
　　　　　　　　　　　　　　Exeunt Uncle, Lance.
Fountaine.　Tis true, he is a knave, I ever thought it.
Harebraine.　And we are fooles, tame fooles.
Bellamore.　　　　　　　　Come lets goe seeke him,
　He shall be hang'd before he colt us basely.

　　　　　　　　　　　　　　　　　　Exeunt.

　　　　　　　Enter Isabella, Luce.　　　　　　[III. iv]

Isabella.　Art sure she loves him?
Luce.　　　　　　　　Am I sure I live?
　And I have clapt on such a commendation
　On your revenge.
Isabella.　　　　Faith, he is a pretty Gentleman.
Luce.　Handsome enough, and that her eye has found out.
Isabella.　He talkes the best they say, and yet the maddest.
Luce.　Has the right way.
Isabella.　　　　　　　How is she?
Luce.　　　　　　　　　　Beares it well,
　As if she cared not, but a man may see
　With halfe an eye through all her forced behaviours,
　And finde who is her *Vallantine.*
Isabella.　　　　　　Come lets goe see her,
　I long to prosecute.
Luce.　　　　　　　By no meanes Mistresse,　10
　Let her take better hold first.
Isabella.　　　　　I could burst now.
　　　　　　　　　　　　　　　　　　Exeunt.

────────────

20 worke.—— Good e'n] S; worke good on Q 1–2, F 2, L
[III.iv]] *no scene division* Q 1–2, F 2, L–C; Scene iii. W–V
2 clapt] Q 2; clap Q 1

Enter Vallentine, Fountaine, Bellamore, Harebraine.   [III. v]

Vallentine.   Upbraide me with your benefits, you Pilchers,
 You shotten-sold, slight fellowes, wast not I
 That undertooke you first from emptie barrells,
 And brought those barking mouthes that gaped like bung-holes
 To utter sense: where got you understanding?
 Who taught you manners and apt carriage
 To ranke your selves? who filed you in fit Tavernes,
 Were those borne with your worships? when you came hether,
 What brought you from the Universities
 Of moment matter to allow you, besides   10
 Your small beere sentences?
Bellamore.   Tis well sir.
Vallentine.   Long cloakes
 With two hand-rapiers, boot-hoses with penny-poses,
 And twentie fooles opinions, who looked on you
 But piping kites that knew you would be prises,
 And Prentises in *Paules* Church-yard, that sented
 Your want of *Brittanes* Bookes.

      Enter Widdow [*and*] Luce.

Fountaine.   This cannot save you.
Vallentine.   Taunt my integretie you whelpes.
Bellamore.   You may talke
 The stocke wee gave you out, but see no further.
Harebraine.   You tempt our patience, we have found you out,
 And what your trust comes to, ye are well feathered,   20
 Thanke us, and thinke now of an honest course,
 Tis time; men now begin to looke, and narrowly
 Into your tumbling trickes, they are stale.

   [III.v]] *no scene division* Q1–2, F2, L–C; Scene iv. W–V
   *2 shotten-sold] S; shotten, sold, Q1–2, F2, L
   8 worships?...hether,] C; ~ ∧ ~ ? ±Q1–2, F2, L–S
   11 beere] S; bare Q1; base Q2, F2, L
   14 kites] S; rites Q1–2, F2, L
   14 prises] S; prising Q1–2, F2, L
   16 [*and*] Luce.] C; *Luce, Harebraine.* Q1–2, F2

Widdow.   Is not that he?
Luce.   Tis he.
Widdow.   Be still and marke him.
Vallentine.   How miserable
  Will these poore wretches be when I forsake um,
  But things have their necessities, I am sorry,
  To what a vomit must they turne againe now,
  To their owne deare dunghill breeding; never hope
  After I cast you off, you men of Motley,   30
  You most undone things below pittie, any
  That has a soule and sixe pence dares releeve you,
  My name shall barre that blessing; theres your cloake sir,
  Keepe it close to you, it may yet preserve you
  A fortnight longer from the foole; your hat, pray be covered,
  And theres the sattin that your worship sent me,
  Will serve you at a sizes yet.
Fountaine.   Nay faith sir,
  You may ene rubbe these out now.
Vallentine.   No such relicke,
  Nor the least ragge of such a sorded weakenesse
  Shall keepe me warme, these breeches are mine owne,   40
  Purchased, and paid for, without your compassion,
  And Christian breeches founded in Blacke Friers,
  And so Ile maintaine um.
Harebraine.   So they seeme sir.
Vallentine.   Onely the thirteene shillings in these breeches,
  And the odde groat, I take it, shall be yours sir,
  A marke to know a knave by, pray preserve it,
  Doe not displease me more, but take it presently,
  Now helpe me off with my bootes.
Harebraine.   We are no groomes sir.
Vallentine.   For once you shall be, doe it willingly,
  Or by this hand Ile make you.
Bellamore.   To our owne sir,   50
  We may apply our hands.

---

*25 How miserable   36 worship] F2; worships Q 1–2
37 a sizcs] (*i.e.,* assizes) Q 2; a sizer Q 1   42 breeches] Q 2; bleeches Q 1

Vallentine.   Theres your hangers,
   You may deserve a strong paire, and a girdle
   Will hold you without buckles; now I am perfect,
   And now the proudest of your worships tell me
   I am beholding to you.
Fountaine.   No such matter.
Vallentine.   And take heede how you pittie me, tis dangerous,
   Exceeding dangerous, to prate of pittie
   Which are the poorer; you are now puppies;
   I without you, or you without my knowledge?
   Be rogues, and so be gone, be rogues and reply not,   60
   For if you doe——
Bellamore.   Onely thus much, and then
   Wee'le leave you, the ayre is farre sharper than our anger sir,
   And these you may reserve to raile in warmer.
Harebraine.   Pray have a care sir of your health.
                              Exeunt Lovers [Widdow *and* Luce].
Vallentine.   Yes hoghounds,
   More than you can have of your wits; tis cold,
   And I am very sensible, extreamely cold too,
   Yet I will not off, till I have shamed these rascalls;
   I have endured as ill heates as another,
   And every way if one could perish my body,
   You'le beare the blame ont; I am colder here,   70
   Not a poore penny left.

              [*Enter*] Uncle *with a bagge* [*and* Lance].

Uncle.   Tas taken rarely,
   And now hees flead he will be ruled.
Lance.   Too him, tew him,
   Abuse him, and nip him close.
Uncle.   Why how now cosen,
   Sunning your selfe this weather?
Vallentine.   As you see sir,
   In a hot fit, I thanke my friends.
Uncle.   But cosen,
   Where are your cloathes man? those are no inheritance,

Your scruple may compound with those I take it,
This is no fashion cosen.
Vallentine.　　　　　　　　Not much followed,
I must confesse; yet Uncle I determine
To trie what may be done next Tearme.
Lance.　　　　　　　　　How came you thus sir,　80
For you are strangely mewd.
Vallentine.　　　　　　Ragges, toyes and triffles,
Fit onely for those fooles that first possessed um,
And to those Knaves they are rendred. Freemen, Uncle,
Ought to appeare like innocent old *Adam*,
A faire Figge-leafe sufficient.
Uncle.　　　　　　　　Take me with you,
Were these your friends, that clear'd you thus?
Vallentine.　　　　　　　　　Hang friends,
And even recknings that make friends.
Uncle.　　　　　　　　I thought till now,
There had beene no such living, no such purchase,
For all the rest is labour, as a list
Of honourable friends, doe not such men as you sir,　90
In liew of all your understandings, travells,
And those great gifts of nature, aime at no more
Than casting off your coates? I am strangely cosend.
Lance.　Should not the towne shake at the cold you feele now,
And all the Gentry suffer interdiction,
No more sence spoken, all things *Goth* and *Vandall*,
Till you be summed againe, velvets and scarlets,
Annointed with gold lace, and cloth of silver
Turned into *Spanish* Cottens for a pennance,
Wits blasted with your bulls, and Tavernes withered,　100
As though the tearme lay at S. *Albones?*
Vallentine.　　　　　　　Gentlemen,
You have spoken long, and levill, I beseech you
Take breath a while and here me; you imagine
Now, by the twirling of your strings, that I
Am at the last, as also that my friends

81 mewd] S; moved Q 1–2, F 2, L　　84 innocent] W; innocents, Q 1

Are flowne like Swallowes after Summer.

Uncle.   Yes sir.

Vallentine.   And that I have no more in this poore pannier,
To raise me up againe above your rents Uncle.

Uncle.   All this I doe beleeve.

Vallentine.   You have no minde to better me.

Uncle.   Yes cosen,   110
And to that end I come, and once more offer you
All that my power is master of.

Vallentine.   A match then,
Lay me downe fiftie pound there.

Uncle.   There it is sir.

Vallentine.   And on it write, that you are pleased to give this,
As due unto my merit, without caution
Of land redeeming, tedious thankes, or thrift
Hereafter to be hoped for.

Uncle.   How?

                    Luce *layes a suite and letter at the doore.*

Vallentine.   Without dareing,
When you are drunke, to rellish of revilings,
To which you are prone in sacke Uncle.

Uncle.   I thanke you sir.

Lance.   Come, come away, let the young wanton play   120
A while, away I say sir, let him goe forward
With his naked fashion, he will seeke you to morrow;
Goodly weather, sultrie hot, sultry, how I sweate.

Uncle.   Farewell sir.   *Exeunt* Uncle *and* Lance.

Vallentine.   Would I sweat too, I am monstrous vext, and cold too;
And these are but thinne pumpes to walke the streetes in;
Cloathes I must get, this fashion will not fadge with me,
Besides, tis an ill Winter weare,—— What art thou;
Yes, they are cloathes, and rich ones, some foole has left um:
And if I should utter—— whats this paper here;   130
Let these be only worne, by the most noble and deserving
    Gentleman *Vallentine*——
Dropt out oth' cloudes; I thinke they are full of gold too;

124 sir.] Q2; Q1 adds *Uncle.* Farewell sir.

Well Ile leave my wonder, and be warme agen,
In the next house Ile shift.

Exit.

Enter Franscisco, Uncle, *and* Lance.

IV. i

Franscisco.   Why doe you deale thus with him? tis unnobly.
Uncle.   Peace cosen peace, you are to tender of him,
  He must be dealt thus with, he must be cured thus,
  The violence of his disease *Francisco,*
  Must not be jested with, tis growne infectious,
  And now strong corasives must cure him.
Lance.   Has had a stinger,
  Has eaten off his Cloathes, the next his skinne comes.
Uncle.   And let it search him to the bones, tis better,
  Twill make him feele it.
Lance.   Where be his noble friends now?
  Will his fantasticall opinions cloath him,   10
  Or the learned Art of having nothing feede him?
Uncle.   It must needes greedely,
  For all his friends have flung him off, he is naked,
  And where to skinne himselfe agen, if I know,
  Or can devise how he should get himselfe lodging,
  His spirit must be bowed, and now we have him,
  Have him at that we hoped for.
Lance.   Next time we meete him
  Cracking of Nuts, with halfe a clocke about him,
  For all meanes are cut off, or borrowing sixe pence,
  To shew his bountie in the pottage Ordinary.   20
Franscisco.   Which way went he?
Lance.   Pox, why should you aske after him,
  You have beene trim'd already, let him take his fortune,
  He spunne it out himselfe, sir, theres no pitty.
Uncle.   Besides some good to you now from this miserie.
Franscisco.   I rise upon his ruines! fie, fie Uncle,

IV.i] *Actus* 4. *Scæna* 1. Q 1–2, F 2
6 must] Q 2; most Q 1   18 clocke] *i.e.,* cloak

Fie honest *Lance*, those Gentlemen were base people,
That could so soone take fire to his destruction.
Uncle.   You are a foole, you are a foole, a young man.

Enter Vallentine.

Vallentine.   Morrow Uncle, morrow *Francke* sweete *Francke* and
  how, and how dee,
  Thinke now, how show matters; morrow Bandogge.
Uncle.   How?   30
Franscisco.   Is this man naked, forsaken of his friends?
Vallentine.   Th'art hansome *Francke*, a pretty Gentleman,
  Ifaith thou lookest well, and yet here may be those
  That looke as hansome.
Lance.   Sure he can conjure, and has
  The devill for his taylor.
Uncle.   New and rich,
  Tis most impossible he should recover.
Lance.   Give him this lucke, and fling him into the Sea.
Uncle.   Tis not he, imagination
  Cannot worke this miracle.
Vallentine.   Yes, yes, tis he,
  I will assure you Uncle, the very he,   40
  The he your wisdome plaid withall,
  I thanke you fort, neyed at his nakednes,
  And made his cold and poverty, your pastime;
  You see I live, and the best can doe no more Uncle,
  And though I have no state, I keepe the streetes still;
  And take my pleasure in the towne, like a poore Gentleman,
  Weare clothes to keepe me warme, poore things they serve me,
  Can make a show too if I list, yes Uncle,
  And ring a peale in my pockets, ding dong, Uncle,
  These are mad foolish wayes, but who can helpe um?   50
Uncle.   I am amazed.
Lance.   Ile sell my coppyhold,
  For since there are such excellent new nothings,
  Why should I labour? is there no fairy haunts him,
  No rat, nor no old woman?

Uncle.   You are *Vallentine.*
Vallentine.   I thinke so, I cannot tell, I have beene cald so,
  And some say christened, why doe you wonder at me,
  And swell, as if you had met a sarjeant fasting,
  Did you ever know desert want? yare fooles,
  A little stoope, there may be to allay him,
  He would grow too ranke else, a small eclipse,   60
  To shaddow him, but out hee must breake, glowingly
  Againe, and with a great luster, looke you Uncle,
  Motion, and Majesty.
Uncle.   I am confounded.
Franscisco.   I am of his faith.
Vallentine.   Walke by his carelesse kinsman,
  And turne againe and walke, and looke thus Uncle,
  Taking some one by the hand, he loves best, leave them
  To the mercy of the hog market, come *Franke,*
  Fortune is now my friend, let me instruct thee.
Franscisco.   Good morrow Uncle, I must needes goe with him.
Vallentine.   Flay me, and turne me out where none inhabits,   70
  Within two houres, I shall be thus againe,
  Now wonder on, and laugh at your owne ignorance.
                         Exeunt Vallentine *and* Franck.
Uncle.   I doe beleeve him.
Lance.   So doe I, and heartily.
  Upon my conscience, bury him starke naked,
  He would rise againe, within two houres imbroidered:
  Sow musterd seedes, and they cannot come up so thicke
  As his new sattens doe, and clothes of silver,
  Theres no striving.
Uncle.   Let him play a while then,
  And lets search out what hand:——
Lance.   I there the game lyes.
                         Exeunt.

Enter Fountaine, Bellamore *and* Harebraine.

Fountaine. Come lets speake for our selves, we have lodg'd him
    sure enough,
  His nakednesse dare not peepe out to crosse us.
Bellamore. We can have no admittance.
Harebraine.   Lets in boldly,
  And use our best arts, who she daines to favour,
  We are all content.
Fountaine.   Much good may doe her with him,
  No civill warres.
Bellamore.   By no meanes, now doe I
  Wonder in what old tod Ivy hee lies whistling
  For meanes, nor clothes hee has none, nor none will trust him,
  We have made that side sure, teach him a new wooing.
Harebraine. Say it is his Uncles spite.
Fountaine.   It is all one Gentlemen,   10
  'Tas rid us of a faire incumbrance, and makes us
  Looke about to our owne fortunes. Who are these?

Enter Isabell *and* Luce.

Isabella. Not see this man yet, well, I shall be wiser:
  But *Luce* didst ever know a woman melt so?
  She is finely hurt to hunt.
Luce.   Peace, the three suitors.
Isabella. I could so titter now and laugh, I was lost *Luce*,
  And I must love, I know not what; O *Cupid*,
  What pretty gins thou hast to halter woodcockes,
  And we must into the Countrey in all hast *Luce*.
Luce. For heavens sake Mistris.
Isabella.   Nay I have done,   20
  I must laugh though; but scholler, I shall teach you.
Fountaine. Tis her sister.
Bellamore.   Save you Ladies.
Isabella.   Faire met Gentlemen,
  You are visiting my sister, I assure my selfe.

       [IV.ii]] W; *no scene division* Q1-2, F2, L-C

Harebraine.   We would faine blesse our eyes.

Isabella.   Behold and welcome,
You would see her?

Fountaine.   Tis our businesse.

Isabella.   You shall see her,
And you shall talke with her.

Luce.   Shee will not see um,
Nor spend a word.

Isabella.   Ile make her fret a thousand,
Nay now I have found the scab, I will so scratch her.

Luce.   She cannot endure um.

Isabella.   She loves um but too dearely,
Come follow me, Ile bring you toth party   30
Gentlemen, then make your owne conditions.

Luce.   She is sicke you know.

Isabella.   Ile make her well, or kill her,
And take no idle answer, you are fooles then,
Nor stand off for her state, sheele scorne you all then,
But urge her still, and though she fret, still follow her,
A widdow must be wonne so.

Bellamore.   Shee speakes bravely.

Isabella.   I would faine have
A brother in law, I love mens company,
And if she call for dinner to avoide you,
Be sure you stay; follow her into her chamber,   40
If she retire to pray, pray with her, and boldly,
Like honest lovers.

Luce.   This will kill her.

Fountaine.   You
Have showed us one way, do but lend the tother.

Isabella.   I know you stand a thornes, come Ile dispatch you.

Luce.   If you live after this——

Isabella.   I have lost my ayme.

                                                    [*Exeunt.*]

*43 lend] *stet* Q1

61

Enter Vallentine *and* Franscisco.

Franscisco.   Did you not see um since?
Vallentine.   No hang um, hang um.
Franscisco.   Nor will you not be seene by um?
Vallentine.   Let um alone *Francke*,
   Ile make um their owne justice, and a jerker.
Franscisco.   Such base discurteous dogge whelpes.
Vallentine.   I shall dogge um,
   And double dog um, ere I have done.
Franscisco.   Will you goe with me,
   For I would faine finde out this peece of bountie,
   It was the widdows man, that I am certaine of.
Vallentine.   To what end would you goe?
Franscisco.   To give thankes sir.
Vallentine.   Hang giving thankes, hast not thou parts deserves it?
   It includes to a further will to be beholding,   10
   Beggers can doe no more at doores; if you
   Will goe there lies your way.
Franscisco.   I hope you will goe.
Vallentine.   No not in ceremony, and to a woman,
   With mine owne father, were hee living *Francke*;
   I would toth Court with beares first, if it be
   That wench, I thinke it is, for tothers wiser,
   I would not be so lookt upon, and laught at,
   So made a ladder for her wit, to climbe upon,
   For tis the tartest tit in Christendome,
   I know her well *Francke*, and have buckled with her,   20
   So lickt, and stroakt, fleard upon, and flouted,
   And showne to Chambermaides, like a strange beast,
   She had purchased with her penny.
Franscisco.   You are a strange man,
   But doe you thinke it was a woman?
Vallentine.   Theres no doubt ont,
   Who can be there to doe it else? besides the manner
   Of the circumstances.

[IV.iii]] W; *no scene division* Q 1–2, F 2, L–C

Franscisco.   Then such courtesies,
Who ever does um sir, saving your owne wisdome,
Must be more lookt into, and better answerd,
Then with deserving slights, or what we ought
To have conferd upon us, men may starve else,   30
Meanes are not gotten now, with crying out
I am a gallant fellow, a good souldier,
A man of learning, or fit to be employed,
Immediate blessings, cease like miracles,
And we must grow, by second meanes; I pray
Goe with me, even as you love me sir.
Vallentine.   I will come to thee, but *Francke*, I will not stay
To heare your fopperies, dispatch those ere I come.
Franscisco.   You will not faile me.
Vallentine.   Some two houres hence expect me.
Franscisco.   I thanke you, and will looke for you.   40

                                        Exeunt.

Enter Widdow, Shorthose, *and* Roger.   [IV. iv]

Widdow.   Who let me in these puppies? you blinde rascals,
You drunken knaves severall.
Shorthose.   Yes forsooth, Ile let um in presently,——
Gentlemen.
Widdow.   Sprecious, you blowne pudding, you bawling rogue.
Shorthose.   I bawle as loud as I can, would you have me fetch um
Upon my backe.
Widdow.   Get um out rascall, out with um, out,
I sweate to have um neare me.
Shorthose.   I should sweate more
To carry um out.
Roger.   They are Gentlemen Madam.
Shorthose.   Shall we get um intoth' butterie, and make um drinke?
Widdow.   Doe any thing, so I be eased.

[IV.iv]] W; *no scene division* Q1–2, F2, L–C
2 severall] *stet* Q1–2, F2, L–S; C–V: *a cryptic stage-direction?*

Enter Isabel, Fountaine, Bellamore, Harebraine.

Isabella.   Now too her sir,
  Feare nothing.
Roger.   Slip a side, boy, I know shee loves um,   10
  Howsoere shee carries it, and has invited um,
  My young Mistris told me so.
Shorthose.   Away to tables then.
                                              Exeunt.

Isabella.   I shall burst with the sport ont.
Fountaine.   You are too curious Madam,
  Too full of preparation, we expect it not.
Bellamore.   Me thinkes the house is hansome, every place decent,
  What neede you be so vext?
Harebraine.   We are no strangers.
Fountaine.   What though we come ere you expected us,
  Doe not we know your entertainements Madam
  Are free, and full at all times?
Widdow.   You are merry Gentlemen.
Bellamore.   We come to be merry Madam, and very merry,   20
  We live to laugh heartily, and now and then Lady
  A little of our old plea.
Widdow.   I am busie,
  And very busie too, will none deliver me.
Harebraine.   There is a time for all, you may be busie,
  But when your friends come, you have as much power Madam.
Widdow.   This is a tedious torment.
Fountaine.   How hansomely
  This title peece of anger shewes upon her,
  Well Madam well, you know not how to grace your selfe.
Bellamore.   Nay every thing she does breedes a new sweetnesse.
Widdow.   I must goe up, I must goe up, I have   30
  A businesse waites upon me, some wine for the Gentlemen.
Harebraine.   Nay, weele goe with you, we never saw your
    chambers yet.
Isabella.   Hold there boyes.

21 We live] 'me ~ Q1; men love Q2, F2, L; Love S; Come C; we love D–V

64

Widdow.　　Say I goe to my prayers.
Fountaine.　　　　　　　　　　　Weele pray with you,
　　And helpe your meditations.
Widdow.　　　　　　　　　　　　This is boystrous,
　　Or say I goe to sleepe, will you goe to sleepe with me.
Bellamore.　　So suddenly before meate will bee dangerous,
　　Wee know your dinners ready Lady, you will not sleepe.
Widdow.　　Give me my Coach, I will take the aire.
Harebraine.　　　　　　　　　　　Weele waite on you,
　　And then your meate after a quickned stomacke.　　　　　40
Widdow.　　Let it alone, and call my steward to mee,
　　And bid him bring his recknings into the Orchard,
　　These unmannerly rude puppies——　　　*Exit* Widdow.
Fountaine.　　　　　　　　　　　Weele walke after you
　　And view the pleasure of the place.
Isabella.　　　　　　　　　　　Let her not rest,
　　For if you give her breath, sheele scorne and floute you,
　　Seeme how she will, this is the way to winne her,
　　Be bold and prosper.
Bellamore.　　　　　　Nay if we doe not tire her——
　　　　　　　　　　　　　　　　　　Exeunt [Lovers].
Isabella.　　Ile teach you to worme me good Lady sister,
　　And peepe into my privacies, to suspect me,
　　Ile torture you, with that you hate, most daintily,　　　50
　　And when I have done that, laugh at that you love most.

Enter Luce.

Luce.　　What have you done, shee chafes and fumes outragiously,
　　And still they persecute her.
Isabella.　　　　　　　　　　　Long may they doe so,
　　Ile teache her to declaime against my pitties,
　　Why is shee not gone out oth' towne, but gives
　　Occasion for men to run mad after her?
Luce.　　I shall be hanged.
Isabella.　　　　　　　　　This in me had beene high treason,
　　Three at a time, and private in her Orchard,
　　I hope sheele cast her reckonings right now.

Enter Widdow.

Widdow.   Well, I shall finde who brought um.   60
Isabella.   Ha, ha, ha.
Widdow.   Why doe you laugh
                                                           sister?
   I feare me tis your tricke, twas neatly done of you,
   And well becomes your pleasure.
Isabella.   What have you done with um?
Widdow.   Lockt um ith Orchard, there Ile make um dance
   And caper too, before they get their liberty,
   Unmannerly rude puppies.
Isabella.   They are somewhat saucy,
   But yet Ile let um out, and once more hound um,
   Why were they not beaten out?
Widdow.   I was about it,
   But because they came as suiters——
Isabella.   Why did you not answer um? 70
Widdow.   They are so impudent they will receive none:
   More yet, how came these in?

Enter Franscisco *and* Lance.

Lance.   At the doore Madam.
Isabella.   It is that face.
Luce.   This is the Gentleman.
Widdow.   Shee sent the money too?
Luce.   The same.
Isabella.   Ile leave you,
   They have some businesse.
Widdow.   Nay you shall stay sister,
   They are strangers both to me: how her face alters.
Isabella.   I am sorry he comes now.
Widdow.   I am glad he is here now though.
   Who would you speake with Gentlemen?
Lance.   You Lady,
   Or your faire sister there, heres a Gentleman,

That has received a benefit.
Widdow.   From whom sir?   80
Lance.   From one of you, as he supposes Madam,
Your man delivered it.
Widdow.   I pray goe forward.
Lance.   And of so great a goodnesse, that he dares not,
Without the tender of his thankes and service,
Passe by the house.
Widdow.   Which is the Gentleman?
Lance.   This, Madam.
Widdow.   Whats your name sir?
Franscisco.   They that know me
Call me *Franscisco* Lady, one not so proud
To scorne, so timely a benefit, nor so wretched,
To hide a gratitude.
Widdow.   It is well bestowed then.
Franscisco.   Your faire selfe, or your sister as it seemes,   90
For what desert I dare not know, unlesse
A hansome subject for your charities,
Or aptnesse in your noble wils to doe it,
Have showred upon my wants, a timely bounty,
Which makes me rich in thankes, my best inheritance.
Widdow.   I am sorry twas not mine, this is the Gentlewoman,
Fie doe not blush, goe roundly to the matter,
The man is a prettie man.
Isabella.   You have three fine ones.
Franscisco.   Then to you deare Lady.
Isabella.   I pray no more Sir, if I may perswade you,   100
Your onely aptnesse to doe this is recompence,
And more then I expected.
Franscisco.   But good Lady——
Isabella.   And for me further to be acquainted with it,
Besides the imputation of vaine glory,
Were greedie thankings of my selfe, I did it
Not to be more affected to; I did it,
And if it happened where I thought it fitted,

I have my end; more to enquire is curious
In either of us, more then that suspicious.

Franscisco.   But gentle Ladie, twill be necessary.   110

Isabella.   About the right way nothing, doe not fright it,
Being to pious use and tender sighted,
With the blown face of complements, it blasts it;
Had you not come at all, but thought thankes,
It had beene too much, twas not to see your person——

Widdow.   A brave dissembling rogue, and how she carries it.

Isabella.   Though I beleeve few handsomer; or heare you,
Though I affect a good tongue well; or try you,
Though my yeares desire a friend, that I relieved you.

Widdow.   A plaguie cunning queane.

Isabella.   For so I carryed it,   120
My ends too glorious in mine eies, and bartred
The goodnesse I propounded with opinion.

Widdow.   Feare her not Sir.

Isabella.   You cannot catch me sister.

Franscisco.   Will you both teach, and tie my tongue up Lady?

Isabella.   Let it suffice you have it, it was never mine,
Whilst good men wanted it.

Lance.   This is a Saint sure.

Isabella.   And if you be
Not such a one restore it.

Franscisco.   To commend my selfe
Were more officious, then you thinke my thankes are,   130
To doubt I may be worth your gift a treason,
Both to mine owne good, and understanding,
I know my mind cleare, and though modesty
Tels me, he that intreates intrudes,
Yet I must thinke something, and of some season,
Met with your better taste, this had not beene else.

Widdow.   What ward for that, Wench?

Isabella.   Alas it never touched me.

Franscisco.   Well gentle Ladie, yours is the first money
I ever tooke upon a forced ill manners.

Isabella.   The last of me, if ever you use other.   140

Franscisco.   How may I doe, and your way to be thought

   A grateful taker?
Isabella.   Spend it and say nothing,
  Your modestie may deserve more.
Widdow.   O sister,
  Will you barre thankefullnesse?
Isabella.   Dogges dance for meate,
  Would you have men doe worse, for they can speake,
  Cry out like Woodmongers, good deeds by the hundreds,
  I did it that my best friend should not know it,
  Wine and vaine glory does as much as I else,
  If you will force my merit, against my meaning,
  Use it in well bestowing it, in showing   150
  It came to be a benefit, and was so;
  And not examining a woman did it,
  Or to what end, in not beleeving sometimes
  Your selfe, when drinke and stirring conversation
  May ripen strange perswasions.
Franscisco.   Gentle Lady,
  I were a base receiver of a curtesie,
  And you a worse disposer, were my nature
  Unfurnished of these foresights. Ladies honours
  Were ever in my thoughts, unspotted ermines,
  Their good deedes holy temples, where the incense   160
  Burnes not to common eyes: your feares are vertuous,
  And so I shall preserve um.
Isabella.   Keepe but this way,
  And from this place to tell me so, you have paid me;
  And so I wish you see all fortune.   *Exit [with Luce].*
Widdow.   Feare not,
  The woman will be thanked, I doe not doubt it.
  Are you so crafty, carry it so precisely?
  This is to wake my feares, or to abuse mee,
  I shall looke narrowly: despaire not Gentlemen,
  There is an houre to catch a woman in,
  If you be wise, so, I must leave you too;   170
  Now will I goe laugh at my suitors.   *Exit.*
Lance.   Sir what courage?

     159 ermines] S; crimes Q 1–2, F 2, L

69

Franscisco.   This woman is a founder, and scites statutes
  To all her benefits.
Lance.   I never knew yet,
  So few yeares and so cunning, yet beleeve me
  She has an itch, but how to make her confesse it,
  For it is a crafty tit, and playes about you,
  Will not bite home, she would faine, but she dares not;
  Carry your selfe but so discreetly Sir,
  That want or wantonnesse seeme not to search you,
  And you shall see her open.
Franscisco.   I do love her,   180
  And were I rich, would give two thousand pound
  To wed her wit but one houre, oh tis a dragon,
  And such a spritely way of pleasure, ha *Lance.*
Lance.   Your ha *Lance* broken once, you would cry, ho, ho, *Lance.*
Franscisco.   Some leaden landed rogue, will have this Wench now,
  When alls done, some such youth will carry her,
  And weare her greasie out like stuffe, some dunce
  That knowes no more but Markets, and admires nothing
  But a long charge at sises: O the fortunes!

Enter Isabel *and* Luce.

Lance.   Comfort your selfe.
Luce.   They are here yet, and alone too,   190
  Boldly upont. Nay Mistresse, I still told you,
  How 'would finde your trust, this tis to venture
  Your charitie upon a boy.
Lance.   Now, whats the matter?
  Stand fast, and like your selfe.
Isabella.   Prethee no more wench.
Luce.   What was his want to you?
Isabella.   Tis true.
Luce.   Or misery,
  Or say he had beene ith' Cage, was there no mercy
  To looke abroad but yours?
Isabella.   I am paid for fooling.

    189 sises] *i.e.*, sizes [= assizes]   190 alone] F2; a love Q1–2

Luce.   Must every slight companion that can purchase
  A shew of povertie and beggerly planet
  Fall under your compassion?
Lance.   Heres a new matter.   200
Luce.   Nay you are served but too well, here he staies yet,
  Yet as I live.
Franscisco.   How her face alters on me?
Luce.   Out of a confidence I hope.
Isabella.   I am glad ont.
Franscisco.   How doe you gentle Lady?
Isabella.   Much ashamed sir,
  But first stand further off me, y'are infectious,
  To finde such vanitie, nay almost impudence
  Where I beleeved a worth: is this your thankes,
  The gratitude you were so mad to make me,
  Your trimme councell Gentlemen?
Lance.   What Lady?
Isabella.   Take your device agen, it will not serve sir,   210
  The woman will not bite, you are finely cosend,
  Droppe it no more for shame.
Luce.   Doe you thinke you are here sir
  Amongst your wastcoateers, your base Wenches
  That scratch at such occasions; you are deluded;
  This is a Gentlewoman of a noble house,
  Borne to a better fame than you can build her,
  And eyes above your pitch.
Franscisco.   I doe acknowledge——
Isabella.   Then I beseech you sir, what could you see,
  Speake boldly, and speake truely, shame the devill,
  In my behaviour of such easinesse   220
  That you durst venture to doe this?
Franscisco.   You amaze me,
  This Ring is none of mine, nor did I droppe it.
Luce.   I saw you droppe it sir.
Isabella.   I tooke it up too,
  Still looking when your modesty should misse it,
  Why what a childish part was this?

207 beleeved] F2; beleeve Q1–2   218 you see] S; 'see Q1–2, F2, L

71

Franscisco.   I vow——
Isabella.   Vow me no vowes, he that dares doe this,
   Has bred himselfe to boldnesse, to forsweare too;
   There take your gugaw, you are too much pampered,
   And I repent my part, as you grow older
   Grow wiser if you can, and so farewell sir.   230
                              Exeunt Isabella *and* Luce.
Lance.   Grow wiser if you can, shee has put it to you,
   Tis a rich Ring, did you droppe it?
Franscisco.   Never,
   Nere see it afore *Lance.*
Lance.   Thereby hangs a taile then:
   What slight shee makes to catch her selfe, looke up sir,
   You cannot lose her if you would, how daintily
   She flies upon the lure, and cunningly
   She makes her stoppes, whistle and she'le come to you.
Franscisco.   I would I were so happie.
Lance.   Maids are clockes,
   The greatest wheele they show, goes slowest to us,
   And makes us hang on tedious hopes; the lesser,   240
   Which are concealed being often oyl'd with wishes
   Flee like desires, and never leave that motion,
   Till the tongue strikes; she is flesh, blood, and marrow,
   Young as her purpose, and soft as pitty;
   No Monument to worship, but a mould
   To make men in, a neate one, and I know
   How ere she appeares now, which is neare enough,
   You are starke blinde if you hit not soone at night;
   Shee would venture fortie pounds more but to feele
   A flea in your shape bite her: drop no more Rings   250
   Forsooth, this was the prettiest thing
   To know her heart by.
Franscisco.   Thou putst me in much comfort.
Lance.   Put your selfe in good comfort, if shee doe
   Not point you out the way, droppe no more rings,
   She'le droppe her selfe into you.

          240 makes us] S; makes Q1; make's Q2, F2, L

                              72

Franscisco.   I wonder my brother comes not.

Lance.   Let him alone,
  And feede your selfe on your owne fortunes; come be frolicke,
  And lets be monstrous wise and full of councell,
  Droppe no more Ringes.

                                                        Exeunt.

            Enter Widdow, Fountaine, Bellamore, Harebraine.   [IV. v]

Widdow.   If you will needes be foolish you must be used so:
  Who sent for you? who entertained you Gentlemen?
  Who bid you welcome hether? you came crowding,
  And impudently bold; presse on my patience,
  As if I kept a house for all Companions,
  And of all sorts; will 'have your wills, will 'vexe me
  And force my liking from you, I never owed you.
Fountaine.   For all this we will dine with you.
Bellamore.   And for all this
  Will have a better answer from you.
Widdow.   You shall never,
  Neither have an answer nor dinner, unlesse you use me   10
  With a more staid respect, and stay your time too.

          Enter Isabella, Shorthose, Roger, Humphrey, Ralph,
                    with dishes of meate.

Isabella.   Forward with the meate now.
Roger.   Come gentlemen march fairely.
Shorthose.   *Roger,* you are a weake Servingman, your white
      broath runnes from you;
  Fie, how I sweate under this pile of Beefe;
  An Elephant can doe more, oh for such a backe now,
  And in these times, what might a man arrive at;
  Goose grase you up, and Woodcocke march behinde thee,
  I am almost foundred.
Widdow.   Who bid you bring the meate yet?

      [IV.v]] W; *no scene division* Q 1–2, F 2, L–C
      6 your] Q 1(c); you Q 1(u)   10 an] Q 2; a Q 1

Away you knaves, I will not dine these two houres,
How am I vext and chafed; goe carry it backe   20
And tell the Cooke, hee's an arrant Rascall,
To send before I called.

Shorthose.   Faces about Gentlemen,
Beate a mournefull march then, and give some supporters,
Or else I perish——   *Exeunt* Servants.

Isabella.   It does me much good
To see her chafe thus.

Harebraine.   Wee can stay Madame, and will stay and dwell here,
Tis good Ayre.

Fountaine.   I know you have beds enough,
And meate you never want.

Widdow.   You want a little.

Bellamore.   We dare to pretend on, since you are curlish,
Wee'le give you physicke, you must purge this anger,   30
It burnes you and decaies you.

Widdow.   If I had you out once
I would be at charge of a percullis for you.

Enter Vallentine.

Vallentine.   Good morrow noble Lady.

Widdow.   Good morrow sir.
How sweetly now he lookes, and how full manly,
What slaves was these to use him so.

Vallentine.   I come
To looke a young man I call brother.

Widdow.   Such a one
Was here sir, as I remember your owne brother,
But gone almost an houre agoe.

Vallentine.   Good e'n then.

Widdow.   You must not so soone sir, here be some Gentlemen,
It may be you are acquainted with um.   40

Harebraine.   Will nothing make him miserable?

Fountaine.   How glorious!

24 else] Q2, esse Q1   29 curlish] *i.e.,* churlish
38 Good] Q2; God Q1

74

Bellamore.   It is the very he, does it raine fortunes,
  Or has hee a familliar?
Harebraine.   How doggedly he lookes too.
Fountaine.   I am beyond my faith, pray lets be going.
Vallentine.   Where are these Gentlemen?
Widdow.   Here.
Vallentine.   Yes I know um
  And will be more famillier.
Bellamore.   Morrow Maddam.
Widdow.   Nay stay and dine.
Vallentine.   You shall stay till I talke with you,
  And not dine neither, but fastingly my fury,
  You thinke you have undone me, thinke so still,
  And swallow that beleefe, till you be company   50
  For Court-hand Clarkes, and starved Atturneyes,
  Till you breake in at playes like Prentices
  For three a groat, and cracke nuts with the schollers
  In penny Roomes agen, and fight for Apples,
  Till you returne to what I found you, people
  Betrai'd into the hands of Fencers, Challengers,
  Toothdrawers bills, and tedious Proclamations
  In Meale-markets, with throngings to see Cutpurses:
  Stirre not, but heare, and marke, Ile cut your throates else,
  Till Waterworkes, and rumours of new Rivers   60
  Rid you againe and runne you into questions
  Who built Theames, till you runne mad
  For Lotteries, and stand there with your tables
  To gleane the golden sentenses, and cite um secretly
  To Servingmen for sound Essayes, till Tavernes
  Allow you but a Towell roome to tipple in,
  Wine that the Bell hath gone for twice, and glasses
  That looke like broken promises, tied up
  With wicker protestations, English Tobacco
  With halfe pipes, nor in halfe a yeare once burnt, and Bisket   70

62 Theames,] C; Theame., Q₁(u); Theamea, Q₁(c)
66–67 in, | Wine] C; in wine Q₁–2, F₂
67 gone] Q₁(c); goe Q₁(u)

That Bawdes have rubb'd their gummes upon like Curralls
To bring the marke againe; till this houre rascalls,
So this most fatall houre will come againe,
Thinke I sit downe the looser.

Widdow.   Will you stay Gentlemen,
A peece of beefe and a cold Capon, thats all,
You know you are welcome.

Harebraine.   That was cast to abuse us.

Bellamore.   Steale off,
The devill is in his anger.

Widdow.   Nay I am sure
You will not leave me so discurteously
Now I have provided for you.

Vallentine.   What doe you heare?
Why doe ye vexe a woman of her goodnesse,   80
Her state and worth; can you bring a faire certificate
That you deserve to be her footmen; husbands, you puppies,
Husbands for Whores and Bawdes, away you wind-suckers;
Doe not looke bigge, nor prate, nor stay, nor grumble,
And when you are gone seeme to laugh at my fury,
And slight this Lady, I shall heare, and know this:
And though I am not bound to fight for women,
As farre as they are good I dare preserve um:
Be not too bold, for if you be Ile swinge you,
Ile swinge you monstrously without all pitty,   90
Your honours now goe, avoide me mainely.

                                        Exeunt [Lovers].

Widdow.   Well sir, you have delivered me, I thanke you,
And with your noblenesse prevented danger
Their tongues might utter, we'll all goe and eate sir.

Vallentine.   No, no, I dare not trust my selfe with women,
Goe to your meate, eate little, take lesse ease,
And tie your body to a daily labour,
You may live honestly, and so I thanke you.   *Exit.*

72 till this houre] C; tell these ~ Q1(c), Q2, F2, L–S; tell these houres Q1(u)
76 *Harebraine.*] C; *Hum.* Q1–2, F2, L–S
79 heare] *i.e.,* here   80 ye] Q2; *omit* Q1   94 we'll] Q2; will Q1

Widdow.　Well goe thy wayes, thou art a noble fellow,
And some meanes I must worke to have thee know it.　　　　100
　　　　　　　　　　　　　Exit [*with* Isabella].

Enter Uncle *and* Merchant.　　　　V. i

Uncle.　Most certaine tis her hands that hold him up,
And her sister relieves *Franke.*
Merchant.　　　　　　I am glad to heare it:
But wherefore doe they not pursue this fortune
To some faire end?
Uncle.　　　　　The women are too craftie,
Vallentine too coy, and *Franke* too bashfull,
Had any wise man hold of such a blessing,
They would strick it out oth' flint but they would forme it.

Enter Widdow *and* Shorthose.

Merchant.　The Widdow sure, why does she stirre so earely?
Widdow.　Tis strange, I cannot force him to understand mee,
And make a benefit, of what I would bring him,　　　　10
Tell my sister ile use any devotions
At home this morning, shee may if shee please goe to Church.
Shorthose.　Hay ho.
Widdow.　And doe you waite upon her with a torch sir.
Shorthose.　Hay ho.
Widdow.　You lasie knave.
Shorthose.　　　　　　Here is such a tincle tanklings
That we can nere lie quiet, and sleepe our prayers out,
Ralph pray emptie my right shooe that you made your
　　Chamberpot,
And burne a little Rosemary int, I must waite upon my Lady.
This morning Prayer has brought me into a consumption,　　　　20
I have nothing left but flesh and bones about me.
Widdow.　You drousie slave, nothing but sleepe and swilling.
Shorthose.　Had you beene bitten with bandogge fleaes, as I have
　　beene,

　　　　V.i] *Actus* 5. *Scæn.* 1. Q1–2, F2　　　14 sir.] F2; ~ ? Q1–2

77

And haunted with the night Mare——
Widdow.   With an Alepot.
Shorthose.   You would have little list to morning Prayers,
Pray take my fellow *Ralph*, hee has a Psalme booke,
I am an ingrum man.
Widdow.   Get you ready quickly,
And when she is ready waite upon her hansomely;
No more, be gone.
Shorthose.   If I doe snore my part out——
                                        Exit Shorthose.

Uncle.   Now to our purposes.
Merchant.   Good morrow Madam.   30
Widdow.   Good morrow Gentlemen.
Uncle.   Good joy and fortune.
Widdow.   These are good things, and worth my thankes, I thanke
   you sir.
Merchant.   Much joy I hope you'le finde, we came to gratulate
Your new knit marriage band.
Widdow.   How?
Uncle.   He's a Gentleman
Although he be my kinsman, my faire Neece.
Widdow.   Neece Sir?
Uncle.   Yes Lady, now I may say so,
Tis no shame to you, I say a Gentleman,
And winking at some light fancies,
Which you most happily may affect him for,
As bravely carried, as nobly bred and managed.   40
Widdow.   Whats all this, I understand you not,
What Neece, what marriage knot?
Uncle.   Ile tell plainely,
You are my Neece, and *Vallentine* the Gentleman
Has made you so by marriage.
Widdow.   Marriage?
Uncle.   Yes Lady,
And twas a noble and a vertuous part,
To take a falling man to your protection,

27 *Widdow.*] Q2; *Short.* Q1

And bay him up againe to all his glories.

Widdow.   The men are mad.

Merchant.   What though he wanted

These outward things, that flie away like shadowes;

Was not his minde a full one, and a brave one?   50

You have wealth enough to give him glosse, and outside;

And he wit enough to give way to love a Lady.

Uncle.   I ever thought he would doe well.

Merchant.   Nay, I knew

How ever he wheel'd about like a loose Carbine,

He would charge home at length, like a brave Gentleman;

Heavens blessing a your heart Lady, wee are so bound to honour you,

In all your service so devoted to you.

Uncle.   Doe not looke so strange Widdow, it must be knowne,

Better a generall joy; no stirring here yet,

Come, come you cannot hide um.

Widdow.   Pray be not impudent,   60

These are the finest toyes, belike I am married then?

Merchant.   You are in a miserable estate in the worlds account else,

I would not for your wealth it come to doubting.

Widdow.   And I am great with child?

Uncle.   No; great they say not,

But tis a full opinion you are with childe,

And great joy among the Gentlemen,

Your husband hath bestirred himselfe fairely.

Merchant.   Alas, we know his private houres of entrance,

How long, and when he staied, could name the bed too

Where hee paid downe his first fruits.

Widdow.   I shall beleeve anon.   70

Uncle.   And we consider for some private reasons,

You would have it private, yet take your owne pleasure;

And so good morrow my best Neece, my sweetest.

Widdow.   No, no, pray stay.

Uncle.   I know you would be with him,

*47 bay] *stet* Q1   54 a] Q1(c); *omit* Q1(u)
54 Carbine] S; Cabine Q1–2, F2, L

Love him, and love him well.
Merchant.   You'le finde him noble,
  This may beget——
Uncle.   It must needes work upon her.

                              Exit Uncle *and* Merchant.
Widdow.   These are fine bobes I faith, married, and with child too,
  How long has this beene I trow? they seeme grave fellowes,
  They should not come to flout; married, and bedded,
  The world take notice too, where lies this May game?   80
  I could be vext extreamely now, and raile too,
  But tis to no end, though I itch a little,
  Must I be scratcht I know not how—— who waites there?

                    Enter Humphrey [*and*] Ralph.

Humphrey.   Madam.
Widdow.   Make ready my Coach quickly, and waite
  You onely; and harke you sir, be secret and speedy,
  Enquire out where he lies.
Ralph.   I shall doe it Madam.

                              Exit [*with* Humphrey].
Widdow.   Married, and got with child in a dreame, tis fine ifaith,
  Sure he that did this, would doe better waking.

                                                Exit.

                Enter Vallentine, Franscisco, Lance,   [V. ii]
                    and a boy with a torch.

Vallentine.   Hold thy Torch hansomely: how dost thou *Francke?*
  Peter Bassell, beare up.
Franscisco.   You have fryed me soundly,
  Sacke doe you call this drinke?
Vallentine.   A shrewd dogge *Francke,*
  Will bite abundantly.
Lance.   Now could I fight,

<hr/>

82 a] Q2; *omit* Q1
*83.1 Humphrey [*and*] Ralph.] *Hum, a servant.* Q1–2, F2
[V.ii]] W; *no scene division* Q1–2, F2, L–C

And fight with thee.

Vallentine.   With me thou man of *Memphis?*

Lance.   But that thou art mine owne naturall Master,
Yet my sacke saies thou art no man, thou art
A Pagan, and pawnest thy land, which a noble cause——

Vallentine.   No armes, no armes, good *Lancelet,*
Deare *Lance,* no fighting here, we will have Lands boy,   10
Livings, and Titles, thou shalt be a Viceroy,
Hang fighting, hang't tis out of fashion.

Lance.   I would faine labour you into your lands againe,
Goe too, it is behoovefull.

Franscisco.   Fie *Lance,* fie.

Lance.   I must beate some body, and why not my Master,
Before a stranger? charity and beating
Begins at home.

Vallentine.   Come thou shalt beate me.

Lance.   I will not be compeld, and you were two Masters,
I scorne the motion.

Vallentine.   Wilt thou sleepe?

Lance.   I scorne sleepe.

Vallentine.   Wilt thou goe eate?

Lance.   I scorne meate, I come for rompering,   20
I come to waite upon my charge discreetely,
For looke you if you will not take your Morgage
Againe, here doe I lie Saint *George,* and so forth.

Vallentine.   And here doe I St. *George,* bestride the Dragon,
Thus with my Lance.

Lance.   I sting, I sting with my taile.

Vallentine.   Doe you so, doe you so Sir, I shall taile you presently.

Franscisco.   By no meanes, doe not hurt him.

Vallentine.   Take his Nellson,
And now rise, thou maiden Knight of *Malligo,*
Lace on thy helmet of inchanted sacke,
And charge againe.

Lance.   I play no more, you abuse me,   30
Will you goe?

7 sacke] Q2; sackes Q1   12 hang't] F2; hang Q1–2   16 a] Q2; *omit* Q1

Franscisco.   Ile bid you good morrow Brother,
For sleepe I cannot, I have a thousand fancies.
Vallentine.   Now thou art arived, goe bravely to the matter,
And doe something of worth *Francke.*
Lance.   You shall heare from us.
                              Exeunt Lance *and* Frank.
Vallentine.   This rogue, if he had beene sober, sure had beaten me,
Is the most tettish knave.

Enter Uncle *and* Merchant: *Merchant with a torch.*

Uncle.   Tis he.
Merchant.   Good morrow.
Vallentine.   Why sir good morrow to you too, and you be so
    lusty.
Uncle.   You have made your brother a fine man, we met him.
Vallentine.   I made him a fine Gentleman, he was a foole before,
Brought up amongst the mist of small beere Brue-houses,   40
What would you have with me?
Merchant.   I come to tell you,
Your latest houre is come.
Vallentine.   Are you my sentence?
Merchant.   The sentence of your state.
Vallentine.   Let it be hangd then,
And let it be hangd hie enough, I may not see it.
Uncle.   A gratious resolution.
Vallentine.   What would you else with me,
Will you goe drinke, and let the world slide Uncle?
Ha, ha, ha, boyes, drinke sacke like whey boyes.
Merchant.   Have you no feeling sir?
Vallentine.   Come hither Merchant:
Make me a supper, thou most reverent Land catcher,
A supper of forty pound.
Merchant.   What then sir.   50
Vallentine.   Then bring thy wife along, and thy faire sisters,
Thy neighbours and their wives, and all their trinkets,
Let me have forty trumpets, and such wine,

*36 Merchant] *May* Q1; Boy Q2, F2   40 mist] S; midst Q2, F2, L

82

Weele laugh at all the miseries of morgage,
And then in state Ile render thee an answer.
Merchant.   What say you to this?
Uncle.   I dare not say nor thinke neither.
Merchant.   Will you redeeme your state, speake to the point sir?
Vallentine.   No, not if it were mine heire in the Turkes gallies.
Merchant.   Then I must take an order.
Vallentine.   Take a thousand,
    I will not keepe it, nor thou shalt not have it,   60
    Because thou camest ith nick, thou shalt not have it,
    Goe take possession, and be sure you hold it,
    Hold fast with both hands, for there be those hounds uncoupled,
    Will ring you such a knell, goe downe in glory,
    And march upon my Land, and cry alls mine;
    Cry as the devil did, and be the devill,
    Marke what an eccho followes, build fine Marchpanes,
    To entertaine Sir Silkworme and his Lady,
    And pull the Chappell downe, to raise a Chamber
    For Mistris Silverpin, to lay her belly in,   70
    Marke what an Earthquake comes, then foolish Merchant
    My tennants are no subjects, they obey nothing,
    And they are people too, never Christned,
    They know no law, nor conscience, theile devoure thee:
    And thou wert all the staple, theile confound thee,
    Within three dayes; no bit nor memory
    Of what thou wert, no not the wart upon thy nose there,
    Shall be ere heard of more, goe take possession,
    And bring thy children downe, to rost like rabbits,
    They love young toasts, and butter, *Bowbell* suckers;   80
    As they love mischiefe, and hate law, they are Canibals:
    Bring downe thy kindred too, that be not fruitfull,
    There be those Mandrakes, that will mollifie um,
    Goe take possession, Ile goe to my Chamber,
    Afore boy goe.
                              Exeunt [Vallentine *and* boy].

56 you] Q2; *omit* Q1   58 No] S; Not Q1–2, F2, L
75 wert all the staple] D; mortall the stople Q1–2, F2, L; art mortal staple S–W

Merchant.　　　　Hees mad sure.

Uncle.　　　　　　　　Hees halfe drunke sure,
　And yet I like this unwillingnesse to loose it,
　This looking backe.

Merchant.　　　　Yes if he did it hansomely,
　But hees so harsh, and strange.

Uncle.　　　　　　　　Beleeve it tis his drinke sir,
　And I am glad his drinke has thrust it out.

Merchant. Cannibals; if ever I come to view his regements,　　90
　If faire termes may be had——

Uncle.　　　　　　　　Hee tels you true sir;
　They are a bunch of the most boystrous rascalls
　Disorder ever made, let um be mad once,
　The power of the whole Country cannot coole um,
　Be patient but a while.

Merchant.　　　　As long as you will sir,
　Before I buy a bargaine of such runts,
　Ile buy a Colledge for Beares, and live among um.

　　　　　　　　　　　　　　　　　　[Exeunt.]

　　　　　Enter Franscisco, Lance, *boy with a torch.*　　　[V. iii]

Franscisco. How dost thou now?

Lance.　　　　　　　Better then I was, and straighter,
　But my heads a hogs' head still; it rowles and tumbles.

Franscisco. Thou wert cruelly paid.

Lance.　　　　　　　I may live to requite it,
　Put a snaffle of sacke in my mouth, and then ride me: very well.

Franscisco. Twas all but sport, Ile tell thee what I meane now,
　I meane to see this wench.

Lance.　　　　　　Where a devill is shee?
　And there were two, 'tweare better.

Franscisco.　　　　　　Doest thou heare
　The bell ring?

Lance.　　Yes, yes.

Franscisco.　　　Then shee comes to prayers,

　　　　[V.iii]] W; *no scene division* Q1–2, F2, L–C

Earely each morning thether: Now if I could but meete her,
For I am of another mettle now.

Enter Isabell, *and* Shorthose *with a torch.*

Lance.   What lights yond?   10
Franscisco.   Ha, tis a light, take her by the hand and Court her.
Lance.   Take her below the girdle, youle never speed else,
  It comes on this way still, oh that I had
  But such an opportunity in a saw pit,
  How it comes on, comes on! tis here.
Franscisco.   Tis she:
  Fortune, I kisse thy hand—— good morrow Lady.
Isabella.   What voyce is that sirrha, doe you sleepe as you goe,
  Tis he, I am glad ont. Why *Shorthose.*
Shorthose.   Yes forsooth, I dreamt, I was going to Church.
Lance.   She sees you as plaine as I doe.
Isabella.   Hold thy Torch up.   20
Shorthose.   Heres nothing but a stall, and a Butchers dogge
  A sleepe int, where did you see the voyce?
Franscisco.   Shee lookes still angry.
Lance.   To her and meet sir.
Isabella.   Here, here.
Franscisco.   Yes Lady, never blesse your selfe, I am but a man,
  And like an honest man, now I will thanke you——
Isabella.   What do you meane, who sent for you, who desired you?
Shorthose.   Shall I put out the Torch forsooth?
Isabella.   Can I not goe
  About my private meditations, hay,
  But such companions as you must ruffle me?
  You had best goe with me sir.
Franscisco.   Twas my purpose.   30
Isabella.   Why what an impudence is this, you had best,
  Being so neare the Church, provide a Priest,
  And perswade me to marry you.
Franscisco.   It was my meaning,
  And such a husband, so loving, and so carefull,

19 I dreamt] V; ~ was ~ Q1–2, F2, L–D

My youth, and all my fortunes shall arrive at——
Harke you.

Isabella.   Tis strange you should be thus unmannerly,
Turne home againe sirrah, you had best now force my man
To leade your way.

Lance.   Yes marry shall a Lady,
Forward my friend.

Isabella.   This is a pretty Riot,
It may grow to a rape.

Franscisco.   Doe you like that better?   40
I can ravish you an hundred times, and never hurt you.

Shorthose. I see nothing, I am asleepe still, when you have done
Tell me, and then Ile wake Mistris.

Isabella.   Are you in earnest Sir,
Doe you long to be hang'd?

Franscisco.   Yes by my troth Lady
In these faire tresses.

Isabella.   Shall I call out for helpe?

Franscisco. No by no meanes, that were a weake tricke Lady,
Ile kisse and stoppe your mouth.

Isabella.   Youle answer all these.

Franscisco. A thousand kisses more.

Isabella.   I was never abused thus,
You had best give out too, that you found me willing,
And say I doted on you.

Franscisco.   Thats knowne already,   50
And no man living shall now carry you from me.

Isabella. This is fine ifaith.

Franscisco.   It shall be tenne times finer.

Isabella. Well seeing you are so valiant, keepe your way,
I will to Church.

Franscisco.   And I will waite upon you.

Isabella. And it is most likely theres a Priest, if you dare venter
As you professe, I would wish you looke about you,
To doe these rude trickes, for you know their recompences,
And trust not to my mercy.

57 their] Q 1(c); the Q 1(u)

86

Franscisco.   But I will Lady.
Isabella.   For Ile so handle you.
Franscisco.   Thats it I looke for.
Lance.   Afore thou dreame.
Shorthose.   Have you done?
Isabella.   Goe on sir,   60
    And follow if you dare.
Franscisco.   If I doe not, hang me.
Lance.   Tis all thine owne boy, and 'twere a million,
    God a mercy Sacke, when would small Beere have done this?

                                    Exeunt.

                Knocking within. Enter Vallentine.   [V. iv]

Vallentine.   Whose that that knockes and bounces, what a devill
        ailes you,
    Is hell broke loose, or doe you keepe an Iron mill?

                        Enter a Servant.

Servant.   Tis a Gentlewoman sir that must needs speak with you.
Vallentine.   A Gentlewoman, what Gentlewoman, what have I to
        doe with Gentlewomen?
Servant.   She will not be answerd Sir.
Vallentine.   Fling up the bed
    And let her in, Ile try how gentle she is——

                                Exit Servant.

    This sacke has fild my head so full of bables,
    I am almost mad; what Gentlewoman should this be,
    I hope she has brought me no butter print along with her
    To lay to my charge, if she have tis all one,   10
    Ile forsweare it.

                Enter Widdow [*and* Servant].

Widdow.   O you're a noble gallant,
    Send of your servant pray.   *Exit* Servant.
Vallentine.   Shee will not ravish mee?

    [V.iv]] W; *no scene division* Q1–2, F2, L–C   11 you're] F2; your Q1–2

                            87

By this light shee lookes as sharpe set as a Sparrow hawke,
What wouldst thou woman?
Widdow.   O you have used me kindely,
And like a Gentleman, this tis to trust to you.
Vallentine.   Trust to me, for what?
Widdow.   Because I said in jeast once,
You were a hansome man, one I could like well,
And fooling, made you beleeve I loved you, and might
Be brought to marry.
Vallentine.   The Widdow is drunke too.
Widdow.   You out of this, which is a fine discretion,   20
Give out the matters done, you have wonne and wed mee,
And that you have put fairely for an heire too,
These are fine rumours to advance my credit;
Ith name of mischiefe what did you meane?
Vallentine.   That you loved me, and that you might be brought
To marry me? why, what a devill
Doe you meane Widdow?
Widdow.   Twas a fine tricke too,
To tell the world though you had enjoyed your first wish,
You missed the wealth you aimed at; that I was poore,
Which is most true, I am, have sold my Lands,   30
Because I love not those vexations,
Yet for mine honors sake, if you must be prating,
And for my credits sake in the Towne——
Vallentine.   I tell thee Widdow,
I like thee ten times better, now thou hast no Lands,
For now thy hopes and cares, lye on thy husband,
If ere thou marryest more.
Widdow.   Have not you married me,
And for this maine cause, now as you report it,
To be your Nurse?
Vallentine.   My Nurse? why what am I growne too,
Give me the glasse, my Nurse.
Widdow.   You nere said truer,
I must confesse I did a little favour you,   40

29 missed] wished Q 1–2, F 2, L–V

88

And with some labour, might have beene perswaded,
But when I found I must be hourely troubled,
With making brawthes, and dawbing your decaies
With swadling, and with stitching up your ruines,
For the world so reports——
Vallentine.   Doe not provoke me.
Widdow.   And half an eye may see——
Vallentine.   Doe not provoke me,
The worlds a lying world, and thou shalt finde it,
Have a good heart, and take a strong faith to thee,
And marke what followes, my Nurse, yes, you shall rocke me:
Widdow Ile keepe you waking.
Widdow.   You are disposed sir.   50
Vallentine.   Yes marry am I Widdow, and you shall feele it,
Nay and they touch my freehold, I am a Tiger.
Widdow.   I thinke so.
Vallentine.   Come.
Widdow.   Whether?
Vallentine.   Any whether.

Sings.

The fits upon me now,
The fits upon me now,
Come quickely gentle Lady,
The fits upon me now,
The world shall know they are fooles,
And so shalt thou doe too,
Let the Cobler meddle with his tooles,
The fits upon me now.   60

                    Take me quickly
While I am in this vaine, away with me,
For if I have but two houres to consider,
All the Widdowes in the world cannot recover me.
Widdow.   If you will, goe with me sir.
Vallentine.   Yes marry will I,
But tis in anger yet, and I will marry thee,
Doe not crosse me; yes, and I will lie with thee,

And get a whole bundle of babies, and I will kisse thee,
Stand still and kisse me hansomely, but do not provoke me,
Stirre neither hand nor foote, for I am dangerous,   70
I drunk sacke yesternight, doe not allure me:
Thou art no widdow of this world, come
In pitty, and in spite Ile marry thee,
Not a word more, and I may be brought to love thee.

Exeunt.

Enter Merchant *and* Uncle *at severall doores.*   [V. v]

Merchant.   Well met agen, and what good newes yet?
Uncle.   Faith nothing.
Merchant.   No fruites of what we sowed?
Uncle.   Nothing I heare of.
Merchant.   No turning in this tide yet?
Uncle.   Tis all flood,
    And till that fall away, theres no expecting.

Enter Franscisco, Isabella, Lance, Shorthose, *a torch.*

Merchant.   Is not this his younger brother.
Uncle.   With a Gentlewoman
    The Widdowes sister, as I live he smiles,
    He has got good hold, why well said *Francke* ifaith,
    Lets stay and marke.
Isabella.   Well you are the prettiest youth,
    And so you have handled me, thinke you ha me sure.
Franscisco.   As sure as wedlocke.
Isabella.   You had best lye with me too.   10
Franscisco.   Yes indeed will I, and get such blacke ey'd boyes.
Uncle.   God a mercy *Francke.*
Isabella.   This is a merry world, poore simple Gentlewomen
    That thinke no harme, cannot walke about their businesse,
    But they must be catcht up I know not how.
Franscisco.   Ile tell you, and Ile instruct you too,
    Have I caught you Mistresse?

[V.v]] W; *no scene division* Q1-2, F2, L-C

Isabella.   Well, and it were
 Not for pure pitty, I would give you the slip yet,
 But being as it is——
Franscisco.   It shall be better.

   Enter Vallentine, Widdow, *and* Ralph *with a torch.*

Isabella.   My sister as I live, your brother with her,
 Sure I thinke you are the Kings takers.   20
Uncle.   Now it workes.
Vallentine.   Nay you shall know I am a man.
Widdow.   I thinke so.
Vallentine.   And such proofe you shall have——
Widdow.   I pray speake softly.
Vallentine.   Ile speake it out Widdow, yes and you shall confesse
   too,
 I am no nurse child, I went for a man, a good one,
 If you can beate me out oth' pit——
Widdow.   I did but jest with you.
Vallentine.   Ile handle you in earnest, and so handle you:
 Nay when my credit cals——
Widdow.   Are you mad?
Vallentine.   I am mad, I am mad.
Franscisco.   Good morrow Sir, I like your preparation.
Vallentine.   Thou hast beene at it *Francke.*   30
Franscisco.   Yes faith, tis done sir.
Vallentine.   Along with me then, never hang an arse, Widdow.
Isabella.   Tis to no purpose sister.
Vallentine.   Well said blackebrowes,
 Advance your Torches Gentlemen.
Uncle.   Yes, yes sir.
Vallentine.   And keepe your ranckes.
Merchant.   *Lance* carry this before him.
Uncle.   Carry it in state.

   Enter Musitians, Fountaine, Harebraine, Bellamore.

Vallentine.   What are you Musitians,
 I know your comming, and what are those behinde you?

Musitian.   Gentlemen that sent us to give the Lady a good morrow.
Vallentine.   O I know them, come boy sing the song I taught you,
 And sing it lustily, come forward Gentlemen, you're welcome,   40
 Welcome, now we are all friends, goe get the Priest ready,
 And let him not be long, we have much businesse:
 Come *Francke* rejoyce with me, thou hast got the start boy,
 But ile so tumble after, come my friends leade,
 Lead chearefully, and let your fiddles ring boyes,
 My follies and my fancies have an end here,
 Display the morgage *Lance,* Merchant ile pay you,
 And every thing shall be in joynt agen.
Uncle.   Afore, afore.
Vallentine.   And now confesse, and know,
 Wit without Money, sometimes gives the blow.   50
            Exeunt.

    40 you're] F2; your Q1–2

TEXTUAL NOTES

I.i

18 vented] Q2 establishes the tradition of 'ventured' (to be rendered as 'ventered' in the conventions of Q1). 'These he would have ventered | Into more manly uses' is the more obvious and intelligible reading. But 'vented' in the sense of *O.E.D. s.v.* vent v² 1.7c 'to spend, get rid of a fortune' remains a distinct possibility and has been retained. (*O.E.D.* cites from Ben Jonson, *Alchemist*, III.iv: 'How doe they live by their wits, there, that have vented | Six times your fortunes?')

I.ii

34–35 march oft | With our faire wedding Colours flying] A passage affected, though not clarified, by the numerous press-corrections in C(o). The separation of 'withour' (Q(u)), which has been accepted, indicates the purely typographical nature of these corrections. Where they change possible copy spellings – 'too' for 'to' (38), 'studied' and 'Studies' for 'studded' [= 'studdied'] (45) and 'Studdies' (48); also 'Fircug' for 'Furcug' (II.ii.37) – or alter the idiom – 'nay's death' for 'nay death' (51) and 'you' for 'he' (57; see below) – they have not been adopted.

Isabella's sense in her syntactically elliptic simile improves with the Q2 emendation of 'without' (34) for 'with' and the recognition by Seward of a compound 'wedding Colours' behind Q1's 'wedding: Colours'. But whether the suitors, upon terms made ('compound' (33)) after their siege, 'march off' (the reading from Q2 onwards) or 'march oft' with those wedding colours, is still open to question. The iterative in 'oft' is attractive enough to be retained.

57 he] Q(c) changes to 'you' and thus incorporates the line in Franscisco's address to Lance. In the uncorrected reading, 'he' refers to Lance and thus marks the line as an aside, or reflection spoken *sotto voce*.

II.ii

1 lookt thee] The transitive construction is possible (*O.E.D., s.v.* look 1.6.d) and is repeatedly used in this play; cf. II.iv.85; IV.v.36.

II.iv

72 *Megeras*] 'Chimeras' (Seward) is an attractive emendation; but the apparently nonsensical term (a malapropism?) may yet be good enough for Lance.

143 I am cosened if after her] Patently a corruption. But Q2 'Or I am cozened else' is equally glibly a cliché substitution with no apparent authority. C's emendation 'I am cozened if—— After her!', ironically setting the stage for a potential confrontation of Franscisco with the Widow's wooers, and Valentine's dupes, may still have most to recommend it.

III.ii

97 nappes] Seward introduces a convincing emendation for competing 'napfes' and napſes' in the early editions. The full plural suffix in Q1 suggests the spelling here constructed.

III.v

2 shotten-sold] I.e., 'shotten-souled'; cf. *O.E.D. s.v.* shotten 3 b.

25 How miserable] Metrically this completes line 23. Line 24, shared by the Widow and Luce, as unobserved listeners to Harebraine's and Valentine's dialogue, is metrically an aside. Cf. IV.iv.60 and 62, and IV.iv.126 and 128.

IV.ii

43 lend] Q2 'lead' undoubtedly makes straighter sense. But 'lend' may be correct in the sense of *O.E.D. s.v.* lend v², 2α 'To give, grant, bestow'.

V.i

47 bay] Q2 emends to 'bouy' (= 'buoy'). But the form may either belong to the variegated hunting terminology in this play, or else denote *O.E.D. s.v.* bay v³, 'To obstruct, dam (water)'.

83.1 Humphrey [*and*] Ralph] Q1: *Hum, a servant.* Q2 takes 'a servant' in apposition to Humphrey and changes Q1 *Ralph* at 86 to *Hum.* But clearly the Widow gives orders to two servants in the scene.

V.ii

36 *Merchant*] From F2 onwards, *May* (Q1–2) is considered a corruption of *Boy.* But if taken as a corruption of *Mer*, it reduces the demand for supernumerary boys to carry torches in the several successive night scenes of the final act.

PRESS-VARIANTS IN Q1

[Copies collated: Bodl¹ (Bodleian Library Malone 243(5)), Bodl² (Bodleian Library Malone 160(4)), BL¹ (British Library 643.g.21), BL² (British Library 644.d.22), BL³ (Wise Collection Ashley 91; supplies Sheet F from Q2), Chap (Chapin Library, Williams College), GU (Glasgow University), KC (King's College, Cambridge), MC (Magdalene College, Cambridge), TC¹ (Trinity College, Cambridge, VI.10.47²), Worc (Worcester College, Oxford); copy compared: TC² (Trinity College, Cambridge, Capell S.4³); copies not seen: Eton College, Sheffield University, Boston Public Library, Clark Library, Library of Congress, Folger Library, Harvard, Newberry Library, New York Public Library, Pierpont Morgan Library, Pforzheimer Collection, Texas, and the private copies of Robert Taylor (Princeton) and Robert Perry.]

SHEET C (*outer forme*)

Corrected: Bodl¹, Bodl², BL², BL³, Chap, GU, KC, MC, TC², Worc
Uncorrected: BL¹, TC¹

Sig. C1
   I.ii.35 with our] withour
   I.ii.38 too?] to?
   I.ii.45 studyed] studded
   I.ii.46 all] a l
   I.ii.48 Studies ,] Studdies,
   I.ii.51 nay's] nay
   I.ii.57 & though you] and ~ he
   I.ii.57 slight,] ~ ∧
Sig. C3
   II.ii.36 Meacockes,] ~ ∧
   II.ii.36 miserable,] ~ ∧
   II.ii.37 Fircug,] Furcug,
Sig. C4ᵛ
   II.iii.22 heard] heare

SHEET F (*inner forme*)

Corrected: Bodl¹, BL¹, BL², GU, KC, MC, TC¹
Uncorrected: Bodl², Chap, TC², Worc

Sig. F2
   III.v.89 labour,] ~ ∧

95

III.v.90 sir₍ₐ₎] ~,
III.v.113 downe] dow
Sig. F3ᵛ
IV.ii.10 Gentlemen,] Gentleman,
Sig. F4
IV.ii.34 off] of

SHEET G

Corrected: Bodl¹, Bodl², BL¹, BL³, Chap, GU, KC, MC, TC¹, TC², Worc
Uncorrected: BL²

Sig. G1ᵛ
IV.iv.49 privacies₍ₐ₎] ~,
Sig. G4
IV.v.6 your] you
c.w. (*out of alignment*)] (*aligned*)

SHEET H

Corrected: Bodl¹, Bodl², BL¹, BL², BL³, Chap, GU, KC, MC, TC¹, TC²
Uncorrected: Worc

Sig. H1
IV.v.62 Theamea,] Theame.,
IV.v.67 gone] goe
IV.v.72 houre] houres
Sig. H2ᵛ
V.i.54 he] h e
V.i.54 a] *omit*
V.i.54 loose] losoe

SHEET I

Corrected: Bodl¹, Bodl², BL¹, BL², Chap, GU, KC, MC, TC¹, TC²
Uncorrected: BL³, Worc

Sig. I1ᵛ
V.iii.57 their] the

I.i

1 *Vallentine?*] Q2; ~ . Q1
3 people?] F2; ~ , Q1–2
12 use‸] Q2; ~ . Q1
26 women?] F2; ~ . Q1–2
34 show.] F2; ~ ; Q1–2
34 lovers:] ~ ‸ Q1–2, F2
37 Towne?] F2; ~ . Q1–2
39 Widdow‸] F2; ~ , Q1–2
40 you——] F2; ~ . Q1–2
52 fort;] ~ , Q1; *om.* Q2, F2
62 next——] C; ~ . Q1–2, F2
64 able——] C; ~ : Q1–2, F2
72 still;] F2; ~ , Q1–2
77 so?] F2; ~ : Q1–2
85 Phew,] Q2; ~ ‸ Q1
86 angry.] Q2; ~ ; Q1
87 people?] Q2; ~ , Q1
88 Why,] F2; ~ ‸ Q1–2
90 um?] F2; ~ : Q1–2
92 bangd] Q2; baugd Q1
92 too?] F2; ~ , Q1–2
94 garlicke,] Q2; ~ ‸ Q1
99 weare?] F2; ~ , Q1–2
103 beauties?] F2; ~ , Q1–2
104 no,] Q2; ~ ‸ Q1
109 next?] F2; ~ , Q1–2
117 state, sir,] Q2; ~ ‸ ~ ‸ Q1
121 pitty?] F2; ~ : Q1–2
123 edifie;] Q2; ~ , Q1

124 withall:] F2; ~ , Q1–2
125 Landlord,] Q2; ~ ‸ Q1
141 breeding:] F2; ~ , Q1–2
148 Carryers;] F2; ~ ‸ Q1–2
148 upont,] Q2; ~ ‸ Q1
152 you?] Q2; ~ , Q1
161 lodging‸] F2; ~ , Q1–2
163 To be] Q2; ~ remoove; and
      when I please to ~ Q1
164 peece‸] F2; ~ , Q1–2
165 here?] F2; ~ . Q1–2
166 last, sir?] F2; ~ ‸ ~ . Q1–2
170 int;] F2; ~ , Q1–2
175 Grasiers?] F2; ~ : Q1–2
180 equall?] F2; ~ . Q1–2
182 money?] F2; ~ , Q1–2
201 these?] F2; ~ : Q1–2
207 ounces?] F2; ~ , Q1–2
209 butchers?] F2; ~ , Q1–2
212 breedes?] F2; ~ ; Q1–2
233 is,] F2; ~ ‸ Q1–2
234 unholsome;] F2; ~ , Q1–2
237 wicked;] F2; ~ , Q1–2
238 selfe;] F2; ~ , Q1–2
239 wanton;] F2; ~ , Q1–2
243 blessings:] ~ , Q1–2, F2
244 woman ——] ~ . Q1–2, F2
249 you:] ~ , Q1–2, F2

I.ii

8 I?] F2; ~ , Q1–2
12 where,] F2; ~ ‸ Q1–2
19 Merchant:] Q2; ~ , Q1
28 faith:] F2; ~ , Q1–2
30 provokers;] L; ~ , Q1–2, F2

35 flying.] F2; ~ , Q1–2
35 Who] Q2; who Q1
37 built] Q2; bult Q1
39 study?] Q2; ~ . Q1
43 me‸ thus?] F2; ~ , ~ ‸ Q1–2

97

44 natures.] F2; ~ , Q1–2
45 studdied] Q2; studded Q1(u);
　studyed Q1(c) .
49 *Lance?*] Q2; ~ . Q1
55 by——] F2; ~ . Q1–2
56 brother——] ~ , Q1–2, F2
57 brother——] ~ : Q1–2, F2
58 gentleman,] F2; ~ ∧ Q1–2

62 you;] F2; ~ , Q1–2
69 wanted?] F2; ~ . Q1–2
70 changes!] F2; ~ , Q1–2
73 thousand!] F2 ~ , Q1–2
75 shadowes∧ by,] S; ~ , ~ ∧
　Q1–2, F2
84 I?] F2; ~ . Q1–2

II.i

1 pitty!] F2; ~ , Q1–2
6 much?] Q2; ~ . Q1
11 afflictions?] F2; ~ : Q1–2
18 gentleman?] Q2; ~ . Q1
22 Knave:] F2; ~ , Q1–2

24 understand:] F2; ~ , Q1–2
26 first;] F2; ~ , Q1–2
26 Councells;] Q2; ~ , Q1
29 it;] ~ , Q1–2, F2
30 wore;] Q2; ~ , Q1

II.ii

7 you:] Q2; ~ , Q1
8 aftergames?] Q2; ~ , Q1
19 um:] Q2; ~ , Q1
20 widdow?] Q2; ~ , Q1
24 answer;] Q2; ~ , Q1
28 in. Marke] Q2; ~ , marke Q1
32 Epitaphs:] Q2; ~ , Q1
33 truth;] F2; ~ , Q1–2
44 discretions;] Q2; ~ , Q1
46 made;] F2; ~ , Q1–2
48 trinkets;] F2; ~ , Q1–2

50 us,] F2; ~ ∧ Q1–2
51–52 cowards. | What] Q2; ~ ,
　what Q1
53 disobedience?] Q2; ~ , Q1
54 yeares?] Q2; ~ ; Q1
54 father:] Q2; ~ , Q1
63 nature. Will] ~ , will Q1–2, F2
74 away;] F2; ~ ∧ Q1–2
88 you?] Q2; ~ . Q1
110 worthy——] C; ~ . Q1–2, F2
115 foolisher:] F2; ~ , Q1–2

II.iii

1 sure?] F2; ~ . Q1–2
2 brother?] F2; ~ . Q1–2
3 truth?] F2; ~ . Q1–2
5 pitty.] L; ~ , Q1–2, F2
7 [1,2]blacke?] F2; ~ . Q1–2
8 him?] F2; ~ . Q1–2
12 man?] F2; ~ . Q1–2
15 kindred?] F2; ~ : Q1–2
16 worth?] F2; ~ . Q1–2
17 live?] F2; ~ . Q1–2

18 brother?] C; ~ . Q1–2, F2
27 *London:*] F2; ~ , Q1–2
30 you∧] Q2; ~ , Q1
34 wit∧] F2; ~ , Q1–2
50 goe——] C; ~ : Q1–2, F2
51 is——] C; ~ : Q1–2, F2
55 sudden?] F2; ~ ; Q1–2
59 wench?] Q2; ~ , Q1
60 this,] Q2; ~ ∧ Q1

II.iv

1 live !] F2; ~ , Q1–2
2 question?] Q2; ~ . Q1
6 *France?*] Q2; ~ , Q1
7 thee?] Q2; ~ : Q1
15 *Francke?*] F2; ~ . Q1–2
16 pound?] Q2; ~ : Q1
21 wretchednesse͵] F2; ~ , Q1–2
25 pound !)] F2; ~ ͵) Q1–2
25 boy?] Q2; ~ : Q1
26 more͵] F2; ~ , Q1–2
27 justifie,] F2; ~ ͵ Q1–2
27 it:] F2; ~ , Q1–2
41 doe?] Q2; ~ . Q1
43 live?] F2; ~ , Q1–2
44 question?] F2; ~ , Q1–2
48 harvests:] F2; ~ , Q1–2
50 Scholler:] F2; ~ , Q1–2
51 live?] F2; ~ , Q1–2
66 wayes?] Q2; ~ . Q1
73 ballads?] Q2; ~ . Q1

79 girles?] Q2; ~ . Q1
83 us?] Q2; ~ . Q1
87 friend?] Q2; ~ . Q1
89 moneths.] ~ ͵ Q1–2, F2
91 penny;] F2; ~ , Q1–2
96 sir?] Q2; ~ . Q1
104 *Franscisco?*] Q2; ~ . Q1
106 it?] Q2; ~ . Q1
114 know——] F2; ~ . Q1–2
116 bagges?] F2; ~ : Q1–2
118 wit,] Q2; ~ ͵ Q1
119 sir,] Q2; ~ ͵ Q1
123 whom?] C; ~ . Q1–2, F2
126 this?] Q2; ~ . Q1
150 *Vallentine* !] F2; ~ . Q1–2
150 so?] Q2; ~ . Q1
154 her?] F2; ~ . Q1–2
155 *Vallentine*——] D; *Valle.* Q1–2, F2
156 *Vallentine.*] L; *Vall.* Q1–2, F2

II.v

8 journey?] F2; ~ . Q1–2
11 Country?] F2; ~ . Q1–2
33 wenches?] F2; ~ . Q1–2
40 um?] F2; ~ , Q1–2

41 plate——] C; ~ : Q1–2, F2
42 fellowes?] F2; ~ . Q1–2
42 boote?] F2; ~ . Q1–2
43 say?] F2; ~ : Q1–2

III.i

2 tongue,] F2; ~ : Q1–2
15 carried.] F2; ~ , Q1–2
28 Mistresse——] C; ~ . Q1–2, F2

41 matter?] Q2; ~ . Q1
71 penny] Q2; peenny Q1
73 for?] F2; ~ . Q1–2
73 time?] Q2; ~ . Q1

III.ii

4 pray:] C; ~ ͵ Q1–2, F2
4 *London*] Q2; London Q1
8 *Highgate*] Q2; Highgate Q1
10 *London*] Q2; London Q1

17 *Bellswagger*] Q2; Bellswagger Q1
22 laugh?] F2; ~ . Q1–2
31 Gentleman?] F2; ~ . Q1–2

99

34 condition,] F2; ~ ₳ Q1–2
38 others?] F2; ~ . Q1–2
39 sure?] F2; ~ : Q1–2
62 else?] F2; ~ , Q1–2
67 proud——] C; ~ : Q1–2, F2
69 us?] Q2; ~ , Q1
70–71 right, |Affronts] F2; ~ ₳ afronts, Q1–2
76 difference?] Q2; ~ , Q1
82 people!] F2; ~ , Q1–2
90 you?] F2; ~ , Q1–2
94 cracke?] Q2; ~ ; Q1
95 Lady,] Q2; ~ . Q1
96 *Mile End*] F2; mile end Q1–2
110 ambushes,] Q2; ~ ₳ Q1
116 Prospectives?] F2; ~ . Q1–2
126 light,] C; ~ ; Q1–2, F2
127 creatures,] Q2; ~ ₳ Q1
130 substance?] F2; ~ ; Q1–2

136 Whoremasters;] D; ~ , Q1–2, F2
151 man,] Q2; ~ ₳ Q1
151 else——] W; ~ , Q1–2, F2
155 come,] Q2; ~ ₳ Q1
160 sir;] Q2; ~ ? Q1
164 monstrous——] F2; ~ . Q1–2
164 strangely——] C; ~ . Q1–2, F2
165 sure?] F2; ~ . Q1–2
172 husbands!] F2; ~ , Q1–2
173 sir,] F2; ~ ; Q1–2
173 example?] F2; ~ , Q1–2
185 Excellent,] Q2; ~ ₳ Q1
196 husbands!] F2; ~ , Q1–2
199 Gentleman:] Q2; ~ , Q1
202 she?] F2; ~ , Q1–2
205 thus?] F2; ~ . Q1–2
213 um?] F2; ~ , Q1–2
214 *Valentine?*] F2; *Velentine*; Q1–2

III.iii

0.1 Lance;] C; *Lance*, Q1–2, F2
1 us?] F2; ~ . Q1–2
3 him?] Q2; ~ . Q1
5 thinke?] F2; ~ . Q1–2

11 him——] F2; ~ . Q1–2
18 yet——] C; ~ . Q1–2, F2
19 us——] W; ~ , Q1–2, F2

III.iv

1 him?] F2; ~ . Q1–2

III.v

8 worships?...hether,] C; ~ ₳ ~ ? Q1–2, F2
20 ye are] yeare Q1–2, F2
28 now,] ~ ₳ Q1–2, F2
59 knowledge?] F2; ~ ₳ Q1–2
76 man?] F2; ~ , Q1–2
83 Knaves] F2; ~ , Q1–2
83 rendred. Freemen,] F2; ~ ₳ freemen₳ Q1–2
86 thus?] F2; ~ . Q1–2

90 sir,] Q2; ~ ₳ Q1
92 nature,] F2; ~ ; Q1–2
93 coates?] F2; ~ , Q1–2
95 interdiction] Q2; intredition Q1
101 *Albones?*] Q2; ~ . Q1
101 Gentlemen,] Q2; ~ ₳ Q1
126 streetes] Q2; steetes Q1

IV.i

1 him?] Q2; ~ ∧ Q1
11 him?] Q2; ~ . Q1
21 why] Q2; Why Q1
25 ruines!] F2; ~ , Q1–2
31 friends?] Q2; ~ . Q1
32 Th'art] Q2; Thar't Q1

50 um?] Q2; ~ . Q1
53 labour?] F2; ~ , Q1–2
54 woman?] F2; ~ , Q1–2
58 want?] Q2; ~ , Q1
73 heartily.] ~ ∧ Q1–2, F2
74 conscience,] F2; ~ ∧ Q1–2

IV.ii

12 these?] Q2; ~ . Q1
14 so?] Q2; ~ , Q1
21 though;] Q2; ~ , Q1

25 her?] F2; ~ : Q1–2
40 stay;] F2; ~ , Q1–2
45 this——] C; ~ . Q1–2, F2

IV.iii

1 since?] C; ~ . Q1–2, F2
2 um?] F2; ~ : Q1–2
6 bountie,] Q2; ~ ∧ Q1
8 goe?] F2; ~ . Q1–2
9 it?] F2; ~ , Q1–2

11 doores;] C; ~ , Q1–2, F2
24 woman?] F2; ~ . Q1–2
25 else?] F2; ~ , Q1–2
31 gotten] Q2; gotton Q1
35 meanes;] C; ~ , Q1–2, F2

IV.iv

1 puppies?] F2; ~ , Q1–2
3 Gentlemen.] F2; gentlemen,
   Q1–2
3 Sprecious,] Q2; Spercious Q1
8 drinke?] F2; ~ . Q1–2
16 vext?] Q2; ~ . Q1
19 times?] F2; ~ . Q1–2
49 privacies,] Q1(u); ~ ∧ Q1(c)
50 hate,] F2; ~ ∧ Q1–2
56 her?] F2; ~ . Q1–2
62 sister?] F2; ~ , Q1–2
64 um?] F2; ~ . Q1–2
69 out?] F2; ~ . Q1–2
70 suiters——] C; ~ . Q1–2, F2
70 um?] F2; ~ . Q1–2
72 in?] F2; ~ . Q1–2
74 too?] F2; ~ . Q1–2
80 sir?] Q2; ~ . Q1
86 This,] Q2; ~ ∧ Q1

102 Lady——] C; ~ . Q1–2, F2
108 end;] Q2; ~ , Q1
109 suspicious.] F2; ~ : Q1–2
113 it;] F2; ~ ∧ Q1–2
115 person——] C; ~ . Q1–2, F2
137 that, Wench?] Q2; ~ ∧ ~ . Q1
142 taker?] F2; ~ . Q1–2
158 foresights.] F2; ~ , Q1–2
161 not∧...eyes:] C; ~ , ... ~ ∧
    Q1–2, F2
164 Feare not,] Q2; feare ~ ∧ Q1
165 it.] F2; ~ , Q1–2
166 precisely?] F2; ~ , Q1–2
168 narrowly:] F2; ~ , Q1–2
171 courage?] Q2; ~ . Q1
189 fortunes!] F2; ~ . Q1–2
195 you?] F2; ~ . Q1–2
197 yours?] Q2; ~ . Q1
200 compassion?] F2; ~ . Q1–2

205 me,] Q2; ~ ‸ Q1
205 infectious,] D; ~ ‸ Q1–2, F2
213 wastcoateers,] F2; wast-|coat-
    eers. Q1–2

221 this?] F2; ~ . Q1–2
225 vow——] C; ~ . Q1–2, F2
228 gugaw,] F2; gu-|gaw‸ Q1–2
240 hopes;] Q2; ~ ‸ Q1

IV.v

33–34 sir. | How] ±F2; ~ , how
    Q1–2
43 familliar?] F2; ~ . Q1–2

72–73 rascalls, |So‸] ~ ‸ so, Q1–2,
    F2
90 pitty] Q2; pittty Q1

V.i

1 tis‸] F2; ~ , Q1–2
5 *Vallentine*] F2; *Vellentine* Q1–2
8 earely?] F2; ~ . Q1–2
24 Mare——] C; ~ . Q1–2, F2
31 and] Q2; aud Q1
33 gratulate‸] Q2; ~ , Q1
34 He's] Q2; Hes Q1
42 knot?] Q2; ~ . Q1

50 one?] Q2; ~ , Q1
55 Gentleman;] Q2; ~ , Q1
58 Widdow,] Q2; ~ ‸ Q1
61 then?] F2; ~ . Q1–2
80 game?] Q2; ~ , Q1
83 how——] W; ~ , Q1–2, F2
85 onely;] C; ~ , Q1–2, F2

V.ii

1 hansomely:] F2; ~ , Q1–2
1 *Francke?*] Q2; ~ , Q1
3 drinke?] Q2; ~ . Q1
5 *Memphis?*] F2; ~ . Q1–2
8 cause——] ~ . Q1–2, F2
16 stranger?] F2; ~ , Q1–2
19 sleepe?] F2; ~ . Q1–2
20 eate?] F2; ~ . Q1–2
27 meanes,] Q2; ~ ‸ Q1
28 *Malligo*] F2; Malligo Q1–2
31 goe?] Q2; ~ . Q1
32 cannot,] Q2; ~ ‸ Q1

32 fancies.] Q2; ~ : Q1
41 me?] Q2; ~ . Q1
42 sentence?] Q2; ~ . Q1
44 it.] Q2; ~ : Q1
46 Uncle?] Q2; ~ , Q1
48 sir?] Q2; ~ . Q1
56 this?] Q2; ~ . Q1
57 sir?] Q2; ~ . Q1
65 mine;] Q2; ~ , Q1
80 *Bowbell*] F2; Bowbell Q1–2
91 had——] C; ~ . Q1–2, F2

V.iii

1 now?] F2; ~ . Q1–2
4 me:] C; ~ ‸ Q1–2, F2
6 shee?] F2; ~ , Q1–2
8 ring?] F2; ~ . Q1–2
10 yond?] F2; ~ . Q1–2
15 on!] F2; ~ , Q1–2

15 she:] F2; ~ , Q1–2
18 ont.] F2; ~ , Q1–2
22 voyce?] F2; ~ . Q1–2
26 you?] F2; ~ ‸ Q1–2
27 forsooth?] F2; ~ . Q1–2
29 me?] F2; ~ , Q1–2

40 better?] F2; ~ , Q1–2
44 hang'd?] F2; ~ . Q1–2
45 helpe?] F2; ~ . Q1–2

60 done?] F2; ~ . Q1–2
61 not,] F2; ~ ˄ Q1–2
63 this?] F2; ~ . Q1–2

V.iv

2 mill?] F2; ~ . Q1–2
12 mee?] F2; ~ , Q1–2
14 woman?] F2; ~ . Q1–2
16 what?] Q2; ~ . Q1
20 this,] F2; ~ ˄ Q1–2
24 meane?] Q2; ~ . Q1
26 me?] F2; ~ , Q1–2

27 Widdow?] Q2; ~ . Q1
33 Towne——] C; ~ . Q1–2, F2
38 ¹Nurse?] F2; ~ . Q1–2
38 ²Nurse?] F2; ~ , Q1–2
45 reports——] C; ~ . Q1–2, F2
46 see——] C; ~ . Q1–2, F2
53 Whether?] F2; ~ . Q1–2

V.v

1 yet?] Q2; ~ . Q1
2 sowed?] Q2; ~ . Q1
3 yet?] Q2; ~ . Q1
17 Mistresse?] F2; ~ . Q1–2
19 is——] C; ~ . Q1–2, F2
23 have——] C; ~ . Q1–2, F2
26 pit——] C; ~ . Q1–2, F2

29 cals——] C; ~ . Q1–2, F2
29 mad?] Q2; ~ . Q1
37 you?] F2; ~ . Q1–2
38 Lady˄] F2; ~ , Q1–2
41 friends,] Q2; ~ ˄ Q1
49 know,] Q2; ~ . Q1

HISTORICAL COLLATION

[Editions collated: Q 1 (Quarto, 1639), Q 2 (Quarto, 1661), F 2 (Folio, 1679), L (Langbaine, 1711), S (Seward, 1750), C (Colman, 1778), W (Weber, 1812), D (Dyce, 1843), V (*Variorum*, ed. R. B. McKerrow, 1805).]

I.i

12 Gentleman] Gent Q 1–2
12 estate] Estate's S
16 Maintaining] maintaine Q 1–2
18 vented] ventured Q 2, F 2, L
44 Reserved, a great Fortune] ~ , and ~ ~ Q 1–2, F 2, L; ~ and ~ ; ~ S–V
52 The...fort;] *om.* Q 2, F 2, L
56 a] *om.* Q 2, F 2, L
56 *Enter...tennants*] ~ *three* ~ Q 1–2, F 2, L–C; ~ Lance *and three* ~ W; ~ Lance *and two* ~ D
66 my] *om.* S–W
96 Can...Stallions,] *om.* Q 1
100 your] you D
101 pots of ale] Oats and Hay S
104 are] *add* all Q 2, F 2, L–D
106 Land] *add* sir Q 2, F 2, L–D

113 broth] both S
115 of] *om.* Q 1–2
115 you have a wit;] you have wit͓ S; ~ ~ ; ~ ~ ͓ C
124 And] to Q 2, F 2, L–C
135 tennants] tenements Q 1, W–D
149 foole] Tool L
157 Tavernes] Tavern's S–C
160 opens] open C, D
172 hindes] hid Q 1
174 I'd shift it] I shifted Q 1, C
183 My] *om.* Q 2, F 2, L
185 other] *om.* Q 2, F 2, L
212 *Andeluria*] *Andeluzia* F 2, L–V
216 beanes] Beasts S
216 *Rumnillo*] *Rumney* S, C
221 finde] *om.* Q 2
224 for] from Q 1
248 estate] state S–V

I.ii

11 satten] sattens Q 2, F 2, L–S
19 and] *om.* Q 2, F 2, L–S
21 essaies͓ a pretty poet,] Essays, ~ ~ ~, Q 2, F 2–V
26 meane] main Q 2, F 2, L–V
34 Without] with Q 1
34 oft] off Q 2, F 2, L–V
35 wedding Colours] ~ : ~ Q 1–2; ~ , ~ F 2, L
43 me͓ thus?] ~ , ~ ͓ Q 1–2

50 titles] tiles S–D
51 Nay] nay's Q 1(c), Q 2, F 2, L–V
57 he] you Q 1(c), Q 2, F 2, L–V
61 The] *om.* Q 1
68 and mind] ~ a ~ Q 1–2, S–W
68 there together] *om.* Q 2, F 2, L–S; there D
75 shadowes͓ by,] ~ , ~ ͓ Q 1–2, F 2, L

79–80 but...cold] but will that   Q2, F2, L
keep him from cold and hunger   82 and] *om.* Q2, F2, L

II.i

18 would] that ~ Q2, F2, L–S

II.ii

1 lookt thee] ~ for ~ Q2, F2,   47 wife] wise Q1–2, F2, L
L–D   60 ham'd] hand Q1
6 Not] no, not Q2, F2, C; no not   94 puppits] Puppet-shows S
to S   95 maide content] ~ will be ~ Q2,
6 nor] or L–S   F2, L–S; maid's ~ C–D
20 wooe] wed D   98 bed agreed,] ~, aged, Q1–2, F2,
29 mens‸ livings,] newes, livings‸   L, C–W; ~ , one Good. S
Q1–2, F2, L   99 the wife] the wise Q2, F2, I
30 Upon] *om.* S   thee wise S
37 Furcug] firecock W   105 your] her Q1–2, F2
42 nothing] nothings Q2, F2, L–V   115 come] comes Q1

II.iii

2, 4 *Isabella.*] *Hare.* Q1–2, F2   48 bith] both Q2
3 *Isabella.*] *om.* Q2; *Hare.* Q1, F2   49 so] *om.* Q2, F2, L–S
22 heare] heard Q1(c), Q2, F2,   49 first] *om.* Q2, F2, L–C
L–V   57 they] thy Q2, F2, L
33 'Is] Is Q1–2

II.iv

6 *France*] frame D   96 spend] spent Q1
8 ²himselfe] him Q2, F2, L–C   106 not you] you not Q2, F2, L
9 his] *om.* Q2, F2, L   133 into] in to F2, L–V
13 Gentlemans] Gentleman Q1   143 I...her,] or I am couzened else,
46 and] *om.* F2, L–S   Q2, F2, L–S; I am cozen'd,
47 Aske] and ask F2, L–S   if—— After her! C–W; I am
57 leven] Levant S   cozen'd, if [not] after her; D–V
61 on *Poules*] ~ St. *Paul's* S   149.1 Lance] *Val.* Q1–2, F2
67 from] o' S   149.2 Harebraine] *Vallentine* Q1–2,
72 *Megeras*] megeras Q1; megera's   F2; *om.* L
Q2, F2, L; Chimeras S–W;   155 *Vallentine*——] *Valle.* Q1; *Val.*
vagaries D–V   Q2, F2, L–W
89 twelve moneths] twelvemonth   156 *Vallentine.*] *Vall.* Q1–2, F2,
Q2, F2, L–V   C–W

II.v

8 Why] Who L
9 now?] now Q 1–2
28 flippery] frippery S–D

30 distillations] distibations Q 1–2,
   F 2, L
37 And] add make S–V

III.i

19 Butcher] butler S–V
29 sometimes] sometime Q 2, F 2,
   L–S
49 me] my Q 1; your Q 2, F 2, L–C
50 follies] Tollies L
60 you] ~ to Q 2, F 2, L–S

60 this] om. S
63 ²know] knows Q 1–2
71 poets] pots Q 1
73 Ist] Its Q 1
77 and] om. Q 2, F 2
78 maine] mean L–S

III.ii

4 from] om. S–W
10 Bike] om. S–V
22 Humphrey.] Short. Q 1–2, F 2,
   L–S
32 feather] fever S–V
36 milde] wild S–W, V; vild D
45 little:] ~ ‸ Q 2, F 2, L
46 grieve] grieved F 2, L–V
60–61 it, | Is] ~ , it is Q 2, F 2; ~ ,
   it is, Sir, ±S
63 like] which ~ S–C
65 His] as his Q 2, F 2, L–S
70–71 right, | Affronts and] ~ ~ ,
   ~ Q 1–2; ~ : ~ are ±C
94 Cases] causes Q 2, F 2, L–C
97 nappes] napfes Q 1–2, F 2, L;
   neives D

116 Prospectives] Perspectives F 2,
   L–W
119 ah] O' F 2, L–V
125 confusions] conclusions Q 1–2,
   F 2, L
127 creatures, next ... malice:]
   ~ ‸ ~ ... ~ : Q 1; ~ : ~ ... ~ ,
   W–V
127 the devills] Devils in S
129 not we] we not C–W
130 beholding] beholden S–W
130 substance] sufferance S–V
147 giddie-eyed,] ~ ‸ F 2, L–D
156 a] of a S, W–D
178 right] ~ good S, D
226 in with] within Q 1

III.iii

6 cause] add he S–V
16 home] whom Q 1

20 Good e'n] good on Q 1–2, F 2, L

III.iv

2 clapt] clap Q 1
8 behaviours] behaviour F 2, L–S

10 prosecute] persecute S–D

III.v

2 shotten-sold] ~ , ~ Q 1–2, F 2, L

7 filed] filled Q 2, F 2, L

11 beere] bare Q 1; base Q 2, F 2, L

14 kites] rites Q 1–2, F 2, L

14 prises] prising Q 1–2, F 2, L

16 *Brittanes*] Breton's S–V

36 worship] worships Q 1–2

37 sizes] sizer Q 1

42 And] a Q 2, F 2, L–S

42 breeches] bleeches Q 1

47 me] *om.* Q 2, F 2, L–S

55 beholding] beholden C–W

58 ²are] or I S–V

69 And...body] And almost every way that one can perish; My | Body S; And every way; if one cold perish me, | Body D–V

70 beare the blame] ~ cold, but they ~ ~ S

81 mewd] moved Q 1–2, F 2, L, W

84 innocent,ʌ] innocents, Q 1–2, F 2 L–C

90 not] *om.* F 2, L–S, D

92 no] *om.* C

113 pound] pounds F 2, L–V

117 *the doore*] *a house door* W

131 these] this L–S

132 cloudes; I thinke] ~ , ~ ~ ! D–V

IV.i

6 must] most Q 1

29–30 how dee, | Thinke now] howʌ d'ye think now S; how, d'ye think now D–V

62 a great] as great a S; a greater W–V

IV.ii

7–8 whistling | For meanes,] ~ ; for means S–V

9 sure, teach] ~ . We'll ~ S–V

32 She] See Q 2

43 lend] lead Q 2, F 2, L–V

IV.iii

8 give thankes sir] give thanks Q 2, F 2, L; give her thanks S

9 parts deserves] part ~ Q 2; ~ deserve F 2, L–D

10 to] *om.* F 2, L–V

11 doores] doore Q 2, F 2, L S

IV.iv

1 me] *om.* Q 2, F 2, L–S

1–2 you...knaves severall] you several blind rascals, drunken knaves S; you...knaves C–V

3 ²you] *om.* Q 2, F 2, L

8 drinke] drunk F 2, L–S

10 boy] bay Q 2

16 so] *om.* Q 2, F 2, L

20 and] *om.* S–C

21 We live] me ~ Q 1; men love Q 2, F 2, L; Love S; Come C

27 title] little Q 2, F 2, L–S, D–V

28 not] *om.* S
68 hound] sound Q2, F2, L
93 wils] will Q2, F2, L–S
114 thought] *add* your S
121 bartred] bettered F2, L–S
132 and] *add* to your S; *add* your D
145 worse,] ~ ? F2, L–W
146 speake,] ~ ? D–V
148 does] do C–D
159 ermines] crimes Q1–2, F2
167 or] not S–C
168 Gentlemen] Gentleman S
182 dragon] paragon S

190 alone] a love Q1–2
192 'would] t'would Q2, F2, L; you would S–V
200 a] *om.* S–W
207 beleeved] beleeve Q1–2
209 Your] This your S
217 eyes] eyres D–V
218 you see] 'see Q1–2, F2
233 see] saw F2, L–V
233 taile] tale W–V
237 stoppes] stoops W–V
244 soft] as soft S–C
248 soone‚ at night;] ~ : ~ ~ ‚S–V
252 putst] puts Q2

IV.v

6 'have] you have C
6 your] you Q1(u)
6 'vexe] you vex C
7 my] a S, D–V
10 an] a Q1
15 doe] *add* no D–V
17 grase] grace V
21 hee's] that he's S
22 Faces] Face F2, L–S
24 Or else I] ~ esse ~ Q1; I or else Q2
29 on] no Q2, F2, L–S
32 percullis] portcullis F2, L–W
35 was] were F2, L–V
38 Good] God Q1

48 fastingly] fasting fly S–C
61 Rid] Ride S–W
62 Theames] Theamea Q1(c); the Thames S–V
67 gone] goe Q1(u)
72 till this houre] tell these ~ Q1(c), Q2, F2, L–S; tell these houres Q1(u)
73 So] For S–V
76 *Harebraine.*] *Hum.* Q1–2, F2, L–S
80 ye] *om.* Q1
90 Ile swinge you] *om.* Q2, F2, L
91 now] *add* may S
94 we'll] will Q1

V.i

11 any] my F2, L–V
14 a] *om.* Q2
27 *Widdow.*] *Short.* Q1
45 ²a] *om.* Q2, F2, L
47 bay] bouy (*i.e.,* buoy) Q2, F2, L–V
54 a] *om.* Q1(u)
54 Carbine] Cabine Q1–2, F2, L
60 um] it S–W

66 And] *add* there's S–C
80 take] takes Q2, F2, L–S
82 a] *om.* Q1
83.1 Humphrey [*and*] Ralph] ~ , *a Servant* Q1–2, F2, L–S; ~ *and another Servant* C; Humphrey W–V
86 *Ralph.*] *Hum.* Q2, F2, L–V

V.ii

7 sacke] sackes Q1
8 which] *add* is S–V
9 ²no armes] nor ~ Q2, F2, L; nor harms S
12 hang't] hang Q1–2
16 a] *om.* Q1
24 And] An Q2
27 his Nellson] this Nelson Q2, F2; this, Nelson L–S
30 I] I'll F2, L–S, D
36 *Merchant*] *May* Q1; Boy F2, L–V
40 mist] midst Q1–2, F2, L, W, D
45 you] *add* have Q2, F2, L–S

50 pound] pounds Q2, F2, L–D
56 you] *om.* Q1
58 No] Not Q1–2, F2, L, D–V
64 a] *om.* Q2
67 what] what what Q2
69 to] and Q2, F2, L–C
71 then] Thou D–V
73 never] were never S–W
75 wert all the staple] mortall the stople Q1–2, F2, L; art mortal staple S–W
90 regements] regiment Q2, F2, L–S

V.iii

10 For...now] now I'm another mettle S
10 of] *om.* L

19 ¹I] *add* was Q1–2, F2, L–D
38 *Lance.*] *Fran.* C
57 their] the Q1(u), Q2, F2, L

V.iv

7 bables] Babels S–C; baubles W–V
13 set as a] set a Q2; set's S
15 tis] is F2, L–S

22 put fairely] ~ ~ put Q2, F2, L
28 wish] *add* which S
29 missed] wished Q1–2, F2, L–V
29 aimed] *add* not C–V

THE PILGRIM

edited by

CYRUS HOY

TEXTUAL INTRODUCTION

The Pilgrim (Greg, *Bibliography*, no. 658) is a work of Fletcher's unaided authorship, and he seems to have written the comedy sometime between 18 September 1621 – when the English version of the play's principal source, Lope de Vega's *El Peregrino en su Patria*, was entered in the Stationers' Register – and New Year's Day, 1622, when the play was performed by the King's Men at Court.[1] There is not a great deal of evidence concerning the play's contemporary reception, but such as there is indicates that it was a popular one. It was acted again at Court on 29 December 1622, and two decades later it was deemed of sufficient value to be included in a list (dated 7 August 1641) of King's Men plays 'which the Lord Chamberlain forbade the printers to publish without the company's consent'.[2] Five years later, on or around 4 September 1646, it was entered in the Stationers' Register by Humphrey Robinson and Humphrey Moseley in their list of some thirty plays that were to comprise the first Beaumont and Fletcher Folio, published in the following year.

R. C. Bald has noted the fact that *The Pilgrim* is one of only eight plays in the 1647 Folio in which there are no 'directions which suggest, even remotely, the specific influence of the prompter'.[3] Not only does the F 1 text lack such directions; it exhibits a number of inconsistencies and unresolved loose ends that make it clear that it was printed from Fletcher's foul papers, and that these had not yet been reduced to the sort of order that could permit them to serve as the basis for a prompt-book. That the father of Pedro, the disguised pilgrim of the title, is named Ferando at I.i.58 and Alonso at II.ii.111 is the least of the textual contradictions with which an editor has to deal.

[1] G. E. Bentley, *The Jacobean and Caroline Stage*, III (Oxford, 1956), 391–3.
[2] *Ibid.* p. 392.
[3] R. C. Bald, *Bibliographical Studies in the Beaumont and Fletcher Folio of 1647* (Oxford, 1938), pp. 109–10.

There is a good deal of uncertainty about the assignment of speeches to supernumeraries, specifically the Outlaws and the various Gentlemen. Roderigo's band consists of six speaking-roles: Jaques, Lopez, and four unnamed Outlaws whose speech-prefixes bear numerals from one to four. This is clear from the evidence of II.ii, where the opening stage-direction brings on Roderigo and four Outlaws, and the four speak in turn during the next forty lines; at II.ii.42.1, they are joined by Lopez and Jaques. At III.i, the initial stage-direction calls for Roderigo, Jaques, Lopez, and three Outlaws, and a fourth one enters at III.i.34.1. The F1 stage-direction refers to him, however, as '2 Outlaw', perhaps because, of the three Outlaws already on stage, only the first has spoken. To this point, matters are reasonably clear, but they become less so in what follows. The F1 stage-direction at III.iii.67.1 reads: '*Enter Rodorigo, and two Outlaw.*' It is not clear whether this refers (as the direction at III.i.34.1 has seemed to do) to the Second Outlaw, or to two Outlaws (as F2 took it to do), but the question, in the event, permits of no answer because in the dialogue that follows Roderigo's entrance at III.iii.67.1, he is found conversing not with any of the Outlaws whose speech-prefixes are mere numerals, but with Lopez, to whom F1 assigns two speeches (at III.iii.68 and 71). The following scene (III.iv) opens with the entrance (according to F1) of '*Iaques, and 1 Out-Law.*' While the first Outlaw is speaking, at III.iv.12, his speech is interrupted by the entrance of '*two Outlawes*' and the final line of his speech is assigned to Lopez, whose presence in the scene had not previously been indicated. The two newly entered Outlaws speak in turn (their speech-prefixes are numbered '*2 Out-l.*' and '*3 Out-l.*'), and Lopez has another speech at III.iv.20. They all leave the stage at that point. Presumably they all enter again a few lines later, at III.iv.35.1, but the F1 stage-direction at this point is not very revealing. It calls merely for the appearance (along with Seberto and Curio) of '*Outlaws, Jaques*', though of the Outlaws who appear, only the first speaks (at III.iv.37), and Jaques has no speeches, while Lopez (not mentioned in the F1 stage-direction) has one (at III.iv.45). The presence of speech-prefixes for Lopez in scenes for which F1's stage-directions have not provided for his presence suggests authorial uncertainty concerning his relation to the rest of the outlaw band. The editorial problem that this poses and the manner in which I have handled it in the present edition are discussed in the Textual Notes on III.iii.67.1; III.iv.0.1; and III.iv.12–14.

The designation of the various Gentlemen is equally trouble-some. In the first place, there are Gentlemen and Gentlemen in the play, as the F2 cast list indicates when it distinguishes the so-called 'Gentleman, of the Country' from three other Gentlemen. An unspecified Gentleman appears with Pedro at the beginning of III.vi (III.v in F1) and offers to show him, obviously a stranger in Segovia, the sights of the city, of which the madhouse is a chief exhibit. Pedro accepts his offer, but when they arrive at the mad-house in the course of the following scene (III.vii.46.1–2), they are now three Gentlemen plus Pedro. The first two Gentlemen are concerned with securing the release of a friend. Their speech-prefixes are clearly designated *1 Gent.* and *2 Gent.* The Gentleman who accompanies Pedro is also called *1 Gent.*, in his first F1 speech-prefix in this scene (III.vii.55). F1 labels his two further speeches (at III.vii.149, 171) simply '*Gent.*' (by now the First and Second Gentlemen have left the scene). The following scene (IV.i) opens with a conversation between Alphonso and an unspecified Gentleman, who tells him that a boy, answering to the description of the disguised Alinda, was recently sent to the neighbouring madhouse.

I think it is evident that the Gentleman who approaches Pedro in III.vi and offers to show him the madhouse, who appears with him there in III.vii and witnesses his rapturous meeting with a seeming boy (and comments on it with amazement at III.vii.149–50), and who tells Alphonso at the beginning of IV.i that a boy very like the one he is seeking is lodged at the local madhouse: I think there can be no doubt that all these Gentlemen are the same Gentleman. He is, I presume, the Gentleman of the Country named in the F2 cast list, and the F2 list is wrong when it makes provision for three other Gentlemen. There are but two others. The evidence of F1 speech-prefixes and stage-directions bears this out. The Gentleman associated with Pedro and Alphonso is always (with the single exception of the speech-prefix at III.vii.55) referred to simply as

'Gentleman' or 'Gent.' Only two other Gentlemen have speaking-roles (those who talk with the madhouse keeper in III.vii.52ff). Their speech-prefixes are numbered *1*. and *2*. There are no F1 speech-prefixes for a Third Gentleman. To refer to the unspecified Gentleman as the Third Gentleman, as some previous editors have done, is to introduce the third (in III.vi) before the first two have appeared (in III.vii). Speech-prefixes in the present edition refer, then, to *Gentleman*, and to *1*. and *2*. *Gentleman*; and it is to be understood that the 'Gentleman' on his own is always the same Gentleman. This will cause the Gentleman to leave the stage at the end of one scene (III.vii) only to return again immediately at the beginning of the next (IV.i), but if one can assume some sort of interval between Acts III and IV in performance, this is not necessarily a problem. And in support of the identification of the Gentleman of III.vi–vii with the Gentleman of IV.i is the fact that, in the course of his visit to the madhouse in III.vii, that Gentleman has seen the supposed boy (the disguised Alinda) there, and so is in possession of the information that the Gentleman of IV.i is passing on to Alphonso as that scene begins.

The Pilgrim was printed in Section 5 of the 1647 Folio, the section assigned to Edward Griffin. It occupies sigs. 5F4 through 5I3 (5I3^v is blank). The evidence of running-titles suggests three-skeleton work for the three quires, with three verso and three recto titles appearing in an orderly sequence:

Verso: I 5F4^v, 5G1^v, 5H1^v, 5I1^v
    III 5G2^v, 5G3^v, 5H2^v, 5H4^v
    V 5G4^v, 5H3^v, 5I2^v

Recto: II 5G1, 5H2, 5I3
    IV 5G2, 5G3, 5H1, 5H3, 5I1, 5I2
    VI 5G4, 5H4

Three compositors seem to have set the F1 text. Their work can be differentiated by means of their mode of abbreviating certain contractions and spelling certain words. Compositor *A* always spells *I'le*; Compositor *B* always spells *Ile*. Compositor *C* almost always spells *I'le* but an occasional *Ile* is found in his share (once on sig. 5G1, four times on sig. 5H4ᵛ). What chiefly distinguishes the work of Compositor *C* from that of the others is his strong preference for *do* to *doe*. In his stint from 5F4 through 5G1ᵛ, Compositor *C* uses *do* nine times, *doe* only three times; in the text that he set from 5H3ᵛ to 5H4ᵛ, *do* appears sixteen times, *doe* not at all. Compositors *A* and *B* use both forms, but each displays a strong preference for *doe*. Compositor *C* is responsible for all occurrences of the spellings *yong* and *bin*; in the portions of the text set by Compositors *A* and *B*, the words appear as *young* and *been*. While Compositors *A* and *B* prefer the spelling *'tis*, Compositor *C* almost always uses the form *tis* (without the apostrophe). Compositors *B* and *C* share the spelling *Mistris*; Compositor *A* spells the word *Mistresse*. Abbreviations for speech-prefixes for the play's Outlaws help to differentiate Compositors *A* and *B*: Compositor *A* spells *Outl.*, Compositor *B* spells *Out-l.* For scene headings, Compositors *A* and *C* always use the form *Scæna*, while Compositor *B* sometimes spells the word *Scena*. From time to time, all three compositors are given to spelling Roderigo's name *Rodorigo*, and throughout the text, all three persistently spell Segovia, *Segonia*. The division of the work of the three compositors in setting the text of *The Pilgrim* seems to be as follows:

Compositor *A*: 5G4–5G4ᵛ (II.ii.344 – III.iv.5); 5H3 (IV.ii.26 (|'*Rod.* It danceth') – 130 ('Christians' |)); 5I2–5I3 (V.iv.32 – V.vi.139.2)

Compositor *B*: 5G2–5G3ᵛ (II.i.69 – II.ii.343); 5H1–5H2ᵛ (III.iv.6 – IV.ii.26 ('see this?' |)); 5I1–5I1ᵛ (IV.iii.187 – V.iv.31)

Compositor *C*: 5F4–5G1ᵛ (I.i.0 – II.i.68); 5H3ᵛ–5H4ᵛ (IV.ii.130 (| '2. Yes') – IV.iii.186)

There are occasional references to *The Pilgrim* in the decades immediately following the Restoration. The title occurs in a list of King's Men plays (dated *c.* 12 January 1669) 'formerly acted at the Blackfryers & now allowed of to his Maᵗᵉˢ Servantes at yᵉ New Theatre.'[1] The publication of a Prologue for *The Pilgrim* in A.B.'s *Covent Garden Drollery* in 1672 suggests a recent revival of the

[1] Bentley, *Jacobean Stage*, III, 392.

play.[1] Sometime around 29 April 1700, *The Pilgrim* was produced
at the Theatre Royal, Drury Lane, in a revision by Sir John
Vanbrugh that closely followed Fletcher's plot while turning his
blank verse into prose and greatly curtailing its rhetorical elabora-
tion.[2] Dryden supplied Vanbrugh's version of the play with a
Prologue, an Epilogue, a 'Song of a *Scholar* and his *Mistresse*,
who being Cross'd by their Friends, fell mad for one another; and
now first meet in *Bedlam*', and a *Secular Masque*. The song of the
Mad Scholar and his Mistress seems most likely to have been
intended for inclusion in the madhouse scene of III.vii.[3] Dryden's
great *Secular Masque* closes the play in Vanbrugh's adaptation, as
the Governor of Segovia invites all the principal personages to
'share with us, an Entertainment the late great Poet of our Age
prepar'd to Celebrate this Day.'[4] Though alive when Vanbrugh's
adaptation had its première at the end of April, Dryden had died
(on 1 May 1700) by the time the printed text appeared in June. The
cast of Vanbrugh's revision included Robert Wilks as Pedro,
George Powell as Roderigo, Benjamin Johnson as Alphonso, and –
in her first major part – Anne Oldfield as Alinda, a role for which
she was greatly acclaimed. Colley Cibber spoke Dryden's Prologue
and Epilogue, and played two small parts (the Mad Englishman and
the Stuttering Cook, the latter a Vanbrugh addition).

Vanbrugh's version of *The Pilgrim* was immensely popular, and
held the stage throughout most of the eighteenth century. According to Bonamy Dobrée, 'it was acted at least twice, often more,
every year until 1733 inclusive',[5] and the play continued to be

[1] *Ibid.* p. 392; *The London Stage: 1660–1800*, Part 1 (1660–1700), ed. William
Van Lennep (Carbondale, Illinois, 1965), p. 187.

[2] For discussion of the date of the première of Vanbrugh's revision of *The Pilgrim*,
see Arthur Colby Sprague, *Beaumont and Fletcher on the Restoration Stage* (Cambridge,
Mass., 1926), pp. 89–91; and Van Lennep, *London Stage*, Part 1, pp. 527–8.

[3] In the 1700 text of Vanbrugh's version, the 'Song of a *Scholar* and his *Mistresse*'
is printed immediately after the play, and before the Masque. For the suggestion that
the song may have served as a necessary interpolation 'between the play and the
masque to allow of stage setting and the grouping of the actors', see Bonamy Dobrée,
The Complete Works of Sir John Vanbrugh (Bloomsbury: The Nonesuch Press
1927), II, 88.

[4] Vanbrugh's revision of *The Pilgrim*, V.v (in Dobrée, *Works of Vanbrugh*, II,
141).

[5] Dobrée, *Works of Vanbrugh*, II, 90–1.

revived throughout the next half century. The volumes of *The London Stage* record performances in 1734, 1738, 1739, 1740, 1741, 1742, 1743, 1748, 1750, 1751, 1752, 1762, 1763, 1780, 1783.[1] By then it must have seemed that the time had come to revise Vanbrugh's revision, a task that was duly undertaken by John Philip Kemble for a production staged at Drury Lane on 26 October 1787, in which Kemble himself acted the role of Pedro.[2] As Herschel Baker has noted, 'Kemble's divagations from Vanbrugh...are almost all made with an eye for brevity and speed of action'; such changes as were not 'motivated solely by his desire for tempo and brevity' were decreed by 'his fastidious omission of indelicate lines'.[3] The production, which ran for six performances (the last on 18 April 1788),[4] was the last revival of *The Pilgrim* on the London stage in the eighteenth century. Kemble's redaction, the text of which was published in November 1787, is a limp bowdlerization of what Baker has astutely called 'Fletcher's cruelly brilliant comedy'.[5]

[1] For post-1733 performances of *The Pilgrim*, see *The London Stage*, Part 3 (1729–1747), ed. Arthur H. Scouten (2 vols., Carbondale, Ill., 1961), I, 396; II, 715, 746, 747, 749, 773, 813, 824, 874, 878, 901, 952–4, 961, 966, 972, 992, 1019, 1056, 1140, 1216, 1240; Part 4 (1747–1776), ed. George Winchester Stone, Jr (3 vols. Carbondale, Ill., 1962), I, 47, 216–17, 219, 229, 313, 338; II, 917, 918, 921, 995; Part 5 (1776–1800), ed. Charles Beecher Hogan (3 vols., Carbondale, Ill., 1968), I, 335, 341, 610.

[2] The 1787 adaptation is sometimes attributed to Thomas King, actor and – at the time – manager of Drury Lane, but Kemble's biographer, Herschel Baker, unhesitatingly assigns it to Kemble (*John Philip Kemble: The Actor in His Theatre* (Cambridge, Mass., 1942), pp. 113ff).

[3] *Ibid.* pp. 116, 117.

[4] *The London Stage*, Part 5, II, 1015, 1016, 1017, 1022, 1023, 1057.

[5] Baker, *Kemble*, p. 114.

Persons Represented in the Play

Governour, of Segovia.
Verdugo, *a Captain under him.*
Alphonso, *an old angry Gentleman.*
Curio, ⎫
Seberto, ⎭ *two Gentlemen, friends to* Alphonso.
Pedro, *the Pilgrim, a noble Gentleman, Servant to* Alinda.
An old Pilgrim.
Lopes, ⎫
Jaques, ⎭ *two Out laws under* Roderigo.   10
Roderigo, *rival to* Pedro, *Captain of the Out-laws.*
A Gentleman, of the Country.
Porter.
Master & ⎫
Keepers, ⎭ *of the Mad folks.*
2 Gentlemen.
4 Peasants.
[*4 Beggars.*]   20
[*4 Out-laws.*]
A Scholar,
A Parson, ⎫
An Englishman, ⎬ *Madmen.*
Jenkin, [*a Welshman*]⎭
Courtiers, [*Citizens, Servants*].

WOMEN.

Alinda, *Daughter to* Alphonso, Pedro's Lady.
Juletta, Alinda's *Maid, a witty Lass.*   30
[*She-*] *Fool.*
Ladies.

The Scene Spain.

The principal Actors were,

Joseph Taylor.	John Lowin.
Nicholas Toolie.	John Underwood.
Robert Benfield.	George Birch.
John Thompson.	James Horn.

Persons...Horn.] F2; *om.* F1   18 *2 Gentlemen*] *3 Gentlemen* F2

THE PILGRIM

Enter Alphonso, Curio, Seberto.

Curio.   Signor *Alphonso*, ye are too rugged to her,
  Believe too full of harshnesse.
Alphonso.   Yes, it seemes so.
Seberto.   A father of so sweet a child, so happy,
  (Fy Sir) so excellent in all endowments,
  In blessednesse of beauty, such a mirror.
Alphonso.   She is a foole, away.
Seberto.   Can ye be angry?
  Can any wind blow rough, upon a blossom
  So faire, and tender? Can a Fathers nature,
  A noble Fathers too——
Alphonso.   All this is but prating: 10
  Let her be rul'd; let her observe my humor,
  With my eyes let her see; with my eares listen;
  I am her Father: I begot her, bred her,
  And I will make her——
Curio.   No doubt ye may compell her,
  But what a mischievous, unhappy fortune
  May wayt upon this wil of yours, as commonly
  Such forcings ever end in hates, and ruines.
Alphonso.   Is't not a man I wish her to? a strong man?
  What can she have? what could she have? a Gentleman?
  A yong man? and an able-man? a rich man?   20
  A handsome man? a valiant man? do you marke me?
  None of your peeced-companions, your pin'd-Gallants,
  That flie to fitters, with every flaw of weather:
  None of your impt bravados: what can she ask more?
  Is not a mettal'd-man fit for a woman?
  A strong chindman? i'le not be foold, nor flurted.

*22 pin'd-Gallants] *stet* F 1–2

Seberto.   I grant ye *Rodorigo* is all these
And a brave Gentleman: must it therefore follow
Upon necessity she must doate upon him?
Will ye allow no liberty in choosing?   30
Curio.   Alas she is tender yet.
Alphonso.   Enough, enough, enough Sir:
She is malliable; shee'l endure the hammer,
And why not that strong workeman that strikes deepest?
Let me know that? she is fifteen, with the vantage,
And if she be not ready now for mannage——
Seberto.   You know he is a banish'd man: an out-Law;
And how he lives: his nature rough, and bloody
By customary rapines: now, her sweet humor
That is as easy as a calme, and peacefull,
All her affections, like the dewes on Roses,   40
Faire as the flowers themselves: as sweet, and gentle:
How would you have these meet?
Alphonso.   A bed, a bed sir:
Let her be the fairest Rose, and the sweetest,
Yet I know this faire rose must have her prickles:
I grant ye *Rodorigo* is an out-Law,
An easie composition cals him in again,
He is a valiant man, and he is a rich man,
And loves the foole: a little rough by custome:
Shee'l like him ten times better. Shee'l doat upon him,
If ere they come to grapling, run mad for him;   50
But there is an other in the wind, some castrell
That hovers over her, and dares her dayly,
Some flickring slave.
Curio.   I dare not think so poorely.
Alphonso.   Something there is, and must be: but I shall sente it
And hunt it narrowly.
Seberto.   I never saw her yet
Make offer at the least glance of affection,
But still so modest, wise.
Alphonso.   They are wise to gull us.
There was a fellow, old *Ferandos* son,

I must confesse handsome, but my enemy,
And the whole family I hate: yong *Pedro*,   60
That fellow I have seen her gaze upon,
And turn, and gaze again, and make such offers
As if she would shoot her eyes like meteors at him:
But that cause stands removed.
Curio.   You need not doubt him,
For long since as 'twas thought on a griev'd conscience,
He left his father, and his friends: more pitty:
For truth reports he was a noble Gentleman.
Alphonso.   Let him be what he wil: he was a begger,
And there i'le leave him.
Seberto.   The more the Court must answer;
But certainly I think, though she might favour him,   70
And love his goodnesse, as he was an honest man:
She never with loose eyes stuck on his person.
Alphonso.   She is so full of conscience too, and charity,
And outward holinesse, she will undoe me:
Relieves more beggers, then an hospitall;
And all poor rogues, that can but say their prayers,
And tune their pipes to Lamentations,
She thinks she is bound to dance to:

        Enter Alinda, *and* Juletta.

                    good morrow to you,
And that's as ye deserve too: you know my mind,
And studdy to observe it: doe it cheerfully,   80
And readily, and home.
Alinda.   I shall obey ye.
But noble sir——
Alphonso.   Come, come, away with your flatteries,
And your fine phrases——
Curio.   Pray ye be gentle to her.
Alphonso.   I know 'em; and know your feates: if you will find me
Noble and loving, seek me in your duty,
You know I am too indulgent.
Seberto.   Alas poor Lady.

Alphonso. To your devotions: I take no good thing from you.
Come Gentlemen; leave pittying, and moaning of her,
And praysing of her vertues: and her whym-whams,
It makes her proud, and sturdy.
Seberto, Curio. Good houres wait on ye. 90
Alinda. I thank ye Gentlemen: I want such comforts:
Exeunt [Alphonso, Curio, Seberto].
I would thank you too father: but your cruelty
Hath almost made me senselesse of my duty,
Yet still I must know: would I had known nothing;
What Poor attend my charity today, wench?
Juletta. Of all sorte, Madam; your open handed bounty
Makes 'em flock every houre: some worth your pitty,
But others that have made a trade of begging.
Alinda. Wench, if they ask it truly, I must give it:
It takes away the holy use of charity 100
To examine wants.
Juletta. I would you would be merry:
A cheerfull-giving hand, as I think, Madam,
Requires a heart as cheerfull.
Alinda. Alas *Juletta,*
What is there to be merry at? what joy now,
Unlesse we foole our own afflictions,
And make them shew ridiculous?
Juletta. Sure Madam,
You could not seeme thus serious, if you were married,
Thus sad, and full of thoughts.
Alinda. Married? to whom, wench?
Thou thinkst if there be a yong handsome fellow,
As those are plentifull, our cares are quenched then. 110
Juletta. Madam, I think a lusty handsome fellow
If he be kind, and loving, and a right one,
Is even as good a pill, to purge this melancholy,
As ever *Galen* gave, I am sure more naturall:
And merrier for the heart, then Wine and Saffron:
Madam, wantone youth is such a Cataplasme.
Alinda. Who has bin thy tutor wench?

Juletta.   Even my own thoughts, Lady:
  For though I be bard the liberty of talking,
  Yet I can think unhappily, and as near the mark, Madam,
  'Faith, marry, and be merry.
Alinda.   Who wil have me?   120
  Who wil be troubled with a tettish Girle?
  It may be proud, and to that vice expencefull?
  Who can assure himselfe, I shall live honest?
Juletta.   Let every man take his fortune.
Alinda.   And o' my conscience
  If once I grow to breeding, a whole Kingdome
  Wil not containe my stock.
Juletta.   The more the merrier:
  'Tis brave to be a mother of new Nations.
Alinda.   Why, I should bury a hundred husbands.
Juletta.   Tis no matter:
  As long as ye leave sufficient men to stock ye.
Alinda.   Is this thy mirth? are these the joyes of marriage?   130
  Away light-headed foole; are these contentments?
  If I could finde a man——
Juletta.   You may a thousand.
Alinda.   Meere men I know I may: and there a woman
  Has liberty, (at least shee'l venture for it,)
  To be a monster and become the time too;
  But to enjoy a man, from whose example
  (As from a compasse) we may steer our fortunes,
  Our actions, and our age; and safe arive at
  A memory that shall become our ashes,
  Such things are few, and far to seek; to finde one   140
  That can but rightly mannage the wild beast, woman,
  And sweetly govern with her. But no more of this, wench,
  Tis not for thy discourse: Lets in, and see
  What poor afflicted wait our charity.   *Exeunt.*

Enter a Porter, *four Beggers, a* Pilgrime,   [I.] ii
    and Pedro [*disguised as a pilgrim*].

Porter.   Stand off, and keep your Rancks: twenty foot further:
    There louse your selves with reason, and discretion.
    The Sun shines warm: the farther still the better,
    Your beasts wil bolt anon, and then tis dangerous.
1. Beggar.   Heaven blesse our Mistris.
Porter.   Does the crack go that way?
    'Twil be o'th' other side anon.
2. Beggar.   Pray ye friend——
Porter.   Your friend? and why your friend? why, goodman turncoat,
    What dost thou see within me, or without me,
    Or what itch dost thou know upon me, tell me,
    That I should be thy friend? what do I look like   10
    Any of thy acquaintance hung in Gibbets?
    Hast thou any Friends, Kindred, or Alliance,
    Or any higher ambition, then an almes-basket?
2. Beggar.   I would be your worships friend.
Porter.   So ye shall Sirra,
    When I quarter the same louse with ye.
3. Beggar.   Tis twelve o'clock.
Porter.   Tis ever so with thee, when thou hast done scratching,
    For that provokes thy stomach to ring noon;
    O the infinite Seas of porridge thou hast swallowd!
    And yet thou lookst as if they had bin but Glisters;
    Thou feedst abundance; thou hadst need of sustenance;   20
    Almes do you call it to relieve these Rascals?
    Nothing but a generall rot of sheep can satisfie 'em.

Enter Alphonso, Curio, Seberto.

Alphonso.   Did not I tel you, how she would undo me?
    What Marts of Rogues, and Beggers?
Seberto.   Tis charity
    Methinks, you are bound to love her for——

Alphonso.   Yes, I warrant ye,
   If men could sale to heaven in porridge pots,
   With masts of Beef, and Mutton, what a voyage should I make?
   What are all these?
1. Beggar.   Poore people, and't like your worship.
2. Beggar. Wretched poor people.
3. Beggar.   Very hungry people.
Alphonso.   And very Lousy.
4. Beggar.   Yes forsooth, so, so.   30
Porter.   I'le undertake five hundred head about 'em,
   And that's no needy Grasier.
Alphonso.   What are you?
Pilgrim.   Strangers that come to wonder at your charity,
   Yet people poore enough to beg a blessing.
Curio.   Use them with favour, sir, their shews are reverent.——
   It seemes ye are holy *Pilgrimes?*
Pilgrim.   Ye ghesse right sir,
   And bound far off, to offer our devotions.
Alphonso.   What make ye this way? we keep no Reliques here,
   Nor holy Shrines.
Pilgrim.   The holiest we ere heard of;
   Ye keep a living monument of goodnesse,   40
   A Daughter of that pious excellence,
   The very Shrines of Saints sinck at her vertues,
   And sweat they cannot hold pace with her pieties,
   We come to see this Lady: not with prophane eyes,
   Nor wanton bloods, to doat upon her beauties,
   But through our tedious wayes to beg her blessings.
Alphonso.   This is a new way of begging, and a neat one,
   And this cries money for reward: good store too;
   These commendations beg not with bag, and bottle;
   Well, well, the sainting of this woman (Gentlemen)   50
   I know what it must come too: these women saints
   Are plaguy heavy saints: they out-waigh a he-saint
   Three thousand thick; I know: I feele.
Seberto.   Ye are more afraid then hurt sir.

   *43 sweat] Seward (*conj.*); swear F 1–2

127

Alphonso [*to Pedro*]. Have you your commendations ready
    too?——
    He bowes, and nods.
Curio.   A handsome well built person.
Alphonso.   What Country-craver are you? nothing but motion?
    A puppet-Pilgrim?
Pilgrim.   Hee's a stranger sir;
    This foure dayes I have traveld in his company,
    But little of his busines, or his Language   60
    As yet, I have understood.
Seberto.   Both yong, and handsome,
    Only the Sun has bin too saucy with him.
Alphonso.   Would ye have money sir, or meat? what kind of
    blessing
    Does your devotion looke for? Still more ducking?
    Be there any saints, that understand by signes only?
    More motion yet? this is the prettiest Pilgrim,
    The pinck of pilgrims: ile be for ye sir;
    Do ye discourse with signes? ye are hartly welcome:
                     [*Takes out a gold piece.*]
    A poor viaticum; very good gold sir;
    But holy men affect a better treasure.   70
    I kept it for your goodnes, but neerthelesse
    Since it can prove but burthensome to your holines,
    And you affect light prayer, fit for carriage,
    I'le put this up againe.
Curio.   Ye are too unreverent.
Alphonso.   Ye talk too broad; must I give way, and wealth too
    To every toy, that carries a grave seeming?
    Must my good angels wait on him? if the proud hilding
    Would yeild but to my wil, and know her duty
    I know what I would suffer.
Seberto.   Good sir, be patient,
    The wrongs ye do these men, may light on you,   80
    Too heavy too: and then you wil wish you had said lesse;
    A comly and sweet usage becomes strangers.

        79 know] F2; knew F1

Alphonso.   We shall have half the Kingdom strangers shortly,
   And this fond prodigality be sufferd;
   But I must be an asse.—— [*To* Porter.] See 'hem relieved,
      sirah;——
   If I were yong again, I would sooner get beare whelps,
   And safer too, then any of these She-saints,
   But I will break her.
Curio.   Such a face for certain.
Seberto.   Me thinks I have seen it too: but we are cozend;
   But fair befall thee Pilgrim, thou lookst lovely.   90
                    Exeunt [Alphonso, Curio, Seberto.]
Porter.   Will ye troop up, ye porridge Regiment?
   Captain Poors quarter wil ye move?

                    Enter Alinda, Juletta.

Alinda.   Ye dull Knave,
   Are not these wretches served yet?
Beggars.   'Blesse my Mistris.
Alinda.   Do you make sport sir, with their miseries?
   Ye drousie rogue.
Porter.   They are too high fed, Madam,
   Their stomacks are a'sleep yet.
Alinda.   Serve 'hem plentifully,
   Or i'le serve you out next: even out o'dores, sirah;
   And serve 'em quickly too.
Beggars.   Heaven blesse the Lady.
Alinda.   Blesse the good end I meane it for.
                    Exeunt [Porter *and*] Beggars.
Juletta [*aside*].   I would I knew it:
   If it be for any mans sake, i'le cry amen too.——   100
   Well Madam, ye have even as pretty a port of pentioners——
Alinda.   Vain-glory would seek more, and handsomer.
   But I appeale to vertue what my end is;
   What men are these?
Juletta.   It seems they are holy Pilgrims:
   That handsome youth should suffer such a pennance,

87 then] them F 1; than F 2   93, 98 s.p. *Beggars*] *Beg.* F 1–2

129

Would I were even the saint they make their vowes too,
How easily I would grant.

Pilgrim.   Heavens grace in-wheele ye:
And all good thoughts, and prayers dwell about ye,
Abundance be your friend; and holy charity
Be ever at your hand, to crown ye glorious.   110

Alinda.   I thank ye sir; peace guid your travels too,
And what you wish for most, end all your trobles;
Remember me by this: and in your prayers
When your strong heart melts, mediate my poor fortunes.

                            [*Gives money.*]

Pilgrim.   All my devotions wait upon your service.

Alinda.   Are ye of this Country, sir?

Pilgrim.   Yes, worthiest Lady,
But far off bred: my fortunes farther from me.

Alinda.   Gentle, I dare believe.

Pilgrim.   I have liv'd freer.

Alinda.   I am no inquisitor, that were too curious:
What ever vow, or pennance puls ye on sir;   120
Conscience, or love, or stubborn disobedience,
The saint ye kneel too, hear, and ease your travels.

Pilgrim.   Yours neer begin: and thus I seal my prayers.   *Exit.*

Alinda.   How constantly this man looks? how he sighes?
Some great affliction hatches his devotions——
Right holy sir:—— how yong, and sweet he suffers?

Juletta [*aside*].   Would I might suffer with him.

Alinda.   He turns from us:
Alas he weeps too: something presses him
He would reveale, but dare not;—— sir, be comforted,
Ye come for that: and take it: if it be want, sir,   130
To me yee appear so worthy of relieving,
I am your steward: speak, and take:—— he's dumb still:
Now as I have a faith this man so stirs me,
His modesty makes me affraid I have trespassed.

Juletta [*aside*].   Would he would stir me too: I like his shape well.

Alinda.   May be he would speak alone: go off *Juletta,*
Afflicted hearts fear their own motions,

Be not far off.

Juletta [*aside*].　　Would I were neerer to him,
A yong smug handsome holines has no fellow.　　　　*Exit.*

Alinda.　　Why do you grieve? do you find your pennance sharp?　140
Or are the vowes ye have made, too mighty for ye?
Do's not the world allure ye to look back
And sorrow for the sweet time ye have lost?
Ye are yong, and fair; be not deluded, sir;
A manly made up heart contemnes these shadows,
And yours appeares no lesse: greifes for your fears,
For houres ill-spent, for wrongs don rash, and rudely,
For fowle contempts, for faiths ill violated,
Become fears well: I dare not task your Goodnes:
And then a sorrow shewes in his true glory　　　　150
When the whole heart is excellently sorry.
I pray ye be comforted.

Pedro.　　　　　　　I am, deer Lady,
And such a comfort ye have cast upon me,
That though I struggle with mine own calamities
Too mighty, and too many for my mannage,
And though, like angry waves, they curld upon me
Contending proudly who should first devour me,
Yet I would stem their danger.

Alinda [*aside*].　　　　He speaks nobly:——
What do ye want?

Pedro.　　　　　All that can make me happy:
I want my selfe.

Alinda.　　　　　Your self? who rob'd ye Pilgrim?　160
[*Aside*] Why does he look so constantly upon me?——
I want my selfe: indeed, you holy wanderers
Are said to seek much: but to seek your selves——

Pedro.　　I seek my self; and am but my selfs-shadow:
Have lost my self; and now am not so noble.

Alinda.　　*I seek my self*: [*Aside*] something I yet remember
That bears that Motto; 'tis not he: he is yonger,
And far more tender:—— for that self-sake (Pilgrim)
Be who it will, take this.　　　　　[*Offers him money.*]

131

Pedro.   Your hand I dare take,
That be far from me, Lady; thus I kisse it,   170
And thus I blesse it too; be constant fair still:
Be good, and live to be a great example.   *Exit.*
Alinda.   One word more (Pilgrim)——has amazd me strangly,
Be constant faire still: tis the posie here: [*Looks at a ring.*]
And here without, *Be good*: he wept to see me.——
Juletta——

                   Enter Juletta.

Juletta.   Madam.
Alinda.   Take this Key, and fetch me
The Marygold Jewell that lies in my little Cabinet:
                                        [*Exit* Juletta.]
I think tis that: what eyes had I, to misse him?
O' me, what thoughts? he had no beard then, and
As I remember well, he was more ruddy.   180
If this be he, he has a manly face yet,
A goodly shape.

              Enter Juletta [*with a jewell*].

Juletta.   Here Madam?
Alinda.   Let me see it:
Tis so, too true: It must be he, or nothing,
He spak the words just as they stand engraved here:
I seek my self, and am but my selfes-shadow:
Alas poor man: didst thou not meet him, *Juletta?*
The Pilgrim, wench?
Juletta.   He went by long ago, Madam.
Alinda.   I forgot to give him something.
Juletta.   'Twas ill done Lady:
For, o' my troth, he is the handsomest man
I saw this many a day: [*Aside*] would he had all my wealth,   190
And me to boote: what ayles she to grow sullen?
Alinda.   Come, I forgot: but I will recompence it.   *Exeunt.*

Enter Alphonso, Curio, Seberto, Juletta, Porter,
and servants.

Alphonso.   Can she slip through a cat-hole? tell me that: resolve me;
Can she fly ith ayre? is she a thing invisible?
Gon, and none know it?

Seberto.   Ye amaz your servants.

Alphonso.   Some pelting rogue has watch'd her houre of itching,
And clawd her; clawd her: do you mark me, clawd her;
Some that I foster up.

Curio.   They are all here, sir.

Alphonso.   Let 'em be where they will, they are arrant rascals,
And by this hand i'le hang 'em all.

Seberto.   Deale calmely:
You will not give 'em time to answer ye.

Alphonso.   I'le choak 'hem: famish 'em: what say you wagtaile?   10
You knew her mind: you were of councell with her,
Tell me: and tell me true.

Curio.   Aske with discretion.

Alphonso.   Discretion? hang discretion, hang ye all:
Let me know where she is.

Juletta.   Would you know o' me sir?

Alphonso.   O' thee sir: I, o' thee sir: what art thou sir?

Juletta.   Hir woman sir, and't like your worship, sir.

Alphonso.   Her baud, her fidle-stick;
Her Lady-fayry, to oyl the dores o' nights,
That they may open with discretion,
Her Gin, her Nut-crack.

Juletta.   Tis very well sir.   20

Alphonso.   Thou liest; tis damnable ill, tis most abhominable:
Will ye confes (Thing)?

Juletta.   Say I were guilty, sir;
I would be hangd before I would confesse:
Is this a World to confesse in?

Curio.   Deale directly.

Juletta.   Yes, if my matter lie direct before me:

17 baud] F2 (bawd); band F1

133

But when I am forc'd, and ferryted——
Alphonso.   Tell me the truth,
  And as I live, i'le give thee a new petticote.
Juletta.   And you would give me ten, I would not tell ye,
  Truths bear a greater price, then you are aware of.
Seberto.   Deale modestly.
Juletta.   I doe not pluck my cloths up.   30
Alphonso.   What say you sirha? you? or you? are ye dumb all?
Porter.   I saw her last night, and't shall like your worship,
  When I serv'd in her Livery.
Alphonso.   What's that, sirha?
Porter.   Her Chamber-pot, and't please ye.
Seberto.   A new Livery.
Alphonso.   Where lay she? who lay with her?
Porter.   In truth not I sir:
  I lay with my fellow *Fredrick*, in the flea-chamber,
  And't like your worship, we are almost worried.
Juletta.   I left her by her self, in her own closet,
  And there I thought she had slept.
Alphonso.   Why lay you from her?
Juletta.   It was her will I should: she is my Mistris,   40
  And my part is obedience.
Alphonso.   Were all the dores lockt?
Porter.   All mine.
1. Servant.   And mine: she could not get out those wayes
  Unles she lept the wals: and those are higher
  Then any womans courage dare aspire at.
Alphonso.   Come, you must know.
Curio.   Conceale it not, but deale plaine.
Juletta.   If I did know, and her trust lay upon me,
  Not all your angers, nor your flatteries
  Should make me speak, but having no more interest
  Then I may well deliver to the aire,
  I'le tell ye what I know, and tell it liberally: 50
  I think she is gon, because we cannot find her;
  I think she is weary of your tyranny,
  And therefore gon: may be she is in love:

May be in love, where you show no great liking,
And therefore gon: May be, some point of conscience,
Or vowd devotion——
Alphonso.   These are nothing, minion;
   You that can aime at these, must know the truth too.
Juletta.   Any more truth then this if I know, hang me,
   Or where to search for it; if I make a lie
   To gaine your love, and envy my best Mistris,   60
   Pin me against a wall, with my heel's upwards.
Alphonso.   Out of my dores.
Juletta.   That's all my poor petition:
   For if your house were gold, and she not in it,
   Sir, I should count it but a cage to whistle in.
Alphonso.   Whore, if she be above ground, I wil have her.
Juletta.   I would live in a cole-pit, then, were I your daughter.
Seberto.   Certaine she dos not know Sir.
Alphonso.   Hang her, hang her:
   She knowes too much: search all the house; all corners,
   And where tis possible she may goe out.

                         Exeunt [Porter *and*] *servants.*
   If I do finde your tricks——
Juletta.   Reward me for 'hem.   70
   Or if I had such tricks you could discover,
   So weak, and sleightly woven, you might look through,
   All the young Girles should hoot me out oth' Parish.
   You are my Master, but ye owne an anger
   Becomes a School-boy, that hath lost his Apples;
   Will ye force things into our knowledges?
Alphonso.   Come hither *Juletta*; thou didst love me.
Juletta.   And do still:
   You are my Ladies father, and I reverence ye.
Alphonso.   Thou wouldst have pleas'd my humor.
Juletta.   Any good way,
   That carried not suspition in't: or flattery,   80
   Or faile of trust.
Alphonso.   Come, come, thou wouldst have——
Juletta.   Stay sir.

Alphonso.   And thou hast felt my bounty for't, and shalt doe.
Dost thou want Clothes or Money?
Juletta.   Both.
Alphonso.   Shalt have both.
Juletta.   But not this way: I had rather be an Adamite
And bring Fig-leaves into fashion again.
If you were young sir,
Handsome, and fitted to a womans appetite;
And I a giddy-headed girle, that car'd for nothing,
Much might be done; then you might fumble with me,
And thinke to grope out matters of some moment,   90
Which now you will put too short for:
For what you have seen hitherto,
And know by me, has been but honest service,
Which I dare pin ith' market-place to answer;
And let the world, the flesh and divell examine it,
And come you in too, I dare stand your strictest.
And so much good may doe you, with your dreames of curtesie.
Alphonso.   This is most monstrous.
Seberto.   Sure she do's not know sir:
She durst not be so confident and guilty.

Enter Porter [*drunk*] *and servants.*

Alphonso.   How now; what newes? what hopes and steps dis-
covered?   100
Speake any thing thats good, that tends to th' matter;
Doe you stand staring still?
1. Servant.   We are no Gods sir,
To say she is here, or there: and what she is doing;
But we have search'd.
Porter.   I am sure she is not ith' Cellar;
For looke you sir, if she had been ith' Cellar——
Alphonso.   I am sure thou hast been there.
Porter.   As I carried the matter,
For I search'd every piece of Wine; yes sure sir,
And every little Terse that could but testifie:

108 Terse] F2; Teresse F1 (*i.e.*, tierce, cask)

And I drew hard to bolt her out.

Alphonso.   Away with him;
Fling him ith' Haymow, let him lie a mellowing;   110
He stinks of Muskadel like an English Christmas:
                    [*Exeunt some of the Servants with* Porter.]
Are these your cares? your services?

2. Servant.   Pray ye heare sir,
We have found where she went out; her very footing.

Alphonso.   Where, where? goe on.

Curio.   Observe then with more staiednesse.

2. Servant.   Searching the garden: at the little Posterne
That opens to the Parke, we first discovered it.

Alphonso.   A little foot?

1. Servant.   It must be hers, or none sir.

Alphonso.   How far beyond that?

2. Servant.   To the Parke it leads us,
But there the ground being hard, we could not marke it.

Alphonso.   She alwaies kept that Key: I was a coxcomb,   120
A foole, an asse, to give a girle that liberty:
Saddle my Horses, rogues, ye drunken varlets:
Your precious diligence lies in Pint-pots,
Your brains in Butts, my horses, ye pin-buttocks.

                              [*Exeunt Servants.*]
You'l beare me company?

Seberto.   We dare not leave ye,
Unlesse we found a quieter soule within ye.

Curio.   If we may do the Lady any service,
Sweet, gentle soule——

Alphonso [*to Servants within*].   I say againe, my horses:——
Are ye so hot? have ye your private pilgrimages?
Must ye be Jumping-Jone? Ile wander with ye: 130
Ile jump ye, and Ile joggle ye: [*to Servants within*] my horses;
And keep me this young Lirry-poope within dores.——
I will discover, dame——

Juletta.   'Tis fit you should sir,
If ye knew what: [*Aside*] Well Love, if thou bee'st with her,
Or what power else that armes her resolution,

137

Conduct her faire, and keepe her from this mad man,
Direct her to her wishes: dwell about her
That no dishonourable end ore-take her,
Danger, or want: and let me try my fortune.
Alphonso.   You know the place we meet in?
Seberto.   We shall hit it.   140
Alphonso.   And as ye are honest Gentlemen, endeavour.
Curio.   We'l search the best we can: if she light in our hands——
Alphonso   Tie her to th' horse taile.
Seberto.   We know how to use her,
But not your way, for all your state.
Alphonso [*to Servants within*].   Make haste there:——
And get you in, and looke to th' house. If you stir out, Damsell,
Or set o' foot any new motion this way,
When I come home, (which shall be suddenly)
You know my mind: if you doe play the rascall,
I have my eyes and eares in sundry places,
If ye doe praunce.
Juletta.   I shall doe that, that's fit, sir: 150
[*Aside*] And fit to crosse your fooleries; Ile faile else.——
And so Ile to my chamber.   *Exit.*
Alphonso.   To your prayers,
And leave your stubborne tricks: She is not far yet,
She cannot be; and we dividing suddenly——
Curio [*aside*].   Keep her from thy hands, I beseech.
Alphonso [*to Servants within*].   Our horses;——
Come cheerfully. Ile teach her to run gadding.

                                        Exeunt.

            Enter Roderigo, *and foure Out-lawes.*   [II.] ii

1. Out-law.   Captaine, y'are not merry.
Roderigo.   We get nothing,
We have no sport; whoring, and drinking spoiles us,
We keep no guards.
2. Out-law.   There come no passengers,
Merchants, nor Gentlemen, nor whosoever,

But we have Tribute.

Roderigo.   And whilst we spend that idlely,
We let those passe that carry the best purchase.
Ile have all search'd and brought in; Rogues, and Beggars,
Have got the tricke now to become Banck-masters.
Ile have none scape: onely my friends, and neighbours,
That may deliver to the King my innocence;   10
Those I would have regarded; tis policy.
But otherwise nor gravities, nor shadows,
Appeare they how they will, that may have purses,
For they shall pay.

3. Out-law.   Ye speake now like a Captaine.
And if we spare, flea us, and coyn our Cassoks;
Will ye looke blith?

Roderigo.   You heare no preparation
The King intends against us yet?

4. Out-law.   Not a word sir.
Good man, he's troubled with matter of more moment,
Hummings of higher nature vex his braines, sir;
Doe not we see his garrisons?

Roderigo.   Who are out now?   20

4. Out-law.   Good fellows sir, that if there be any purchase stirring
Will strike it dead; *Jaques* and *Lopez*, Lads
That know their quarters, as they know their knapsaks;
And will not off.

Roderigo.   Where is the boy ye brought me?
A pretty lad, and of a quicke capacity,
And bred up neatly.

1. Out-law.   He's within at meat, sir,
The knave is hungry: yet he seasons all
He eates or drinkes with many teares and sighings,
The saddest appetite I ever look'd on.

Roderigo.   The boy is young, tis feare and want of company   30
He knows and loves: use him not rough, nor harshly,
He will be quickly bold; Ile entertaine him:
I want a pretty Boy to waite upon me,

And when I am sad or sleepy, to prate to me;
Besides there's something in his face, I like well.
And still the more I looke, more like; let him want nothing,
And use him gently, all.
2. *Out-law.*   Here's a small Box, sir,
We tooke about him, which he griev'd to part with,
May be some wealth.
Roderigo.   Alas, some little money
The poore knave carried to defray his lodgings,   40
Ile give it him againe, and adde unto it.
'Twere sin to open such a petty purchase.
        Enter Lopez *and* Jaques, *with* Pedro [*in his pilgrim disguise*].
How now, who is this? what have you brought me Souldiers?
Lopez.   We know not wel what: a strange staring fellow,
Sullen enough I am sure.
Roderigo.   Where tooke ye him?
Jaques.   Upon the skirt o'th wood, viewing, and gaping,
And sometime standing still, as if he had meant
To view the best accesses to our quarters;
Money he has enough: and when we threatned him,
He smil'd, and yeilded; but not one word utter'd.   50
Lopez.   His habit saies he's holy: if his heart
Keep that proportion too, 'tis best ye free him,
We keep his Wallet here: I am sure tis heavy.
Roderigo.   Pilgrime: come hither sir; Are you a Pilgrime?
A piece of pretty holinesse: doe you shrinke sir?
A smug young Saint. What Countrey were you born in?
Ye have a Spanish face: In a dumb Province?
And had your mother too this excellent vertue?
No tongue do you say? sure she was a matchlesse woman;
What a fine family is this man sprung from!   60
Certaine he was begotten in a calme,
When all was husht: the Midwife was dumb Midnight;
Are ye seal'd up? or doe you scorne to answer?
Ye are in my hands, and I have medicines for ye
Can make ye speake: pull off his Bonnet, Souldiers;

        *44 staring] Dyce; staving F 1–2

140

Ye have a speaking face.

Lopez.　　　　　　　　　　I am sure a handsome:

This Pilgrime cannot want She-Saints to pray to.

Roderigo.　　Stand neerer: ha?

Pedro.　　　　　　　　　Come, do your worst; I am ready.

Roderigo.　　Is your tongue found?—— Go off, and let me talk
　　with him;

And keepe your watches round.

All.　　　　　　　　　　We are ready Captaine.　　　70

　　　　　　　　[*Exeunt all except* Roderigo *and* Pedro.]

Roderigo.　　So: now what are ye?

Pedro.　　　　　　　　　Am I?

My habit shewes me what I am.

Roderigo.　　　　　　　　Thy heart

A desperate foole, and so thy fate shall tell thee;

What devill brought thee hither? for I know thee.

Pedro.　　I know thou dost: and since it is my fortune

To light into thy fingers; I must thinke too

The most malicious of all devils brought me,

Yet some men say thou art Noble.

Roderigo.　　　　　　　　　Not to thee,

That were a benefit to mocke the giver:

Thy father hates my friends, and family,　　　　　　　80

And thou hast been the heire of all his malice.

Can two such stormes meet then, and part with kissing?

Pedro.　　You have the mightier hand.

Roderigo.　　　　　　　　And so Ile use it.

Pedro.　　I cannot hinder ye: lesse can I beg

Submissive at his knees that knows not honour;

That bears the stamp of man, and not his nature;

Ye may doe what ye please.

Roderigo.　　　　　　　　I will doe all.

Pedro.　　And when you have done all, which is my poore ruine,

(For farther your base malice cannot venture)

Dishonours selfe will cry you out a coward.　　　　　90

Hadst thou been brave, and noble and an Enemy,

　　　　81 his] Dyce; this F 1–2

141

Thou wouldst have sought me whilst I carried Armes,
Whilst my good Sword was my profession,
And then have cried out *Pedro*, I defie thee;
Then stuck *Alphonso's* quarrell on the point,
The mercenary anger thou serv'st under
To get his daughter. Then thou shouldst have brav'd me,
And arm'd with all thy families hate, upon me
Done something worthy feat: Now poore and basely
Thou setst Toyles to betray me; and like the Pesant,   100
That dares not meet the Lyon in the face,
Digst crafty pit-fals: Thou sham'st the Spanish honour:
Thou hast neither poynt of man, nor conscience in thee.
Roderigo.   Sir, sir, y'are brave; ye plead now in a Sanctuary;
You think your Pilgrimes bulwarke can defend ye:
You will not finde it so.
Pedro.   I looke not for't.
The more unhallowed soule hast thou to offer it.
Roderigo.   When you were bravest, sir, and your Sword sharpest,
I durst affront ye: when the Court Sunne guilded ye,
And every cry was the young hopefull *Pedro*,   110
Alonsos sprightly sonne; then durst I meet ye,
When you were Master of this fame, and fashion,
And all your glories in the full Meridian,
The Kings proof-favour buckled on your body;
Had we then come to competition,
Which I have often sought——
Pedro.   And I desired too.
Roderigo.   You should have seen this Sword, how ere you sleight it,
And felt it too; sharper then sorrow felt it,
In execution quicker then thy scornes;
Thou shouldst have seen all this, and shrunke to see it.   120
Then like a Gentleman I would have us'd thee,
And given thee the faire fortune of thy being,
Then with a Souldiers Arme I had honour'd thee;
But since thou stealst upon me like a Spie,
And thiefe-like thinkst that holy case shall carry thee

*111 *Alonsos* sprightly sonne] *stet* F 1–2

142

Through all my purposes, and so betray me,
Base as your act, thy end be, and I forget thee.
Pedro.   What poore evasions thou buildst on, to abuse me?
The goodnesse of a man nere taught these principles.
I come a Spie? durst any Noble spirit   130
Put on this habit, to become a Traitor?
Even in an Enemy shew me this antipathy
Where there is Christian faith, and this not reverenced:
I come a Spie? no *Roderigo*, no,
A hater of thy person, a maligner?
So far from that, I brought no malice with me,
But rather when I meet thee, teares to soften thee;
When I put on this habit, I put off
All fires, all angers, all those starts of youth
That clapt too ranke a biasse to my being,   140
And drew me from the right marke all should aime at;
Instead of stubborne steele, I put on prayers;
For rash and hasty heats, a sweet repentance:
Long weary steps, and vows, for my vain-glories.
O *Roderigo*.
Roderigo.   If thy tongue could save thee,
Prating be thy baile, thou hast a rare benefit.——
Souldiers, come out, and bring a halter with ye;——
Ile forgive your holy habit sir, but Ile hang you.

Enter Outlaws, Lopez, Jaques.

1. Out-law.   Wherefore this halter Captaine?
Roderigo.   For this traytor.
Go, put it on him, and then tie him up.   150
1. Out-law.   Do you want a Band sir? This is a course wearing,
Twill sit but scurvily upon this collar;
But patience is as good as a French Pickadell.
Lopez.   What's his fault, Captaine?
Roderigo.   Tis my will he perish,
And thats his fault.
Pedro.   A Captaine of good government.

127 your] you F 1; the F 2

Come Souldiers, come, ye are roughly bred, and bloody,
Shew your obedience, and the joy ye take
In executing impious commands;
Ye have a Captaine seales your liberall pardons,
Be no more Christians, put religion by,   160
Twill make ye cowards: feele no tendernesse,
Nor let a thing call'd conscience trouble ye;
Alasse, twill breed delay. Beare no respect
To what I seem: were I a Saint indeed,
Why should that stagger ye? You know not holinesse:
To be excellent in evill, is your goodnesse;
And be so, twill become ye: have no hearts,
For feare you should repent: that will be dangerous:
For if there be a knocking there, a pricking,
And that pulse beate backe to your considerations,   170
How ye have laid a stiffe hand on Religion——
Roderigo.   Trusse him I say.
Pedro.   And violated faith——
Roderigo.   Heare him not prate.
Pedro.   Why, what a thing will this be?
What strange confusion then will breed among ye?
Roderigo.   Will none of ye obey?
Pedro.   What devils vex ye?
The feares ye live in and the hourely dangers
Will be delights to these: those have their ends,
But these outlive all time, and all repentance:
And if it creep into your conscience once,
Be sure ye locke that close.
Roderigo.   Why stand ye gazing?   180
Pedro.   Farewell sleep, peace, all that are humane comforts,
Better ye had been Trees, or Stones, and happier;
For those die here, and seeke no further being,
Nor hopes, nor punishments.
Roderigo.   Rots take ye Rascals.
Jaques.   What would you have us do?
Roderigo.   Dispatch the prater.
Jaques.   And have religious blood hang on our consciences?

144

We are bad enough already: sins enough
To make our graves even loath us.
Roderigo.   No man love me?
Lopez.   Although I be a thiefe, I am no hangman;
They are two mens trades, and let another execute.   190
Lay violent hands on holy things?
Roderigo.   Base Cowards,
Put to your powers, ye Rascals, I command ye.
Holy, or unholy, if I say it,
Ile have it done.
1. Out-law.   If I do't, let me starve for't.
2. Out-law.   Or I.
3. Out-law.   Or I: we will obey things handsome,
And bad enough, and over doe obedience:
But to be made such instruments of mischiefe——
Jaques.   I have done as many villanies as another,
And with as little reluctation,
Let me come cleare of these, and wipe that score off.   200
Put me upon a felt and known perdition?
Roderigo.   Have ye conspir'd, ye slaves?
Pedro.   How vildly this showes,
In one that would command anothers temper,
And beare no bound in's own?
Roderigo.   Am I thus jaded?
Pedro.   Is it my life thou long'st for *Roderigo*?
And can no sacrifice appease thy malice,
But my blood spilt? Doe it thy selfe, dispatch it;
And as thou takst the whole revenge unto thee,
Take the whole sin upon thee; and be mighty,
Mighty in evill, as thou art in anger: 210
And let not these poore wretches houle for thy sake.
Those things that in thine owne glasse seeme most monstrous,
Wouldst thou abuse their weak sights with, for amiable?
Is it, thou thinkst to feare me with thy terrors,
And into weake condition draw my vertue?
If I were now to learn to die I would sue to thee:
Or did I feare death, then I would make thee glorious.

But knowing what, and how far I can suffer;
And all my whole life being but deaths preface,
My sleep but at next doore——
Roderigo.   Are ye so valiant?   220
Ile make ye feele: Ile make ye know, and feele too;
And Rascals, you shall tremble. Keepe him here,
And keep him safe too: if he scape your guards——
Pedro.   Feare not, I will not.
Roderigo.   As I live, ye die for't;
I will not be thus baffled.   *Exit.*
Jaques.   What a divel have ye done, Pilgrim? or what mischief
Have you conspir'd, that he should rage and rave thus?
Have you kild his father, or his mother? or strangled any of his
    kindred?
Lopez.   Has he no sisters? Have you not been bouncing
About their belly-pieces?
Jaques.   Why should that be dangerous   230
Or any way deserve death? is it not naturall?
Bar us the Christian liberty of women,
And build us up with brick, take away our free-stone.
1. Out-law.   Because thou art holier then he, upon my conscience
He dos not envy thee: that's not his quarrell;
For, look you, that might be compounded without praiers.
Lopez.   Nor that thou seemst an honester man: for here
We have no trading with such Tinsell-stuffe;
To be an excellent thiefe, is all we aime at.
Wilt thou take a spit and stride, and see if thou canst outrun us?   240
Pedro.   I scorn to shift his fury, keepe your obedience;
For though your government admit no president,
Keep your selves carefull in't.
Jaques.   Thou wilt be hang'd then.
Pedro.   I cannot die with fewer faults upon me.
2. Out-law.   Tis ten to one he wil shoot him: for the devil's in him
If he hang him himselfe.
Lopez.   He has too proud a nature:
He will compell some one.

243 wilt] F2; will F1

146

Jaques.   I am confident.

Lopez.   And so are all I thinke.

Pedro.   Be not molested,
  If I must die, let it not trouble you;
  It stirs not me: It is the end I was born for.   250
  Onely this honest office I desire ye,
  (If there be curtesie in men of your breed)
  To see me buried; not to let his fury
  Expose my body to the open violence
  Of beasts, and fowles: so far I urge humanity.

      Enter Roderigo, Alinda [*disguised as a boy*].

Jaques.   He shall not deny us that: we'l see ye under ground
  And give ye a volley of as good cups of Sacke,
  For that's our Discipline.

Lopez.   He comes againe,
  As high in rage as ever; the boy with him.

1. Out-law.   Will he compell the child?

Lopez.   He is bent to doe it,   260
  And must have somebody.

Roderigo.   If thou lov'st me doe it:
  Love me, or love me not, I say thou shalt doe it:
  Stare not, nor stagger, sirra; if ye deny me——
  Doe you see this Rogue?

Alinda.   What would ye have me doe sir?
  [*Aside*] Heavens goodnesse blesse me.

Roderigo.   Doe? why hang the Rascall,
  That would hang me.

Alinda.   I am a boy, and weake, sir.

Roderigo.   Thou art strong enough to tie him to a Bough,
  And turn him off: come, thou shalt be my Jewell,
  And Ile allow thee horse, and all thy pleasures,
  And twenty gallant things: Ile teach thee armes too;   270
  Make thee mine heire.

Alinda.   Let me inherit death first.

Roderigo.   Make me not angry, sirha.

Alinda.   Which is the man, sir?

Ile pluck up the best heart I can yet.
Roderigo.   Feare not,
  It is my will: That in the Pilgrimes coate there,
  That devill in the Saints skin.
Alinda [*aside*].   Guard me goodnesse.
Roderigo.   Dispatch him presently.
Pedro.   I wait your worst, sir.
Jaques.   Will the boy doe it? Is the rogue so confident?
  So young, so deep in blood?
Lopez.   He shakes, and trembles.
Pedro.   Dost thou seeke more coles still to sear thy conscience,
  Worke sacred innocence, to be a devill?   280
  Doe it thy selfe for shame, thou best becomst it.
Roderigo.   Sirha, I scorn my finger should be filde with thee;
  And yet Ile have it done: this child shall strangle thee,
  A crying Girle, if she were here should master thee.
Alinda [*aside*].   How should I save him? how my self from
    violence?
Pedro.   Leave your tongue-valour, and dispatch your hate, sir;
  The patience of my death, shall more torment thee,
  (Thou painted honour, thou base man made backward)
  Then all my life has fear'd thee.
Roderigo.   Gag him, sirha.
Jaques.   The Boy looks cheerfully now: sure he will do it.   290
Lopez.   He will mall him else.
Alinda.   Are ye prepar'd to die, sir?
Pedro.   Yes boy, and ready; prethee to thy businesse.
Alinda.   Why are ye then so angry? so perplext, sir?
  Patience wins Heaven, and not the heat of passion.
  Why doe you rayle?
Lopez.   The boy's a pretty Priest.
Pedro.   I thank ye gentle child, you teach me truely.
Alinda.   You seem to feare too.
Pedro.   Thou seest more, then I feel, boy.
Alinda.   You tremble sure.
Pedro.   No sure boy, tis thy tendernesse:
  Prethee make haste, and let that gulph be satisfied.

Alinda.   Are ye so willing to goe to it?
Pedro.   Most willing: 300
  I would not borrow from his curtesie
  One houre of life, to gaine an age of glory.
Alinda.   And is your reckoning straight sir?
Pedro.   As straight as truth, boy:
  I cannot go more joyfully to a wedding.
Alinda.   Then to your prayers: Ile dispatch ye presently.
  [*Aside*] Now guid my tongue, thou blessednesse.
Roderigo.   A good boy.
Alinda.   But harke ye sir, one word; and pray ye resolve me.
  Let me speake privately.
Roderigo.   What wouldst thou have child?
                         [*They withdraw from the others.*]
Alinda.   Shall this man die?
Roderigo..   Why dost thou make that question?
Alinda.   Pray ye be not angry: if he must, Ile doe it.   310
  But must he now?
Roderigo.   What else? who dare reprieve him?
Alinda.   Pray ye thinke againe; and as your injuries
  Are great, and full, you suffer from this fellow,
  Doe not ye purpose so to suit your vengeance?
Roderigo.   I doe, and must.
Alinda.   You cannot if he die now.
Roderigo.   Cannot?
Alinda.   No, cannot: be not vext, you'l finde it:
  I have considered, and I know it certaine,
  Ye suffer below him: lose all your angers.
Roderigo.   Why my best boy?
Alinda.   I love, and tender ye,
  I would not tell ye else. Is that revenge,   320
  To sleight your cause, and Saint your enemy,
  Clap the Doves wings of downy peace unto him,
  And let him soare to Heaven, whilst you are sighing?
  Is this revenge?
Roderigo.   I would have him die.
Alinda.   Prepar'd thus?

149

The blessing of a father never reach'd it:
His contemplation now scornes ye, contemnes ye,
And all the tortors ye can use. Let him die thus;
And these that know and love revenge will laugh at ye:
Here lies the honour of a wel-bred anger,
To make his enemy shake and tremble under him;   330
Doubt: nay, almost despaire, and then confound him.
This man ye rocke asleep, and all your rages
Are Requiems to his parting soule, meere Anthems.

Roderigo.   Indeed he is strongly built.
Alinda.   You cannot shake him;
And the more waight ye put on his foundation,
Now as he stands, ye fixe him still the stronger;
If ye love him, honour him, would heape upon him
Friendships and benefits beyond example,
Hope him a Star in Heaven, and there would stick him,
Now take his life.

Roderigo.   I had rather take mine own, Boy.   340
Alinda.   Ile ease him presently.
Roderigo.   Stay, be not hasty.
Alinda [*aside*].   Blesse my tongue still.
Lopez.   What has the boy done to him?
How dull, and still he lookes?
Alinda.   You are a wise man.
And long have buckled with the worlds extremities,
A valiant man, and no doubt know both fortunes,
And would ye work your Master-peece thus madly,
Take the bare name of honour, that will pitty ye
When the world knows ye have prey'd on a poor Pilgrim?
Roderigo.   The Boy has staggard me: what would'st thou have
    me?
Alinda.   Have ye? do you not feel Sir? do's it not stir ye?   350
Doe you aske a child? I would have ye do most bravely,
Because I most affect ye: like your selfe Sir,
Scorn him, and let him goe; seem to contemne him,
And now ye have made him shake, seale him his pardon.
When he appears a subject fit for Anger,

And fit for you, his pious Armour off,
His hopes no higher then your sword may reach at,
Then strike, and then ye know revenge; then take it.
[*Aside*] I hope I have turn'd his mind.
Roderigo.   Let the foole goe there,
  I scorn to let loose so base an anger   360
  May light on thee: See me no more, but quit me;
  And when we meet again——
Pedro.   I'le thank ye Captaine.   *Exit.*
Alinda.   Why this was like your selfe: [*aside*] but which way
    goes he?
  Shall we ne're happy meet?
Roderigo.   I am drowsie; Boy,
  Goe with me, and discourse: I like thy company
  O Child! I love thy Tongue.
Alinda.   I shall waite on ye.
                 Exeunt [*Alinda* and *Roderigo*].
Lopez.   The Boy has don't: a Plaguey witty Rascall.
  And I shall love him terribly.
Jaques.   'Twas he most certaine,
  For if ye marke, how earnest he was with him,
  And how he labour'd him.
Lopez.   A cuning villaine,   370
  But a good Rogue; This Boy will make's all honest.
1. Out-law.   I scarce beleeve that: but I like the Boy well.
  Come, let's to Supper; then upon our watches.
Lopez.   This Pilgrim scap'd, a joyfull one.
Jaques.   Let's Drink round,
  To the Boyes health, and then about our businesse.
                          Exeunt.

Enter Roderigo, Jaques, Lopez, *and three Out-Lawes.*   III. i

Roderigo.   None of you know her?
Jaques.   Alas Sir, we never saw her:
  Nor ever heard of her, but from your report.

        *374 scap'd,] ~ ₐ F 1–2

Roderigo. No happy eye?

Lopez. I doe not think 'tis she, Sir,
Methinks a woman dares not.

Roderigo. Thou speak'st poorely,
What dares not woman, when she is provok'd?
Or what seemes dangerous to Love, or fury?
That it is she, this has confirm'd me certain,
These Jewels here, a part of which I sent her,
And though unwilling, yet her Father wrought her
To take, and weare.   10

Lopez. A wench, and we not know it?
And among us? where were our understandings?
I could have ghess'd unhappily: have had some feeling
In such a matter: Here are as pretty fellowes,
At the discovery of such a Jigambob:
A handsome wench too? Sure we have lost our faculties,
We have no motions: what should she doe here, Sir?

Roderigo. That's it that troubles me: O that base Rascall!
There lies the misery: how cunningly she quit him,
And how she urg'd? Had ye been constant to me,
I ne're had suffer'd this.   20

1. Out-law. Ye might have hang'd him:
And would he had been hang'd, that's all we care for't:
So our hands had not don't.

Roderigo. She is gone again too,
And what care have ye for that? gone, and contemn'd me;
Master'd my will, and power, and now laughs at me.

Lopez. The devill that brought her hither, Sir I thinke
Has carryed her back again invisible,
For we ne're knew, nor heard of her departure.

Jaques. No living thing came this night through our watches.
She went with you.

Roderigo. Was by me till I slept,   30
But when I wak'd, and call'd: O my dull pate here,
If I had open'd this when it was given me,
This Roguy Box.

Lopez. We could but give it ye.

Roderigo.   Pilgrime? a Pox o' Pilgrimes, there the game goes,
  There's all my fortune fled; I know it, I feele it.

      Enter Alphonso, *and* Second Outlaw.

Alphonso.   Bring me unto thy Captain: where's thy Captain?
  I am founder'd, melted, some fairy thing or other
  Has led me dauncing; the devill has haunted me
  Ith' likenesse of a voyce: give me thy Captaine.
2. Out-law.   He's here Sir, there he stands.
Alphonso.   How do'st thou Captain?
  I have been fool'd and jaded, made a doggebolt.   40
  My daughters runne away: I have been haunted too,
  I have lost my horse; I am hungry, and out of my wits also.
Roderigo.   Come in; I'le tell you what I know: strange things,
  And take your ease; I'le follow her recovery:
  These shall be yours the whil'st, and do ye service.
Alphonso.   Let me have drinke enough: I am almost choak'd too.
Roderigo.   You shall have any thing; what think you now,
  Souldiers?
Jaques.   I think a woman, is a woman that's any thing.
  The next we take, we'l search a little neerer,
  We'l not be boyed again with a paire of breeches.   50
                                  Exeunt.

      Enter Juletta [*disguised as a boy*].   [III.] ii

Juletta.   He's gone in here: This is *Roderigo's* quarter,
  And i'le be with him soone: I'le startle him,
  A little better then I have done: All this long night
  I have led him out o'th way, to try his patience,
  And made him sweare, and curse; and pray, and sweare againe,
  And cry for anger; I made him leave his horse too,
  Where he can never find him more; whistled to him,
  And then he would run through thick and thin, to reach me,
  And down in this ditch; up again, and shake him,
  And swear some certaine blessings; then into that bush   10

    34.1 Second Outlaw] Dyce; 2 *Outlaw* F 1; 2 *Out-laws* F 2

Pop goes his pate, and all his face is comb'd over,
And I sit laughing: a hundred tricks, I have serv'd him:
And I will double em, before I leave him;
I'le teach his anger to dispute with women.
But all this time, I cannot meet my Mistresse,
I cannot come to comfort her; that grieves me,
For sure she is much afflicted: till I doe,
I'le haunt thy Ghost *Alphonso*; I'le keep thee waking,
Yes, I must get a Drum: I am villanous weary,   20
And yet i'le trot about these villages
Till I have got my will, and then have at ye.
I'le make your anger drop out at your elbowes ere I leave ye.

                                                        Exit.

Enter Seberto, *and* Curio.

Seberto.   'Tis strange, in all the circuit we have ridden,
    We cannot crosse her: no way light upon her.
Curio.   I doe not think she is gone thus far, or this way,
    For certain if she had, we should have reach'd her,
    Made some discovery: heard some news; we have seen nothing.
Seberto.   Nor passed by any body that could promise any thing.
    She is certainly disguis'd, her modesty
    Durst never venture else.
Curio.   Let her take any shape,
    And let me see it once, I can distinguish it.   10
Seberto.   So should I think too: has not her father found her?
Curio.   No, i'le be hang'd then; he has no patience
    Unlesse she light in's teeth, to looke about him.
    He guesses now, and chafes and frets like Tinsell.
Seberto.   Let him goe on, he cannot live without it.
    But keep her from him, heaven: where are we *Curio*?
Curio.   In a wood I think, hang me if I know else.
    And yet I have ridden all these Coasts, at all houres,
    And had an aime.
Seberto.   I would we had a guid.

        6 passed] Sympson; passe F 1-2   18 an aime] F 2; and aime F 1

Curio.   And if I be not much awry *Seberto*,
  Not far off should be *Rodorigo's* quarter,   20
  For in this Fastnes if I be not cozen'd,
  He and his Out-laws live.
Seberto.   This is the place then
  We appointed him to meet in.
Curio.   Yes, I thinke so.
            Enter Alinda [*in boy's disguise*].
Seberto.   Would we could meet some living thing: what's that
    there?
Curio.   A Boy, I think, stay; why may not he direct us?
Alinda.   I am hungry, and I am weary, and I cannot find him.
  Keep my wits heaven, I feele 'em wavering,
  O God my head.
Seberto.   Boy, dost thou heare, thou stripling?
Alinda.   Now they will teare me, torture me, now *Roderigo*
  Will hang him without mercy; ha!
Curio.   Come hither.   30
  A very pretty Boy: what place is this, child?
  And whether dost thou travell? How he stares!
  Some stubborn Master has abus'd the Boy,
  And beaten him: how he complaines! Whether goest thou?
Alinda.   I goe to *Segovia* Sir, to my sick Mother,
  I have been taken here by drunken theeves,
  And (O my bones;) I have been beaten Sir,
  Mis-us'd, and rob'd: extreamly beaten Gentlemen,
  O God, my side!
Seberto.   What beasts would use a Boy thus?
  Look up, and be of good cheer.
Alinda.   O, I cannot.   40
  My back, my back, my back.
Curio.   What theeves?
Alinda.   I know not.
  But they call the Captaine *Roderigo*.
Curio.   Look ye,
  I knew we were there abouts.

43 knew] F2; know F1

Seberto.   Do'st thou want any thing?
Alinda.   Nothing but ease, but ease, Sir.
Curio.   There's some mony,
   And get thee to thy Mother.
Alinda.   I thank ye Gentlemen.
Seberto.   This was extreamely foule, to vex a Child thus.
   Come, let's along, we cannot loose our way now.
                               Exit [*with* Curio].
Alinda.   Though ye are honest men, I feare your fingers,
   And glad I am got off; O how I tremble!
   Send me but once within his armes dear Fortune,   50
   And then come all the world: what shall I do now?
   'Tis almost night again, and where to lodge me,
   Or get me meat, or any thing, I know not.
   These wild woods, and the fancies I have in me,
   Will run me mad.

         Enter Juletta [*in her boy's disguise, with a drum*].

Juletta.   Boy, Boy.
Alinda [*aside*].   More set to take me?
Juletta.   Do'st thou heare Boy? thou pointer.
Alinda [*aside*].   'Tis a Boy too,
   A Lacky Boy: I need not feare his feircenesse.
Juletta.   Canst thou beat a Drum?
Alinda.   A Drum?
Juletta.   This thing, a drum here.
   Didst thou never see a Drum: Canst thou make this grumble?
Alinda [*aside*].   *Julettas* face, and tongue; Is she run mad too?   60
   Here may be double craft:—— I have no skill in't.
Juletta.   I'le give thee a Royall but to goe along with me.
Alinda.   I care not for thy Royall, I have other businesse,
   Drum to thy selfe, and daunce to it.
Juletta.   Sirha, Sirha.
   Thou scurvy Sirha; thou snotty-nos'd scab, do'st thou heare me?
   If I lay downe my Drum——
Alinda [*aside*].   Here comes more Company,
   I feare a plot, heaven send me fairely from it.   *Exit.*

Enter Rodorigo, Jaques *and* Lopez [*carrying a pilgrim's gown and a sword*].

Juletta [*aside*].   Basto; who's here?   [*She steps aside.*]
Lopez.   Captain, do you need me farther?
Roderigo.   No not a foot: give me the gowne: the sword now.
                                        [*He puts them on.*]
Juletta [*aside*].   This is the devill theef, and if he take me,   70
    Woe be to my Gally-gaskins.
Lopez.   Certaine Sir,
    She will take her patches of, and change her habit.
Roderigo.   Let her do what she please: No, no *Alinda*
    You cannot cozen me againe in a Boyes figure,
    Nor hide the beauty of that face in patches,
    But I shall know it.
Juletta [*aside*].   A Boy his face in patches?
Roderigo.   Nor shall your tongue againe bewitch mine Anger.
    If she be found ith' woods, send me word presently,
    And i'le returne; she cannot be farre gone yet:
    If she be not, expect me, when ye see me,   80
    Use all your service to my friend *Alphonso*,
    And have a care to your businesse: farewell,
    No more, farewell.
            Exeunt [Roderigo *one way*, Jaques *and* Lopez *the other*].
Juletta.   I am heartily glad thou art gone yet.
    This Boy in patches, was the Boy came by me,
    The very same, how hastily it shifted?
    What a mopp'-eyed asse was I, I could not know her,
    This must be she, this is she, now I remember her,
    How loth she was to talk too, how she fear'd me?
    I could now pisse mine eyes out for meer anger:
    I'le follow her, but who shall vex her father then?   90
    One flurt at him, and then I am for the voyage.
    If I can crosse the Captain too: Come Tabor.   *Exit.*

*67.1 Jaques *and* Lopez] *and two Outlaw* F 1; *and two Outlaws* F 2
68 farther] F 2; Father F 1   72 of] *i.e.*, off

Enter Jaques, *and* Lopez.   [III.] i

Jaques.   Are they all set?
Lopez.   All, and each quarter quiet.
Jaques.   Is the old man asleep?
Lopez.   An houre agoe Sir.
Jaques.   We must be very carefull in his absence,
    And very watchfull.
Lopez.   It concerns us neerely,
    He will not be long from us.
Jaques.   No, he cannot.
Lopez.   A little heate of love, which he must wander out,
    And then again: harke.   *Drum a far off.*
Jaques.   What?
Lopez.   Tis not the wind sure:
    That's still and calme; no noyse, nor flux of waters.
Jaques.   I heare a Drum, I thinke.
Lopez.   That that; it beats againe now.
Jaques.   Now it comes neerer: sure we are surprized, sir;   10
    Some from the Kings command: we are lost, we are dead all.
Lopez.   Hark, hark, a charge now: my Captaine has betray'd us,
    And left us to this ruine, run away from us.
    Another beates o'that side.

Enter two Out-lawes.

1. Out-law.   Fly, flie, *Jaques,*
    We are taken in a toyle: snapt in a pitfall;
    Methinks I feele a Sword already shave me.
2. Out-law.   A thousand horse and foot, a thousand pioners,
    If we get underground, to fetch us out againe;
    And every one an Axe to cut the woods downe.
Lopez.   This is the dismalst night——
                                        Exeunt.

*0.1 Lopez] Dyce; *1* Out-Law F 1–2
1, 2, 4, 6, 7, 9, 12 s.p. *Lopez]* Dyce; *1* Outl. F 1–2
*12–14 *Lopez.* Hark...side] Dyce; *1* Outl. Hark...from us. | *Lop.* Another...
side F 1–2
    14 s.p. *1. Out-law]* Dyce; *2* Out-l. F 1–2
    17 s.p. *2. Out-law]* Dyce; *3* Out-l $_\Lambda$ F 1–2

Enter Alphonso [*half-dressed.*]

Alphonso.   Where's my nag now?   20
And what make I here to be hang'd? What devill
Brought me into this danger? Is there nere a hole,
That I may creep in deep enough, and die quickly?
Nere an old ditch to choke in? I shall be taken
For their Commander now, their Generall,
And have a commanding Gallows set up for me
As high as a May-pole; and nasty Songs made on me,
Be printed with a Pint-pot and a dagger.
They are all kill'd by this time: Can I pray?
Let me see that first: I have too much feare to be faithfull.   30
Where's all my State now? I must go hunt for daughters;
Daughters, and damsels of the Lake, damned daughters.
A hundred Crownes for a good tod of Hay,
Or a fine hollow Tree, that would containe me;
I heare 'em comming: I feele the nooze about me.

Enter Seberto, Curio, *Outlaws*, [Lopez], Jaques.

Seberto.   Why do you fear, and fly? here are no Souldiers;
None from the King to vex ye.
1. Out-law.   The Drum, the Drum, sir.
Curio.   I never saw such Pigeon-hearted people:
What Drum? what danger? who's that that shakes behind there:
Mercy upon me sir, why are ye fear'd thus?   40
Alphonso.   Are we all kill'd, no mercy to be hoped for?
Am I not shot do you think?
Seberto.   You are strangely frighted,
Shot with a fiddle stick: who's here to shoot ye?
A Drum we saw indeed, a boy was beating it,
And hunting Squirrels by Moon-light.
Lopez.   Nothing else, sir?
Curio.   Not any thing: no other person stirring.
Alphonso.   O that I had that boy: this is that Devill,
That fairy rogue, that haunted me last night;
H'as sleeves like Dragons wings.

159

Seberto.   A little Foot-boy.

Alphonso.   Come, let's go in, and let me get my clothes on;   50
  If ere I stay here more to be thus martyr'd——
  Did ye not meet the wench?

Seberto.   No sure, we met her not.

Alphonso.   She has been here in boyes apparrell, Gentlemen,
  A gallant thing, and famous for a Gentlewoman,
  And all her face patcht over for discovery:
  A pilgrime too, and thereby hangs a circumstance,
  That she hath playd her master-prize, a rare one.
  I came too short.

Curio.   Such a young boy we met sir.

Alphonso.   In a gray hat.

Curio.   The same: his face all patcht too.

Alphonso.   Twas she, a rot run with her; she: that ranck she;   60
  Walk in, Ile tell ye all: and then we'l part again,
  But get some store of Wine: this fright sits here yet.

                                                    Exeunt.

                        Enter Juletta.   [III. v

Juletta.   What a fright I have put 'em in; what a brave hurry.
  If this doe bolt him, Ile be with him againe
  With a new part, was never play'd; Ile ferk him.
  As he hunts her, so ile hunt him: Ile claw him.
  Now will I see if I can crosse her footing:
  Yet still ile watch his water, he shall pay for't;
  And when he thinks most malice, and meanes worse,
  Ile make him know the Mare's the better Horse.   *Exit.*

                Enter Pedro [*disguised*], *and a* Gentleman.   [III.

Gentleman.   Ye are a stranger sir, and for humanity,
  Being come within our walls, I would shew you something.
  Ye have seen the Castle?

              III.v] Dyce; *scene unmarked in* F 1–2
              III.vi] *Scena quinta.* F 1; SCENE V. F 2

                            160

Pedro.   Yes sir, tis a strong one,
And well maintain'd.
Gentleman.   Why are you still thus sad, sir?
How doe ye like the walkes?
Pedro.   They are very pleasant;
Your Town stands coole and sweet.
Gentleman.   But that I would not
Affect you with more sadnesse, I could shew ye
A place worth view.
Pedro.   Showes seldome alter me sir;
Pray ye speake it, and then shew it.
Gentleman.   Tis a house here
Where people of all sorts, that have been visited   10
With lunacies and follies waite their cures:
There's fancies of a thousand stamps and fashions,
Like flies in severall shapes buze round about ye,
And twice as many gestures; some of pitty,
That it would make ye melt to see their passions:
And some as light againe, that would content ye.
But I see sir, your temper is too modest,
Too much inclin'd to contemplation,
To meet with these?
Pedro.   You could not please me better;
And I beseech you sir, doe me the honour   20
To let me waite upon ye.
Gentleman.   Since ye are willing,
To me it shall be a pleasure to conduct ye.
Pedro. I never had such a mind yet to see misery.   *Exeunt.*

Enter two [madhouse] Keepers.   [III. vii]

1. Keeper. Carry mad *Besse* some meat, she rores like Thunder;
And tie the Parson short, the Moone's ith full,
H'as a thousand Pigs in's braines: Who lookes to the Prentize?
Keep him from women, he thinks h'as lost his Mistris;
And talke of no silke stuffes, 'twill runne him horn mad.

12 There's] F2; Their's F1   III.vii] *Scena sexta,* F1; SCENE VI. F2

2. Keeper.   The Justice keeps such a stirre yonder with his Charges,
And such a coyle with warrants.
1. Keeper.   Take away his Statutes;
The divell has possest him in the likenesse
Of penall Lawes: keep him from Aquavite,
For if that spirit creep into his corum,   10
He will commit us all: how is it with the Scholler?
2. Keeper.   For any thing I see, he's in his right wits.
1. Keeper.   Thou art an asse; in's right wits, goodman coxcomb?
As though any man durst be in's right wits, and be here.
It is as much as we dare be that keep 'em.

Enter English madman.

English Madman.   Give me some drink.
1. Keeper.   O, there's the English man.
English Madman.   Fill me a thousand pots, and froth 'em, froth
'em.
Down o' your knees, ye rogues, and pledge me roundly;

> *One, two, three, and foure;*
> *We shall be all merry within this houre.*   20

To the great Turke.
1. Keeper.   Peace, peace, thou Heathen drunkard;
These English are so Malt-mad, there's no medling with 'em;
When they have a fruitfull yeere of Barly there,
All the whole Island's thus.
English Madman.   A Snuff, a snuff, a snuff,
A lewd notorious snuff: giv't him againe, boy.

Enter Shee-*foole.*

She-fool.   God-ye-good even, Gaffer.
2. Keeper.   Who let the Foole loose?
1. Keeper.   If any of the mad-men take her, she is pepper'd,
They'l bounce her loynes.
She-fool.   Will ye walke into the cole house?
1. Keeper.   She is as leacherous too as a she-ferret.

*19–20 *One, two...this houre.*
26, 28, 31, 33, 34, 36, 37, 47, 51 s.p. *She-fool*] Fool (*Foole*) F 1–2

2. Keeper. Who a vengeance looks to her? Go in *Kate,*   30
Ile give thee a fine Apple.
She-fool.   Will ye busse me?
And tickle me, and make me laugh?
1. Keeper.   Ile whip ye.
English Madman. Foole, foole, come up to me foole.
She-fool.   Are ye peeping?
English Madman. Ile get thee with five fooles.
She-fool.   O fine, O dainty.
English Madman. And thou shalt lie in in a horse-cloth, like a
    Lady.
She-fool. And shall I have a Coach?
English Madman.   Drawn with foure Turkeys,
And they shall tread thee too.
She-fool.   We shall have egges then;
And shall I sit upon 'em?
English Madman.   I, I, and they shall be all addle,
And make an admirable Tanzey for the divell.
Come come away, I am taken with thy love foole,   40
And will mightily belabour thee.
1. Keeper. How the foole bridles? how she twitters at him?
These Englishmen would stagger a wise-woman.
If we should suffer her to have her will now,
We should have all the women in *Spaine* as mad as she here.
2. Keeper. They would strive who should be most fool: away with
    her.

> *Enter* Master [*of the madhouse*], *three* Gentlemen,
>   *a mad* Scholler, *and* Pedro [*disguised*].

She-fool. Pray ye stay a little: lets heare him sing, h'as a fine
    breast.
1. Keeper. Here comes my Master; to the spit ye whore,
And stir no more abroad, but tend your businesse;
You shall have no more sops ith' pan else, nor no porrige: 50
Besides, Ile whip your breech.
She-fool.   Ile goe in presently.

50 You] F2; Your F1

163

[*Exeunt two* Keepers, English Madman, *and* She-fool.]

1. Gentleman.   Ile assure ye sir, the Cardinal's angry with ye
For keeping this young man.

Master.   I am heartily sorry.
If ye allow him sound, pray ye take him with ye.

Gentleman [*to Pedro*].   This is the place, and now observe their
    humors.

2. Gentleman.   We can find nothing in him light, nor tainted;
No startings, nor no rubs, in all his answers,
In all his Letters nothing but discretion,
Learning, and handsome stile.

Master.   Be not deceived sir,
Marke but his looke.

1. Gentleman.   His griefe, and his imprisonment   60
May stamp that there.

Master.   Pray talke with him again then.

2. Gentleman.   That will be needlesse, we have tride him long
    enough,
And if he had a taint we should have met with't.
Yet to discharge your care——

Pedro.   A sober youth:
Pity so heavy a crosse should light upon him.

2. Gentleman.   You finde no sicknesse?

Scholar.   None sir, I thank Heaven,
Nor nothing that diverts my understanding.

1. Gentleman.   Doe you sleep a nights?

Scholar.   As sound, and sweet, as any man.

2. Gentleman.   Have ye no fearfull dreams?

Scholar.   Sometimes, as all have
That go to bed with raw and windy stomacks;   70
Else, I am all one piece.

1. Gentleman.   Is there no unkindnesse
You have conceiv'd from any friend or parent?
Or scorne from what ye lov'd?

Scholar.   No, truely sir:
I never yet was master of a faith

55 s.p. *Gentleman*] *1* Gent. F 1–2

164

So poore, and weake, to doubt my friend or kindred,
And what love is, unlesse it lie in learning
I thinke I am ignorant.

1. Gentleman.   This man is perfect,
A civiller discourser I nere talk'd with.

Master.   You'l finde it otherwise.

2. Gentleman.   I must tell ye true sir,
I thinke ye keep him here to teach him madnesse.   80
Here's his discharge from my Lord Cardinall;
And come sir, goe with us.

Scholar.   I am bound unto ye,
And farewell Master.

Master.   Farewell *Stephano*,
Alas poore man.

1. Gentleman.   What flaws, and whirles of weather,
Or rather storms have been aloft these three daies;
How darke, and hot, and full of mutiny!
And still grows lowder.

Master.   It has been stubborn weather.

2. Gentleman.   Strange work at Sea, I fear me there's old tumbling.

1. Gentleman.   Blesse my old unkles Barke, I have a venture.

2. Gentleman.   And I more then I would wish to lose.   90

Scholar.   Doe you feare?

2. Gentleman.   Ha! how he lookes?

Master.   Nay, marke him better Gentlemen.

2. Gentleman.   Mercy upon me: how his eyes are altered?

Master.   Now tell me how ye like him: whether now
He be that perfect man ye credited?

Scholar.   Doe's the Sea stagger ye?

Master.   Now ye have hit the nick.

Scholar.   Doe ye feare the billowes?

1. Gentleman.   What ailes him? who has stir'd him?

Scholar.   Be not shaken,
Nor let the singing of the storm shoot through ye,
Let it blow on, blow on: let the clouds wrastle,
And let the vapours of the earth turn mutinous,   100
The Sea in hideous mountaines rise and tumble,

165

Upon a Dolphins back Ile make all tremble,
For I am *Neptune.*
Master.   Now what think ye of him?
2. Gentleman.   Alas poore man.
Scholar.   Your Barke shall plough through all,
And not a Surge so saucy to disturbe her.
Ile see her safe, my power shall saile before her.

> *Down ye angry waters all,*
> *Ye loud whistling whirlwinds fall;*
> *Down ye proud Waves, ye stormes cease;*
> *I command ye, be at peace.*   110
> *Fright not with your churlish Notes,*
> *Nor bruise the Keele of Bark that flotes:*
> *No devouring Fish come nigh,*
> *Nor Monster in my Empery,*
> *Once shew his head, or terror bring;*
> *But let the weary Saylor sing:*
> *Amphitrite with white armes*
> *Strike my Lute, Ile sing thy Charmes.*

Master.   He must have Musicke now: I must observe him;
His fit will grow to full else.   *Musick, Song.*
2. Gentleman.   I must pitty him.   120
Master.   Now he will in himselfe most quietly,
And clean forget all, as he had done nothing.
                                        [*Exit* Scholar.]
1. Gentleman.   We are sorry, sir: and we have seen a wonder;
From this houre we'l believe, and so we'l leave ye.
                              Exeunt [1. *and* 2. Gentlemen].
Pedro.   This was a strange fit.
Master.   Did ye marke him sir?
Pedro.   He might have cozen'd me with his behaviour.
Master.   Many have sworn him right, and I have thought so:
Yet on a sudden, from some word, or other,
When no man could expect a fit, he has flown out:

---

*107–118 *Down ye angry waters...Charmes.*
118 *thy*] Sympson; *om.* F 1–2

I dare not give him will.

Pedro.   Pray Heaven recover him.   130

Enter Alinda [*disguised*].

Alinda.   Must I come in too?

Master.   No, my pretty Lad;
  Keep in thy chamber Boy: 'shalt have thy supper.

Pedro.   I pray ye what is he sir?

Master.   A strange boy, that last night
  Was found i'th' Town, a little craz'd, distracted,
  And so sent hither.

Pedro.   How the pretty knave looks,
  And playes, and peepes upon me! Sure such eyes
  I have seen, and lov'd: what fair hands? certainly——

Master.   Good sir, you'l make him worse.

Pedro.   I pray believe not.
  Alas, why should I hurt him? How he smiles!
  The very shape, and sweetnesse of *Alinda*:   140
  Let me look once againe: were it in such clothes
  As when I saw her last; this must be she.
  How tenderly it stroakes me?

Master.   Pray ye be mild sir;
  I must attend elsewhere.

Pedro.   Pray ye be secure sir.   *Exit* [Master].
  What would ye say? How my heart beates and trembles?
  He holds me hard by th' hand; O my life, her flesh too!
  I know not what to think: her teares, her true ones;
  Pure orient teares: Hark, doe you know me little one?

Alinda.   O *Pedro Pedro*!

Pedro.   O my soule!

Gentleman [*aside*]   What fit's this?
  The Pilgrimes off the hooks too.

Alinda.   Let me hold thee,   150
  And now come all the world, and all that hate me.

Pedro.   Be wise, and not discovered: O how I love ye!
  How doe ye now?

149, 171 s.p. *Gentleman*] *Gent.* F 1–2

167

Alinda.   I have been miserable;
But your most vertuous eyes have cur'd me, *Pedro*:
Pray ye thinke it no immodesty, I kisse ye,
My head's wild still.
Pedro.   Be not so full of passion,
Nor do not hang so greedily upon me;
Twill be ill taken.
Alinda.   Are ye weary of me?
I will hang here eternally, kisse ever,
And weep away for joy.

Enter Master.

Master.   I told ye sir,   160
What ye would doe: for shame doe not afflict him;
You have drawn his fit upon him fearfully:
Either depart, and presently; Ile force ye else.
Who waits within?

Enter two Keepers to fetch 'em off.

Pedro.   Alas good sir——
Master.   This is the way never to hope recovery.
Stay but one minute more, Ile complaine to the Governour.
Bring in the boy: doe you see how he swels, and teares himselfe?
Is this your cure? Be gon; if the boy miscarry
Let me nere find you more, for ile so hamper ye——   170
Gentleman.   You were too blame: too rash.
Pedro.   Farewell for ever.
        Exeunt [Master *and* Keepers *with* Alinda *on one side*,
                Pedro *and* Gentleman *on the other*].

Enter Alphonso, Gentleman, [*followed by*] Juletta   IV. i
        [*disguised, and listening*].

Gentleman.   You are now within a mile oth' Towne sir: if my
        businesse

166 s.p. *Master*] Langbaine; *om.* F 1; F 2 *assigns lines* 165–166 *to* Pedro, *and lines*
167–170 *to* Master

Would give me leave, I would turne and waite upon ye;
But for such Gentlemen as you enquire of,
Certaine, I saw none such: But for the boy ye spoke of,
I will not say tis he, but such a one;
Just of that height——

Alphonso.   In such clothes?

Gentleman.   I much mistake else,
Was sent in th'other night, a little maddish,
And where such people waite their cures.

Alphonso.   1 understand ye.

Gentleman.   There you may quickly know.

Alphonso.   I thanke ye sir.

Juletta [*aside*].   So doe I to: and if there be such a place,   10
I aske no more; but you shall heare more of me.
She may be there, and you may play the tyrant;
Ile see what I can doe: I am almost foundred
In following him; and yet Ile never leave him,
Ile crawle of all foure first; my cause is meritorious,
And come what can come——

Gentleman.   All you have told me is certaine;
Complexion, and all else.

Alphonso.   It may be she then;
And ile so fumble her: Is she growne mad now?
Is her blood set so high? Ile have her madded,
Ile have her worm'd.

Juletta [*aside*].   Marke but the end, old Master,   20
If thou beest not sicke oth' Bots within these five hours,
And kickst and roar'st; Ile make ye fart fire, Signior.

                    Enter Alinda, [*disguised*] *as a foole.*

Gentleman.   Here's one oth' house, a foole, an idiot sir;
May be she is going home; she'l be a guide to ye:
And so I kisse your hand.

Alphonso.   I am your servant.

                              Exit [Gentleman].

Alinda [*aside*].   O now I am lost, lost, lost, Lord, how I tremble!
My father, arm'd in all his hates and angers;
This is more misery then I have scap'd yet.

                    169

Alphonso.   Foole, foole.

Alinda [*aside*].   He knows me not;—— will ye give
me two-pence?

And gaffer, here's a Crow-flower, and a Dazie;   30
I have some pie in my pocket too.

Alphonso.   This is an arrant foole,
An ignorant thing.

Alinda [*aside*].   Believe so, and I am happy.

Alphonso.   Dost thou dwell in *Sigovia*, foole?

Alinda.   No no, I dwell in Heaven.
And I have a fine little house, made of Marmalad.
And I am a lone woman, and I spin for Saint *Peter*;
I have a hundred little children, and they sing Psalmes with me.

Alphonso.   Tis pity this pretty thing should want understanding.
But why doe I stand talking with a coxcombe?
If I doe finde her, if I light upon her,   40
Ile say no more. Is this the way to th' Town, foole?

Alinda.   You must goe over the top of that high steeple, Gaffer——

Alphonso.   A plague o' your fooles face.

Juletta [*aside*].   No, take her counsell.

Alinda.   And then you shall come to a River twenty mile over,
And twenty mile and ten: and then you must pray, Gaffer;
And still you must pray, and pray——

Alphonso.   Pray Heaven deliver me
From such an asse, as thou art.

Alinda.   Amen, sweet Gaffer:
And fling a sop of Suger-cake into it;
And then you must leap in naked——

Juletta [*aside*].   Would he would believe her.   50

Alinda.   And sink seven daies together; can ye sinck gaffer?

Alphonso.   Yes coxcombe, yes; prethee farewell: a pox on thee.
A plague o' that foole too, that set me upon thee.

Alinda.   And then Ile bring you a sup of Milke shal serve ye:
I am going to get Apples.

Alphonso.   Go to th' devill:
Was ever man tormented with a puppy thus?
Thou tell me news? thou be a guide?

Alinda.   And then Nunkle——

Alphonso.   Prethee keepe on thy way (good Naunt)—— I could
    rayle now
  These ten houres at mine owne improvidence:——
  Get Apples, and be choak'd: farewell.   *Exit.*

Alinda.   Farewell Nuncle.   60

Juletta [aside].   I rejoyce in any thing that vexes him;
  And I shall love this foole extreamly for't:
  Could I but see my Mistris now, to tell her
  How I have truely, honestly wrought for her,
  How I have worne my selfe away, to serve her.——
  Foole, there's a Royall for the sport thou mad'st me,
  In crossing that old foole, that parted from thee.

Alinda [aside].   Thou art honest sure; but yet thou must not
    see me:——
  I thanke ye little Gentleman: Heaven blesse ye
  And ile pray for ye too: pray ye keep this Nutmeg,   70
  Twas sent me from the Lady of the Mountaine,
  A golden Lady.

Juletta.   How prettily it prattles.

Alinda.   Tis very good to rub your understanding:
  And so good night: the Moone's up.

Juletta.   Pretty innocent.

Alinda [aside].   Now fortune, if thou dar'st do good, protect me.
                                                            Exit.

Juletta.   Ile follow him to yond Towne: he shall not scape me:
  Stay, I must counterfeit a Letter by the way first,
  And one that must carry some credit with it: I am wide else,
  And all this to no purpose that I ayme at.
  A Letter must be had, and neatly handled: 80
  And then if Goodwife fortune doe not faile me,
  Have at his skirts: I shall worse anger him
  Then ever I have done, and worse torment him.
  It do's me good to thinke how I shall conjure him,
  And crucifie his crabbednesse: he's my Master,
  But that's all one: Ile lay that on the left hand.
  He would now persecute my harmlesse Mistris,

A fault without forgivenesse, as I take it;
And under that bold banner flies my vengeance,
A meritorious war, and so Ile make it.   90
I'th' name of Innocence, what's this the foole gave me?
She said twas good to rub my understanding.
What strange concealment? Bread, or Cheese, or a Chesnut?
Ha! tis a Ring: a pretty Ring, a right one:
A ring I know too! the very same Ring:
O admirable Blockhead! O base eyes!
A Ring my Mistris tooke from me, and wore it;
I know it by the Posie: *Prick me, and heale me.*
None could deliver this, but she her selfe too:
Am I twice sand-blind? twice so neer the blessing   100
I would arrive at? and block-like never know it?
I am veng'ance angry, but that shal light on thee,
And heavily, and quickly, I pronounce it:
There are so many crosse waies, there's no following her:
And yet I must not now: 1 hope she is right still,
For all her outward shew, for sure she knew me;
And in that hope, some few houres Ile forget her.   *Exit.*

Enter Roderigo [*disguised as a pilgrim*].   [IV.] i

Roderigo.   She is not to be recovered, which I vex at;
And he beyond my veng'ance, which torments me:
O! I am fool'd and sleighted, made a Rascall;
My hopes are flutterd, as my present fortunes:
Why should I wander thus and play the coxcomb?
Tire out my peace and pleasure for a Girle?
A Girle that scorns me too? a thing that hates me?
And considered at the best, is but a short breakfast
For a hot appetite: why should I walke, and walke thus,
And fret my selfe, and travell like a Carrier,   10
And peep, and watch? want Meat, and Wine, to cherish me,
When thousand women may be had, ten thousand,
And thank me too, and I sit still: well, trim Beauty

4 flutterd] Weber; flatterd F 1–2   5 coxcomb] F 2; coxcomes F 1

And Chastity, and all that seem to ruin me,
Let me not take ye; let me not come neer ye,
For Ile so trim ye: Ile so bussell with ye;
Tis not the name of Virgin shall redeem ye,
Ile change that property: nor teares, nor angers:
I beare a hate about me scorns those follies.
To finde this villaine too, for there's my main prize;   20
And if he scape me then——

                    Enter Alinda [*in fool's disguise*].

Alinda [*aside*].   Is not that *Pedro?*
    Tis he, tis he: O!
Roderigo.   What art thou?
Alinda [*aside*].   Ha? now, now, now,
    O now most miserable.
Roderigo.   What a' devill art thou?
Alinda [*aside*].   No end of my mis-fortunes, Heaven?
Roderigo.   What Anticke?
    Speake Puppet, speake.
Alinda [*aside*].   That habit to betray me?
    Ye holy Saints, can ye see this?
Roderigo [*aside*].   It danceth:
    The devill in a fooles Coat, is he turn'd Innocent?
    What mops, and mowes it makes: heigh, how it frisketh,
    Is't not a Faiery? or some small hobgoblin?
    It has a mortall face, and I have a great mind to it,   30
    But if it should prove the devill then.
Alinda.   Come hither.
Roderigo [*aside*].   I think 'twill ravish me, it is a handsome thing,
    But horribly Sun-burnt, what's that it points at?
Alinda.   Do'st thou see that Starre there, that, just above the
        Sunne;
    Prethe goe thither, and light me this Tobacco,
    And stop it with the hornes o'th' Moone.
Roderigo [*aside*].   The thing's mad,

    21 scape] Sympson; snap F 1-2   29 Is't not] F2; Is't it not F 1

Abhominably mad, her braines are butter'd.——
Goe sleep, foole, sleep.
Alinda.   Thou canst not sleep so sweetly:
For so I can say my Prayers, and then slumber.

> *I am not proud, nor full of wine,*   40
> *This little Flowre will make me fine:*
> *Cruell in heart, for I shall crie,*
> *If I see a Sparrow dye:*
> *I am not watchfull to doe ill,*
> *Nor glorious to pursue it still:*
> *Nor pittilesse to those that weepe;*
> *Such as are, bid them goe sleep.*

Doe, doe, do, and see if they can.
Roderigo [*aside*].   It said true,
I feele it sinke into me forcibly.
Sure 'tis a kind of Sibill, some mad Prophet.   50
I feel my wildnesse bound, and fetter'd in me.
Alinda.   Give me your hand, and i'le tell you what's your fortune.
Roderigo.   Here: prethee speake.
Alinda.   Fie, fie, fie, fie, fie.
Wash your hands, and pare your Nailes, and look finely,
You shall never kisse the Kings daughter else.
Roderigo.   I wash 'em daily.
Alinda.   But still you fowle 'em faster.
Roderigo [*aside*].   This goes neerer.
Alinda.   You'll have two wives.
Roderigo.   Two wives?
Alinda.   I, two fine gentle-women.
Make much of 'em: for they'l stick close to you Sir:
And these two, in two dayes.
Roderigo.   That's a fine Riddle.   60
Alinda.   Today you shall wed sorrow,
And repentance will come tomorrow.
Roderigo [*aside*].   Sure she's inspired.
Alinda.   I'le sing ye a fine Song Sir.

174

> *He called down his merry men all,*
> *By one, by two, by three,*
> William *would faine have been the first,*
> *But now the last is he.*

Roderigo [*aside*].   Tis the meer Chronicle of my mis-haps.

Alinda.   I'le bid you good ev'n: for my Boat staies for me yonder,
And I must Sup with the Moone to night in the Mediterraneum.   70
                                                        Exit.

Roderigo.   When fools, and mad-folks shall be tutors to me,
And feele my sores, yet I unsensible;
Sure it was set by Providence upon me
To steer my heart right: I am wondrous weary,
My thoughts too, which adde more burthen to me:
I have been ill, and (which is worse) pursu'd it,
And still runne on: I must thinke better, nobler,
And be another thing, or not at all.
Still I grow heavier, heavier, heaven defend me:
I'le lye down, and take rest: and goodnes guard me.   80

Enter four Pesants.

1. Peasant.   We have scap'd today well: certain, if the Out-laws
Had known we had been stirring, we had paid for't.

2. Peasant.   Plague on 'em, they have rob'd me thrice.

3. Peasant.   And me five times:
Beside they made my daughter one of us too,
An arrant Drum: O, they are the lewdest Rascals,
The Captaine such a damn'd peece of iniquitie:
But we are farre enough of on 'em, that's the best on't,
They cannot heare.

4. Peasant.   They'le come to me familiarly
And eat up all I have: drinke up my wine too,
And if there be a Servant that contents 'em,   90
Let her keele hold, they'll give her Stowage enough:
We have no Children now, but Theeves, and Outlawes.

---

*64–67 He called . . . last is he.   68 Tis] Sympson; This F 1–2
87 of] *i.e.*, off   90 contents] F 2; content F 1

The very Brats in their Mothers bellies have their qualities.
They'll steale into the world.

1. Peasant.   Would we had some of 'em here.

2. Peasant.   I, o' that condition we could Master 'em,
They are sturdy knaves.

3. Peasant.   A devill take their sturdinesse,
We can neither keep our wives from 'em, nor our States,
We pay the Rent, and they possesse the benefit.

1. Peasant.   What's this lies here? is it drunk, or sober?
It sleeps, and soundly too.

2. Peasant.   'Tis an old woman   100
That keepes sheepe here abouts: it turns, and stretches.

4. Peasant.   Do's she keep sheep with a sword?

3. Peasant.   It has a Beard too.

1. Peasant.   Peace, peace: It is the devill *Roderigo*,
Peace of all hands, and looke.

2. Peasant.   'Tis he.

3. Peasant.   Speake softly.

4. Peasant.   Now we may fit him.

3. Peasant.   Stay, stay: let's be provident.

1. Peasant.   Kill him, and wake him then.

4. Peasant.   Let me come to him,
Ev'n one blow at his pate, if ere he wake more——

3. Peasant.   So, so, so, lay that by.

                              [*They take* Roderigo's *sword.*]

2. Peasant.   I must needs kill him.
It stands with my reputation.

3. Peasant.   Stand off, I say:
And let us some way make him sure; then torture him.   110
To kill him presently, has no pleasure in't.
Has been tormenting of us, at least this twelve moneth.

Roderigo.   Oh me!

All.   He comes: he comes.

4. Peasant.   Has he no Guns about him?

3. Peasant.   Softly again: no, no: take that hand easily,
And tye it fast there: then to th' other bough there.

112 tormenting] F2; tormented F1

176

Fast, fast, and easie least he wake.

> [*They tie* Roderigo *to a tree.*]

2. Peasant.   Have we got ye?
This was a benefit we never aym'd at.
3. Peasant.   Out with your knives, and let's carve this Cock-theefe,
Daintily carve him.
1. Peasant.   I would he had been used thus
Ten year agoe; we might have thought we had children.   120
3. Peasant.   O, that Sir *Nicholas* now our Priest were here.
What a sweet Homily would he say over him,
For ringing all in, with his wife in the Bell-frey?
He would stand up stiffe girt: Now pounce him lightly,
And as he rores, and rages, let's goe deeper:
Come neere: you are dym ey'd: on with your spectacles.
Roderigo.   O, what torments me thus? what slaves, what villaines?
O spare me, doe not murther me.
3. Peasant.   We'll but tickle ye,
You have tickled us at all points.
4. Peasant.   Where are his Emblemes?
Roderigo.   As ye are men, and Christians——
2. Peasant.   Yes we hear ye,   130
And you shall here of us too.
Roderigo.   Oh no mercy?

> *Enter* Pedro [*disguised*].

Pedro.   What noyse is this? what rore? I cannot find her,
She is got free again: but where, or which way?
Roderigo.   O' villains, beasts.
Pedro.   Murdring a man, ye rascals?
Ye inhumane slaves, off, off, and leave this cruelty,
Or as I am a Gentleman: do ye brave me?
Then have among ye all, ye slaves, ye cowards.
[*To Roderigo*]   Take up that sword, and stand: stay ye base
   rascals,
Ye cut-throate rogues.
All.   Away, away.   *Exeunt Pesants.*

139 s.d. *Pesants*] *Pes.* F 1–2

177

Pedro. Ye dog-whelps.

Roderigo [*aside*]. O' I am now more wretched far, then ever. 140

Pedro [*aside*]. A violence to that habit? ha? *Roderigo*,
What makes he here, thus clad? is it repentance,
Or only a fair shew to guild his mischiefes?

Roderigo [*aside*]. This benefit has made me shame to see him,
To know him, blush.

Pedro. You are not much hurt?

Roderigo. No Sir;
All I can call a hurt, sticks in my conscience,
That pricks, and tortures me.

Pedro. Have ye considerd
The nature of these men, and how they us'd ye?
Was it fair play? did it appear to you handsom?

Roderigo. I dare not speak: or if I do, tis nothing 150
Can bring me off, or justifie me.

Pedro. Was it noble
To be o're-layd with odds, and violence?
Manly, or brave in these thus to oppresse ye?
Do you blush at this, in such as are meer rudenes,
That have stopt soules, that never knew things gentle?
And dare you glorifie worse in your self sir?
Ye us'd me with much honour, and I thank ye,
In this I have requited some: ye know me:
Come turne not back, ye must, and ye shall know me;
Had I bin over seasond with base anger, 160
And suited all occasions to my mischiefes,
Bore no respect to Honesty, Religion,
No faith, no common tie of man, humanity,
Had I had in me, but given reines, and licence
To a tempestuous will, as wild as winter,
This day, know *Roderigo*, I had set
As small a price upon thy life, and fortunes,
As thou didst lately on mine innocence;
But I reserve thee to a nobler service.

Roderigo. I thank ye, and i'le studdy more to honour ye: 170

142 clad] F2; lad F1   143 guild] Sympson; guid F1; guile F2

178

You have the nobler soule, I must confesse it,
And are the greater master of your goodnes.
Though it be impossible I should now recover,
And my rude will grow handsome in an instant,
Yet touching but the purenes of your mettle,
Something shall shew like gold, at least shall glister,
That men may hope, although the mine be rugged,
Stony, and hard to work: yet time, and honour
Shall find and bring forth that, that's rich and worthy.

Pedro.   I'le trie that: and to th' purpose: ye told me sir   180
In noble emulation (so I take it;
I'le put your hatred far off, and forget it)
You had a faire desire to try my valour:
You seemd to court me to it; you have found a time,
A weapon in your hand, an equall enemy,
That, as he puts this off, puts of all injuries,

                              [*Removes his pilgrim's gown.*]

And only now for honors sake defies ye:
Now, as you are a man, I know you are valiant,
As you are gentle bred, a souldier fashioned.

Roderigo.   His vertue startles me. I dare fight *Pedro.*   190

Pedro.   And as you have a Mistris that you honor,
Mark me, a Mistris——

Roderigo.   Ha?

Pedro.   A handsome Mistris,
As you dare hold your self deserving of her——

Roderigo [*aside*].   Deserving? what a word was that to fire me?

Pedro.   I could compell ye now without this circumstance,
But i'le deale free, and fairely, like a Gentleman:
As ye are worthy of the name ye carry,
A daring man——

Roderigo [*aside*].   O that I durst not suffer:
For all I dare do now, implies but pennance.

Pedro.   Now do me noble right.

Roderigo.   I'le satisfy ye: 200
But not by th' sword: pray ye hear me, and allow me;

186 of] *i.e.*, off   201 sword] F 2; word F 1

179

I have bin rude: but shall I be a monster,
And teach my sword to hurt that that preserved me?
Though I be rough by nature, shall my name
Inherit that eternall staine of barbarous?
Give me an enemy, a thing that hates ye,
That never heard of yet, nor felt your goodnes,
That is one main antipathy to sweetnes;
And set me on, you cannot hold me coward:
If I have ever err'd 'thas bin in hazard: 210
The temper of my sword starts at your vertue,
And will flie off, nay it will weep to fight ye;
Things excellently mingled, and of pure nature,
Hold sacred love, and peace with one another.
See how it turnes.

Pedro.   This is a strange conversion:
And can ye faile your Mistris? can ye grow cold
In such a case?

Roderigo.   Those heats that they adde to us,
(O noble *Pedro*) let us feele 'em rightly,
And rightly but consider how they move us.

Pedro.   Is not their honour ours?

Roderigo.   If they be vertuous;   220
And then the sword ads nothing to their lustre,
But rather cals in question what's not doubted:
If they be not, the best swords, and best valours
Can never fight 'em up to fame again:
No, not a Christian war, and that's held pious.

Pedro [*aside*].   How bravely now he is tempered? I must fight,
And rather make it honorable, then angry.——
I would not taske those sins to me committed.

Roderigo.   You cannot sir: you have cast those by; decarded 'em,
And in a noble mind, so low and loosely   230
To look back, and collect such lumps, and lick 'em
Into new horrid formes agen——

Pedro [*aside*].   Still braver.

210 'thas bin in] F 2; 'th as in F 1   212 fight] Colman; light F 1–2
*229 decarded] *stet* F 1

Roderigo.   To fight, because I dare, were worse, and weaker
  Then if I had a woman in my cause, sir,
  And more proclaim'd me foole; yet I must confesse
  I have bin covetous of all occasions,
  And this I have taken upon trust, for noble,
  The more shame mine; devise a way to fight thus,
  That like the wounded aire no blood may issue,
  Nor where this sword shall enter, no lost spirit,   240
  And set me on: I would not scar that body,
  That vertuous, valiant body, nor deface it
  To make the Kingdom mine: if one must bleed,
  Let me be both the sacrifice, and altar,
  And you the Priest; I have deserv'd to suffer.
Pedro.   The noble *Roderigo*, now I call ye,
  And thus my love shall ever count, and hold ye.
Roderigo.   I am your servant sir: and now this habit,
  Devotion, not distrust shall put upon me.
  I'le wait upon your fortunes, that's my way now,   250
  And where you grieve, or joy, i'le be a partner.
Pedro.   I thank ye sir, I shall be too proud of ye;
  O I could tell ye strange things.
Roderigo.   I ghesse at 'em,
  And I could curse my self, I made 'em stranger;
  Yet my mind sayes, you are not far from happines.
Pedro.   It shall be welcome; come, lets keep us thus still,
  And be as we appear: Heavens hand may blesse us.

                                         Exeunt.

   Enter Alphonso, Master [*of the madhouse*] *and* Keepers.   [IV.] iii

Master.   Yes sir, here be such people: but how pleasing
  They will appear to you——
Alphonso.   Pray let me see'm.
  I come to that end: pray let me see 'em all.
Master.   They will confound ye sir, like bels rung backward
  They are nothing but confusion, and meer noyses.

Alphonso.   May be I love a noyse: but hark ye sir,
Have ye no boyes, handsome yong boyes?
Master.   Yes one sir,
A very handsome boy.
Alphonso.   Long here?
Master.   But two dayes;
A little crazed: but much hope of recovery.
Alphonso.   I, that boy, let me see: may be I know him;   10
That boy, I say: [*aside*] This is the boy he told me of,
And it must needs be she.—— That boy I beseech ye sir,
That boy I come to see.
Master.   And ye shall see him:
Or any els, but pray be not too violent.
Alphonso.   I know what to do, I warrant ye: I am for all fancies:
I can talk to 'em, and dispute.
1. Keeper.   As madly?
For they be very madde sir.
Alphonso.   Let 'em be horne mad.
1. Keeper.   We have few Citizens: they have bedlames of their
own sir,
And are mad at their own charges.
Alphonso.   Who lies here?
Master.   Pray ye do not disturb 'em sir, here lie such youths   20
Will make you start if they but dance their trenchmores.
Fetch out the boy, sirha.   [*Exeunt* 1. *and* 2. Keepers.]

Shake Irons within [*and Enter*] English Madman,
Scholler, Parson.

Hark!
Alphonso.   Heigh boyes.
English Madman.   Bownce,
Clap her o'th Star-bord: bounce: top the can, *Jenkin.*
Scholar.   Dead ye dog, dead: do ye quarrell in my Kingdom?
Give me my trident.
English Madman.   Bownce, 'twixt wind and water,
Loaden with Mackrels: O brave meat.

*23 *Jenkin*] stet F 1–2

Scholar.   My Sea horses!
  I'le charge the Northern wind, and break his bladder.
Parson.   I'le sell my bels, before 1 be out-brav'd thus.
Alphonso.   What's he? what's he?
Master.   A parson sir, a parson,
  That run madde for tythe Goslings.
Alphonso.   Green sawce cure him.   30
Parson.   I'le curse ye all, i'le excommunicate ye:
  Thou English heretique, give me the tenth pot.
English Madman.   Sue me, i'le drink up all, bownce I say once
    more!
  O, have I split your mizen? Blow, blow thou West wind,
  Blow till thou rive, and make the Sea run roaring.
  I'le hisse it down againe with a bottle of Ale.
Scholar.   Triton, why Triton!
English Madman.   Tritons drunk with metheglin.
Scholar.   Strike, strike the surges, strike!
English Madman.   Drink, drink, tis day light;
  Drink, didle, didle, didle, drink, *Parson*, proud *Parson*:
  A pigs tayle in thy teeth, and I defie thee.   40
Parson.   Give me some porridge, or i'le damne thee English.
Alphonso.   How comes this English madde man here?
Master.   Alas thats no question: they are mad every where sir;
  Their fits are coole now: let 'em rest.
Alphonso.   Madde Gallants:
  Most admirable mad: I love their fancies.

     Enter [1. *and* 2.] Keepers *and* Shee-foole
      [*in Alinda's boy's disguise*].

1. Keeper.   Ye stinking whore: who knew of this? who lookd to
    him?
  Pox take him, he was sleepy when I left him.
2. Keeper.   Certain he made the foole drunk.
Master.   How now who's this here?
  Where is the boy?
1. Keeper.   The boy sir?

     45 fancies] Sympson; faces F 1–2

183

Master.   I, the boy, sir.
1. Keeper.   Here's all the boyes we founde.
Master.   These are his cloths.   50
But wher's the boy?
She-fool.   The boy is gone a maying,
Hee'l bring me home a Cuckowes nest; do ye hear *Master*?
I put my cloths off, and I dizend him,
And pind a plum in's forehead, and a feather,
And buss'd him twice, and bid him go seek his fortune:
He gave me this fine money, and fine wine too,
And bid me sop: and gave me these trim cloths too,
And put 'em on.
Alphonso.   Is this the boy you would shew?
She-fool.   I'le give you two pence Master.
Alphonso.   Am I foold of all sides?
I met a foole i'th woods, they said she dwelt here,   60
In a long pied coat.
Master.   That was the very boy, sir.
She-fool.   I, I, I, I gave him leave to play forsooth,
Hee'l come again tomorrow, and bring pescods.
Master.   I'le bring your bones.
Alphonso.   Pox o' your fooles, and bedlams,
Plague o' your owls and apes.
Master.   Pray ye sir, be tamer,
We cannot help this presently: but we shal know.
[*To the Keepers*] I'le recompence your cares too.
Alphonso.   Know me a pudding!
You juggle, and ye fidle: fart upon ye:
I am abused.
Master.   Pray ye sir——
Alphonso.   And I will be abused sir,
And you shall know I am abused.

[*Enter*] Welch mad-man.

Welsh Madman.   Whaw, Master Keeper.   70
Alphonso.   Pox o' thy whawes, and thy whyms, pox o' thy urship.

54 plum] F2; plumb F1   *63 pescods] *stet* F1; peascods F2

Welsh Madman.   Give me some Ceeze, and Onions: give me some
   wash-brew,
   I have—in my bellies: give me abundance,
   Pendragon was a Shentleman, marg you sir,
   And the Organs at *Rixum* were made by revelations,
   There is a spirit blowes, and blowes the bellowes,
   And then they sing.
Alphonso.   What Moon-calf's this? what dreame?
Master.   Pray ye sir observe him,
   He is a mountaineere, a man of Goteland.
Welsh Madman.   I will beate thy face as black as a blew-clout,   80
   I will leave no more sheet in thine eyes.
Master.   He will not hurt ye.
Welsh Madman.   Give me a great deale of guns: thou art the
   devils,
   I know thee by thy tayles: poor *Owen*'s hungry,
   I will pig thy bums full of bullets.
Alphonso.   This is the rarest rascall,
   He speakes as if he had butter-milk in's mouth.
   Is this any thing a kin to th'English?
Master.   The elder brother, sir,
   He run mad because a rat eate up's cheese.   90
Alphonso.   H'ad a great deale of reason sir.
Welsh Madman.   *Basilus manus*, is for an old codpice, mark ye.
   I will borrow thy urships whore, to seale a Letter.
Master.   Now he growes villanous.
Alphonso.   Methinks he's best now.
Master.   Away with him.
Alphonso.   He shall not.
Master.   Sir, he must.
Welsh Madman.   I will sing, and dance:
   Do anything.
Alphonso.   Wilt thou declaime in greek?
Master.   Away with the foole, and whip her soundly sirah.
She-fool.   I'le tell no more tales.   *Exit* [*with* 1. Keeper].
Alphonso.   Or wilt thou fly i'th ayre?

75 *Rixum*] *i.e.*, Wrexham

185

English Madman.   Do, and i'le catch thee,
  And like a wisp of hay, i'le whirle, and whirle thee,   100
  And puffe thee up: and puff thee up.
Scholar.   I'le save thee,
  And thou shalt fall into the Sea, soft, softly.
Welsh Madman.   I'le get upon a mountaine and call my
    Countrymen.
Master.   They all grow wild: away with him for heaven sake——
  Sir, ye are much too blame.
Alphonso.   No, no, tis brave sir,
  Ye have cozend me; i'le make you madde.
Master.   In with him,
  And lock him fast.

[Exit 2. Keeper with all the Madmen.]

Alphonso.   I'le see him in his lodging.   *Exit*.
Master.   What meanes this Gentleman?

Enter Juletta [disguised].

Juletta.   He's in: have at him.
  Are you the Master, sir?
Master.   What would you with him?
Juletta.   I have a busines from the Duke of *Medina*,   110
  Is there not an old Gentleman come lately in?
Master.   Yes, and a wild one too; But not a prisoner.
Juletta.   Did you observe him well? tis like he may be.
Master.   I have seen younger men of better temper
Juletta.   You have hit the cause I come for: ther's a letter,
  Pray ye peruse it well: [*aside*] I shall be wi' ye;
  And sodainly, I fear not: finely, daintely,
  I shall so feed your fierce vexation,
  And raise your worships stormes: I shall so niggle ye,
  And juggle ye, and fiddle ye, and firck ye: 120
  I'le make ye curse the houre ye vext a woman;
  I'le make ye shake, when our sex, are but sounded:
  For the Lords sake, we shall have him at; I long to see it
  As much as for my wedding night: I gape after it.

121 ye vext] F2; yet vext F1

Master.   This Letter sayes the Gentleman is lunatique;
   I half suspected it.
Juletta.   Tis very true sir,
   And such prancks he has plaid.
Master.   He's some great man,
   The Duke commands me with such care to look to him,
   And if he grow too violent, to correct him,
   To use the speediest meanes for his recovery,   130
   And those he must finde sharpe.
Juletta.   The better for him.
Master.   How got ye him hither?
Juletta.   With a train, I told him:
   He's in love with a boy, there lies his mellancholly.
Master.   Hither he came to seek one.
Juletta.   Yes, I sent him,
   Now had we dealt by force, we had never brought him.
Master.   Here was a boy.
Juletta.   He saw him not?
Master.   He was gon first.
Juletta.   It is the better; looke you to your charge well:
   Ile see him lodged, for so the duke commanded me;
   He will be very rough.
Master.   We are usd to that sir,
   And we as rough as he, if he give occasion.   140
Juletta.   You will find him gainfull, but be sure ye curb him,
   And get him if ye can fairely to his lodging;
   I am afraid ye will not.
Master.   We must sweat then.

               Enter Alphonso [*and* 2. Keeper].

Alphonso.   What dost thou talk to me of noyses? I'le have more
       noyse,
   I'le have all loose, and all shall play their prizes;
   Thy Master has let loose the boy I lookt for,
   Basely convaid him hence.
2. Keeper.   Will ye go out sir?

   *132 told] *stet* F 1–2   147, 155 s.p. 2. *Keeper*] *Keep.* F 1–2

Alphonso. I will not out: I will have all out with me,
I'le have thy Master in; he's only madde here.
And rogues, ile have ye all whipt:

> [*Madmen*] *shake irons* [*within*].
> heigh mad boyes, mad boyes. 150

Juletta. Do you perceive him now?
Master.   Tis too apparant.
Juletta [*aside*].   I am glad she is gon: he raves thus.
Master.   Do you hear sir,
Pray will ye make lesse stir, and see your chamber?————
Call in more help; and make the closset ready.
2. *Keeper.*   I thought he was mad: ile have one long lash at ye.

> [*Exit.*]

Alphonso.   My chamber? where my chamber? why my chamber?
Wher's the young boy?
Master.   Nay pray ye sir be more modest
For your own credit sake: the people see ye,
And I would use ye with the best.
Alphonso.   Best, hang ye,
What dost thou think me madde?
Master.   Pray, and be civill,   160
Heaven may deliver ye.
Alphonso.   Into a rogues hands.
Master.   You do but draw more misery upon ye,
And adde to your disease.
Alphonso.   Get from me.
Master.   No sir,
You must not be left so: bear your self civilly,
And twill be better for ye: swell not, nor chafe not.
Alphonso.   I am a Gentleman, and a neighbour, rascall.
Master.   A great deale the more pity: I have heard of ye.
Juletta [*aside*].   Excellent Master.
Master.   The Duke is very tender too.
Alphonso.   Am I lunatique? am I run madde?
What dost thou talk to me of Dukes, and Devils,   170
Why do the people gape so?
Master.   Do not anger 'em,

But go in quietly, and slip in softly,
They will so tew ye, els, I am commanded sir.
Alphonso.   Why, prethee why?
Master.   Ye are dog-mad: you perceive it not,
Very far madde: and whips wil scant recover ye.
Alphonso.   Ha! whips?
Master.   I, whips, and sore whips, and ye were a Lord sir,
If ye be stubborne here.
Alphonso.   Whips? what am I grown?
Juletta [*aside*].   O I could burst: hold, hold, hold, hold o'both
    ends,
How he lookes, pray heaven, he be not madde indeed.   180
Alphonso.   I do not perceive I am so; but if you think it——
Nor I'le be hangd if't be so.
              Irons brought in [*by* 1. *and* 2. Keepers].
Master.   Do you see this sir?
Down with that devill in ye.
Alphonso [*aside*].   Indeed I am angry,
But ile containe my selfe: O I could burst now,
And teare my selfe, but these rogues will torment me:
Madde in mine old dayes? make mine owne afflictions?
Master.   What doe you mutter sir?
Alphonso.   Nothing, sir, nothing;
I will goe in, and quietly, most civilly:
And good sir, let none of your tormentors come about me,
You have a gentle face; they look like Dragons.   190
Master.   Be civill and be safe: come, for these two daies
Ye must eate nothing neither: twill ease your fits sir.
Alphonso.   Twill starve me sir; but I must beare it joyfully.
I may sleepe?
Master.   Yes, a little: go in with these men.
Alphonso.   O miserable me!
Master.   Ile follow presently.
                    Exit [Alphonso *with two Keepers*].
You see tis done sir.
Juletta.   Ye have done it handsomely,
And ile inform the Duke so: Pray ye attend him,

Let him want nothing, but his will.
Master.   He shall not,
    And if he be rebellious——
Juletta.   Never spare him:
    H'as flesh, and hide enough, he loves a whipping.   200
Master.   My service to his Grace.
Juletta.   I shall commend it.——

                                            Exit [Master].

    So, thou art fast: I must goe get some fresh roome
    To laugh, and caper in: O how it tickles me!
    O how it tumbles me with joy! thy mouths stopt:
    Now if I can doe my Mistris good, I am Sainted.   *Exit.*

                    Enter Seberto, Curio.   V. i

Seberto.   Now, o' my conscience, we have lost him utterly,
    He's not gon home: we heard from thence this morning,
    And since our parting last at *Rodorigo's,*
    You know what ground we have travel'd.
Curio.   He's asleep sure:
    For if he had been awake, we should have met with him:
    'Faith let's turn back, we have but a fruitlesse journey;
    And to hope further of *Alindas* recovery,
    (For sure she'l rather perish then returne)
    Is but to seeke a Moth i'th Sunne.
Seberto.   We'l on sure;
    Something we'l know, some cause of all this fooling,   10
    Make some discovery.
Curio.   Which way shall we cast then,
    For all the Champion Country, and the villages,
    And all those sides?
Seberto.   We'l crosse these woods awhile then:
    Here if we faile, we'l gallop to *Segovia,*
    And if we light of no news there, heare nothing,
    We'l even turn fairly home, and coast the other side.
Curio.   He may be sicke, or faln into some danger;

                    *9 Moth] *stet* F 1–2

                            190

He has no guide, nor no man to attend him.
Seberto.   He's well enough, he has a travel'd body,
  And though he be old, he's tough, and will endure well;   20
  But he is so violent to finde her out,
  That his anger leads him a thousand wild-goose chases:
  Ile warrant he is well.
Curio.   Shall we part company?
Seberto.   By no means, no: that were a sullen businesse:
  No pleasure in our journey: Come, let's crosse here first,
  And where we finde the paths, let them direct us.   *Exeunt.*

         Enter Juletta, Alinda [*both disguised*].   [V.] ii

Juletta.   Why are you still so fearfull of me, Lady?
  So doubtfull of my faith, and honest service,
  To hide your selfe from me, to fly my company?
  Am I not yours? all yours? by this light you shake still;
  Do ye suspect me false? did I ever faile ye?
  Doe you think I am corrupted? base? and treacherous?
  Lord, how ye look! Is not my life tyde to ye?
  And all the power I have to serve, and honour ye?
  Still do ye doubt? still am I terrible?
  I will not trouble ye: good Heaven preserve ye,   10
  And send ye what ye wish: I will not see ye,
  Nor once remember I had such a Mistris.
  I will not speak of ye, nor name *Alinda*,
  For feare you should suspect I would betray ye:
  Goodnesse and peace conduct ye.
Alinda.   Prethee pardon me,
  I know thou art truly faithfull: and thou art welcome,
  A welcome partner to my miseries;
  Thou knowst I love thee too.
Juletta.   I have thought so, Lady.
Alinda.   Alas, my feares have so distracted me
  I durst not trust my selfe.
Juletta.   Come, pray ye think better,   20
  And cast those by: at least consider, Lady,

191

How to prevent 'em: pray ye put off this fooles coate;
Though it have kept ye secret for a season,
Tis known now, and will betray ye; your arch enemy
Roderigo is abroad: many are looking for ye.

Alinda.   I know it: and those many I have cozen'd.

Juletta.   You cannot still thus.

Alinda.   I have no meanes to shift it.

Juletta.   I have: and shift you too. I lay last night
At a poore widows house here in the Thicket,
Whether I will conduct ye, and new shape ye,   30
My selfe too to attend ye.

Alinda.   What meanes hast thou?
For mine are gone.

Juletta.   Feare not, enough to serve ye;
I came not out so empty.

Alinda.   Prethee tell me,
(For thou hast stroke a kind of comfort through me,)
When saw'st thou *Roderigo*?

Juletta.   Even this morning,
And in these woods: take heed, h'as got a new shape.

Alinda.   The habit of a Pilgrime? yes, I know it,
And I hope shall prevent it; was he alone?

Juletta.   No Madam, and which made me wonder mightily,
He was in company with that handsome Pilgrime,   40
That sad sweet man.

Alinda.   That I forgot to give to?

Juletta.   The same, the very same, that you so pittied,
A man as fit to suit his villanies——

Alinda.   And did they walke together?

Juletta.   Wondrous civilly.

Alinda.   Talke, and discourse?

Juletta.   I thinke so, for I saw 'em
Make many stands, and then embrace each other.

Alinda.   The Pilgrime is betraid, a *Judas* dwels with him,
A *Sinon*, that will seem a Saint to choake him.
Canst thou but shew me this?

34 stroke] *i.e.*, struck   45 saw] F2; see F1   48 *Sinon*] F2; *Simon* F1

192

Juletta [*aside*].　　　　　　　Lord how she trembles!——
　　Not thus, for all the world, ye are undone then;　　　　50
　　But let's retire, and alter, then we'l walke free;
　　And then ile shew ye any thing.
Alinda.　　　　　　　　　Come, good wench,
　　And speedily: for I have strang faiths working,
　　As strange feares too, ile tell thee all my life then.
Juletta.　Come quick, ile conduct ye, and still serve ye,
　　And doe not feare; hang feare, it spoiles all projects.
　　This way; Ile be your guide.　　　　　　　*Exeunt*.

　　　　　Enter Governour, Verdugo, *Citizens*.　　　　[V.] iii

Governor.　Use all your sports, all your solemnities;
　　Tis the Kings day tomorrow,
　　His birth day, and his marriage, a glad day,
　　A day we ought to honour, all.
1. Citizen.　　　　　　　　We will sir,
　　And make *Segovia* ring with our rejoycings.
Governor.　Be sumptuous, but not riotous; be bounteous,
　　But not in drunken Bacchanals: free to all strangers,
　　Easie, and sweet in all your entertainments,
　　For tis a Royall day admits no rudenesse.
2. Citizen.　Your Lordship will do us the honour to be here your　10
　　selfe,
　　And grace the day?
Governor.　　　　　　　Tis a maine part of my service.
3. Citizen.　I hope your honour has taken into your consideration
　　The miseries we have suffered by these Out-laws,
　　The losses, howrly feares; the rude abuses
　　Strangers that travell to us are daily loaden with;
　　Our daughters, and our wives complaints.
Governor.　　　　　　　　　I am sorry for't,
　　And have Commission from the King to ease it:
　　You shall not be long vext.
1. Citizen.　　　　　　Had we not wals, sir,
　　And those continually man'd too with our watches,

We should not have a bit of meat to feed us.   20
And yet they are our friends, and we must think so,
And entertaine 'em so sometimes, and feast 'em,
And send 'em loden home too, we are lost else.

2. Citizen.   They'l come to Church amongst us, as we hope
   Christians,
   When all their zeale is but to steale the Chalices;
   At this good time now, if your Lordship were not here,
   To awe their violence with your authority,
   They would play such gambals!

Governor.   Are they grown so heady?

2. Citizen.   They would drink up all our Wine, pisse out our
   Bonfires;
   Then, like the drunken Centaures, have at the fairest,   30
   Nay, have at all: fourscore and ten's a Goddesse,
   Whilst we, like fooles, stand shaking in our cellars.

Governor.   Are they so fierce upon so little sufferance?
   Ile give 'em such a purge, and suddenly.
   Verdugo, after this solemnity is over
   Call on me for a charge of men, of good men,
   To see what house these knaves keep: of good souldiers,
   As sturdy as themselves: that dare dispute with 'em,
   Dare walk the woods as well as they, as fearlesse,
   But with a better faith belabour 'em;   40
   Ile know what claim they have to their possession.
   Tis pity of their Captaine *Roderigo*,
   A wel-bred Gentleman, and a good souldier,
   And one, his Majesty has some little reason
   To thank, for sundry services, and faire ones;
   That long neglect bred this, I am sorry for him.

Verdugo.   The hope of his estate keeps backe his pardon;
   There's divers waspes, that buz about that honey-box,
   And long to lick themselves full.

Governor.   True *Verdugo*,
   Would he had but the patience to discerne it,   50
   And policy to wipe their lips.

Verdugo.   To fetch him in sir,

By violence, he being now no infant,
Will aske some bloody crowns. I know his people
Are of his owne choice men, that will not totter,
Nor blench much at a Bullet; I know his order,
And though he have no multitude, h'as manhood;
The elder-twin to that too, staid experience.
But if he must be forced, sir,——
Governor.   There's no remedy,
Unlesse he come himselfe.
Verdugo.   That will be doubtfull.
Did you never hear yet of the Noble *Pedro*?   60
Governor.   I cannot by no means; I think he's dead sure;
The Court bewailes much his untimely losse:
The King himselfe laments him.
Verdugo.   He was sunke;
And if he be dead, he died happily,
He buried all he had in the Kings service,
And lost himselfe.
Governor.   Well: if he be alive, Captaine,
(As hope still speaks the best) I know the Kings mind
So inwardly and full, he will be happy.
Come, to this preparation; when that's done,
The Outlaws expedition is begun.   70
1. Citizen.   We'l contribute all to that, and help our selves too.

                                        Exeunt.

                    Enter Rodorigo, Pedro.   [V.] iv

Roderigo.   How sweet these solitary places are? how wantonly
The wind blowes through the leafes, and courts, and playes
    with 'em?
Will ye sit down, and sleep? the heat invites ye.
Harke how yond purling stream dances, and murmurs,
The Birds sing softly too: pray take some rest, sir.
[*Aside.*] I would faine wooe his fancie to a peace,
It labours high and hastily upon him;——

                    71 s.p. *1. Citizen*] Dyce; *Cit.* F 1-2

                    195

Pray ye sit, and Ile sit by.

Pedro.   I cannot sleep friend,
I have those watches here admit no slumbers.
Saw ye none yet?

Roderigo.   No creature.

Pedro.   What strange Musicke   10
Was that we heard afar off?

Roderigo.   I cannot guesse;
Twas loud, and shrill: sometimes it shew'd hard by us,
And by and by the sound fled as the wind does;
Here's no inhabitants.

Pedro.   It much delighted me.

Roderigo.   They talke of Faeries, and such demi-devils,
This is as fine a place to dance their gambols——

Musick and [singing of] Birds [within].

Pedro.   Methought I heard a voyce.

Roderigo.   They can sing admirably,
They never lose their maiden-heads: [*aside*] I would foole any
   way
To make him merry now:—— methinks yond rocks yonder
Shew like inchanted Cels, where they inhabit.   20

Musick afar off. [Singing of] Pot Birds.

Pedro.   Tis here againe, harke gentle *Roderigo*,
Hark, hark: O sweet, sweet, how the Birds record too!
Marke how it flies now every way. O love,
In such a harmony art thou begotten,
In such soft Ayre, so gentle, lul'd and nourish'd.
O my best Mistris!

Roderigo [aside].   How he weeps! deere Heaven
Give him his hearts content, and me forgive too.
I must melt too.

Pedro.   The Birds sing lowder, sweeter,
And every note they emulate one another.
Lie still and heare: These when they have done their labours,   30

18 way] F2; away F1   *20.1 *Pot Birds*] stet F1–2

196

Their pretty ayres, fall to their rests, enjoy 'em.
Nothing rocks Love asleep, but death.

Enter Alinda *and* Juletta, *like old women.*

Roderigo.   Who are these?
Pedro.   What?
Roderigo.   Those there, those, those things that come upon us,
Those grandame things, those strange antiquities.
Did not I say these woods begot strange wonders?
Juletta.   Now ye may view 'em.
Alinda.   Ha?
Juletta.   The men ye long'd for,
Here they are both: now ye may boldly talke with 'em,
And never be ghess'd at: be not afraid, nor faint not;   40
They wonder at us; let's maintaine that wonder;
Shake not, but what ye purpose doe discreetly,
And from your tongue i'le take my part.
Alinda.   Ha?
Juletta.   There:
Before ye, there, doe not turne coward Mistresse,
If ye doe love, carry your Love out handsomely.
Alinda.   'Tis he and *Roderigo*; what a peace
Dwels in their faces, what a friendly calme
Crownes both their soules?
Roderigo.   They show as if they were mortall,
They come upon us still.
Pedro.   Be not afraid, man,
Let 'em be what they wil, they cannot hurt us.   50
Roderigo.   That thing ith' Button'd-Cap lookes terribly.
She has Guns in her eyes, the devils Ingeneer.
Pedro.   Come, stand, and let's goe meet 'em.
Roderigo.   Goe you first.
I have lesse faith: when I have said my Prayers——
Pedro.   There needs no feare, haile reveren'd dames.
Alinda.   Good ev'en.
What doe ye seeke?

37 woods] F 2; words F 1   49 s.p. *Pedro*] F 2; *Alin.* F 1

Pedro.   We would seek happier fortunes.
Roderigo [*aside*].   That little devill has maine need of a Barber,
    What a trim beard she has?
Alinda.   Seek 'em, and make 'em.
    Lie not still, nor longer here,
    Here inhabits naught but feare.   60
    Be constant good, in faith be clear,
    Fortune will waite ye every where.
Pedro.   Whether should we goe? for we beleeve thy Reverence,
    And next obey.
Alinda.   Goe to *Segovia.*
    And there before the Altar pay thy vowes,
    Thy gifts, and Prayers: unload thy heavines,
    Tomorrow shed thy teares, and gaine thy suit,
    Such honest noble showres, ne're wanted fruit.
Juletta [*to Roderigo*].   Stand you out too.
Roderigo [*aside*].   I shall be hang'd, or whipt now:
    These know, and these have power.
Juletta.   See how he shakes.   70
    A secure conscience never quakes,
    Thou hast been ill; be so no more,
    A good retreat is a great store.
    Thou hast commanded men of might,
    Command thy selfe, and then thou art right.
Alinda.   Command thy will: thy foule desires.
    Put out and quench thy unhallowed fires:
    Command thy mind, and make that pure;
    Thou art wise then, valiant, and secure.
    A blessing then thou maist beget.   80
Juletta.   A curse else that shall never set
    Will light upon thee: Say thy Prayers,
    Thou hast as many sins, as haires.
    Thou art a Captain, let thy men
    Be honest, have good thoughts, and then
    Thou maist command, and lead in chiefe,
    Yet thou art bloody, and a thiefe.

85 have good] Sympson; and good F 1–2

198

Roderigo.   What shall I doe? I doe confesse.
Alinda.   Retire,
  And purge thee perfect in his fire:
  His life observe; live in his Schoole,   90
  And then thou shalt put off the foole.
Juletta.   Pray at *Segovia* too, and give
  Thy Offrings up, repent, and live.
Alinda.   Away, away: enquire no more,
  Doe this, ye are rich, else fooles, and poore;   *Musicke within.*
  [*Aside to Juletta*] What Musick's this?
Juletta [*aside to Alinda*].   Retire! 'tis some neat Joy,
  In honour of the Kings great day: they wonder,
  This comes in right to confirme their reverence.
  Away, away, let them admire, it makes
  For our advantage: how the Captaine shakes?   100
                        Exeunt [Alinda *and* Juletta].
Pedro.   This was the Musick.
Roderigo.   Yes, yes, how I sweat!
  I was never so deserted; sure these woods
  Are onely inhabited with rare dreames, and wonders;
  I would not be a knave againe, a villaine:
  Lord, how I loath it now: for these know all Sir,
  And they would finde me out.
Pedro.   They are excellent women,
  Deepe in their knowledge, friend.
Roderigo.   I would not be traytor,
  And have these of my Jury; how light I am,
  And how my heart laughes now me thinkes within me?
  Now I am Catechiz'd, I would ever dwell here,   110
  For here is a kinde of Court of Reformation;
  Had I beene stubborn friend——
Pedro.   They would have found it.
Roderigo.   And they they would have handled me a new way,
  The devils dump had been danced then.
Pedro.   Let's away
  And doe their great Commands, and do 'em handsomely:

                  111 here] F2; there F1

                        199

Contrite, and true, for I beleeve *Roderigo*,
And constantly beleeve, we shall be happy.
Roderigo.　So you doe well; fall edge or flat o' my side,
　　All I can stagger at is the Kings Anger,
　　Which if it come, I am prepar'd to meet it.　　　　　　　120
Pedro.　The King has mercy, friend, as well as Justice:
　　And when you fall: no more.
Roderigo.　　　　　　　　　I hope the fairest.　　　*Exeunt.*

　　　　　Enter Master [*of the madhouse*], Seberto, Curio.　　　[V.] v

Curio.　We have told ye what he is: what time we have sought him:
　　His nature, and his name: the seeming Boy too,
　　Ye had here, how, and what; by your own relation,
　　All circumstances we have cleer'd: That the Duke sent him
　　We told ye how impossible; he knowes him not;
　　That he is mad himselfe, and therefore fit
　　To be your Prisoner, we dare swear against it.
Seberto.　Take heed Sir, be not madder then you would make him;
　　Though he be rash, and suddain (which is all his wildenes),
　　Take heed ye wrong him not: he is a Gentleman,　　　　　10
　　And so must be restor'd and cleer'd in all points;
　　The King shall be a Judge else.
Curio.　　　　　　　　　　'Twas some trick
　　That brought him hither: the Boy, and letter counterfeit,
　　Which shall appear, if ye dare now detain him.
Master.　I dare not Sir; nor will not: I beleeve ye,
　　And will restore him up: had I known sooner
　　H'ad been a neighbour, and the man you speak him,
　　(Though as I live, he carried a wild seeming)
　　My Service, and my selfe had both attended him:
　　How I have us'd him, let him speake.
Seberto.　　　　　　　　　　Let's in, and visit him:　　　20
　　Then to the holy Temple: there pay our duties,
　　And so wee'le take our leaves.
Master.　　　　　　　　　I'le waite upon ye.　　　*Exeunt.*

*122 fall: no more] *stet* F 1–2

An Altar prepar'd: Solemne Musick.
Enter Governour, Verdugo, *Courtiers, Ladies, etc.*

Governor.   This to devotion sacred be,
  This to the Kings prosperity,
  This to the Queen, and Chastity.   *Musick.*
Verdugo.   These Oblations first we bring
  To purge our selves: These to the King.
  To love, and beautie these: now sing.   *Musick.*
Ladies.   Holy Altar, daigne to take
  These for our selves: For the Kings sake
  And honour these: These sacred lye
  To Vertue, Love, and Modesty,   10
  Our wishes to Eternity.   *Musick.*

Enter Pedro *and* Roderigo.

Pedro.   For our selves first, thus we bend,
  Forgive us heaven, and be our friend:
Roderigo.   And happy fortune to us send.
Pedro.   To the King, honour, and all Joy,
  Long, and happy from annoy.
Roderigo.   Prosperous be all his dayes,
  Every new houre, a new praise.
Pedro.   Every minute thus be secne,
Both.   And thousand honours Crowne the Queene.   *Musick.* 20

Enter Alphonso, Curio, Seberto.

Seberto.   Come to the Altar: let us do our duties.
Alphonso.   I have almost forgot a Church.
Curio.   Kneele reverently.
Alphonso.   For my lost wits (let me see)
  First I pray: and secondly
  To be at home againe, and free,
  And if I travell more, hang me.
  For the King, and for the Queene,
  That they may be wise, and seene
  Never in the Mad-mans Inne.

For my daughter, I would pray   30
But she has made a holly-day,
And needs not my devotion now;
Let her take her own course (heaven,)
Whether it be od, or even,
And if that please not, take her you.   *Musick.*

Enter Alinda, *and* Juletta *like Shepheardesses.*

Seberto.   A short, and sweet Meditation: what are these here?
Alinda.   Haile to this sacred place.
Juletta [*aside to Alinda*].   They are all here, Madam:
    No violence dare touch here; be secure:
    My Bilbo Master too: how got he loose againe?
    How lamentably he lookes: he has had discipline.   40
    I dare not let him know my prancks.   [*They kneel.*]
Seberto.   'Tis she sure.
Curio.   'Tis certainly.
Pedro.   Ha! doe I dazell?
Roderigo.   'Tis the faire *Alinda.*
Governor.   What wonder stand these strangers in?
Roderigo.   Her woman by her,
    The same Sir, as I live.
Alphonso.   I had a daughter,
    With such a face once: such eyes and nose too,
    Ha, let me see, 'tis wondrous like *Alinda,*
    Their devotion ended, I'le marke 'em and neerer.
    And she had a Filly that waited on her:
    Just with such a favour: Doe they keepe Goats now?   50
Alinda.   Thus we kneele, and thus we pray
    A happy honour, to this day,
    Thus our Sacrifice we bring
    Ever happy to the King.
Juletta.   These of Purple, Damask, greene,
    Sacred to the vertuous Queene
    Here we hang.
Alinda.   As these are now

35.1 *Shepheardesses*] Weber; *Shepheards* F 1–2

Her glories ever spring, and show.
These for our selves: our hopes, and loves,
Full of pincks, and Ladies gloves,   60
Of hartes-ease too, which we would faine
As we labour for, attaine;
Heare me heaven, and as I bend,
Full of hope: some comfort send.
Juletta.   Heare her: heare her: if there be
A spotles Sweetnes, this is she.   *Musick.*
Pedro.   Now *Roderigo* stand.
Roderigo.   He that devides ye
Devides my life too.
Governor.   *Pedro*, Noble *Pedro.*
Doe not you know your friend?
Pedro.   I know, and honour ye.
Governor.   Lady this leave i'le crave, pray be not angry,   70
I will not long devide you: how happy *Pedro*,
Would all the Court be now, might they behold thee?
Might they but see you thus, and thus embrace you?
The King will be a joyfull man beleeve it
Most joyfull, *Pedro.*
Pedro.   I am his humble Servant.
Nay, good Sir, speake your will, I see you wonder;
One easie word from you——
Alphonso.   I dare say nothing;
My tongue's a new tongue Sir, and knowes his tither,
Let her doe what she please, I dare doe nothing,
I have been damn'd for doing. Will the King know him?   80
That fellow there, will he respect and honour him?
He has been look'd upon they say: will he own him?
Governor.   Yes certainly and grace him, ever honour him,
Restore him every way, he has much lamented him.
Alphonso.   Is't your will too? This is the last time of asking.
Roderigo.   I am sure, none else shall touch her, none else enjoy her,
If this, and this hold.
Alphonso.   You had best begin the game then, I have no title in her,
Pray take her, and dispatch her, and commend me to her,

And let me get me home, and hope I am sober: 90
Kisse, kisse, it must be thus: stand up *Alinda*,
I am the more Childe, and more need of blessing.
Ye had a waiting woman, one *Juletta*,
A pretty desperate thing, just such another
As this sweet Lady; we call'd her nimble chaps.
I pray is this the party?

Juletta.   No indeed Sir,
She is at home; I am a little Foot-Boy,
That walke a nights, and fright old Gentlemen;
Make 'em loose Hats and Cloakes.

Alphonso.   And Horses too.

Juletta.   Sometimes I doe Sir, teach 'em the way through ditches;   100
And how to breake their worships shins, and noses
Against old broken Stiles, and Stumps.

Alphonso.   A fine art;
I feele it in my bones yet.

Juletta.   I am a Drum Sir,
A Drum at mid-night, ran tan tan tan tan Sir,
Do you take me for *Juletta*? I am a Page Sir,
That brought a letter from the Duke of *Medina*
To have one senior *Alphonso*, just such another
As your old worship worm'd for running mad Sir.
Alas, you are mistaken.

Alphonso.   Thou art the devill,
And so thou hast used me.

Juletta.   I am any thing,   110
An old woman, that tels fortunes——

Roderigo.   Ha!

Juletta.   And frights good people,
And sends them to *Segovia* for their fortunes:
I am strange ayers, and excellent sweet voyces.
I am any thing, to doe her good beleeve me:
She now recovered, and her wishes crown'd
I am *Juletta* againe, pray sir forgive me.

Alphonso.   I dare not doe otherwise, for fear thou should'st still
follow me,

Prethee be forgiven, and I prethee forgive me too:
And if any of you will marry her——
Juletta.   No I beseech you Sir;
My Mistresse is my husband, with her I'le dwell still,   120
And when you play any more prancks you know where to
    have me.
Pedro.   You know him Sir.
Governor.   Know him, and much lament him:
The Kings incens'd much, much Sir, I can assure you.
Pedro.   Noble Governour——
Governor.   But since he is your friend, and now appeares,
In honour of this day, and love to you sir:
I'le try the power I have, to the pinch i'le put it;
Here's my hand *Roderigo*, I'le set you faire again.
Roderigo.   And here's mine, to be true, and full of Service.
Governor.   Your people too, shall have their generall pardons,   130
We'll have all peace and love.
Roderigo.   All shall pray for you.
Governor.   To my house now, and suite you to your worths;
Off with these weeds, and appeare glorious:
Then to the Priest, that shall attend us here,
And this be stil'd Loves new and happy yeare.
Roderigo.   The Kings and Queenes, two noble honors meet,
To grace this day, two true loves at their feet.
Alphonso.   Well well, since wedding will come after wooing,
Give me some Rose-Mary, and let's be going.
                                                        Exeunt

FINIS

TEXTUAL NOTES

I.i

22 pin'd-Gallants] Dyce declared 'pinn'd' to be the true reading, and so rendered it in his modern-spelling text. He compared IV.iii.54 ('pind a plum in's forehead'), where F 1-2 read as here and the meaning is 'pinned'. But they are 'pinned' gallants only on the most superficial level (i.e., with reference to their elaborate dress, the various articles of which are held together with pins). This is the outward and visible sign of their physical fragility; their bodies are held together by physicians' plasters and so they are constantly vulnerable to collapse. In a word, they are diseased, and this brings another word ('pined', *O.E.D.*, *v.*, 3) into play. Another sense of 'pined', meaning 'starved' (*O.E.D.*, *v.*, 2), is also present and suggests that the gallants are impoverished. 'Pin'd' meaning 'starved' is frequent in Fletcher. Cf. *The Spanish Curate*, II.i (F 1647; p. 29a): 'a young Clerk | A half pin'd-puppy that would write for a Royall'; and II.i (F 1647; p. 30a): 'Produce some few pind-Butter prints, that scarce hold | The christening'. And *The Sea Voyage*, II.i (F 1647; p. 8a): 'I left in yonder desart | A Virgin almost pind.'

I.ii

0.1 a Pilgrime] This presumably is the '*old Pilgrim*' of the F2 cast list (line 8), but the character is never designated 'old' either in stage-directions or speech-prefixes of F 1-2.

43 sweat] 'Swear', the reading of F 1-2, implies an articulate utterance hardly to be expected of shrines. Seward's conjectural emendation 'sweat' is logically necessary and imagistically right; the image of stone altars or shrines sweating as a sign of sympathy with some extraordinary example of virtue or horror at some display of depravity is a common one. In the *Nativity Ode*, Milton, commenting on the consternation that seizes on the pagan deities and their priestly servants at the dawning of a higher power, extends their dismay to the very stones of their shrines, where 'the chill marble seems to sweat' (line 195). Here, as in the present passage, the sweating shrines bear witness to their tutelary spirits' recognition that they are being outdone by a force greater than they are. For an example of the stones of a holy place sweating in horror at an act of violence, cf. *The Knight of Malta*, IV.ii (F 1647; p. 90b, a Fletcher scene); 'doe you creep behind the Altar? | Looke how it sweats, to shelter such a rascal.' Cf. as well *The Double Marriage*, II.iii (F 1647; p. 28b, a Fletcher scene); 'The

206

memory and monuments of good men | Are more then lives, and tho their Tombs want tongues, | Yet have they eyes, that daily sweat their losses'; and *Thierry and Theodoret*, I.i.157–8 (a Fletcher scene): 'tell my tale so subtilly | That the cold stones shall sweat, and statues mourne'.

II.ii

44 staring] F1–2 'staving' has never been adequately explained. Seward accounted for it from the pilgrim's staff that Pedro might be supposed to have in his hand, but this seems merely a guess. Earlier in the passage from *The Knight of Malta* quoted in the preceding note, Fletcher has made reference to 'a dog stav'd' (i.e., beaten with staves: 'Thou art a dogge, I will make thee sweare, a dog stav'd, | A mangy Cur-dogge; doe you creep behind the Altar?'), but this sheds no apparent light on 'staving' here. Dyce's emendation 'staring' is orthographically plausible, and accords with the description (line 46, below) of Pedro ' Upon the skirt o'th wood, viewing, and gaping'.

111 *Alonsos* sprightly sonne] Pedro's father was named Ferando at I.i.58.

374 scap'd,] The pointing is Weber's, and makes clear the sentence's meaning: 'Now that this pilgrim has escaped and not been hanged, our supper will be a joyful one.'

III.iii

67.1 Jaques *and* Lopez] The F1 stage-direction reads '*Enter Rodorigo, and two Outlaw.*' This raises the question whether Roderigo enters with one other person (the Second Outlaw) or with two others ('*two Outlaws*' as F2 has it). The F1 stage-direction is crowded into the right-hand margin beside the two halves of line 66, so that lack of space could account for the omission of the plural '*s*' from '*Outlaw*'. And if the F1 stage-direction referred only to the Second Outlaw, it seems more likely that he would have been designated by the numeral '*2*' (as in the similar stage-direction – '*Enter Alphonso, and 2 Outlaw*' – at III.i.34.1) than by the word '*two*'. The most plausible assumption is that two Outlaws enter with Roderigo here. That one of them is Lopez is evident from the F1 speech-prefixes that follow in this scene at lines 68 and 71. That Jaques is also on hand is to be inferred from the familiarity that he exhibits with Roderigo's plans in the dialogue that opens the following scene, where he is named in the initial stage-direction. Jaques is there conversing with what F1 labels *1 Outl.*, and two telltale speech-prefixes labelled *Lop.* indicate who that outlaw is. It seems clear, then, that two Outlaws, Lopez and Jaques, receive Roderigo's orders at the end of the present scene, and that the same two are discovered trying to carry them out at the beginning of the following scene. See Textual Notes on III.iv.0.1 and 12–14, below.

III.iv

0.1 Lopez] F1–2 bring on Jaques and '*1 Out-Law*' here, but that the Outlaw is Lopez is indicated by two speech-prefixes bearing his abbreviated name later in the F1–2 text of this scene: one at line 14 (see the following note), the other at line 20. See the preceding note.

12–14 *Lopez*. Hark...side] F1–2 assign lines 12–13 ('Hark...from us') to *1 Outl.*, and the words 'Another beates o'that side' (line 14) to *Lop.*, of whose presence in the scene there has been no previous indication. Between lines 13 and 14, F1–2 print the stage-direction, '*Enter two Out-lawes*'. That Lopez is not one of these is clear from the fact that both he and they have speeches assigned them in the following passage: *1. Out-law* speaks at lines 14–16, *2. Out-law* speakes at lines 17–19, and Lopez speaks again at line 20. Prefixes for the speeches of the First and Second Outlaws occur in F1–2, as, respectively, *2* and *3 Out-l.*, thus adding their number to the *1 Out-Law* who has been on stage since the beginning of the scene. The text reflects the First Outlaw in process of taking on the character of Lopez, as speech-prefixes for him are accordingly changed, though F1–2 do not always record the change accurately. The speech-prefix *Lop.* that occurs in F1–2 at the beginning of line 14 must have been intended to stand at the beginning of line 12; there is no reason to suppose that lines 12–13 were designed to be spoken by one character, and the words 'Another beates o'that side' (line 14) by another.

III.vii

19–20 *One, two...this houre.*] Old Merrythought sings this refrain in *The Knight of the Burning Pestle*, III, 485–6.

107–118 *Down ye angry waters...Charmes.* Music for what has been taken to be a variant text of this song is given in John Wilson's *Cheerfull Ayres or Ballads* (Oxford, 1660), pp. 112–13. The text in Wilson is as follows:

> Downe Be still you Seas,
> water your dread master please,
> Downe downe I say
> or be silent as the day,
> you that fling and roare a loft
> Whistling winds be still and soft,
> not an Angry look let fly,
> you proud Mountains Fall and dye.
> Tumble no more,
> nor kick nor Roare,

> nor trouble her Keele
> to make her reele,
> but safe from Surges, Rocks and Sand,
> Kisse her and Stroake her, and set her a Land.

Manuscript versions of the song with this alternative text are preserved in the New York Public Library (Drexel MS 4041, no. 17, fols. 11ᵛ–12) and in the Edinburgh University Library (Music MS Dc. 1. 69. 71). The text of the latter is identical with the words in Wilson. Variants between the text of MS Dc. 1. 69 and that of Drexel 4041 are recorded by John Cutts, who wonders if this song preserved in the manuscripts is the one called for in the stage-direction at line 120, below, but not printed in either the F1 or F2 texts of *The Pilgrim* (*La Musique de Scène de la Troupe de Shakespeare*, 2nd rev. ed. (Paris: Editions du Centre National de la Recherche Scientifique, 1971), p. 175). Cutts gives music for the song on p. 89.

IV.ii

64–67 *He called...last is he.*]   The fifteenth stanza of the ballad of 'The Knight and Shepherd's Daughter':

> He called down his merry men all,
>   By one, by two, and by three;
> Sweet William was us'd to be the first,
>   But now the last comes hee.

Francis James Child (ed.), *The English and Scottish Popular Ballads* (Boston and New York: Houghton, Mifflin and Company, 1886), II, 460. Old Merrythought quotes stanza twenty-three of this ballad in *The Knight of the Burning Pestle*, II, 475–8.

229 decarded]   According to Nares' *Glossary*, 'to discard, to cast away a card out of a hand in playing'; hence, 'to set aside, get rid of'.

IV.iii

23 *Jenkin*]   The stage-direction '*Shake Irons within.* | *Engl. mad-m.* | *Scholler, Parson.*' (printed at line 22 in the present edition) is printed on three lines in the right-hand margin of F1 (beside the words 'hark', 'boyes', 'Bownce') and ends just above the word '*Jenkin*' at the end of line 23. This marginal cluster of italicized names caused the compositor of F2 to regard Jenkin as one more of the number of those making their entrance along with the English Madman, the Scholar and the Parson, with the result that Jenkin's name was removed from the dialogue of line 23 and appended to the stage-direction that precedes it. Later editors, while recognizing that Jenkin (the Welsh Madman who eventually appears at

line 70) does not enter here, have (except for Langbaine and Sympson) followed F2 in dropping Jenkin's name from line 23. This is unwarranted. The English Madman is addressing him, though given the lunatic nature of the dialogue here it would be hard to say whether the words 'top the can' are supposed to be directed to Jenkin off-stage or to his imagined presence with the rest.

63 pescods]   For this variant form of 'peascods', cf. Philip Massinger, *The City Madam*, I.ii.53–5: 'I flatter not my mercers wife, nor feast her | With the first cherries, or pescods, to prepare me | Credit with her husband'.

132 told]   The verb 'toll' or 'tole' (*O.E.D.*, vb. trans. 1) meaning 'to entice, draw on', is frequent in Fletcher. Cf. *The Faithful Shepherdess*, I.i.119; *The Loyal Subject*, IV.v.94; *The Scornful Lady*, II.i.36.

V.i

9 Moth]   For 'moth' as an Elizabethan form of 'mote', cf. Shakespeare, *King John*, IV.i (lines 1668–72 of C. Hinman's facsimile of the 1623 Shakespeare Folio): '*Art.* Is there no remedie? | *Hub.* None, but to lose your eyes. | *Art.* O heauen: that there were but a moth in yours, | A graine, a dust, a gnat, a wandering haire, | Any annoyance in that precious sense'.

V.iv

20.1 *Pot Birds*]   Nares, noting the present appearance of the term, could 'only conjecture [it] to mean the sound of birds, imitated by a pot of water, and a quill', and *O.E.D.* can do no better than this: 'a theatrical imitation of the notes of birds (? by blowing through a pipe in a pot or vessel of water)'. Jane Hodgart of the Cambridge University Press has drawn my attention to an Edwardian allusion to the same or a similar technique in E. Nesbit's *The Phoenix and the Carpet* (George Newnes: London, 1904), ch. 4, where reference is made to a 'chorus of singing birds that was done behind a screen with glass tubes and glasses of water'. Cf. *The Wild-Goose Chase*, III.i.442.

122 fall: no more]   Sympson (though preserving the F1–2 assignment of all three words to Pedro) suggested breaking off Pedro's speech with the words 'when you fall——' and giving the words 'no more' to Roderigo, to be followed by his affirmation ('I hope the fairest') of line 122, and editors since his time have adopted the arrangement he suggested. In this reading, when Pedro alludes to the possibility that Roderigo may again fall from the path of virtue, Roderigo interrupts with a strong assertion that all that is behind him. But this is editorial meddling, for the F1 arrangement is entirely satisfactory, and indeed subtly superior to later editorial efforts at improvement. In F1, Pedro interrupts himself: he starts

to make reference to the possibility of a future lapse on Roderigo's part, but stops himself; 'no more' of that, he says in effect. Roderigo's reply is appropriately modest. He hopes for the best, but does so without protesting too much. It should be noted that, while F 2 retains F 1's assignment of 'fall: no more' to Pedro, it opens the way to future editorial tendencies to view his speech as interrupted, for F 2 inserts a dash after 'no more'.

PRESS-VARIANTS IN F1 (1647)

[Copies collated: Hoy (personal copy of Cyrus Hoy, Rochester, N.Y.), ICN (Newberry Library, IU¹ (University of Illinois, copy 1), IU² (copy 2), MB (Boston Public Library), MH (Harvard University), MnU (University of Minnesota), MWiW-C (Chapin Library, Williams College), NcD (Duke University), NIC (Cornell University), NjP (Princeton University), PSt (Pennsylvania State University), RoU (University of Rochester), ViU¹ (University of Virginia, copy 1), ViU² (copy 2), WaU (University of Washington), WMU¹ (University of Wisconsin–Milwaukee, copy 1), WMU² (copy 2), WMU³ (copy 3), WMU⁴ (copy 4), WU (University of Wisconsin–Madison).]

SHEET 5Fi (*inner forme*)

Corrected: MH, RoU
Uncorrected: the rest

Sig. 5F4
   I.i.60 *Pedro*] *Pearo*

EMENDATIONS OF ACCIDENTALS

I.i

I.i] *Actus Primus——Scæna Prima.*] F 1–2

9 too——] ~ ? F 1–2

14 her——] F 2; ~ . F 1

15 mischievous] F 2; misceivous F 1

27 *Rodorigo*] *Rodorgio* F 1; *Roderigo* F 2

31 Enough, enough] F 2; ~ ˄ ~ F 1

45 *Rodorigo*] *Redorigo* F 1; *Roderigo* F 2

57 us.] F 2; ~ , F 1

60 family I hate: yong *Pedro*,] F 2; ~ , ~ ~ ˄ ~ ~ : F 1

78 s.d.] *printed in margin at end of lines 75–77 in* F 1; *following line 75 in* F 2

82 sir——] ~ . F 1–2

83 phrases——] ~ , F 1; ~ . F 2

87 you.] F 2; ~ ˄ F 1

91.1] *in margin beside* wait on ye. (*line 90*) *in* F 1–2

109 fellow,] F 2; ~ ˄ F 1

130 s.p. *Alinda*] F 2; (*Alin.*); *Alm.* F 1

132 man——] F 2; ~ . F 1

I.ii

I.ii] *Scæna Secunda.* F 1; SCENE II. F 2

6 o'th' other] F 2; o'th o'ther F 1

6 friend——] ~ . F 1–2

7 turncoat,] ~ ˄ F 1–2

11 hung] F 2; hoong F 1

22.1] *printed in margin at end of lines 21–24 in* F 1; *following line 21 in* F 2

35 reverent.——] ~ , ˄ F 1–2

55 too?——] ~ ? ˄ F 1–2

85 asse.——] ~ , ˄ F 1–2

85 sirah;——] ~ ; ˄ F 1–2

90.1 *Exeunt*] *Exit* F 1–2

92 s.d.] *printed in margin at end of line 91–92 in* F 1; *following line 92 in* F 2

92 s.d. Alinda, Juletta] F 2; ~ ˄ ~ F 1

99 s.d. *Exeunt*] *Ex.* F 1 (*on line 102*) *and* F 2 (*on line 103*)

99 s.d. *Beggers*] *printed in margin at end of line 103 in* F 1–2

100 too.——] ~ , ˄ F 1; ~ . ˄ F 2

101 pentioners——] ~ . F 1–2

125 devotions——] ~ , F 1–2

126 sir:——] ~ : ˄ F 1; ~ , ˄ F 2

129 not;——] ~ ; ˄ F 1–2

132 take:——] ~ : ˄ F 1; ~ ; ˄ F 2

148 contempts,] F 2; ~ ˄ F 1

158 nobly:——] ~ : ˄ F 1; ~ ; ˄ F 2

161 me?——] ~ ? ˄ F 1–2

162 *I want my selfe*] F 2; *rom.* F 1

162 wanderers] F 2; wounderers F 1

163 selves——] F 2; ~ . F 1

166 *I seek my self*] F 2; *rom.* F 1

168 tender:——] ~ : ˄ F 1; ~ ; ˄ F 2

170 Lady;] ~ , F 1–2

173 (Pilgrim)——] (Pilgrim)˄ F 1–2

174 *Be constant faire still*] F2; rom.
  F1
175 *Be good*] F2; rom. F1
175 me.——] ~ ₍ₐₐ₎ F1; ~ . ₍ₐ₎ F2
176 *Juletta*——] ~ : F1; ~ . F2

181 yet,] F2; ~ ₍ₐ₎ F1
182 s.d.] *on line* 180 *in* F1; *following
  line* 180 *in* F2
185 *I seek . . . shadow*] rom. F1–2
187 Pilgrim,] F2; ~ ₍ₐ₎ F1

II.i

II.i] *Actus Secundus. Scæna Prima.*
  F1–2
17 - stick;] F2; - ~ . F1
22 (Thing)?] (Thing?) F2;
  (Thing) ₍ₐ₎ F1
22 guilty] F2; gulty F1
22 sir;] F2; ~ ? F1
26 ferryted——] ~ . F1–2
32 worship,] F2; ~ ₍ₐ₎ F1
36 - chamber,] F2; - ~ ₍ₐ₎ F1
42 s.p. *1. Servant*] *Ser.* F1–2
50 know,] F2; ~ : F1
50 liberally:] ~ , F1–2
56 devotion——] ~ . F1–2
59 it;] ~ , F1–2
69 out.] ~ , F1–2
70 tricks——] ~ . F1–2

71 tricks₍ₐ₎ . . . discover,] ~ , . . . ~ ₍ₐ₎
  F1–2
81 have₍ₐ₎——] F2; ~ . F1
99.1] *after* monstrous. (*line* 98) *in*
  F1–2
114 Where, where] F2; ~ ₍ₐ₎ ~ F1
114 with] F2; wth F1
128 soule——] ~ . F1–2
128 horses:——] ~ : ₍ₐ₎ F1; ~ , ₍ₐ₎ F2
132 dores.]—— ~ , ₍ₐ₎ F1–2
133 dame——] ~ . F1–2
142 hands——] ~ . F1–2
144 there:——] ~ : ₍ₐ₎ F1; ~ ; ₍ₐ₎ F2
151 else.——] ~ . ₍ₐ₎ F1; ~ : ₍ₐ₎ F2
154 suddenly——] ~ . F1–2
155 horses;——] ~ ; ₍ₐ₎ F1–2
156.1 *Exeunt*] F2; *Exit* F1

II.ii

II.ii] *Scena secunda.* F1; SCENE II.
  F2
22, 42.1 *Lopez*] F2; *Loper* F1
29 on.] ~ ; F1–2
46 viewing] F2; veiwing F1
69 found?——] ~ ? ₍ₐ₎ F1–2
98 hate, upon me₍ₐ₎] ~ ₍ₐ₎ ~ ~, F1;
  ~ ₍ₐ₎ ~ thee, F2
116 sought——] ~ . F1–2
146 benefit.——] ~ . ₍ₐ₎ F1–2
147 ye;——] ~ ; ₍ₐ₎ F1–2
148.1 Lopez] *Loper* F1–2
172 faith——] ~ , F1; ~ . F2

197 mischiefe——] ~ . F1–2
220 doore——] ~ . F1–2
242 government] F2; governmennt
  F1
263 me——] ~ , F1–2
354 pardon.] ~ , F1–2
357 at,] F2; ~ ₍ₐ₎ F1
362 again——] ~ . F1–2
366.1 *Exeunt*] *Exit* F1–2
371 This] 'This F1–2
372 well.] F2; ~ ₍ₐ₎ F1
374 scap'd,] ~ ₍ₐ₎ F1–2

III.i

III.i] *Actus Tertius. Scæna prima.*
F 1–2
0.1 *Lopez*] F 2; *Loper* F 1
28 watches.] F 2; ~ ˏ F 1
33 o'] F 2; O F 1
33 Pilgrimes,] F 2; ~ ˏ F 1

34.1 *in margin beside the two halves*
of line 32 in F 1; *following first*
half of line 32 in F 2
43 things,] ~ ˏ F 1–2
44 recovery:] ~ , F 1–2

III.ii

III.ii] *Scæna secunda.* F 1;
SCENE II. F 2

14 women.] F 2; ~ , F 1

III.iii

III.iii *Scæna Tertia.* F 1; SCENE
III. F 2
4 her,] F 2; ~ ˏ F 1
21 Fastnes] F 2 (fastness); Fastwes
F 1
23.1 *in margin beside* place then
(*line* 22) *in* F 1; *following* place
then (*line* 22) *in* F 2
25 us?] F 2; ~ . F 1
30 ha!] ~ : F 1; ~ ? F 2
33 abus'd] F 2; abu'd F 1
35 *Segovia*] F 2; *Segonia* F 1
37 Sir,] ~ . F 1–2

55 s.d.] *in margin at end of lines* 52–
3 *in* F 1; *following line* 52 *in* F 2
56 Boy?] F 2; ~ ; F 1
61 craft:——] ~ :ˏ F 1–2
65 Sirha] F 2 (Sirrha); Sitha F 1
66 Drum——] ~ . F 1–2
67.1 *Enter . . . Lopez*] *in margin be-*
side the two halves of line 66 *in*
F 1; *following* my Drum (*line* 66)
in F 2
77 Anger.] ~ , F 1–2
79 yet:] F 2; ~ , F 1
91 voyage.] ~ , F 1–2

III.iv

III.iv *Scæna quarta.* F 1; SCENE
IV. F 2
6 out,] ~ . F 1–2
9 That . . . now.] F 1–2 *line:* That
that; | It . . . now.

12 us,] F 2; ~ . F 1
14 s.d.] *following line* 13 *in* F 1–2
20 s.d. *Exeunt*] *Exit* F 1–2
22 hole,] F 2; ~ ? F 1
62.1 *Exeunt*] *Ex.* F 1–2

III.v

III.v] *scene unmarked in* F 1–2

III.vi

III.vi] *Scæna quinta.* F 1; SCENE
V. F 2

11 cures:] ~ , F 1–2

215

III.vii

III.vii] *Scena sexta.* F 1; SCENE VI. F 2
4 Mistris;] F 2; ~ , F 1
19–20 *One . . . houre*] *one line in rom. in* F 1–2
24 A Snuff, a snuff, a snuff,] ~ ~ , ~ ~ , ~ ~ . F 1–2
26 Gaffer] F 2; Goffer F 1
95 stagger] F 2; staggger F 1
101 tumble,] ~ ₐ F 1–2
102 back,] ~ , F 1–2
118 *Strike*] F 2; *srike* F 1
119 him;] ~ . F 1; ~ , F 2
124.1 *Exeunt*] *Exit* F 1–2
130.1] *after* give him will. (*line* 130) *in* F 1–2
139 smiles!] F 2; ~ ? F 1
144 s.d.] *in margin beside* attend elsewhere. *in* F 1–2
165 sir——] ~. F 1–2

IV.i

IV.i *Actus quartus. Scæna prima.* F 1–2
6 height——] ~ . F 1–2
16 come——] ~ . F 1–2
29 not;——] ~ ;ₐ F 1–2
33 *Sigovia*] F 2; Sigonia F 1
42 Gaffer——] ~ . F 1–2
46 pray——] ~ . F 1–2
47 Gaffer:] ~ . F 1–2
49 naked——] ~ . F 1–2
54 serve] F 2; sarve F 1
58 Naunt)——] Naunt)ₐ F 1–2
59 improvidence:——] ~ :ₐ F 1–2
65 her.——] ~ .ₐ F 1–2
68 me:——] ~ :ₐ F 1–2
71 Mountaine,] F 2; ~ . F 1
84 him,] F 2; ~ . F 1

IV.ii

IV.ii] *Scena secunda.* F 1; SCENE II. F 2
21 then——] ~ . F 1–2
32–34 I think . . . the Sunne;] F 1–2 *line:* I think . . . me, | It . . . Sunburnt, | What's . . . at? | Do'st . . . there, | That, . . . the Sunne;
37 butter'd.——] ~ ,ₐ F 1–2
54 finely,] F 2; ~ ₐ F 1
58 I,] F 2; ~ ₐ F 1
59 Sir:] F 2; ~ ₊ F 1
64 *all*,] F 2 ~ ₐ F 1
74 weary,] F 2; ~ . F 1
79 heavier, heaven] F 2; ~ ₐ ~ F 1
80.1] *in margin beside lines* 78–79 *in* F 1; *following line* 78 *in* F 2
84 too] ~ ₐ F 1–2
95 o'] O' F 1
107 more——] ~ . F 1–2
130 Christians——] ~ ₐ F 1; ~ . F 2
131 mercy?] ~ . F 1–2
131.1] *in margin beside* Where are his Emblemes? (*line* 129) *in* F 1; *centred on a separate line beneath these words in* F 2
145 blush.] F 2; ~ ? F 1
180 to th'] F 2; to 'th F 1
181–182 emulationₐ (so . . . forget it)ₐ] ~ , ₐ ~ . . . ~ ~ ₐ, F 1–2
192 Mistris——] ~ . F 1–2
193 her——] ~ . F 1–2
198 man——] ~ . F 1–2
223 not,] F 2; ~ : F 1
227 angry.——] ~ ,ₐ F 1–2

232 agen——] F2; ~ . F1

249 me.] ~ , F1–2

252 ye;] ~ , F1–2

IV.iii

IV.iii] *Scæna Tertia.* F1; SCENE III. F2

1 pleasing,] F2; ~ , F1

2 you——] ~ . F1–2

10 I,] F2; ~ , F1

12 she.——] ~ :, F1; ~ ;, F2

16 madly?] ~ : F1; ~ ; F2

22 sirha.] ~ : F1; ~ ; F2

22 s.d. *Shake Irons...Parson] in margin to right of line 22 in* F1; *after* Hark (*line 22) in* F2

22 Hark!] F2; ~ . F1

26 horses!] ~ . F1; ~ ; F2

33 more!] ~ , F1–2

37 Triton!] ~ . F1–2

38 strike!] ~ . F1–2

43 Alas...sir] F1–2 *line:* Alas... question: | They...sir

45.1–45.2] *in margin to right of the two halves of line 44 in* F1; *after* let 'em rest. (*line 44) in* F2

49 I,] F2; ~ , F1

52 *Master?*] F2; ~ , F1

59 sides] F2; sidies F1

67 pudding!] ~ . F1; ~ , F2

69 sir——] ~ . F1–2

71 Pox...urship] F1–2 *line:* Pox ...whyms, | Pox...urship

87 mouth.] ~ , F1–2

92 ye.] ~ , F1–2

97 Away...sirah] F1–2 *line:* Away...foole, | And...sirah

104 sake——] ~ , F1–2

108 him.] ~ , F1–2

115 letter,] F2; ~ , F1

117 finely] F2; finley F1

125 lunatique;] ~ , F1; ~ , F2

138 me;] ~ , F1; ~ , F2

142 lodging;] ~ , F1–2

143.1 *in margin to right of line 142 and first half of line 143 in* F1; *following line 142 in* F2

144 noyse,] F2; ~ , F1

146 for,] F2; ~ , F1

150 s.d. *shake irons] in margin of lines 148–149 in* F1; *following line 148 in* F2

153 chamber?——] ~ ,, F1–2

156 why my chamber?] F2; ~ ~ ~ , F1

159 ye,] F2; ~ , F1

172 softly,] ~ , F1–2

174 not,] F2; ~ , F1

177 I,] ~ , F1–2

178 grown?] F2; ~ . F1

181 it——] ~ , F1–2

182 s.d.] *in margin beside* this sir? (*line 182) in* F1–2

185 me:] ~ , F1–2

195.1 *in margin beside* miserable me! (*line 195) in* F1–2

201 it.——] ~ . F1–2

201.1] *in margin beside* Grace. (*line 201) in* F1–2

V.i

V.i *Actus Quintus. Scæna prima.* F1–2

14 *Segovia,*] Segonia. F1; *Segovia.* F2

15 nothing,] ~ ; F1–2

V.ii

V.ii] *Scæna secunda.* F1; SCENE
II. F2
0.1 *Enter*] F2; *Enteo* F1
2 service,] ~ ? F1–2

34 me,] ~ . F1–2
43 villanies——] ~ . F1–2
49 trembles!——] ~ !ᴧ F1–2

V.iii

V.iii] *Scena tertia.* F1; SCENE III.
F2
1–2 Use...tomorrow] F1–2 *line:*
Use...sports | All...tomorrow
2 tomorrow,] F2; ~ . F1

5 *Segovia*] F2; Segonia F1
15 with;] ~ ᴧ F1; ~ , F2
28 gambals!] ~ . F1–2
47 pardon;] ~ , F1–2
53 people,] F2; ~ . F1

V.iv

V.iv] *Scæna Quarta.* F1; SCENE
IV. F2
7 him;——] ~ ;ᴧ F1–2
16 gambols,——] ~ .—— F1–2
19 now:——] ~ :ᴧ F1–2
29 another.] F2; ~ ? F1
32 asleep] F2; asleeep F1
32.1] *following line 30 in* F1–2
34 What?] ~ . F1–2
39 boldly] F2; boldy F1
43–44 And...Mistresse] F1–2

line: And...part. | Ha? | There
...Mistresse
58 'em.] ~ , F1–2
64, 92 *Segovia*] F2; Segonia F1
95 s.d.] *in margin to right of lines
93–94 in* F1; *on line 93 in* F2
96 Retire!] ~ ? F1–2
100.1 *Exeunt*] *Exit* F1–2
112 friend——] ~ . F1–2
118 o' my] F2; O my F1
118 side,] ~ ; F1–2

V.v

V.v] *Scæna quinta.* F1; SCENE V.
F2
0.1 Seberto, Curio] F2; ~ : ~ F1

3 what;] ~ ᴧ F1–2
9 wildenes),] wildenes)ᴧ F1–2
19 him:] ~ ᴧ F1–2

V.vi

V.vi] *Scæna Sexta.* F1; SCENE
VI. F2
1–20 This...Queene] *ital. in*
F1–2
10 Modesty,] F2; ~ ᴧ F1

12 bend,] F2; ~ ᴧ F1
17 dayes,] ~ ᴧ F1–2
23–35 For...you] *ital. in* F1–2
26 me.] F2; ~ , F1
32 now;] ~ ᴧ F1–2

34 even,] F2; ~ . F1

35 s.d.] *on line* 34 *in* F1–2

50 Just...now] F1–2 *line:* Just... favour, | Doe...now?

50 favour:] F2; ~ , F1

51–66 Thus...she] *ital. in* F1–2

55 Damask, greene,] ~ ₐ ~ ₐ F1–2

58 show.] F2; ~ , F1

75 joyfull,] F2; ~ ₐ F1

76–77 Nay...you——] *prose in* F1–2

76 wonder;] ~ , F1–2

77 nothing;] ~ ₐ F1–2

80 doing. Will] doing, will F1–2

86 enjoy her,] ~ ~ . F1–2

102 art;] ~ . F1–2

111 fortunes——] ~ . F1–2

111 Ha!] ~ . F1–2

112 *Segovia*] F2; *Segonia* F1

119 you₍ will] F2; ~ , ~ F1

119 her——] ~ . F1–2

124 Governour——] ~ . F1–2

HISTORICAL COLLATION

[NOTE: The F1 (Folio 1647) copy-text has been collated with the following editions: F2 (Folio 1679), L (*Works*, 1711, ed. Gerard Langbaine the younger and others), S (*Works*, 1750, ed. Theobald, Seward and Sympson; *The Pilgrim* edited by Sympson); C (*Works*, 1778, ed. George Colman the younger), W (*Works*, 1812, ed. Henry Weber), D (*Works*, 1843–6, ed. Alexander Dyce). No variants in *you–ye–you* are noted unless they originate in F2, and no colloquial contractions not originating in F2 unless metrical differences might result.]

Title

THE PILGRIM] THE PILGRIM. A COMEDY. F2

I.i

0.1 Curio, Seberto] Curio, *and*
    Seberto F2+
2 Believe] Believe't S, C
9 Fathers] father W
19 could] wou'd S, C
22 pin'd] pined W; pinn'd D
25 Is] Is't S+

35 mannage] marriage L, S
60 *Pedro*] *Pearo* F1(u), F2
77 tune] turn C, W
96 sorte] sorts F2, S, C, W, D
116 wantone] a wanton S+
121 tettish] pettish F2
142 with] *om*. C

I.ii

3 farther] further C, W, D
19 Glisters] clisters C
29 s.p. *2. Beggar*] *1 Beg*. F2
33 that come] that are come W
43 sweat] swear F1–S
68 hartly] heartily F2, C, W, D
73 And you] And that you F2
75 Ye talk too broad] *words assigned
    to Curio in* C
79 know] knew F1, L
87 then] them F1

114 mediate] meditate F2
141 ye have] ye've F2, S; you've C;
    you have W, D
146 appeares] appear F2
146 fears] errors D
149 fears] tears S–D
167 he is] he's F2, S, C
183 so, too true] so true F2
184 engraved] engraven F2
191 grow sullen] grow so sullen F2

II.i

2 ith] in the F2
3 Ye] You F2
8 'em] *om.* F2
17 baud] band F1, L
29 bear] bears C
70 'hem] 'em F2+
74 ye] you F2
85 Fig-leaves] Fig-tree leaves F2
93 know] known S, C, W
103 and what] or what F2

108 Terse] Teresse F1; Teress L;
　　Tierce S–D
118 s.p. *2. Servant]* *1 Serv.* F2
130 Jumping-Jone] jumping, Joan
　　F2
131 joggle] juggle F2
143 Tie] I'll tye F2
143 th' horse] the horse F2
147 shall] will F2

II.ii

13 that] they F2
20 not we] we not W
30 s.p. *Roderigo] om.* F1–S
31 nor] and F2
32 Ile entertaine] *Rod.* Ile entertain
　　L, S
44 staring] staving F1–W
53 We] We'll S, C, W
72 Thy heart] Thou art S
81 his] this F1–L
89 farther] further C
98 me] thee F2
101 dares] dare C, W

111 *Alonsos]* Fernando's C; Fer-
　　ando's W, D
127 your] you F1, L, S; the F2, C–D
137 to] so L
146 Prating] Or prating S
152 sit] fit F2
193 Holy] For holy S
202 vildly] vilely F2, C, W; wildly L
216 sue to thee] sue thee F2
233 away] 'way S
243 wilt] will F1
281 Doe it] Do't F2
348 on] upon S

III.i

16 motions] notions S *conj.,* C
34.1 Second Outlaw] *2 Outlaw* F1;

2 *Out-laws* F2–W

III.ii

4 led] let F2

III.iii

6 passed] passe F1–L
18 an aime] and aime F1
30 him] me F2

43 knew] know F1
53 know] now F2
62, 63 Royall] Ryal L, C, W

67.1 Jaques *and* Lopez] *two Out-*
law F 1; *two Outlaws* F 2–W;
Lopez *carrying a pilgrim's gown*
and a sword, and another Out-
law D

68 farther] Father F 1, L; further C
86 mopp'-eyed] mop-eyed F 2–S;
mope-eyed C–D
89 mine] my W

III.iv

0.1 Lopez] *1 Out-Law* F 1–2; *one*
Out-law L–S; *First Outlaw* C–W
1, 2, 4, 6, 7, 12 s.p. *Lopez*] 1 *Out-l.*
F 1–W
9 s.p. *Lopez*] 1 *Out-l.* F 1–C;
2 *Out.* W

14 Another] *Lop.* Another F 1–W
14 s.p. *1. Out-law*] 2 *Out-l.*
F 1–W
17 2. *Out-law*] 3 *Out-l.* F 1–W
24 in] me W

III.v

III.v] *no scene division in* F 1–W

III.vi

III.vi] III.v *in* F 1–W
0.1 *a* Gentleman] *Third Gentle-*
man W

12 There's] Their's F 1; There L, S;
Their C, W

III.vii

III.vii] III.vi *in* F 1–W
20 *be all*] all be F 2, C, W
25.1 Shee-foole] Kate D (*so too in*
speech-prefixes for this character)
26 Gaffer] Goffer F 1, L
35 lie in in a] lie in a F 2–S
46.1–46.2 *a mad* Scholler] Stephano
D (*so too in speech-prefixes for*
this character)
50 You] Your F 1

55 s.p. *Gentleman*] 1 *Gent.* F 1–S;
Third Gentleman C–D
112 *flotes*] *flats* W
118 *thy*] om. F 1–L
124 we'l leave] will leave W
149, 171 s.p. *Gentleman*] *Third Gentle-*
man S–D
166 s.p. *Master*] om. F 1–2
167 Stay] *Mast.* Stay F 2

IV.i

22.1 *as a foole*] *in* Kate's *clothes* D
66 Royall] ryal L–W

98 *Prick me, and heale me*] om. F 2

222

IV.ii

4 flutterd] flatterd F1–C
5 coxcomb] coxcomes F1
21 scape] snap F1–L, W
42 *shall*] *will* F2
68 Tis] This F1–L
71 shall] will F2
90 contents] content F1, L
105 s.p. *3. Peasant*] 4. S
112 tormenting] tormented F1
119 s.p. *1. Peasant*] 2. F2
120 year] years L–W
142 clad] lad F1
143 guild] guid F1; guile F2, C; guide L, W

173 should] would F2
177 mine] mind F2
201 sword] word F1, L
210 'thas bin in] 'th as in F1
212 fight] light F1–S; light on W
215 See] *Pedro*. See C
221 the sword] their sword W
229 decarded] discarded F2, S–W
240 this] the F2, C
241 scar] scare F2
248 s.p. *Roderigo*] *om*. F1
256 us] up F2

IV.iii

12 needs] need F2
17 they be] they are F2, C, W
18 s.p. *1. Keeper*] 2 *Keep*. S, C
23 *Jenkin*] *om*. F2, C–D (F2 *prints the name after* Parson, *in s.d. at line* 22; *see Textual Note on* IV.iii.23)
26 Mackrels] Mackrel F2, C
45 admirable] admirably S
45 fancies] faces F1–L
45.1 Shee-foole] *She-fools* F2; Kate D (*so in speech-prefixes*)
54 plum] plumb F1, L–W
67 cares] Care F2, S, C
85 pig] peg F2
92 *Basilus manus*] *Besar las manos* S–W

92 codpice] Codpiss F2; cod-piece L–W
92 mark] marg C, W
104 heaven] Heavens F2, W
113 he may be] it may be he F2
121 ye vext] yet vext F1; you vex'd C–D
132 told] tole'd C, W; tol'd D
147, 155 s.p. *2. Keeper*] *Keep*. F1–W
169 I lunatique] I a lunatic S, W
174 you perceive it] yet perceive't S, D; yet perceive it C, W
177 and ye] an you C–D
186 mine old] my old L, S

V.i

9 Moth] moat C, D

12 Champion] champaign C, W

V.ii

27 still thus] still do thus F2
34 stroke] struck F2–D

45 saw] see F1
48 *Sinon*] *Simon* F1, L

V.iii

V.iii] V.ii *in* L, S
12 s.p. *3. Citizen*] *Cit.* L; *1 Cit.*
S

24 amongst] 'mongst S; among C,
W
71 s.p. *1. Citizen*] *Cit.* F 1–W

V.iv

2 leafes] leaves F 2–D
11 afar] 'far S
16 as fine a place] a fine place F 2
18 way] away F 1, L, S
19 methinks] methink F 2
19 yond rocks yonder] yon rocks
C, W
20.1 *Pot*] *om.* W, D
37 woods] words F 1
48 if] *om.* S
49 s.p. *Pedro*] *Alin.* F 1

59 longer] linger S *conj.*, C–D
69 whipt now] whip'd know L;
whip'd I know S
85 have good] and good F 1–L
105 Lord, how] O how F 2
111 here] there F 1, L, S
118 o' my] O my F 1
122 fall: no more. | *Roderigo.* I
hope] fall— | *Rod.* No More: I
hope Sympson *conj.*, C–D

V.v

22 ye] you F 2

V.vi

4 Oblations] *Obligations* L
7 s.p. *Ladies*] *First Lady* D
9 honour these] honour, these L,
W, D; Honour's, these S, C
35.1 *Shepheardesses*] *Shepheards*
F 1–C

49 a Filly that] a Filly too that
S–W
60 Ladies gloves] Lady-gloves
S–W
99 loose] lose F 2, C–D

THE
WILD-GOOSE CHASE

edited by
FREDSON BOWERS

TEXTUAL INTRODUCTION

The Wild-Goose Chase (Greg, *Bibliography*, no. 706) is generally regarded as the sole work of John Fletcher.[1] The earliest date that can be associated with it is the Christmas holidays 1621, when it was played at Court.[2] On 24 January 1622 payment was made for the comedy, among six plays acted before the Court, probably but not certainly a result of the holiday performance. That the play was popular is suggested by its choice by Sir George Herbert as his perquisite for the receipts of two chosen plays per year on the second day after revival: on 6 November 1632 he received the very large sum of £15 for *The Wild-Goose Chase* as his winter selection. The play was listed on 7 August 1641 among the King's Men's plays that the Lord Chamberlain forbade printers to publish without the company's consent. On [4] September 1646 it headed the original inscription of the list of plays Humphrey Robinson and Humphrey Moseley entered in the Stationers' Register in preparation for the Folio of 1647. However, copy had not been found, and in the address to the readers of the Folio Moseley states that among the previously unpublished plays he is now printing,

> One only Play I must except (for I meane to deale openly) 'tis a COMEDY call'd the *Wilde-goose Chase*, which hath beene long lost, and I feare irre-coverable; for a *Person of Quality* borrowed it from the *Actors* many yeares since, and (by the negligence of a Servant) it was never return'd; therefore now I put up this *Si quis*, that whosoever hereafter happily meetes with it, shall be thankfully satisfied if he please to send it home.

A copy was found, eventually, probably just before the entry on 12 April 1652 by Moseley in the Stationers' Register, where it is conventionally listed (as also on the titlepage) as by Beaumont as well as Fletcher.

---

[1] Cyrus Hoy, 'The Shares of Fletcher and his Collaborators in the Beaumont and Fletcher Canon (1)', *Studies in Bibliography*, VIII (1956), 132, 145.

[2] This and all other historical information about the play is drawn from G. E. Bentley, *The Jacobean and Caroline Stage*, III (Oxford, 1967), 425–30.

The resulting 1652 Folio, as Bentley remarks, 'is one of the most handsome and elaborate issues of a single play in the time'. In format it appears to have been designed to go with, and even to be bound with, the 1647 Folio, although the pages are set in single column instead of the double columns of the Folio. Bentley offers evidence that the cast provided in 1652 cannot have been the one for the original production in 1621 or earlier. For instance, Swanston did not join the King's Men until 1624; Trigg and Hammerton were acting boys' roles in 1631 and 1632 respectively and would have grown out of female parts by then if they had acted as early as 1621. Alexander Gough would have been only seven years old by 1621. A terminal date is established by the death of Shank in 1635/6. The cast, then, is most logically to be associated with the 1632 revival, after which, at some indeterminate time, the company's copy (whether the only one cannot be established) was lent to and not returned by the person of quality.

The Wild-Goose Chase was printed in folio, with the collation 2°: [A]² a² B–P², 32 leaves, $1 (+ a2, I2, K2) signed; pp. [i–viii] 1–56.

The play was printed in two sections, probably in two different shops. The first section of the text comprises Sheets B–G (I.i.0.1–III.i.18); the second, Sheets H–P (III.i.19–V.vi.108). The printer of the preliminary sheets [A] and a cannot be identified positively. If he were the first printer then each shop would have been responsible for eight sheets. However, the presence of press-variants in Sheet a (as in the work from the second shop) suggests that the assignments were unequal and that the second shop printed at least Sheet a, although Sheet A could have been printed by either shop.[1] The paper is the same in each section. (No printer's name appears in the imprint.)

The running-titles of Sheets B–G are '*The Wild-Goofe-Chafe.*' whereas in H–P the spelling is '*The Wilde-Goofe Chafe.*' In the first section the catchword includes the first dialogue word after the speech-prefix on sigs. F1, F1ᵛ, F2ᵛ, and G1ᵛ but on sigs. C1

---

[1] In the title to Jephson's commendatory verses, the original misprint '*CHASE*' (after '*WILD-*') was corrected by a cancel slip '*GOOSE*' pasted over the error and still present in various copies.

and G1 only the prefix appears. On sig. D1 the catchword 'And' appears in error for the following word '*Mir*. And' on D1ᵛ. In the second section the prefix alone serves as catchword on sigs. H1ᵛ, I2ᵛ, L2ᵛ, N1ᵛ, and O1ᵛ. The first word of the dialogue is added to the prefix to form the catchword on sigs. I1, I1ᵛ, I2, K1ᵛ, K2, N2ᵛ, O2ᵛ, P1, and P2. Several errors appear. On K1ᵛ the catchword is '*Ser*. Now', but Mirabel's speech 'Now I know him.', which ends K1ᵛ, is continued as the first line of K2 (a speech that should have been a single line although metrically uneven) 'Know him now plain.' The Servant's speech then follows as the second line on K2, beginning '*Ser*. I have discharg'd' (III.i.433–4). This is the odder confusion, since it appears to have come in the work of the same compositor, presumably setting in sequence, but possibly in reverse order. On sig. N2, by the same workman, the catchword 'For' has no relation to any preceding or following text, and the speech appears to continue without a gap from 'You see, before they are married, what Moriscoes,' on N2 to 'What Masques, and Mummeries they put upon us,' on N2ᵛ (V.ii.7–8). It is possible that a line has dropped out but the evidence may suggest some odd catchword error instead. On D1 the catchword is 'And', which omits the speech-prefix found in the first line on the next page, '*Mir*. And get two Boyes at every birth?' The same catchword error is found in the second section on M2ᵛ, where the catchword '*Certain*' omits the speech-prefix of the first line on N1, '*Ca-Last*. Certain she knowes ye not, yet loves to see ye'. A minor variant appears in the catchword on sig. K2 '*Lug*. Then', when the following words on K2ᵛ are '*Leug*. Then', but this difference in the spelling of the prefix comes between the work of two compositors.

In both sections, 52 lines of text are set on each page (plus signature–catchword line), but abruptly beginning with sig. O2 (V.ii.²128) with Belleur's speech 'Now we shall have you:' the text is set in a smaller type with 61 lines to the page, obviously to save ending on the recto of a single leaf Q1, with consequent expense of paper. In typography each section uses the old long ſ but does not observe the old u–v or i–j conventions. Each section was set using two skeleton-formes per sheet (with one exception). In the first section the most identifiable running-title appears regularly on B_2^v–C_2^v–D_2^v–E_2^v–F_2^v–G_2^v. In the second section, Sheet H (the first printed) was machined using only one skeleton-forme, but for Sheet I a second skeleton was constructed, which printed the outer formes of Sheets I–L and O–P and the inner formes of Sheets M–N. The most obviously identifiable running-title can be traced as H_1^v–H_2^v–I_1^v–K_1^v–L_1^v–M_2^v–N_2^v–O_1^v–P_1^v. Characteristic of the first section is the setting of all entrance-directions to the right margin, opposite lines of text, except for the first direction in each scene. In Sheet B the directions are set in italic and the names in roman, but beginning with C the setting is in the reverse, the direction in roman and the names in italic. In the second section the directions are to the right in sigs. I_1, I_2^v, K_1, K_2, L_2^v, M_1, M_1^v, N_2^v, O_1, and P_1^v; however, internal entrance-directions are centred in H_1, I_1, I_2, K_1^v, and L_2. Both compositors are irregular in this positioning of the direction in respect to the following speech.

Despite the alteration of the typography of directions between Sheets B and C, the characteristics of the first section are so even that the only hypothesis justified by the evidence is that one compositor set the whole of the text. On the contrary, two compositors set the second section. Very slight indications of crowding, with a few anomalies, suggest but do not demonstrate that copy was cast off and set by formes in the first section as well as in the second. In the second the schedule of work shows considerable irregularity but sometimes the two compositors each set a page apiece of a forme, as in Sheets N and P, and sometimes each set both pages of a single forme, as in Sheet L. Other sheets may have been set with three pages by one compositor and one by the other.

Except for five pages in which the contraction does not appear, the two compositors may be distinguished by the variant *Ile* (a few times, *I'le*) set by Compositor *X* or the *I'll* set by Compositor *Y*. Except for two pages, M_1^v and O_2^v, which contain one aberrant spelling but can be assigned on other evidence, this distinction is constant. Compositor *X* set *Ile* on sigs. H_1, H_1^v (1 *Ile*, 2 *I'le*), I_2^v (4 *I'le*), K_2^v, L_1^v, L_2, M_1^v (3 *Ile*, 1 *I'll*), M_2, M_2^v, N_1, N_1^v, O_1^v, P_1, and P_1^v. Compositor *Y* set *I'll* on sigs. I_2, K_1, K_1^v,

K2, L1, L2^v, N2, N2^v, O1, O2, O2^v (2 *I'll*, 1 *Ile*), P2, and P2^v. The validity of this identification can be confirmed by other evidence. The most valuable is that of the *do–doe* variant. Compositor *X* in general preferred *doe* but set a smaller number of *do* forms always on the same page with *doe*. For example, *X*'s *doe* is found on H1^v(4), I2^v(2), K2^v(3), L2(1), M1^v(1), M2(1), M2^v(1), N1(2), P1(1), and P1^v(1). On certain of these pages, he set *do* as well: K2^v(2), M1^v(3), M2(2), M2^v(4), P1(1). On the other hand, in Compositor *Y*'s pages, identified by *I'll*, no *doe* spelling ever appears, and *do* is constant on I2(2), K1(1), L1(1), L2^v(5), O1(1), O2(1), O2^v(2), P2(3), and P2^v(3). The same distinction holds for *goe–go*. Compositor *Y* never sets *goe*, and *go* appears on I2(1), K1^v(1), N2^v(1), O2(4). On the other hand, Compositor *X* has a distinct preference for *goe*, which he set on H2^v(1), K2^v(1), L1^v(1), L2(2), M2(1), N1(1), N1^v(2), P1(3), and P1^v(1). He set *go* only on M2(1) and M2^v(1). In his pages identified by *I'll* spellings, Compositor *Y* set only the spelling *Lady*, as on I2(1), K1^v(2), K2(1), and P2(1). Compositor *X* also sets *Lady*, as on K2^v(1), L1^v(3), M1^v(1), M2(2), P1(1), and P1^v(1); but he admitted *Ladie*, as on K2^v(2), L2(2), N1(1), and P1^v(1). Except on the anomalous sig. P2^v, where two long dashes appear in the text, one before a half-line, Compositor *Y* never uses a long dash even for broken-off speech, nor does Compositor *X*. On the other hand, on identified sigs. H1, L2, N1, and O1^v Compositor *X* places a long dash before the exit-direction at the right. Compositor *X* prefers the speech-prefix alone as catchword, as on H1^v, I2^v, N1^v, but on P1 he adds the following word. Compositor *Y* sets prefix plus following word on I2, K1^v, K2, N2^v, O2^v, and P2^v. Compositor *X* sets the longer prefix form *Ori.* for *Oriana* on H1^v, M2^v, N1^v, P1, P1^v. His single short form *Or.* occurs on M2^v along with six *Ori.* forms. Compositor *Y* sets the short form *Or.* exclusively, as on K1, K1^v, K2, O2^v, P2, and P2^v. Compositor *X* sets a few pronominal forms in double -*ee*-, as *wee'll* on H1, H1^v, L2, P1^v and *shee'll* on N1, as well as the conventional forms, whereas *Y* never sets such double -*ee*- forms. In stage-directions, Compositor *X* ordinarily sets the names in italic and *Y* in roman. In their *Ile–I'll*-identified pages, *X* sets the italic names on I2^v, K2^v, L2, M2, P1, and P1^v, and *Y* on

K1, K2, L2^v, O2, and O2^v. However, in side directions on N2^v and the odd P2^v, Compositor Y set names in italic. The name is in roman on moot M1. Signature N2 is anomalous. Its first direction, near the head, introduces V.i with roman names, but V.ii, eight lines from the foot, has italic names in the entrance, a sign, just possibly, that X finished a Y page, perhaps beginning with the new scene. In connection with the speech-prefix *Leug.–Lug.*, another anomalous page, although readily explained, is Y's sig. K2, which contains both. But Y, who is consistent elsewhere with *Lug.*, was obviously influenced by the spelling in the IV.i entrance-direction, in which he seems to have followed his copy spelling *Leugier* and so set *Leug.* for the very first prefix after the entrance, although changing to his customary *Lug.* in line 10 and the following catchword. On the other hand, early in his stint X favours *Leug.*, as on H1, H1^v, and K2^v. Possibly by chance, the form *Rosaluce* in stage-directions appears only in X's work, on H1, L2, M2, and P1^v.

A few pieces of typographical evidence help in confirming the identification. A roman capital 'M' (which starts on the moot page I1^v (III.i.240)) has a unique break in its left leg, at the top, extending to remove the serif. This same sort occurs again in K2 and N2^v, pages set by Y. Y's sigs. P2 and P2^v are linked by the appearance of a badly damaged capital 'I', the peculiarities of which have given rise to editorial misreading at V.vi.30 (see Textual Note) on P2. An odd short capital 'I' type, from a different fount, comes in Y's cases on I2, K1, K1^v, and N2^v. Two capital italic I sorts are mixed in the case with roman 'I'. These appear first in Y's K1^v, K2, and N2^v, but also in X's K2^v. Debatable M1 also has them. A shortage of italic capital R sorts is a characteristic of X's case, owing to the drain placed upon the character by the speech-prefixes for Rosalura. This shortage shows up immediately on sig. H1 and, after coming again on the two moot pages H2^v and M1, continues on X's M2, M2^v, N1, and N1^v. On all his pages Y is able to set italic *Ros.* except on sig. L2^v, where after five consecutive *Ros.* prefixes, he sets three with a roman 'R', a single prefix with italic R intervening before the last two roman R*os*. A single swash italic M appears in X's work on sigs. H1^v, I2^v, L2, N1^v. On N2 it occurs in the prefix for V.ii.[21], the lower part of Y's page that on the basis of the italic

names in the entrance-direction had been suggested as the work of
X taking over to finish the page, but it also comes once on *Y*'s
sig. O 1. Five pages of text do not contain either *Ile* (*I'le*) or *I'll*
as identifiers: these are sigs. H 2 (III.i.100–43), H 2ᵛ (III.i.144–86),
I 1 (III.i.187–223), I 1ᵛ (III.i.224–¹264), and M 1 (IV.ii.356–90). Of
these, H 2ᵛ can be assigned to *X* on sufficient evidence. In H 2ᵛ
on III.i.177 occurs the spelling *goe*, which *X* favours but which *Y*
does not admit. The appearance twice of *greifes* in lines 174–5
can be associated with *greive* on *X*'s sig. K 2ᵛ (*grieve* on *Y*'s L 1)
and possibly with *X*'s *Preist* on L 1ᵛ, whereas *Y* never transposes
these vowels. The *-que* spelling *publique* in line 168 can be matched
by *Heritique* in *X*'s sig. H 1ᵛ but nowhere else in the text. In line
184 *deer* (for 'dear') also occurs on N 1 but never in *Y*, and *cleer*
in line ¹186 appears again in *X*'s L 1ᵛ, N 1, and P 1ᵛ but not in *Y*.
Three appearances of *Lady* on the page are neutral since *X* may
set this spelling as well as *Ladie*. The evidence for sig. I 1ᵛ is strong
for assignment to *Y*. Most prominent is the typographical evidence
of the broken 'M' already remarked, as also found in *Y*'s case on
K 2 and N 2ᵛ. Fairly strong is *Y*'s characteristic addition of the first
word after the speech-prefix in the catchword. The spelling *endebted*
in line 237 may be paralleled by *enterview* on *Y*'s sig. O 1. We also
find the spelling *curtesie*, line 230, which is also found on *Y*'s O 2ᵛ
and P 2ᵛ, as well as *discurteous* on N 2ᵛ. Compositor *X* sets *courtesie*
on K 2ᵛ but also *curteous* once on sig. O 1ᵛ. The *Lady* form appears
five times, and we have one *do*.

These assignments leave only sigs. H 2, I 1, and M 1 as less certain. Because of the single skeleton-forme used to impose Sheet H,
with two-skeleton printing to follow for Sheet I and the rest, it
would be convenient if all of Sheet H could be assigned to Compositor *X*, who can be identified on H 1 and H 1ᵛ with some certainty, and with almost equal certainty on H 2ᵛ, despite its lack of
the *Ile* evidence. However, H 2 has no positive evidence for *X* and
at least some negative evidence against him and in favour of *Y*.
The strongest evidence is the use of roman for the name in the
entrance-direction in line 135. There is also the negative evidence
against *X* in the spellings *go*, *near*, and *clear*, as well as *we'll* (as
against *wee'll* five times on the preceding page H 1ᵛ, which should

have been set by formes with H2). The chief positive evidence for
Y as the compositor of sig. I1 rests on the characteristic use of the
first word after the prefix used as catchword, and the use of roman
names in the entrance-direction at III.i.215. Otherwise, the evidence
is negative against X. For example, there are the spellings *grieve* and
clear especially, since *Lady* alone is insufficient indication. Also negative is the italic setting of *England*: Y always sets the names of countries in italic whereas X is irregular and twice sets roman for italic.

Signature M1 has its difficulties. On the one hand it appears to
be linked with Compositor Y from its use of the roman name in
the stage-direction in IV.ii.70, its six *do* spellings without a single
doe, and its two italic capital I types, which had appeared in Y's
pages K1^v, K2, and after an occurrence in X's K2^v, again in Y's
N2^v. On the other hand, the shortage of italic capital W on M1,
which led to the substitution of roman 'W' for the women's speech-
prefixes at IV.ii.81, ^{2}83, and 85, is preceded by the expedient of
capital VV for the *1. Woman* at line ^{2}77. On X's M1^v the first
prefix for one of the women comes in the second line (IV.ii.^{2}91)
and is again *1. VVo.*, seemingly linked with the shortage on M1;
however, lower, in line 112, the prefix *Wo.* employs a normal italic
sort. Four of the ten prefixes *Ros.* in M1 use a roman capital 'R'.
This shortage of italic R for Rosalura's prefix had shown up on
X's H2^v and was to appear again in his M2 and M2^v (though not
in his M1^v). Yet Compositor Y, whose stock of italic R was usually
sufficient, had begun to run short on L2^v toward the foot of the
page and substituted three roman sorts with one intervening italic.
This evidence, thus, appears to be a stand-off. The spelling *neer*
(i.e., *neerer*, IV.ii.^{2}64) is more characteristic of X than of Y and
appears again on X's N1^v. Amidst this contradictory evidence it
may appear that the use of the roman name in the stage-direction
and the unusually large uses of *do* (with no *doe* spelling) on M1
may swing the balance in Y's favour, especially since the four pages
of Sheet M would otherwise have been set exclusively by X.

Granted the validity of the assignment of these five pages, we
end with the following compositorial assignments for the second
section. Compositor X set sigs. H1, H1^v, H2^v, I2^v, K2^v, L1^v, L2,
M1^v, M2, M2^v, N1, N1^v, O1^v, P1, P1^v, and very likely a few lines

at the foot of Y's sig. N2. Compositor Y set sigs. H2, I1, I1^v,
I2, K1, K1^v, K2, L1, L2^v, N2 (upper part), N2^v, O1, O2, O2^v,
P2, and P2^v. As remarked, sig. P2^v (V.vi.^{2}72–108) is anomalous in
its characteristics. Signature M1 remains uncertain but is probably
Y's. In terms of the act–scene–line-numbering of the present text,
Compositor X set III.i.19–99; III.i.144–$3$186; III.i.^{2}302–46; IV.i.310–
52; IV.i.100–IV.ii.16; V.ii.0.1–7(?); V.ii.88–$1$128; V.iv.^{2}25–V.vi.27.
Compositor Y, correspondingly, set III.i.100–43; III.i.187–$1$302;
III.i.^{1}347–IV.i.^{2}10; IV.i.53–99; IV.ii.17–$2$56; IV.iii.^{2}158–V.i.24;
V.ii.8–49; V.ii.50–87; V.ii.^{2}128–V.iv.^{1}25; V.vi.28–108. Y perhaps
set M1, IV.ii.356–IV.iii.^{1}158.

The nature of the manuscript copy that lies behind the 1652
first edition poses a difficult problem. We have Humphrey Moseley's
statement that he could not print the play in the 1647 Folio, since
the actors had lent it to a person of quality, who by the negligence
of a servant had failed to return it. This statement, if strictly accu-
rate, suggests that the company had preserved only a single copy
of the play, which obviously would have been the prompt-book.
But whether the company would have provided the person of
quality with the actual prompt-book (presumably after the 1632
revival) is at least arguable; and it is clear that not all prompt-books
had been preserved, since a large number of plays in the 1647 Folio
are printed from other copy. Moreover, we have no evidence that
the manuscript that was eventually discovered and printed by the
actors Lowin and Taylor was the copy once possessed by the person
of quality or else some other document that had been lost. If the
play had been lent 'many yeares since', the discovered copy could
have been anything. It is only a fairly natural inference (or wishful
thinking) that the lost had been found, over the passage of some
years, and that the person of quality's copy had indeed turned up.[1]

[1] It is difficult not to associate the loss of the play with the lending to the person
of quality. Odd as it would be to lend the prompt-book itself, the company may have
done so to an important personage if no further immediate performance after the
1632 revival were contemplated. Of course, Moseley's 'many yeares since' may
mean anything. If during the early years of the Commonwealth the play had been
lent from the players' stock, the loan of the prompt-book, the single copy, would
be understandable. Despite certain problems, there are signs of prompt-book origin,
or at least of the marking of a copy by the book-keeper in preparation for the final
book. In general, the odds may favour the prompt-book itself.

The listing of the play among the King's Men's plays on 7 August 1641 for which the Lord Chamberlain forbade publication without the company's consent does not signify that the company at that time had a copy, for it would have wished to suppress publication even were the copy lost to them. It would seem clear, also, that Moseley's inclusion of the play in his mass entry of 4 September 1646 for his Folio had no connection with his possession of the copy.

Wanting external evidence, we are forced back into what internal evidence may suggest, which in this case is not entirely enlightening. One feature of the print is that it contains no descriptive directions whatever but confines itself strictly to the simple record of entrances and exits (one entrance-direction being omitted and a character left out of another). The positioning of the entrance-directions in both sections of the print suggests that ordinarily they were written to the right of the text, in prompt-book style. How faithful the printer was in following the exact placement of the first line of these directions in relation to the text cannot be demonstrated, but comparison with the centred directions suggests that the positioning was fairly exact and that the entrance would be placed a few lines before the first speech of the entering character. But evidence of this nature as suggesting prompt copy, while suggestive perhaps, is scarcely to be trusted.

An oddity occurs in the side entrance-direction at III.i.314 for Lugier's appearance as 'Leverdure, des Lugier, Mr. Illiard.' The des is a misreading of alias, as found in the opening direction for the scene, 'Leverdure, alias, Lugier'. The specification of Hilliard Swanston as Lugier (agreeing with the preliminary cast of characters) cannot represent an original entry in the prompt-book, since Swanston did not join the company until 1624, three years after the first production, although it could have been made in the original book, or a revision, for the November 1632 revival. The theatrical purpose of so identifying Lugier at this point is obscure, however, for his first appearance in the play had been as early as I.ii.[1]

---

[1] It would be mere speculation that the addition of the actor's name was a jotting made by the two entrepreneurs, Lowin and Taylor, in the process of making up a *dramatis personæ* to print. But we have no evidence about the provenance or the writer of the list of characters, which being for the 1632 production may have come to Lowin and Taylor complete.

Of more significance, however, is the mistaken identification of Lugier as in disguise in his dialogue with de Gard at the opening of III.i and then the repetition of his disguise as that of Leverdure when, in fact, at III.i.314 he does enter, disguised, for his encounter with Mirabel. Moreover, Mirabel calls him a 'youth', and is previously unacquainted with him, both contrary to the Factor's later statements (V.ii.76–7) about Leverdure as Mirabel's old merchant who supplied him with money. It would seem that we have both in III.i.o.1 and III.i.314 a positive error, or change of plan not rectified, and, curiously enough, Lugier as Leverdure is indicated by the variant speech-prefix *Lev.* for *Lug.* at III.i.347, on sig. K1, second line, set by a different compositor from the one who had set the entrance at III.i.314 on sig. I2ᵛ, and hence referable to copy even though the rest of the prefixes on K1 are *Lug.*

The spelling of the names in the *Drammatis Personæ* very likely has small authority in respect to the forms of the original manuscript, and in certain spellings of names it conforms to nothing in the text. Whether this list was supplied by Lowin and Taylor, or was theatrical in origin, is not to be proved, except that the laudatory notices of the performances of several actors sound like the puffing of Lowin and Taylor. The actors' names show that the list could not refer to the original production but instead to the 1632 revival. Whoever made it up did not recall the names of the boy(s) who played Petella and Mariana (doubtless a doubled part).¹

In the text itself two particular oddities stand out. In all stage-directions in the first section Nantolet is given as *Natolet* (prefixes *Na.*) and he is twice called *Natolet* in the text at I.i.71, 150. Yet once in II.i.89 he is *Nantolet* in the text. Thereafter his name does not appear in the first section; throughout the second section he is always *Nantolet* (prefixes *Nan.* or *Nant.*). On his first introduction in the entrance-direction for I.iii Lugier is *Lugien*, possibly a misreading, since in his next appearance in III.i he is *Lugier*. In the first section Lugier's speech-prefixes are *Lug.* However, when the second section begins on sig. H1, with Compositor *X*, the prefixes shift to *Leug.*, as also on H1ᵛ until his exit. At this point, no matter

¹ Nevertheless, Bentley (*Jacobean Stage*, III, 427) remarks, 'The cast published in this edition is one of the most complete of the time and much the most elaborate.'

which page he set first, Compositor X was setting without benefit of any stage-direction: he would have no idea who the character was or how named, and thus his prefixes *Leug.* should reproduce copy. It is worth notice that copy again appears to be reproduced in the entrance-direction for IV.i (sig. K2) where he is *Leugier*. This is the first time Compositor Y had set his name, and the first speech-prefix *Leug.* is perhaps influenced by this immediately preceding direction, for another below and in the catchword is *Lug.*, which would not seem to be a compositorial variant but the copy form. Yet when X sets K2^v, the next page, the one prefix before his exit is *Leug.* again, the form that X had previously set. Nevertheless, in the entrance-direction for IV.ii (set by X) he is *Lugier*, and this spelling together with the prefix *Lug.* is invariable thereafter in the work of both compositors. It may seem possible that the copy itself varied between *Leugier* and *Lugier* (and perhaps even *Lugien*).

Other variant spelling of names also seems referable to copy, at least in part. In the entrance for I.i, Oriana's brother is *de Gard* but in the centred first prefix he is *De Gard*. However, the prefixes in I.i are all *de Ga.*, becoming *de G.* as the scene progresses. In his entrance in I.iii he is again *de Gard*, with prefixes of *de G.*, and so in his entrance and speeches in II.i (varying in prefixes between *de Ga.* and *de G.*). When Compositor X then continues III.i at the start of the second section he uses the prefixes *de Gr.* but when Y sets the re-entrance later in III.i (sig. K1) his name is hyphenated for the first time *De-Gard* and his one prefix on the page has also the capitalized *De* and the hyphen, *De-G.*, the prefix form that continues on sigs. K1^v–K2, also set by Y. In the entrance to IV.iii on M2, set by X, the form is *de-Gard* on re-entrance but the prefixes are capitalized as *De-G.*, changing on X's sig. N1 to *de-Ga.* In Y's page N2 the entrance form is *De-Gard* for V.i and the prefixes correspond as *De-G.*, but on Y's sig. P2^v the entrance is *de-Gard*. Here certainly there is some compositorial as well as copy variation: in the first section the name is not hyphenated and is usually in the form *de Gard*, whereas in the second section both compositors hyphenate the name (except on its first introduction in X's work in III.i). Whether it is *De* or *de* is a matter of indifference to either compositor, but the form has a tendency to stay constant within a stint.

The problem of hyphenation is also present for La-Castre, as well as the problem whether the compositors favoured *La-Castre* or *la-Castre* in directions and prefixes. In the first section he is *La-Castre* on entrance in I.i, but (perhaps under the influence of the *de Gard* form) the prefixes are not hyphenated, as in *La Ca.* or *La C.* The same forms are repeated in I.iii (hyphenated in direction but unhyphenated in prefixes) but after two pages the compositor on sig. D1 set a full stop *La.Ca.* three times and *La C.* twice, not in sequence, although for the rest of the scene the prefixes are the standard *La C.* In the second section his first entrance is for IV.iii (sig. M2 set by *X*) where he is *la-Castre* with the prefix *le-Cast.* on the same page but *la-Ca.* on the next. However, on sig. N1 Compositor *X* changes the prefix (after an initial typo *Ca-Last.*) to capitalized *La-Cast.* In the re-entrance within IV.iii on sig. N1ᵛ (*X*) he is *la.Castre* with a prefix *la-Cast*; yet on *Y*'s sig. N2 the entrance for V.ii has *La castre* and the unhyphenated prefix *La Cast.* for the immediately following prefix. Overpage on N2ᵛ, however, *Y* set the prefixes *la-Cast.*, as also in the scene's continuation on sig. O1. The next appearance is in V.iii, as a mute, where in his entrance, set by *Y*, he is *le-Castre*.

Lylia-Biancha in the first section starts out in the entrance for I.iii as *Lylia-Biancha*; her first prefix (far removed) is *Lyl.*, the form repeated throughout the scene. Her entrance within II.ii is as *Lilia*, with prefixes *Lil.* or *Li.* in the scene. In the second section, within III.i on sig. H1 set by *X*, she has changed to *Lelia*, with prefixes *Lel.*, the same prefix holding when *Y* takes over on H2, and so on for both compositors in this scene. In the entrance for IV.i on *Y*'s sig. K2 she is again *Lelia*, prefixes *Lel.*, and again this prefix carries over when *X* starts his stint. However, on her entrance in IV.ii on *Y*'s(?) sig. M1 she is *Lilia*, although her prefixes on the next page (*X*'s) are *Lel.* Her first entrance in IV.iii is as *Lelia*, prefixes *Lel.*, but her re-entrance, still in *X*'s pages, is as *Bianch.*, her prefix *Lil.* In *Y*'s sig. O2 her entrance-direction for V.iii is *Lillia*, prefix *Lil.*, forms that persist in the work of both compositors for the rest of the scene.

Rosalura starts out in the first section as *Rosa Lieura* in the entrance for I.iii. In II.iii she has changed on entrance to *Rosalura*. In the second section the entrance form *Rosaluce* in III.i, IV.ii, IV.iii, and V.iii is all in the work of Compositor *X* and seems to be a misreading, such as his *Leverduce* on sig. I 2ᵛ. It is unfortunate that Compositor *Y* abbreviates her name as *Rosalu.* in her entrance for V.iii (sig. O 2), thus effectively preventing a comparison with *X*. Mirabel is almost always *Mirabell* except for a few scattered *Mirabel* forms. Bellure starts out in the entrance for I.ii as *Belleure* but everywhere else he is *Bellure* in the work of both compositors.

Some evidence points towards variant forms of names both in directions and in prefixes as associated with scene division, and hence of the influence of copy. Certainly, not all can be compositorial preference although there is perhaps enough of this to prevent any attempt to itemize the forms in the copy. All that can be said is that the manuscript under the print must have lacked uniformity, although the differences between the first and second sections in respect to some forms suggest variable degrees of fidelity to copy in the three compositors involved in setting this play. Because of the confusion of forms, the editor has chosen to reproduce the names in the stage-directions as they appear in all their copy-text variety, but to make the spellings of the speech-prefixes uniform according to some probabilities of copy-preference. All directions are set in italic, with names in roman, without regard for the typography of the Folio copy-text. All side directions are centred; but because of some possible ambiguity about their placement, directions have been moved to a position immediately before the character's first speech, as is most convenient in a reading edition.

There can be no guarantee that the manuscript that Lowin and Taylor discovered in 1652 was the same as that borrowed by the person of quality, although the likelihood is great. All we can know is that Moseley did not find the prompt-book or any other copy in what remained of the company's files, from which he seems to have collected most if not all of the manuscripts for his 1647 Folio. In *The Wild-Goose Chase* the bareness of the directions is of small evidence either for working papers, intermediate copy, or the prompt-book itself, although the placement of directions at the side suggests a prompt-book. However, the confusion about Lugier as Leverdure may point to an earlier stage for the manuscript than the prompt-book unless it resulted from inept editing, as indicated in one of the two crucial directions by the presence of the actor's name. On the other hand, such editing would not, apparently, account for the single *Lev.* prefix among those for *Lug.*, and it may be wiser to speculate that some change of plan in the original copy, never ironed out, is to blame. Beyond this point speculation seems useless except for the remark that the concurrence of both sections in certain unusual spellings suggests that only one hand may be found in the underlying manuscript copy.

The copy-text is of necessity the Folio of 1652 (F°), the closest to original authority, since the Second Folio of 1679 (F2) is a simple reprint and none of its variants shows any indication of outside authority.

No source for the play is known.

The documentary form of the copy-text has been drawn from a collation of the following copies: British Library (644. k. 28), Bodleian Library, copy 1 (Mal. 25[6]) and copy 2 (2° H. 1.g. Art. Seld.), University of Chicago, copies 1 and 2, Harvard University, and Princeton University. In the observed copies the minor press-variants have been observed only in the second section and in preliminary Sheet a. In either section proof-reading could not have been very careful, on the evidence of the number of misprints that were not corrected.

THE DEDICATION.

To the Honour'd, Few, Lovers of

Drammatick Poesie.

Noble Spirits!

It will seem strange to you that we should beg a Pardon from you before you know a Crime committed; But such is our *harsh Fate*, that we shall want as much of your *Mercie* to the forgiving of this sad presumption of offering to your view these few *poor* sheets, the *Rich Remains* of our too-long-since lost Friend, M^r. *FLETCHER*, as we shall your favourable *Acceptance*, and *Incouragement* in it. The Play was of so Generall a receiv'd Acceptance, that (he *Himself* a *Spectator*) we have known him un-concern'd, and to have wisht it had been none of His; He, as well as the *throng'd Theatre* (in despight of his innate Modesty) Applauding this *rare issue of his Brain.* His *Complacencie* in his own Work, may be, perhaps no Argument to you of the Goodness of the Play, any more than our *Confidence* of it; and we do not expect our *Encomium* can do any thing with you, when the Play it self is so near: That will *commend* it self unto you. And now Farewell our *Glory!* Farewell your *Choice Delight*, most noble Gentlemen! Farewell th' *Grand Wheel* that set *Us* smaller Motions in Action! Farewell the Pride and Life o'th' Stage! Nor can we (though in our Ruin) much repine that we are so little, since *He* that gave us being is no more.

Generous Soules!

'Tis not unknown unto you All, how by a cruell Destinie we have a long time been *Mutes* and *Bound*, although our Miseries have been sufficiently *Clamorous* and *Expanded*, yet till this happy opportunitie, never durst vex your open Ears and Hands: But this we're confident of will be the surest Argument for your *Noblesses*.

242

What an Ingenious Person of Qualitie once spake of his *Amours*, we apply to our necessities,

> *Silence in Love betrays more Wo*
> *Than Words, though ne'r so Wittie:*
> *The* Beggar *that is DUMB, you know,*
> *Deserves a DOUBLE PITTIE.*

But be the *Comœdie* at your *Mercy* as *We* are. Onely we wish, that you may have the same *kind Joy* in *Perusing* of it, as we had in the *Acting*.

So *Exeunt*
Your Gratefull Servants,

JOHN LOWIN,
JOSEPH TAYLOR.

On the best, last, and only
remaining *Comedy* of Mr.
FLETCHER.

I'm un-o'reclowded too! Clear from the Mist!
The blind *and late* Heaven's Ey's *Great* Oculist
Obscur'd *with the* False Fiers *of his Sceme*
Not halfe those Souls are Lightned by this Theme.
   Unhappy Murmurers that still repine
(*After th'*Eclipse *our Sunne doth brighter shine*)
Recant your False Grief and your True joyes knowe,
Your Bliss is Endles as you fear'd your Woe!
What Fort'nate Flood *is this? what storm of Witt?*
Oh who would live *and not* orewhelm'd *in it?*   10
No more a Fatall Diluge *shall be hurl'd,*
This Inundation *hath* sav'd *the World.*
   Once more the Mighty FLETCHER *doth arise*
Roab'd in a Vest, Studded with Starrs and Eyes
Of all his former Glories; His last Worth
Imbroydered with what yet Light e're brought forth.
See! in this glad Farewell he doth appeare
Stuck with the Constellations *of his* Sphere,
Fearing we num'd fear'd no Flagration
Hath curled all his Fyres in this one ONE,   20
Which (as they guard his hallowed Chast Urn)
The dull approaching Hereticks do burn.
   FLETCHER *at his Adieu Carouses thus*
To the Luxurious Ingenious.
A Cleopatra *did of Old out-vie*
Th'un-numbred dishes of her Anthonie
When (He at th'emptie Board a Wonderer)
Smiling shee call's for Pearl *and* Vineger;
First pledges Him in's Breath, then at one Draught
Swallowes Three Kingdomes *off to* His best Thought.   30
   Hear Oh ye Valiant Writers *and subscribe!*

244

(*His* Force *set by*) *y'are* Conquer'd *by this* Bribe;
Though you Hold out your selves, *He doth commit*
In this a Sacred Treason *on your Witt;*
Although in Poems desperately Stout,
Give up; *This Overture must* buy you out.
   Thus with some Prodigall Us'rer 't doth fare
That keepes his Gold still veyl'd, *his steel-breast* bare,
That doth exclude his Coffers all but's Eye
And his Ey's Idoll the Wing'd Deitie;   40
That cannot lock his Mines *with half the Art*
As some Rich Beauty *doth his* wretched heart:
Wild at his reall Poverty, and so wise
To winne her, turnes Himselfe into a Prise.
*First startles Her with th'*Emerald-Mad-lover,
The Rubie-Arcas; *lest thee should recover*
Her das'led Thought a Diamond *He throwes*
Splendid in all the bright Aspatia's *woes;*
Then to summe up the Abstract *of his store*
He flings a Rope *of* Pearl *of* Forty *more.*   50
Ah see! the stag'ring Vertue faints! *which He*
Beholding, darts his Wealth's Epitome,
And now to Consumate her wished Fall
Shewes this one Carbuncle *that darkens All.*

RICHARD LOVELACE.

ON

Mr. FLETCHERS

excellent Play,

THE

WILD-GOOSE CHASE.

Me thinkes I see thy *angred ashes* rise
FLETCHER; I feel them smarting in my eyes.
Methinks thou sayst what would this rimer have,
He *raises me*, yet *gives my fame a grave?*

245

Me thinkes (like that *Old Moralist's* Complaint
What ill of mine has gain'd this ill mans prayse?)
I hear thee say, sure this Play has some taint
That this ill Poet gives his withered bayes?
Perhaps this good *Philosophers* life began
To make the *ill* man *good*; As in a man   10
To love the good's a step to being so,
Love to thy *Muse* may be to me so too;
Then I shall know how to commend thy Muse
When her own self the prayses shall infuse:
Till then I must sit down, confess the *wonder*,
'Bove which I *cannot* go, and *won't* goe *under*.
But where's the prayse (you'l say) to *FLETCHERS* wit?
I would ha giv'n but had no Offering fit.
Then let these lines be thought to *FLETCHERS* Muse
Not an *Encomium*, but an *Excuse*.   20

NORREYS JEPHSON.

An Epigram upon the Long lost and fortunately recovered
WILD-GOOSE CHASE, and as seasonably bestowed on
Mr. *JOHN LOWEN* and Mr. *JOSEPH TAYLOR*,
for their best advantage.

In this late dearth of wit, when *Jose* and *Jack*
Were hunger-bit, for want of fowl and Sack,
His nobleness found out this happy meanes
To mend their dyet with these *WILD-GOOSE* scenes,
By which he hath revived in a day
Two Poets, and two Actors with one Play.

W. E.

16 goe] F°(u); go F°(c)
18 giv'n ₐ] F°(u); ~ , F°(c)

To the incomparable Mr. *FLETCHER*,
upon his excellent Play, The
WILD-GOOSE CHASE.

Sole Soul of *Drammas*, thou who only art
Whole in the whole, and whole in ev'ry *Part.*
Thy *fury* every scene with spirit warmes,
And that same *spirit* every line *informes.*
No *Commas* ly intranc't, and rise up sense
Three, four lines off, such is thy *Influence.*
Thy woords are all *alive*; and thou ne're writ
Things to come to themselves, nor *Types* of *Wit,*
All lives, and is fulfill'd. And for thy *Plot*
When ere we read *we have, and have it not,*   10
And glad to be deceiv'd, finding thy Drift
T'excell our guess at every turn, and shift,
Some new *Meanders* still do put us out,
Yet find that nearest what we thought *about.*
Through all *Intrigu's* we are securely lead,
And all the way we pass w'ave hold o'th' thread,
Which a long while we *feel* not, till thy Close
Winding the *Bottom* up the *Bottom* showes.

H: HARINGTON.

On Mr. *FLETCHERS Wild-Goose Chase recovered.*

This sprightly *Posthume*, whom our pious fear
Bewail'd as if it an *abortive* were
(And out of sense of that, no *gen'rous breast*
But a forsaken lover's grief exprest)
Hath forc'd his way thorough the *pangs* of *Fate,*
And in his *infancy*'s at *mans estate.*
Thus that *Fam'd flood* that's *plung'd* into a grave

5 intranc't] F°(u); intranc'd F°(c)

For many leagues, at length *exalts* his wave;
Leapes from his Sepulcher, and proudly slides
Through's banks in deeper, more expanded tides;   10
Till to his watry Center he hath got
By wrigling twines, subtile as *FLETCHER'S plot*.
That 'tis a sacred birth from hence we know,
It doth by *buriall*, more *glorious* grow:
For Saints by persecution thrive; and none
Is Martyr'd, but's *opprest* into a *throne*.
There reign he to Time's end! while we from this,
Doe calculate his *Apotheosis*,

JAMES RAMSEY.

DRAMMATIS PERSONÆ.

DE-GARD, A Noble stayd Gentleman that being newly lighted from his Travells, assists his sister *Oriana* in her chase of *Mirabell* the *Wild-Goose*. — Acted by Mr. *Robert Benfield.*

LA-CASTRE, the Indulgent Father to *Mirabell*. — Acted by Mr. *Richard Robinson.*

MIRABELL, the *Wild-Goose*, a Travayl'd Monsieur, and great defyer of all Ladies in the way of Marriage, otherwise their much loose servant, at last caught by the despis'd *Oriana*. — Incomparably Acted by Mr. *Joseph Taylor.* 10

PINAC, his fellow Traveller, of a lively spirit, and servant to the no lesse sprightly *Lillia-Bianca*. — Admirably well Acted by Mr. *Thomas Pollard.*

BELLEUR, Companion to both, of a stout blunt humor, in love with *Rosalura*. — Most naturally Acted by Mr. *John Lowin.*

NANTOLET, Father to *Rosalura* and *Lillia-Bianca*. — Acted by Mr. *William Penn.*

LUGIER, the rough and confident Tutor to the Ladies, and chiefe Engine to intrap the *Wild-Goose*. — Acted by Mr. *Hilliard Swanston.* 20

ORIANA, the faire betroth'd of *Mirabell*, and wittie follower of the *Chase*. — Acted by Mr. *Stephen Hammerton.*

ROSALURA ⎱ the Aërie Daughters — *William Trigg.*
LILLIA-BIANCA ⎰ of *Nantolet*. — *Sander Gough.*

PETELLA, their waiting-woman.

Their SERVANT. — Mr. *Shanck.*

MARIANA, an English Courtezan.

A young FACTOR. — [Acted] by Mr. *John Hony-man.*

PAGE. 30

SERVANTS.

*26–27 PETELLA.... Their SERVANT. Mr. *Shanck*.] PETELLA, their waiting-woman. Their Servant Mr *Shanck*. F°

249

SINGING-BOY[.]
TWO MERCHANTS.
PRIEST.
FOURE WOMEN.

THE SCENE PARIS.

THE
WILD-GOOSE-CHASE

Enter Monsieur de Gard *and a Foot-boy.*

de Gard. Sirha, you know I have rid hard; Stir my Horse well,
And let him want no Litter.
Boy.   I am sure I have run hard,
Would some body would walk me, and see me Litterd;
For I think my fellow-Horse, cannot in reason
Desire more rest, nor take up his Chamber before me.
But we are the Beasts now, and the Beasts are our Masters.
de Gard. When you have don, step to the Ten-Crown
        Ordinary——
Boy. With all my heart, Sir, For I have a Twenty-Crown
    stomach.
de Gard. And there bespeak a dinner.
Boy.   Yes Sir, presently.
de Gard. For whom, I beseech you, Sir?
Boy.   For my self, I take it Sir. 10
de Gard. In truth ye shall not take it, 'tis not meant for you,
    Ther's for your Provender: Bespeak a Dinner
    For Mounsieur *Mirabell*, and his Companions,
    They'll be in Town within this houre. When you have don,
        Sirha,
    Make ready all things at my Lodging, for me,
    And wait me there.
Boy.   The Ten-Crown *Ordinary?*
de Gard. Yes Sir, if you have not forgot it.
Boy.   I'll forget my feet first;
    'Tis the best part of a Foot-mans faith.   *Exit Boy.*
de Gard.   These youths
    For all they have been in *Italy*, to learn thrift,

8 a] F2; *om.* F°

251

And seem to wonder at mens lavish waies,   20
Yet they cannot rub off old friends, their French ytches;
They must meet sometimes to disport their Bodies
With good Wine, and good Women; and good store too.
Let 'em be what they will, they are Armd at all points
And then hang saving, let the Sea grow high.
This *Ordinarie* can fit 'em of all Sizes,
They must salute their *Countrie* with old customes.

Enter La-Castre *and* Oriana.

Oriana. Brother.
de Gard.   My dearest sister.
Oriana.   Welcom, welcom:
  Indeed ye are welcom home, most welcom.
de Gard.   Thank ye,
  You are grown a handsome woman *Oriana*   30
  (Blush at your faults), I am wondrous glad to see ye.
  Monsieur *La-Castre*: Let not my Affection
  To my fair Sister, make me held unmannerly:
  I am glad to see ye well, to see ye lustie,
  Good health about ye, and in fair company,
  Beleeve me, I am proud——
La-Castre.   Fair Sir, I thank ye:
  Monsieur *de Gard*, you are welcom from your journey,
  Good men have stil good welcom: give me your hand, Sir.
  Once more, you are welcom home: you look still younger.
de Gard. Time has no leasure to look after us,   40
  We wander, every where: Age cannot find us.
La-Castre. And how does all?
de Gard.   All well, Sir; and all lusty.
La-Castre. I hope my Son be so, I doubt not Sir,
  But you have often seen him in your journeis,
  And bring me some fair Newes.
de Gard.   Your Son is well, Sir,
  And grown a proper Gentleman: he is well, and lustie,
  Within this eight hours, I took leave of him,

*25 saving, let...high.] Sympson; ~ . Let... ~ , F°, F 2

252

And over-eyd him, having some slight busines
That forc'd me out o'th' way: I can assure you
He will be here to night.

La-Castre.   Ye make me glad Sir,   50
For o' my faith, I almost long to see him,
Me thinks he has been away——

de Gard.   'Tis but your tenderness;
What are three yeares? a love-sick wench will allow it!
His friends that went out with him are come back too;
Beleure, and young *Pinac*: he bid me say little,
Because he meanes to be his own glad Messenger.

La-Castre.   I thank ye for this newes, Sir, he shalbe welcom,
And his friends too: Indeed I thank you heartily:
And how (for I dare say, you will not flatter him)
Has *Italy* wrought on him? ha's he mew'd yet   60
His wild fantastick Toyes? they say that Climate
Is a great purger of those humorous Fluxes.
How is he improved, I pray ye?

de Gard.   No doubt Sir, well.
H'as born himself a full, and noble Gentleman,
To speak him farther, is beyond my Charter.

La-Castre.   I am glad to hear so much good: Come, I see
You long to enjoy your Sister: yet I must intreat ye
Before I go, to sup with me to night
And must not be deni'd.

de Gard.   I am your servant.

La-Castre.   Where you shall meet fair, merry, and noble Company, 70
My neighbour *Nantolet*, and his two fair daughters.

de Gard.   Your supper's season'd well, Sir. I shall wait upon ye.

La-Castre.   Till then I'll leave ye: and y'are once more welcom.
                                        Exit.

de Gard.   I thank ye, noble Sir. Now *Oriana*,
How have ye done since I went? Have ye had your health well?
And your mind free?

Oriana.   You see I am not bated;
Merry, and eat my meat.

*48 over-eyd] *stet* F°–F2   71, 150 *Nantolet*] *Natolet* F°, F2

253

de Gard.   A good preservative.
And how have you been us'd? You know *Oriana*,
Upon my going out, at your request,
I left your Portion in *La-Castres* hands,   80
(The main Means you must stick to) for that reason
(And 'tis no little one) I ask ye, Sister,
With what humanitie he entertains ye,
And how ye find his curtesie?
Oriana.   Most ready.
I can assure you, Sir, I am us'd most nobly.
de Gard.   I am glad to hear it: But I pre'thee tell me,
(And tell me true) what end had you *Oriana*,
In trusting your money here? He is no Kinsman,
Nor any tie upon him of a Guardian;
Nor dare I think ye doubt my prodigality.   90
Oriana.   No, certain, Sir, none of all this provoked me;
Another private reason.
de Gard.   'Tis not private,
Nor carryed so: 'tis common (my fair Sister)
Your love to *Mirabell*; your blushes tell it:
'Tis too much known, and spoken of too largely;
And with no little shame I wonder at it.
Oriana.   Is it a shame to love?
de Gard.   To Love undiscreetly:
A Virgin should be tender of her honour,
Close, and secure.
Oriana.   I am as close as can be,
And stand upon as strong and honest guards too,   100
Unless this Warlike Age need a Port-cullis:
Yet I confess, I love him.
de Gard.   Hear the people.
Oriana.   Now I say hang the people: He that dares
Believe what they say, dares be mad, and give
His Mother, nay his own Wife up to Rumor;
All grounds of truth they build on, is a Tavern,
And their best censure's Sack, Sack in abundance:
For as they drink, they think: they ne'r speak modestly

Unless the wine be poor, or they want money.
Beleeve them? beleeve *Amadis de Gaul*,   110
The *Knight* o'th' *Sun*, or *Palmerin* of *England*;
For these, to them, are modest, and true stories.
Pray understand me; if their tongues be truth,
And if in *Vino veritas* be an Oracle,
What woman is, or has been ever honest?
Give 'em but ten round cups, they'll swear *Lucretia*
Dy'd not for want of power to resist *Tarquine*,
But want of Pleasure, that he stayd no longer:
And *Portia*, that was famous for her Pietie
To her lov'd Lord, they'll face ye out, dy'd o'th' pox.   120
de Gard.   Well, there is something, Sister.
Oriana.   If there be, Brother,
'Tis none of their things, 'tis not yet so monstrous;
My thing is Mariage: And at his return
I hope to put their squint-eyes right again.
de Gard.   Mariage? 'tis true: his father is a rich man;
Rich both in land and money: he his heir,
A young and handsom man, I must confess too;
But of such qualities, and such wild flings,
Such admirable imperfections, Sister,
(For all his travaile, and bought experience)   130
I should be loth to own him for my brother:
Me thinks a rich mind in a state indifferent
Would prove the better fortune.
Oriana.   If he be wild,
The reclaming him to good, and honest (brother)
Will make much for my honor; which, if I prosper,
Shall be the study of my love, and life too.
de Gard.   Ye say well; would he thought as well, and loved too.
He mary? he'll be hang'd first: he knows no more
What the conditions and the ties of Love are,
The honest purposes and grounds of Mariage,   140
Nor will know, nor be ever brought t'endeavour,
Than I do how to build a Church; he was ever
A loose and strong defier of all order,

His Loves are wanderers, they knock at each door,
And tast each dish, but are no residents:
Or say he may be brought to think of Mariage
(As 't will be no small labour) thy hopes are strangers.
I know there is a labour'd match, now follow'd,
(Now at this time, for which he was sent for home too)
Be not abus'd, *Nantolet* has two fair daughters,   150
And he must take his choice.
Oriana.   Let him take freely;
For all this I despair not: my mind tells me
That I, and onely I, must make him perfect;
And in that hope I rest.
de Gard.   Since y'are so confident,
Prosper your hope: I'll be no adversary:
Keep your self fair and right, he shall not wrong ye.
Oriana.   When I forget my vertue, no man know me.

                                                    Exeunt.

                Enter Mirabell, Pinac, Belleure, *and Servants.*   [I.] ii

Mirabell.   Welcom to *Paris* once more, Gentlemen:
We have had a merry, and a lusty Ord'nary,
And wine, and good meat, and a bounsing Reckning;
And let it go for once; 'Tis a good physick:
Only the wenches are not for my dyet,
They are too lean and thin; their embraces brawn-fall'n.
Give me the plump Venetian, fat, and lusty,
That meets me soft and supple; smiles upon me,
As if a cup of full wine leap'd to kiss me;
These slight things I affect not.
Pinac.   They are ill built;   10
Pin-buttockt, like your dainty Barbaries,
And weak i'th' pasterns; they'l endure no hardness.
Mirabell.   There's nothing good, or handsom, bred amongst us;
Till we are travail'd, and live abroad, we are coxcombs:
Ye talk of *France*, a slight, unseason'd Country;
Abundance of gross food, which makes us block-heads:

                            256

We are fair set-out indeed, and so are fore-horses.
Men say we are great Courtiers, men abuse us:
We are wise, and valiant too, *non credo Signior*:
Our women the best Linguists, they are Parrats;   20
O' this side the *Alpes* they are nothing but meer Drollaries:
Ha, *Roma la Santa, Italie* for my money:
Their policies, their customs, their frugalities,
Their curtesies so open, yet so reserved too,
As when ye think y'are known best, ye are a stranger;
Their very pick-teeth speak more man than we do,
And season of more salt.

Pinac.   'Tis a brave Country;
Not pester'd with your stubborn precise puppies,
That turn all usefull, and allow'd contentments
To scabs and scruples; hang 'em Capon-worshippers.   30

Bellure.   I like that freedom well, and like their women too,
And would fain do as others do; but I am so bashfull,
So naturally an Ass: Look ye, I can look upon 'em,
And very willingly I go to see 'em,
(There's no man willinger) and I can kiss 'em,
And make a shift——

Mirabell.   But if they chance to flout ye,
Or say ye are too bold; fie Sir remember;
I pray sit farther off;——

Bellure.   'Tis true, I am humbled,
I am gone, I confess ingenuously I am silenced,
The spirit of Amber cannot force me answer.   40

Pinac.   Then would I sing and dance.

Bellure.   You have wherewithall, Sir.

Pinac.   And charge her up again.

Bellure.   I can be hang'd first:
Yet where I fasten well, I am a tyrant.

Mirabell.   Why, thou darst fight?

Bellure.   Yes, certainly, I dare fight;
And fight with any man, at any weapon,
Would th'other were no more; but, a pox on't,
When I am sometimes in my height of hope,

And reasonable valiant that way, my heart harden'd,
Some scornfull jest or other, chops between me
And my desire: What would ye have me to do then, Gentlemen? 50
Mirabell.   *Belleure*, ye must be bolder: Travell three years,
And bring home such a baby to betray ye
As bashfulness? a great fellow, and a souldier?
Bellure.   You have the gift of impudence, be thankful;
Every man has not the like talent: I will study
And if it may be reveal'd to me——
Mirabell.   Learn of me,
And of *Pinac*: no doubt you'll find imployment;
Ladies will look for Courtship.
Pinac.   'Tis but fleshing,
But standing one good brunt or two: ha'st thou any mind to
   mariage?
Wee'll provide thee some soft-natur'd wench, that's dumb too. 60
Mirabell.   Or an old woman that cannot refuse thee in charity.
Bellure.   A dumb woman, or an old woman, that were eager,
And car'd not for discourse, I were excellent at.
Mirabell.   You must now put on boldness, there's no avoyding it;
And stand all hazards; fly at all games bravely;
They'll say you went out like an Ox, and return'd like an Ass
   else.
Bellure.   I shall make danger sure.
Mirabell.   I am sent for home now,
I know it is to mary, but my father shall pardon me:
Although it be a witty ceremony,
And may concern me hereafter in my gravitie;   70
I will not lose the freedom of a Traveller;
A new strong lusty Bark cannot ride at one anchor;
Shall I make divers suits to shew to the same eyes?
'Tis dull, and home-spun: Study severall pleasures,
And want employments for 'em? I'll be hang'd first;
Tie me to one smock? make my travels fruitless?
I'll none of that: For every fresh behaviour,
By your leave, father, I must have a fresh Mistris,

69 witty] *stet* F⁰–F2

258

And a fresh favour too.

Bellure.   I like that passingly;
As many as you will, so they be willing;   80
Willing and gentle, gentle.

Pinac.   There's no reason
A Gentleman, and a Traveller, should be clapt up,
For 'tis a kind of Bilboes to be maryed
Before he manifest to the world his good parts:
Tug ever like a rascall at one oar?
Give me the Italian liberty.

Mirabell.   That I study;
And that I will enjoy: Come, go in Gentlemen,
There mark how I behave my self, and follow.

                                    Exeunt.

Enter La-Castre, Nantolet, Lugier, Rosa Lieura, Lylia-Biancha.   [I.] iii

La-Castre.   You and your beauteous daughters are most welcom,
Beshrew my blood they are fair ones; welcom Beauties,
Welcom sweet birds.

Nantolet.   They are bound much to your curtesies.

La-Castre.   I hope we shall be nearer acquainted.

Nantolet.   That's my hope too.
For certain, Sir, I much desire your Alliance.
You see 'em, they are no Gipseis, for their breeding,
It has not been so coarse, but they are able
To rank themselves with women of fair fashion;
Indeed they have been trained well.

Lugier.   Thank me.

Nantolet.   Fit for the heirs of that state I shall leave 'em;   10
To say more, is to sell 'em. They say your son
Now he has travail'd must be wondrous curious,
And choice in what he takes: These are no coarse ones;
Sir, here's a merry wench, let him look to himself,   [Rosalure.]
(All heart, y'faith) may chance to startle him;

83 Bilboes] Sympson; Bæboes F°–F2, L   85 a] F2; at a F°
o.1 Nantolet, Lugier] *Natolet, Lugien* F°, F2   5 For] F2; *Na.* For F°

259

For all his care, and travail'd caution,
May creep into his eye; if he love Gravitie,
Affect a solemn face, there's one will fit him.   [Lylia-Biancha.]
La-Castre.   So young, and so demure?
Nantolet.   She is my daughter,
   Else I would tell you, Sir, she is a Mistris   20
   Both of those manners, and that modesty,
   You would wonder at: She is no often speaker,
   But when she does, she speaks well; Nor no Reveller,
   Yet she can dance, and has studied the Court Elements,
   And sings, as some say, handsomly; if a woman,
   With the decencie of her sex, may be a Scholar,
   I can assure ye, Sir, she understands too.
La-Castre.   These are fit Garments, Sir.
Lugier.   Thank them that cut 'em:
   Yes, they are handsom women; they have handsom parts too;
   Prettie becoming parts.
La-Castre.   'Tis like they have, Sir.   30
Lugier.   Yes, yes, and handsom Education they have had too:
   Had it abundantly; they need not blush at it;
   I taught it, I'll avouch it.
La-Castre.   Ye say well, Sir.
Lugier.   I know what I say, Sir, and I say but right, Sir.
   I am no trumpet of their commendations
   Before their father; else I should say farther.
La-Castre.   Pray ye, what's this Gentleman?
Nantolet.   One that lives with me, Sir;
   A man well bred and learn'd, but blunt and bitter,
   Yet it offends no wise man; I take pleasure in't:
   Many fair gifts he has, in some of which   40
   That lie most easie to their understandings,
   H'as handsomly bred up my girls, I thank him.
Lugier.   I have put it to 'em, that's my part, I have urg'd it,
   It seems they are of years now to take hold on't.
Nantolet.   He's wondrous blunt.
La-Castre.   By my faith I was afraid of him:

*43 *Lugier.*] Sympson; *om.* F°–F 2, L

260

　Does he not fall out with the Gentlewomen sometimes?
Nantolet.　No, no; he's that way moderate, and discreet, Sir.
Rosalura.　If he did, we should be too hard for him.
Lugier.　　　　　　　　　　　　　　Wel said Sulphur:
　Too hard for thy husbands head, if he wear not armour.
Nantolet.　Many of these bickrings, Sir.
La-Castre.　　　　　　　I am glad they are no Oracles: 50
　Sure, as I live, he beats them, he's so puisant.

　　　Enter Mirabell, Pinac, [Bellure,] de Gard, *and* Oriana.

Oriana.　Well, if ye do forget——　　[*They speak coming on.*]
Mirabell.　　　　　　　　　Pre'thee hold thy peace;
　I know thou art a prettie wench; I know thou lov'st me,
　Preserve it till we have a fit time to discourse on't,
　And a fit place: I'll ease thy heart, I warrant thee:
　Thou seest I have much to do now.
Oriana.　　　　　　　　　　I am answer'd, Sir:
　With me ye shall have nothing on these conditions.
de Gard.　Your father, and your friends.
La-Castre.　　　　　　　You are welcom home, Sir;
　'Bless ye, ye are very welcom. 'Pray know this Gentleman,
　And these fair Ladies.
Nantolet.　　　　　　Monsieur *Mirabell*,　　　　　　60
　I am much affected with your fair return, Sir;
　You bring a generall joy.
Mirabell.　　　　　　　　I bring you service,
　And these bright beauties, Sir.
Nantolet.　　　　　　　　Welcom home, Gentlemen,
　Welcom, with all my heart.
Bellure, Pinac.　　　　　　We thank ye, Sir.
La-Castre.　Your friends will have their share too.
Bellure.　　　　　　　　　　　　Sir, we hope
　They'll look upon us, though we shew like strangers.
Nantolet.　Monsieur *de-Gard*, I must salute you also,
　And this fair Gentlewoman: you are welcom from your Travell
　　too.
　All welcom, all.

de Gard.   We render ye our loves, Sir;
   The best wealth we bring home: By your favours, Beauties: 70
   One of these two, you know my meaning.   [*Aside to* Oriana.]
Oriana.   Well Sir;
   They are fair and handsom, I must needs confess it;
   And let it prove the worst, I shall live after it,
   Whilst I have meat and drink, Love can not starve me;
   For if I dye o'th' first fit, I am unhappy,
   And worthy to be buried with my heels upward.
Mirabell.   To mary, Sir?   [*Speaks apart.*]
La-Castre.   You know I am an old man,
   And every hour declining to my grave,
   One foot already in, more sons I have not,
   Nor more I dare not seek whilst you are worthy,   80
   In you lies all my hope, and all my name,
   The making good or wretched of my memory,
   The safety of my state.
Mirabell.   And you have provided
   Out of this tenderness these handsom Gentlewomen,
   Daughters to this rich man, to take my choice of?
La-Castre.   I have, dear son.
Mirabell.   'Tis true, ye are old, and feebled;
   Would ye were young again, and in full vigor;
   I love a bounteous fathers life, a long one,
   I am none of those that when they shoot to ripeness,
   Do what they can to break the boughs they grew on: 90
   I wish ye many years, and many riches,
   And pleasures to enjoy 'em: But for Mariage,
   I neither yet beleeve in't, nor affect it,
   Nor think it fit.
La-Castre.   You will render me your reasons?
Mirabell.   Yes, Sir, both short and pithy; and these they are:
   You would have me mary a Mayd?
La-Castre.   A Mayd? what else?
Mirabell.   Yes, there be things called Widdows, dead-mens Wills,
   I never lov'd to prove those; nor never long'd yet

     84 these...Gentlewomen] F 2; this...Gentlewoman F°

To be buried alive in another mans cold Monument.
And there be Maids appearing, and Maids being: 100
The appearing, are fantastick things, meer shadows;
And if you mark 'em well, they want their heads too;
Onely the world, to cosen mystie eyes,
Has clapt 'em on new faces. The Mayds being,
A man may venture on, if he be so mad to mary;
If he have neither fear before his eyes, nor fortune;
And let him take heed how he gather these too;
For look ye, father, they are just like Melons,
Musk-Melons are the Emblems of these Mayds;
Now they are ripe, now cut 'em, they taste pleasantly,   110
And are a dainty fruit, digested easily:
Neglect this present time, and come to morrow,
They are so ripe they are rotten gon, their sweetness
Run into humour, and their taste to surfeit.

La-Castre.   Why these are new ripe son.
Mirabell.   I'll try them presently,
And if I like their taste——
La-Castre.   'Pray ye please your self, Sir.
Mirabell.   That liberty is my due, and I'll maintain it.
Lady, what think you of a handsom man now?
Rosalura.   A wholsom too, Sir?
Mirabell.   That's as you make your bargain.
A handsom, wholsom man then, and a kind man,   120
To chear your heart up, to rejoyce ye, Lady?
Rosalura.   Yes, Sir, I love rejoycing.
Mirabell.   To ly close to ye?
Close as a cockle? keep the cold nights from ye?
Rosalura.   That will be lookt for too, our bodies ask it.
Mirabell.   And get two Boyes at every birth?
Rosalura.   That's nothing,
I have known a Cobler do it, a poor thin Cobler;
A Cobler out of mouldy cheese perform it,
Cabbage, and coarse black bread: me thinks a Gentleman
Should take foul scorn to have a Nawl out-name him.

99 another] F2; anothers F°   *115 new] now F°–F2

Two at a birth? why every House-dove has it: 130
That man that feeds well, promises as well too,
I should expect indeed something of worth from.
Ye talk of two?
Mirabell [*aside*].   She would have me get two dozen,
Like Buttons, at a birth.
Rosalura.   You love to brag, Sir.
If you proclame these offers at your Mariage,
Ye are a pretty timber'd man, take heed,
They may be taken hold of, and expected,
Yes, if not hoped for at a higher rate too.
Mirabell.   I will take heed, and thank ye for your counsell:
Father, what think ye?
La-Castre.   'Tis a merry Gentlewoman; 140
Will make, no doubt, a good wife.
Mirabell.   Not for me:
I mary her, and happily get nothing;
In what a state am I then, Father? I shall suffer
For any thing I hear to the contrary, *more majorum,*
I were as sure to be a Cuckold, Father,
A Gentleman of Antler.
La-Castre.   Away, away fool.
Mirabell.   As I am sure to fail her expectation,
I had rather get the pox than get her babies.
La-Castre.   Ye are much too blame; if this do not affect ye,
Pray try the other; she is of a more demure way. 150
Bellure [*aside*].   That I had but the audacitie to talk thus!
I love that plain-spoken Gentlewoman admirably,
And certain I could go as near to please her,
If down-right doing—— She has a per'lous countenance,
If I could meet one that would beleeve me,
And take my honest meaning without circumstance——
Mirabell.   You shall have your will, Sir, I will try the other,
But 'twill be to small use. I hope, fair Lady
(For methinks in your eyes I see more mercy)
You will enjoyn your Lover a less penance; 160

*143 then, Father?] Colman; ~ ? ~ , Fº–F2

264

And though I'll promise much, as men are liberall,
And vow an ample sacrifice of service,
Yet your discretion, and your tenderness,
And thriftiness in Love, good housewives carefulnes
To keep the stock entire——
Lylia-Biancha.   Good Sir, speak louder,
That these may witness too ye talk of nothing,
I should be loth alone to bear the burthen
Of so much indiscretion.
Mirabell.   Heark ye, heark ye;
Od's-bobs, you are angry, Lady.
Lylia-Biancha.   Angry? no, Sir;
I never own'd an anger to lose poorly.   170
Mirabell.   But you can love, for all this, and delight too,
For all your set-austeritie, to hear
Of a good husband, Lady?
Lylia-Biancha.   You say true, Sir:
For by my troth, I have heard of none these ten year,
They are so rare, and there are so many, Sir,
So many longing-women on their knees too,
That pray the droping down of these good husbands,
The droping down from heaven: for they are not bred here,
That you may ghess at all my hope, but hearing——
Mirabell.   Why may not I be one?
Lylia-Biancha.   You were near 'em once, Sir,   180
When ye came ore the *Alpes*; those are near heaven;
But since ye mist that happiness, there's no hope of ye.
Mirabell.   Can ye love a man?
Lylia-Biancha.   Yes, if the man be lovely;
That is, be honest, modest: I would have him valiant,
His anger slow, but certain for his honor;
Travail'd he should be, but through himself exactly;
For 'tis fairer to know manners well, than Countries;
He must be no vain talker, nor no Lover
To hear himself talk, they are brags of a wanderer,
Of one finds no retreict for fair behaviour;   190
Would ye learn more?

Mirabell.   Yes.

Lylia-Biancha.   Learn to hold your peace then,
   Fond girls are got with tongues, women with tempers.

Mirabell.   Women, with I know what; but let that vanish:
   Go thy way good-wife *Bias*; sure thy husband
   Must have a strong Philosophers stone, he will ne'r please thee
      else.
   Heer's a starcht peece of Austeritie: do you hear, father?
   Do you hear this morall Lecture?

La-Castre.   Yes, and like it.

Mirabell.   Why there's your judgment now; there's an old bolt
     shot:
   This Thing must have the strangest observation,
   Do you mark me (father?) when she is maryed once,   200
   The strangest custom too of admiration
   On all she do's and speaks, 'twill be past sufferance;
   I must not lie with her in common language,
   Nor cry, have at thee *Kate*, I shall be hist then;
   Nor eat my meat without the sawce of Sentences,
   Your powder'd beef, and problemes, a rare dyet;
   My first son, Monsieur *Aristotle*, I know it,
   Great Master of the Metaphysicks, or so;
   The second *Solon*, and the best Law-setter;
   And I must look Egyptian God-fathers,   210
   Which will be no small trouble: My eldest daughter
   Sapho, or such a fidling kind of Poetess,
   And brought up, *invita Minerva*, at her needle.
   My dogs must look their names too, and all Spartan,
   Lelaps, *Melampus*; no more *Fox* and *Baudiface*.
   I maryed to a sullen set of Sentences?
   To one that weighs her words and her behaviours
   In the Gold-weights of discretion? I'll be hang'd first.

La-Castre.   'Pre'thee reclame thy self.

Mirabell.   'Pray ye give me time then;
   If they can set me any thing to play at,   220
   That seems fit for a Gamester, have at the fairest
   Till I see more, and try more.

La-Castre.   Take your time then,
 I'll bar ye no fair liberty: Come Gentlemen,
 And Ladies, come; to all once more a welcom,
 And now let's in to supper.
Mirabell.   How do'st like 'em?
Pinac.   They are fair enough, but of so strange behaviors.
Mirabell.   Too strange for me; I must have those have mettle,
 And mettle to my mind: Come let's be merry.
Bellure.   'Bless me from this woman: I would stand the Cannon
 Before ten words of hers.
de Gard.   Do you find him now?   230
 Do you think he will be ever firm?
Oriana.   I fear not

                                        Exeunt.

                 Enter Mirabell, Pinac, Bellure.   II. i

Mirabell.   Ne'r tel me of this happiness, 'tis nothing;
 The state they bring with being sought to scurvey,
 I had rather make mine own play, and I will do.
 My happiness is in mine own content,
 And the despising of such glorious trifles,
 As I have done a thousand more. For my humour
 Give me a good free fellow, that sticks to me,
 A joviall fair companion; there's a Beauty:
 For women, I can have too many of them;
 Good women too, as the Age reckons 'em,   10
 More than I have employment for.
Pinac.   You are happy.
Mirabell.   My only fear is, that I must be forced
 Against my nature, to conceal my self.
 Health, and an able body are two jewels.
Pinac.   If either of these two women were offer'd to me now,
 I would think otherwise, and do accordingly:
 Yes, and recant my heresies, I would Sir;
 And be more tender of opinion,

                 *2 sought to] *stet* F°–F 2

And put a little of my travail'd Libertie
Out of the way, and look upon 'em seriously.   20
Me-thinks this grave-carried wench——
Bellure.   Me-thinks the other,
The home-spoken Gentle-woman, that desires to be fruitfull,
That treats of the full mannage of the matter,
For there lies all my aim; that wench, me-thinks
If I were but well set-on; for she is affable,
If I were but hounded right, and one to teach me;
She speaks to th' matter, and comes home to th' point:
Now do I know I have such a body to please her,
As all the kingdom cannot fit her with, I am sure on't;
If I could but talk my self into her favour.
Mirabell.   That's easily done.   30
Bellure.   That's easily said, would 'twere done;
You should see then how I would lay about me;
If I were vertuous, it would never grieve me,
Or any thing that might justifie my modesty,
But when my nature is prone to do a charitie,
And my calfs-tongue will not help me——
Mirabell.   Will ye go to 'em?
They cannot but take it curteously.
Pinac.   I'll do my part,
Though I am sure 'twil be the hardest I e'r plaid yet,
A way I never try'd too, which will stagger me,
And if it do not shame me, I am happy.   40
Mirabell.   Win 'em, and wear 'em, I give up my interest.
Pinac.   What say ye, Monsieur *Bellure?*
Bellure.   Would I could say,
Or sing, or any thing that were but handsom,
I would be with her presently.
Pinac.   Yours is no venture;
A merry ready wench.
Bellure.   A vengeance squibber;
She'll fleer me out of faith too.

*19 of] Langbaine; off F°–F2
25 affable] Sympson(*qy*), C; a fable F°–F2

268

Mirabell.   I'll be near thee;
Pluck up thy heart, I'll second thee at all brunts;
Be angry if she abuse thee, and beat her a little;
Some women are won that way.
Bellure.   Pray be quiet,
And let me think: I am resolv'd to go on;   50
But how I shall get off again——
Mirabell.   I am perswaded
Thou wilt so please her, she will go neer to ravish thee.
Bellure. I would 'twere come to that once: Let me pray a little.
Mirabell. Now for thine honor *Pinac*; board me this modesty,
Warm but this frozen snow-ball, 'twill be a conquest
(Although I know thou art a fortunate Wencher,
And hast done rarely in thy daies) above all thy ventures.
Bellure. You will be ever neer?
Mirabell.   At all necessities,
And take thee off, and set thee on again, Boy;
And cherish thee, and stroak thee.
Bellure.   Help me out too?   60
For I know I shall stick i'th' mire: if ye see us close once,
Be gone, and leave me to my fortune, suddainly,
For I am then determin'd to do wonders.
Farewell, and fling an old shooe: how my heart throbs?
Would I were drunk: Farewell *Pinac*; heaven send us
A joyfull and a merry meeting, man.
Pinac.   Farewell,
And chear thy heart up; and remember *Bellure*
They are but women.
Bellure.   I had rather they were Lyons.
Mirabell. About it; I'll be with you instantly.
                    Exeunt [Pinac, Bellure].

                    Enter Oriana.

Shall 1 ne'r be at rest? no peace of conscience?   70
No quiet for these creatures? Am I ordain'd
To be devour'd quick by these she-Canibals?
Here's another they call handsom, I care not for her,

I ne'r look after her: When I am half tipled
It may be I should turn her, and peruse her,
Or in my want of women, I might call for her;
But to be haunted when I have no fancie,
No maw to th' matter—— Now, why do you follow me?

Oriana. I hope, Sir, 'tis no blemish to my vertue,
Nor need you (out of scruple) ask that question,   80
If you remember ye, before your Travell
The contract you ty'd to me: 'tis my love, Sir,
That makes me seek ye, to confirm your memory,
And that being fair and good, I cannot suffer:
I come to give ye thanks too.

Mirabell.   For what 'prethee?

Oriana. For that fair peece of honesty ye shew'd, Sir,
That constant nobleness.

Mirabell.   How? for I am short headed.

Oriana. I'll tell ye then; for refusing that free offer
Of Monsieur *Nantolets*; those handsom Beauties,
Those two prime Ladies, that might well have prest ye,   90
If not to have broken, yet to have bow'd your promise.
I know it was for my sake, for your faith sake,
You slipt 'em off: your honesty compell'd ye.
And let me tell ye, Sir, it shew'd most handsomly.

Mirabell. And let me tell thee, there was no such matter:
Nothing intended that way of that nature;
I have more to do with my honesty than to fool it,
Or venture it in such leak-barks as women;
I put 'em off, because I lov'd 'em not,
Because they are too queazie for my temper,   100
And not for thy sake, nor the Contract sake,
Nor vows, nor oathes; I have made a thousand of 'em,
They are things indifferent, whether kept or broken;
Meer veniall slips, that grow not near the Conscience;
Nothing concerns those tender parts; they are trifles;
For, as I think, there was never man yet hop'd for
Either constancie, or secrecie, from a woman,
Unless it were an Ass ordain'd for sufferance;

Nor to contract with such can be a Tie-all;
So let them know again; for 'tis a Justice,   110
And a main point of civill policie,
Whate're we say or swear, they being Reprobates,
Out of the state of faith, we are clear of all sides,
And 'tis a curious blindness to beleeve us.
Oriana.   You do not mean this sure?
Mirabell.   Yes sure, and certain,
And hold it positively, as a Principle,
As ye are strange things, and made of strange fires and fluxes,
So we are allow'd as strange wayes to obtain ye,
But not to hold; we are all created Errant.
Oriana.   You told me other tales.
Mirabell.   I not deny it;   120
I have tales of all sorts for all sorts of women,
And protestations likewise of all sizes,
As they have vanities to make us coxcombs;
If I obtain a good turn, so it is,
I am thankfull for it: if I be made an Ass,
The mends are in mine own hands, or the Surgeons,
And there's an end on't.
Oriana.   Do not you love me then?
Mirabell.   As I love others, heartily I love thee,
When I am high and lusty, I love thee cruelly:
After I have made a plenteous meal, and satisfi'd   130
My senses with all delicates, come to me,
And thou shalt see how I love thee.
Oriana.   Will not you mary me?
Mirabell.   No, certain, no, for any thing I know yet;
I must not lose my liberty, dear Lady,
And like a wanton slave cry for more shackles.
What should I mary for? Do I want any thing?
Am I an inch the farther from my pleasure?
Why should I be at charge to keep a wife of mine own,
When other honest maryed men will ease me?
And thank me too, and be beholding to me: 140

109 Tie-all] Weber; Tiall F⁰–F2   *126 mends] *stet* F⁰–F2

Thou thinkst I am mad for a Maiden-head, thou art cozen'd;
Or if I were addicted to that diet
Can you tell me where I should have one? thou art eighteen now,
And if thou hast thy Maiden-head yet extant,
Sure 'tis as big as Cods-head: and those grave dishes
I never love to deal withall: Do'st thou see this book here?
Look over all these ranks; all these are Women,
Mayds, and pretenders to Maiden-heads; these are my conquests,
All these I swore to mary, as I swore to thee,
With the same reservation, and most righteously,   150
Which I need not have don neither; for alas they made no scruple,
And I enjoy'd 'em at my will, and left 'em:
Some of 'em are maried since, and were as pure mayds again,
Nay o' my conscience better than they were bred for;
The rest fine sober women.

Oriana.   Are ye not asham'd, Sir?

Mirabell. No by my troth, Sir; there's no shame belongs to it;
I hold it as commendable to be wealthy in pleasure,
As others do in rotten sheep, and pasture.

Oriana. Are all my hopes come to this? is there no faith?
No troth? nor modesty in men?

Enter de Gard.

de Gard.   How now Sister,   160
Why weeping thus? did I not prophesie?
Come tell me why——

Oriana.   I am not well; 'pray ye pardon me.

Exit.

de Gard. Now Monsieur *Mirabell*, what ails my Sister?
You have been playing the wag with her.

Mirabell.   As I take it,
She is crying for a cod-peece; is she gone?
Lord, what an Age is this? I was calling for ye,
For as I live I thought she would have ravish'd me.

de Gard.   Ye are merry Sir.

Mirabell. Thou know'st this book, *de Gard*, this Inventory.

de Gard. The Debt-book of your Mistrisses, I remember it.

Mirabell.   Why this was it that anger'd her; she was stark mad   170
   She found not her name here, and cry'd down-right,
   Because I would not pitty her immediately,
   And put her in my list.
de Gard.   Sure she had more modesty.
Mirabell.   Their modesty is anger to be over-done;
   They'll quarrell sooner for precedence here,
   And take it in more dudgen to be slighted,
   Than they will in publique meetings; 'tis their nature:
   And alass 1 have so many to dispatch yet,
   And to provide my self for my affairs too,
   That in good faith——
de Gard.   Be not too glorious foolish;   180
   Summe not your Travails up with vanities,
   It ill becomes your expectation:
   Temper your speech, Sir; whether your loose story
   Be true, or false (for you are so free, I fear it)
   Name not my Sister in't; I must not hear it;
   Upon your danger name her not: I hold her
   A Gentlewoman of those happy parts and carriage,
   A good mans tongue may be right proud to speak her.
Mirabell.   Your Sister, Sir? d'ye blench at that? d'ye cavill?
   Do you hold her such a peece, she may not be play'd withall?   190
   I have had an hundred handsomer and nobler,
   Has su'd to me too for such a curtesie:
   Your Sister comes i'th' rear: since ye are so angry,
   And hold your Sister such a strong Recusant,
   I tell ye I may do it, and it may be will too,
   It may be have too; there's my free confession;
   Work upon that now.
de Gard.   If I thought ye had, I would work,
   And work such stubborn work, should make your heart ake;
   But I beleeve ye, as I ever knew ye,
   A glorious talker, and a Legend maker   200
   Of idle tales, and trifles; a depraver
   Of your own truth; their honours fly about ye;
   And so I take my leave, but with this caution,

Your sword be surer than your tongue, you'll smart else.
Mirabell.   I laugh at thee, so little I respect thee;
And I'll talk louder, and despise thy Sister;
Set up a Chamber-maid that shall out-shine her,
And carry her in my Coach too, and that will kill her.
Go get thy Rents up, go.
de Gard.   Ye are a fine Gentleman.   *Exit.*
Mirabell.   Now have at my two youths, I'll see how they do,   210
How they behave themselves, and then I'll study
What wench shall love me next, and then I'll loose her.

                                                  Exit.

Enter Pinac *and a Servant.*   [II.] ii

Pinac.   Art thou her servant, saist thou?
Servant.   Her poor creature,
But servant to her horse, Sir.
Pinac.   Canst thou shew me
The way to her chamber? or where I may conveniently
See her, or come to talk to her?
Servant.   That I can, Sir;
But the question is whether I will or no.
Pinac.   Why I'll content thee.
Servant.   Why I'll content thee then; now ye come to me.
Pinac.   There's for your diligence.
Servant.   There's her chamber, Sir;
And this way she comes out; stand ye but here, Sir,
You have her at your prospect, or your pleasure.
Pinac.   Is she not very angry?
Servant.   You'll find that quickly: 10
'May be she'll call ye sawcy scurvey fellow,
Or some such familiar name: 'may be she knows ye,
And will fling a Piss-pot at ye, or a Pantofle,
According as ye are in acquaintance: if she like ye,
'May be she'll look upon ye, 'may be no,
And two moneths hence call for ye.
Pinac.   This is fine.
She is monstrous proud then?

Servant.   She is a little haughtie;
   Of a small body, she has a mind well mounted.
   Can ye speak Greek?
Pinac.   No certain.
Servant.   Get ye gon then;   20
   And talk of stars, and firmaments, and fire-drakes,
   Do you remember who was *Adams* School-master,
   And who taught *Eve* to spin? she knowes all these,
   And will run ye over the beginning o'th' world
   As familiar as a Fidler.
   Can ye sit seven hours together, and say nothing?
   Which she will do, and when she speaks speak Oracles;
   Speak things that no man understands, nor her self neither.
Pinac.   Thou mak'st me wonder.
Servant.   Can ye smile?
Pinac.   Yes willingly:
   For naturally I bear a mirth about me.
Servant.   She'll ne'r endure ye then; she is never merry;   30
   If she see one laugh, she'll swound past Aquavitæ:
   Never come near her, Sir; if ye chance to venture,
   And talk not like a Doctor, you are damn'd too;
   I have told ye enough for your Crown, and so good speed ye.
                                                Exit.

Pinac.   I have a pretty task, if she be thus curious,
   As sure it seems she is; if I fall off now,
   I shall be laugh'd at fearfully; if I go forward,
   I can but be abus'd, and that I look for,
   And yet I may hit right, but 'tis unlikely.
   Stay, in what mood and figure shall I attempt her?   40
   A careless way? no, no, that will not waken her;
   Besides, her gravity will give me line still,
   And let me lose my self; yet this way often
   Has hit, and handsomly. A wanton method?
   I, if she give it leave to sink into her consideration;
   But there's the doubt: if it but stir her blood once,
   And creep into the crannies of her phansie,
   Set her a gog: but if she chance to slight it,

And by the pow'r of her modesty fling it back,
I shall appear the arrantst Rascal to her,   50
The most licentious knave, for I shall talk lewdly.
To bear my self austerely? rate my words,
And fling a generall gravitie about me,
As if I meant to give Laws? but this I cannot do,
This is a way above my understanding;
Or if I could, 'tis ods she'll think I mock her;
For serious and sad things are ever still suspicious.
Well, I'll say something.
But learning I have none, and less good manners,
Especially for Ladies; well, I'll set my best face;   60
I hear some coming; this is the first woman
I ever fear'd yet, the first face that shakes me.

                                           [*Stands apart.*]

Enter Lilia, Petella.

Lylia-Biancha.   Give me my hat *Petella*, take this veil off,
   This sullen cloud, it darkens my delights;
   Come wench be free, and let the Musick warble,
   Play me some lusty measure.   [*Musick.*]
Pinac.   This is she sure,
   The very same I saw, the very woman,
   The Gravitie I wonder'd at: Stay, stay,
   Let me be sure; ne'r trust me, but she danceth,
   Summer is in her face now, and she skippeth: 70
   I'll go a little nearer.
Lylia-Biancha.   Quicker time fellows,
   I cannot find my legs yet, now *Petella*.
Pinac.   I am amaz'd, I am founder'd in my fancie.

Enter Mirabell.

Mirabell.   Hah, say ye so; is this your gravitie?
   This is the austeritie ye put upon ye?
   I'll see more o' this sport.   [*Stands on the other side.*]
Lylia-Biancha.   A Song now;
   Call in for a merry, and a light Song,

276

Enter a man.

And sing it with a liberall spirit.
Man.   Yes, Madam.
Lylia-Biancha.   And be not amaz'd sirha, but take us for your own
  company.
                                        [*Man sings and exits.*]
  Let's walk our selves; come wench, would we had a man or two. 80
Pinac.   Sure she has spi'd me, and will abuse me dreadfully,
  She has put on this for the purpose; yet I will try her.
                                                  [*Advances.*]
  Madam, I would be loth my rude intrusion,
  Which I must crave a pardon for——
Lylia-Biancha.   O ye are welcom,
  Ye are very welcom, Sir, we want such a one;
  Strike up again: I dare presume ye dance well:
  Quick, quick, Sir, quick, the time steals on.
Pinac.   I would talk with ye.
Lylia-Biancha.   Talk as ye dance.   [*Dance.*]
Mirabell.   She'll beat him off his legs first.
  This is the finest Masque.
Lylia-Biancha.   Now how do ye, Sir?
Pinac.   You have given me a shrew'd heat.
Lylia-Biancha.   I'll give ye a hundred. 90
  Come sing now, sing; for I know ye sing well.
  I see ye have a singing face.
Pinac.   A fine Modesty!
  If I could she'd never give me breath,
  Madam would I might sit and recover.
Lylia-Biancha.   Sit here, and sing now,
  Let's do things quickly, Sir, and handsomly,
  Sit close wench, close, begin, begin.   *Song.*
Pinac.   I am lesson'd.
Lylia-Biancha.   'Tis very pretty y'faith, give me some wine now.
Pinac.   I would fain speak to ye.
Lylia-Biancha.   You shall drink first, believe me:
  Here's to ye a lusty health.

Pinac.   I thank ye Lady.
Would I were off again; I smell my misery;   100
I was never put to this rack; I shall be drunk too.
Mirabell.   If thou be'st not a right one, I have lost mine aim much:
I thank heaven that I have scap'd thee: To her *Pinac*;
For thou art as sure to have her, and to groan for her——
I'll see how my other youth does; this speeds trimly:
A fine grave Gentlewoman, and worth much honour.   *Exit.*
Lylia-Biancha.   Now? how do ye like me, Sir.
Pinac.   I like ye rarely.
Lylia-Biancha.   Ye see, Sir, though sometimes we are grave and
   silent,
And put on sadder dispositions,
Yet we are compounded of free parts, and sometimes too   110
Our lighter, airie, and our fierie mettles
Break out, and shew themselves; and what think you of that, Sir?
Pinac.   Good Lady sit, for I am very weary;
And then I'll tell ye.
Lylia-Biancha.   Fie, a young man idle:
Up, and walk; be still in action.
The motions of the body are fair beauties,
Besides 'tis cold; ods-me Sir, let's walk faster.
What think ye now of the Lady *Felicia?*
And *Bella-fronte* the Dukes fair daughter? ha?
Are they not handsom things? there is *Duarta*,   120
And brown *Olivia*.
Pinac.   I know none of 'em.
Lylia-Biancha.   But brown must not be cast away, Sir; if young
   Lelia
Had kept her self till this day from a husband,
Why what a Beauty, Sir? you know *Ismena*
The fair Jem of Saint *Germins?*
Pinac.   By my troth I do not.
Lylia-Biancha.   And then I know you must hear of *Brisac*,
How unlike a Gentleman——
Pinac.   As I live I have heard nothing.
Lylia-Biancha.   Strike me another Galliard.

Pinac.   By this light I cannot;
  In troth I have sprain'd my leg, Madam.
Lylia-Biancha.   Now sit ye down, Sir,
  And tell me why ye came hither, why ye chose me out?   130
  What is your business? your errant? dispatch, dispatch;
  'May be ye are some Gentlemans man, and I mistook ye,
  That have brought me a Letter, or a haunch of Venison,
  Sent me from some friend of mine.
Pinac.   Do I look like a Carrier?
  You might allow me what I am, a Gentleman.
Lylia-Biancha.   Cry'ye mercie, Sir, I saw ye yesterday,
  You are new come out of Travail, I mistook ye;
  And how do's all our impudent friends in *Italie?*
Pinac.   Madam, I came with duty, and fair curtesie,
  Service, and honour to ye.
Lylia-Biancha.   Ye came to jeer me: 140
  Yee see I am merry, Sir, I have chang'd my coppy:
  None of the Sages now, and 'pray ye proclame it,
  Fling on me what aspersion you shall please, Sir,
  Of wantonness, or wildness, I look for it;
  And tell the world I am an hypocrite,
  Mask in a forc'd and borrow'd shape, I expect it;
  But not to have you beleev'd; for mark ye, Sir,
  I have won a nobler estimation,
  A stronger tie by my discretion
  Upon opinion (how ere you think I forced it)   150
  Than either tongue or art of yours can slubber,
  And when I please I will be what I please, Sir,
  So I exceed not Mean; and none shall brand it
  Either with scorn or shame, but shall be slighted.
Pinac.   Lady, I come to love ye.
Lylia-Biancha.   Love your self, Sir.
  And when I want observers, I'll send for ye:
  Heigh, ho; my fit's almost off, for we do all by fits, Sir:
  If ye be weary, sit till I come again to ye.   *Exit.*

*146 Mask] *stet* F°–F 2   *151 art] *stet* F°–F 2
  156 I'll] F 2; 'll F°

Pinac.   This is a wench of a dainty spirit; but hang me if I know
    yet
Either what to think, or make of her; She had her will of me,   160
And baited me abundantly, I thank her.
And I confess I never was so blurted,
Nor never so abus'd; I must bear mine own sins;
Ye talk of Travails, here's a curious Country,
Yet I will find her out, or forswear my facultie.

                                                          Exit.

            Enter Rosalura, *and* Oriana [*and* Petella].   [II.] iii

Rosalura.   Ne'r vex your self, nor grieve; ye are a fool then.
Oriana.   I am sure I am made so: yet before I suffer
    Thus like a girl, and give him leave to triumph———
Rosalura.   You say right; for as long as he perceives ye
    Sink under his proud scornings, he'll laugh at ye:
    For me, secure your self; and for my Sister,
    I partly know her mind too: howsoever
    To obey my Father we have made a tender
    Of our poor beauties to the travail'd *Monsieur*;
    Yet two words to a bargain; he slights us   10
    As skittish things, and we shun him as curious.
    'May be my free behaviour turns his stomach,
    And makes him seem to doubt a loose opinion.
    I must be so sometimes, though all the world saw it.
Oriana.   Why should not ye? Are our minds only measur'd?
    As long as here ye stand secure———
Rosalura.   Ye say true;
    As long as mine own conscience makes no question,
    What care I for Report: That woman's miserable
    That's good or bad for their tongues sake: Come let's retire.
    And get my veil wench: By my troth your sorrow,   20
                              [*Exit* Petella; *brings veil.*]
    And the consideration of mens humorous maddings,
    Have put me into a serious contemplation.

            159–160 This...me,] stet F°, F 2

                              280

Oriana.   Come 'faith, let's sit and think.
Rosalura.   That's all my business.

                Enter Bellure, *and after him* Mirabell.

Mirabell.   Why standst thou peeping here? thou great slug,
   forward.
Bellure.   She is there, peace.
Mirabell.   Why standst thou here then,
   Sneaking, and peaking, as thou would'st steal linnen?
   Hast thou not place and time?
Bellure.   I had a rare speech
   Studied, and almost ready, and your violence
   Has beat it out of my brains.
Mirabell.   Hang your rare speeches,
   Go me on like a man.
Bellure.   Let me set my Beard up.   30
   How has *Pinac* performed?
Mirabell.   He has won already:
   He stands not thrumming of caps thus.
Bellure.   Lord, what should I ail?
   What a cold I have over my stomach; would I had some Hum.
   Certain I have a great mind to be at her:
   A mighty mind.
Mirabell.   On fool.
Bellure.   Good words, I beseech ye;
   For I will not be abused by both.
Mirabell.   Adieu, then,
   I will not trouble you, I see you are valiant,
   And work your own way.
Bellure.   Hist, hist, I will be rul'd,
   I will y'faith, I will go presently:
   Will ye forsake me now and leave me i'th' suds: 40
   You know I am false-hearted this way; I beseech ye,
   Good sweet *Mirabell*; I'll cut your throat if ye leave me,
   Indeed I will sweet heart.

   23.1 *Enter*...Mirabell.] Enter *Mirabell* and *Bellure*. F° (*at right, opposite lines*
   22–123)

Mirabell.   I will be ready,
   Still at thine elbow; take a mans heart to thee,
   And speak thy mind: the plainer still the better.
   She is a woman of that free behaviour,
   Indeed that common curtesie, she cannot deny thee;
   Go bravely on.
Bellure [advances].   Madam——keep close about me,
   Still at my back. Madam, sweet Madam.
Rosalura.   Ha;
   What noise is that, what saucy sound to trouble me?   50
Mirabell.   What sayd she?
Bellure.   I am saucy.
Mirabell.   'Tis the better.
Bellure.   She comes; must I be saucie still?
Mirabell.   More saucie.
Rosalura.   Still troubled with these vanities? heaven bless us;
   What are we born to? would ye speak with any of my people?
   Go in, Sir, I am busie.
Bellure.   This is not she sure:
   Is this two children at a Birth? I'll be hang'd then:
   Mine was a merry Gentlewoman, talkt daintily,
   Talkt of those matters that befitted women;
   This is a parcell-pray'r-book; I'm serv'd sweetly;
   And now I am to look too; I was prepar'd for th'other way.   60
Rosalura.   Do you know that man?
Oriana.   Sure I have seen him, Lady.
Rosalura.   Me-thinks 'tis pitty such a lusty fellow
   Should wander up and down and want employment.
Bellure.   She takes me for a Rogue: you may do well Madam,
   To stay this wanderer, and set him a work, forsooth,
   He can do something that may please your Ladiship.
   I have heard of women that desire good breedings,
   Two at a birth, or so.
Rosalura.   The fellow's impudent.
Oriana.   Sure he is crazed.
Rosalura.   I have heard of men too that have had good manners;   70
   Sure this is want of grace; indeed 'tis great pitty

The young man has been bred so ill; but this lewd Age
Is full of such examples.
Bellure.   I am founder'd,
And some shall rue the setting of me on.
Mirabell.   Ha? so bookish, Lady, is it possible?
Turn'd holy at the heart too? I'll be hang'd then:
Why this is such a feat, such an activitie,
Such fast and loose: a veyl too for your knavery?
O dio, dio!
Rosalura.   What do you take me for, Sir?
Mirabell.   An hypocrite, a wanton, a dissembler,   80
How e're ye seem, and thus ye are to be handled.
Mark me *Bellure*, and this you love, I know it.
Rosalura.   Stand off, bold Sir.
Mirabell.   You wear good clothes to this end,
Jewels, love Feasts, and Masques.
Rosalura.   Ye are monstrous saucie.
Mirabell.   All this to draw on fools? and thus, thus Lady,
Ye are to be lull'd.
Bellure.   Let her alone, I'll swinge ye else,
I will y'faith; for though I cannot skill o' this matter
My self, I will not see another do it before me,
And do it worse.
Rosalura.   Away, ye are a vain thing;
You have travail'd far Sir, to return again   90
A windy and poor Bladder: you talk of women,
That are not worth the favour of a common one;
The grace of her grew in an Hospitall:
Against a thousand such blown fooleries
I am able to maintain good womens honours,
Their freedoms, and their fames, and I will do it.
Mirabell.   She has almost struck me dumb too.
Rosalura.   And declame
Against your base malicious tongues; your noyses;
For they are nothing else: You teach behaviours?
Or touch us for our freedoms? teach your selves manners,   100
Truth and sobriety, and live so clearly

283

That our lives may shine in ye; and then task us:
It seems ye are hot, the suburbs will supply ye,
Good women scorn such Gamesters; so I'll leave ye.
I am sorry to see this; 'faith Sir live fairly.

        Exeunt [Rosalura *and* Oriana].

Mirabell. This woman, if she hold on, may be vertuous,
 'Tis almost possible: we'll have a new day.
Bellure. Ye brought me on, ye forced me to this foolery;
 I am sham'd, I am scorn'd, I am flurted; yes, I am so:
 Though I cannot talk to a woman like your worship,   110
 And use my phrases, and my learned figures,
 Yet I can fight with any man.
Mirabell.   Fie.
Bellure.   I can, Sir,
 And I will fight.
Mirabell.   With whom?
Bellure.   With you, with any man;
 For all men now will laugh at me.
Mirabell.   Pre'thee be moderate.
Bellure. And I'll beat all men. Come.
Mirabell.   I love thee dearly.
Bellure. I will beat all that love, Love has undone me;
 Never tell me, I will not be a History.
Mirabell. Thou art not.
Bellure.   'Sfoot I will not; give me room,
 And let me see the proudest of ye jeer me,
 And I'll begin with you first.
Mirabell.   'Pre'thee *Bellure*;   120
 If I do not satisfie thee——
Bellure.   Well, look ye do:
 But now I think on't better, 'tis impossible;
 I must beat some body, I am maul'd my self,
 And I ought in Justice——
Mirabell.   No, no, no, ye are couzen'd;
 But walk, and let me talk to thee.
Bellure.   Talk wisely,

    116 will] Sympson; *om.* F°–F2

284

And see that no man laugh upon no occasion;
For I shall think then 'tis at me.
Mirabell.   I warrant thee.
Bellure.   Nor no more talk of this.
Mirabell.   Do'st think I am maddish?
Bellure.   I must needs fight yet; for I find it concerns me,
A pox on't, I must fight.   130
Mirabell.   Y'faith thou shalt not.

                                             Exeunt.

                 Enter De Gard, *and* Lugier.   III. i

de Gard.   I know ye are a Scholar, and can do wonders.
Lugier.   There's no great Scholarship belongs to this, Sir;
What I am, I am; I pitty your poor Sister,
And heartily I hate these Travellers,
These Gim-cracks, made of Mops, and Motions:
There's nothing in their houses here but humings;
A Bee has more brains. I grieve, and vex too
The insolent licentious carriage
Of this out-facing fellow, *Mirabell*,
And I am mad to see him prick his plumes up.   10
de Gard.   His wrongs you partly know.
Lugier.   Do not you stir, Sir,
Since he has begun with wit, let wit revenge it;
Keep your sword close, wee'll cut his throat a new way.
I am asham'd the Gentlewoman should suffer
Such base lewd wrongs.
de Gard.   I will be rul'd, he shall live,
And left to your revenge.
Lugier.   I, I, I'll fit him:
He makes a common scorn of handsom women;
Modesty, and good manners are his May-games:
He takes up Maidenheads with a new Commission;
The Church warrant's out of date: follow my Counsell   20
For I am zealous in the Cause.

          0.1 Lugier] Langbaine; *Leverdure, alias, Lugier* F°, F 2

de Gard.   I will, Sir;
   And will be still directed: for the truth is
   My Sword will make my sister seem more monstrous:
   Besides there is no honor won on Reprobates.
Lugier.   You are ith' right: The slight he has shew'd my Pupills
   Setts me a fire too: goe Ile prepare your Sister,
   And as I told ye——
de Gard.   Yes all shalbe fit, Sir.
Lugier.   And seriously, and handsomely.
de Gard.   I warrant ye.
Lugier.   A little councell more.
de Gard.   'Tis well.
Lugier.   Most stately.
   See that observ'd; and then——
de Gard.   I have ye every way.   30
Lugier.   Away then and be ready.
de Gard.   With all speed Sir.   *Exit.*

Enter Lelia, Rosalura, Oriana.

Lugier.   Wee'll learne to travell too, may be beyond him.
   Good day, Faire beauties.
Lylia-Biancha.   You have beautified us.
   We thank ye Sir, ye have set us off most gallantly
   With your grave precepts.
Rosalura.   We expected Husbands
   Out of your Documents, and taught behaviours;
   Excellent Husbands, thought men would run starck mad on us,
   Men of all Ages, and all States: we expected
   An Inundation of desires, and Offers,
   A Torrent of trym Suitors: all we did,   40
   Or said, or purpos'd to be Spels about us,
   Spells to provoake.
Lylia-Biancha.   Ye have provoak'd us finely,
   We follow'd your directions, we did rarely,
   We were Stately, Coy, Demure, Careless, Light, Giddy,
   And plai'd at all points: This you swore would Carry.
Rosalura.   We made Love, and Contemn'd Love. Now seemd holy

286

With such a reverent put-on Reservation
Which could not misse according to your Principles,
Now gave more hope again, Now close, Now publick,
Still up and down, we beate it like a Billowe;   50
And ever those Behaviours you read to us,
Subtile, and new. But all this will not help us.

Lylia-Biancha.   They help to hinder us of all Acquaintance,
They have frighted off all Friends: what am I better
For all my Learning, if I love a Dunce,
A handsome dunce? to what use serves my Reading?
You should have taught me what belongs to Horses,
Doggs, dice, Hawkes, Banketts, masks, free and faire Meetings,
To have studied Gownes and Dressings.

Lugier.   Ye are not mad sure.

Rosalura.   We shalbe if we follow your encouragements;   60
I'le take mine own way now.

Lylia-Biancha.   And I my Fortune.
We may live Maids else till the Moon drop Milstones;
I see your modest Women are tak'en for Monsters,
A Dowry of good breeding is worth nothing.

Lugier.   Since ye take it so toth' heart, pray'ye give me leave yet
And ye shall see how I'le convert this Heretique;
Mark how this *Mirabell*——

Lylia-Biancha.   Name him no more:
For, though I long for a husband, I hate him,
And would be marryed sooner to a Monkey,
Or to a Jack of Straw, then such a Juggler.   70

Rosalura.   I am of that minde too; he is too nimble,
And plays at fast and loose too learnedly
For a plain-meaning Woman; that's the truth on't.
Here's one too, that we love well, would be angry;
And reason why: No, no, we will not trouble ye
Nor him, at this time: may he make you happy.
We'll turn our selves loose now, to our faire Fortunes,
And the down-right way.

Lylia-Biancha.   The winning-way wee'll follow,
Wee'll bait, that men may bite fair, and not be frighted;

Yet wee'll not be carryed so cheap neither: wee'll have som
    sport,   80
Some mad-Morrysse or other for our money (Tutor.)

Lugier.   'Tis like enough: prosper your own Devices;
    Ye are old enough to Choose: But for this Gentlewoman
    So please her, give me leave.

Oriana.   I shall be glad Sir,
    To finde a Friend, whose pity may direct me.

Lugier.   Ile doe my best, and faithfully deale for ye;
    But then ye must be ruled.

Oriana.   In all, I vow to ye.

Rosalura.   Doe, doe: he has a lucky hand somtimes, Ile assure ye:
    And hunts the recovery of a lost Lover deadly.

Lugier.   You must away straight.

Oriana.   Yes.

Lugier.   And Ile instruct ye: 90
    Here ye can know no more.

Oriana.   By your leave, sweet Ladies,
    And all our Fortunes, arive at our own wishes.

Lylia-Biancha.   Amen, Amen.

Lugier.   I must borrow your man.

Lylia-Biancha.   'Pray take him;
    He is within: to doe her good, take any thing,
    Take us, and all.

Lugier.   No doubt he may finde Takers;
    And so wee'll leave ye to your own disposes.

                      Exeunt [Lugier, Oriana].

Lylia-Biancha.   Now which way, Wench.

Rosalura.   Wee'll goe a brave way; fear not:
    A safe and sure way too: and yet a by-way,
    I must confess I have a great minde to be marryed.

Lylia-Biancha.   So have I too, a grudging of good-will that way; 100
    And would as fain be dispatch'd. But this Monsieur
    Quicksilver ——

Rosalura.   No, no: we'll bar him, by, and Mayne: Let him
    trample;
    There is no safety in his Surquedrie:

An Army-Roiall of Women, are too few for him,
He keeps a Journall of his Gentleness,
And will go near to print his fair Dispatches,
And call it his Triumph over Time and Women:
Let him pass out of memory: what think ye
Of his two Companions?
Lylia-Biancha.   *Pinac* methinks is reasonable;
A little Modestie he has brought home with him,   110
And might be taught in time some handsome duty.
Rosalura.   They say he is a Wencher too.
Lylia-Biancha.   I like him better:
A free light Touch or two becomes a Gentleman,
And sets him seemly off: so he exceed not,
But keep his Compass clear, he may be lookt at;
I would not marry a man that must be taught,
And conjur'd up with Kisses; the best Game
Is plaid still by the best Gamesters.
Rosalura.   Fie upon thee!
What talk hast thou?
Lylia-Biancha.   Are not we alone, and merry?
Why should we be asham'd to speak what we think? thy *Gentleman*   120
The tall fat-Fellow; he that came to see thee.
Rosalura.   Is't not a goodly man?
Lylia-Biancha.   A wondrous goodly!
'Has weight enough I warrant thee: Mercy upon me;
What a Serpent wilt thou seem under such a *St. George.*
Rosalura.   Thou are a Fool; give me a man brings Mettle,
Brings substance with him; needs no Brothes to Lard him:
These little Fellows shew like Fleas in boxes,
Hop up and down, and keep a stir to vex us;
Give me the puissant Pike, take you the small Shot.
Lylia-Biancha.   Of a great thing I have not seen a Duller,   130
Therefore methinks, sweet Sister——
Rosalura.   Peace: he's modest:
A bashfulness, which is a point of grace, Wench:
But when these Fellows come to moulding, Sister,

*126 Lard] Lare F° +

289

To heat, and handling: as I live, I like him;
And methinks I could form him.

Enter Mirabell.

Lylia-Biancha.   Peace: the Fire-drake.
Mirabell.   'Bless ye sweet Beauties: sweet incomparable Ladies:
   Sweet wits: sweet humours: 'Bless you, Learned Lady,
   And you, most holy Nun; 'Bless your Devotions.
Lylia-Biancha.   And 'bless your brains, Sir, your most pregnant
      brains, Sir,
   They are in Travail, may they be delivered   140
   Of a most hopefull Wild-Goose.
Rosalura.   'Bless your manhood:
   They say ye are a Gentleman of Action,
   A fair accomplish'd man; and a rare Engineer,
   You have a trick to blow-up Maidenheads,
   A subtle trick, they say abroad.
Mirabell.   I have Lady.
Rosalura.   And often glory in their Ruines.
Mirabell.   Yes forsooth;
   I have a speedy trick: please you to try it:
   My Engine will dispatch ye instantly.
Rosalura.   I would I were a Woman, Sir, fit for ye,
   As there be such, no doubt, may Engine you too;   150
   May with a Counter-mine blow up your valour:
   But in good faith, Sir, we are both too honest;
   And the plague is, we cannot be perswaded:
   For, look ye: if we thought it were a glory
   To be the last of all your lovely Ladies——
Mirabell.   Come, come; leave prating: this has spoil'd your
      Market;
   This pride, and pufft-up heart, will make ye fast (Ladies)
   Fast, when ye are hungry too.
Rosalura.   The more our pain, Sir.
Lylia-Biancha.   The more our health, I hope too.
Mirabell.   Your behaviours
   Have made men stand amaz'd; those men that lov'd ye;   160

Men of fair States and parts; your strange conversions
Into I know not what, nor how, nor wherefore;
Your scorns of those that came to visit ye;
Your studied Whim-whams; and your fine set Faces:
What have these got ye? proud, and harsh opinions:
A Travail'd-*Monsieur*, was the strangest Creature,
The wildest Monster to be wondred at:
His Person made a publique Scoff, his Knowledge,
(As if he had been bred 'mongst Bears or Bandoggs)
Shunn'd and avoided: his conversation snuft at.   170
What Harvest brings all this?
Rosalura.   I pray ye proceed, Sir.
Mirabell.   Now ye shall see in what esteem a Travailer,
An understanding Gentleman, and a Monsieur
Is to be held, and to your greifes confes it,
Both to your greifes, and gaules.
Lylia-Biancha.   In what I pray ye, Sir?
We would be glad to understand your Excellence.
Mirabell. ˌ Goe on, (sweet Ladies) it becomes ye rarely.
For me, I have blest me from ye, scoff on, seriously,
And note the Man ye mock'd: you, (Lady Learning)
Note the poore Traveller, that came to visit ye,   180
That flat unfurnish'd Fellow: note him throughly,
You may chance to see him soon.
Lylia-Biancha.   'Tis very likely.
Mirabell.   And see him Courted, by a Travell'd Lady,
Held deer, and honour'd by a vertuous virgin,
May be a Beautie, not far short of yours, neither:
It may be, cleerer.
Lylia-Biancha.   Not unlikely.
Mirabell.   Younger:
As killing eyes as yours: a wit as poynant:
May be, a State to that may top your Fortune;
Enquire how she thinks of him, how she holds him;
His good parts; in what precious price already;   190

161 conversions] Sympson; conventions F⁰–F2
*188 to] *i.e.*, too, *perhaps, as in* Sympson + (− D)

Being a stranger to him, how she courts him;
A stranger to his Nation too, how she dotes on him:
Enquire of this; be sick to know: Curse, Lady,
And keep your Chamber: cry, and curse, a sweet one,
A thousand in yearly land; well bred; well friended:
Travell'd, and highly followed for her fashions.

Lylia-Biancha.   'Bless his good Fortune, Sir.

Mirabell.   This scurvy fellow;
I think they call his name *Pinac*; this serving-man
That brought ye Venison, as I take it, Madam;
Note but this Scab; 'tis strange that this course creature,   200
That has no more set off, but his jugglings,
His travell'd tricks——

Lylia-Biancha.   Good, sir, I grieve not at him,
Nor envy not his Fortune: yet I wonder,
He's handsom; yet I see no such perfection.

Mirabell.   Would I had his Fortune: for 'tis a woman
Of that sweet temper'd nature, and that judgment,
Besides her state, that care, clear understanding,
And such a wife to bless him.

Rosalura.   Pray ye whence is she?

Mirabell.   Of *England* and a most accomplish'd Lady,
So modest that mens eies are frighted at her,   210
And such a noble carriage.

Enter a Boy.

                                    How now Sirrah?

Boy.   Sir, the great English Lady.

Mirabell.   What of her, sir?

Boy.   Has newly left her Coach, and coming this way,
Where you may see her plain: Monsieur *Pinac*,
The onely man that leades her.

Enter Pinac, Mariana, *and Attendants.*

Mirabell.   He is much honored;
Would I had such a favour: now vex Ladies,
Envy, and vex, and raile.

Rosalura.   Ye are short of us, Sir.
Mirabell.   'Bless your fair Fortune, sir.
Pinac.   I Nobly thank ye.
Mirabell.   Is she married, friend?
Pinac.   No, no.
Mirabell.   A goodly Lady;
  A sweet and delicate Aspect: mark, mark, and wonder.   220
  Hast thou any hope of her?
Pinac.   A little.
Mirabell.   Follow close then:
  Loose not that hope.
Pinac.   To you, Sir.   [*She curtesies.*]
Mirabell.   Gentle Lady.
Rosalura.   She is fair indeed.
Lylia-Biancha.   I have seen a fairer, yet she is well.
Rosalura.   Her clothes fit handsome too.
Lylia-Biancha.   She dresses prettily.
Rosalura.   And by my faith she is rich; she looks stil sweeter.
  A well-bred woman, I warrant her.
Lylia-Biancha.   Do you hear, Sir;
  May I crave this Gentlewomans name?
Pinac.   *Mariana*, Lady.
Lylia-Biancha.   I will not say I ow ye a quarel Monsieur
  For making me your stale: a noble Gentleman
  Would have had more curtesie; at least, more faith,   230
  Then to turn of his mistris at first trial:
  You know not what respect I might have shew'd ye;
  I finde ye have worth.
Pinac.   I cannot stay to answer ye;
  Ye see my charge: I am beholding to ye
  For all your merry tricks ye put upon me,
  Your bobs, and base accounts: I came to love ye,
  To woo ye, and to serve ye; I am much endebted to ye
  For dancing me off my legs; and then for walking me;
  For telling me strange tales I never heard of,

220 wonder.] F° (u); ~ ! F° (c)   229 stale] F° (u); Stale F° (c)
231 of] *i.e.*, off *as in* F2

293

More to abuse me; for mistaking me,   240
When ye both knew I was a Gentleman,
And one deserv'd as rich a match as you are.

Lylia-Biancha. Be not so bitter, Sir.

Pinac.   You see this Lady:
She is young enough, and fair enough to please me,
A woman of a loving minde, a quiet,
And one that weighs the worth of him that loves her,
I am content with this, and bless my Fortune;
Your curious Wits, and Beauties——

Lylia-Biancha.   Faith see me once more.

Pinac. I dare not trouble ye.

Lylia-Biancha.   May I speak to your Lady?

Pinac. I pray ye content your self: I know ye are bitter,   250
And in your bitterness, ye may abuse her;
Which if she comes to know, (for she understands ye not)
It may breed such a quarrel to your kindred,
And such an indiscretion fling on you too;
For she is Nobly friended.

Lylia-Biancha. [aside].   I could eat her.

Pinac. Rest as ye are, a modest noble Gentlewoman,
And afford your honest neighbours som of your prayers.

                              Exeunt [Pinac, Mariana].

Mirabell. What think you now?

Lylia-Biancha.   Faith she's a pretty Whiting;
She has got a pretty catch too.

Mirabell.   You are angry;
Monstrous angry now; grievously angry;   260
And the pretty heart does swell now.

Lylia-Biancha.   No in troth, sir.

Mirabell. And it will cry anon; a pox upon it:
And it will curse it self: and eat no meat, Lady;
And it will sigh.

Lylia-Biancha. Indeed you are mistaken;
It will be very merry.

Rosalura.   Why, sir, do you think

264 sigh] Sympson(*qy*); fight F°–F2

There are no more men living, nor no handsomer
Then he, or you? By this light there be ten thousand,
Ten thousand thousand: comfort your self, dear Monsieur,
Faces, and Bodies, Wits, and all Abilliments
There are so many we regard 'em not.   270
Mirabell.   That such a noble Lady, I could burst now.
So far above such triffles.

Enter Bellure, *and two Gentlemen.*

Bellure.   You did laugh at me,
And I know why ye laughed.
1. Gentleman.   I pray ye be satisfied;
If we did laugh, we had some private reason,
And not at you.
2. Gentleman.   Alas, we know you not, sir.
Bellure.   I'll make you know me; set your faces soberly;
Stand this way, and look sad; I'll be no May-game;
Sadder; demurer yet.
Rosalura.   What's the matter? What ailes this Gentleman?
Bellure.   Go off now backward, that I may behold ye;   280
And not a simper on your lives.   [*Exeunt Gentlemen.*]
Lylia-Biancha.   He's mad sure.
Bellure.   Do you observe me too?
Mirabell.   I may look on ye.
Bellure.   Why do you grin? I know your minde.
Mirabell.   You do not.
You are strangely humorous: Is there no mirth, nor pleasure,
But you must be the object?
Bellure.   Mark, and observe me; where ever I am nam'd,
The very word shall raise a general sadness,
For the disgrace this scurvy woman did me;
This proud pert thing; take heed ye laugh not at me;
Provoke me not, take heed.
Rosalura.   I would fain please ye;   290
Do any thing to keep ye quiet.

272 triffles.] F°(u); ~ ? F° (c)
281 your] F2; you F°

Bellure.   Hear me,
  Till I receive a satisfaction
  Equall to the disgrace, and scorn ye gave me;
  Ye are a wreatched woman: till thou woo'st me,
  And I scorn thee asmuch, as seriously
  Gear, and abuse thee; ask what Gill thou art;
  Or any baser name; I will proclaim thee;
  I will so sing thy vertue; so be-paint thee——
Rosalura. Nay, good sir, be more modest.
Bellure.   Do you laugh again?
  Because ye are a woman ye are lawless,   300
  And out of compass of an honest anger.
Rosalura. Good sir, have a better belief of me.
Lylia-Biancha.   Away deare sister.
                 Exeunt [Rosalura, Lylia-Biancha].
Mirabell. Is not this better now, this seeming madness,
  Then falling out with your friends.
Bellure.   Have I not frighted her?
Mirabell. Into her right wits, I warrant thee: follow this humor,
  And thou shalt see how prosperously 'twil guide thee.
Bellure. I am glad I have found a way to woo yet, I was afraid once
  I never should have made a civill Suiter.
  Well, I'le about it still.   *Exit.*
Mirabell.   Doe, doe, and prosper.
  What sport do I make with these fools? What pleasure   310
  Feeds me, and fats my sides at their poor innocence?
  Wooing and wiving, hang it: give me mirth,
  Witty and dainty mirth: I shall grow in love sure
  With mine own happy head.

        Enter Lugier [*disguised*].

          Who's this? To me, Sir?
  What youth is this?
Lugier.   Yes, Sir, I would speak with you,
  If your name be Monsieur *Mirabel.*

    314 Lugier] *Leverduce, des Lugier, Mr. Illiard* F°

Mirabell.   Ye have hit it.
  Your businesse, I beseech yee.
Lugier.   This it is, Sir.
  There is a Gentlewoman hath long time affected yee,
  And lov'd ye dearly.
Mirabell.   Turn over, and end that story,
  'Tis long enough: I have no faith in women, Sir.   320
Lugier.   It seems so, Sir: I do not come to woo for her,
  Or sing her praises, though she well deserve 'em.
  I come to tell ye, ye have been cruel to her,
  Unkind and cruell, falser of faith, and carelesse,
  Taking more pleasure in abusing her,
  Wresting her honour to your wild disposes,
  Then noble in requiting her affection:
  Which, as ye are a man, I must desire ye
  (A Gentleman of rank) not to persist in;
  No more to load her fair name with your injuries.   330
Mirabell.   Why, I beseech ye, Sir?
Lugier.   Good Sir, I'le tell ye.
  And I'le be short: I'le tell yee, because I love ye,
  Because I would have you shun the shame may follow:
  There is a noble man, new come to Town, Sir,
  A noble and a great man that affects her,
  A Countreyman of mine, a brave *Savoyan*,
  Nephew to th' Duke, and so much honours her,
  That 'twill be dangerous to pursue your old way,
  To touch at any thing concerns her honour,
  Believe, most dangerous; her name is *Oriana*,   340
  And this great man will marry her: take heed, Sir;
  For howsoev'r her brother, a staid Gentleman,
  Lets things passe upon better hopes, this Lord, Sir,
  Is of that fiery, and that poynant metall,
  (Especially provok'd on by affection)
  That 'twill be hard: but you are wise.
Mirabell.   A Lord, sir?
Lugier.   Yes, and a noble Lord.
Mirabell.   'Send her good fortune.

This will not stir her Lord; a Baronness,
Say ye so; say ye so: by'r Lady, a brave title;
Top, and top gallant now; 'save her great Ladiship.　　　350
I was a poor servant of hers, I must confess, Sir,
And in those daies, I thought I might be jovy,
And make a little bold to call in to her:
But *Basto*; now, I know my rules and distance;
Yet, if she want an Usher; such an implement;
One that is throughly pac'd; a clean made gentleman;
Can hold a hanging up with approbation;
Plant his Hat formally, and wait with patience;
I do beseech you, sir——

Lugier.　　　　　　　　　　Sir, leave your scoffing;
And as ye are a Gentleman, deal fairly:　　　　　　360
I have given ye a friends councel, so I'll leave ye.

Mirabell.　　But hark ye, hark ye, sir; is't possible
I may beleeve what you say?

Lugier.　　　　　　　　　You may chuse, sir.

Mirabell.　　No Baites? No Fish-hooks, sir? No Gins? No Nooses?
No Pitfals to catch Puppies?

Lugier.　　　　　　　　　I tell ye certain;
You may beleeve; if not, stand to the danger.　　*Exit.*

Mirabell.　　A Lord of *Savoy* saies he? The Dukes Nephew?
A man so mighty? By'r Lady a fair marriage;
By my faith, a handsom Fortune: I must leave prating;
For to confess the truth, I have abused her,　　　　370
For which I should be sorry; but that will seem scurvy;
I must confess, she was ever since I knew her
As modest, as she was fair: I am sure she lov'd me;
Her means good; and her breeding excellent;
And for my sake she has refus'd fair matches:
I may play the fool finely. Stay who are these?

Enter De-Gard [*disguised as the Lord*], Oriana, *and Attendants.*

'Tis she, I am sure; and that the lord it should seem,
He carries a fair Port; is a handsom man too:

353 in to] C; into F°–F2　　　368 By'r Lady] C; By 'Lady F°–F2

298

I do begin to feel, I am a Coxcomb.

Oriana.   Good my Lord, chuse a nobler: for I know   380
    I am so far below your rank and Honor,
    That what ye can say this way, I must credit,
    But spoken to beget your self sport: Alas, Sir,
    I am so far off, from deserving you,
    My Beauty so unfit for your Affection,
    That I am grown the scorn of common Railers,
    Of such injurious Things, that when they cannot
    Reach at my person, lie with my reputation:
    I am poor besides.

de Gard.   Ye are all wealth and goodness;
    And none but such as are the scum of men,   390
    The Ulcers of an honest State; Spight-weavers,
    That live on poyson onely, like swoln Spiders,
    Dare once profane such excellence, such sweetness.

Mirabell.   This man speaks loud indeed.

de Gard.   Name but the men, Lady;
    Let me but know these poor, and base depravers;
    Lay but to my revenge their persons open,
    And you shall see how suddenly, how fully
    For your most Beautious sake, how direfully
    I'll handle their despights. Is this thing one?
    Be what he will.

Mirabell.   Sir.

de Gard.   Dare your malicious tongue, sir?   400

Mirabell.   I know you not; nor what ye mean.

Oriana.   Good my Lord.

de Gard.   If he, or any he——

Oriana.   I beseech your Honor.
    This Gentleman's a stranger to my knowledge,
    And no doubt, sir, a worthy man.

de Gard.   Your mercy;
    But had he been a tainter of your Honor;
    A blaster of those beauties raign within ye——
    But we shall finde a fitter time: dear Lady,

       405 he] F2; ye F°   405 a tainter] F2; attaint F°

As soon as I have freed ye from your Guardian,
And done some honour'd offices unto ye,
I'll take ye with those faults the world flings on ye;   410
And dearer then the whole world I'll esteem ye.   *Exeunt.*
Mirabell.   This is a thundring Lord; I am glad I scap'd him:
How lovingly the wench disclaim'd my villany?
I am vext now heartily that he shall have her;
Not that I care to marry, or to lose her;
But that this Bilbo-Lord shall reap that Maiden-head
That was my due; that he shall rig and top her;
I'de give a thousand Crowns now, he might miss her.

Enter a Servant [Lilia-Biancha's *man*].

Servant [*aside*].   Nay, if I bear your blowes, and keep your
        councel,
    You have good luck, Sir; I'll teach ye to strike lighter.   420
Mirabell.   Come hether, honest Fellow; canst thou tell me
    Where this great Lord lies? This *Savoy* Lord? Thou met'st him;
    He now went by thee certain.
Servant.   Yes, he did, Sir;
    I know him; and I know you are fool'd.
Mirabell.   Come hether.
    Here's all this, give me truth.
Servant.   Not for your money;
    (And yet that may do much) but I have been beaten:
    And by the worshipful Contrivers beaten, and I'll tel ye;
    This is no Lord, no *Savoy* Lord.
Mirabell.   Go forward.
Servant.   This is a Trick, and put upon ye grosly
    By one *Lugier*; the Lord is Monsieur *De-Gard*, Sir;   430
    An honest Gentleman, and a neighbour here;
    Their ends you understand better then I, sure.
Mirabell.   Now I know him. Know him now plain.
Servant.   I have discharg'd my Colours; so God by ye, sir.   *Exit.*
Mirabell.   What a purblinde Puppy was I; now I remember him.
    All the whole cast on's face, though 'twere umber'd,

411 *Exeunt.*] F 2; *om.* F°   *434 Colours] *stet* F°–F 2

And mask'd with patches: what a dunder-whelp
To let him domineer thus: how he strutted,
And what a load of Lord he clapt upon him?
Would I had him here again, I would so bounce him,   440
I would so thank his Lordship for his lewd plot:
Do they think to carry it away, with a great band made of bird-
    pots
And a pair of pin-buttockt breeches?

Enter De-Gard, Oriana, *etc.*

                                   Ha! 'Tis he again.
He comes, he comes, he comes; have at him.

Sings.   My *Savoy* Lord, why dost thou frown on me?
            And will that favour never sweeter be?
            Wilt thou I say, for ever play the fool?
            De-Gard, be wise, and *Savoy* go to School.

My Lord *De-Gard*, I thank ye for your Antick,
My Lady bright, that will be sometimes Frantick;   450
You worthy Train, that wait upon this Pair,
'Send you more wit, and they a bouncing Baire;
And so I take my humble leave of your honors.   *Exit.*
de Gard.   We are discover'd, there's no remedy;
Lelia-Biancha's man upon my life,
In stubbornness, because *Lugier* corrected him.
(A shameless Slave——plague on him for a Rascal.)
Oriana.   I was in a perfect hope; the bane on't is now,
He will make mirth on mirth, to persecute us.
de Gard.   We must be patient; I am vext to the proof too.
I'll try once more; then if I fail: Here's one speaks.   460
Oriana.   Let me be lost, and scorn'd first.
de Gard.   Well, we'll consider.
Away, and let me shift; I shall be hooted else.
                                        Exeunt.

450 sometimes] F2; sometime F°
452 Baire] *i.e.*, bairn
457 Slave——plague] Sympson (~ ! ~); Slaves-plague F°-F2

301

Enter Leugier, Lelia, *Servant [carrying a willow garland]*.   IV. i

Lugier.   Faint not; but do as I direct ye, trust me;
Beleeve me too, for what I have told ye, (Lady)
As true as you are *Lelia*, is Authentick;
I know it; I have found it; 'tis a poor courage
Flies off for one repulse; these Travellers
Shall finde before we have done, a home-spun wit,
A plain French understanding may cope with 'em;
They have had the better yet, thank your sweet Squire, here;
And let 'em brag: You would be reveng'd?
Lylia-Biancha.   Yes surely.
Lugier.   And married too?
Lylia-Biancha.   I think so.
Lugier.   Then be Counsel'd; 10
You know how to proceed: I have other Irons
Heating as well as yours: and I will strike
Three blowes with one Stone home, be rul'd, and hapie;
And so I leave yee. Now is the time.
Lylia-Biancha.   I am ready. [*Exit* Lugier.]
If he doe come to dor me——
Servant.   Will ye stand here,
And let the people think, ye are God knows what, Mistris,
Let Boyes, and Prentizes presume upon ye?
Lylia-Biancha.   Pre'thee hold thy peace.
Servant.   Stand at his dore, that hates ye?
Lylia-Biancha.   Pre'thee leave prating.
Servant.   'Pray ye goe to th' Tavern. Ile give ye a Pint of wine
      there;
If any of the Mad-cap Gentlemen should come by   20
That take up women upon speciall warrant,
You were in a wise case now.

Enter, Mirabell, Pinac, Mariana, *Priest, Attendants.*

Lylia-Biancha.   Give me the Garland,
And wait you here.

0.1 *Servant*] C; Servants Fº   *15 dor me——] Sympson; do me. Fº–F2

302

Mirabell.   She is here to seeke thee, Sirrah.
  I told thee what would follow; she is mad, for thee;
  Shew, and advance. So early stirring Lady,
  It shewes a busie mind, a fancie troubled:
  A willowgh Garland too. Is't possible,
  'Tis pitty so much Beautie should lie mustie,
  But 'tis not to be help'd now.
Lylia-Biancha.   The more's my Miserie.
  Good fortune to ye (Ladie) you deserve it: 30
  To me, too late Repentance; I have sought it:
  I doe not envy, though I greive a little,
  You are Mistris of that happiness, those Joyes
  That might have bin, had I bin wise: but fortune——
Pinac.   She understands ye not, 'pray ye doe not trouble her;
  And do not crosse me like a Hare thus, 'tis as ominous.
Lylia-Biancha.   I come not to upbraid your Levitie,
  Though ye made shew of Love, and though I lik'd ye,
  To claime an Interest; we are yet both Strangers,
  But what we might have bin, had you persever'd, Sir,   40
  To be an eye-sore to your loving Lady——
  This garland shewes, I give my self forsaken;
  (Yet She must pardon me, 'tis most unwillingly:)
  And all the power and interest I had in ye;
  As I perswade my self, somewhat ye Lov'd me;
  Thus patiently I render up, I offer
  To her that must enjoy ye; and so blesse ye:
  Onely, I heartily desire this Courtesie,
  And would not be denide: to wait upon ye
  This day, to see ye tide, then no more trouble ye.   50
Pinac.   It needs not, Ladie.
Lylia-Biancha.   Good Sir, grant me so much.
Pinac.   'Tis privat, and we make no Invitation.
Lylia-Biancha.   My presence, sir, shall not proclaim it publick.
Pinac.   May be 'tis not in Town.
Lylia-Biancha.   I have a Coach, sir,
  And a most ready will to do you service.

51 needs] F2; need F°

303

Mirabell.   Strike now or never; make it sure: I tell thee,
　She will hang her self; if she have thee not.
Pinac.   'Pray ye, sir,
　Entertain my noble mistris: onely a word or two
　With this importunate woman, and I'll relieve ye.
　Now ye see what your flings are, and your fancies,   60
　Your States, and your wild stubbornes, now ye finde
　What 'tis to gird and kick at mens fair services,
　To raise your pride to such a pitch, and glory,
　That goodness shews like Gnats, scorn'd under ye.
　'Tis ugly, naught, a self-will in a woman,
　Chain'd to an over-weening thought, is Pestilent,
　Murthers fair Fortune first; Then fair opinion!
　There stands a Patern, a true patient Patern,
　Humble, and sweet.
Lylia-Biancha.   I can but grieve my ignorance.
　Repentance some say too, is the best Sacrifice;   70
　For sure, Sir, if my chance had been so happy,
　(As I confess I was mine own destroyer)
　As to have arrived at you; I will not prophesie,
　But certain, as I think, I should have pleas'd ye;
　Have made ye as much wonder at my curtesie,
　My love, and duty, as I have dishearten'd ye.
　Some hours we have of youth, and some of folly;
　And being free-born Maides, we take a liberty,
　And to maintain that, sometimes we strain highly.
Pinac.   Now ye talk reason.
Lylia-Biancha.   But being yoak'd, and govern'd,   80
　Married, and those light vanities purg'd from us;
　How fair we grow, how gentle, and how tender
　We twine about those loves that shoot-up with us?
　A sullen woman fear, that talks not to ye;
　She has a sad and darkn'd soul, loves dully:
　A merry and a free wench, give her libertie;
　Beleeve her in the lightest form she appears to ye;
　Beleeve her excellent, though she despise ye;
　Let but these fits and flashes pass, she will shew to ye,

As Jewels rub'd from dust, or Gold new burnish'd: 90
Such had I been, had you beleev'd.

Pinac.   Is't possible?

Lylia-Biancha.   And to your happiness, I dare assure ye
If True love be accounted so; your pleasure,
Your will, and your command had ty'd my Motions:
But that hope's gone; I know you are young and giddy,
And till you have a Wife can govern with ye,
You saile upon this world-Sea, light and empty;
Your Bark in danger daily; 'tis not the name neither
Of Wife can steer ye; but the noble nature,
The diligence, the Care, the Love, the Patience: 100
She makes the Pilat, and preserves the Husband,
That knowes, and reckons every Ribb, he is built on;
But this I tell ye, to my shame.

Pinac.   I admire ye,
And now am sorry, that I ayme beyond ye.

Mirabell.   So, so, so: faire and softly. She is thine own (Boy)
She comes now, without Lure.

Pinac.   But that it must needes
Be reckon'd to me as a wantonnesse,
Or worsse, a Madnesse, to forsake a Blessing,
A Blessing of that hope——

Lylia-Biancha.   I dare not urge ye;
And yet, deare Sir——

Pinac.   'Tis most certain, I had rather,   110
If 'twere in mine owne Choice, for you are my Country-woman,
A Neighbour here borne by me, She a Stranger;
And who knowes how her Friends——

Lylia-Biancha.   Doe as you please, Sir:
If ye be fast, not all the world: I love ye,
'Tis most true: and cleer, I would perswade ye;
And I shall love ye still.

Pinac.   Goe, get before me:
So much ye have won upon me: doe it presently:
Here's a Preist ready: Ile have you.

Lylia-Biancha.   Not now, Sir,

No, you shall pardon me: advance your Lady,
I dare not hinder your most high preferment,   120
'Tis honor enough for me, I have unmask'd ye.

Pinac.   How's that.

Lylia-Biancha.   I have caught ye, Sir; alas, I am no States-woman,
Nor no great Traveller, yet I have found ye,
I have found your Lady too: your beauteous Lady;
I have found her Birth, and Breeding too: her disciplin:
Who brought her over, and who kept your Lady:
And when he laid her by, what vertuous Nunnery
Received her in: I have found all these: are ye blanck now,
Methinks such travel'd wisdomes should not foole thus: 130
Such excellent Indiscretions.

Mirabell.   How could she know this?

Lylia-Biancha.   'Tis true she is English borne: but most part
    French now,
And so I hope you will find her, to your comfort,
Alas, I am ignorant of what She cost ye:
The price of these hired Clothes I doe not know Gentlemen;
Those Jewells are the Broakers, how ye stand bound for 'em.

Pinac.   Will you make this good?

Lylia-Biancha.   Yes, yes, and to her face, Sir,
That she is an English whore, a kind of fling dust,
One of your London Light o' Loves: a right one;
Came over in thin Pumps, and half a Petticote,   140
One fall, and one Smock, with a broken Haberdasher;
I know all this, without a Conjurer:
Her name is Jumping-*Jone*, an ancient Sin-Weaver;
She was first a Ladies Chamber-maid, there slip'd
And broke her leg above the knee: departed
And set up shop her self. Stood the fierce Conflicts
Of many a furious Tearme; there lost her Colours,
And last shipt over hither.

Mirabell.   We are betray'd.

Lylia-Biancha.   Doe you come to fright me with this Misterie?
To stirre me with a stink none can endure, Sir?   150

*135 Clothes, ... Gentlemen;] stet F°–F2   *141 fall] faith F°, F², L +

I pray ye proceed, the Wedding will becom ye,
Who gives the Lady? you? an excellent Father:
A carefull man, and one that knows a Beautie.
'Send ye faire shipping, Sir, and so Ile leave ye;
Be wise and manly, then I may chance to love ye.   *Exit.*

Mirabell.   As I live I am asham'd, this wench has reach'd me,
Monstrous asham'd, but there's no remedie,
This skew'd-eyde Carren——

Pinac.   This I suspected ever,
Come, Come, uncase, we have no more use of ye;
Your Clothes must back againe.

Mariana.   Sir, ye shall pardon me: 160
'Tis not our English use to be degraded:
If you will visit me and take your venture,
You shall have pleasure for your properties;
And so sweet heart——   [*Exit.*]

Mirabell.   Let her goe, and the Devill goe with her:
We have never better luck with these preludiums:
Come, be not daunted: think she is but a woman,
And let her have the devills witt, wee'll reach her.

                                    Exeunt.

              Enter Rosalura, *and* Lugier   [IV.] ii

Rosalura.   Ye have now redeem'd my good opinion (Tutor)
And ye stand faire again.

Lugier.   I can but labour,
And sweat in your Affaires: I am sure *Bellure*
Wilbe here instantly, and use his Anger,
His wonted harshness.

Rosalura.   I hope he will not beate me.

Lugier.   No sure; he has more manners: be you ready.

Rosalura.   Yes, yes, I am: and am resolv'd to fit him,
With patience to out-doe all he can offer;
But how do's *Oriana?*

Lugier.   Worse, and worse still:
There is a sad house for her: she is now   10

        0.1 Rosalura] Rosaluce F°: Rosalure F 2

                    307

Poore Ladie, utterly distracted.
Rosalura.   Pittie:
   Infinite pittie: 'tis a handsom Ladie,
   That *Mirabel*'s a Beast, worse then a Monster,
   If this affliction work not.

                    Enter Lelia-Biancha.

Lylia-Biancha.   Are ye readie?
   Bellure is comming on, here, hard behind me,
   I have no leysure to relate my Fortune.
   Onely I wish you may come off as handsomely,
   Upon the sign you know what.   *Exit.*
Rosalura.   Well, well, leave me.

                    Enter Bellure.

Bellure.   How now?
Rosalura.   Ye are welcome, sir.
Bellure.   'Tis well ye have manners:
   That Curtsy again, and hold your Countenance staidly;   20
   That look's too light; take heed: so, sit ye down now,
   And to confirm me that your gall is gone,
   Your bitterness dispers'd, for so I'll have it;
   Look on me stedfastly; and whatsoe'er I say to ye,
   Move not, nor alter in your face, ye are gon then;
   For if you do express the least distaste,
   Or shew an angry wrinkle; mark me, woman,
   We are now alone, I will so conjure thee:
   The third part of my Execution
   Cannot be spoke.
Rosalura.   I am at your dispose, sir.   30
Bellure.   Now rise, and woo me a little, let me hear that faculty;
   But touch me not; nor do not lie, I charge ye.
   Begin now.
Rosalura.   If so mean and poor a Beauty
   May ever hope the grace——

                    20 Curtsy] F° (u); Curt'sy F° (c)

                              308

Bellure.   Ye Cog, ye flatter
 Like a lew'd thing, ye lie: may hope that grace?
 Why, what grace canst thou hope for? Answer not,
 For if thou dost, and lyest again, I'll swindge thee;
 Do not I know thee, for a pestilent woman?
 A proud at both ends? Be not angry;
 Nor stir not o' your life!

Rosalura.   I am counseld, sir.   40

Bellure. Art thou not now, (confess, for I'll have the truth out)
 As much unworthy of a man of merit,
 Or any of ye all? Nay of meer man?
 Though he were crooked, cold, all wants upon him;
 Nay of any dishonest thing, that bears that figure;
 As Devils are of mercy?

Rosalura.   We are unworthy.

Bellure. Stick to that truth, and it may chance to save thee;
 And is it not our bounty that we take ye?
 That we are troubled, vex'd, or tortur'd with ye?
 Our meer, and special bounty?

Rosalura.   Yes.

Bellure.   Our pitty,   50
 That for your wickedness we swindge ye soundly;
 Your stubborness and stout hearts, we be-labour ye?
 Answer to that?

Rosalura.   I do confess your pitty.

Bellure. And dost not thou deserve in thine own person?
 (Thou Impudent, thou Pert; do not change countenance!)

Rosalura. I dare not, sir.

Bellure.   For if ye do——

Rosalura.   I am setled.

Bellure. Thou Wag-tail, Peacock, Puppy; look on me:
 I am a Gentleman.

Rosalura.   It seems no less, sir.

Bellure. And darest thou in thy Surquedry——

Rosalura.   I beseech ye.   60
 It was my weakness, sir; I did not view ye;
 I took not notice of your noble parts;

Nor call'd your person, nor your proper fashion.

Bellure. This is some amendes yet.

Rosalura. I shall mend, sir, daily.
And study to deserve.

Bellure. Come a little neerer:
Canst thou repent thy Villany?

Rosalura. Most seriously.

Bellure. And be asham'd?

Rosalura. I am asham'd.

Bellure. Cry.

Rosalura. It will be hard to do, sir.

Bellure. Cry now instantly;
Cry monstrously, that all the Town may hear thee;
Cry seriously; as if thou hadst lost thy Monkey;
And as I like thy Tears——

Rosalura. Now.

Enter Lilia *and four women laughing.*

Bellure. How? How? do ye jear me? 70
Have ye broke your bounds again Dame?

Rosalura. Yes, and laugh at ye;
And laugh most heartily.

Bellure. What are these, Whirl-winds?
Is Hell broke loose, and all the Furies flutter'd?
Am I greas'd once again?

Rosalura. Yes indeed are ye;
And once again ye shall be, if ye quarrel:
Do you come to vent your fury on a Virgin?
Is this your manhood, sir?

1. Woman. Let him do his best:
Let's see the utmost of his indignation:
I long to see him angry: come, proceed, sir.
Hang him, he dares not stir; a man of Timber. 80

2. Woman. Come hither to fright Maids, with thy Bul-faces?
To threaten Gentlewomen? Thou a man? A May-pole.
A great dry Pudding.

*62 call'd. . .proper fashion] *stet* F⁰–F2

3. Woman.　　　　　　Come, come, do your worst, sir;
Be angry if thou dar'st.
Bellure.　　　　　　The Lord deliver me.
4. Woman.　Do but look scurvily upon this Lady,
Or give us one foul word. We are all mistaken;
This is some mighty Dairy-Maid in mans clothes.
Lylia-Biancha.　I am of that minde too.
Bellure.　　　　　　　　What will they do to me?
Lylia-Biancha.　And hired to come and abuse us; a man has
manners;
A Gentleman, Civility, and Breeding:　　　　　　90
Some Tinkers Trull with a beard glew'd on.
1. Woman.　　　　　　　Let's search him;
And as we finde him——
Bellure.　　　　　Let me but depart from ye,
Sweet Christian women.
Lylia-Biancha.　　　　Hear the Thing speak, Neighbours.
Bellure.　'Tis but a small request: if ere I trouble ye,
If ere I talk again of beating Women,
Or beating any thing that can but turn to me;
Or ever thinking of a handsom Lady
But vertuously and well: of ever speaking
But to her honor: This I'le promise ye,
I will take Rhubarb; and purge Choler mainly,　　　　100
Abundantly Ile purge.
Lylia-Biancha.　　　　Ile send ye Brothes, Sir.
Bellure.　I will be laugh'd at, and endure it patiently,
I will doe any thing.
Rosalura.　　　　Ile be your Bayle then:
When ye com next to woo, 'pray ye com not boistrously
And furnish'd like a Bear-ward.
Bellure.　　　　　　No in truth, forsooth.
Rosalura.　I sented ye long since.
Bellure.　　　　　　I was to blame, sure;
I will appear a Gentleman.
Rosalura.　　　　　'Tis the best for ye,
For a true noble Gentleman's a brave thing;

Upon that hope we quit ye: You fear seriously?

Bellure.   Yes truly do I; I confess I fear ye,   110
And honor ye, and any thing.

Rosalura.   Farewel then.

1. Woman.   And when ye come to woo next bring more mercy.
                              Exeunt [all the women].

Bellure.   A Dary-Maid? A Tinkers-Trull: Heaven bless me:
Sure if I had provok'd 'em, they had quarter'd me.
I am a most ridiculous Ass, now I perceive it:
A Coward, and a Knave too.

Enter two Gentlemen.

1. Gentleman.   'Tis the mad Gentleman.
Let's set our Faces right.

Bellure.   No, no, laugh at me;
And laugh aloud.

2. Gentleman.   We are better manner'd, sir.

Bellure.   I do deserve it; call me Patch, and Puppy,
And beat me if you please.

1. Gentleman.   No indeed: We know ye.   120

Bellure.   'Death, do as I would have ye.

2. Gentleman.   Ye are an Ass then;
A Coxcomb, and a Calf.

Bellure.   I am a great Calf:
Kick me a little now: Why, when? Sufficient:
Now laugh aloud, and scorn me; so good buy'ye;
And ever when ye meet me laugh.

Gentlemen.   We will, sir.

                              Exeunt.

Enter Nantolet, la-Castre, de-Gard, Lugier, Mirabell.   [IV.] ii

Mirabell.   Your Patience, Gentlemen; why do ye bait me?

Nantolet.   Is't not a shame you are so stubborn-hearted,
So stony and so dull to such a Lady,
Of her Perfections, and her Misery?

        112 *1. Woman.*] *Wo.* F⁰–F2

Lugier.   Does she not love ye? does not her distraction
  For your sake only, her most pityed Lunacie
  Of all but you, shew ye? does it not compell ye?
Mirabell.   Soft and fair, Gentlemen, pray ye proceed temperately.
Lugier.   If ye have any feeling, any sense in ye,
  The least touch of a noble heart——
La-Castre.   Let him alone;   10
  It is his glory that he can kill Beauty,
  Ye bear my Stamp, but not my Tenderness;
  Your wild unsavoury Courses set that in ye!
  For shame be sorry, though ye cannot Cure her,
  Shew something of a Man, of a fair Nature.
Mirabell.   Ye make me Mad.
de Gard.   Let me pronounce this to ye,
  You take a strange felicity in slighting
  And wronging Women; which my poor sister feels now;
  Heavens hand be gentle on her: Mark me, Sir,
  That very hour she dyes; there's small hope otherwise;   20
  That minute you and I must grapple for it;
  Either your life or mine.
Mirabell.   Be not so hot, Sir,
  I am not to be wrought on by these Policies;
  In truth I am not; Nor do I fear the Tricks,
  Or the high sounding Threats of a *Savoyen*:
  I glory not in Cruelty; ye wrong me;
  Nor grow up water'd with the Tears of Women;
  This let me tell ye, howsoe're I shew to ye
  Wilde, as you please to call it; or self-will'd;
  When I see cause, I can both doe, and suffer,   30
  Freely, and feelingly, as a true Gentleman.

Enter Rosalura *and* Lelia.

Rosalura.   O pity, pity; thousand thousand pities!
Lylia-Biancha.   Alas, poor soul! she will die; she is grown sensless;
  She will not know, nor speak now.

*13 set] *stet* F°–F2
31.1, 136.1 Rosalura] *Rosaluce* F°; Rosalure F2

Rosalura. Die for Love,
And Love of such a Youth? I would die for a Dog, first.
He that kils me, Ile give him leave to eat me;
Ile know men better ere I sigh for any of 'em.

Lylia-Biancha. Ye have don a worthy act, Sir; a most famous;
Ye have kild a Maid the wrong way; ye are a conqueror.

Rosalura. A Conqueror? a Cobler, hang him Sowter;   40
Goe hide thy self for shame; so lose thy Memory;
Live not 'mongst Men; thou art a Beast, a Monster;
A Blatant Beast.

Lylia-Biancha. If ye have yet any honestie,
Or ever heard of any; take my Counsell;
Off with your Garters; and seek out a Bough,
A handsom Bough; (for I would have ye hang like a Gentleman;)
And write some dolefull matter to the world,
A warning to hard-hearted men.

Mirabell. Out Kitlings:
What Catterwalling's here? what gibbing?
Do you think my heart is softned with a black Santis;   50
Shew me some Reason.

Enter Oriana *on a bed.*

Rosalura. Here then, here is a reason.

Nantolet. Now, if ye be a man, let this sight shake ye.

La-Castre. Alas poor Gentlewoman! do ye know me Lady?

Lugier. How she looks up and stares.

Oriana. I know ye very well:
You are my Godfather; and that's the Monsieur.

de Gard. And who am I?

Oriana. You are *Amadis de Gaule*, Sir.
Oh, oh, my heart! were you never in love, sweet Lady?
And do you never dream of Flowres and Gardens;
I dream of walking Fires: take heed, It comes now,
Who's that? pray stand away; I have seen that face sure;   60
How light my head is.

Rosalura. Take some rest.

50 Santis] *i.e.*, Sanctus

Oriana.   I cannot.
  For I must be up to morrow, to go to Church:
  And I must dress me, put my new Gown on,
  And be as fine to meet my Love: Heigh ho!
  Will not you tell me where my Love lies buried?
Mirabell.   He is not dead: beshrew my heart she stirs me.
Oriana.   He is dead to me.
Mirabell.   Is't possible my Nature
  Should be so dampnable, to let her suffer;
  Give me your hand.
Oriana.   How soft you feel; how gentle?
  Ile tell ye your fortune, Friend.
Mirabell.   How she stares on me?   70
Oriana.   You have a flattring face; but 'tis a fine one;
  I warrant you may have a hundred Sweet-hearts:
  Will ye pray for me? I shall die to morrow;
  And will ye ring the Bells?
Mirabell.   I am most unworthy;
  I doe confess unhappy; doe you know me?
Oriana.   I would I did.
Mirabell.   Oh fair tears; how ye take me.
Oriana.   Do you weep too? you have not lost your Lover?
  You mock me: Ile go home and pray.
Mirabell.   Pray ye pardon me:
  Or if it please ye to consider justly,
  Scorn me; for I deserve it: Scorn, and shame me: 80
  Sweet *Oriana.*
Lylia-Biancha.   Let her alone; she trembles.
  Her fits will grow more strong, if ye provoke her.
La-Castre.   Certain she knowes ye not; yet loves to see ye:
  How she smiles now?

[Enter Bellure.]

Bellure.   Where are ye? oh, why doe not ye laugh: come, laugh
      at me;
  Why a devill, art thou sad, and such a subject,
  Such a ridiculous subject, as I am

315

Before thy face?

Mirabell.   Pre'thee put off this Lightnes,
This is no time for mirth, nor place: I have us'd too much on't:
I have undon my self and a sweet Ladie,   90
By being too Indulgent to my Foolery
Which truly I repent: looke here.

Bellure.   What ayles she.

Mirabell.   Alas she is mad.

Bellure.   Mad?

Mirabell.   Yes, too sure: for me too.

Bellure.   Dost thou wonder at that? by this good light, they are
   all so;
   They are coz'ning mad, they are brawling mad, they are proud
   mad.
   They are all, all mad: I came from a world of mad women,
   Mad as march Hares: get 'em in Chaines, then deale with 'em.
   There's one that's mad: she seemes well, but she is dog mad:
   Is she dead do'st think?

Mirabell.   Dead? heaven forbid.

Bellure.   Heaven further it.
   For till they be key-cold dead, there's no trusting of 'em: 100
   What ere they seeme, or howsoere they carry it,
   Till they be chap-falne, and their Tongues at peace,
   Nayl'd in their Coffins sure, Ile ne're beleeve 'em,
   Shall I talk with her?

Mirabell.   No, deer friend, be quiet;
   And be at peace a while.

Bellure.   Ile walk a side,
   And come again anon: But take heed to her:
   You say she is a woman?

Mirabell.   Yes.

Bellure.   Take great heed:
   For if she doe not Cozen thee, then hang me:
   Let her be mad, or what she will, shee'll cheate thee.   *Exit.*

Mirabell.   Away wild Foole: how vild this shewes in him now?   110
   Now take my faith, before ye all I speake it,
   And with it, my repentant Love.

La-Castre.   This seemes well.
Mirabell.   Were but this Lady cleere again, whose sorrowes
   My very hart melts for; were she but perfect
   (For thus to marry her, would be two Miseries,)
   Before the richest, and the noblest Beautie,
   France, or the world could shew me, I would take her;
   As she is now, my Teares, and praires shall wed her.
de Gard.   This makes some small emends.
Rosalura.   She beckens to ye,
   To us too, to goe off.
Nantolet.   Let's draw aside all.   [*Exeunt.*]   120
Oriana.   Oh my best friend: I would faine——
Mirabell.   What? she speakes well,
   And with another voice.
Oriana.   But I am fearfull,
   And shame a little, stops my tongue——
Mirabell.   Speake boldly.
Oriana.   Tell ye, I am well, I am perfect well, 'pray ye mock not;
   And that I did this to provoke your Nature,
   Out of my infinite, and restles Love,
   To win your pitty: pardon me.
Mirabell.   Goe forward;
   Who set ye on?
Oriana.   None, as I live, no Creature.
   Not any knew, or ever dreamt, what I meant:
   Will ye be mine?
Mirabell.   'Tis true, I pittie ye;   130
   But when I marry ye, ye must be wiser;
   Nothing but Tricks? devises?
Oriana.   Will ye shame me?
Mirabell.   Yes, marry will I: Come neer, Come neer, a Miracle;
   The Woman's well: she was only mad for Mariage,
   Stark mad to be ston'd to death; give her good Councel,
   Will this world never mend? are ye caught, Damsell?

       Enter Bellure, la-Castre, Lugier, Nantolet, de-Gard,
               Rosalura, [Lelia-]Biancha.

                              317

Bellure.   How goes it now?

Mirabell.   Thou art a kind of Prophet,
   The woman's well again; and would have gull'd me,
   Well, excellent well: and not a Taynt upon her.

Bellure.   Did not I tell ye? Let 'em be what can be;   140
   Saints, Devills, any thing, they will abuse us;
   Thou wert an Asse to beleeve her so long: a Coxcomb;
   Give 'em a minute, they'll abuse whole Millions.

Mirabell.   And am not I a rare Phisitian, Gentlemen?
   That can cure desperate mad Mindes?

de Gard.   Be not insolent.

Mirabell.   Well, goe thy waies: from this howre, I disclame thee,
   Unless thou hast a Trick above this: then Ile love thee.
   Ye owe me for your Cure; pray have a Care of her,
   For fear she fall into Relaps; Come *Bellure*,
   We'll set up Bills, to Cure diseased virgins.   150

Bellure.   Shall we be merry?

Mirabell.   Yes.

Bellure.   But Ile no more projects;
   If we could make 'em mad, it were some Mastery.

                           Exeunt [Mirabell, Bellure].

Lylia-Biancha.   I am glad she is well again.

Rosalura.   So am I, certain;
   Be not ashamed.

Oriana.   I shall never see a man more.

de Gard.   Come, ye are a foole: had ye but told me this Trick,
   He should not have gloried thus.

Lugier.   He shall not long neither.

La-Castre.   Be rul'd, and be at peace: ye have my Consent,
   And what powre I can work with.

Nantolet.   Come, leave blushing;
   We are your Friends; an honest way compell'd ye;
   Heaven will not see so true a love unrecompenc'd;   160
   Come in, and slight him too.

Lugier.   The next shall hit him.

                                                       Exeunt.

318

Enter De-Gard, *and* Lugier.   V. i

de Gard.   'Twill be discover'd.
Lugier.   That's the worst can happen:
  If there be any way, to reach, and work upon him;
  Upon his nature suddenly, and catch him: That he loves,
  Though he dissemble it, and would shew contrary,
  And will at length relent: I'll lay my Fortune,
  Nay more, my life.
de Gard.   Is she won?
Lugier.   Yes, and ready,
  And my designments set.
de Gard.   They are now for Travel,
  All for that Game again: they have forgot wooing.
Lugier.   Let 'em; we'll travel with 'em.
de Gard.   Where's his Father?
Lugier.   Within; he knows my minde too, and allows it;   10
  Pitties your Sisters Fortune most sincerely;
  And has appointed, for our more assistance,
  Some of his secret Friends.
de Gard.   'Speed the plowgh.
Lugier.   Well said;
  And be you serious too.
de Gard.   I shall be diligent.
Lugier.   Let's break the Ice for one, the rest will drink too
  (Beleeve me, sir) of the same Cup; my young Gentlewomen
  Wait but who sets the Game a foot; though they seem stubborn,
  Reserv'd, and proud now, yet I know their hearts,
  Their pulses, how they beat, and for what cause, Sir;
  And how they long to venture their Abilities   20
  In a true Quarrel; Husbands they must, and will have,
  Or Nunneries, and thin Collations
  To cool their bloods; Let's all about our business,
  And if this faile, let Nature work.
de Gard.   Ye have arm'd me.
                              Exeunt.

319

Enter Mirabel, Nantolet, La castre. [V.] ii

La-Castre.   Will ye be wilful then?

Mirabell.   'Pray, sir, your pardon,
For I must Travel: lie lazy here;
Bound to a Wife; Chain'd to her subtleties,
Her humors, and her wills, which are meer Fetters;
To have her today pleas'd, to morrow peevish,
The third day mad, the fourth rebellious;
You see, before they are married, what Moriscoes,
What Masques, and Mummeries they put upon us,
To be ty'd here, and suffer their Lavolto's?

Nantolet.   'Tis your own seeking.

Mirabell.   Yes, to get my freedom;   10
Were they as I could wish 'em——

La-Castre.   Fools, and Meacocks,
To endure what you think fit to put upon 'em:
Come, change your minde.

Mirabell.   Not before I have chang'd air (Father)
When I know women worthy of my company,
I will return again and wait upon 'em;
Till then (dear Sir) I'll amble all the world over,
And run all hazards, misery, and poverty,
So I escape the dangerous Bay of Matrimony.

Enter Pinac *and* Bellure.

Pinac.   Are ye resolv'd?

Mirabell.   Yes certain; I will out again.

Pinac.   We are for ye, sir; we are your servants once more;   20
Once more we'll seek our fortune in strange Countries;
Ours is too scornful for us.

Bellure.   Is there ne'er a Land
That ye have read, or heard of, (for I care not how far it be,
Nor under what Pestiferous Star it lies)
A happy Kingdom, where there are no Women?
Nor have been ever? Nor no mention
Of any such lewd Things, with lewder qualities?

For thether would I Travel; where 'tis Fellony
To confess he had a Mother: a Mistris, Treason!

La-Castre.   Are you for Travel too?

Bellure.   For any thing;   30
For living in the Moon, and stopping hedges,
E'er I stay here to be abus'd, and baffell'd.

Nantolet.   Why did ye not break your minds to me? They are my
     daughters;
And sure I think I should have that command over 'em,
To see 'em well bestow'd: I know ye are Gentlemen,
Men of fair Parts and States; I know your Parents;
And had ye told me of your fair Affections:
Make but one Tryal more; and let me second ye.

Bellure.   No I'll make Hob-nailes first, and mend old Kettles:
Can ye lend me an Armor of high proof, to appear in,   40
And two or three field pieces to defend me?
The Kings Guard are meer Pigmeys.

Nantolet.   They will not eat ye.

Bellure.   Yes, and you too, and twenty fatter Monsieurs,
If their high stomacks hold: They came with Chopping-knives,
To cut me into Rands, and Surloyns, and so powder me.
Come, shall we go?

Nantolet.   You cannot be so discurteous
(If ye intend to go) as not to visit 'em,
And take your leaves.

Mirabell.   That we dare do, and civilly,
And thank 'em too.

Pinac.   Yes, sir, we know that honesty.

Bellure.   I'll come i'th Rear, forty foot off, I'll assure ye,   50
With a good Gun in my hand; I'll no more Amazons,
I mean, no more of their frights; I'll make my three legs,
Kiss my hand twice; and if I smell no danger;
If the enterview be clear, may be I'll speak to her;
I'll ware a privy coat too; and behind me,
To make those parts secure, a Bandog.

La-Castre.   You are a merry Gentleman.

Bellure.   A wary Gentleman, I do assure ye;

I have been warn'd, and must be arm'd.

La-Castre.   Well, Son,
These are your hasty thoughts, when I see you are bent to it,
Then I'll beleeve, and joyn with ye; So we'll leave ye: 60
[*Aside.*]   There's a Trick will make ye stay.

Nantolet [*aside*].   I hope so.
                                    Exeunt [la-Castre, Nantolet].

Mirabell.   We have won immortal Fame now, if we leave 'em.

Pinac.   You have, but we have lost.

Mirabell.   *Pinac*, Thou are cozen'd;
I know they Love ye; and to gain ye handsomly,
Not to be thought to yeeld, they would give millions;
Their Fathers willingness, that must needs shew ye.

Pinac.   If I thought so——

Mirabell.   Ye shall be hang'd, ye Recreant,
Would ye turn Renegado now?

Bellure.   No let's away, Boyes,
Out of the Air, and tumult of their Villanies;
Though I were married to that Grashopper,   70
And had her fast by th' legs I should think she would cozen me.

Enter a young Factor.

Factor.   Monsieur *Mirabel*, I take it?

Mirabell.   Y'are ith' right, sir.

Factor.   I am come to seek ye, sir; I have been at your Fathers,
And understanding you were here——

Mirabell.   Ye are welcome:
May I crave your name?

Factor.   *Fosse*, Sir, and your servant;
That you may know me better, I am Factor
To your old Merchant, *Leverdure.*

Mirabell.   How do's he?

Factor.   Well, sir, I hope: he is now at *Orleance*,
About some business.

Mirabell.   You are once more welcom.
Your Master's a right honest man; and one   80

68 now] F2; no F°

322

I am much beholding too, and must very shortly
Trouble his love again.
Factor.   You may be bold, sir.
Mirabell.   Your business if you please now?
Factor.   This it is, sir.
I know ye well remember in your Travel
A *Genoa* Marchant.
Mirabell.   I remember many.
Factor.   But this man, sir, particularly; your own benefit
Must needs imprint him in ye: one *Alberto*;
A Gentleman you sav'd from being Murther'd
A little from *Bollonia*,
I was then myself in *Italie*, and supplide ye,   90
Though happely, you have forgot me now.
Mirabell.   No, I remember ye,
And that *Alberto* too: a noble Gentleman:
More to remember, were to thanck myself, Sir.
What of that Gentleman?
Factor.   He is dead.
Mirabell.   I am sorry.
Factor.   But on his death bed, leaving to his Sister
All that he had beside some Certaine Jewells,
Which with a Ceremony, he bequeathd to you,
In grateful memory: he commanded strictly
His Sister, as she lov'd him and his peace,
To see those Jewells safe, and true deliverd;   100
And with them, his last Love. She, as tender
To observe this wil, not trusting friend, nor Servant,
With such a weight, is come her self to *Paris*
And at my Masters House.
Mirabell.   You tell me a wonder.
Factor.   I tell ye a truth, Sir: She is young, and handsom,
And well attended: of much State, and Riches;
So loving, and obedient to her Brother;
That on my Conscience, if he had given her also,
She would most willingly have made her tender.
Mirabell.   May not I see her?

323

Factor.   She desires it hartily.   110

Mirabell.   And presently?

Factor.   She is now about some Business,
Passing Accompts of some few debts here owing,
And buying Jewells of a Merchant.

Mirabell.   Is she wealthie?

Factor.   I would ye had her, Sir, at all adventure.
Her Brother had a main State.

Mirabell.   And faire too?

Factor.   The prime of all those parts of *Italie*,
For Beautie, and for Curtesie.

Mirabell.   I must needs see her.

Factor.   'Tis all her Business, Sir. Ye may now see her,
But to morrow will be fitter for your visitation;
For she is not yet prepared.

Mirabell.   Onely, her sight, Sir.   120
And when you shall think fit for further visit.

Factor.   Sir, ye may see her; and Ile wayt your Coming.

Mirabell.   And Ile be with ye instantly. I know the house,
Mean time, my love, and thanks, Sir.

Factor.   Your poore Servant.

                                     Exit.

Pinac.   Thou hast the strangest Luck: What was that *Alberto*?

Mirabell.   An honest noble Marchant, 'twas my chance
To rescue from some Rogues had almost slain him;
And he in kindness to remember this.

Bellure.   Now we shall have you,
For all your protestations, and your forwardness,
Finde out strange Fortunes in this Ladies eyes,   130
And new enticements to put off your journey;
And who shall have honor then?

Mirabell.   No, no, never fear it:
I must needs see her, to receive my Legacy.

Bellure.   If it be tide up in her smock, Heaven help thee:
May not we see too?

Mirabell.   Yes, afore we go:
I must be known my self e'er I be able

To make thee welcom: wouldst thou see more women?
I thought you had been out of love with all.
Bellure.   I may be,
I finde that, with the least encouragement:
Yet I desire to see whether all Countries   140
Are naturally possess'd with the same spirits;
For if they be, I'll take a Monastery,
And never Travel; for I had rather be a Frier,
And live mewed up, then be a fool, and flouted.
Mirabell. Well, well, I'll meet ye anon; then tell you more,
     Boys;
How e'er, stand prepar'd, prest for our journey;
For certain, we shall go, I think, when I have seen her,
And view'd her well.
Pinac.   Go, go, and we'll wait for ye;
Your fortune directs ours.
Bellure.   You shall finde us ith' Tavern,
Lamenting in Sack and Suger for our losses;   150
If she be right Italian, and want servants,
You may prefer the properest man. How I
Could worry a woman now?
Pinac.   Come, come, leave prating;
Ye may have enough to do, without this boasting.

                                              Exeunt.

          Enter Lugier, de-Gard, Rosalura *and* Lillia.   [V.] iii

Lugier.   This is the last adventure.
de Gard.   And the happiest,
As we hope too.
Rosalura.   We should be glad to finde it.
Lylia-Biancha.   Who shall conduct us thither?
Lugier.   Your man is ready,
For I must not be seen; no, nor this Gentleman;
That may beget suspicion: all the rest
Are people of no doubt; I would have ye, Ladies,

                137 thee] F2; thou F°

                      325

Keep your old liberties, and as we instruct ye:
Come, look not pale; you shall not lose your wishes;
Nor beg 'em neither: but be your selves, and happy.

Rosalura.   I tell ye true, I cannot hold off longer,   10
Nor give no more hard language.

de Gard.   You shall not need.

Rosalura.   I love the Gentleman, and must now show it;
Shall I beat a propper man out of heart?

Lugier.   There's none advises ye.

Lylia-Biancha.   'Faith I repent me too.

Lugier.   Repent, and spoil all.
Tell what ye know, ye had best.

Lylia-Biancha.   I'll tell what I think;
For if he ask me now, if I can love him,
I'll tell him yes, I can: The man's a kinde man;
And out of his true honesty affects me;
Although he plaid the fool, which I requited;
Must I still hold him at the staves end?

Lugier.   You are two strange women.   20

Rosalura.   We may be, if we fool still.

Lugier.   Dare ye beleeve me?
Follow but this advice I have set you in now,
And if ye lose: would ye yeeld now so basely?
Give up without your honors saved?

de Gard.   Fie, Ladies.
Preserve your freedom still.

Lylia-Biancha.   Well, well, for this time.

Lugier.   And carry that full state.

Rosalura.   That's as the winde stands:
If it begin to chop about, and scant us;
Hang me, but I know what Ile do: come direct us,
I make no doubt, we shall do handsomly.

de Gard.   Some part o'th' way, we'll wait upon ye, Ladies;   30
The rest your man supplies.

Lugier.   Do well, I'll honor ye.

                              Exeunt.

18 affects] F2; affect F°

Enter Factor *and* Mirabel, Oriana [*disguised*] *and*   [V.] iv
two Merchants [*above*].

Factor.   Look ye, Sir, there she is, you see how busie;
   Methinks you are infinitely bound to her, for her journey.
Mirabell.   How gloriously she shews? She is a tall woman.
Factor.   Of a fair Size, sir. My Master not being at home,
   I have been so out of my wits, to get her company:
   I mean, sir, of her own fair Sex, and fashion.
Mirabell.   A far off, she is most fair too.
Factor.   Neer, most Excellent.
   At length, I have entreated two fair Ladies,
   And happily you know 'em: the young daughters
   Of Monsieur *Nantolet.*
Mirabell.   I know 'em well, sir.   10
   What are those? Jewels?
Factor.   All.
Mirabell.   They make a rich shew!
Factor.   There is a matter of ten thousand pounds too
   Was owing here: you see those Merchants with her;
   They have brought it in now.
Mirabell.   How handsomly her shape shews?
Factor.   Those are still neate: your Italians are most curious:
   Now she looks this way.
Mirabell.   She has a goodly presence.
   How full of curtesie? Well, sir, I'll leave ye.
   And if I may be bold to bring a friend or two;
   Good noble Gentlemen——
Factor.   No doubt, ye may, sir.
   For you have most command.
Mirabell.   I have seen a wonder.   *Exit.* 20
Oriana.   Is he gon?
Factor.   Yes.
Oriana.   How?
Factor.   Taken to the utmost.
   A wonder dwels about him.
Oriana.   He did not guess at me?

Factor.   No, be secure; ye shew another woman.
　He is gone to seek his friends.
Oriana.   Where are the Gentlewomen?

Enter Rosalura, Lillia, *Servant.*

Factor.　　　　　　　　　Here, here, now they are come,
　Sit still, and let them see ye.
Rosalura.　　　　　　　　Pray ye, where's my friend, Sir?
Factor.   She is within, Ladies, but here's another Gentlewoman;
　A stranger to this Towne: so please you visit her,
　'Twill be well taken.
Lylia-Biancha.　　　　Where is she?
Factor.　　　　　　　　There, Above; Ladies.
Servant.   'Bless me: what Thing is this? two Pinacles,   30
　Upon her pate! Is't not a glode to catch Wood-cocks?
Rosalura.   Peace, ye rude knave.
Servant.　　　　　　　What a bouncing Bum she has too?
　There's Saile enough for a Carreck.
Rosalura.　　　　　　　What is this Lady?
　For as I live, she is a goodly woman.
Factor.   Ghess, ghess.
Lylia-Biancha.　　　　I have not seen a nobler Presence.
Servant.   'Tis a lustie wench: now could I spend my forty-pence,
　With all my heart, to have but one fling at her;
　To give her but a washing blow.
Lylia-Biancha.　　　　　　Ye Rascall.
Servant.   I that's all a man has, for's goodwill: 'twil be long
　　enough,
　Before ye cry come *Anthonie*, and kiss me.   40
Lylia-Biancha.   Ile have ye whipt.
Rosalura.　　　　　　　Has my friend seen this Lady?
Factor.   Yes, yes, and is well known to her.
Rosalura.   I much admire her Presence.
Lylia-Biancha.　　　　　　Soe do I too:
　For I protest, she is the handsomest,

25 Rosalura] *Rosaluce* Fº; Rosalure F2　　26 my friend] *i.e.*, Oriana
31 glode] *i.e.*, glade (*O.E.D.*)　　　　34 she is] Dyce; she's Fº–F2

328

The rarest, and the newest to mine eie
That ever I saw yet.
Rosalura.   I long to know her;
My friend shall doe that kindness.
Oriana.   So she shall Ladies.
Come, pray ye come up.
Rosalura.   O, me.
Lylia-Biancha.   Hang me if I knew her:
Were I a man my self, I should now love ye;
Nay, I should doate.
Rosalura.   I dare not trust mine eies;   50
For as I live ye are the strangest alter'd:
I must come up to know the truth.
Servant.   So must I, Lady;
For I am a kind of unbeleever too.
Lylia-Biancha.   Get ye gon, Sirrah;
And what ye have seen, be secret in: you are paid else;
No more of your long tongue.
Factor.   Will ye goe in Ladies,
And talke with her. These venturers will come strait:
Away with this fellow.
Lylia-Biancha.   There, Sirrah, goe, disport ye.
Servant.   I would the Trunck-hos'd woman would goe with me.

                                        Exeunt.

                  Enter Mirabel, Pinac, Bellure.   [V.] v

Pinac.   Is she so glorious handsome?
Mirabell.   You would wonder:
Our Women look like Gipsies, like Gills to her:
Their Clothes and fashions beggerly, and Bankrupt:
Base, old, and scurvy.
Bellure.   How lookes her face?
Mirabell.   Most heavenly:
And the becoming-motion of her Bodie
So setts her off.
Bellure.   Why then we shall stay.

                         329

Mirabell.   Pardon me:
  That's more then I know: if she be that Woman,
  She appeares to be——
Bellure.   As 'tis impossible.
Mirabell.   I shall then tell ye more.
Pinac.   Did ye speake to her?
Mirabell.   No, no, I onely saw her: She was busie: 10
  Now I goe for that end: And mark her (Gentlemen)
  If she appear not to ye, one of the sweetest,
  The handsomest: the fayrest, in behaviour.
  We shall meet the two wenches there too, they come to visit her,
  To wonder, as we doe.
Pinac.   Then we shall meet 'em.
Bellure.   I had rather meet two Beares.
Mirabell.   There you may take your leaves, dispatch that business,
  And as ye find their humours——
Pinac.   Is your Love there too?
Mirabell.   No certain, she has no great heart to set out againe.
  This is the house, Ile usher ye?
Bellure.   Ile bless me,   20
  And take a good heart if I can.
Mirabell.   Come, nobly.

                                              Exeunt.

              Enter Factor, Rosalura, Lillia, Oriana [, *Boy*].   [V.] vi

Factor.   They are come in: Sit you two off, as Strangers,
  There Ladie: where's the Boy? be readie, Sirrha,
  And cleere your Pipes, the Musick now: they enter.

           Musick, then Enter Mirabell, Pinac *and* Bellure.

Pinac.   What a State she keepes? how far off they sit, from her?
  How rich she is, I marry, this shewes bravely.
Bellure.   She is a lusty wench: and may allure a good man,
  But if she have a Tongue, Ile not give two pence for her:
  There sits my Fury: how I shake to see her.

          0.1 Rosalura] *Rosaluce* F°; Rosalure F 2

                              330

Factor.   Madam this is the Gentleman.
Mirabell.   How sweet she kisses?
She has a Spring dwells on her lipps: a paradize: 10
   This is the Legacie?

Song

From the honor'd dead I bring
Thus his love and last offring.
Take it nobly, 'tis your due,
From a friendship ever true.
From a faith &c.

Oriana.   Most noble Sir,
   This from my now dead Brother, as his love,
   And gratefull memory of your great benefit:
   From me my thanks, my wishes, and my Service.
   Till I am more acquainted I am silent,   20
   Onely I dare say this, you are truly noble.
Mirabell.   What should I think?
Pinac.   Think ye have a handsome fortune,
   Would I had such another.
Rosalura.   Ye are well mett Gentlemen;
   We heare ye are for Travell?
Pinac.   Ye heare true, Ladie,
   And come to take our Leaves.
Lylia-Biancha.   Wee'll along with ye,
   We see you are growne so witty by your Journey,
   We cannot choose but step out too: This Lady,
   We mean to wait upon as far as *Italy.*
Bellure.   I'll travel into *Wales*; amongst the Mountains,
   I hope they cannot finde me.
Rosalura.   If you go further;   30
   So good, and free society we hold ye,
   We'll jog along too.
Pinac.   Are ye so valiant Lady?
Lylia-Biancha.   And we'll be merry, Sir, and laugh.

*30 I] *stet* Fº–F2

Pinac.   It may be
  We'll go by Sea.
Lylia-Biancha.   Why 'tis the onely voyage;
  I love a Sea-voyage, and a blustring Tempest;
  And let all split.
Pinac.   This is a dainty Damosel:
  I think 'twill tame ye: can ye ride post?
Lylia-Biancha.   O excellently: I am never weary that way:
  A hundred mile a day is nothing with me.
Bellure.   I'll travel under ground: do you hear (sweet Lady?)   40
  I finde it will be dangerous for a woman.
Rosalura.   No danger, sir, I warrant; I love to be under.
Bellure.   I see she will abuse me all the world over:
  But say we pass through *Germany*, and drink hard?
Rosalura.   We'll learn to drink and swagger too.
Bellure.   She'll beat me.
  Lady, I'll live at home.
Rosalura.   And I'll live with thee;
  And we'll keep house together.
Bellure.   I'll keep hounds first;
  And those I hate right hartily.
Pinac.   I go for *Turky*,
  And so it may be up into *Persia*.
Lylia-Biancha.   We cannot know to much, I'll travel with ye.   50
Pinac.   And you'll abuse me?
Lylia-Biancha.   Like enough.
Pinac.   'Tis dainty.
Bellure.   I will live in a bawdy-house.
Rosalura.   I dare come to ye.
Bellure.   Say, I am dispos'd to hang my self?
Rosalura.   There I'll leave ye.
Bellure.   I am glad I know how to
  Avoid ye.
Mirabell.   May I speak yet?
Factor.   She beckons to ye.
Mirabell.   Lady, I could wish, I knew to recompence,
  Even with the service of my life, those paines,

332

And those high favours you have thrown upon me;
Till I be more desertful in your eye;
And till my duty shall make known I honor ye: 60
Noblest of Women, do me but this favour,
To accept this back again, as a poor testimony.

Oriana.   I must have you too with 'em; else the Will,
That says they must rest with ye, is infring'd, sir;
Which pardon me, I dare not do.

Mirabell.   Take me then;
And take me with the truest love.

Oriana.   'Tis certain,
My Brother lov'd ye dearly, and I ought
As dearly to preserve that love. But, Sir;
Though I were willing; these are but your Ceremonies.

Mirabell.   As I have life, I speak my soul.

Oriana.   I like ye.   70
But how you can like me, without I have Testimony,
A Stranger to ye——

Mirabell.   I'll marry ye immediately.
A fair State, I dare promise ye.

Bellure.   Yet she'll cozen thee.

Oriana.   Would some fair Gentlemen durst promise for ye.

Mirabell.   By all that's good——

Enter la-Castre, Nantolet, Lugier, *and* de-Gard.

All.   And we'll make up the rest, Lady.

Oriana.   Then *Oriana* takes ye; nay, she has caught ye;
If ye start now let all the World cry shame on ye:
I have out Travell'd ye.

Bellure.   Did not I say she would cheat thee?

Mirabell.   I thank ye, I am pleas'd ye have deceived me;
And willingly I swallow it, and joy in't;   80
And yet perhaps I knew ye: whose plot was this?

Lugier.   He is not asham'd that cast it: he that executed
Followed your Fathers will.

Mirabell.   What a world's this,

81 knew] Sympson; know F⁰–F 2

333

Nothing but craft, and cozenage?

Oriana. Who begun, sir?

Mirabell. Well; I do take thee upon meer Compassion;
And I do think, I shall love thee. As a Testimony,
I'll burn my book and turn a new leafe over.
But these fine clothes you shall wear still.

Oriana. I obey you, sir, in all.

Nantolet. And how! How, daughters! What say you to these
Gentlemen?
What say ye, Gentlemen, to the Girles?

Pinac. By my troth——if she can love me—— 90

Lylia-Biancha. ——How long?

Pinac. Nay, if once ye love——

Lylia-Biancha. Then take me,
And take your chance.

Pinac. Most willingly, ye are mine, Lady:
And if I use ye not, that ye may love me——

Lylia-Biancha. A Match y'faith.

Pinac. Why now ye travel with me.

Rosalura. How that thing stands?

Bellure. It will, if ye urge it.
'Bless your five wits.

Rosalura. Nay, 'prethee stay, I'll have thee.

Bellure. You must ask me leave first.

Rosalura. Wilt thou use me kindly;
And beat me but once a week?

Bellure. If ye deserve no more.

Rosalura. And wilt thou get me with child?

Bellure. Dost thou ask me seriously?

Rosalura. Yes indeed do I. 100

Bellure. Yes, I will get thee with child: Come presently,
And't be but in revenge, I'll do thee that curtesie.
Well, if thou wilt fear God, and me; have at thee.

Rosalura. I'll love ye, and I'll honor ye.

Bellure. I am pleas'd then.

Mirabell. This *Wild-Goose-Chase* is done, we have won o' both
sides.

Brother, your love: and now to Church of all hands;
Let's lose no time.
Pinac.   Our Travelling, lay by.
Bellure.   No more for *Italy*; for the *Low-Countries*, I.

                                                        Exeunt.

                    FINIS.

                *108 I] Sympson; *om.* Fº–F2

335

TEXTUAL NOTES

DRAMMATIS PERSONAE

PETELLA...*Shanck*.] The descriptive phrase 'their waiting-woman' sufficiently identifies Petella. In F°, however, 'Their Servant Mr *Shanck*.' is printed as a unit on the same line but after a space. This duplication appears to be a compositorial misunderstanding that has misled editors. John Shanck was a well-known comedian, specializing in clown's parts, and therefore should be assigned the role of the loose-talking impertinent Servant to the two daughters (although properly Servant only to Lilia-Biancha, since in II.ii he calls himself her groom). G. E. Bentley (*Jacobean Stage*, II (1941), 562ff) apparently accepts Shanck as taking the part of Petella, instead, and he speculates that Shanck was allowed to gag her lines, this being a mute part. Dyce first suggested that 'Their Servant' might be the Servant to Lilia-Biancha, but he felt that Shanck probably doubled the role with that of Petella. Neilson conflates the entry and makes Petella the servant played by Shanck; Spencer assigns Petella to Shanck and omits mention of a servant; Bentley's edition, alone, separates Petella from the Servant and lists each as an individual, but his descriptive cast of characters is his own and omits the actors' names. It is perhaps significant that no actor is assigned the part of Mariana or of Petella. That some boy played Petella, not the mature comedian John Shanck, should be obvious; that this boy doubled the parts of Petella and Mariana, and probably one of the four women, is probable.

I.i

25 saving, let...high.] The F° punctuation, which begins a new sentence with 'Let', thus associates 'Let the Sea grow high' with 'This *Ordinarie* can fit 'em of all Sizes', a not impossible meaning, something like: when the wine flows freely, both high and low ('all Sizes') are suited by this expensive ordinary. But the usual editorial view that puts 'Let the Sea grow high' in apposition to 'And then hang saving' is probably correct, on the analogy of V.vi.35–6: 'I love a Sea-voyage, and a blustring Tempest; | And let all split.' The transposition of the punctuation effects this sense.

I.ii

48 over-eyd]   Since Weber, 'over-hied' has been the universal emendation; nevertheless, it is so suspect as almost certainly to be wrong. F° 'over-eyd' (F2 'over-ey'd') is listed in *O.E.D.* under various senses such as 'to cast one's eye over', 'to watch', 'observe', which are appropriate here: whereas *O.E.D.* cites 'over-hied' as 'to overtake by hastening after', and notes only the emended reading in the *Chase* as the sole example for 'to leave behind by hastening on', a quite contrary sense, and adds the superfluous comment 'rare'. It seems clear that in contemporary usage 'over-hied' cannot mean what the editors think it does. On the other hand, by 'over-eyd' de Gard is assuring La-Castre that when he took leave of his son not eight hours since, he observed that Mirabel was well and lusty and will presumably be so upon his arrival. In context 'And over-eyd him' is essentially parenthetical and the main sense runs 'I took leave of him, ... having some slight busines | That forc'd me out o'th' way'.

I.iii

43 *Lugier*.]   This supplying of a missing speech-prefix seems required not only by the sense but also by the speech-prefix '*Na.*' before line 45, which should indicate (if it is correct) that some other speaker has intervened between it and the preceding Na. in line 37. Nevertheless, it is somewhat dashing that sig. C2 ends with line 42 and the catchword 'I' without prefix, just as the following word on C2ᵛ is 'I' without prefix, indicating that the error more likely arose in the copy than with the compositor, even though he could have marked his copy wrongly. (On sig. D1 the catchword is simply 'And', but the following word on sig. D1ᵛ has the necessary prefix '*Mir.* And'. Elsewhere in this first section, the catchwords consist of the prefix alone or the prefix and the first word of the dialogue.) The language of lines 43–4 suggests strongly that the speaker is Lugier, not the father. It should be noted that the other option to supplying Lugier's prefix is to give 'He's wondrous blunt' to La-Castre, whose prefix appears in the line below. This is a more desperate and less desirable expedient.

115 new]   F° 'now', accepted by all editors, makes sense in connection with lines 110–11, but not with the use of 'ripe' in line 113. Mirabel's discourse has emphasized the transitory ripeness of a melon (and a young woman). It follows that La-Castre's response that Nantolet's daughters are *now* ripe has little pertinence to Mirabel's contrast between ripeness today and rottenness tomorrow. On the other hand, 'new' is pertinent since it implies that the young daughters will keep their freshness longer than Mirabel implies. The subject is not specifically directed to the greenness of melons and women as implied by 'now', but about what happens after they have

337

reached ripeness. In secretary hand 'o' and 'e' are, of course, readily confused.

143 then, Father?] F⁰ 'then? Father, | I shall suffer' makes sense but, despite line 140¹, with 'Father' also beginning a sentence ('Father, what think ye?'), it produces a rhythm unlike that found with the more characteristic placement of 'Father' in the sentence in lines 145, 196, 200, as well as V.ii.13.

II.i

2 sought to] Modern editors Neilson, Spencer, and Bentley follow Colman and Weber as taking this as 'sought-to'. The rest, including Dyce, follow F⁰ without comment. The variant spelling 'to' for 'too' is a possible interpretation but is not encouraged by any other example of this spelling in the first printed section of the play.

19 of] Despite the concurrence of F 2 with F⁰ 'off', Langbaine emended to 'of', in which he has been followed by all editors. Because of the frequent confusion of 'of' and 'off' the emendation seems called for, especially when 'out of the way' completes the clause. At this point no specific proposals for further travel have been made, as they are later. Hence although the idiom seems possible, the sense of 'reschedule' or 'delay' in 'put off' is not pertinent.

126 mends] Editors since Colman (except Spencer) have printed ''mends', which may be right, but since a pun seems intended, the original 'mends' as the primary meaning seems sufficiently satisfactory.

II.ii

146 Mask] This reading of F⁰ and of all editors can be right only if one assumes that the F⁰ omission of a comma after 'hypocrite' in line 145 is an error and supplies it from F 2. This traditional emendation of line 145, involving the elision of 'that I' at the start of line 146, is certainly the simplest; otherwise one would need to read 'Maskt' or 'Mask'd' without preceding comma.

151 art] Sympson's probable sophistication of 'act' was followed up to Dyce. But no need exists to emend, in view of *O.E.D.* subst. III.13 defining the word 'art' as 'skilful', 'crafty' or 'artificial' conduct, or under 14 as an 'artifice', 'contrivance', 'strategem', 'wile', 'trick', 'cunning device'.

159–160 This...me,] The relining 'This...but | Hang...think | Or... me,' which Sympson started, has been accepted by every editor except Spencer. It is true that the F⁰ lines have many extra syllables (although such looseness can be matched elsewhere), and it is true that the page (sig. G 1) is very crowded and the reduction of three lines to two may have been a compositorial necessity in dealing with improperly cast-off copy. On the

338

other hand, if in line 159 'This is' is pronounced '''Tis', the line is by no means uncharacteristically loose for Fletcher, and line 160 presents no real metrical difficulties. It is perhaps best to be conservative here although admitting the possibility of compositorial relining to save space.

III.i

126 Lard]　F⁰, F 2 'Lare' is not identifiable in *O.E.D.* as a word with any application here despite its retention by Neilson (although he queries 'lard'), Walley–Wilson and Bentley, with a definition of 'to fatten'. Jokes about broths for men usually involve suggestions of building up their physical sexual abilities.

188 to]　All editors following Sympson's lead have quite naturally taken 'to' in context as 'too', a common variant spelling. This is very possibly the meaning; however, it should be noted that 'to' could also mean 'in addition to your wit' and still make sense, though more strained than 'too'.

434 Colours]　Sympson emended to 'Choler', a reading followed by some editors, including the conservative Spencer, but not Neilson, who only queries 'choler'. The plural, while nearer to F⁰ 'Colours', is not so idiomatic as the singular. One cannot say positively that this emendation is wrong, but it is suspect, especially when one considers 'there lost her Colours' (IV.i.147) applied to Mariana, although in a punning and figurative sense for defeat, and set by the same compositor. 'Discharge' may be taken in a military sense, as in the discharge of a cannon and thence to the more general notion of 'relieve myself of', although the sense of 'dismiss' is as probable, especially in the sense of *O.E.D.* vb 4d, or of 'to get rid of', 'do away with, abolish', or of 10a 'to clear off or acquit oneself of (an obligation) by fulfillment or performance'. 'Colours' may mean 'pretenses', and the sense of 'I have got rid of my pretences (in the plot) and am now an honest man' is not impossible. (It is true, however, that we have not seen the Servant as part of the plot, although he has been taken over by Lugier from his mistress for the purpose and knows all about the scheme.) But the word may also mean allegiance, the standard (flag) under which he has served. It is not, then, impossible to defend the original text. The Servant enters threatening retaliation for his beating, and in consequence reveals the plot to Mirabel. He then departs, satisfied that he has repaid the beating by repudiating his service to the cause of the plotters. The problem is perhaps clarified by two quotations from *Wit Without Money*. In the first, at II.iv.92, Shorthose says, 'You stirre my colour', a clear pun on the reddening in the face caused by choler; yet in III.ii.213 a passage reads, 'and coward like doe you lose your colours to um?', an apparent reference to defeat and the relinquishment of one's standard, although a distant reference to cowardly pallor may just possibly be present. What the two together suggest is that 'colours' could be used in

its simple military sense, in the plural, but in the singular as a pun on 'choler'. If so, at III.i.434 a punning double meaning might be present but the plural encourages the military sense as the primary one.

IV.i

15 dor me——] The full stop after 'ready' in the line above seems to have no bearing on whether F⁰'s 'do' is corrupt, or Sympson's emendation 'dor' to be preferred, for in either case the sentence need not be run on, and a new sentence can start with 'If'. The full stop, however, enforces the emendation of the F⁰ full stop after 'me' to a dash signifying broken-off speech; but in the sentence no problem is created since neither compositor uses the dash for this purpose. The original can, of course, be defended. 'If he doe come to do me' plus editorial dash allows Lilia-Biancha to finish the sentence in any way, such as 'if he comes to insult me, or to triumph over me', etc. The two different spellings of 'doe' (Compositor *X*'s favourite) and 'do' may have no significance even in the same line, since *X* does admit a number of 'do' forms, and indeed the same variation is found below in lines 35–6. If Sympson's emendation had been made merely as an ingenious guess, out of the blue, conservative editing would suggest its rejection. But 'If he doe come to do——' is not entirely natural, and 'dor' is strongly supported by *A Wife for a Month*, IV.v.4: 'To give her such a dor'. With this example, an editor may opt for the emendation 'dor' here.

135 Clothes_∧ . . . Gentlemen;] The syntax is not wholly clear here. It could be straightened out if one were to place a colon after 'Clothes' and a comma after 'Gentlemen', thus making 'Those Jewells are the Broakers' substantially parenthetical and 'I doe not know Gentlemen' to apply to 'how ye stand bound for 'em'. But this is not entirely natural and it seems better to retain the original relationship and to assume maximum elision: I do not know the price of the clothes; moreover, those jewels that come from the brokers, I do not know how you stand obligated, or in surety, for them.

141 fall] F⁰ 'one faith', followed by all editors in lieu of an acceptable substitute, was thought corrupt by Colman, who is quoted by Dyce. Weber, also quoted by Dyce, noted, 'The text seems to imply "possessing just as much faith and as large a stock of linen as a bankrupt haberdasher," whose credit is destroyed and his goods seized by the law.' This explanation is surely strained, for it is odd indeed to interpolate in this series anything but another article of female attire. The emendation 'fall', proposed here, may fit the purpose, defined by *O.E.D.* subst. VI.23 as an article of dress: (a) 'a band or collar worn falling flat round the neck in fashion during the seventeenth century' or (less likely) (b) 'a kind of veil worn by women, *esp.* one hanging from the front of the bonnet'.

IV.ii

62 call'd...fashion]   The Dyce emendation adopted by modern editors
reads 'fashion proper'. Smoother sense is made thus but a question of
idiom does arise. It may seem better to concentrate on 'call'd'. In context
with line 61 the sense is clear: Rosalura had not taken sufficient notice of
Belleur's parts, person, and fashion. In that context 'call'd' should follow
in some sort on 'take notice'. Under vb 11 *O.E.D.* provides, 'to name',
'give a name or designation to', and under 11.11a 'to give a name or title
to', 'to name', and in 11b 'to style', 'designate', 'term', 'address as',
'speak of as', 'to reckon', 'consider'. The Dyce emendation is less attractive when we have these other legitimate possibilities for meaning.

IV.iii

13 set]   As Spencer substantially remarks, although Mason's suggestion
of 'let' ('to hinder, suppress') is plausible and possibly even right (since
it refers most directly to 'Tenderness' in the preceding line, it is still
possible for 'set' to refer back to Mirabel's glory that he can kill beauty,
in which case line 12 would need to be largely parenthetical.

V.vi

30 I hope]   The reading of F⁰ has been doubted by most editors after
Colman and emended to 'In'. It is true that some mark has printed close
up against the upright of the capital 'I', but this mark seems to be an
imperfectly cast type. A keen eye could see the shadow of an 'n', but (1)
it would be a physical impossibility for an 'n' type to print so close to the
'I' since the first limb of the supposed 'n' would be covered by the upright
of the 'I'; (2) the height of this supposed 'n' is lower than that in the
regular fount. It is also of some interest that F2 took the reading to be
'I'. The final evidence, however, is the appearance of this same defective
type from V.vi.30 (sig. P2) in V.vi.88 'I obey' on sig. P2ᵛ. With the
suggestion of a printed 'n' thus removed, the only virtue of an unsupported
emendation to 'In' is that it goes better with the F⁰ punctuation of line 29,
'*Wales*...Mountains;', but a simple transposition of semicolon and comma
straightens out the crux.

108 I]   One of the arguments for the universal adoption of 'I', first added
by Sympson, is the fact that a comma follows '-*Countries*'; but given the
frequency of improper terminal punctuation in this section, the argument
would be worthless. Metrically, either reading is acceptable. The best
reason for the emendation is the fact that it closes the play with a couplet
and makes the last line less abrupt.

PRESS-VARIANTS IN F° (1652)

[Copies collated: BL (British Library, 644. k. 28), Bodl¹ (Mal. 25[6]), Bodl²
(2° H. 1.g. Art. Seld.), ICU¹ (University of Chicago, copy 1), ICU² (University of Chicago, copy 2), MH (Harvard University), NjP (Princeton University)]

GATHERING a (*inner forme*)

Uncorrected: BL, Bodl¹

Sig. a1ᵛ (Jephson)
  6 prayfe?)] prayfe?
 15 down,] down
 16 *won't*] *wont*
 16 go] goe
 18 giv'n,] giv'n
Sig. a2 (Harington)
  5 intranc'd] intranc't
 signature a2] a

GATHERING I (*inner forme*)

Uncorrected: Bodl¹

Sig. I1ᵛ
 III.i.229 Stale] ftale
 III.i.245 quiet] quit
Sig. I2
 III.i.272 triffles?] triffles.

GATHERING I (*outer forme*)

Uncorrected: BL, Bodl¹⁻²

Sig. I1
 III.i.188 Fortune;] Fortune
 III.i.191 him;] him,
 III.i.192 too,] too:
 III.i.195 thoufand] thofand
 III.i.198 *Pinac;*] *Pinac,*

III.i.204 perfection.] perfection
III.i.220 wonder!] wonder.
Sig. I2ᵛ
III.i.327 affection:] affection.
III.i.333 follow:] follow,

GATHERING K (*inner forme*)

Uncorrected: Bodl¹

Sig. K2
III.i.454 remedy;] remedy

GATHERING L (*outer forme*)

Uncorrected: Bodl¹

Sig. L1
IV.i.55 ſervice.] ſervice,
IV.i.68 Patern] Hatern
Sig. L2ᵛ
IV.ii.19 manners] manner
IV.ii.20 Curt'ſy] Curfy
IV.ii.40 counſeld] counſel
IV.ii.47 thee] the
IV.ii.49 vex'd] vez'd

EMENDATIONS OF ACCIDENTALS

Lovelace Commendation

45 –lover,] ~ ‸ F⁰   51 Vertue] Uertue F⁰

Jephson Commendation

3 have,] ~ ‸ F⁰

Harington Commendation

12 shift,] ~ . F⁰   16 o'th'] 'oth' F⁰
15 *Intrigu's*] *Intriqu's* F⁰

I.i

I.i] Actus Primus. Scena Pri-   26 Sizes,] F 2; ~ ‸ F⁰
   ma. F⁰, F 2   27.1 *Enter. . . .*] F⁰ *places at right,*
 1 *et seq. de Gard.*] s.p. are forms   *opposite lines 26–27*
   of *de Ga.*   32 Monsieur] F 2; *Monsieur* F⁰
 5 me.] ~ , F⁰, F 2   36 et seq. *La-Castre.*] s.p. are forms
 7 *Ordinary*——] ~ . F⁰, F 2   of *La Cas.*
 8 Twenty-Crown ‸] ~ ‸ ~ - F⁰;   38 men ‸] ~ , F⁰, F 2
   ~ ‸ ~ ‸ F 2   53 it!] ~ ? F⁰; ~ : F 2
13, 37 Mounsieur] *Mounsieur* F⁰, F 2   65 Charter.] F 2; ~ , F⁰
16 *Ordinary*] F 2; Ordinary F⁰   70 Company,] ~ . F⁰, F 2
20 mens lavish] F 2; menslavish F⁰   154 confident,] F 2; ~ ‸ F⁰

I.ii

I.ii] Scena Secunda. F⁰; SCENE   51 *Belleure*] *Belvere* F⁰, F 2
   II. F 2   56 me——] ~ . F⁰, F 2
 7 Venetian] *Venetian* F⁰, F 2   68 me:] ~ , F⁰, F 2
12 i'th'] F 2; i'th F⁰   86 Italian] *Italian* F⁰, F 2
22 Ha,] F 2; ~ ‸ F⁰

I.iii

I.iii] Scena Tertia. F°; SCENE III. F2
  1 *La-Castre.*] s.p. are forms of *La Ca.* except line 94, *La. Ca.*
  3 *Nantolet.*] s.p. are *Na.*
  42 H'as] F2; Has F°
  48 *Rosalura.*] s.p. are *Ros.*
  51.1 *Enter . . .*] F° *places at right, opposite lines 49–51;* F2 *centres as line 48.1*
  58–60 You . . . Ladies.] F°, F2 *line:* You . . . Sir; | 'Bless . . . welcom.

| 'Pray . . . Gentleman, | And . . . Ladies.
  60, 67 Monsieur] F2; *Monsieur* F°
  70–71 Beauties: . . . two,] ~ , . . . ~ : F°, F2
  119 Sir?] ~ . F°, F2
  154 doing—— She] doing——she F°, F2
  156 circumstance——] ~ . F°, F2
  165 *Lylia-Biancha.*] s.p. are *Lyl.*
  228 let's] F2; lets F°

II.i

II.i] *Actus Secundus. Scene Prima.* F°, F2
  21 wench——] ~ . F°, F2
  36 me——] ~ . F°, F2
  42, 89, 163 Monsieur] F2; *Monsieur* F°
  61 i'th'] 'ith' F°; i'th F2

129 cruelly:] F2; ~ ₐ F°
  159 there] F2: their F°
  160 *Enter . . .*] F° *places in two lines at right, opposite lines 158–159;* F2 *centres as line 158.1*
  160 *de Gard.*] s.p. are forms of *de Ga.*

II.ii

II.ii] Scena Secunda. F°; SCENE II. F2
  62.1 *Enter* Lilia, Petella.] F° *places in two lines at right, opposite lines 60–61;* F2 *centres as line 60.1*

63 *Lylia-Biancha.*] s.p. are forms of *Lil.*
  73.1 *Enter . . .*] F° *places at right, opposite line* 71; F2 *centres as* 71.1
  120 there is] F2; thereis F°
  145 hypocrite,] F2; ~ ₐ F°

II.iii

II.iii] Scena Tertia. F° SCENE III. F2
  9 Monsieur] F2; *Mousieur* F°
  12 'May] ₐ ~ F°, F2

16 secure——] ~ . F°, F2
  38 rul'd,] F2; ~ ₐ F°
  105.1 *Exeunt.*] *Exit.* F°, F2

III.i

III.i] *Actus Tertius, Scena Prima.* F°, F2

1 *de Gard.*] s.p. in III.i, sig. G2ᵛ are *de Ga.*; sig. H1 are *de Gr.*; sigs. H1–K2 forms of *De-G.*

3 *Lugier.*] s.p. in sig. G2ᵛ are *Lug.*; sigs. H1–I2ᵛ are *Leug.*; on sig. K1 after *Lev.* (III.i.347) are *Lug.*

20 Church ʌ] F2; ~ , F°

27 ye——] ~ . F°, F2

30 then——] ~ . F°, F2

31 ʌ *Exit.*] F2; ——*Exit.* F°

31.1 Rosalura] F2; *Rosaluce* F°

32 him.] F2; ~ ʌ F°

33 *Lylia-Biancha.*] F° s.p. are *Lel.*

37 us,] F2; ~ ʌ F°

49 again,] ~ . F°, F2

56 Reading?] F2; ~ , F°

58 Meetings,] F2; ~ ʌ F°

59 sure.] F2; ~ , F°

61 now.] F2; ~ : F°

67 *Mirabell*——] F2; ~ . F°

73 that's] F2; thats F°

81 mad-Morrysse] *possibly* Mad. Morrysse F°

90 away] *possibly* a way F°

96 *Exeunt.*] F2; *Exit.* F°

101 *Quicksilver*——] ~ . F°, F2

115 Compassʌ clear,] ~ , ~ ʌ F°, F2

124 *St.*] *St*ʌ F°; S. F2

125 Mettle,] F2; ~ . F°

131 Sister——] ~ - F°

135 *Enter* Mirabell.] F° *places to right, opposite line* 134; F2 *centres as line* 134.1

138 Devotions.] F2; ~ , F°

143 fair] F2; fare F°

155 Ladies——] ~ . F°, F2

173 understanding] F2; under standing F°

176 Excellence.] F2; ~ ʌ F°

177 rarely.] F2; ~ ʌ F°

182 likely.] F2; ~ ʌ F°

185 neither:] ~ ʌ F°, F2

186 unlikely.] F2; ~ ʌ F°

187 poynant:] ~ ʌ F°, F2

202 tricks——] ~ . F°, F2

211 *Enter a Boy.*] F° *places to right of line* 210; F2 *centres as line* 211.1

223 I...well.] F°, F2 *line:* I...yet | She is well.

247 Fortune;] ~ , F°, F2

248 Beauties——] ~ . F°, F2

257.1 *Exeunt.*] *Exit.* F°, F2

267 you?] ~ ; F°; ~ , F2

267 thousand,] ~ ʌ F°; ~ ? F2

272 *Enter....*] F°, F2 *centre as line* 270.1

279 What's...Gentlemen?] F°, F2 *line:* What's...matter? | What ...Gentleman?

280 Go] F2; go F°

286 Mark...nam'd,] F°, F2 *line:* Mark...me; | Where...nam'd,

286 nam'd,] ~ ; F°, F2

293–294 me; ...woman:] ~ : ... ~ ; F°, F2

295 asʌ seriouslyʌ] F2; ~ , ~ , F°

298 thee——] ~ , F°; ~ . F2

302.1 *Exeunt.*] *Exit.* F°, F2

306 'twil] *possibly* 't wil F°

314 *Enter....*] F° *places to right, opposite lines* 311–313; F2 *centres as line* 311.1

354 *Basto*; now,] Basto, ~ ; F°, F2

357 upʌ with approbation;] ~ ; ~ ~ ʌ F°, F2

358 patience;] ~ ʌ F°, F2

359 sir——] ~ . F°, F2

402 he——] ~ . F°, F2

406 ye——] ~ ; F°, F2

418 I'de] F2; Ide F°

433 Now...plain.] F 2 *line:* Now
...him. | Know...plain. (F⁰
c.w. *Ser.* Know)

442 -pots∧] ~ . F⁰, F 2

443 *Enter...* .] F⁰ *places to right,*
opposite lines 444–445; F 2 *centres*
as line 444.1

443 again.] *point doubtful in* F⁰;
wanting in F 2

455 *Lelia-Biancha's*] ~ , ~ F⁰; ~ ∧
~ F 2

458 now,] F 2; ~ ; F⁰

461 Here's] F 2; Hear's F⁰

IV.i

IV.i] ACTUS *Quartus.* Scæn. 1. F⁰;
Actus Quartus. Scena Prima. F 2

1, 10 *Lugier.*] *Leug.* F⁰ (c.w. *Lug.*
Then)

10 *Lylia-Biancha*] s.p. are *Lel.*

17 ye?] F 2; ~ . F⁰

29 Miserie.] F 2; ~ ∧ F⁰

31 me,] F 2; ~ : F⁰

34 fortune——] ~ . F⁰, F 2

37 upbraid∧ your Levitie,] ~ , ~
~ ∧ F⁰; ~ ∧ ~ ~ ∧ F 2

38 ye,] ~ ∧ F⁰, F 2

41 Lady——] ~ ; F⁰, F 2

44 ye:] F 2; ~ ? F⁰

47 ye;...ye:] ~ :...~ ; F⁰, F 2

51 Good∧] F 2; ~ , F⁰

63 glory,] ~ ∧ F⁰, F 2

64 ye.] ~ , F⁰, F 2

67 opinion!] ~ ? F⁰; ~ : F 2

76 ye.] ~ , F⁰, F 2

89 ye,] ~ ; F⁰, F 2

91 possible?] F 2; ~ . F⁰

95 hope's] F 2; hopes F⁰

100 Patience:] ~ , F⁰, F 2

109 hope——] ~ . F⁰, F 2

110 yet, deare∧] F 2; ~ ∧ ~ , F⁰

110 Sir——] ~ . F⁰, F 2

113 Friends——] ~ ? F⁰, F 2

113–114 Sir:...fast,] ~ ,...~ : F⁰;
~ ,...~ ; F 2

118 Not] F 2; not F⁰

134 what∧] F 2; ~ , F⁰

138 dust,] F 2; ~ ∧ F⁰

139–140 one;...Pumps,] ~ ,...~ ;
F⁰; ~ ,...~ , F 2

140 Petticote] Petcicote F⁰; Petticoat
F 2

153 Beautie.] ~ , F⁰, F 2

155 ∧*Exit.*] F 2; ——*Exit.* F⁰

158 Carren——] ~ . F⁰, F 2

160 Clothes∧] F 2; ~ , F

164 heart——] ~ . F⁰, F 2

167.1 *Exeunt.*] F 2; ——*Exit.* F⁰

IV.ii

IV.ii] *Scæn* 2. F⁰; SCENE II. F 2

3 *Bellure*∧] F 2; ~ : F⁰

4 Anger,] F 2; ~ ∧ F⁰

13 Monster,] F 2; ~ . F⁰

14 *Lelia-Biancha*] ~ , ~ F⁰; ~ ∧ ~
F 2

14 *Lylia-Biancha.*] s.p. are *Lel.*

21 look's] F 2; looks F⁰

34 grace——] ~ . F⁰, F 2

40 life!] ~ ? F⁰; ~ . F 2

53 Answer∧] ~ , F⁰, F 2

55 countenance!] ~ ? F⁰; ~ . F 2

56 do——] ~ . F⁰, F 2

59 Surquedry——] ~ ? F⁰, F 2

70 Tears——] ~ . F⁰, F 2

88 *Lylia-Biancha.*] F⁰ s.p. on sig.
M 1 are *Lil.*; on M 1ᵛ at line 93
is *Lel.*

92 him——] ~ . F°, F 2
116 Enter... .] F° places to right,

opposite lines 114–115; F 2 centres
as line 112.1

IV.iii

IV.iii] Scæn. 3. F°; SCENE III.
   F 2
10 heart——] ~ . F°, F 2
10 La-Castre.] s.p. are forms of la-
   Cast. except line 10 le-Cast. and
   line 82 Ca-Last.
16 de Gard.] s.p. are forms of de-
   Ga. except line 16 De-G.
31.1 Enter... .] F 2; F° places to
   right, opposite lines 30–31
38 Lylia-Biancha.] s.p. are Lel.
41 hide] F 2; hid F°
64 Heigh] F 2; Heig F°
82 her.] F 2; ~ ; F°
83 ye:] F 2; ~ ∧ F°
84 now?] ~ : F°; ~ ! F 2
93 Mad?] F 2; ~ . F° (point doubtful)
93 sure:] ~ ∧ F°, F 2

97 Hares] F 2; Haires F°
100 'em:] ~ ∧ F°; ~ , F 2
104 her?] F 2; ~ . F°
106 her:] ~ ∧ F°; ~ , F 2
109 thee.] F 2; ~ ∧ F°
109 ∧Exit.] F 2; ——Exit∧ F°
116 richest] F 2; rishest F°
117 France] F 2; France F°
117 me,...her;] ~ ;...~ ∧ F°, F 2
121 faine——] ~ . F°, F 2
123 tongue——] ~ . F°, F 2
124 well,] F 2; ~ . F°
134 Woman's] F 2; Womans F°
136.1 Biancha] Bianth. F°; Bianca F 2
149 Bellure,] ~ ∧ F°, F 2
153 certain;] ~ ∧ F°; ~ , F 2
155 Come,] ~ ∧ F°, F 2
155 a foole] F 2; ~ afoole F°

V.i

V.i] Actus Quintus. Scæn. 1. F°;
   Actus Quintus. Scena Prima. F 2
1 de Gard.] s.p. are De-G.

10 too,] F° point doubtful; ~ ∧ F 2
17 ∧stubborn] F 2; 'stubborn F°

V.ii

V.ii] Scæn. 2. F°; SCENE II. F 2
1 La-Castre.] s.p. here (sig. N 2)
   is La Cast.; elsewhere in V.ii is
   la-Cast. (sigs. N 2ᵛ, O 1)
11 'em——] ~ . F°, F 2
18.1 Enter... .] F° places to right,
   opposite lines 17–18; F 2 centres
   as line 17.1
23 heard] F 2; head F°
29 Treason!] ~ ? F°; ~ . F 2
34 'em,] F 2; ~ ? F°
51 Amazons] F 2; Amazous F°

57 Gentlemen,...ye;] ~ ;...~, F°
   F 2
58 have] F 2; Have F°
67 so——] ~ . F°, F 2
68 let's] F 2; lets F°
74 here——] ~ . F°, F 2
76 better,] ~ ; F°, F 2
94 dead.] F 2; ~ : F°
95 Sister∧] F 2; ~ . F°
113 Merchant.] F 2; ~ , F°
113 wealthie?] F 2; ~ . F°
115 had∧] F 2; ~ , F°

116 *Italie*] F 2; Italie F°
124 Servant.] F 2; ∼ ∧ F°
124 ∧*Exit.*] F 2; ——*Exit.* F°
128 you,] F 2; ∼ : F°
138 all.] F 2; ∼ : F°
139 that,] F 2; ∼ ∧ F°

144 flouted.] F 2; ∼ : F°
147 her,] F 2; ∼ . F°
152–153 You…now?] You…man. |
     How…now? F°, F 2
154 boasting.] F 2; ∼ ∧ F°

V.iii

V.iii] Scæn. 3. F°; SCENE III. F 2
0.1 Rosalura] *Rosalu.* F°, F 2
1 *de Gard.*] s.p. are *de-G.*
3 *Lylia-Biancha.*] s.p. are *Lil.*

3 ready,] F 2; ∼ . F°
29 handsomly.] F 2; ∼ : F°
31 supplies.] F 2; ∼ : F°

V.iv

V.iv] Scæn. 4. F°; SCENE IV. F 2
11 shew !] ∼ ? F°, F 2
16 goodly] F 2; gooly F°
19 Gentlemen——] ∼ . F°, F 2
32 rude∧] F 2; ∼ , F°
35 *Lylia-Biancha.*] s.p. are *Lil.*

46 ever∧] F 2; ∼ , F°
48 me.] F 2; ∼ , F°
50 not∧] F 2; ∼ , F°
51 alter'd:] ∼ ∧ F°; ∼ , F 2
58 woman∧] F 2; ∼ , F°
58.1 *Exeunt.*] *Exit.* F°, F 2

V.v

V.v.] Scæn. 5. F°; SCENE V. F 2
8 be——] ∼ . F°, F 2
10 busie:] F 2; ∼ ∧ F°
12 appear∧] F 2; ∼ , F°

13 behaviour.] ∼ , F°; ∼ : F 2
18 humours——] ∼ . F°, F 2
21 can.] F 2; ∼ : F°
21 nobly.] F 2; ∼ ∧ F°

V.vi

V.vi] Scæn. 6. F°; SCENE VI. F 2
2 Sirrah,] F 2; ∼ ∧ F°
3.1 *Musick,*] ∼ . F°; ∼ ∧ F 2
10 paradize:] F 2; ∼ ∧ F°
11 Legacie?] ∼ . F°, F 2
16+ (= 11) noble∧] F 2; ∼ , F°
19 Service.] F 2; ∼ , F°
29 *Wales*;…Mountains,] ∼ ,…
     ∼ ; F°, F 2
33 *Lylia-Biancha.*] s.p. are *Lil.*
38 ∧O] F 2; 'O F°
47 we'll] F 2; We'll F°
48 hartily.] F 2; ∼ : F°

54–55 I…ye.] *one line in* F°, F 2
72 *ye*——] ∼ . F°, F 2
75 good—] ∼ ∧ F°; ∼ . F 2
78 Did] F 2; did F°
79 pleas'd∧] ∼ , F°, F 2
83–84 What…cozenage?] *one line
     in* F°, F 2
84 sir?] F 2; ∼ . F°
90, 93 me——] ∼ . F°, F 2
91 love——] ∼ . F°, F 2
96 'prethee] F 2; 'prethe F°
104 ye.] F 2; ∼ : F°

HISTORICAL COLLATION

[NOTE: The following editions are herein collated for substantives: F⁰ (Folio 1652), F2 (Folio 1679), L (*Works*, 1711, ed. Gerard Langbaine the Younger and others), S (*Works*, 1730, ed. Theobald, Seward, and Sympson), C (*Works*, 1778, ed. George Colman the Younger), W (*Works*, 1812, ed. Henry Weber), D (*Works*, rev. ed. 1877, ed. Alexander Dyce), N (*The Chief Elizabethan Dramatists*, ed. William Allan Neilson, 1911), WH (*Early Seventeenth-Century Plays 1600–1642*, ed. Harold R. Walley and John H. Wilson, 1930), H (*Elizabethan Plays*, ed. Hazelton Spencer, 1933), B (*The Development of English Drama*, ed. G. E. Bentley, 1950). J. Monck Mason, *Comments on the Plays of Beaumont and Fletcher* (1798), has been consulted.]

Dedication] *om.* F2 (− C, D)　　　　Commendatory Poems] *om.* F2 (− C, D)

Lovelace Commendation

3 *Sceme*] scheme D　　　　　　25 A] As D (after *Lucasta*, 1659)

I.i

8 With...stomach.] F2, L–W *line:* With...Sir, | For...sto-mach.
8 a] *om.* F⁰
14 They'll...Sirha,] F2, L, S *line:* They'll...houre. | When... Sirha,
15 Lodging] lodgings W

25 saving, let...high.] ~ . Let... ~ , F⁰, F2, L
33 held] be held F2, C, W, H
48 over-eyd] over-rid S(*qy*), C; over-hied W+
71, 150 *Nantolet*] *Natolet* F⁰, F2
114 And] As W
130 and] and his S

I.ii

47 am] was F2, L
50 And...Gentlemen?] L *lines:* And my desire: | What... Gentlemen?

51 ye] you F2, L–B(−H)
69 witty] weighty S–B(−H)
83 Bilboes] Bæboes F⁰, F2, L
85 a] at a F⁰

I.iii

0.1 Nantolet, Lugier] *Natolet, Lugien* F°, F2
5 For] *Na.* For F°
9 Indeed] *La Ca.* Indeed S
33 Ye] You F2, L–D, B
43 *Lugier.*] *om.* F°, F2, L
45 *Nantolet.*] *om.* F2, L
70 The...Beauties:] *om.* S
84 these...Gentlewomen] this...Gentlewoman F°
99 another] anothers F°
107 gather] gathers F2, L, S
113 gon] grown S(*qy*)
115 new] now F°, F2, L+

121, 122, 123, 136, 140 ye] you F2, L–D, B
128 bread] thread W
129 a Nawl] an Awl F2, L+(−D, B)
143 then, Father?] ~ ? ~ , F°, F2, L–S, H
155 would] would but S
174 year] years F2, L–D, B
178 here] there F2, L
179 hope, but] hope's but D(*qy*)
193 that] this F2, L, S
221 fairest,] ~ ! C, W; ~ , D–B
222 I] then C, W
224 a] *om.* F2, L

II.i

17 would] would fain F2, L
19 of] off F°, F2
25 affable] a fable F°, F2, L
36 And] Then S
45 squibber] squib her L
72 quick] quickly L
98 leak-] ~ ‸ F°, F2, L+

109 Tie-all] Tiall F°, F2, L, C, W, D; tie S
126 mends] 'mends C–B(−H)
139 men] mens S–W
145 ²as] as a L
192 Has] Have F2, L+
202 about] above S(*qy*), C, W, D(*qy*)

II.ii

24–25 As...nothing?] C *lines:* As ...ye | Sit...nothing?
57–58 For...something.] W *lines:* For...still|Suspicious...something.
57 ever] *om.* S
73 fancie] fancies F2, L
77.1 *man*] Singing Boy W, D, B
93–94 If...recover.] W *lines:* If ...would | I...recover.
107 Now?] *om.* W
115 Up] Up, up S

127 have] *om.* W
138 do's] do F2, L+(−H)
151 art] Act S, C, D
156 I'll] 'll F°
159–160 This...me,] S+(−H) *line:* This...but | Hang...think, | Or...me,
160 ¹of] *om.* L
162 blurted] blurred F2, L, S
163 never] ever F2, L–W
163 mine] my C

II.iii

15 our] not C, W
39, 130 y'faith] 'faith F2, L
65 a] at L–W

87 y'faith] 'faith F2, L, S
100 touch] task C, W
116 will] *om.* F°, F2; I'll H

III.i

0.1 Lugier] *Leverdure,* alias, *Lugier* F°, F2 (alias‸)
126 Lard] Lare F°, F2, L+
140 Travail] Travel F2, L–W, B
161 conversions] conventions F°, F2, L
213 and] and's S
264 sigh] fight F°, F2, L, S(*but qy* sigh), C
281 your] you F°
309 about] be about L, S
311 Feeds...innocence?] S, C *line:* Feeds me, | And...innocence?
314 Lugier] *Leverduce, des Lugier, Mr. Illiard.* F°, F2 (*alias*)
324 falser] false C–D, B
353 in to] into F°, F2, L, S
368 By'r Lady] By 'Lady F°, F2, L, D–B

401 ye] you F2, L–D, B
405 he] ye F°
405 a tainter] attaint F°
434 Colours] Choler S–W, WH, H
434 by ye] b'y ye F2, L; be wi' you C, W, B; b' wi' you D; be wi' ye WH
443–444 And...him.] WH *line:* And...Ha! | 'Tis...him.
443–444 Ha!...him.] S, C *line:* Ha! 'Tis he | Again...him.; W *lines:* Ha! | 'Tis...him.
450 sometimes] sometime F°
452 they] them C–B(–H)
457 slave——plague] Slaves-plague F°, F2 (~ ‸ ~) L, H; Slave! plague S–B(–H)
458 a] *om.* W

IV.i

0.1 *Servant*] *Servants* F°, F2, L, S
15 dot] do F°, F2, L
51 needs] need F°
61 finde] mind F2, L
82 tender‸] ~ , F2, L–D, B; ~ ! N, WH

97 world-Sea] wold-Sea F2, L; World's Sea S–B(–H)
111 mine] my F2, L–W
116, 117 ye] you F2, L–D, B
141 fall] faith, F°, F2, L+

IV.ii

0.1 Rosalura] *Rosaluce* F°
20 staidly] steadily L
39 A] And S
41 out] on't H(*qy*)
44 cold] old D(*qy*)

52 stout] your stout F2, L–W
61 not] no F2, L, S
62 call'd] skill'd S(*qy*); marked C; culled W; conned *or* scanned Mason (*qy*)

62 proper fashion] fashion proper
   D–B
67 now] *om.* F 2, L
73 Furies‸] ~ ? C
104 ²ye] *om.* F 2, L, S
112 *1. Woman.*] *Wo.* F°, F 2, L–B

121 Ye] You F 2, L–D, B
124 good buy'ye] good b'ye F 2, L,
   N; God b'ye S, C; God b' wi'
   you C, D, WH, B; good buy
   ye H

IV.iii

13 set] let D (*after* Mason), N, WH,
   B
53, 70, 85 ye] you F 2, L–D, B
57 you] ye F 2, L–W
72 may] *om.* S
85 not] *om.* F 2, L

86 Why] What F 2, L, S
94 good] *om.* F 2, L
96 all mad] ~ - ~ D(*qy*)
118 is now] now is L–W
149 Relaps] a relapse W

V.ii

2 lie] I lie D(*qy*)
16 amble] ramble C
29 he] ye L, S
45 Rands] rounds C
68 now] no F°
77 *Leverdure*] *Le Verdure* S
101–102 And...Servant,]   S–D,

WH, B *line:* And...to | Ob-
   serve...Servant,
102 this] his F 2, L, S, D–B
104 And] And's S
124 *Exit.*] *Exit* Alberto. F 2
125 *Alberto*] *om.* F 2
137 thee] F 2; thou F°

V.iii

7 as] do as L–W

18 affects] affect F°

V.iv

31 glode] glade W (*after* Mason), D,
   WH, B
34 she is] she's F°, F 2, L, H

38 a] one B
38 washing] swashing C–D, WH
51 strangest] strangliest L

V.v

14 We...her,] S *lines:* We...two | Wenches...her,

V.vi

30 I] In C, W, N–B

54 There...ye.] S *lines:* There I'll |
Leave ye.

54–55 I...ye.] *one line in* F⁰, F 2,
L–B

56 Lady...recompence,] S *lines:*
Lady | I...recompence,

74 Gentlemen] Gentleman F 2, L–B

81 knew] know F⁰, F 2, L

108 I] *om.* F⁰, F 2, L

A WIFE FOR A MONTH

edited by
ROBERT KEAN TURNER

TEXTUAL INTRODUCTION

Apparently written shortly before, *A Wife for a Month* (Greg, *Bibliography*, no. 665) was licensed by Sir Henry Herbert on 27 May 1624. Herbert's entry attributes the work to Fletcher alone, and the Prologue speaks of the author in the singular; despite random attributions to Beaumont and Fletcher, there has never been a serious question of Fletcher's sole authorship. The play was performed at Court on 9 February 1636/7, and as it was included among the pieces forbidden by the Lord Chamberlain to be printed without the company's consent, it was evidently still in the repertory of the King's Men in 1641.[1]

In September 1646, *A Wife for a Month* was entered in the Stationers' Register along with the other copies that were to be included in the Beaumont and Fletcher Folio, and when that collection was published in the following year the play appeared as the third in Section 6 (F4–I2ᵛ), following *The Queen of Corinth* and *Women Pleas'd* and preceding *Wit at Several Weapons*. The printing of this section has recently been studied by Iain Sharp,[2] who discovered that its printer, previously unknown, was Moses Bell and that the formes containing *A Wife for a Month* were typeset by two compositors, probably in the following sequence:

Compositor	–	B	–	B	A	A	B	A	B	A	B	A
Forme	F1ᵛ:4		F1:4ᵛ		G2ᵛ:3		G2:3ᵛ		G1ᵛ:4		G1:4ᵛ	

Compositor	A	B	A	B	A	B	A	B	B	–	B	–
Forme	H2ᵛ:3		H2:3ᵛ		H1ᵛ:4		H1:4ᵛ		I2ᵛ:3		I2:3ᵛ	

Compositor	B	A	–	B	–
Forme	I1ᵛa	I1ᵛb:4		I1:4ᵛ	

---

[1] See Gerald Eades Bentley, *The Jacobean and Caroline Stage*, III (Oxford, 1956), 422–5. The play's authorship was studied anew by Cyrus Hoy in 'The Shares of Fletcher and his Collaborators in the Beaumont and Fletcher Canon (1)', *Studies in Bibliography*, VIII (1956), 129–46.

[2] I am grateful to Dr Sharp for allowing me to see his unpublished paper on Section 6. According to his findings, the regular order of printing was from the inside of the quire to the outside (i.e., $2ᵛ:3, 2:3ᵛ, etc.) and Compositor B is most

Thus Compositor *A* set II.ii.19–IV.iii.34, including the passage printed in the Appendix of this edition, and V.iii.125–80, and Compositor *B* the rest, including the Prologue and the Epilogue. Judging from the substantive and semi-substantive errors found in the takes of each – those which seem compositorial in character – the two workmen were of about equal proficiency, each making two or three mistakes a page, on the average. Neither was especially competent when it came to punctuating. These opinions might be modified, however, if we knew more about the effect of proof-reading on the printed text. Collation of twenty-one copies of F1 turned up but one variant, 'turue' for 'turne' at IV.iii.4, and it in only one copy;[1] indeed, in all Section 6, collation of seventeen copies has revealed only three variants reasonably certain to have resulted from press-correction. This one, then, may have originated with the incorrect replacement of a pulled type, in which case 'turne' would be the earlier reading. Strictly speaking, one cannot tell whether the pages of *A Wife for a Month* are all corrected, all uncorrected or a mixture of the two, although considering the general state of the text, the first is perhaps the best guess.

At first glance the F1 version appears neat enough; the compositors seem in general to have rendered faithfully what they found in their copy. In that manuscript, however, there was in some sections a play still being composed, and the aberrations caused by authorial changes and reworking were translated into

firmly distinguished from *A* by his preference for medial *Ile* as opposed to *ile* and for spaces before semi-colons (which he employs more often than *A*) and before question-marks. Because of the implications of type-recurrence evidence, I differ slightly from Dr Sharp in assigning 6G2^v and 6I1^{v}b to *A*.

[1] Bodleian Library B.1.8.Art., University Library Cambridge Acton a.Sel.19 and SSS. 10.8, Cyrus Hoy's copy, Newberry Library, University of Illinois 822/B38/1647 and q822/B38/1647 c.2, Boston Public Library, University of Minnesota Library, Duke University Library, Cornell University Library, Princeton University Ex 3623.1/1647q c.2, Pennsylvania State University Library, University of Virginia 570973 and 217972, University of Washington, University of Wisconsin–Madison, and University of Wisconsin–Milwaukee c.1–4. Virginia 570973 reads 'turue'. In the Pennsylvania State copy James P. O'Donnell found some annotations that seem to be 'prompt notes representing an early stage of readying the [play] for production'. None affects one's interpretation of the text. See 'Some Beaumont and Fletcher Prompt Annotations', *Publications of the Bibliographical Society of America*, LXXIII (1979), 334–7.

print. From time to time F1 shows Fletcher revising as he goes along and in one instance beginning to develop action in a certain way, becoming dissatisfied, and then striking out in a new direction. As far as is now known, Fletcher based *A Wife for a Month* on no specific source. Langbaine comments, 'The Character and Story of *Alphonso* and his Brother *Frederick's* Carriage to him, much resembles the History of *Sancho* the Eighth, King of *Leon*. I leave the Reader to the perusal of his Story in *Mariana*, and *Louis de Mayerne Turquet*'.[1] Langbaine seems to have in mind Sancho II of Castile and his brother Alphonso VI of León and Castile, but the resemblence between the story of the Spanish kings and Fletcher's plot is remote. Eugene M. Waith suggests that the account of the evil King Ferrand in Thomas Danett's translation of *The Historie of Philip de Commines* (1596) served as an inspiration for Fletcher's Frederick and that there are in the play some faint echoes of Neapolitan history.[2] Yet it is probably true that even if a specific source should be discovered Fletcher's own work would remain a major influence. To mention but a few parallels, the situation of the amorous bride and the reluctant bridegroom of the wedding-night scene (III.iii) reverses the similar scene in *The Maid's Tragedy*; the poisoned Alphonso's volcanic sufferings (IV.iv) are anticipated by those of the sleepless Thierry in *Thierry and Theodoret* (V.ii); and the honest courtiers have appeared before in *Philaster*. My notion is that when he began to write *A Wife for a Month* Fletcher was on such familiar ground that he needed to imagine little more than the general outline of the plot, experience providing the details of its development as he proceeded.[3]

[1] Gerard Langbaine, *An Account of the English Dramatic Poets* (Oxford, 1691), p. 216. Turquet says that according to earlier accounts Don Sancho, having overcome him in battle, 'dispossest his brother D. *Alphonso* of the Kingdome of Leon, and forced him to become a Monke, and to take upon him the habit of Saint *Benet*' (*The Generall Historie of Spaine*, trans. Edward Grimeston (London, 1612), p. 241). This occurs in Turquet's Liber 8, which may account for Langbaine's assignment of the wrong numeral to his Sancho. Juan de Mariana (*Historia General de España* (Madrid, 1617), 1 : 428) tells roughly the same tale as Turquet. Some details in II.iv may have been borrowed from Jonson; see the textual note on II.iv.11–12.

[2] *The Pattern of Tragicomedy in Beaumont and Fletcher* (New Haven, 1952), pp. 16n, 163.

[3] Alphonso's sufferings were compared not only with Valentinian's but also with the death scene in *King John* by Seward (*The Works of Francis Beaumont and John*

The most prominent signs of revision during composition are found in the following passages:

II.v.42–8

Concluding his argument in favour of dying young, in F1 Valerio adds after line 43 'Wee'l have a rouse before we go to bed friends'. At this point it apparently occurred to Fletcher that he should prepare further for the masque which is to follow in II.vi, this event having been mentioned only once before and then in passing (II.iv.12). He thus wrote a few lines about the masque and the dancing to come, after which he repeated Valerio's line about rousing before bed as line 47. If he cancelled the first use of this line, the cancellation was not observed.

II.v.50–II.vi.25.3

A conversation between Valerio and the three courtiers is broken off when music is heard. In F1 II.v concludes with these lines (Valerio is speaking):

> You shall have all Gloves presently.   *Exit.*
>   *Men.*   We attend Sir, but first we must looke to'th
> Doores.   *Kn[o]cking within.*
> The King has charged us.   *Exeunt.*

II.vi begins with speeches by two door-keeping servants who are having trouble controlling the crowd seeking admission to the room in which the masque will be presented. They are soon joined by the three courtiers and Tony the fool for twenty lines or so of comic dialogue ending with 'hark, the King comes' (line 25). These words imply the regular entrance of the king and the party attending the wedding of Evanthe and Valerio in the temple, yet the F1 stage-direction (II.vi.25.1ff) seems to call for a discovery:

Fletcher (London, 1750), I, xxxiff), and Clifford Leech (*The John Fletcher Plays* (Cambridge, Mass., 1962), pp. 100–4) finds similarities to *Henry VIII* in the Frederick–Queen–Evanthe triangle and in *A Wife for a Month*'s doorkeeping scene (II.vi). The latter he compares with *Henry VIII*, V.iv, a scene attributed to Fletcher by Hoy (*Studies in Bibliography*, xv (1962), 76ff).

A Curtaine drawne.

The King, Queene, Valerio, Evanthe, Ladies, Attendants,
Camillo, Cleanthes, Sorano, Menallo.

A Maske.

Cupid descends....

Camillo, Cleanthes, and Menallo are Valerio's courtier friends.
They are already on stage.

F1's confusion seems to result from an incomplete revision.
Evidently Fletcher's first idea was to send the three courtiers off
to the temple with Valerio, and II.v may have ended with the
pentameter

You shall have all Gloves presently.
Men. We attend Sir. *Ex.*

Fletcher also planned, one imagines, to begin II.vi with

Enter two Servants.

1 *Serv.* What a noyse.... *Knocking within.*

and to continue with comic door-keeping dialogue after the manner
of *The Maid's Tragedy* I.ii, the servants perhaps being augmented
by Tony – all this a rowdy prologue to the masque, which is the
main business of the scene. Why Fletcher subsequently decided the
courtiers were needed in the door-keeping sequence one can only
guess, but his means of introducing them into it is reasonably clear:
to Menallo's final speech in II.v he added the pentameter (mislined
in F1) 'But first we must looke to'th Doores. The King has charged
us'. This addition rendered the original *exeunt* redundant – it is
translated in F1 into an inappropriate *exit* for Valerio at II.v.51 –
and it seems also to have displaced the *Knocking within*, which
applies to the action of II.vi. Having made this change, he should
have removed the courtiers from the stage-direction preliminary
to the masque, but he neglected to do so. In fact, he also neglected
to change the direction from a discovery to a regular entrance as
the last line of his new dialogue – 'hark, the King comes' – implies
it is.[1]

---

[1] As the discovery space, with properties, is required for III.i, the next scene, its
employment here may have been awkward, yet presumably between this scene and

III.ii.119–III.iii.1

Having been told by Sorano that he is forbidden to make love to his bride, Valerio is left to pray for the relief of his suffering. Sorano has exited just before. The scene closes, and III.iii opens upon Frederick and Sorano, the latter reporting the effect the prohibition has had upon the hapless bridegroom. F1 renders the beginning of Valerio's soliloquy (III.ii.119ff) as

> Heaven be not angry, and I have some hope yet,
> And when you please, and how allay my miseries.
> *Enter Frederick.*

Despite the entrance the speech continues for eight lines, concluding with 'And when you please, and how, allay my miseries' once again (III.ii.127). Here it seems likely that Fletcher at first intended to conclude III.ii with the initial occurrence of this line, and to begin III.iii with Frederick alone. This proving unsatisfactory for some reason, Fletcher decided to bring Sorano as well into the opening of III.iii. As Sorano, however, had exited from III.ii only at line 118, the new scheme required that Valerio's speech should be lengthened. The first occurrence of III.ii.127 and *Enter Frederick* should have been cancelled; if a direction bringing both Frederick and Sorano on at III.iii.0.1 was ever written, it has been lost.

IV.ii.1ff

Fletcher seems to have begun this scene with only one situation in mind, a confrontation of Frederick and Valerio during which the former would be further revealed as a despicable tyrant and the latter as an honourable and courageous sufferer. Having written the dialogue for this encounter, the playwright was struck by a different inspiration, parallel scenes of Frederick's attempt upon Valerio's honour and Cassandra's upon Evanthe's, but to make the latter situation possible he needed Cassandra to become Frederick's

that there would have been an act interval during which properties could have been set. The apparent discrepancy here between a discovery and a regular entrance may thus be only an oversight, a failure to carry through the alterations made to the opening of II.vi.

instrument. He retained the first two lines of the scene (they send Podrano to fetch Valerio), inserted *Enter Cassandra* beneath them, and then presumably cancelled the original Frederick–Valerio dialogue, a cancellation that was not observed.[1] Fletcher then wrote the Frederick–Cassandra section (IV.ii.3–40) and revised the Frederick–Valerio interview along different lines from the first version, salvaging what he could from it, specifically lines 46–53 (cf. lines [10–19], Appendix). Cassandra's ineffectual seduction of Evanthe he handled in IV.iii.

V.iii.157–73

Valerio supposedly dead, the Lawyer, Physician, Captain, and Cutpurse seek Evanthe's hand, but their courtship swiftly concludes when they learn the consequences of marrying her. At V.iii.157 Evanthe tries to bring matters to an end. F1 has

> *Evan.* Come, your sentence, let me dye, you see Sir,
> None of your valiant men dare venture on me,
> A moneth's a dangerous thing.
>
> *Enter Valerio disguis'd.*
>
> *Fred.* Away with her, let her dye instantly.

But Evanthe is not taken away, and the disguised Valerio does nothing. Instead, Evanthe continues to address Frederick:

> Will you then be willing
> To dye at the time prefixt, that I must know too. . . .

Plainly there has been an omission. Very likely Frederick has once again offered to marry Evanthe counting on her acceptance because it will save her life, and Evanthe has accepted him but on the condition he has set for the others, his death at the month's end. Evanthe's speech continues from V.iii.159 through 172, and then Frederick's earlier line – 'Away with her, let her dye instantly' (V.iii.173) – is repeated. What seems to have happened here is that Fletcher first concluded this segment of the action with Evanthe's request for death, Frederick's angry order for her execution, and immediately upon that Valerio's entrance. It then

---

[1] These lines may be found in the Appendix, pp. 481–2.

struck him that the situation could be given one last twist, Frederick's offer of marriage and Evanthe's fatal acceptance. This idea Fletcher developed, but in what F1 prints Frederick's proposal has been lost. The first occurrence of line 173 should have been cancelled and Valerio's entrance should have been inserted before line 174, but the tidying-up was not done.

These instances of revision are marked by obvious irregularities in the text. It stands to reason, then, that the play contains other revisions not so marked or less clearly so, although in these cases the traces one thinks he sees may be those only of authorial carelessness or misinterpretation by some agent of transmission. At I.ii.49 it is suspicious that F1 omits Podrano from the stage-direction and gives him a speech apparently Camillo's. At I.ii.103 the stage-direction *Exit Lords* seems odd because Podrano is but a servant. In V.iii Castruchio's exits and re-entrances are by no means clear. The entrance-directions at III.iii.96.1 and V.iii.72 are placed eight lines higher by F1, possibly because some material was inserted after them. Whether or not these anomalies reveal more of Fletcher's revising hand, however, there seems little question that behind F1 lay an authorial manuscript considerably worked over.

Yet the F1 copy seems not to have been this manuscript directly but a transcript of it. According to Hoy's count, *A Wife for a Month* contains 176 of Fletcher's favourite *ye*'s, a lower number than any other of the unaided plays except *The Woman's Prize* (133), and Hoy suggests that the reduction from what was likely to have been a higher original number could have resulted from the intervention of Edward Knight, who was actively employed as book-keeper of the King's Men by 1624.[1] The F1 text does in fact have a few features that may be characteristic of Knight: 'gent.' stands not only for 'gentlemen' but also, unusually, for 'gentlewoman' (II.vi.16), as it does in Knight's transcript of *The Honest Man's Fortune*;[2] the spelling of *off* is 'of' as it is in one of Knight's addi-

---

[1] Hoy, *Studies in Bibliography*, VIII (1956), 141, 145.
[2] See J. Gerritsen (ed.), *The Honest Man's Fortune*, Groningen Studies in English 3 (Groningen, 1952), p. cvi.

tions to *The Soddered Citizen* (MSR, line 2210), in *The Hones, Man's Fortune* (I.i.234), and in his transcript of *Bonduca* (MSR*t* lines 487, 1336, 1560, etc.); and the spelling of *too* is occasionally 'to' as it is occasionally in *Bonduca* (lines 121, 897). What is remarkable is that if he copied Fletcher's draft, Knight preserved in his rendition many of the discrepancies the draft contained. While some of Fletcher's alterations may have baffled Knight, it looks as though he never set out to create a finished product; instead, he copied more or less everything he saw, perhaps because nearly every word – right or wrong, redundant or not – might be useful subsequently.[1] His version could not have served as the prompt-book; it must have been intended to furnish a reasonably clean, although unfinished, text for literary revision, after which the prompt copy would be inscribed from it. And there are a few signs that alterations were made on the transcript. At II.vi.4.1 F1's repetition involving Tony – *Tony following, and Foole following* – is unlikely to be a scribal lapse; it is a compositor's confusion arising from the substitution of a personal for a generic name. Similarly, the garble at III.ii.115 most probably is a compositor's attempt to deal with an unclear cancellation and substitution. But one imagines that most of the changes made to the transcript would have been deletions of discarded material or the repositioning of misplaced parts, both done so as to be clear to Knight but not always clear to the printer.[2]

The second and last seventeenth-century edition of *A Wife for a Month* appeared in the Folio of 1679. The editor of this collection, as usual, supplied the names of the principal actors: Joseph Taylor, Richard Robinson, Nicholas Tooley, Robert Benfield, John Underwood, and George Birch. This list is wrong in including Tooley, who had died almost a year before *A Wife for a Month* was

---

[1] In his prompt-book transcript of *Beggars' Bush*, 'Knight made a minimum effort to exercise his personal judgment in straightening out various of the tangles in the directions and the action and was generally content to copy what he found with the addition only of directions for properties and noises' (Fredson Bowers, '*Beggars Bush:* A Reconstructed Prompt-Book and Its Copy', *Studies in Bibliography*, XXVII (1974), 131).

[2] The evidence for revision is discussed more fully in my 'Revisions and Repetition-Brackets in *A Wife for a Month*', *Studies in Bibliography*, XXXVI (1983), 178–90.

licensed; it is also curious that John Lowin's name does not appear, as Lowin was performing regularly at the time of the play's first production. As Bentley points out, the cast may be that of another play altogether or it may be the right cast with some names omitted and one mistaken.[1] In either case the list does not inspire confidence in the accuracy of the F2 editor in this instance.

Nor do the changes he made to the text suggest very strongly that he had access to a version other than F1's. He or the F2 compositor improved the punctuation and repaired some obviously incorrect readings. Several of his alterations – e.g., 'face' to 'fann' (IV.ii.15) and 'what...him?' to 'that...him.' (IV.iii.132) – are shrewd and apparently right, but none seems beyond the capacity of a thoughtful reader. F1's repetition of II.v.47 is allowed to stand, its duplicate entrances for the three courtiers at II.vi.4.1 and II.vi.25.3 are retained, and the two versions of the meeting between Frederick and Valerio in IV.ii are reproduced. F1's early entrance of Frederick (without Sorano) after III.ii.119 and the repetition of III.ii.127 before the false entrance troubled him; his response was simply to eliminate the development of Valerio's speech (lines 120–6), recreating the problem of Sorano's entrance into III.iii. In general, F2 is the source of occasional improvements to the text, but the edition has no major effect upon it. An adaptation, Thomas Scot's *The Unhappy Kindness: Or A Fruitless Revenge* (London, 1697), although it follows *A Wife for a Month* fairly closely in some scenes, is ignored as making no contribution to the textual tradition of Fletcher's play.

Virginia Haas helped a great deal with the apparatus of this edition, and Bertram L. O'Neill very kindly answered my questions about court tennis. I am grateful to them and to the College of Letters and Science of the University of Wisconsin–Milwaukee for continued support. Unfortunately I did not learn of David Rush Miller's 1981 Tulane University dissertation, 'John Fletcher's "A Wife for a Moneth": A Critical Old-Spelling Edition', in time to make use of it.

[1] Bentley, *Jacobean Stage*, III, 423–4.

Prologue

You are welcome Gentlemen, and would our Feast
Were so well season'd, to please every Guest;
Ingenuous appetites, I hope we shall,
And their examples may prevaile in all
(Our noble friends); who writ this, bid me say,
He had rather dresse, upon a Triumph day,
My Lord Mayers Feast, and make him Sawces too,
Sawce for each severall mouth, nay further go,
He had rather build up those invincible Pyes
And Castle Custards that afright all eyes,   10
Nay eat 'em all, and their Artillery,
Then dresse for such a curious company
One single dish; yet he has pleas'd ye too,
And you have confest he knew well what to do;
Be hungry as you were wont to be, and bring
Sharpe stomacks to the stories he shall sing,
And he dare yet, he saies, prepare a Table
Shall make you say well drest, and he well able.

4–5 *all*ᴧ *(Our…friends);*| Dyce; *all*ᴧ *(Our…friends)*ᴧ F1; *all.*ᴧ *Our…friend,*ᴧ
F2

367

Alphonso, *true heir to the throne of* Naples, *elder Brother to* Frederick.
Frederick, *the reigning King, unnatural and libidinous Brother to*
  Alphonso.
Sorano, *a Lord, Brother to* Evanthe, Frederick's *wicked instrument.*
Valerio, *a noble young Lord, servant to* Evanthe.
Camillo, ⎫
Cleanthes, ⎬ *three honest Court Lords.*
Menallo, ⎭
Rugio, *a Lord* ⎫ *friends to* Alphonso.
Marco, *a Fryer* ⎭
Podrano, *a necessary creature to* Sorano.
Tony, *King* Frederick's *knavish foole.*
Castruchio, *Captain of the Cittadel, an honest man.*
Lawyer.
Physician.
Captain.
Cutpurse.
Citizens, Fryers, Guard, Attendants.

WOMEN.

Queen, *to* Frederick, *a vertuous Lady.*
Evanthe, *sister to* Sorano, *the chaste Wife of* Valerio, *or a Wife for
  a Moneth.*
Cassandra, *an old Bawd, Waiting-woman to* Evanthe.
Three City-Wives.
Ladies.

MASKERS.

Cupid.	Desire.	Distrust.	Ire.
Graces.	Delight.	Jealousy.	Poverty.
Fancy.	Hope.	Care.	Despair.
	Fear.		

The Scene Naples.]

Persons] based on the list in F 2

A WIFE FOR A MONETH.

Enter King Frederick, Sorano, Valerio, Camillo,
Cleanthes, Menallo, *and Attendants.*

Sorano. Will your Grace speak?
Frederick. Let me alone *Sorano,*
   Although my thoughts seeme sad, they are welcome to me.
Sorano. You know I am private as your secret wishes,
   Ready to fling my soule upon your service,
   Ere your command be on't.
Frederick. Bid those depart.
Sorano. You must retire my Lords.
Camillo. What new design
   Is hammering in his head now?
Cleanthes. Lets pray heartily
   None of our heads meet with it, my wife's old,
   That's all my comfort.
Menallo. Mine's ugly, that I am sure on,
   And I think honest too, 'twould make me start else.   10
Camillo. Mine's troubled in the Country with a feaver,
   And some few infirmities else; he looks againe,
   Come let's retire, certaine 'tis some she businesse,
   This new Lord is imployed.
Valerio [aside]. I'le not be far off,
   Because I doubt the cause.
         Exeunt Lords. [*Manet* Valerio, *retired.*]
Frederick. Are they all gone?
Sorano. All but your faithfull servant.
Frederick. I would tell thee,
   But 'tis a thing thou canst not like.
Sorano. Pray ye speak it,
   Is it my head? I have it ready for ye, Sir:

*14 This...imployed] *stet* F 1–2

Is't any action in my powre? my wit?
I care not of what nature, nor what followes.   20
Frederick.   I am in love.
Sorano.   That's the least thing of a thousand,
   The easiest to atchieve.
Frederick.   But with whom *Sorano*?
Sorano.   With whom you please, you must not be deny'd, Sir.
Frederick.   Say it be with one of thy Kinswomen.
Sorano.   Say with all,
   I shall more love your Grace, I shall more honour ye,
   And would I had enough to serve your pleasure.
Frederick.   Why 'tis thy Sister then, the faire *Evanthe*,
   Ile be plain with thee.
Sorano.   Ile be as plaine with you Sir,
   She brought not her perfections to the world,
   To lock them in a case, or hang 'em by her,   30
   The use is all she breeds 'em for, she is yours, Sir.
Frederick.   Dost thou meane seriously?
Sorano.   I meane my Sister,
   And if I had a dozen more, they were all yours:
   Some Aunts I have, they have been handsome women,
   My mother's dead indeed, and some few cozens
   That are now shooting up, we shall see shortly.
Frederick.   No, 'tis *Evanthe*.
Sorano.   I have sent my man unto her,
   Upon some businesse to come presently
   Hither, she shall come; Your Grace dare speak unto her?
   Large golden promises, and sweet language, Sir,   40
   You know what they worke, she is a compleat Courtier,
   Besides Ile set in.
Frederick.   She waights upon my Queene,
   What jealousie and anger may arise,
   Incensing her?
Sorano.   You have a good sweet Lady,
   A woman of so even and still a temper,
   She knows not anger; say she were a fury,

24 with all] Langbaine; withall F1; withal F2

370

I had thought you had been absolute, the great King,
The fountaine of all honours, place and pleasures,
Your will and your commands unbounded also;
Go get a paire of beads and learne to pray, Sir.   50

Enter Servant.

Servant.   My Lord, your servant staies.
Sorano.   Bid him come hither,
And bring the Lady with him.   [*Exit* Servant.]
Frederick.   I will wooe her,
And either lose my selfe, or win her favour.
Sorano.   She is comming in.
Frederick.   Thy eyes shoot through the doore,
They are so piercing, that the beames they dart
Give new light to the roome.

Enter Podrano *and* Evanthe.

Evanthe.   Whether dost thou go?
This is the Kings side, and his private lodgings,
What businesse have I here?
Podrano.   My Lord sent for ye.
Evanthe.   His lodgings are below, you are mistaken,
We left them at the staire-foot.
Podrano.   Good sweet Madam——   60
Evanthe.   I am no Counsellor, nor important Sutor,
Nor have no private businesse through these Chambers,
To seek him this way, o' my life thou art drunke,
Or worse then drunke, hir'd to convey me hither
To some base end; now I looke on thee better,
Thou hast a bawdy face, and I abhor thee,
A beastly bawdy face, Ile go no further.
Sorano.   Nay shrink not back, indeed you shall good Sister,
Why do you blush? the good King will not hurt ye,
He honours ye, and loves ye.
Evanthe.   Is this the businesse?   70

*47 absolute,] F2; ~ ᴧ F1   48 place] Colman (Sympson); playes F1–2
56 Podrano] *Podramo* F1–2   61 important] *i.e.*, importunate (Mason)

371

Sorano.   Yes, and the best you ever will arive at,
   If you be wise.
Evanthe.   My Father was no bawd Sir,
   Nor of that worshipfull stock as 1 remember.
Sorano.   You are a foole.
Evanthe.   You are that I shame to tell ye.
Frederick.   Gentle *Evanthe*——
Evanthe.   The gracious Queen Sir
   Is well and merry, heaven be thanked for it,
   And as I think she waites you in the Garden.
Frederick.   Let her wait there, I talk not of her Garden,
   I talk of thee sweet flower.
Evanthe.   Your Grace is pleasant,
   To mistake a nettle for a rose.
Frederick.   No Rose,   80
   Nor Lilly, nor no glorious Hyacinth
   Are of that sweetnesse, whitenesse, tendernesse,
   Softnesse, and satisfying blessednesse
   As my *Evanthe.*
Evanthe.   Your Grace speakes very feelingly,
   I would not be a hansome wench in your way Sir,
   For a new gowne.
Frederick.   Thou art all hansomnesse,
   Nature will be asham'd to frame another
   Now thou art made, thou hast rob'd her of her cunning,
   Each severall part about thee is a beauty.
Sorano.   Do you heare this Sister?
Evanthe.   Yes unworthy Brother,   90
   But all this will not do.
Frederick.   But love *Evanthe*,
   Thou shalt have more then words, wealth, ease, and honours,
   My tender wench.
Evanthe.   Be tender of my credit,
   And I shall love you Sir, and I shall honour ye.
Frederick.   I love thee to injoy thee my *Evanthe*,
   To give thee the content of love.
Evanthe.   Hold, hold Sir,

372

Ye are to fleet, I have some businesse this way,
Your Grace can nere content.
Sorano.   You stubborne toy.
Evanthe.   Good my Lord *Bawd* I thank ye.
Frederick.   Thou shalt not go, beleeve me sweet *Evanthe*,   100
So high I will advance thee for this favour,
So rich and potent I will raise thy fortune,
And thy friends mighty——
Evanthe.   Good your Grace be patient,
I shall make the worst honourable wench that ever was,
Shame your discretion, and your choyce.
Frederick.   Thou shalt not.
Evanthe.   Shall I be rich do you say, and glorious,
And shine above the rest, and scorne all beauties,
And mighty in command?
Frederick.   Thou shalt be any thing.
Evanthe.   Let me be honest too, and then ile thank ye.
Have you not such a title to bestow too?   110
If I prove otherwise, I would know but this Sir,
Can all the power you have or all the riches,
But tye mens tongues up from discoursing of me,
Their eyes from gazing at my glorious folly,
Time that shall come from wondering at my impudence,
And they that read my wanton life, from curses?
Can you do this? have ye this magick in ye?
This is not in your powre, though you be a Prince Sir
(No more then evill is in holy Angels)
Nor I, I hope; get wantonnesse confirm'd   120
By Act of Parliament an honesty,
And so receiv'd by all, ile harken to ye.
Heaven guide your Grace.   [*Offers to go.*]
Frederick.   *Evanthe*, stay a little,
Ile no more wantonnesse, ile marry thee.
Evanthe.   What shall the Queene do?
Frederick.   Ile be divorsed from her.

97 to] *i.e.,* too
*118–119 Sir (No...Angels)] Weber (Mason) *substantially*; ~ , ~ ... ~ , F 1–2

Evanthe.   Can you tell why? what has she done against ye?
Has she contrived a treason gainst your Person?
Abus'd your bed? does disobedience urge ye?
Frederick.   That's all one, 'tis my will.
Evanthe.   'Tis a most wicked one,
  A most absurd one, and will show a Monster;   130
  I had rather be a Whore, and with lesse sin,
  To your present lust, then Queen to your unjustice.
  Yours is no love, Faith and Religion fly it,
  Nor has no taste of faire affection in it,
  Some hellish flame abuses your faire body,
  And hellish furies blow it (looke behinde ye);
  Divorse ye from a woman of her beauty,
  Of her integrity, her piety?
  Her love to you, to all that honours ye,
  Her chast and vertuous love, are these fit causes?   140
  What will you do to me, when I have cloyd ye?
  You may finde time out in eternity,
  Deceit and violence in heavenly Justice,
  Life in the grave, and death among the blessed,
  Ere staine or brack in her sweet reputation.
Sorano.   You have fool'd enough, be wise now, and a woman,
  You have shew'd a modesty sufficient,
  If not too much for Court.
Evanthe.   You have shew'd an impudence,
  A more experienc'd bawd would blush and shake at;——
  You will make my kindred mighty?
Frederick.   Prethee heare me.   150
Evanthe.   I do Sir, and I count it a great offer.
Frederick.   Any of thine.
Evanthe.   'Tis like enough you may clap honour on them,
  But how 'twill sit, and how men will adore it,
  Is still the question. Ile tell you what they'l say Sir,
  What the report will be, and 'twill be true too,
  And it must needs be comfort to your Master,

136 it (looke behinde ye);] Dyce; ~ ; ~ ~ ~ , ∧ F1–2
*157 Master] *stet* F1–2

These are the issues of her impudence:
Ile tell your Grace, so deare I hold the Queene,
So deare that honour that she nurs'd me up in,   160
I would first take to me, for my lust, a Moore,
One of your Gally-slaves, that cold and hunger,
Decrepid misery, had made a mock-man,
Then be your Queene.
Frederick.   You are bravely resolute.
Evanthe.   I had rather be a Leapar, and be shun'd,
And dye by peeces, rot into my grave,
Leaving no memory behind to know me,
Then be a high Whore to eternity.
Frederick.   You have another Gamster I perceive by ye,
You durst not slight me else.
Sorano.   Ile finde him out,   170
Though he lye next thy heart hid, Ile discover him,
And ye proud peat, Ile make you curse your insolence.
Valerio [aside].   Tongue of an Angell, and the truth of Heaven,
How am I blest!   *Exit* Valerio.
Sorano [aside to him]. *Podrano* go in hast
To my Sisters Gentlewoman, you know her well,
And bid her send her Mistris presently
The lesser Cabinet she keeps her Letters in,
And such like toyes, and bring it to me instantly.
Away.
Podrano.   I am gone.   *Exit.*

          Enter the Queene *with two Ladies.*

Sorano.   The Queene.
Frederick.   Lets quit the place,
She may grow jealous.   *Exeunt* Frederick [*and*] Sorano.   180
Queene.   So suddenly departed, what's the reason?
Doe's my approach displease his Grace? are my eyes
So hatefull to him? or my conversation
Infected, that he flies me?——faire *Evanthe,*

          174 Podrano] Podramo F1–2
          181 Queene.] F2; Mar. F1 (*through rest of scene*)

          375

Are you there? then I see his shame.

Evanthe.   'Tis true Madam,
  'Thas pleas'd his Goodnesse to be pleasant with me.

Queene.   'Tis strange to finde thy modesty in this place,
  Doe's the King offer faire? doe's thy face take him?
  Nere blush *Evanthe*, 'tis a very sweet one,
  Doe's he raine gold, and precious promises   190
  Into thy lap? will he advance thy fortunes?
  Shalt thou be mighty wench?

Evanthe.   Never mock Madam;
  'Tis rather on your part to be lamented,
  At least reveng'd; I can be mighty, Lady,
  And glorious too, glorious and great, as you are.

Queene.   He will marry thee?

Evanthe.   Who would not be a Queene, Madam?

Queene.   'Tis true *Evanthe*, 'tis a brave ambition,
  A golden dreame, that may delude a good minde,
  What shall become of me?

Evanthe.   You must learne to pray,
  Your age and honour will become a Nunnery.   200

Queene.   Wilt thou remember me?   *Weeps.*

Evanthe.   She weeps.——   [*Kneels.*]
                                        Sweet Lady
  Upon my knees I aske your sacred pardon,
  For my rude boldnesse; and know, my sweet Mistris,
  If e're there were ambition in *Evanthe*,
  It was and is to do you faithfull duties;
  'Tis true I have been tempted by the King,
  And with no few and potent charmes, to wrong ye,
  To violate the chaste joyes of your bed,
  And those not taking hold, to usurpe your state;
  But she that has been bred up under ye,   210
  And daily fed upon your vertuous precepts,
  Still growing strong by example of your goodnesse,
  Having no errant motion from obedience,
  Flyes from these vanities, as meere illusions;
  And arm'd with honesty, defies all promises.

In token of this truth, I lay my life downe
Under your sacred foot, to do you service.
Queene.   Rise my true friend,   [*Raises her.*]
                    thou vertuous bud of beauty,
Thou Virgins honour, sweetly blow and flourish,
And that rude nipping winde, that seeks to blast thee,   220
Or taint thy root, be curst to all posterity;
To my protection from this houre I take ye,
Yes, and the King shall know——
Evanthe.   Give his heat way, Madam,
And 'twill go out againe, he may forget all.
                                        Exeunt.

                    Enter Camillo, Cleanthes, *and* Menallo.   [I. ii]

Camillo.   What have we to do with the times? we cannot cure em;
Let 'em go on, when they are swolne with surfets
They'le burst and stink, then all the world shall smell 'em.
Cleanthes.   A man may live a bawd, and be an honest man.
Menallo.   Yes, and a wise man too, 'tis a vertuous calling.
Camillo.   To his owne wife especially, or to his sister,
The neerer to his owne blood, still the honester;
There want such honest men, would we had more of 'em.
Menallo.   To be a villaine is no such rude matter.
Camillo.   No, if he be a neat one, and a perfect,   10
Art makes all excellent, what is it Gentlemen,
In a good cause to kill a dozen coxcombs?
That blunt rude fellowes call good Patriots?
Nothing, nor ne're look'd after.
Menallo.   'Tis ene as much,
As easie too, as honest, and as cleer,
To ravish Matrons, and deflowre coy wenches,
But here they are so willing, 'tis a complement.
Cleanthes.   To pull down Churches with pretention
To build 'em fairer, may be done with honour,
And all this time beleeve no God.
Camillo.   I think so,   20

                                        377

'Tis faith enough if they name him in their angers,
Or on their rotten Tombs ingrave an Angell;
Well, brave *Alphonso*, how happy had we been,
If thou had'st rain'd!

Menallo.   Would I had his disease,
Tyed like a Leprosie to my posterity,
So he were right againe.

Cleanthes.   What is his Melady?

Camillo.   Nothing but sad and silent melancholly,
Laden with griefes and thoughts, no man knows why neither;
The good *Brandino*, Father to the Princes,
Used all the art and industry that might be,   30
To free *Alphonso* from this dull calamity,
And seat him in his rule; he was his eldest
And noblest too, had not faire nature stopt in him,
For which cause this was chosen to inherit,
Frederick the yonger.

Cleanthes.   Doe's he use his brother
With that respect and honour that befits him?

Camillo.   He is kept privately, as they pretend,
To give more ease and comfort to his sicknesse;
But he has honest servants, the grave *Rugio*,
And Fryer *Marco*, that waight upon his Person,   40
And in a Monastery he lives.

Menallo.   'Tis full of sadnesse,
To see him when he comes to his fathers Tombe,
As once a day that is his Pilgrimage,
Whilst in devotion the Quire sings an Antheme:
How piously he kneeles, and like a Virgin
That some crosse fate had cozen'd of her Love,
Weeps till the stubborne Marble sweats with pitty,
And to his grones the whole Quire beares a *Chorus.*

Camillo.   So do I too.

29 Princes] Sympson (Theobald); Princesse F 1–2
*48–49 *Chorus. | Camillo. So do I too. | Enter...Cabinet, and* Podrano.] F 2 *(with
stage-direction after line 48 and Camillo's entire speech following, assigned to him);
Chorus. | Enter...Cabinet. | Pod. So do I too.* F 1 *(stage-direction and speech placed
as in F)* 2

Enter Frederick, Sorano *with the Cabinet, and* Podrano.

                    The King with his contrivers,
This is no place for us.   *Exeunt* Lords.   50
Frederick.   This is a Jewell,
Lay it aside, what Paper's that?
Podrano.   A Letter,
But 'tis a womans, Sir, I know by the hand,
And the false authography, they write old Saxon.
Frederick.   May be her ghostly mothers, that instructs her.
Sorano.   No, 'tis a cozens, and came up with a great Cake.
Frederick.   What's that?
Sorano.   A paire of Gloves the Duchesse gave her,
For so the outside saies.
Frederick.   That other Paper?
Sorano.   A charme for the tooth-ach, here's nothing but Saints and
    Crosses.
Frederick.   Look in that box, me thinks that should hold secrets.
Podrano.   'Tis paint and curles of haire, she begins to exercise.   60
A glasse of water too, I would faine taste it,
But I am wickedly afraid 'twill silence me,
Never a Conduit Pipe to convey this water.
Sorano.   These are all Rings, deaths heads and such mementoes
Her Grandmother, and worme-eaten Aunts left to her,
To tell her what her beauty must arive at.
Frederick.   That, that?
Podrano.   They are written Songs Sir, to provoke young Ladies;
Lord, here's a prayer booke, how these agree?
Here's a strange Union.
Sorano.   Ever by a surfeit   70
You have a julip set to coole the Patient.
Frederick.   Those, those?
Sorano.   They are Verses: *to the blest* Evanthe.
Frederick.   Those may discover, reade them out *Sorano.*
Sorano [*reades*].

        49 *and* Podrano] *om.* F 1; *and* Podramo F 2
        *60–63 'Tis . . . water.] *stet* F 1–2

To the blest Evanthe.

Let those complaine, that feeles Loves cruelty,
　And in sad Legents write their woes,
With Roses gently 'has corrected me,
　My war is without rage or blowes;
　　My Mistris eyes shine faire on my desires,
　　And hope springs up inflam'd with her new fires.　　80

No more an Exile will I dwell,
　With folded armes, and sighs all day,
Reckoning the torments of my hell,
　And flinging my sweet joyes away;
　　I am call'd home againe to quiet peace,
　　My Mistris smiles, and all my sorrowes cease.

Yet what is living in her eye,
　Or being blest with her sweet tongue,
If these no other joyes imply?
　A golden Give, a pleasing wrong:　　90
　　To be your owne but one poore Moneth, I'd give
　　My youth, my fortune, and then leave to live.

Frederick. This is my rivall, that I knew the hand now.
Sorano. I know it, I have seene it, 'tis *Valerio's,*
　That hopefull Gentlemans that was brought up
　With ye, and by your charge nourisht and fed
　At the same Table, with the same allowance.
Frederick. And all this curtesie to ruine me?
　Crosse my desires? had better have fed humblier,
　And stood at greater distance from my fury:　　100
　Go for him quickly, finde him instantly,
　Whilst my impatient heart swells high with choller;
　Better have lov'd despaire, and safer kist her.
　　　　　　　　　Exeunt Sorano *and* Podrano.

87 *eye*] F2; *eyes* F1　　90 *Give*] *i.e.*, gyve
*103.1 *Exeunt...Podrano*] Colman (Podramo); *Exit Lords* F1–2±

Enter Evanthe *and* Cassandra.

Evanthe.   Thou old weak foole, dost thou know to what end,
   To what betraying end he got this Casket?
   Durst thou deliver him without my Ring,
   Or a command from mine own mouth, that Cabinet
   That holds my heart? you unconsiderate asse,
   Thou brainlesse Ideot.
Cassandra.   I saw you go with him,
   At the first word commit your person to him,   110
   And made no scruple; he is your brothers Gentleman,
   And for any thing I know, an honest man;
   And might not I upon the same security
   Deliver him a box?
Evanthe.   A Bottle-head.
Frederick [aside].   You shall have cause to chafe, as I will handle it.
Evanthe.   I had rather thou hadst delivered me to Pirats,
   Betraid me to uncurable diseases,
   Hung up my Picture in a Market place,
   And sold me to wilde bawds.
Cassandra.   As I take it Madam,
   Your Maidenhead lyes not in that Cabinet,   120
   You have a closer, and you keep the key too,
   Why are you vext thus?
Evanthe.   I could curse thee wickedly,
   And wish thee more deformed then age can make thee;
   Perpetuall hunger, and no teeth to satisfie it,
   Waight on thee still, nor sleep be found to ease it:
   Those hands that gave the Casket, may the Palsie
   For ever make unusefull, even to feed thee;
   Long winters, that thy bones may turne to Isicles
   No Hell can thaw againe, inhabit by thee.
   Is thy care like thy body, all on crookednesse?   130
   How scurvily thou criest now, like a drunkard!
   Ile have as pure teares from a durty spout:

*110 the] F2; their F1   *119 wilde] *stet* F1–2   130 on] *i.e.*, one
131 now,...drunkard!] Colman (~ !...~ !); ~ ?...~ , F1–2

Do, sweare thou didst this ignorantly, sweare it,
Sweare and be damn'd, thou halfe witch.
Cassandra.   These are fine words,
  Well Madam, Madam.
Evanthe.   'Tis not well thou mummy,
  'Tis impudently, basely done, thou durty——
Frederick. Has your young sancitity done railing, Madam,
  Against your innocent Squire? do you see this Sonnet?
  This loving Script? do you know from whence it came too?
Evanthe. I do, and dare avouch it pure and honest.   140
Frederick. You have private Visitants, my noble Lady,
  That in sweet numbers court your goodly vertues,
  And to the height of adoration.
Evanthe.   Well Sir,
  There's neither Heresie nor Treason in it.
Frederick. A Prince may bed at the doore, whilst these feast with
    ye;
  A favour or a grace, from such as I am,
  Course, common things——

Enter Valerio *and* Podrano.

                     You are welcome; pray come neer, Sir,
  Do you know this paper?
Valerio [*aside*].   I am betray'd;——I do Sir,
  'Tis mine, my hand and heart,——if I die for her,   [*Aside.*]
  I am thy Martyr, Love, and time shall honour me.   150
Cassandra. You sawcy Sir, that came in my Ladies name,
  For her guilt Cabinet, you cheating Sir too,
  You scurvy Usher, with as scurvy leggs,
  And a worse face, thou poore base hanging holder,
  How durst thou come to me with a lye in thy mouth?
  An impudent lye——
Podrano.   Hollow, good *Jill*, you hobble.
Cassandra. A stinking lye, more stinking then the teller,
  To play the pilfring knave? there have been rascals

---

*146–147 am, ...things——] Sympson; ~ . . . . ~ . F1; ~ , . . . ~ . F2
*154 hanging holder] *stet* F1–2

Brought up to fetch and carry like your Worship,
That have been hang'd for lesse, whipt there are daily,   160
And if the Law will do me right——
Podrano.   What then old Maggot?
Cassandra.   Thy mother was carted younger; Ile have thy hide,
Thy mangy hide, embroder'd with a dog-whip,
As it is now with potent Pox, and thicker.
Frederick.   Peace, good antiquity, Ile have your bones else
Ground into Gunpowder to shoot at Cats with,
One word more, and Ile blanch thee like an Almond;
There's no such cure for the she-falling-sicknesse,
As the powder of a dried bawds skin, be silent.——
You are very prodigall of your service here, Sir,   170
Of your life more it seemes.
Valerio.   I repent neither,
Because your Grace shall understand it comes
From the best part of love, my pure affection,
And kindled with chaste flame, I will not fly from it;
If it be error to desire to marry,
And marry her that sanctity would dote on,
I have done amisse; if it be a Treason
To graft my soule to vertue, and to grow there,
To love the tree that beares such happinesse
(Conceive me, Sir, this fruit was ne're forbidden),   180
Nay, to desire to taste too, I am Traytor;
Had you but plants enough of this blest Tree, Sir,
Set round about your Court to beautifie it,
Deaths twice so many, to dismay the approachers,
The ground would scarce yeeld graves to noble Lovers.
Frederick.   'Tis well maintain'd, you wish and pray to fortune,
Here in your Sonnet, and she has heard your prayers,
So much you dote upon your owne undoing,
But one Month to injoy her as your wife,
Though at the expiring of that time you die for't.   190
Valerio.   I could wish many, many ages Sir,
To grow as old as time in her imbraces,
If heaven would grant it, and you smile upon it;

But if my choice were two houres, and then perish,
I would not pull my heart back.
Frederick.   You have your wish,
  To morrow I will see you nobly married,
  Your Month take out in all content and pleasure;
  The first day of the following Month you dye for't;
  Kneele not, not all your prayers can divert me;——
  Now marke your sentence, mark it scornfull Lady,   200
  If when *Valerio*'s dead, within twelve houres,
  For that's your latest time, you finde not out
  Another husband on the same condition
  To marry you againe, you dye your self too.
Evanthe.   Now you are mercifull, I thank your Grace.
Frederick.   If when you are married, you but seek to scape
  Out of the Kingdome, you, or she, or both,
  Or to infect mens minds with hot commotions,
  You dye both instantly;——will you love me now Lady?
  My tale will now be heard, but now I scorne ye.   210
                    Exeunt. Manent Valerio, *and* Evanthe.
Evanthe.   Is our faire love, our honest, our intire,
  Come to this hazard?
Valerio.   'Tis a noble one,
  And I am much in love with malice for it,
  Envy could not have studied me a way,
  Nor fortune pointed out a path to honour,
  Straighter and nobler, if she had her eyes:
  When I have once injoyed my sweet *Evanthe*,
  And blest my youth with her most deere imbraces,
  I have done my journey here, my day is out,
  All that the world has else is foolery,   220
  Labour, and losse of time; what should I live for?
  Think but mans life a moneth, and we are happy.
  I would not have my joyes grow old for any thing;
  A paradise, as thou art my *Evanthe*,
  Is only made to wonder at a little,
  Enough for humane eyes, and then to wander from.
  Come do not weep, sweet, you dishonour me,

Your teares and griefes but question my ability,
Whether I dare dye: Do you love intirely?
Evanthe.   You know I do.
Valerio.   Then grudge not my felicity.   230
Evanthe.   Ile to the Queene.
Valerio.   Do any thing that's honest,
But if you sue to him, in death I hate you.

                              [*Exeunt severally.*]

          Enter Camillo, Cleanthes, *and* Menallo.   II. i

Camillo.   Was there ever heard of such a marriage?
Menallo.   Marriage and hanging go by destiny,
'Tis the old proverb, now they come together.
Cleanthes.   But a month married, then to lose his life for't?
I would have a long month sure that payes the Souldiers.
Camillo.   Or get all the Almanacks burnt, that were a rare trick,
And have no month remembered.

          Enter Tony *with Urinall.*

                              How now *Tony?*
Whose water are you casting?
Tony.   A sick Gentlemans,
Is very sick, much troubled with the stone,
He should not live above a month by his Urine,   10
About Saint *Davids* day it will go hard with him,
He will then be troubled with a paine in his neck too.
Menallo.   A pestilent foole;——when wilt thou marry *Tony?*
Tony.   When I mean to be hangd, and 'tis the surer contract.
Cleanthes.   What think you of this marriage of *Valerios?*
Tony.   They have given him a hot custard,
And meane to burn his mouth with it; had I knowne
He had been given to die honourably,
I would have helpt him to a wench, a rare one,
Should have kill'd him in three weeks, and sav'd the sentence.   20

*5 long...Souldiers] *stet* F 1–2   *8–34 A...hanging.] *stet* F 1–2
9 Is] *i.e.,* he's   *11 Saint *Davids* day] *stet* F 1–2

Camillo.   There be them would have spared ten days of that too.
Tony.   It may be so, you have women of all vertues;
　There be some Guns that I could bring him too,
　Some Morter-peeces that are plac'd i'th Suburbs,
　Would teare him into quarters in two houres;
　There be also of the race of the old Cockatrices,
　That would dispatch him with once looking on him.
Menallo.   What Month wouldst thou chuse *Tony*, if thou hadst
　The like fortune?
Tony.　　　　　　I would chuse a mull'd Sack month,
　To comfort my belly, for sure my back   30
　Would ake for't, and at the months end I would be
　Most dismally drunk, and scorn the gallows.
Menallo.   I would chuse March, for I would come in like a Lion.
Tony.   But you'ld go out like a Lamb, when you went to hanging.
Camillo.   I would take April, take the sweet o'th year,
　And kisse my wench upon the tender flowrets,
　Tumble on every Greene, and as the birds sung,
　Embrace and melt away my soule in pleasure.
Tony.   You would go a Maying gayly to the gallowes.
Cleanthes.   Prethee tell us some newes.
Tony.　　　　　　　　　Ile tell ye all I know,   40
　You may be honest and poore fooles, as I am,
　And blow your fingers ends.
Camillo.　　　　　　　That's no newes foole.
Tony.   You may be knaves then, when you please, starke knaves,
　And build faire houses, but your heires shall have none of 'em.
Menallo.   These are undoubted.
Tony.　　　　　　　Truth is not worth the hearing,
　Ile tell you newes then, There was a drunken Saylor,
　That got a Marmaid with childe as she went a milking,
　And now she sues him in the bawdy Court for it,
　The infant Monster is brought up in Fish-street.
Camillo.   I, this is somthing.   50
Tony.   Ile tell you more, There was a fish taken,

---

　23 too] *i.e.,* to, *probably*　　　　*25 quarters] F 2; quartets F 1
*48 bawdy Court] *stet* F 1–2

A monstrous fish, with a sword by his side, a long sword,
A pike in's neck, and a gun in's nose, a huge gun,
And letters of Mart in's mouth, from the Duke of *Florence*.

Cleanthes. This is a monstrous lye.

Tony.   I do confesse it;
Do you think I would tell you truths, that dare not heare 'em?
You are honest things, we Courtiers scorn to converse with.

                                                    Exit.

Camillo. A plaguy foole, but lets consider Gentlemen,
Why the Queen strives not to oppose this sentence,
The Kingdomes honour suffers in this cruelty.   60

Menallo. No doubt the Queen, though she be vertuous,
Winks at the marriage, for by that only meanes
The Kings flame lessens to the youthfull Lady,
If not goes out; within this month, I doubt not,
She hopes to rock a sleep his anger also;
Shall we go see the preparation?
'Tis time, for strangers come to view the wonder.

Camillo. Come, lets away, send my friends happier weddings.

                                                    Exeunt.

                    Enter Queen *and* Evanthe.   [II. ii]

Queen. You shall be merry, come, Ile have it so,
Can there be any nature so unnoble?
Or anger so unhumane to pursue this?

Evanthe. I feare there is.

Queen.   Your feares are poore and foolish,
Though he be hasty, and his anger death,
His will like torrents, not to be resisted,
Yet Law and Justice go along to guide him;
And what Law or what Justice can he finde
To justifie his will? what Act or Statute,
By Humane or Divine establishment,   10
Left to direct us, that makes marriage death?
Honest faire wedlock? 'twas given for increase,
For preservation of mankinde I take it;

He must be more then man then, that dare break it;
Come dresse ye handsomly, you shall have my Jewels,
And put a face on that contemnes base fortune,
'Twill make him more insult to see you fearfull,
Outlooke his anger.

Evanthe.   O my *Valerio*!
Be witnesse my pure minde, 'tis thee I grieve for.

Queen.   But shew it not, I would so crucifie him   20
With an innocent neglect of what he can do,
A brave strong pious scorne, that I would shake him;
Put all the wanton *Cupids* in thine eyes,
And all the graces on that nature gave thee,
Make up thy beauty to that height of excellence
(Ile help thee, and forgive thee) as if *Venus*
Were now againe to catch the God of Warre,
In his most rugged anger; when thou hast him
(As 'tis impossible he should resist thee)
And kneeling at thy conquering feet for mercy,   30
Then shew thy vertue, then againe despise him
And all his power, then with a looke of honour,
Mingled with noble chastity, strike him dead.

Evanthe.   Good Madam dresse me,
You arme me bravely.

Queen.   Make him know his cruelty
Begins with him first, he must suffer for it,
And that thy sentence is so welcome to thee,
And to thy noble Lord, you long to meet it.
Stamp such a deep impression of thy beauty
Into his soule, and of thy worthinesse,   40
That when *Valerio* and *Evanthe* sleep
In one rich earth, hung round about with blessings,
He may run mad, and curse his act; be lusty,
Ile teach thee how to die too, if thou fear'st it.

Evanthe.   I thank your Grace, you have prepar'd me strongly,
And my weak minde.

Queen.   Death is unwelcome never,
Unlesse it be to tortur'd mindes and sick soules,

That make their own Hells; 'tis such a benefit
When it comes crown'd with honour, shews so sweet too;
Though they paint it ugly, that's but to restraine us,   50
For every living thing would love it else,
Fly boldly to their peace, ere nature call'd 'em;
The rest we have from labour, and from trouble,
Is some incitement, every thing alike,
The poore slave that lies private has his liberty,
As amply as his Master, in the Tombe,
The earth as light upon him, and the flowers
That grow about him, smell as sweet, and flourish;
But when we live with honour to our ends,
When memory and vertue are our mourners,   60
What pleasure's there? they are infinite *Evanthe*;
Onely, my vertuous wench, we want our sences,
That benefit we are barr'd, 'twould make us proud else,
And lazy to look up to happier life,
The blessings of the people would so swell us.

Evanthe.   Good Madam dresse me, you have drest my soul,
The merriest Bride ile be for all this misery,
The proudest to some eyes too.

Queen.   'Twill do better,
Come shrink no more.

Evanthe.   I am too confident.

                                                Exeunt.

                Enter Frederick *and* Sorano.   [II. iii]

Sorano.   You are too remisse and wanton in your angers,
You mold things hansomly, and then neglect 'em;
A powerful Prince should be constant to his power still,
And hold up what he builds, then people fearc him;
When he lets loose his hand, it shews a weaknesse,
And men examine or contemne his greatnesse;
A scorne of this high kinde should have cal'd up

---

*56 the] Seward *conj.*; that F 1–2   59 live] Dyce *conj.*; love F 1–2
60 vertue] F 2; vertues F 1

389

A revenge equall, not a pitty in you.

Frederick.   She is thy sister.

Sorano.   And she were my mother,
Whilst I conceive she has you wrong'd, I hate her,   10
And shake her neernesse off; I study, Sir,
To satisfie your angers that are just,
Before your pleasures.

Frederick.   I have done that already,
I feare has pull'd to many curses on me.

Sorano.   Curses or envies, on *Valerio's* head
(Would you take my counsell, Sir) they should all light,
And with the weight, not only crack his scull,
But his faire credit; the exquisite vexation
I have devis'd (so please you give way in't,
And let it worke) shall more afflict his soule,   20
And trench upon that honour that he brags of,
Then feare of death in all the frights he carries;
If you sit downe here they will both abuse ye,
Laugh at your poore relenting powre, and scorne ye;
What satisfaction can their deaths bring to you,
That are prepar'd and proud to dye, and willingly,
And at their ends will thank you for that honour?
How are you nearer the desire you aim at?
Or if it be revenge your anger covets,
How can their single deaths give you content, Sir?   30
Petty revenges end in blood, sleight angers,
A Princes rage should finde out new diseases
Death were a pleasure to, to pay proud fooles with.

Frederick.   What should I do?

Sorano.   Adde but your power unto me,
Make me but strong by your protection,
And you shall see what joy, and what delight,
What infinite pleasure this poore month shall yeeld him,
Ile make him wish he were dead on's marriage day,

32–33 diseases_∧ . . . to,] Weber (*with a comma after* diseases; *from* Mason: diseases _∧); diseases, . . . too, F 1–2
37 month] F 2; mouth F 1

390

Or bedrid with old age, ile make him curse,
And cry and curse, give me but power.
Frederick.   You have it,   40
  Here take my Ring, I am content he pay for't.
Sorano.   It shall be now revenge, as I will handle it,
  He shall live after this to beg his life too;
  Twenty to one by this thread, as ile weave it,
  Evanthe shall be yours.
Frederick.   Take all authority,
  And be most happy.
Sorano.   Good Sir, no more pitty.

                                     Exeunt.

     Enter Tony, *three* Citizens, *and three* Wives.   [II. iv]

1. Wife.   Good Master *Tony*, put me in.
Tony.   Where do you dwell?
1. Wife.   Forsooth, at the sign of the great Shoulder of Mutton.
Tony.   A hungry man would hunt your house out instantly,
  Keep the dogs from your doore; Is this Lettice Ruffe your
  husband?
  A fine sharp sallet to your signe.
2. Wife.   Will you put me in too?
3. Wife.   And me, good Master *Tony.*
Tony.   Put ye all in?
  You had best come twenty more; you think 'tis easie,
  A tricke of legerdemaine, to put ye all in,
  'Twould pose a fellow that had twice my body,
  Though it were all made into chines and fillets.   10
2. Wife.   Puts into'th wedding, Sir, we would fain see that.
1. Wife.   And the brave Masque too.
Tony.   You two are pretty women,——
  Are you their husbands?
2. Citizen.   Yes, for want of better.
Tony.   I think so too, you would not be so mad else
  To turne 'em loose to a company of young Courtiers,

    *4 Lettice] stet F 1–2   *11–12 Puts...too] stet F 1–2

That swarme like Bees in May, when they see young
   wenches;——
You must not squeak.
3. Wife.   No Sir, we are better tutor'd.
Tony.   Nor if a young Lord offer you the curtesie——
2. Wife. We know what 'tis, Sir.
Tony.   Nor you must not grumble,
If you be thrust up hard, we thrust most furiously.   20
3. Wife. We know the worst.
Tony.   Get you two in then quietly,
And shift for your selves;——   [*Exeunt* 2. *and* 3. Wife.]
                we must have no old women,
They are out of use, unlesse they have petitions,
Besides they cough so loud they drown the Musick,——
You would go in too, but there is no place for ye,
I am sorry for't, go and forget your wives,
Or pray they may be able to suffer patiently.
You may have Heires may prove wise Aldermen,
Go, or ile call the Guard.
3. Citizen.   We will get in,
Wee'l venture broken pates else.
Tony.   'Tis impossible,   30
You are too securely arm'd;——
               Exeunt Citizens *and* Woman.
               how they flock hether,
And with what joy the women run by heapes
To see this Marriage! they tickle to think of it,
They hope for every moneth a husband too;
Still how they run, and how the wittals follow 'em,
The weake things that are worne between the leggs,
That brushing, dressing, nor new naps can mende,
How they post to see their owne confusion!
This is a merry world.

Enter Frederick.

---

*21 3. Wife.] 1. W. F1–2±   *31 securely arm'd] *stet* F1–2
31 Exeunt...Woman] Weber; 'Exit Citiz. and Women' after else. line 30 F1–2±

Frederick.   Looke to the doore sirra,
Thou art a foole, and may'st do mischiefe lawfully.   40
Tony.   Give me your hand, you are my brother Foole,
You may both make the Law, and mar it presently.
Do you love a wench?
Frederick.   Who does not foole?
Tony.   Not I,
Unlesse you will give me a longer lease to marry her.
Frederick.   What are all these that come, what businesse have they?
Tony.   Some come to gape, those are my fellow fooles;
Some to get home their wives, those be their own fooles;
Some to rejoyce with thee, those be the times fooles;
And some I feare to curse thee, those are poore fooles,
A sect; people calls them honest.

>   *Enter* Cassandra, *an old Lady, passing over.*

                              Looke, looke King, look,   50
A weather-beaten Lady new carin'd.
Frederick.   An old one.
Tony.   The glasses of her eyes are new rub'd over,
And the worm-eaten records in her face are daub'd up neatly;
She lays her breasts out too, like to poch'd eggs
That had the yelkes suckt out; they get new heads also,
New teeth, new tongues, for the old are all worne out,
And as 'tis hoped, new tayles.
Frederick.   For what?
Tony.   For old Courtiers,
The young ones are too stirring for their travells.
Frederick.   Go leave your knavery, and helpe to keepe the doore
     well,
I will have no such presse.
Tony.   Lay thy hand a thy heart King.   60
Frederick.   Ile have ye whipt.
Tony.   The Foole and thou are parted.
>   *Exit.*

<hr>

*50 sect;] set‸ F1–2   *54 to] *stet* F1–2
*60 Lay...King.] *stet* F1–2

Frederick.   *Sorano* work, and free me from this spell,
'Twixt love and scorne there's nothing felt but hell.

Exit.

Enter Valerio, Camillo, Cleanthes, Menallo, *and Servants.*   [II. v]

Valerio.   Tye on my Scarfe, you are so long about me,——
Good my Lords help,——give me my other Cloke,
That Hat and Feather,——Lord what a Taylor's this,
To make me up thus straight, one sigh would burst me,
I have not roome to breath,——come button, button,
Button, apace.
Camillo.   I am glad to see you merry Sir.
Valerio.   'Twould make you merry had you such a wife,
And such an age to injoy her in.
Menallo.   An age Sir?
Valerio.   A moneth's an age to him that is contented,
What should I seeke for more?——give me my sword.——   10
Ha my good Lords, that every one of you now
Had but a Lady of that youth and beauty
To blesse your selves this night with, would ye not?
Pray ye speak uprightly.
Cleanthes.   We confesse ye happy,
And we could well wish such another Banquet,
But on that price my Lord——
Valerio.   'Twere nothing, else,
No man can ever come to aime at Heaven,
But by the knowledge of a Hell.——These shooes are heavy,
And if I should be call'd to dance they'l clog me,
Get me some pumps;——ile tell ye brave *Camillo*,   20
And you deare friends, the King has honour'd me,
Out of his gracious favour has much honour'd me,
To limit me my time; for who would live long?
Who would be old? 'tis such a wearinesse,
Such a disease, that hangs like lead upon us;
As it increases, so vexations,

4 straight] *i.e.*, strait   *10 What...more?] *stet* F 1–2

394

Griefes of the minde, paines of the feeble body,
Rhumes, coughs, catarrs, we are but our living coffines;
Beside, the faire soules old too, it growes covetous,
Which shewes all honour is departed from us,   30
And we are earth againe.
Cleanthes.   You make faire use Sir.
Valerio.   I would not live to learne to lye *Cleanthes*
For all the world, old men are prone to that too;——
Thou that hast been a Souldier *Menallo*,
A noble Souldier, and defied all danger,
Adopted thy brave arme the heire to victory,
Would'st thou live so long till thy strength forsooke thee?
Till thou grew'st only a long tedious story
Of what thou hadst been? till thy sword hung by,
And lazie Spiders fill'd the hilt with cobwebs?   40
Menallo.   No sure, I would not.
Valerio.   'Tis not fit ye should,
To dye a young man is to be an Angell,
Our great good parts, put wings unto our soules:——
Pray ye tell me, ist a hansome Maske we have?
Camillo.   We understand so.
Valerio.   And the young gentlemen dance?
Cleanthes.   They do Sir, and some dance well.
Valerio.   They must before the Ladies,
Wee'l have a rouse before we go to bed friends,
A lusty one, 'twill make my blood dance too.
Camillo.   Ten if you please.
Valerio.   And wee'l be wondrous merry,
                                        Musick.

They stay sure, come, I heare the Musick forward,   50
You shall have all Gloves presently.
Menallo.   We attend Sir,

---

39 hung] Dyce; hang F 1–2
43 Our...soules:——] *followed in* F 1–2 *by a duplicate of line* 47, *which* Colman
first omits. See p. 360.
*43 unto] F 2; to F 1   *46 must₍ₐ₎] *stet* F 1–2
*50 Musick₍ₐ₎] *stet* F 1–2

But first we must looke to'th Doores. The King has charged us.
Exeunt severally.

Enter two Servants. *Knocking within.*   [II. vi]

1. Servant. What a noyse do you keepe there,——call my fellowes
A the Guard;——you must cease now untill the King be enter'd,
He is gone to'th Temple now.
2. Servant.   Looke to that back doore,
And keep it fast, they swarme like Bees about it.

Enter Camillo, Cleanthes, Menallo; Tony *following.*

Camillo. Keepe back those Citizens, and let their wives in,
Their hansome wives.
Tony.   They have crowded me to Vergis,
I sweat like a Butter-box.
1. Servant.   Stand further off there.
Menallo. Take the women aside, and talk with 'em in privat,
Give 'em that they came for.
Tony.   The whole Court cannot do it;
Besides, the next Maske if we use 'em so,   10
They'l come by millions to expect our largesse;
We have broke a hundred heads.
Cleanthes.   Are they so tender?
Tony. But 'twas behinde, before they have all murrions.
Camillo. Let in those Ladies, make 'em roome for shame there.
Tony. They are no Ladies, there's one bald before 'em,
A gentlewoman bald? they are curtall'd queanes in hired clothes,
They come out of *Spaine* I think, they are very sultry.
Menallo. Keep 'em in breath for an Embassadour,
Me thinks my nose shakes at their memories.   *Knocks within.*
What bounsing's that?

---

*52.1 *Exeunt severally.*] ' *Exit.*' *after* presently., *line* 51, *and* ' *Exeunt.*' *after line* 52
F 1–2
*0.1 *Knocking within.*] Colman; *after* Doores., II.v.52 F 1–2
4.1 *following.*] F 2; *following, and Foole following.* F 1
13 murrions] *i.e.,* morions, helmets, *playing on* murrains
*16 gentlewoman] Weber (Mason); gent. F 1–2

2. *Citizen* (*within*).   I am one of the Musick Sir.   20
3. *Citizen* (*within*).   I have sweet-meats for the banquet.
Camillo.   Let 'em in.
Tony.   They lye my Lord, they come to seeke their wives,
  Two broken Citizens.
Camillo.   Breake 'em more, they are but brusled yet.——
  Bold Rascalls, offer to disturbe your wives?
Cleanthes.   Lock the doores fast,   [*Musick*.]
                    the Musick, hark, the King comes.

Enter the King [Frederick], Queene, Valerio, Evanthe,
  Sorano, *Ladies, Attendants*; Camillo, Cleanthes,
  Menallo *wait upon them*.

A Maske.

A Curtaine drawne. Cupid *descends* [*in a Chariot*], *the* Graces
  sitting by him, Cupid *being bound the* Graces
  unbinde him, he speakes.

Cupid.   Unbinde me, my delight, this night is mine,
  Now let me looke upon what Stars here shine,
  Let me behold the beauties, then clap high
  My cullor'd wings, proud of my Diety;
  I am satisfied, binde me agen, and fast,   30
  My angry Bow will make too great a waste
  Of beauty else: now call my Maskers in,
  Call with a Song, and let the sports begin;
  Call all my servants, the effects of love,
  And to a measure let them nobly move.

The Graces *sing*.

Come you servants of proud love,
  Come away:

*20–21 2. *Citizen* (*within*). ....3. Citizen (within).] Within. ... Within. F 1–2
*23 brusled] *stet* F 1–2
*25.1–25.3 Enter...them] *The King, Queene, Valerio, Evanthe, Ladies, Attendants,
Camillo, Cleanthes, Sorano, Menallo* F 1–2
  25.5 A Curtaine drawne.] *Dyce; as line* 25.1 F 1–2   25.6 bound] *i.e., blindfolded*
  34 servants,] *Colman;* ~ ₍ F 1–2   35.1 *The* Graces *sing.*] *Weber; om.* F 1–2

Fairely, nobly, gently move,
Too long, too long you make us stay;
Fancy, Desire, Delight, Hope, Feare,   40
Distrust and Jealousie, be you too here;
Consuming Care, and raging Ire,
And Poverty in poore attire,
March fairely in, and last Despaire;
Now full Musick strike the Aire.

Enter the Maskers, Fancy, Desire, Delight, Hope, Feare,
Distrust, Jealousie, Care, Ire, Poverty, Despaire,
they dance, after which Cupid *speakes.*

Cupid.   Away, I have done, the day begins to light,——
                              [*Exeunt Maskers.*]
   Lovers, you know your fate, good night, good night.
                  Cupid *and the* Graces *ascend in the Chariot.*

Frederick.   Come to the Banquet, when that's ended Sir,
   Ile see you a bed, and so good night; be merry,
   You have a sweet bed-fellow.
Valerio.   I thanke your Grace,   50
   And ever shall be bound unto your noblenesse.
Frederick.   I pray I may deserve your thankes, set forward.
                              Exeunt.

Enter divers Monkes, Alphonso [*supported*] *going to*   III. i
   the Tombe, Rugio *and Frier* Marco *discover the Tombe*
   and a Chaire.

Marco.   The night growes on, lead softly to the Tombe,
   And sing not till I bid ye; let the Musick
   Play gently as he passes.
Rugio.   O faire picture,
   That wert the living hope of all our honours,
   How are we banisht from the joy we dreamt of!
   Will he ne're speak more?

45.2 *Poverty,*] Sympson (Theobald), *om.* F 1–2

398

Marco.   'Tis full three moneths Lord *Rugio*,
Since any articulate sound came from his tongue,——
Set him downe gently.   [Alphonso] *sits in a Chaire.*
Rugio.   What should the reason be Sir?
Marco.   As 'tis in nature with those loving Husbands,
That sympathize their wives paines, and their throwes   10
When they are breeding (and 'tis usuall too,
We have it by experience) so in him Sir,
In this most noble spirit that now suffers;
For when his honour'd Father good *Brandino*
Fell sick, he felt the griefes, and labour'd with them,
His fits and his disease he still inherited,
Grew the same thing, and had not nature check'd him,
Strength, and ability, he had dyed that houre too.
Rugio.   Embleme of noble love!
Marco.   That very minute
His fathers breath forsooke him, that same instant,   20
(A rare example of his piety,
And love paternall) the Organ of his tongue
Was never heard to sound againe; so neare death
He seekes to waite upon his worthy Father,
But that we force his meat, he were one body.
Rugio.   He points toth' Tombe.
Marco.   That is the place he honours,
A house I feare he will not be long out of.
He will toth' Tombe, good my Lord lend your hand;
                        [*They leade* Alphonso.]
Now sing the Funerall Song, and let him kneele,
For then he is pleas'd.   [*Musick.*] *A Song.*
Rugio.   Heaven lend thy powerfull hand,   30
And ease this Prince.
Marco.   He will passe back againe.
                                        Exeunt.

17–18 nature...ability] *i.e.*, nature, strength, and ability checked him

Enter Valerio.

Valerio.   They drink abundantly, I am hot with wine too,
    Lustily warme, ile steale now to my happinesse,
    'Tis midnight, and the silent houre invites me,
    But she is up still, and attends the Queene;
    Thou dew of wine and sleep hang on their eye-lids,
    Steep their dull sences in the healths they drink,
    That I may quickly finde my lov'd *Evanthe*.
    The King is merry too, and dranke unto me,
    Signe of faire peace, O this nights blessednesse!
    If I had forty heads I would give all for it.   10
    Is not the end of our ambitions,
    Of all our humane studies, and our travells,
    Of our desires, the obtaining of our wishes?
    Certaine it is, and there man makes his Center.
    I have obtain'd *Evanthe*, I have married her,
    Can any fortune keep me from injoying her?
    I have my wish, what's left me to accuse now?

Enter Sorano.

    I am friends with all the world, but thy base malice;
    Go glory in thy mischiefes thou proud man,
    And cry it to the world thou hast ruin'd vertue;   20
    How I contemne thee and thy petty malice,
    And with what scorne I looke downe on thy practice!
Sorano.   You'l sing me a new Song anon *Valerio*,
    And wish these hot words——
Valerio.   I despise thee fellow,
    Thy threats, or flatteries, all I fling behinde me;
    I have my end, I have thy noble Sister,
    A name too worthy of thy blood; I have married her,
    And will injoy her too.
Sorano.   'Tis very likely.
Valerio.   And that short moneth I have to blesse me with her
    Ile make an age, ile reckon each embrace   30
    A yeare of pleasure, and each night a Jubilee,

Every quick kisse a Spring; and when I meane
To lose my selfe in all delightfulnesse,
Twenty sweet Summers I will tye together
In spight of thee, and thy malignant Master:
I will dye old in love, though young in pleasure.

Sorano.   But that I hate thee deadly, I could pitty thee,
Thou art the poorest miserable thing
This day on earth; ile tell thee why *Valerio*,
All thou esteemest, and build'st upon for happinesse,   40
For joy, for pleasure, for delight is past thee,
And like a wanton dreame already vanisht.

Valerio.   Is my love false?

Sorano.   No, she is constant to thee,
Constant to all thy misery she shall be,
And curse thee too.

Valerio.   Is my strong body weakn'd,
Charm'd, or abus'd with subtle drink? speak villaine.

Sorano.   Neither, I dare speake, thou art still as lusty
As when thou lov'dst her first, as strong and hopefull;
The month thou hast given thee is a month of misery,
And where thou think'st each hower shall yeeld a pleasure,   50
Looke for a killing paine, for thou shalt finde it;
Before thou dyest, each minute shall prepare it,
And ring so many knells to sad afflictions;
The King has given thee a long moneth to dye in,
And miserably dye.

Valerio.   Undo thy Riddle,
I am prepar'd what ever fate shall follow.

Sorano.   Dost thou see this Ring?

Valerio.   I know it too.

Sorano.   Then marke me,
By vertue of this Ring this I pronounce to thee,
'Tis the Kings will.

Valerio.   Let me know it suddenly.

Sorano.   If thou dost offer to touch *Evanthes* body   60
Beyond a kisse, though thou art married to her,
And lawfully as thou think'st may'st injoy her,

That minute she shall dye.
Valerio.   O Devill——
Sorano.   If thou discover this command unto her,
    Or to a friend that shall importune thee,
    And why thou abstainest, and from whose will, ye all perish,
    Upon the self-same forfeit: are ye fitted Sir?
    Now if ye love her, ye may preserve her life still,
    If not, you know the worst, how falls your month out?
Valerio.   This tyranny could never be invented   70
    But in the schoole of Hell, earth is too innocent;
    Not to injoy her when she is my wife?
    When she is willing too?
Sorano.   She is most willing,
    And will run mad to misse; but if you hit her,
    Be sure you hit her home, and kill her with it
    (There are such women that will dye with pleasure):
    The Axe will follow else, that will not faile
    To fetch her Maiden-head, and dispatch her quickly;
    Then shall the world know you are the cause of Murther,
    And as 'tis requisite your life shall pay for't.   80
Valerio.   Thou dost but jest, thou canst not be so monstrous
    As thou proclaim'st thy selfe; thou art her Brother,
    And there must be a feeling heart within thee
    Of her afflictions; wert thou a stranger to us,
    And bred amongst wilde rocks, thy nature wilde too,
    Affection in thee as thy breeding, cold,
    And unrelenting as the rocks that nourisht thee,
    Yet thou must shake to tell me this; they tremble
    When the rude sea threatens divorce amongst 'em,
    They that are sencelesse things shake at a tempest;   90
    Thou art a man——
Sorano.   Be thou too then, 'twill try thee,
    And patience now will best become thy noblenesse.
Valerio.   Invent some other torment to afflict me,
    All, if thou please, put all afflictions on me,
    Study thy braines out for 'em; so this be none
    I care not of what nature, nor what cruelty,

Nor of what length.

Sorano.   This is enough to vex ye.

Valerio.   The tale of *Tantalus* is now prov'd true,
And from me shall be registred Authentick;
To have my joyes within my armes, and lawfull,   100
Mine owne delights, yet dare not touch. Even as
Thou hatest me Brother, let no young man know this,
As thou shalt hope for peace when thou most needest it,
Peace in thy soule; desire the King to kill me,
Make me a traitor, any thing, ile yield to it,
And give thee cause so I may dye immediatly;
Lock me in Prison where no Sun may see me,
In walls so thick no hope may ere come at me;
Keep me from meat, and drink, and sleep, ile blesse thee;
Give me some damned potion to deliver me,   110
That I may never know my selfe againe, forget
My Country, kindred, name and fortune; last,
That my chaste love may never appeare before me,
This were some comfort.

Sorano.   All I have I have brought ye,
And much good may it do ye my deare Brother,
See ye observe it well; you will finde about ye
Many eyes set, that shall o're-looke your actions,
If you transgresse, ye know, and so I leave ye.   [*Exit.*]

Valerio.   Heaven be not angry, and I have some hope yet,
Looke on my harmelesse youth Angels of pitty,   120
To whom I kneele; be mercifull unto me,
And from my bleeding heart wipe off my sorrowes,
The power, the pride, the malice and injustice
Of cruell men are bent against mine innocence.
You that controwle the mighty wills of Princes,

---

*115 good...ye] F2; may it do ye with it F1
*119–121 Heaven...me,] Colman (Sympson *conj. approx.*); *in* F1 *line* 119 *is
followed by* And when you please, and how allay my miseries. [*cf. line* 127] | *Enter
Frederick.* | , *then lines* 121 *and* 120 *in that order;* F2 *marks Valerio's exit at line* 119
and omits all to entrance at III.iii.o.1.
*119 and] stet F1–2

403

And bow their stubborne armes, look on my weaknesse,
And when you please, and how, allay my miseries.

Exit.

Enter Frederick *and* Sorano. [III. iii]

Frederick.   Hast thou been with him?
Sorano.   Yes, and given him that Sir
  Will make him curse his Birth; I told ye which way:
  Did you but see him Sir, but look upon him,
  With what a troubled and dejected nature
  He walkes now in a mist, with what a silence,
  As if he were the shrowd he wrapt himselfe in,
  And no more of *Valerio* but his shadow,
  He seekes obscurity to hide his thoughts in,
  You would wonder and admire, for all you know it;
  His jollity is downe, valed to the ground Sir,   10
  And his high hopes of full delights and pleasures
  Are turn'd tormenters to him, strong diseases.
Frederick.   But is there hope of her?
Sorano.   It must fall necessary
  She must dislike him, quarrell with his person,
  For women once deluded are next Devills,
  And in the height of that opinion Sir,
  You shall put on againe, and she must meet ye.
Frederick.   I am glad of this.
Sorano.   Ile tell ye all the circumstance
  Within this houre, but sure I heard your Grace,
  To day as I attended, make some stops,   20
  Some broken speeches, and some sighs between,
  And then your Brothers name I heard distinctly,
  And some sad wishes after.
Frederick.   Ye are i'th right Sir,
  I would he were as sad as I could wish him,
  Sad as the earth.

Sorano.   Would ye have it so?
Frederick.   Thou hearest me,
  Though he be sick with small hope of recovery,
  That hope still lives, and mens eyes live upon it,
  And in their eyes their wishes; my *Sorano*,
  Were he but cold once in the tombe he dotes on,
  As 'tis the fittest place for melancholly,   30
  My Court should be another Paradice,
  And flow with all delights.
Sorano.   Go to your pleasures,
  Let me alone with this, hope shall not trouble ye,
  Nor he three dayes.
Frederick.   I shall be bound unto thee.
Sorano.   Ile do it neatly too, no doubt shall catch me.

        Enter Valerio, Camillo, Cleanthes, Menallo.

Frederick.   Be gone, they are going to bed, ile bid good night to
    'em.
Sorano.   And mark the man, you'le scarce know 'tis *Valerio. Exit.*
Camillo.   Cheere up my noble Lord, the minutes come,
  You shall injoy the abstract of all sweetnesse,
  We did you wrong, you need no wine to warme ye,   40
  Desire shoots through your eyes like sudden wild-fires.
Valerio.   Beshrew me Lords, the wine has made me dull,
  I am——I know not what.
Frederick.   Good pleasure to ye,
  Good night and long too, as you finde your appetite
  You may fall too.
Valerio [*to* Frederick].   I do beseech your Grace,
  For which of all my loves and services
  Have I deserved this?
Frederick.   I am not bound to answer ye.
Valerio.   Nor I bound to obey in unjust actions.
Frederick.   Do as you please, you know the penalty,
  And as I have a soule it shall be executed;   50
  Nay look not pale, I am not used to feare Sir,
  If you respect your Lady,——good night to ye.   *Exit.*

                        405

Valerio [aside]. But for respect to her and to my duty,
That reverent duty that I owe my Soveraigne,
Which anger has no power to snatch me from,
The good night should be thine; good night for ever:——
The King is wanton Lords, he would needs know of me
How many nick chases I would make to night.
Menallo. My Lord, no doubt you'l prove a perfect gamester.
Valerio. Faith no, I am unacquainted with the pleasure,   60
Bungle a set I may,——how my heart trembles,   *[Aside.]*
And beats my breast as it would breake his way out!——
Good night my noble friends.
Cleanthes.   Nay we must see you
Toward your bed my Lord.
Valerio.   Good faith it needs not,
'Tis late, and I shall trouble you.
Camillo.   No, no,
Till the Bride come Sir.
Valerio.   I beseech you leave me,
You will make me bashfull else, I am so foolish,
Besides, I have some few devotions Lords,
And he that can pray with such a book in's armes——
Camillo. Wee'l leave ye then, and a sweet night wait upon ye.   70
Menallo. And a sweet issue of this sweet night crown ye.
Cleanthes. All nights and dayes be such till you grow old Sir.
Valerio. I thank ye,   *Exeunt* Lords.
                    'tis a curse sufficient for me,
A labour'd one too, though you meane a blessing.
What shall I do? I am like a wretched Debtor,
That has a summe to tender on the forfeit
Of all he is worth, yet dare not offer it.
Other men see the Sun, yet I must wink at it;
And though I know 'tis perfect day, deny it:
My veines are all on fire, and burne like *Ætna*,   80
Youth and desire beat larums to my blood,
And adde fresh fuell to my warme affections.
I must injoy her, yet when I consider,

When I collect my selfe, and weigh her danger,
The Tyrants will, and his powre taught to murther,
My tender care controlls my blood within me,
And like a cold fit of a peevish Ague
Creepes to my soule, and flings an Ice upon me,
That locks all powres of youth up but prevention;
O what a blessednesse 'twere to be old now,   90
To be unable, bed-rid with diseases,
Or halt on Crutches to meet holy *Hymen*;
What a rare benefit! but I am curst,
That that speakes other men most freely happy,
And makes all eyes hang on their expectations,
Must prove the bane of me, youth and ability.

> *Enter* Queene, Evanthe, Ladies, *and* [Tony *the*] *Foole.*

She comes to bed, how shall I entertaine her?
Tony.   Nay I come after too, take the foole with ye,
For lightly he is ever one at Weddings.
Queene.   *Evanthe*, make ye unready, your Lord staies for ye,   100
And prethee be merry.
Tony.   Be very merry, Chicken,
Thy Lord will pipe to thee anon, and make thee dance too.
Lady.   Will he so, good-man asse.
Tony.   Yes goody filly,
And you had such a Pipe, that piped so sweetly,
You would dance to death, you have learnt your sinque a pace.
Evanthe.   Your Grace desires that that is too free in me,
I am merry at the heart.
Tony.   Thou wilt be anon,
The young smug Boy will give thee a sweet cordiall.
Evanthe.   I am so taken up in all my thoughts,
So possest Madam with the lawfull sweets   110
I shall this night partake of with my Lord,
So far transported (pardon my immodesty)——

---

*89 That...prevention;] *stet* F 1   96.1 *Enter...Foole.*] *after line* 88 F 1–2
*99 lightly] *stet* F 1–2
105 sinque a pace] *i.e.,* cinquepace, *punning on* sink apace

Valerio [*aside*].   Alas poore wench, how shall I recompence thee?
Evanthe.   That though they must be short, and snatcht away too,
  E're they grow ripe, yet I shall far prefer 'em
  Before a tedious pleasure with repentance.
Valerio [*aside*].   O how my heart akes.
Evanthe.   Take off my Jewells Ladies,
  And let my Ruffe loose, I shall bid good night to ye,
  My Lord staies here.
Queene.   My wench, I thank thee heartily,
  For learning how to use thy few houres hansomly,   120
  They will be yeares I hope; off with your Gowne now,——
  Lay downe the bed there!
Tony.   Shall I get into it
  And warme it for thee? a Fooles fire is a fine thing,
  And I'll so busse thee.
Queene.   Ile have ye whipt ye rascall.
Tony.   That will provoke me more,——ile talke with thy
    husband,
  He's a wise man I hope.
Evanthe.   Good night deare Madam,
  Ladies, no further service, I am well,
  I do beseech your Grace to give us this leave;
  My Lord and I to one another freely,
  And privately, may do all other Ceremonies,   130
  Woman and Page wee'l be to one another,
  And trouble you no farther.
Tony.   Art thou a wise man?
Valerio.   I cannot tell thee *Tony*, aske my neighbours.
Tony.   If thou beest so, go lye with me to night,
  (The old foole will lye quieter then the young one,
  And give thee more sleep), thou wilt looke to morrow else
  Worse then the prodigall foole the Ballad speakes of,
  That was squeez'd through a horne.
Valerio.   I shall take thy counsell.
Queene.   Why then good night, good night my best *Evanthe*,

125 more,——] Dyce; ~ , ∧ F1–2
*131 Woman] Sympson; Women F1–2

408

My worthy maid, and as that name shall vanish,　　　140
　A worthy wife, a long and happy;——follow sirra.
Evanthe.　That shall be my care, goodnesse rest with your Grace.
Queene.　Be lusty Lord, and take your Lady to ye,
　And that power that shall part ye be unhappy.
Valerio.　Sweet rest unto ye, to ye all sweet Ladies;
　Tony good night.
Tony.　　　　　　　　Shall not the Foole stay with thee?
Queene.　Come away Sirra.　　　　　*Exeunt* Queene, Ladies.
Tony.　　　　　　　　How the Foole is sought for!

　　　Sweet Malt is made of easie fire,
　　　A hasty horse will quickly tire,
　　　A sudden leaper sticks i'th mire,　　　150
　　　Phlebotomy and the word *lye nier*,
　　　Take heed of, friend, I thee require;
　　　This from an Almanack I stole,
　　　And learne this lesson from a foole.

Good night my Bird.
Evanthe.　　　　　　Good night wise Master *Tony*;　*Exit* Tony.
　Will ye to bed my Lord? Come, let me help ye.
Valerio.　To bed *Evanthe*? art thou sleepy?
Evanthe.　　　　　　　　　No,
　I shall be worse if you look sad upon me,
　Pray ye let's to bed.
Valerio.　　　　　I am not well my love.
Evanthe.　Ile make ye well, there's no such Phisick for ye　　　160
　As your warme Mistris armes.
Valerio.　　　　　　Art thou so cunning?
Evanthe.　I speake not by experience, pray ye mistake not;
　But if you love me——
Valerio.　　　　　I do love so dearely,
　So much above the base bent of desire
　I know not how to answer thee.
Evanthe.　　　　　　To bed then,
　There I shall better credit ye; fie my Lord,

154 learne] F2 (learn); learnt F1　　　166 ye] F2; yea F1

Will ye put a maid too't, to teach ye what to do?
An innocent maid? Are ye so cold a Lover?
Intruth you make me blush, 'tis midnight too,
And 'tis no stolne love, but authorised openly,   170
No sin we covet, pray let me undresse ye,
You shall help me; prethee sweet *Valerio*,
Be not so sad, the King will be more mercifull.

Valerio.   May not I love thy minde?

Evanthe.   And I yours too,
'Tis a most noble one, adorn'd with vertue;
But if we love not one another really,
And put our bodies and our mindes together,
And so make up the concord of affection,
Our love will prove but a blinde superstition:
This is no schoole to argue in my Lord,   180
Nor have we time to talke away allow'd us,
Pray let's dispatch, if any one should come
And finde us at this distance, what would they think?
Come, kisse me and to bed.

Valerio.   That I dare do,
And kisse againe.

Evanthe.   Spare not, they are your owne Sir.

Valerio.   But to injoy thee is to be luxurious,
Too sensual in my love, and too ambitious;
[*Aside*] O how I burne!——to pluck thee from the stalke,
Where now thou grow'st a sweet bud and a beauteous,
And bear'st the prime and honour of the Garden,   190
Is but to violate thy spring, and spoile thee.

Evanthe.   To let me blow, and fall alone would anger ye.

Valerio.   Let's sit together thus, and as we sit
Feed on the sweets of one anothers soules,
The happinesse of love is contemplation,
The blessednesse of love is pure affection,
Where no allay of actuall dull desire,
Of pleasure that partakes with wantonnesse,
Of humane fire that burnes out as it kindles,
And leaves the body but a poore repentance,   200

Can ever mix; let's fixe on that *Evanthe*,
That's everlasting, the tother casuall;
Eternity breeds one, the other Fortune,
Blinde as her selfe, and full of all afflictions.
Shall we love vertuously?

Evanthe.   I ever loved so.

Valerio.   And only think our love? the rarest pleasure,
And that we most desire, let it be humane,
If once injoyed growes stale, and cloyes our appetites;
I would not lessen in my love for any thing,
Nor finde thee but the same in my short journey,   210
For my loves safety.

Evanthe.   Now I see I am old Sir,
Old and ill-favour'd too, poore and despis'd,
And am not worth your noble Fellowship,
Your fellowship in Love; you would not else
Thus cunningly seeke to betray a maid,
A maid that honours you thus piously,
Strive to abuse the pious love she brings ye.
Farewell my Lord, since ye have a better Mistris,
For it must seeme so, or ye are no man,
A younger, happier, I shall give her roome,   220
So much I love ye still.

Valerio.   Stay my *Evanthe*,
Heaven beare me witnesse, thou art all I love,
All I desire, and now have pitty on me,
I never lyed before; forgive me Justice,   [*Aside.*]
Youth and affection stop your eares unto me.

Evanthe.   Why do you weep? if I have spoke too harshly,
And unbeseeming, my beloved Lord,
My care and duty, pardon me.

Valerio.   O heare me,
Heare me *Evanthe*;——I am all on torture   [*Aside.*]
And this lye tears my conscience as I vent it;——   230
I am no man.

Evanthe.   How Sir?

*202 the tother] *stet* F 1–2

411

Valerio.   No man for pleasure,
No womans man.
Evanthe.   Goodnesse forbid my Lord,
Sure you abuse your selfe.
Valerio.   'Tis true *Evanthe*;
I shame to say you will finde it.   *Weepes.*
Evanthe [*aside*].   He weepes bitterly,
'Tis my hard fortune, blesse all young maids from it;——
Is there no help my Lord in Art will comfort ye?
Valerio.   I hope there is.
Evanthe.   How long have you been destitute?
Valerio.   Since I was young.
Evanthe [*aside*].   'Tis hard to dye for nothing,——
Now you shall know 'tis not the pleasure Sir,
(For I am compell'd to love you spiritually)   240
That women aime at I affect ye for,
'Tis for your worth; and kisse me, be at peace,
Because I ever loved ye I still honour ye,
And with all duty to my Husband follow ye;
Will ye to bed now? ye are asham'd it seemes;
Pigmalion prayed and his cold stone took life,
You do not know with what zeale I shall aske Sir,
And what rare miracle that may worke upon ye;
Still blush? prescribe your Law.
Valerio.   I prethee pardon me,
To bed, and ile sit by thee, and mourne with thee,   250
Mourne both our fortunes, our unhappy ones:
Do not despise me, make me not more wretched,
I pray to heaven when I am gone *Evanthe*,
As my poore date is but a span of time now,
To recompense thy noble patience,
Thy love and vertue with a fruitfull husband,
Honest and honourable.
Evanthe.   Come, you have made me weep now,
All fond desire dye here, and welcome chastity,
Honour and chastity! do what you please Sir.   *Exeunt.*

243 honour] F 2; honour'd F 1

Enter at one doore Rugio, *and Frier* Marco; *at
the other doore* Sorano, *with a little glasse violl.*

Rugio.   What ailes this peece of mischief to looke sad?
   He seemes to weep too.
Marco.   Something is a hatching,
   And of some bloody nature too Lord *Rugio*,
   This Crocadile mournes thus cunningly.
Sorano.   Haile holy Father,
   And good day to the good Lord *Rugio*,
   How fares the sad Prince I beseech ye Sir?
Rugio.   'Tis like you know, you need not aske that question,
   You have your eyes and watches on his miseries
   As neare as ours, I would they were as tender.
Marco.   Can you do him good? as the King and you appointed
      him,   10
   So he is still, as you desir'd I think too,
   For every day he is worse (Heaven pardon all!)
   Put off your sorrow; you may laugh now Lord,
   He cannot last long to disturbe your Master,
   You have done worthy service to his Brother,
   And he most memorable love.
Sorano.   You do not know Sir
   With what remorse I aske, nor with what wearinesse
   I grone and bow under this load of honour,
   And how my soule sighs for the beastly services,
   I have done his pleasures.   [*Weepes.*]
                         These be witnesse with me,   20
   And from your piety beleeve me Father,
   I would as willingly unclothe my selfe
   Of title (that becomes me not I know;
   Good men, and great names best agree together),
   Cast off the glorious favours, and the trappings
   Of sound and honour, wealth and promises,
   His wanton pleasures have flung on my weaknesse,

         20 These] *i.e.,* these tears   *26 sound] *stet* F 1-2

                         413

And chuse to serve my Countries cause and vertues,
Poorely and honestly, and redeeme my ruines,
As I would hope remission of my mischiefes.   30
Rugio.   Old and experienc'd men my Lord *Sorano*,
Are not so quickly caught with gilt hypocrisie;
You pull your clawes in now and fawne upon us,
As Lyons do to intice poore foolish beasts;
And beasts we should be too if we beleeved ye,
Go exercise your Art——
Sorano.   For heaven sake scorne me not,
Nor adde more hell to my afflicted soule
Then I feele here; as you are honourable,
As you are charitable looke gently on me,
I will no more to Court, be no more Devill,   40
I know I must be hated even of him
That was my Love now, and the more he loves me
For his foule ends, when they shall once appeare to him,
Muster before his conscience and accuse him,
The fouler and the more falls his displeasure,
Princes are fading things, so are their favours.   *He weeps agen.*
Marco.   His heart is toucht sure with remorce.
Sorano.   See this,
And give me faire attention, good my Lord
And worthy Father see, within this violl
The remedy and cure of all my honour,   50
And of the sad Prince, lyes.
Rugio.   What new trick's this?
Sorano.   'Tis true, I have done Offices abundantly
Ill and prodigious, to the Prince *Alphonso*,
And whilst I was a knave I sought his death too.
Rugio.   You are too late convicted to be good yet.
Sorano.   But Father, when I felt this part afflict me,
This inward part, and call'd me to an audit
Of my misdeeds and mischiefes——

28 vertues] *i.e.*, virtue's, *probably*
46–47 favours. . . .His] Dyce *conj.*; favours. | *Mar.* He weeps agen, his F 1–2
57 part] F 2; *om.* F 1

414

Marco.   Well, go on Sir.

Sorano.   O then, then, then, what was my glory then Father?
   The favour of the King, what did that ease me?   60
   What was it to be bow'd to by all creatures?
   Worshipt, and courted, what did this availe me?
   I was a wretch, a poore lost wretch.

Marco.   Still better.

Sorano.   Till in the midst of all my griefe I found
   Repentance, and a learned man to give the meanes to it,
   A Jew, an honest and a rare Phisition,
   Of him I had this Jewell; 'tis a Jewell,
   And at the price of all my wealth I bought it:
   If the King knew it I must lose my head,
   And willingly, most willingly I would suffer: 70
   A childe may take it, 'tis so sweet in working.

Marco.   To whom would you apply it too?

Sorano.   To the sick Prince,
   It will in halfe a day dissolve his melancholly.

Rugio.   I do beleeve, and give him sleep for ever.
   What impudence is this, and what base malice,
   To make us instruments of thy abuses?
   Are we set here to poison him?

Sorano.   Mistake not,
   Yet I must needs say, 'tis a noble care,
   And worthy vertuous servants; if you will see
   A flourishing estate againe in *Naples*,   80
   And great *Alphonso* reigne that's truly good,
   And like himselfe able to make all excellent,
   Give him this drink, and this good health unto him.   *Drinks.*
   I am not so desperate yet to kill my selfe,
   Never looke on me as a guilty man,
   Nor on the water as a speedy poison:
   I am not mad, nor laid out all my treasure,
   My conscience and my credit to abuse ye;
   How nimbly and how cheerefully it workes now
   Upon my heart and head, sure I am a new man,   90
   There is no sadnesse that I feele within me,

But as it meets it, like a lazie vapour
How it flyes off. Here, give it him with speed,
You are more guilty then I ever was,
And worthier of the name of evill subjects,
If but an houre you hold this from his health.

Rugio. 'Tis some rare vertuous thing sure, he is a good man,
It must be so, come, let's apply it presently,
And may it sweetly work.

Sorano.   Pray let me heare on't,
And carry it close my Lords.

Marco.   Yes, good *Sorano.*   100

           Exeunt Rugio, Marco.

Sorano.   Do my good fooles, my honest pious coxcombs,
My wary fooles too, have I caught your wisedomes?
You never dream't I knew an Antidote,
Nor how to take it to secure mine owne life;
I am an asse? go, give him the fine cordiall,
And when you have done go dig his grave, good Frier,
Some two houres hence we shall have such a bawling,
And roaring up and downe for Aquavitæ,
Such rubbing, and such nointing, and such cooling,
I have sent him that will make a bonefire in's belly,   110
If he recover it, there is no heat in Hell sure.

             Exit.

     Enter Frederick *and* Podrano.   [IV. ii

Frederick.   *Podrano?*
Podrano.   Sir.
Frederick.   Call hither Lord *Valerio,*
And let none trouble us.
Podrano.   It shall be done Sir.   *Exit.*

      Enter Cassandra.

*105 I...asse?] I...asse, F1-2
*2 *Exit.*] F1 follows with *Enter Cassandra.* and forty-five lines omitted here. See
Appendix, pp. 481-2.

Frederick.   Come hither Time, how does your noble Mistris?

Cassandra.   As a Gentlewoman may do in her case that's newly
    married Sir:
  Sickly sometimes, and fond, an't like your Majesty.

Frederick.   She is breeding then?

Cassandra.   She wants much of her cullour,
  And has her qualmes as Ladies use to have Sir,
  And her disgusts.

Frederick.   And keeps her chamber?

Cassandra.   Yes Sir.

Frederick.   And eats good Broaths and Jellies?

Cassandra.   I am sure she sighs Sir,
  And weepes, good Lady.

Frederick.   Alas good Lady for it,   10
  She should have one could comfort her *Cassandra*,
  Could turne those teares to joyes, a lusty comforter.

Cassandra.   A comfortable man does well at all houres,
  For he brings comfortable things.

Frederick.   Come hither,
  And hold your fann between, you have eaten Onions,——
  Her breath stinks like a Fox, her teeth are contagious,
  These old women are all Elder-pipes,——do ye mark me?
                                        Gives a Purse.

Cassandra.   Yes Sir, but does your Grace think I am fit,
  That am both old and vertuous?

Frederick.   Therefore the fitter, the older still the better,   20
  I know thou art as holy as an old Cope,
  Yet upon necessary use——

Cassandra.   'Tis true Sir.

Frederick.   Her feeling sence is fierce still, speake unto her,
  You are familiar; speake I say unto her,
  Speake to the purpose; tell her this, and this.   [*Whispers.*]

Cassandra.   Alas, she is honest, Sir, she is very honest,
  And would you have my gravity——

Frederick.   I, I,

3 *Frederick.*] F2; *om.* F1   *5 fond, an'tₐ] Dyce (Sympson); ~ ₐ on't, F1–2
15 fann] F2; face F1   *17 Elder-pipes] *stet* F1–2

Your gravity will become the cause the better,
Ile looke thee out a Knight shall make thee a Lady too,
A lusty Knight, and one that shall be ruled by thee,   30
And adde to these, ile make 'em good; no mincing,
Nor ducking out of nicity good Lady,
But do it home, wee'l all be friends to, tell her;
And such a joy——

Cassandra.　　　　　　That's it that stirs me up Sir,
I would not for the world attempt her chastity,
But that they may live lovingly hereafter.

Frederick.　For that I urge it too.

Cassandra.　　　　　　　　A little evill
May well be suffered for a generall good, Sir,
Ile take my leave of your Majesty.

Frederick.　　　　　　Go fortunately,
Be speedy too.　　　　　　　　*Exit* [Cassandra.]

Enter Valerio.

　　　　　Here comes *Valerio*,   40
If his affliction have allayed his spirit
My work has end. Come hither Lord *Valerio*,
How do you now?

Valerio.　　　　　Your Majesty may ghesse,
Not so well, nor so fortunate as you are,
That can tye up mens honest wills and actions.

Frederick.　You have the happinesse you ever aim'd at,
The joy, and pleasure.

Valerio.　　　　　　Would you had the like Sir.

Frederick.　You tumble in delights with your sweet Lady,
And draw the minutes out in deare embraces,
You lead a right Lords life.

Valerio.　　　　　　　Would you had tryed it,   50
That you might know the vertue but to suffer,
Your anger, though it be unjust and insolent

30 thee] F2; her F1　　33 to] *i.e.,* too　　*46–53 You...Sir.] stet F1–2
50 lead] F1 (second version); live F1 (first version); *om.* F2
52 Your] F1 (first version); If F1 (second version); *om.* F2

Sits hansomer upon you then your scorne, Sir.
Frederick.   You cleerly see now brave *Valerio*
What 'tis to be the rivall to a Prince,
To interpose against a raging Lion;
I know you have suffer'd, infinitely suffer'd,
And with a kind of pitty I behold it,
And if you dare be worthy of my mercy,
I can yet heale you (yeeld up your *Evanthe*)   60
Take off my sentence also.
Valerio.   I fall thus low Sir,   [*Kneels.*]
My poore sad heart under your feet I lay,
And all the service of my life.
Frederick.   Do this then,
For without this 'twill be impossible,
Part with her for a while.
Valerio.   You have parted us,
What should I do with that I cannot use Sir?
Frederick.   'Tis well consider'd, let me have the Lady,
And thou shalt see how nobly ile befriend thee,
How all this difference——
Valerio.   Will she come, do you think Sir?
Frederick.   She must be wrought, I know she is too modest,   70
And gently wrought, and cunningly.
Valerio.   'Tis fit Sir.
Frederick.   And secretly it must be done.
Valerio.   As thought.
Frederick.   Ile warrant ye, her honour shall be faire still,
No soyle nor staine shall appeare on that, *Valerio*,
You see a thousand that beare sober faces,
And shew of as in-imitable modesties;
You would be sworn to, that they were pure Matrons,
And most chaste maids; and yet to augment their fortunes
And get them noble friends——
Valerio.   They are content Sir,
In private to bestow their beauties on 'em.   80
Frederick.   They are so, and they are wise, they know no want for't,

76 of] *i.e.*, off   77, 92 to] *i.e.*, too

419

Nor no eye sees they want their honesties.
Valerio. If it might be carried thus——
Frederick.   It shall be Sir.
Valerio [*aside*]. Ile see you dead first,——with this caution,
  Why sure I think it might be done.
Frederick.   Yes, easily.
Valerio. For what time would your Grace desire her body?
Frederick. A moneth or two, it shall be carried still
  As if she kept with you, and were a stranger,
  Rather a hater of the Grace I offer:
  And then I will returne her with such honour——   90
Valerio [*aside*]. 'Tis very like——I dote much on your honour.
Frederick. And load her with such favour to, *Valerio*——
Valerio [*aside*]. She never shall claw off,——I humbly thank ye.
Frederick. Ile make ye both the happiest, and the richest,
  And the mightiest too——
Valerio.   But who shall work her Sir?
  For on my conscience she is very honest,
  And will be hard to cut as a rough Diamond.
Frederick. Why you must work her, any thing from your tongue,
  Set off with golden and perswasive language,
  Urging your dangers too——
Valerio.   But all this time   100
  Have you the conscience Sir to leave me nothing,
  Nothing to play withall?
Frederick.   There be a thousand,
  Take where thou wilt.
Valerio.   May I make bold with your Queene?
  She is uselesse to your Grace as it appeares Sir,
  And but a loyall wife that may be lost too;
  I have a mind to her, and then 'tis equall.
Frederick.   How Sir?
Valerio. 'Tis so Sir, thou most glorious impudence,
  Have I not wrongs enow to suffer under,
  But thou must pick me out to make a monster?
  A hated wonder to the world? Do you start   110
  At my intrenching on your private liberty,

420

And would you force a hye-way through mine honour,
And make me pave it too? but that thy Queene
Is of that excellence in honesty,
And guarded with Divinity about her,
No loose thought can come neare, nor flame unhollowed,
I would so right my selfe.
Frederick.   Why take her to ye,
I am not vext at this, thou shalt injoy her,
Ile be thy friend if that may win thy courtesie.
Valerio.   I will not be your Bawd though, for your Royalty.   120
Was I brought up, and nourisht in the Court,
With thy most Royall Brother and thy selfe,
Upon thy Fathers charge, thy happy Fathers,
And suckt the sweetnesse of all humane Arts,
Learnt armes and honour to become a rascall;
Was this the expectation of my youth,
My growth of honour? Do ye speak this truly,
Or do ye try me Sir? for I beleeve not,
At least I would not, and me thinks 'tis impossible
There should be such a Devill in a Kings shape,   130
Such a malignant Fiend.
Frederick.   I thank ye Sir,
To morrow is your last day, and looke to it,
Get from my sight, away.
Valerio.   Ye are,——Oh,
My heart's too high and full to think upon ye.   *Exeunt.*

Enter Evanthe *and* Cassandra.   [IV. iii]

Evanthe.   You think it fit then, mortified *Cassandra*,
That I should be a Whore?
Cassandra.   Why a whore, Madam?
If every woman that upon necessity
Did a good turne (for there's the maine point, mark it)
Were term'd a whore, who would be honest, Madam?

*116 unhollowed] *stet* F 1
120 Bawd‸ though,] Dyce (~ , ~ ,); ~ ‸ ~ ‸ F 1; ~ , ~ ‸ F 2

Your Lords life and your owne are now in hazard,
Two precious lives may be redeem'd with nothing,
Little or nothing; say an houres or dayes sport,
Or such a toy, the end to it is not wantonnesse
(That we call lust that maidens lose their fame for)   10
But a compell'd necessity of honour,
Faire as the day, and cleare as innocence,
Upon my life and conscience a direct way——

Evanthe.   To be a rascall.

Cassandra.   'Tis a kinde of Rape too,
That keeps you cleare, for where your will's compell'd,
Though you yeeld up your body you are safe still.

Evanthe.   Thou art grown a learned Bawd, I ever look'd
Thy great sufficiency would breake out.

Cassandra.   You may,
You that are young and faire scorne us old creatures,
But you must know my yeares ere you be wise Lady,   20
And my experience too; say the King loved ye?
Say it were nothing else?

Evanthe.   I marry wench,
Now thou comest to me.

Cassandra.   Doe you thinke Princes favours are such sleight things,
To fling away when you please? there be young Ladies
Both faire and honourable, that would leap to reach 'em,
And leap aloft too.

Evanthe.   Such are light enough;
I am no Valter, wench, but canst thou tell me,
Though he be a King, whether he be sound or no?
I would not give my youth up to infection.   30

Cassandra.   As sound as honour ought to be, I think Lady;
Go too, be wise, I do not bid you try him;
But if he love you well, and you neglect him,
Your Lords life hanging on the hazard of it,
If you be so wilfull proud——

Evanthe.   Thou speakest to the point still;
But when I have lyen with him, what am I then, Gentlewoman?

9 not] Sympson; *om.* F1-2

Cassandra.   What are you? why the same you are now, a Woman,
  A vertuous woman, and a noble woman,
  Touching at what is noble, you become so.
  Had *Lucrece* e're been thought of, but for *Tarquin?*   40
  She was before a simple unknowne woman,
  When she was ravisht, she was a reverent Saint;
  And do you think she yeelded not a little?
  And had a kinde of will to have been re-ravisht?
  Believe it yes: There are a thousand stories
  Of wondrous loyall women, that have slipt,
  But it has been e're the ice of tender honour,
  That kept 'em coole still to the world; I think
  You are blest, that have such an occasion in your hands
  To beget a Chronicle, a faithfull one.   50
Evanthe.   It must needs be much honour.
Cassandra.   As you may make it, infinite and safe too,
  And when 'tis done, your Lord and you may live
  So quietly and peaceably together,
  And be what you please.
Evanthe.   But suppose this, wench,
  The King should so delight me with his company,
  I should forget my Lord, and no more look on him.
Cassandra.   That's the maine hazard, for I tell you truly,
  I have heard report speak, is an infinite pleasure,
  Almost above beliefe: there be some Ladies,   60
  And modest to the world too, wondrous modest,
  That have had the blessednesse to try his body,
  That I have heard proclaime him a new *Hercules.*
Evanthe.   So strongly able?
Cassandra.   There will be the danger,
  You being but a young and tender Lady,
  Although your minde be good, yet your weak body,
  At first encounter too, to meet with one
  Of his unconquer'd strength——
Evanthe.   Peace thou rude bawde,
  Thou studied old corruptnesse, tye thy tongue up,

Your hired base tongue; is this your timely counsell?   70
Dost thou seeke to make me dote on wickednesse?
Because 'tis ten times worse then thou deliver'st it?
To be a whore, because he has sufficiency
To make a hundred? O thou impudence,
Have I relieved thy age to mine owne ruine?
And worne thee in my bosome to betray me?
Can yeares and impotence win nothing on thee
That's good and honest, but thou must go on still?
And where thy blood wants heat to sin thy selfe,
Force thy decreped will to make me wicked?   80
Cassandra.   I did but tell ye——
Evanthe.   What the damned'st woman,
The cunning'st and the skilful'st bawd comes short of:
If thou had'st liv'd ten ages to be dam'd in,
And exercised this art the Devill taught thee,
Thou could'st not have exprest it more exactly.
Cassandra.   I did not bid you sin.
Evanthe.   Thou wood'st me to it,
Thou that art fit for prayer and the grave,
Thy body earth already, and corruption,
Thou taught'st the way; go follow your fine function,
There are houses of delight, that want good Matrons,   90
Such grave instructors, get thee thither monster,
And read variety of sins to wantons,
And when they rore with paines, learne to make playsters.
Cassandra.   This we have for our good wills.
Evanthe.   If e're I see thee more,
Or any thing that's like thee, to affright me,
By this faire light ile spoile thy bawdery,
Ile leave thee neither eyes nor nose to grace thee;
When thou wantest bread, and common pitty towards thee,
And art a starving in a ditch, think of me,
Then die, and let the wandering bawds lament thee;   100
Be gone, I charge thee, leave me.

Enter Frederick.

Cassandra.   You'l repent this.

                                      Exit [*weeping*].

Frederick [*aside*].   She's angry, and t'other crying too, my suit's
    cold;——
    Ile make your heart ake, stubborne wench, for this;
    Turne not so angry from me, I will speak to you,
    Are you growne proud with your delight, good Lady,
    So pamper'd with your sport, you scorne to know me?

Evanthe.   I scorne ye not, I would you scorn'd not me, Sir,
    And forc't me to be weary of my duty,
    I know your Grace, would I had never seene ye.

Frederick.   Because I love you, because I dote upon ye,   110
    Because I am a man that seeke to please ye?

Evanthe.   I have man enough already to content me,
    As much, as noble, and as worthy of me,
    As all the world can yeeld.

Frederick.   That's but your modesty,
    You have no man (nay never look upon me,
    I know it Lady) no man to content ye,
    No man that can, or at the least that dare,
    Which is a poorer man, and neerer nothing.

Evanthe.   Be nobler, Sir, inform'd.

Frederick.   Ile tell thee, wench,
    The poore condition of this poorer fellow,   120
    And make thee blush for shame at thine owne errour,
    He never tendred yet a husbands duty,
    To thy warme longing bed.

Evanthe [*aside*].   How should he know that?

Frederick.   I am sure he did not, for I charg'd him no,
    Upon his life I charg'd him, but to try him;
    Could any brave or noble spirit stop here?
    Was life to be prefer'd before affection?
    Lawfull, and long'd for too?

Evanthe.   Did you command him?

Frederick.   I did in policy to try his spirit.

Evanthe.   And could he be so dead cold to observe it?   130

    102–103 cold;——...this;] F₂ (~ . ₄ ... ~ ;);~ ; ₄ ... ~ ; F₁

                                   425

Brought I no beauty? nor no love along with me?
Frederick.   Why that is it that makes me scorne to name him.
   I should have lov'd him, if he had venter'd for't,
   Nay, doted on his bravery.
Evanthe.   Onely charg'd?
   And with that spell sit downe? dare men fight bravely
   For poore slight things, for drink or ostentation?
   And there indanger both their lives and fortunes,
   And from their lawfull Loves fly off with feare?
Frederick.   'Tis true,
   And with a cunning base feare too to abuse thee;
   Made thee believe, poore innocent *Evanthe*,   140
   Wretched young girle, it was his impotency;
   Was it not so? deny it.
Evanthe.   O my anger,
   At my yeares to be cozen'd with a young man!
Frederick.   A strong man too, certaine he lov'd ye deerly.
Evanthe.   To have my shame and love mingled together,
   And both flung on me like a wait to sinke me;
   I would have dyed a thousand times.
Frederick.   So would any,
   Any that had the spirit of a man;
   I would have been kill'd in your armes.
Evanthe.   I would he had been,
   And buried in mine armes, that had been noble,   150
   And what a monument would I have made him!
   Upon this breast he should have slept in peace,
   Honour, and everlasting love his mourners;
   And I still weeping till old time had turn'd me,
   And pittying powers above, into pure christall.
Frederick.   Hadst thou lov'd me, and had my way been stuck
   With deaths, as thick as frosty nights with stars,
   I would have ventur'd.
Evanthe [aside].   Sure there is some trick in't;
   Valerio ne're was coward.
Frederick.   Worse then this too,

   132 that...him.] F2; what...him? F1   *138 from] for F1–2

Tamer, and seasoning of a baser nature,   160
He set your woman on ye to betray ye,
Your bawdy woman, or your sin solicitor
(I pray but think what this man may deserve now)
I know he did, and did it to please me too.

Evanthe.   Good Sir afflict me not too fast, I feele
I am a woman, and a wrong'd one too,
And sensible I am of my abuses,
Sir, you have loved me——

Frederick.   And I love thee still,
Pitty thy wrongs, and dote upon thy person.

Evanthe.   To set my woman on me, 'twas too base Sir.   170

Frederick.   Abominable vilde.

Evanthe.   But I shall fit him.

Frederick.   All reason and all Law allowes it to ye,
And ye are a foole, a tame foole, if you spare him.

Evanthe.   You may speake now, and happily prevaile too,
And I beseech your Grace be angry with me.

Frederick.   I am, at heart.——She staggers in her faith, [*Aside.*]
And will fall off I hope, Ile ply her still.——
Thou abused innocence, I suffer with thee,
If I should give him life, he would still betray thee;
That foole that feares to dye for such a beauty,   180
Would for the same feare sell thee unto misery!
I do not say he would have been bawd himself too.

Evanthe [*aside*].   Follow'd thus far? nay then I smell the malice,
It tasts too hot of practis'd wickednesse,
There can be no such man, I am sure no Gentleman:
Shall my anger make me whore, and not my pleasure?
My sudden unconsiderate rage abuse me?
Come home againe, my frighted faith, my vertue,
Home to my heart againe:——he be a bawd too?

Frederick.   I will not say, he offered faire, *Evanthe.*   190

Evanthe.   Nor do not dare, 'twill be an impudence,
And not an honour, for a Prince to lye;
Fie Sir, a person of your ranke to trifle,

*182 I...say] *stet* F1-2   *190 faire,] Langbaine; ~ ∧ F1-2

427

I know you do lye.
Frederick.   How!
Evanthe.   Lye shamefully,
And I could wish my selfe a man but one day,
To tell you openly you lye too, basely.
Frederick.   Take heed wilde foole.
Evanthe.   Take thou heed thou tame Devill,
Thou all *Pandora's* box in a Kings figure,
Thou hast almost whor'd my weake beliefe already,
And like an Engineer blowne up mine honour;   200
But I shall countermine, and catch your mischiefe,
This little Fort you seeke, I shall man nobly,
And strongly too, with chaste obedience
To my deere Lord, with vertuous thoughts that scorne ye.
Victorious *Tameris* nere won more honour
In cutting off the Royall head of *Cyrus*,
Then I shall do in conquering thee; farewell,
And if thou canst be wise, learne to be good too,
'Twill give thee nobler lights then both thine eyes do;
My poore Lord and my selfe are bound to suffer,   210
And when I see him faint under your sentence,
Ile tell ye more, it may be then Ile yeeld too.
Frederick.   Foole, unexampled shall my anger follow thee!
                              Exeunt [severally].

            Enter Rugio, *and Fryer* Marco, *amazed.*   [IV. iv

Rugio.   Curse on our sights, our fond credulities,
A thousand curses on the slave that cheated us,
The damn'd slave.
Marco.   We have e'ne sham'd our service,
Brought our best cares and loyalties to nothing,
'Tis the most fearefull poyson, the most potent

---

*205   *Tameris*] stet F1
*213   Foole, unexampled‸] Dyce; ~ , ~ , F1; ~ ‸ ~ , F2
1   Curse] Sympson; Curst F1–2   *1 sights] stet F1–2
*4   cares] Dyce *conj.*; care F1–2

(Heaven give him patience); oh it works most strongly,
And teares him Lord.
Rugio.   That we should be so stupid,
   To trust the arrant'st villaine that e're flatter'd,
   The bloodiest too, to believe a few soft words from him,
   And give way to his prepar'd teares.
Alphonso (*within*).   Oh, oh, oh.
Rugio.   Harke Fryer *Marco*, 10
   Harke, the poore Prince, that we should be such blockheads,
   As to be taken with his drinking first!
   And never think what Antidotes are made for!
   Two wooden sculls we have, and we deserve to be hang'd for't,
   For certainly it will be laid to our charge;
   As certaine too, it will dispatch him speedily;
   Which way to turne, or what to——
Marco.   Let's pray,
   Heavens hand is strong.
Rugio.   The Poysons strong, you would say.
   Would any thing——

Enter Alphonso, *carried in a Couch by two Fryers.*

                He comes, let's give him comfort.
Alphonso.   Give me more ayre, ayre, more ayre, blow, blow, 20
   Open thou Easterne gate, and blow upon me,
   Distill thy cold dewes, O thou icy Moone,
   And, rivers, run through my afflicted spirit,
   I am all fire, fire, fire, the raging dog star
   Raines in my blood, oh which way shall I turne me?
   Ætna and all his flames burne in my head,
   Fling me into the Ocean or I perish:
   Dig, dig, dig till the springs fly up,
   The cold, cold springs, that I may leap into 'em,
   And bathe my scorcht limbs in their purling pleasures; 30
   Or shoot me up into the higher Region,
   Where treasures of delicious snow are nourisht,

     19 *in a Couch*] *in a Coach* F 1; *on a Couch* F 2
     23 And, rivers,] Dyce; ~ ∧ ~ ∧ F 1–2

And banquets of sweet haile.

Rugio.   Hold him fast Fryer,
O how he burnes!

Alphonso.   What, will ye sacrifice me?
Upon the Altar lay my willing body,
And pile your wood up, fling your holy incense;
And as I turne me you shall see all flame,
Consuming flame; stand off me, or you are ashes.

Both [Rugio *and* Marco].   Most miserable wretches.

Alphonso.   Bring hither charity
And let me hug her, Fryer, they say she's cold,   40
Infinite cold, devotion cannot warme her;
Draw me a river of false lovers teares
Cleane through my breast, they are dull, cold, and forgetfull,
And will give ease, let Virgins sigh upon me,
Forsaken soules, their sighs are precious,
Let them all sigh: oh hell, hell, hell, oh horror.

Marco.   To bed, good Sir.

Alphonso.   My bed will burne about me,
Like *Phaeton*, in all consuming flashes
I am inclosed, let me fly, let me fly, give roome;
Betwixt the cold beare, and the raging Lyon   50
Lyes my safe way; O for a cake of ice now,
To clap unto my heart to comfort me;
Decrepid winter hang upon my sholders,
And let me weare thy frozen Isicles
Like Jewels round about my head, to coole me;
My eyes burne out, and sinke into their sockets,
And my infected braine like brimstone boyles,
I live in hell, and severall furies vex me;
O carry me where no Sun ever shew'd yet
A face of comfort, where the earth is christall,   60
Never to be dissolv'd, where nought inhabits
But night and cold, and nipping frosts, and winds
That cut the stubborne rocks, and make them shiver;
Set me there friends.

45 their] Sympson; the F 1–2   *50 Betwixt...Lyon] *stet* F 1–2

Rugio.   Hold fast, he must to bed Fryer,
  What scalding sweats he has!
Marco.   He'le scalld in hell for't,
  That was the cause.
Alphonso.   Drinke, drinke, a world of drinke,
  Fill all the cups, and all the antick vessels,
  And borrow pots, let me have drinke enough,
  Bring all the worthy drunkards of the time,
  The experienc'd drunkards, let me have them all,   70
  And let them drinke their worst, Ile make them Ideots;
  Ile lye upon my Back and swallow Vessels,
  Have Rivers made of cooling wine run through me,
  Not stay for this mans health, or this great Princes,
  But take an Ocean, and begin to all; oh, oh.
Marco. He cooles a little, now away with him,
  And to his warme bed presently.
Alphonso.   No drinke?
  No winde? no cooling aire?
Rugio.   You shall have any thing.——
  His hot fit lessens, Heaven put in a hand now,
  And save his life;——there's drink Sir in your chamber,   80
  And all coole things.
Alphonso.   Away, away, lets fly to 'em.
                    Exeunt [carrying Alphonso].

                Enter Valerio *and* Evanthe.   [IV. v]

Evanthe. To say you were impotent, I am asham'd on't,
  To make your self no man, to a fresh maid too,
  A longing maid, upon her wedding night also,
  To give her such a dor.
Valerio.   I prethee pardon me.
Evanthe. Had you been drunke, 'thad been excusable,
  Or like a Gentleman under the Surgeons hands,
  And so not able, there had been some colour,
  But wretchedly to take a weaknesse to ye,
  A fearefull weaknesse, to abuse your body,

                    431

And let a lye worke like a spell upon ye,   10
A lye, to save your life——
Valerio.   Will you give me leave sweet?
Evanthe.   You have taken too much leave, and too base leave too,
     To wrong your Love; hast thou a noble spirit?
     And canst thou looke up to the peoples loves,
     That call thee worthy, and not blush *Valerio?*
     Canst thou behold me that thou hast betraid thus?
     And no shame touch thee?
Valerio.   Shame attend the sinfull,
     I know my innocence.
Evanthe.   Ne're think to face it, that's a double weaknesse,
     And shewes thee falser still; the King himselfe,   20
     Though he be wicked, and our Enemy,
     But juster then thou, in pitty of my injuries,
     Told me the truth.
Valerio.   What did he tell *Evanthe?*
Evanthe.   That but to gaine thy life a fortnight longer,
     Thy lov'd poore life, thou gav'st up all my duties.
Valerio.   I sweare 'tis false, my life and death are equall,
     I have weigh'd 'em both, and finde 'em but one fortune,
     But Kings are men, and live as men, and dye too,
     Have the affections men have, and their falsehoods;
     Indeed they have more power to make 'em good;   30
     The King's to blame, it was to save thy life wench,
     Thy innocent life, that I forebore thy bed,
     For if I had toucht thee thou hadst dyed, he swore it.
Evanthe.   And was not I as worthy to dye nobly?
     To make a story for the times that follows,
     As he that married me? what weaknesse, Sir,
     Or dissability do you see in me,
     Either in minde or body, to defraud me
     Of such an opportunity? Do you think I married you
     Only for pleasure, or content in lust?   40
     To lull you in mine armes, and kisse you hourely?
     Was this my end? I might have been a Queen, Sir,

19 face] *i.e.,* outface   *22 thou] Dyce; thine F1; thou art F2

If that had caught me, and have knowne all delicates,
There's few that would have shun'd so faire an offer;
O thou unfaithfull fearefull man, thou hast kill'd me,
In saving me this way, thou hast destroy'd me,
Rob'd me of that thy love can never give more;
To be unable, to save me? O misery!
Had I been my *Valerio*, thou *Evanthe*,
I would have lyen with thee under a Gallowes,   50
Though the Hangman had been my *Hymen*, and the furies
With iron whips and forks, ready to torter me,
I would have hug'd thee too, though hell had gap'd at me;
Save my life! that expected to dye bravely,
That would have woo'd it too! Would I had married
An *Eunuch*, that had truly no ability,
Then such a fearefull lyar! thou hast done me
A scurvy curtesie, that has undone me.

Valerio.   Ile do no more, since you are so nobly fashion'd,
Made up so strongly, Ile take my share with ye,   60
Nay Deere, Ile learne of you.

Evanthe [*aside*].   He weeps too, tenderly;
My angers gone,——good my Lord pardon me,
And if I have offended, be more angry,
It was a womans flash, a sudden valour,
That could not lye conceal'd.

Valerio.   I honour ye
By all the rights of holy marriage,
And pleasures of chaste love, I wonder at ye,
You appeare the vision of a Heaven unto me,
Stuck all with stars of honour shining cleerly,
And all the motions of your minde celestiall;   70
Man is a lumpe of earth, the best man spiritlesse,
To such a woman; all our lives and actions
But counterfeits in *Arras* to this vertue;
Chide me againe, you have so brave an anger,
And flowes so nobly from you, thus deliver'd,

48 unable,] Sympson; ~ ₐ F1-2   61 too,] Colman; ~ ₐ F1-2
73 counterfeits in *Arras*] *i.e., pictures in tapestry* (Dyce)

433

That I could suffer like a childe to heare ye,
Nay make my self guilty of some faults to honour ye.
Evanthe.   Ile chide no more, you have rob'd me of my courage.
And with a cunning patience checkt my impudence;
Once more forgivenesse!   *She kneeles.*
Valerio.   Will this serve *Evanthe?*   80
                                    [*Raises her.*] *Kisses her.*
And this my love? Heavens mercy be upon us;
But did he tell no more?
Evanthe.   Only this trifle:
You set my woman on me, to betray me;
'Tis true, she did her best, a bad old woman,
It stir'd me Sir.
Valerio.   I cannot blame thee, Jewell.
Evanthe.   And me thought when your name was sounded that
    way——
Valerio.   He that will spare no fame, will spare no name Sweet;
Though as I am a man, I am full of weaknesse,
And may slip happily into some ignorance,
Yet at my yeeres to be a bawd, and cozen   90
Mine owne hopes with my Doctrine——
Evanthe.   I beleeve not,
Nor never shall; our time is out to morrow.
Valerio.   Let's be too night then full of fruitfulnesse,
Now we are both of one minde, let's be happy,
I am no more a wanting man *Evanthe,*
Thy warme embraces shall dissolve that impotence,
And my cold lye shall vanish with thy kisses;
You houres of night be long, as when *Alcmena*
Lay by the lusty side of *Jupiter;*
Keep back the day, and hide his golden beames,   100
Where the chaste watchfull morning may not finde 'em;
Old doting *Tython* hold *Aurora* fast,
And though she blush the day-break from her cheeks,
Conceale her still; thou heavy Waine stand firme,
And stop the quicker revolutions;
Or if the day must come, to spoile our happinesse,

434

Thou envious Sunne peepe not upon our pleasure,
Thou that all Lovers curse, be farre off from us.
Evanthe.   Then let's to bed, and this night in all joyes
And chaste delights——

Enter Castruchio *with Guard.*

Castruchio.   Stay, I must part ye both;   110
It is the Kings command, who bids me tell ye,
To morrow is your last houre.
Valerio.   I obey, Sir,
In Heaven we shall meet, Captaine, where King *Frederick*
Dare not appeare to part us.
Castruchio.   Mistake me not,
Though I am rough in doing of my Office,
You shall finde, Sir, you have a friend to honour ye.
Valerio.   I thank ye Sir.
Evanthe.   Pray Captaine tell the King,
They that are sad on Earth, in Heaven shall sing.   *Exeunt.*

Enter Fryer Marco, *and* Rugio.   V. i

Rugio.   Have you writ to the Captaine of the Castle?
Marco.   Yes, and charged him
Upon his soules health, that he be not cruell,
Told him *Valerio's* worth among the people,
And how it must be punisht in posterity,
Though he scape now.
Rugio.   But will not he, Fryer *Marco,*
Betray this to the King?
Marco.   Though he be stubborne,
And of a rugged nature, yet he is honest,
And honours much *Valerio.*
Rugio.   How doe's *Alphonso?*
For now me thinks my heart is light againe,
And pale feare fled.
Marco.   He is as well as I am;   10
The Rogue against his will has sav'd his life,

435

A desperate poyson has re-cur'd the Prince.

Rugio. To me 'tis most miraculous.

Marco. To me too,
Till I consider why it should do so,
And now I have found it a most excellent Physick,
It wrought upon the dull cold misty parts,
That clog'd his soule (which was another poyson,
A desperate too) and found such matter there,
And such abundance also to resist it,
And weare away the dangerous heat it brought with it,　　　20
The pure blood and the spirits scap'd untainted.

Rugio. 'Twas Heavens high hand, none of *Sorano's* pitty.

Marco. Most certaine 'twas, had the malitious villaine
Given him a cooling poyson, he had paid him.

Enter Castruchio.

Rugio. The Captain of the Castle.

Marco. O ye are welcome,
How doe's your Prisoner?

Castruchio. He must go for dead;
But when I do a deed of so much villany,
Ile have my skin pull'd o're mine eares, my Lord,
Though I am the Kings, I am none of his abuses;
How doe's your Royall Charge? that I might see once.　　　30

Marco. I pray see now, you are a trusty Gentleman.

Enter Alphonso, *and Fryers.*

Alphonso. Good Fathers, I thanke Heaven, I feele no sicknesse.

Castruchio. He speaks againe.

Alphonso. Nothing that barres the free use of my spirit,
Me thinks the ayre's sweet to me, and company
A thing I covet now——*Castruchio.*

Castruchio. Sir,——
He speaks, and knowes, for Heaven sake break my pate Lord,
That I may be sure I sleep not.

Alphonso. Thou wert honest,
Ever among the rank of good men counted.

436

I have been absent long out of the world,   40
A dreame I have lived, how doe's it looke *Castruchio*?
What wonders are abroad?
Castruchio.   I fling off duty
To your dead Brother, for he is dead in goodnesse,
And to the living hope of brave *Alphonso*,
The noble heire of nature, and of honour,
I fasten my Allegeance.
Marco.   Softly Captaine,
We dare not trust the ayre with this blest secret,——
Good Sir, be close againe, heaven has restor'd ye,
And by miraculous meanes, to your faire health,
And made the instrument your enemies malice,   50
Which doe's prognosticate your noble fortune;
Let not our carelesse joy lose you againe, Sir,
Help to deliver ye to a further danger,
I pray you passe in, and rest a while forgotten,
For if your brother come to know you are well againe,
And ready to inherit as your right,
Before we have strength enough to assure your life,
What will become of you? and what shall we
Deserve in all opinions that are honest,
For our losse of judgement, care, and loyalty?   60
Rugio.   Deere Sir, passe in, Heaven has begun the worke,
And blest us all, let our indeavours follow,
To preserve this blessing to our timely uses,
And bring it to the noble end we aime at;
Let our cares worke now, and our eyes pick out
An houre to shew ye safely to your Subjects,
A secure houre.
Alphonso.   I am counsell'd; ye are faithfull.
Castruchio.   Which houre shall not be long, as we shall handle it.
Once more the tender of my duty.
Alphonso.   Thank ye.
Castruchio.   Keep you the Monastery.
Rugio.   Strong enough Ile warrant ye. 70
                                                Exeunt.

Enter [Tony] *the Foole, and* Podrano.

Podrano.   Who are all these that crowde about the Court Foole?
    Those strange new faces?
Foole.   They are Suitors Coxcombe,
    Dainty fine Suitors to the widow Lady,
    Thou hadst best make one of 'em, thou wilt be hang'd as
      handsomly
    At the Moneths end, and with as much joy follow'd
    (And 'twere to morrow), as many mourning bawds for thee,
    And holy Nuns, whose vestall fire ne're vanishes,
    In sackcloth smocks, as if thou wert Heire apparent
    To all the impious Suburbs, and the sink-holes.
Podrano.   Out you base rogue.
Foole.   Why dost abuse thy selfe?   10
    Thou art to blame, I take thee for a Gentleman,
    But why doe's not thy Lord and Master marry her?
Podrano.   Why, she is his sister.
Foole.   'Tis the better Foole,
    He may make bold with his owne flesh and blood,
    For a my conscience there's none else will trust him,
    Then he may pleasure the King at a dead pinch too,
    Without a *Mephestophilus*, such as thou art,
    And ingrosse the royall disease like a true Subject.
Podrano.   Thou wilt be whipt.
Foole.   I am sure thou wilt be hangd,
    I have lost a Ducket else, which I would be loath   20
    To venter without certainty. They appeare.

Suitors [*Lawyer, Physitian, Captain, and Cutpurse*] *pass by.*

Podrano.   Why these are rascals.
Foole.   They were meant to be so,
    Doe's thy Master deserve better kinred?
Podrano.   Ther's an old Lawyer,
    Trim'd up like a Gally Foist, what would he do with her?
Foole.   As Userers do with their Gold, he would looke on her,

21.1 *Suitors pass by.*] F2; *om.* F1

438

And read her over once a day, like a hard report,
Feed his dull eye, and keepe his fingers itching;
For any thing else, she may appeale to a Parliament,
Sub Pæna's and *Post Teas* have spoil'd his Codpeece;
There's a Physitian too, older then he,   30
A *Gallen Gallenatius*, but he has lost his spurres,
He would be nibling too.
Podrano.   I marked the man,
If he be a man.
Foole.   Has much a do to be so,
Searecloths and Sirrops glew him close together,
He would fall a peeces else; mending of she patients,
And then trying whether they be right or no
In his owne person (there's the honest care an't)
Has mollifi'd the man; if he do marry her,
And come but to warme him well at *Cupids* bonfire,
He will bulge so subtilly and suddenly,   40
You may snatch him up by parcels, like a Sea Rack:
Will your Worship go, and looke upon the rest, Sir,
And heare what they can say for themselves?
Podrano.   I'le follow thee.
                                            Exeunt.

                Enter Camillo, Menallo, Cleanthes, Castruchio.   [V. iii]

Camillo.   You tell us wonders.
Castruchio.   But I tell you truths,
They are both well.
Menallo.   Why are not we in Armes then?
And all the Island given to know——
Castruchio.   Discreetly
And privately it must be done, 'twill misse else,
And prove our ruines; most of the noble Citizens

---

29 *Post Teas*] Sympson (*Posteas*); *Post Kaes* F1–2
31 A] Weber (Sympson); And F1–2
31 *Gallenatius*] i.e., *gallinaceus*, cock-like
*41 Rack] *stet* F1–2   *3 Island] *stet* F1–2

Know it by me, and stay the houre to attend it,
Prepare your hearts and friends, let their's be right too,
And keepe about the King to avoid suspition;
When you shall heare the Castle Bell, take courage,
And stand like men, away, the King is comming.   10
                        Exeunt Lords.   [*Manet* Castruchio.]

                    Enter Frederick *and* Sorano.

Frederick.   Now Captain, what have you done with your Prisoner?
Castruchio.   He is dead, Sir, and his body flung i'th Sea,
    To feed the fishes, 'twas your will, I take it,
    I did it from a strong Commission,
    And stood not to capitulate.
Frederick.   'Tis well done,
    And I shall love you for your faith. What anger
    Or sorrow did he utter at his end?
Castruchio.   Faith little, Sir, that I gave any eare to,
    He would have spoke, but I had no Commission
    To argue with him, so I flung him off;   20
    His Lady would have seene, but I lockt her up,
    For feare her womans teares should hinder us.
Frederick.   'Twas trusty still. I wonder, my *Sorano*,
    We heare not from the Monastery; I believe
    They gave it not, or else it wrought not fully.
Castruchio.   Did you name the Monastery?
Frederick.   Yes, I did Captaine.
Castruchio.   I saw the Fryer this morning, and Lord *Rugio*,
    Bitterly weeping, and wringing of their hands,
    And all the holy men hung downe their heads.
Sorano.   'Tis done, Ile warrant ye.
Castruchio.   I asked the reason.   30
Frederick.   What answer hadst thou?
Castruchio.   This in few words, Sir,
    Your Brothers dead, this morning he deceased,
    I was your servant, and I wept not, Sir,
    I knew 'twas for your good.
Frederick.   It shall be for thine too,

                                440

Captaine, indeed it shall.——O my *Sorano*,
Now we shall live.
Sorano.   I, now there's none to trouble ye.
Frederick.   Captaine, bring out the woman, and give way
  To any Suitor that shall come to marry her,
  Of what degree soever.
Castruchio.   It shall be done, Sir.
                              Exit Captaine [Castruchio].
Frederick.   O let me have a lusty Banquet after it,   40
  I will be high and merry.

      Enter Evanthe, Camillo, Cleanthes, Menallo, [Tony *the*] *Foole*,
                    Castruchio.

Sorano.   There be some Lords
  That I could counsell ye to fling from Court, Sir,
  They pry into our actions, they are such
  The foolish people call their Countries honours,
  Honest brave things, and stile them with such Titles,
  As if they were the patternes of the Kingdome,
  Which makes them proud, and prone to looke into us,
  And talk at randome of our actions;
  They should be yours, lovers of your commands,
  And followers of your will, bridles and curbs   50
  To the hard headed Commons that maligne us;
  They come here to do honour to my sister,
  To laugh at your severity, and fright us;
  If they had power, what would these men do?
  Do you heare, Sir, how privily they whisper?
Frederick.   I shall silence 'em,
  And to their shames, within this weeke *Sorano*,
  In the meane time have patience.
Sorano.   How they leere,
  And looke upon me as I were a Monster
  And talk and jeere! How I shall pull your plumes, Lords,

*41 *Enter*. . .Castruchio.] *stet* F 1
49 be yours, lovers] Dyce; be your lovers F 1; be lovers F 2
57 leere] Colman; jeere F 1-2

How I shall humble ye within these two daies,   60
Your great names, nor your Country cannot save ye.
Frederick.   Let in the Suitors.   [*Exit* Castruchio.]
                                    Yet submit, Ile pardon ye,
You are halfe undone already, do not winde
My anger to that height, it may consume ye,
And utterly destroy thee, faire *Evanthe*:
Yet I have mercy.
Evanthe.   Use it to your bawds,
To me use cruelty, it best becomes ye,
And shewes more Kingly: I contemne your mercy,
It is a cozening, and a bawdy mercy;
Can any thing be hoped for, to relieve me?   70
Or is it fit I thank you for a pitty,
When you have kill'd my Lord?

                    Enter Lawyer, Physitian, Captain, Cutpurse.

Frederick.   Who will have her?
Evanthe.   My teares are gone,
My teares of love to my deere *Valerio*,
But I have fill'd mine eyes againe with anger,
O were it but so powerfull to consume ye;
My tongue with curses I have arm'd against ye,
With Maiden curses, that Heaven crownes with horrors,
My heart set round with hate against thy tyranny;
O would my hands could hold the fire of Heaven,
Wrapt in the thunder that the Gods revenge with,   80
That like sterne Justice I might fling it on thee;
Thou art a King of Monsters, not of men,
And shortly thou wilt turne this Land to Devills.
Frederick.   Ile make you one first, and a wretched Devill,——
Come, who will have her?
Lawyer.   I an't like your Majesty, I am a Lawyer,
I can make her a Joynter of any mans Land in *Naples*,

                    62 *Exit* Castruchio.] Dyce; *om.* F 1–2
                    72 *Enter*...Cutpurse.] Dyce; *after line* 64 F 1–2
                    87 Joynter] *i.e.,* jointure

                                    442

And she shall keepe it too, I have a trick for it.

Foole.   Canst thou make her a Joynter of thine honesty?
Or thy ability, thou lewd abridgement?   90
Those are non-suted and flung o're the barre.

Physitian.   An't please your Majesty to give me leave,
I dare accept her; and though old I seeme, Lady,
Like *Eason*, by my art I can renew
Youth and ability.

Foole.   In a powdring Tub
Stew thy selfe tender againe, like a Cock Chicken,
The broth may be good, but the flesh is not fit for doggs sure.

Captaine.   Lady, take me, and Ile maintaine thine honour,
I am a poore Captaine, as poore people call me,
Very poore people, for my Souldiers   100
They are quartered in the outsides of the City,
Men of ability, to make good a high way;
We have but two grand Enemies that oppose us,
The *Don Gout*, and the Gallowes.

Foole.   I believe ye,
And both these you will binde her for a Joynter;
Now Signior *Firke.*

Cutpurse.   Madam, take me and be wise,
I am rich and nimble, and those are rare in one man,
Every mans pocket is my Treasury,
And no man weares a Sute but fits me neatly;
Clothes you shall have, and weare the purest Linnen,   110
I have a tribute out of every Shop, Lady;
Meat you shall eat (I have my Caters out too)
The best and lustiest, and drinke good Wine, good Lady,
Good quickening Wine, Wine that will make you caper.
And at the worst——

Foole.   It is but capring short, Sir,
You seldome stay for Agues or for Surfets,
A shaking fit of a whip sometimes o're takes ye,
Marry you dye most commonly of chokings,
Obstructions of the halter are your ends ever;

104 *Don Gout*] *i.e.*, Spanish gout, syphilis

443

Pray leave your horne and your knife for her to live on.　　120
Evanthe.　Poore wretched people, why do you wrong your selves?
　Though I fear'd death, I should feare you ten times more,
　You are every one a new death, and an odious,
　The earth will purifie corrupted bodies,
　You'le make us worse, and stinke eternally.
　Go home, go home, and get good Nurces for you,
　Dreame not of wives.
Frederick.　　　　　You shall have one of 'em,
　If they dare venter for ye.
Evanthe.　　　　　They are dead already,
　Crawling diseases that must creep into
　The next grave they finde open, are these fit husbands　130
　For her you have loved Sir? though you hate me now,
　And hate me mortally, as I hate you,
　Your noblenesse (in that you have done otherwise,
　And named *Evanthe* once as your poore Mistris)
　Might offer worthier choice.
Frederick.　　　　　Speake, who dare take her
　For one moneth, and then dye?
Physitian.　　　　　Dye Sir?
Frederick.　　　　　I, dye Sir,
　That's the condition.
Physitian.　　　　One moneth is too little
　For me to repent in for my former pleasure,
　And go still on, unlesse I were sure she would kill me,
　And kill me delicately before my day,　　140
　Make it up a yeare, for by that time I must dye,
　My body will hold out no longer.
Frederick.　　　　　No Sir,
　It must be but a moneth.
Lawyer.　　　　Then farewell Madam,
　This is like to be a great yeare of dissention
　Among good people, and I dare not lose it,
　There will be money got.
Captaine.　　　　Blesse your good Ladiship,

*120 horne...knife] *stet* F1-2　　　*139 And] Mason; To F1-2

444

There's nothing in the grave but bones and ashes,
In Tavernes there's good wine, and excellent wenches,
And Surgeons while we live.
Cutpurse.   Adieu sweet Lady,
Lay me when I am dead neare a rich Alderman,   150
I cannot pick his Purse; no, ile no dying,
Though I steale Linnen, ile not steale my shrowde yet.
All [*Suitors*].   Send ye a happy match.   *Exeunt.*
Foole.   And you all halters,
You have deserved 'em richly.——These do all Villanies,
And mischiefes of all sorts, yet those they feare not:
To flinch where a faire wench is at the stake!
Evanthe.   Come, your sentence, let me dye, you see Sir,
None of your valiant men dare venture on me,
A moneth's a dangerous thing.
                    . . . .
                    Will you then be willing
To dye at the time prefixt? that I must know too,   160
And know it beyond doubt.
Frederick.   What if I did wench?
Evanthe.   On that condition if I had it certaine,
I would be your any thing, and you should injoy me,
How ever in my nature I abhor you,
Yet as I live I would be obedient to you;
But when your time came how I should rejoyce,
How then I should bestir my selfe to thanke ye!
To see your throat cut, how my heart would leap Sir!
I would dye with you, but first I would so torter ye,
And cow you in your end, so dispise you,   170
For a weak and wretched coward, you must end sure;
Still make ye feare, and shake, dispised, still laugh at ye.
Frederick.   Away with her, let her dye instantly.

Enter Valerio *disguis'd.*

159 *See note* 173.1   171 coward...sure] *i.e.*, coward that you must surely end
*173.1 *Enter* Valerio *disguis'd.*] Colman; *after* thing, *line* 159, *the stage-direction
being followed by a duplicate of line* 173 *and the speech-prefix* 'Evan.' *before* Will, *line*
159 F 1–2

Camillo.   Stay, there's another, and a Gentleman,
  His habit shewes no lesse, may be his businesse
  Is for this Ladies love.
Frederick.   Say why ye come Sir,
  And what you are.
Valerio.   I am discended nobly,
  A Prince by birth, and by my trade a Souldier,
  A Princes fellow; *Abidos* brought me forth,
  My Parents Duke *Agenor*, and faire *Egla*,   180
  My businesse hither to renew my love
  With a young noble spirit, call'd *Valerio*;
  Our first acquaintance was at Sea, in fight
  Against a Turkish man of War, a stout one,
  Where Lyon-like I saw him shew his valour,
  And as he had been made of compleat vertue,
  Spirit, and fire, no dreggs of dull earth in him.
Evanthe [*aside*].   Thou art a brave Gentleman, and bravely
  speakest him.
Valerio.   The Vessell dancing under him for joy,
  And the rough whisling winds becalm'd to view him,   190
  I saw the childe of honour, for he was young,
  Deale such an Almes amongst the spightfull pagans
  (His towring sword flew like an eager Falcon)
  And round about his reach invade the Turks:
  He had intrencht himselfe in his dead quarryes;
  The silver Cressents on the tops they carried
  Shranke in their heads to see his rage so bloody,
  And from his fury suffered sad ecclipses;
  The game of death was never plaid more nobly,
  The meager theefe grew wanton in his mischiefes,   200
  And his shrunke hollow eyes smil'd on his ruines.
Evanthe [*aside*].   Heaven keepe this Gentleman from being a
  Suitor,
  For I shall ne're deny him, he's so noble.

179 *Abidos*] F 2; *Abidig* F 1
*180 My...*Egla*,] F 2; *line repeated* F 1 (*Agenor*ᴧ)
*188 *aside*] *see Textual Notes*   *196 the tops] *stet* F 1-2

Valerio.   But what can last long? strength and spirit wasted,
   And fresh supplies flew on upon this Gentleman,
   Breathlesse and weary with oppression,
   And almost kill'd with killing: 'twas my chance
   In a tall Ship I had to view the fight;
   I set into him, entertain'd the Turke,
   And for an houre gave him so hot a breakfast,   210
   He clapt all linnen up he had to save him,
   And like a Lovers thought he fled our fury;
   There first I saw the man I lov'd, *Valerio*,
   There was acquainted, there my soul grew to him,
   And his to me, we were the twins of friendship.
Evanthe [*aside*].   Fortune protect this man, or I shall ruine him.
Valerio.   I made this voyage to behold my friend,
   To warme my love anew at his affection;
   But since I landed, I have heard his fate,
   My Fathers had not been to me more cruell: 220
   I have lamented too, and yet I keepe
   The treasure of a few teares for you Lady,
   For by description you were his *Evanthe*.
Evanthe.   Can he weep that's a stranger to my story?
   And I stand still and looke on? Sir, I thanke ye;
   If noble spirits after their departure,
   Can know, and wish, certaine his soule gives thanks too;
   There are your teares againe, and when yours faile Sir,
   Pray ye call to me, I have some store to lende ye.
   Your name?
Valerio.   *Urbino.*
Evanthe.   That I may remember,   230
   That little time I have to live, your friendships,
   My tongue shall study both.
Frederick.   Do you come hither,
   Only to tell this story Prince *Urbino*?
Valerio.   My businesse now is, Sir, to wooe this Lady.
Evanthe.   Blessing defend ye; Do you know the danger?
Valerio.   Yes, and I feare it not, danger's my play-fellow,
   Since I was man 'thas been my best companion,——

I know your doome, 'tis for a Moneth you give her,
And then his life you take that marries her.

Frederick. 'Tis true, nor can your being borne a Prince,   240
If you accept the offer, free you from it.

Valerio. I not desire it, I have cast the worst,
And even that worst to me is many blessings;
I lov'd my friend, not measur'd out by time,
Nor hired by circumstance of place and honour,
But for his wealthy selfe and worth I lov'd him,
His minde and noble mold he ever mov'd in,
And woe his friend because she was worthy of him,
The only relick that he left behinde, Sir;
To give his ashes honour: Lady take me,   250
And in me keepe *Valerio's* love alive still,
When I am gone, take those that shall succeed me,
Heaven must want light, before you want a husband,
To raise up Heires of love and noble memory,
To your unfortunate——

Evanthe.   Am I still hated?
Hast thou no end, O fate, of my affliction?
Was I ordained to be a common Murdresse?
And of the best men too? Good Sir——

Valerio [aside].   Peace Sweet,
Looke on my hand.

Evanthe.   I do accept the Gentleman,——
I faint with joy.   [*Aside.*]

Frederick.   I stop it, none shall have her,   260
Convey this stranger hence.

Valerio. I am no stranger.——

          [*Throws off disguise as bell rings within.*]
                    Harke to the bell, that rings,
Harke, harke, proud *Frederick*, that was King of mischief,
Harke, thou abhorred man, dost thou heare thy sentence?
Doe's not this bell ring in thine eares thy ruine?

Frederick. What bell is this?

Camillo.   The Castle bell: Stand sure Sir,

248 woe] *i.e.*, woo

448

And move not, if you do you perish.
Menallo.　It rings your knell;——*Alphonso*, King *Alphonso*.
All.　*Alphonso*, King *Alphonso*.
Frederick.　　　　　　　　　I am betraid,
　　Lock fast the Palace.
Camillo.　　　　　　　We have all the keyes, Sir.　　　　270
　　And no doore here shall shut without our Licence.
Cleanthes.　Do you shake now Lord *Sorano*? no new trick?
　　Nor speedy poyson to prevent this businesse?
　　No bawdy meditation now to fly to?
Frederick.　Treason, Treason, Treason.
Camillo.　　　　　　　　　　Yes, we heare ye,
　　And we have found the Traytor in your shape, Sir,
　　Wee'l keep him fast too.

Enter Alphonso, *Rugio*, Marco, *Castruchio, Queene, with Guard.*

Frederick.　　　　　　　Recover'd! then I am gone,
　　The Sun of all my pompe is set and vanisht.
Alphonso.　Have you not forgot this face of mine, King *Frederick*?
　　Brother I am come to see you, and have brought　　280
　　A Banquet to be merry with your Grace;
　　I pray sit downe, I do beseech your Majesty
　　And eat, eat freely, Sir; why do you start?
　　Have you no stomack to the meat I bring you?
　　Dare you not taste? have ye no Antidotes?
　　You need not feare; *Sorano*'s a good Apothecary,
　　Me thinks you looke not well,——some fresh wine for him,
　　Some of the same he sent me by *Sorano*;——
　　I thank you for't, it sav'd my life, I am bound to ye,
　　But how 'twill worke on you——I hope your Lordship　　290
　　Will pledge him too, me thinks you looke but scurvily,
　　And would be put into a better colour,
　　But I have a canded Toad for your good Lordship.
Sorano [*aside*].　Would I had any thing that would dispatch me,
　　So it were downe, and I out of this feare once.
Frederick.　Sir, thus low as my duty now compells me,
　　　　　　　　　　　　　　　[*He and* Queene *kneele.*]

449

I do confesse my unbounded sinnes, my errours,
And feele within my soule the smarts already;
Hide not the noble nature of a brother,
The pitty of a friend, from my afflictions;   300
Let me a while lament my misery,
And cast the load off of my wantonnesse,
Before I finde your fury, then strike home
(I do deserve the deepest blow of Justice)
And then how willingly, O death, Ile meet thee.

Alphonso.   Rise, Madam, those sweet tears are potent speakers,
And brother live, but in the Monastery,
Where I lived, with the selfe same silence too,
Ile teach you to be good against your will brother,
Your tongue has done much harme, that must be dumbe now;   310
The daily pilgrimage to my fathers Tombe
(Teares, sighs, and groanes, you shall weare out your daies with,
And true ones too) you shall performe deare brother;
Your diet shall be slender to inforce these;
To light a pennance, Sir.

Frederick.   I do confesse it.

Alphonso.   *Sorano* you shall——

Sorano [*aside*].   How he studies for it,
Hanging's the least part of my pennance certaine.

                                    Evanthe *kneeles.*

Alphonso.   What Lady's that that kneeles?

Castruchio.   The chaste *Evanthe.*

Alphonso.   Sweet, your petition?

Evanthe.   'Tis for this bad man, Sir,
Abominable bad, but yet my brother.   320

Alphonso.   The bad man shall attend as bad a Master,
And both shall be confin'd within the Monastery;
His ranke flesh shall be pull'd with daily fasting,
But once a week he shall smell meat, he will surfet else,
And his immodest minde compell'd to prayer;
On the bare bords he shall lye, to remember
The wantonnesse he did commit in beds;

            315 To] *i.e.,* too   *323 pull'd] *stet* F 1-2

                        450

And drinke faire water, that will ne're inflame him;
He sav'd my life, though he purpos'd to destroy me,
For which Ile save his, though I make it miserable: 330
Madam, at Court I shall desire your company,   [*To* Queene.]
You are wise and vertuous, when you please to visit
My brother *Frederick*, you shall have our Licence,——
My deere best friend, *Valerio*.
Valerio.   Save *Alphonso*.
Omnes.   Long live *Alphonso*, King of us, and *Naples*.
Alphonso.   Is this the Lady that the wonder goes on?
Honour'd sweet maid, here take her my *Valerio*,
The King now gives her, she is thine owne without feare:
Brother, have you so much provision that is good?
Not season'd by *Sorano* and his Cooks?   340
That we may venture on with honest safety,
We and our friends?
Frederick.   All that I have is yours, Sir.
Alphonso.   Come then, let's in, and end this Nuptiall,
Then to our Coronation with all speed:
My vertuous maid, this day Ile be your Bride-man,
And see you bedded to your owne desires too;
Beshrew me Lords, who is not merry hates me,
Onely *Sorano* shall not beare my cup:
Come, now forget old paines and injuries,
As I must do, and drowne all in faire healths;   350
That Kingdom's blessed, where the King begins
His true love first, for there all loves are twins.

                                        Exeunt Omnes.

                    *328 water,] *stet* F 1–2

Epilogue.

We have your favours Gentlemen, and you
Have our indeavours, (deere friends grudge not now,)
There's none of you, but when you please can sell
Many a lame Horse, and many a faire tale tell;
Can put off many a maid unto a friend,
That was not so since the action at *Mile-end*;
Ours is a Virgin yet, and they that love
Untainted flesh, we hope our friends will prove.

6 Mile-end] stet F 1–2

TEXTUAL NOTES

Persons Represented

Persons] The F2 dramatis personæ describes Frederick as the 'usurper' of Alphonso's kingdom, but, as Dyce points out, Frederick was chosen to succeed his father because of Alphonso's disqualifying melancholy and did not gain the crown illegally (I.ii.27–35). Weber notes, 'The queen has been nameless hitherto, but in the first folio, *Mar.* is prefixed to her speeches in the first act, and I have ventured to name her *Maria* upon this testimony.' In the present edition, however, she is called Queen; she is one, and *Maria* is uncertain. The name of Sorano's servant does not occur in any other Elizabethan play, and I have been unable to find it elsewhere. It is spelled out six times in F1, as *Podramo* at I.i.56 (F4; Compositor *B*) and I.i.174 (F4ᵛ; *B*) and as *Podrano* at I.ii.147 (G1ᵛ; *B*); IV.ii.0.1 and 1 (H2; *A*), and V.ii.0.1 (I1; *B*). The variation occurs only in *B*'s work, *Podramo* being on the first and second pages he typeset and *Podrano* on the fourth and – much later – the thirteenth and last. I believe *B* misread the name the first time he saw it and repeated his error when he shortly afterwards came upon the name again. Subsequently he got the name right, as did *A* when he encountered it.

In F1 the scene is mentioned several times as Naples (IV.i.80; V.iii.87; V.iii.335) and once as an island (V.iii.3), the last, as Sympson notes, apparently Fletcher's mistake, an easy one as the action has reference to no specific location.

I.i

14 This...imployed] Sympson emends to 'employ'd in'. A note contributed to Colman's edition by J. N. (John Nichols?) explains, however, that the construction is 'as this new lord is employed'.

47 absolute,] F2's comma is probably right, but it is not impossible that 'absolute' is an adverb – 'completely, unreservedly'.

118–119 Sir (No...Angels)] Mason notes that 'Nor I, I hope' (line 120) means 'Nor am I, I hope, in your power.' Editors subsequent to him punctuate as does F1, but accept Mason's interpretation.

157 Master] I.e., Sorano, Frederick's instructor in vice (Mason). J. N. (John Nichols?) believed the line is addressed to Sorano (Colman's edition).

I.ii

48–49 *Chorus*...Podrano.] The stage-direction may have been written in
such a way that its last word – *Podrano* – was mistaken by the F1 compositor for a speech-prefix, or F1's *Pod.* may be the vestige of an earlier
layer of composition. See the textual note on I.ii.103.1. If the manuscript
continued 'So...us.' (lines 49–50) to Menallo, which is not impossible,
the compositor's error is easier to imagine, but it also may be that the
compositor thought the manuscript speech-prefix at line 49 to have been
replaced by *Podrano*, as F2's correction implies. At least it is clear the
lines do not belong to Cleanthes, who is the asker of questions about
Alphonso's condition, not one who has groaned with the monastic choir.
It is also possible that Podrano rather than Sorano should carry the cabinet
(i.e., that the stage-direction should read *Sorano, and Podrano with the
Cabinet*). This complicates the mechanics of the mistake, however, and
because at I.i.178 Sorano has ordered Podrano to 'bring it to me instantly',
the cabinet may already have been delivered to him.

60–63 'Tis...water.] The water is a cosmetic lotion (*O.E.D.*, *sb.* 16),
and such concoctions contained strange ingredients. Podrano's last line
seems to mean either 'This water never came through [*O.E.D.*, Convey,
v. 8.a] a pipe from a regular water supply [conduit = aqueduct, canal;
O.E.D., *sb.* 1]' or 'who will never be a conduit pipe to convey this water'
rather than 'Is there no conduit pipe to take this water away?' For the
infinitive in place of a preposition and a gerund (here 'for conveying'),
see E. A. Abbott, *A Shakesperian Grammar* (London, 1879), §356. Evanthe
probably 'begins to exercise' in the sense of practising herself in the
cosmetic arts (*O.E.D.*, Exercise, *v.* 5.b).

103.1 *Exeunt*...Podrano] F1's direction is wrong because Podrano is no
lord, the discrepancy perhaps being a bit of authorial or scribal carelessness.
It is somewhat strange, however, that this stage-direction substantially
duplicates that at line 50, a possible indication that lines 50–103 were re-
written and inserted.

110 the] F2's reading seems right, as 'their' would imply that Cassandra
knows Podrano's words to be Frederick's and Sorano's. She does not
know this, and Podrano's instructions came only from Sorano in any case.
In the next line, however, F2's change to 'make' is a sophistication, an
unnecessary regularizing of the tense.

119 wilde] 'Licentious, dissolute, loose' (*O.E.D.*, *adj.* 7.b).

146–147 am,...things——] Sympson notes:

'The Sense here is easy enough, but the Expression labours. I would read,

> *A Favour or a Grace, for such as I am*
> *Course common things——You're welcome*, &c.

i.e. such common things as I am are not worthy of a Grace, &c.'

Regarding this, Colman comments, 'We see no difficulty here, either of *sense* or *expression*', and the later editors agree by remaining silent on the point. The sentence may be supposed to end 'you hold to be', yet it is not entirely clear whether 'course, common things' refers to Frederick, as Sympson thought, to the favour or grace, or to those who supposedly feast with Evanthe. I think there was an omission between 'am' and 'Course'. Cf. notes on IV.v.22 and V.iii.173.1.

154 hanging holder] I.e., 'an attendant' (*O.E.D.*, Hanging, *vbl. sb.* 8). Dyce compares *The Wild-Goose Chase*, III.i: 'if she want an usher...one that...Can hold a hanging up with approbation' (ed. 1845).

II.i

5 long...Souldiers] Weber notes: 'It would appear that the pay of soldiers in the Low Countries was sometimes increased by paying them for more days than the month or the week contains'; he cites parallels in *The Witch of Edmonton* (ed. Fredson Bowers, III.i.40) and *The Fair Maid of the Inn* (ed. F. L. Lucas, IV.ii.107). Dyce adds *Hudibras*, 2.1.513, and Lucas *Anything for a Quiet Life*, I.i.246–7. As Lucas remarks: 'The captain would thus be able to keep back more of his men's pay.'

8–34 A...hanging.] Many of the witticisms turn on the idea of a man's killing himself because of sexual longing or exertion, with associated innuendoes. 'Stone' (line 9) is lithiasis (*O.E.D.*, 10), to which 'go hard with' makes punning reference, but also 'testicle' (*O.E.D.*, 11). Marrying and hanging are, of course, conventionally linked, as in line 2 (Tilley W232), but hanging is the surer contract (line 14) because wives play false. Firearms and lethal or fiery women are frequently compared (e.g., *The Knight of the Burning Pestle*, ed. Hoy, v, 101ff), and a mortar-piece (line 24) is 'a short piece of ordnance with a large bore' (*O.E.D.*). The cocka-trice, the legendary creature whose looks kill, is also a harlot (*O.E.D.* 3). March's proverbial lion (Tilley M641) may also have sexual overtones; a 'lioness', at least, was a harlot (Farmer, *Slang*, 3).

11 Saint *Davids* day] The allusion is to the English custom of hanging or burning the effigy of a Welshman on St David's Day, 1 March (see T. F. Thiselton-Dyer, *Folk-Lore of Shakespeare* (New York, 1884), p. 304). Theobald believed the reference indicates the play to have been 'acted about the latter End of *January*' (Sympson ed.), which Weber interprets to mean that the play's action is supposed to occur at that time.

25 quarters] F1's reading is a literal error. The *O.E.D.*'s earliest citation of 'quartet' in any sense is dated 1790.

48 bawdy Court] A church court in which offences against canon law were tried, frequently moral offences.

II.ii

56 the] All editors have kept F1's 'that', but only with some effort. Heath (Dyce ed.) argues that *'that* is by way of emphasis, the tomb which attracts the eyes of spectators', Weber believes the Queen points to a tomb from the window, and Dyce thinks the word refers to the idea of the tomb 'implied in what has been previously said concerning death, &c.' But, as Mason observes, the idea is general rather than particular, and 'that' could have been carried down from line 55.

II.iv

4 Lettice] A whitish-grey fur, punning on 'lettuce'.

11–12 Puts...too] Weber observes the similarity between this situation and a part of Jonson's *Love Restored*, performed 6 January 1612. There are several coincidences. In the masque Robin Goodfellow describes the difficulty he encountered in gaining entry to the hall even though he shifted into a variety of shapes:

'Then I pretended to be a musician [see II.vi.20]. . . . I saw a fine citizens wife, or two, let in; and that figure provok'd mee exceedingly to take it: which I had no sooner done, but one o' the *Blackguard* had his hand in my vestrie. . . . He thought he might be bold with me, because I had not a husband in sight to squeake to [cf. line 17].'
(Herford and Simpson (eds.), VII, 379–80)

21 *3. Wife.*] Two of the wives are young and pretty and will be admitted; the third is old and ugly and will not be. Assuming that 1. Citizen is matched with 1. Wife and so on, one of the pretty wives must be 3. because of her husband's insistence upon following her at line 29. The other is probably 2. because of 2. Citizen's reply at line 13 and because she and 3. are the two instructed by Tony in lines 17–20. This line, therefore, should be 3.'s, as 1., by elimination, is the wife Tony rejects. It follows that 2. and 3. Citizens are the two who try to gain admission at II.vi.20–1.

31 securely arm'd] The joke seems to be on two senses of 'armed': 'of animals: furnished with horns', as in 'The arm'd Rhinoceros' of *Macbeth* 1378 (*O.E.D.*, *ppl. a.*¹ 2.b), and the heraldic significance, 'represented with...horns' (sense 5). 'Securely' probably means 'certainly' (*adv.* 3) as well as 'safely' (armoured with thick skulls).

31 *Exeunt...*Woman] Regarding F1's *Women*, cf. note on III.iii.131.

50 sect;] For F1's 'set‸' Seward conjectured 'Yet' and Sympson 'And yet'. Colman reads with F1, glossing '*A set people* may signify "*formal, precise* people that call those poor fools honest;" or that "people call those poor fools an honest set."' His first interpretation could possibly be right, although the *O.E.D.* does not substantiate the meaning he finds in 'set'

except by extension (see *ppl. a.*, especially 5 and 6). Mason rejects this reading but elaborates upon Colman's second by recommending a comma after 'set' and citing V.iii.41ff – 'There be some Lords... | The foolish people call their Countries honours, | Honest brave things', which, as he says, alludes to the same persons Tony mentions here. The difficulty with this is that the *O.E.D.*'s earliest illustration of 'set' in the sense required (*sb.² 2*: 'A...group associated by community of...interests') is dated 1682. *The English Dialect Dictionary* gives a meaning that might do – 'A good quantity' – but in the illustrations the noun is always modified and usually plural, as in 'no great sets' (*sb. 19*). It thus seems best to accept Mason's idea but to emend 'set' to the closely related 'sect' (*sb.¹ 6*: 'A school of opinion...more or less jestingly'), a word in use from the early seventeenth century. Cf. Cynthia's 'see...a greater Majestie, Betweene our sect and us' (*The Maid's Tragedy*, I.ii.272–4).

54 to]   Usually interpreted, possibly correctly, as 'two'. Cf. 'They looke like potch'd Eggs with the soules [i.e., 'sowls' – here, I presume, the meat of eggs] suckt out, Empty and full of wind' (*Queen of Corinth*, F 1:6 B 1a).

60 Lay...King.]   'Lay thy hand a thy heart' is 'take it to heart, consider it seriously' as in Capulet's 'Thursday is neare, lay hand on heart, advise' (*Rom.* 2237). The joke seems to turn on the indecent meaning of 'presse'; cf. *The Faithful Friends*, MSR, lines 533–5.

II.v

10 What...more?]   Probably 'what should I seek more for?'; possibly 'what, should I seek for more?'

43 unto]   As Valerio has been speaking quite even verse, F 2 is probably right to regularize this line. The F 1 compositor may have been thrown off stride by the addition that immediately follows, or have carried down 'to' from the preceding line.

46 must_∧]   Editors since Colman add a comma, but the line remains ambiguous – 'they must dance well before the ladies dance' or 'they must dance well because the ladies will be watching'. As the masque makes no provision for the Ladies to be taken out, the latter meaning is apparently intended.

50 Musick_∧]   Editors since Sympson add punctuation, which makes 'forward' a command. The word, however, means 'well advanced, nearly finished' (*O.E.D., a. adv.* and *sub. 5*).

52.1 *Exeunt severally.*]   F 1's *Exit* at line 51, which appears to apply to Valerio, is probably a vestige of a revision; see p. 360. *Severally* is justified by the fact that Valerio will join the wedding party whereas the Lords will attend the doors of the hall in which the masque is to be presented.

II.vi

0.1 *Knocking within.*]   Between II.v and II.vi the scene shifts from Valerio's quarters to the hall, and it is the doors of this that are under assault by the Citizens. The stage-direction seems to have been displaced in F1 because of a revision. See pp. 360f.

16 gentlewoman]   Although 'Gentl.' and 'gent.' stand for 'gentlemen' at I.ii.11; II.i.58; and II.v.45, here, as Mason conjectured, 'gentlewoman' is intended. See p. 364. Weber notes: 'The baldness alluded to was the consequence of venereal disease.' Weber also thinks the queans are 'curtall'd' because they are dressed in 'the short mantles anciently worn by prostitutes'; it is more likely that their hair is cut short ('Our women cut their hair like men, The cock's ore-master'd by the hen': 'An Excellent Medley' in J. Payne Collier, *Broadside Black-letter Ballads* (1868), p. 119).

20–21 2. *Citizen* (*within*)....3. *Citizen* (*within*).]   See the textual notes on II.iv.11–12 and II.iv.21.

23 brusled]   I.e., roughed up. The *O.E.D.*, citing only this line, defines the word, doubtfully, as 'to crack; to bruise a little', but *The English Dialect Dictionary* gives 'to push roughly'.

25.1–25.3 *Enter...them*]   The F1 direction seems to call for a discovery rather than for a regular entrance, a matter about which Fletcher appears to have changed his mind, as he also did about including the three courtiers in the wedding party. The direction was not revised, however. Following Dyce's lead, I have provided an entrance to the main stage, and it seems natural for the three Lords to leave their door-keeping to join the other courtiers. *A Curtain drawne* perhaps should be omitted, but I have retained it on the assumption that a masque scene might be employed which should not be revealed until the spectators have arranged themselves. See pp. 360f.

III.ii

115 good...ye]   F1's reading conflates 'much good may it do ye' with 'much may ye do with it', one of these expressions being a cancelled first shot. As far as meaning is concerned, there is little to choose, but the order of F1's words suggests that 'much [*good* an insertion missed] may it do ye [*with it* a deletion not observed]' was the reading as it was revised. This is also F2's version.

119–121 Heaven...me,]   F1's anticipation of line 127 and perhaps its transposition of lines 120 and 121 appear to result from a revision incorrectly handled. See p. 362. Weber believes that lines 120–7 were a theatrical cut carelessly restored in F1. See the textual note on V.iii.173.1.

119 and]   The idiom may seem odd, and the word, possibly an error for 'as' or 'for', could have been carried down from line 118. Yet 'and' could be used to mark 'the predicted consequence or fulfilment of...a

458

hypothesis put imperatively, or elliptically' (*O.E.D.*, *conj.* 8.b). With 'and' taken in this sense, Valerio means: 'Heaven, if you be not angry, then I have some hope yet.'

126 armes] Mason notes, 'I think we should read stubborn *aims*...as stubborn is an epithet more applicable to the mind than the body', and Dyce supports his conjecture, adducing 'arm' mistaken for 'aim' in *Tro.* 1218 and 3475 and *2H6* 2882 as well as 'aim' correctly employed in *Cor.* and *Ham.* (see Dyce's *Remarks on Mr. J. P. Collier's and Mr. C. Knight's Editions of Shakespeare* (London, 1844), pp. 152–3). Editors of Shakespeare have not agreed, however, that 'arm' is wrong in any of the instances cited, nor does it seem to be here. 'Armes' by metonymy means 'strengths', which stand in contrast to Valerio's weakness. Sympson rather confusingly remarks that '*Armes*...is plainly corrupted', although in his transcription of the F1 passage and his correction of it he prints '*Armes*' and 'Arms'. He actually means F1's erroneous 'armrs'.

III.iii

58–61 nick...set] The bawdy puns are on terms used in real tennis. 'Chase' refers to the second impact of a ball not returned, the value of the shot being 'determined by the nearness of the spot of impact to the end wall' (*O.E.D.*, *sb.*[1] 7); the 'nick' is the junction of the wall and floor (*Supp. to O.E.D.* (1976), *sb.*[1] 1.d). A 'nick chase' would be a second impact at that angle. According to Bertram L. O'Neill of the U.S. Court Tennis Association, the term is correct but very rarely used today; 'a chase better than three' would be a modern equivalent. The *O.E.D.* does not notice 'nick' as 'pudendum', but the usage was common bawdry; see, for example, Marston, *1 Antonio and Mellida*, ed. Hunter, Ind. 60, and Chapman, *The Widow's Tears*, ed. Ornstein, III.i.95. 'Gamester' (cf. I.i.169) and 'set' (a unit of six games, as in lawn tennis) also had salacious overtones.

89 That...prevention;] All editors have adopted F2's pointing, a colon after 'up' and a dash after 'prevention'. Mason objected that the last words are nonsense and that the dash means nothing; he wished to emend 'but' to 'by', but his proposal was rejected by Weber and Dyce. Both, one assumes, believe the prevention is the senile impotence described in the lines following, but F1 is more satisfactory than this. It seems to mean that Valerio's tender care for Evanthe is stronger than (controls) his passion and locks up all his energetic powers but self-control, the power to forestall or baffle (prevent) Frederick's murderous designs.

99 lightly] I.e., 'commonly' (Mason), 'merrily', and probably also 'wantonly' (cf. *O.E.D.*, Light, *a.*[1] 14.b), although the *O.E.D.* does not notice the adverb in this sense until 1745.

131 Woman] Regarding F1's mistake, cf. II.iv.31. 'Woman' here means 'waiting-woman'.

202 the tother] Although he knew this to be an acceptable form, Dyce prefers Langbaine's change to 'the other' because of 'the other' in the next line, but the inconsistency does not seem very important. In other occurrences (e.g., *The Faithful Shepherdess*, II.i.28, and *The Island Princess*, F1:3N4ᵛa) 'the tother' takes three syllables as it evidently does here, although two would make the line more regular.

IV.i

26 sound] Although no editor has questioned it, the word seems odd in this context, but it is probably authentic. It could mean either 'mere audible effect, without significance' (*O.E.D.*, *sb.*³ 4.a), linking with 'promises', or possibly 'fame' (*sb.*³ 5), but the *O.E.D.* gives no example of the latter sense in which 'sound' is used absolutely.

105 I...asse?] Evidently '*I* am an ass?' – derisively.

IV.ii

2 *Exit*.] The forty-five lines that follow in F1 and subsequent editions are an early version of the interview between Frederick and Valerio. Fletcher rewrote it as lines 40–134. See pp. 362–3 and 481–2.

5 fond, an't,] Cf. V.iii.86 (Dyce).

17 Elder-pipes] The allusion may be to tobacco pipes made of elder or alder wood or to water pipes made of alder logs bored hollow, that wood being notably resistant to decay in damp. As the pipes grew old (elder), presumably they grew foul.

46–53 You...Sir.] Because they substantially duplicate lines [10–19] of the first version of this part of the scene, these lines are omitted by F2 and subsequent editions. See pp. 362–3 and 481.

116 unhollowed] The *O.E.D.* does not recognize 'hollow' as a spelling of 'hallow', but in *Titus Andronicus*, Q 1594, one finds 'vnhollow, and bloodstained hole' (D4ᵛ), which F1 changes to 'vnhallow'd' (963). See also *The English Dialect Dictionary* (*s.v.* Hallow).

IV.iii

47 e're] 'Coole', line 48, means 'unimpassioned', hence 'chaste' (cf. *O.E.D.*, Cold, *a.* 7.b and 7.c); Cassandra's argument is that many supposedly virtuous women have slipped with great men, but the men's auras of greatness have preserved the women's reputations – 'touching at what is noble', the women have become so. F1's 'on' may have been induced by the idea of slipping on ice, scarcely intelligible in this context, and perhaps no word should be substituted for it, yet 'on' could also have been a misreading of 'ere'. 'Tender' here probably means 'subject to

subtle interpretation' (cf. *O.E.D.*, *a*.6) rather than 'fragile, easily wounded'.
'E're', of course, is 'ever', as in line 40.

138 from]   Of the many meanings of 'for', 'because of, on account of a
thing' (*O.E.D.*, *prep.* and *conj.* 21.b) or 'in consequence of' (22) may be
possibilities here, but neither accords very well with what Evanthe is
saying. The word may have been repeated from line 136.

182 I...say]   Because of Evanthe's answer, Colman suggests that the words
should be 'I dare say', but Weber points out Frederick's 'I will not say'
at line 190. Weber continues: Frederick 'evidently goes gradually and
artfully to work, afraid of Evanthe's suspicions being roused by an accu-
sation too downright, and seems insidiously to retract his first assertions,
to gain her confidence more strongly'.

190 faire,]   I.e., 'clearly, distinctly, plainly' (*O.E.D.*, *adv.* 9.d).

205 *Tameris*]   I.e., Tomyris, queen of the Massagetae. Herodotus says she
decapitated the dead body of Cyrus and plunged the head into a bag
of blood so he might have his fill of it.

213 Foole, unexampled$_\wedge$]   'The modern editors point, "*Fool unexampled,
shall*," &c.: but the epithet "*unexampled*" belongs to "*anger*" (which
Heath did not perceive, when, in his *M.S. Notes*, he proposed altering
"*shall*" to "*still*")' (Dyce).

IV.iv

1 sights]   Colman adopted 'light', Sympson's conjecture (i.e., 'our easi-
ness in Believing'), but Mason remarks, 'They curse their sights, because
it was their eyes deceived them. They gave no credit to Sorano, until
they saw him drink the poison.'

4 cares]   Cf. V.i.65 (Dyce).

50 Betwixt...Lyon]   In his preface to the *Works* of 1750, Seward, writing
after Sympson's text was printed, remarks: 'The learned Reader need not
be told that the *Bear* and the *Lion* here...stand for the *frigid* and the
torrid Zones, and betwixt the two Means the *temperate Zone*.' He goes on
to argue that 'a Man wrapt in Flames' would want to be in the frigid zone
only and to recommend that the line become '"Twixt the cold Bears, far
from the raging Lion', a reading Colman adopted. Mason, however,
defends F1: 'The allusion is to the story of Phaeton, and particularly to
this line': *medio tutissimus ibis* ('In the middle is the safest path'; Ovid,
Metamorphoses, ed. Frank Justus Miller, II.137). Coleridge, incensed,
adds: 'This Mr. Seward is a blockhead of the provoking species. In his
itch for correction, he forgot the words – "lies my safe way!" The Bear
is the extreme pole, and thither would he travel over the space contained
between it and "the raging lion"' (*The Literary Remains* (London, 1836),
II, 314–15). Coleridge is not exactly right. The 'cold beare' is the constellation Ursa Major (see Golding's gloss on *Metamorphoses* II.171) and the

'raging Lyon' the Zodiacal constellation Leo (11.81); Alphonso is figuratively reiterating the idea of 'in the middle'.

IV.v

22 thou] F2's 'thou art' for F1's apparently impossible 'thine' seems wrong because the reading creates an uncharacteristic hexameter, and Dyce's 'thou' allows the line to remain a pentameter if '-er then thou' is taken as an anapaest. Instead of a misreading, as these emendations seem to assume, the problem may lie in the omission of one or more words after F1's correct 'thine'. Cf. notes on I.ii.146–7 and V.iii.173.1.

V.ii

41 Rack] Evidently 'wrack'. The spelling is not recognized by the O.E.D., but it is given by The English Dialect Dictionary (s.v. Wrack, sb.¹ and v.¹).

V.iii

3 Island] Sympson notes: 'As the Scene is throughout at Naples, this Expression, if not a Corruption, is a flagrant Oversight.' It seems unquestionably the latter.

41 Enter . . . Castruchio.] This stage-direction may be improperly placed and it may not specify exactly the right characters. At lines 37–9 Castruchio has been sent to fetch Evanthe; nothing has been said of the three Lords and Tony. Evanthe must be on stage when Frederick speaks to her at line 62, and the Lords are probably, but not certainly, present when Sorano mentions their whispering at line 55. F2 and Langbaine place the direction as does F1, but from the characters named exclude Castruchio, saving him for re-entrance at V.iii.277. Neither edition provides anyone in particular to execute Frederick's order to admit the Suitors at line 62. Sympson agrees approximately, but, a bit confused, brings Evanthe on again with the Suitors, whose entrance he moves to follow line 61. Colman follows Sympson in having Evanthe enter twice, but he restores the Suitors' direction to line 64.1. Weber brings on the three Lords only after line 51 and Evanthe, the Suitors, and Tony after line 62. Dyce's solution is to bring on the Lords and Tony after line 51 and Castruchio with Evanthe after line 61. Castruchio goes for the Suitors at line 62; they enter without him at line 72 upon the conclusion of Evanthe's speech. Dyce's arrangement has much to recommend it, yet if the Lords enter as Frederick stops speaking in line 41, their dirty looks at the tyrannical pair could motivate Sorano's speech. They might well attend Evanthe, as in F1 and, as she may be supposed under orders to attend Frederick, the brief time between Castruchio's exit and re-entrance poses no problem.

As Castruchio is acting as chamberlain ('give way | To any Suitor', lines 37–8), it is appropriate that he should admit the Suitors to the presence, but he need not accompany them.

120 horne...knife] Dyce notes: 'Pick-pockets were said to place a case, or thimble, of horn on their thumbs, to support the edge of the knife in the act of cutting purses.'

139 And] Mason, who recommended 'And' for F1's 'To', is about right that F1's line is 'not sense as it stands'; the syntax is at least unusual, for the Physician apparently means 'A month is too little for me to repent for my former pleasures [those mentioned by Tony at V.ii.35–8] and continue in the same pleasures with Evanthe.' The 'And' seems necessary. Weber adds it to F1's 'To', which makes the line slightly irregular and disregards the possibility that F1's 'To' was induced by the 'to' in the preceding line. Weber suspects 'one or more lines are lost', but there is no reason for believing that.

173.1 *Enter* Valerio *disguis'd*.] F1's repetition of line 173 directly after this stage-direction signals the beginning of an inserted passage, but, as Sympson remarks, a speech of Frederick's seems to have been omitted. Evanthe's 'Will...doubt' (lines 159–61) does not follow 'A moneth's a dangerous thing'; it is probably her reply to another proposal by Frederick that she should marry him. See p. 363. Although he agrees that the duplicate of line 173 should not, as in F1, precede 'Will you then be willing' (line 159), Colman thinks that instead of lines having been lost Frederick whispers his proposal to Evanthe after she says 'A moneth's a dangerous thing.' Weber and Dyce believe that the F1 lines between 'A moneth's a dangerous thing' and line 173, like III.ii.120–7, were theatrical cuts imperfectly restored in F1.

180 My...*Egla*,] The first version is the last line of I1ᵛb, set by Compositor *A*, and the second the first line of I2a, set by Compositor *B*. *A* misunderstood where *B* began. See p. 357.

188 *aside*] Evanthe apparently is not addressing Valerio. Cf. lines 202–3 and 216.

196 the tops] I.e., the crowns of their helmets. Possibly '*their* tops', 'the' having been repeated from the first word in the line.

323 pull'd] That Sorano's rank (fat, licentious, or corrupt) flesh will be 'pulled' with fasting may be wrong: all the appropriate senses of 'pull' (e.g., 'strip' or 'pluck' (*O.E.D.*, *v.* 5) or 'tear off' (10)) imply force, whereas what seems wanted is a less violent verb – e.g., 'pall' ('enfeeble, weaken' (*v.* 7)), 'peel' ('strip skin' (*v.* 3)), or 'pill' (–'peel'). None of these, however, offers much improvement in meaning, and perhaps 'ranke' also carries the subsidiary meaning 'overgrown' (*a.* 5, 10), like weeds requiring pulling.

328 water,] Colman and later editors change the comma to a semicolon to make 'that' a demonstrative pronoun, a very possible interpretation.

Epilogue

6 *Mile-end*] As Weber points out, Mile End is mentioned in *Monsieur
Thomas* in the title, probably invented, of a ballad, 'The landing of the
Spaniards at *Bow*, With the bloudy battell at *Mile-end*' (III.iii.45–6), and
in *The Knight of the Burning Pestle* Mistress Merrythought remembers
Mile End as the site of a 'pitch-field' between 'the naughty *Spaniels* and
the *English-men*' (II, 71–2), evidently a mock battle for training the
militia. The same event may be alluded to here. The 'action' possibly is
bawdy as well, for Mile End was a place of fairs, shows, hangings, and
presumably seductions.

EMENDATIONS OF ACCIDENTALS

I.i

I.i] Actus primus, Scæna prima. F 1–2±
5 depart] F 2; depatt F 1
6–7 What...now?] *one line* F 1–2
14–15 I'le...cause.] *one line* F 1–2
15 *Exeunt*] *Ex.* F 1–2
17–18 Pray...Sir:] *one line* F 1–2
51–52 Bid...him.] *one line* F 1–2
60 Madam——] ~ , F 1–2
61 Sutor,] F 2; ~ . F 1
71–72 Yes...wise.] *one line* F 1–2
75 *Evanthe*——] ~ . F 1–2
80–81 No...Hyacinth] *one line* F 1–2
90–91 Yes...do.] *one line* F 1–2
92 honours,] F 2; honors∧ F 1 (|)
96–98 Hold...content] F 1–2 *line:* Hold...fleet, | I...content
103 mighty——] ~ . F 1–2
104 worst] F 2; wo st F 1
111 Sir,] ~ ; F 1–2

116 life,] ~ ∧ F 1–2
149 at;——] ~ ; ∧ F 1–2
150 mighty?] ~ . F 1–2
158 *These...impudence:*] roman F 1–2
165 Leapar] Leopar F 1; Leper F 2
174 blest!] F 2; ~ ? F 1
178–179 And...Away.] *one line* F 1–2
178 instantly] F 2; Instantly F 1
179–180 Lets...jealous.] *one line* F 1–2
180 *Exeunt*] *Exit* F 1; *Ex.* F 2
184 me?——] ~ ? ∧ F 1–2
194 reveng'd;...mighty,] ~ ,... ~ ∧ F 1–2
196 thee?] F 2; ~ . F 1
201 weeps.——] ~ . ∧ F 1–2
208–209 bed,...state;] ~ ;...~ , F 1; ~ ; ...~ ; F 2
218 vertuous∧] F 2; ~ , F 2

I.ii

11 Gentlemen,] F 2; Gentl. F 1
14–15 'Tis...cleer,] *one line* F 1–2
18 pretention∧] F 2; ~ , F 1
20–21 I...angers,] *one line* F 1–2
24 rain'd!] F 2; ~ ? F 1
32 rule;] ~ , F 1–2
67 that?] ~ . F 1–2
70–71 Ever...Patient.] *one line* F 1–2
70 surfeit] F 2; sufeit F 1
72 those?...Verses:] ~ . ... ~ ∧ F 1–2

73 Those...*Sorano.*] F 1–2 *line:* Those...discover, | Reade... *Sorano.*
74 *Sorano.*] *om.* F 1–2
74 Evanthe.] F 2; ~ , F 1
77 *me,*] F 2; ~ ; F 1
87 *eye,*] ~ ? F 1
95–96 That...fed] F 1–2 *line:* That ...ye, | And...fed
106–108 Ring,...mouth,...heart?] F 2; ~ ?...~ ?...~ , F 1
113–114 And...box?] *one line* F 1–2

465

121 closer] Closer F 1–2
123 thee;] ~ , F 1–2
134–135 These...Madam.] *one line*
     F 1–2
147 *Enter...Podrano.*] *after line* 146
     F 1–2
148 betray'd;——] ~ ; ᴧ F 1–2
149 heart,——] ~ , ᴧ F 1–2
156–158 lye——...knave?] ~ ?
     ...~ , F 1; ~ ?...~ ? F 2
160 daily,] F 2; ~ ᴧ F 1
166–167 with,...Almond;] ~ ;...
     ~ , F 1–2
169 silent.——] ~ , ᴧ F 1; ~ . ᴧ F 2
172 your] F 2; Your F 1

174 it;] ~ , F 1–2
179 that] F 2; thar F 1
179–180 happinesse (Conceive...
     forbidden),] ~ ; ~ ...~ ᴧ ; F 1–
     2
184 so many] F 2; somany F 1
199 me;——] ~ ; ᴧ F 1–2
202 that's] F 2; thar's F 1
209 instantly;——] ~ ; ᴧ F 1–2
210.1 *Manent* ᴧ] F 2; ~ , F 1
213–214 'Tis...it,] *one line* F 1–2
221 time;] F 2; ~ , F 1
232 him, in death ᴧ] F 2; ~ ᴧ ~ ~ ,
     F 1

II.i

II.i] Actus Secundus. *Scæna Prima.*
     F 1–2±
7 *Enter...Urinall*] *after line* 5 F 1–
     2 (*Ent* F 1)
13 foole;——] ~ ; ᴧ F 1–2
16–20 They...sentence.] *prose* F 1–
     2

28–32 What...gallows.] *prose* F 1–
     2
33 March] *March* F 1–2
35 April] *April* F 1–2
49 Fish] F 2; fish F 1
58 Gentlemen,] F 2; Gentl. F 1
64 out;] F 2; ~ , F 1

II.ii

25–26 excellence (Ile...thee)] ~ ,
     ~ ...~ , F 1–2
28 anger;] ~ , F 1–2
38 you] F 2; You F 1

49 too;] ~ , F 1; ~ ! F 2
58 flourish;] ~ , F 1; ~ . F 2
68–69 'Twill...more.] *one line* F 1–
     2

II.iii

15–16 head (Would...Sir)] ~ , ~
     ...~ , F 1–2
19–20 devis'd (so...worke)] ~ , ~
     ...~ , F 1–2

43 too;] ~ , F 1–2
45–46 Take...happy.] *one line* F 1–
     2

II.iv

2 Shoulder] F 2; shoulder F 1
4–5 Keep...signe.] *prose* F 1–2
6–8 Put...in] F 1–2 *line:* Put...
     you | Think...in

12–13 You...husbands?] *one line*
     F 1–2
12 women,——] ~ , ᴧ F 1–2
14 would] F 2; wouid F 1

466

16 wenches;——] ~ ; ˄ F 1–2
21 the] F 2; tne F 1
22 selves;——] ~ ; ˄ F 1–2
24 Musick,——] ~ , ˄ F 1–2 ±
29–30 We...else.] *one line* F 1–2
31 arm'd;——] ~ ; ˄ F 1–2

33 Marriage!] F 2; ~ ? F 1
38 confusion!] ~ ? F 1–2
43–44 Not...her.] *one line* F 1–2
47 their wives] F 2; theit wives F 1
49 fooles,] F 2; ~ . F 1
50 *Lady,*] ~ ˄ F 1–2

II.v

1–5 me,—— ... help,—— ...
  Feather,——...breath,——]
  F 1–2 *om. dashes*
10 more?——...sword.——] ~ ?
  ˄...~ . ˄ F 1–2
16 nothing,] ~ ˄ F 1–2
18–20 Hell.——...pumps;——]
  ~ . ˄...~ ; ˄ F 1–2
23 time;] ~ , F 1–2

25 us;] ~ ˄ F 1; ~ . F 2
33 too;——] ~ ; ˄ F 1–2
34 Souldier ˄ *Menallo,*] ~ , ~ ˄ F 1;
  ~ , ~ , F 2
43 soules:——] ~ : ˄ F 1–2
45 gentlemen] gent. F 1–2
49.1 *Musick.*] *on line* 48 F 1–2
51–52 We...us] F 1–2 *line:*
  We...Doores. | The...us

II.vi

0.1 *Knocking*] F 2; *Knacking* F 1
1–2 there,——...Guard;——]
  ~ , ˄...~ ; ˄ F 1–2 ±
2–3 A...now] F 1–2 *line:* A...
  be | Enter'd...now
3–4 Looke...it] F 1–2 *line:* Looke
  ...fast, | They...it
4.1 *Enter*] F 2; *Entrr* F 1
4.1 Menallo;] ~ , F 1–2
16 bald?] ~ , F 1–2

18–19 Embassadour,...memories.]
  ~ . ... ~ , F 1–2
19 *Knocks within.*] *after line* 18 F 1–
  2
23 yet.——] ~ . ˄ F 1–2
24 wives?] F 2; ~ . F 1
32 else:] ~ , F 1–2
46 light,——] ~ , ˄ F 1–2
48, 52 *Frederick*] *King* F 1–2

III.i

III.i] Actus Tertius. *Scæna Prima.*
  F 1–2 ±
4 honours,] ~ ; F 1–2
5 of!] ~ ? F 1–2
7 tongue,——] ~ , ˄ F 1–2

11–12 breeding (and...experi-
  ence)] ~ , ~...~ ˄ F 1; ~ ,
  ~...~ ; F 2
21–22 (A...paternall)] ˄ ~...~ ,
  F 1–2

III.ii

15 *Evanthe*] F 2; *Enanthe* F 1
17.1 *Enter* Sorano.] *after line* 16
  F 1–2

22 practice!] F 2; ~ . F 1
48 lov'dst] F 2; lovsdst F 1
48 hopefull;] ~ , F 1–2

467

50 pleasure,] F 2; ~ ∧ F 1 (|)
51 it;] ~ ∧ F 1–2
67 forfeit:...Sir?] F 2; ~ ∧...~ , F 1
75–76 it (There...pleasure):] ~ ; ~...~ ∧: F 1–2
81 monstrous] F 2; moostrous F 1
95 'em;] ~ , F 1–2

101–102 Mine...this] F 1–2 line: Mine...touch. | Even...this
104 soule;] ~ , F 1–2
112 Country,] F 2; ~ ∧ F 1
113 appeare] F 2; appeate F 1
118 transgresse,] ~ ∧ F 1–2
121 kneele;] ~ ∧ F 1; om. F 2
126 armes] armrs F 1; om. F 2

III.iii

2 way:] ~ , F 1; ~ . F 2
9 admire,...it;] ~ ∧...~ , F 1–2
19 Grace,] ~ ∧ F 1–2
28 eyes] s barely prints in some copies of F 1
32–34 Go...dayes] F 1–2 line: Go ...this, | Hope...dayes
35.1 Enter...Menallo.] after line 34 F 1–2
35.1 Cleanthes] F 2; Cleanthas F 1
40 wrong,] F 2; ~ ∧ F 1
43 am——] ~ ∧ F 1–2
52 Lady,——] ~ , ∧ F 1–2
56 ever:——] ~ , ∧ F 1; ~ . ∧ F 2
61–62 may,——...out!——] ~ , ∧...~ ∧∧ F 1; ~ :∧...~ !∧ F 2
63–64 Nay...Lord.] one line F 1–2
65–66 No...Sir.] one line F 1–2
75 do?] F 2; ~ , F 1
88 me,] F 2; ~ . F 1
93 benefit!...curst,] F 2; ~ ,... ~ ∧ F 1
96 me, youth∧] ~ ∧ ~ , F 1; ~ , ~ , F 2
107–108 Thou...cordiall.] prose F 1–2
112 immodesty] F 2; immmodesty F 1
112 immodesty∧)——] ~ ∧)∧ F 1; ~.)∧ F 2
121 now,——] ~ ,∧ F 1–2
122 there!] ~ ? F 1–2

122–123 Shall...thing,] one line F 1–2
123 thee?]F 2; ~ , F 1
128 leave;] ~ , F 1–2
135–136 (The...sleep),] ∧ ~... ~ ∧, F 1–2
138 squeez'd] F 2; sqeez'd F 1
141 happy;——] ~ ;∧ F 1–2
142 That...Grace.] F 1–2 line: That ...care, | Goodnesse...Grace.
147–154 How...foole] F 1–2 line: How...fire, | A...mire, | Phlebotomy...require; | This ...foole
147 for!] F 2; ~ , F 1
151 lye nier] roman F 1–2
152 of, friend,] ~ ∧ ~ ∧ F 1–2
157 Evanthe?] ~ , F 1–2
157–158 No,...me,] one line F 1–2
166 fie] F 2; sie F 1
172 Valerio,] ~ ; F 1–2
184–185 That...againe.] one line F 1–2
188 burne!——] ~ ! ∧ F 1–2
201 mix;] ~ , F 1–2
206 love?] ~ ; F 1–2
214 Love;] ~ , F 1–2
216 piously,] ~ ; F 1–2
227 unbeseeming,] F 2; ~ ∧ F 1
229–230 Evanthe;——...it;——] ~ ; ∧...~ ; ∧ F 1–2
231–233 No...selfe] F 1–2 line: No ...man, | Goodnesse...selfe

235 it;——] ~ ; ∧ F1–2 259 chastity!] ~ , F1–2
238 nothing,——] ~ , ∧ F1–2

IV.i

IV.i] Actus Quartus. *Scæna Prima.*
  F1–2±
0.1 Marco;] ~ , F1–2
12 all!)] ~ ∧)F1–2
13 sorrow;] ~ , F1–2
20 pleasures. These] ~ , these F1–
  2
23–24 title (that...together),] ~ ,
  ~...~ ∧ ; F1–2
29 ruines] F2; rulnes F1
32 hypocrisie;] ~ , F1–2
36 Art——] ~ . F1–2
47–48 See...Lord] *one line* F1–2
48 attention,...Lord∧] ~ ∧...~ ,
  F1–2

51 Prince,] ~ ∧ F1–2
53 Ill∧ and prodigious,] ~ , ~ ~ ∧
  F1; ~ ∧ ~ ~ ∧ F2
70 suffer:] ~ , F1–2
77–78 Mistake...care,] *one line* F1–
  2
82 excellent,] ~ ; F1–2
90 man,] F2; ~ ∧ F1
92 it,] F2; ~ ∧ F1
95 subjects,] F2; ~ : F1
99–100 Pray...Lords.] *one line*
  F1–2
100.1 *Exeunt*] *Exit* F1; *Ex.* F2
102 wisedomes?] F2; ~ , F1

IV.ii

1–2 Call...us.] *one line* F1–2
9 Broaths] Brooths F1; Broths F2
9 Jellies?] ~ . F1–2
9–10 I...Lady.] *one line* F1–2
14–15 Come...Onions,——] *one
  line* F1–2
15 Onions,——] ~ ,∧ F1–2
17 pipes,——] ~ , ∧ F1–2
17 me?] F2; ~ . F1
19 vertuous?] F2; ~ . F1
22 use——] F2; ~ . F1
27–28 I, I...better,] *one line* F1–2
30–31 thee,...good;] ~ ;...~ ,
  F1; ~ ,...~ , F2
33 to,] F2; ~ ∧ F1
37–38 A...Sir,] *one line* F1–2
39–40 Go...*Valerio*,] *one line* F1–
  2
40 too.] ~ , F1; ~ : F2
40 *Exit.* | *Enter* Valerio.] *after*
  Majesty., *line* 39 F1–2

60 you (yeeld...*Evanthe*)] ~ ; ~
  ...~ , F1–2
63–64 Do...impossible,] *one line*
  F1–2
69 difference——] F2; ~ . F1
77 to, that∧] ~ ∧ ~ , F1 (*doubtful*);
  ~ ∧ ~ ∧ F2
83 thus——] ~ . F1–2
84 first,——] ~ , ∧ F1–2
91 like——] ~ ∧ F1–2
92 to,] F2; ~ ∧ F1
93 off,——] ~ , ∧ F1–2±
95–97 Sir?...Diamond.] F2; ~ ,
  ...~ ? F1
100 too——] ~ . F1–2
102–103 There...wilt.] *one line* F1–
  2
103–106 Queene?...equall.] ~ ,...
  ~ ? F1–2
133–134 Ye...ye.] *one line* F1–2
133 are,——] ~ , ∧ F1; ~ ∧——F2

IV.iii

1 then,] F2; ~ ˌ F1
4 turne (for...it)] ~ , ~...~ ,
   F1–2
9 wantonnesseˌ] ~ . F1–2
13 wayˌ——] F2; ~ . —— F1
22–23 I...me.] *one line* F1–2
35 proud——] ~ . F1–2
48–50 That...one] F1–2 *line:* That
   ...blest, | That...Chronicle, |
   A faithfull one
48 world;] ~ , F1; ~ . F2
68 strength——] ~ . F1–2
80 wicked?] F2; ~ . F1
81 ye——] ~ . F1–2
97 thee;] ~ , F1; ~ . F2
101 *Enter* Frederick.] *after line* 98
   F1–2
111 ye?] ~ . F1–2
115–116 man (nay...Lady)] ~ , ~
   ...~ , F1–2
126 here] r *does not print in some
   copies of* F1
138–139 'Tis...thee;] *one line* F1–2
141 girle,] F2; *comma doubtful in* F1

142–143 O...man!] *one line* F1–2
146 me;] ~ , F1–2
151 him!] ~ ? F1–2
155 above,] ~ ˌ F1–2
158–159 Sure...coward.] *one line*
   F1–2
162–163 solicitor (I...now)] ~ : ~
   ...~ , F1–2±
168 me——] ~ . F1–2
168–169 And...person.] *one line*
   F1–2
170 me,] ~ ˌ F1–2
176 am,] ~ ˌ F1–2
176–177 heart.——...still.——]
   ~ . ˌ...~ . ˌ F1–2
178 thee,] F2; ~ ˌ F1
181 misery!] ~ ? F1; ~ . F2
189 againe:——] ~ : ˌ F1–2±
192 honour,] ~ ˌ F1–2
194 How!] ~ ? F1–2
194–195 Lye...day,] *one line* F1–2
197 *Evanthe.*] F2; *Fvan.* F1
213 thee!] ~ ? F1–2

IV.iv

5–6 potent (Heaven...patience);]
   ~ , ~...~ ˌ ; F1–2
10 *Alphonso (within)*] *Within Alphonso* F1–2±
10–11 Harke...blockheads,] *one
   line* F1–2
12–13 first!...for!] F2; ~ ?... ~
   ? F1
14 for't,] ~ ; F1–2
16 speedily;] ~ , F1–2
17–18 Lets...strong.] *one line* F1–
   2
33–34 Hold...burnes!] *one line*
   F1–2

34 What,] ~ ˌ F1–2
35–36 body,...incense;] F2; ~ ?
   ...~ ? F1
38 flame;] ~ , F1–2
64–65 Hold...has!] *one line* F1–2
65 has!] ~ ? F1–2
65–66 He'le...cause.] *one line* F1–
   2
71–72 Ideots;...Vessels,] ~ ,...
   ~ ; F1–2
77–78 No...aire?] *one line* F1–2
78 thing.——] ~ . ˌ F1–2
80 life;——] ~ ; ˌ F1–2
81 *Alphonso.*] F2; *Alpb.* F1

IV.v

11 life——] ~ . F 1–2
17–18 Shame...innocence.] *one line*
   F 1–2
38 body,] ~ ? F 1–2
39 such] F 2; Such F 1
43–44 delicates,...offer;] ~ ;...
   ~ , F 1; ~ ;...~ . F 2
49 *Evanthe*] F 2; *Evantbe* F 1
55 too!] ~ ? F 1; ~ : F 2
57 lyar!] ~ , F 1–2
62 gone,——] ~ , ∧ F 1–2

65–66 I...marriage,] *one line* F 1–
   2
80 forgivenesse!] ~ ? F 1–2
82–83 Only...me;] *one line* F 1–2
90 bawd,] *comma barely prints in*
   F 1
91–92 I...morrow.] *one line* F 1–2
110 *Enter...Guard.*] *after line* 108
   F 1–2
114–115 Mistake...Office,] *one line*
   F 1–2

V.i

V.i] Actus Quintus. *Scæna Prima.*
   F 1–2±
5–6 But...King?] *one line* F 1–
   2
6–7 Though...honest,] *one line*
   F 1–2
13–14 To...so,] *one line* F 1–2
17–18 soule (which...too)] ~ , ~
   ...~ , F 1–2
24.1 *Enter* Castruchio.] *after line* 23
   F 1–2
25–26 O...Prisoner?] *one line* F 1–
   2

31.1 *Enter...Fryers.*] *after line* 28
   F 1–2
36 now——] ~ ∧ F 1; ~ , F 2
36–37 Sir,——...Lord,] *one line*
   F 1–2
36 Sir,——] ~ , ∧ F 1–2
38–39 honest,...counted.] ~ ....
   ~ , F 1; ~ ,...~ , F 2
42–43 I...goodnesse,] *one line* F 1–
   2
46–47 Softly...secret,——] *one*
   line F 1–2
47 secret,——] ~ , ∧ F 1–2

V.ii

5–6 follow'd (And...morrow),]
   ~ , ~ ...~ ∧ ; F 1–2
10 selfe?] F 2; ~ , F 1
20–21 I have...appeare] F 1–2 *line:*
   I have...venter | Without...
   appeare F 1–2
22–23 They...kinred?] *one line*
   F 1–2

23 Doe's] F 2 (does); doo's F 1
32–33 I...man.] *one line* F 1–2
36 no∧] F 2; ~ , F 1
37 person (there's...an't)] ~ , ~
   ...~ , F 1–2
42–43 Sir,...themselves?] ~ ?...
   ~ . F 1–2

V.iii

1–2 But...well.] *one line* F1–2
3–4 Discreetly...else,] *one line* F1–2
10.2 *Enter...Sorano.*] *after line* 8 F1–2
35 shall.——] ~ . ˏ F1–2
39.1 *Captaine*] *Cap.* F1; *Cast.* F2
48 actions;] ~ , F1–2
50–51 will,...us;] ~ ;...~ , F1–2
56 shames,] ~ ˏ F1–2
57–58 How...Monster] *one line* F1–2
58–59 Monsterˏ...jeere!] ~ ?... ~ , F1; ~ ?...~ ? F2
59 Lords,] ~ ˏ F1–2
64 ye,] F2; ~ . F1
65–66 And...mercy.] *one line* F1–2
71–72 Or...Lord?] *one line* F1–2
71–72 fitˏ...Lord?] ~ ?...~ . F1–2
72 Captain,] ~ ˏ F1–2
74–75 anger,...ye;] ~ ;... ~ , F1; ~ ;...~ . F2
84 Devill,——] ~ , ˏ F1–2
94–95 Like...ability.] *one line* F1–2
104–105 I...Joynter;] *one line* F1–2
106 *Firke*] firke F1–2±
111 Lady;] ~ , F1–2
112 eat (I...too)] ~ , ~ ...~ , F1–2
127–128 You...ye.] *one line* F1–2
131 Sir?] F2; ~ , F1
133–134 noblenesse (in...Mistris)] ~ ˏ ~ ...~ , F1–2±
133 otherwise] F2; oeherwise F1
135–136 Speake...dye?] *one line* F1–2
136–137 I...condition.] *one line* F1–2

142–143 No...moneth.] *one line* F1–2
146–147 Blesse...ashes,] *one line* F1–2
151 Purse;] ~ , F1–2
153–154 And...richly.——] *one line* F1–2
154 richly.——] ~ ˏ ˏ F1; ~ . ˏ F2
154–155 These...not:] *one line* F1–2
155 And] F2; an F1
155 not:] ~ ˏ F1; ~ , F2
156 stake!] ~ . F1–2
160 prefixt?] F2; ~ , F1
162 condition] F2; conditfon F1
167 ye!] ~ ˏ F1–2
168 Sir!] F2; ~ , F1
176–177 Say...are.] *one line* F1–2
177–178 I...Souldier,] *one line* F1–2
179 fellow;] ~ , F1–2
190 him,] ~ ; F1–2
192–193 pagans (His...Falcon)] ~ , ~ ...~ , F1–2
194 Turks:] *Turks,* F1–2
207 killing:] ~ , F1–2
209 Turke,] F2; ~ . F1
219–220 fate,...cruell:] ~ :...~ , F1–2
229–230 Pray...name?] *one line* F1–2
232–233 Do...*Urbino?*] *one line* F1–2
237 companion,——] ~ , ˏ F1–2
250 honour:] ~ , F1–2
255–256 Am...affliction?] *one line* F1–2
258 Sir——] F2; ~ . F1
258–259 Peace...hand.] *one line* F1–2
259–260 I...joy.] *one line* F1–2
259 Gentleman,——] ~ , ˏ F1–2

260–261 I...hence.] *one line* F 1–2
266–267 The...perish.] *one line* F 1–2
268 knell;——] ~ ; ₄ F 1–2
269–270 I...Palace.] *one line* F 1–2
277 *Enter...Guard.*] *after line* 275 F 1–2
283 Sir;] ~ , F 1–2
285 Antidotes] F 2; *Antidotes* F 1

287–288 well,——...*Sorano;*——]
  ~ , ₄...~ ; ₄ F 1–2
296 thus] Thus F 1–2
303–304 home (I...Justice)] ~ , ~
  ...~ , F 1–2
311–313 Tombe   (Teares...too)]
  ~ , ~...~ , F 1–2
314–315 Your...Sir.] *one line* F 1–2
333 Licence,——] ~ , ₄ F 1–2

Epilogue

8 prove.] followed by *Here endeth A Wife for a Moneth.* F 1

HISTORICAL COLLATION

[Included are substantive and semi-substantive differences from the present text as well as a few notes on the variant lineation of troublesome passages. Except for those introduced by F2, modernizations (e.g., *ye–you, further–farther, reverend–reverent*) and insignificant changes in the wording and position of stage-directions are ignored. Only the originators of conjectural readings are acknowledged. The + sign indicates the agreement of all editions after the one to which the reading is attributed and − (minus) exceptions to this. The readings of eight editions and two commentaries have been collated, as follows:

F1   *Comedies and Tragedies* (1647).
F2   *Fifty Comedies and Tragedies* (1679).
L   *Works* (1711), with introduction by Langbaine.
Q   *A Wife for a Month*, 1717.
S   *Works* (1750), edited by Theobald, Seward, and Sympson (*A Wife for a Month* by Sympson).
C   *Works* (1778), edited by Colman.
M   J. Monck Mason, *Comments on the Plays of Beaumont and Fletcher* (London, 1798).
W   *Works* (1812), edited by Weber.
D   *Works* (1843–6), edited by Dyce.
De   [E.] K. Deighton, *The Old Dramatists* (Westminster, 1896).

Heath's MS notes are quoted from Dyce's edition.]

Prologue

4–5 all, (*Our noble friends*);] all   noble friend, F2, L, Q, C, W;
(*Our noble friends*) F1; *all. Our*   all, Our noble Friend, S

I.i

5 your command be] you com-   24 with all] withall F1–2
   mand me W   37 unto] to S
14 imploved] employ'd in S   38–39 presently, Hither,] ∼ , ∼ ,
15 *Exeunt* Lords.] *Ex.* F2; *Exit.*   S, C
   L, Q, S   44 her?] ∼——C, W, D

474

47 absolute,] ~ ₄ F 1
48 place] playes F 1–2, L, Q, S;
    Pains *or* Honours; Pains and
    Pleasures | Waiting your Will,
    and your Commands unbounded
    or Place S *conj.*
56 Podrano] *Podramo* F 1+
118–119 Sir (No...Angels)] ~ , ~
    ...~ , F 1+
132 unjustice] injustice F 2+

136 it (looke behinde ye);] ~ ; ~ ~
    ~ , ₄ F 1+ (−D)
157 Master] Minister Seward *conj. in*
    S
172 proud] pound L, Q
174 *Podrano*] *Podramo* F 1+
179 Queene] Maria W, D
181 *Queene.*] *Mar.* F 1, W, D
    (*through rest of scene*)

I.ii

6 to] *om.* S
20–21 God...him] gods...'em
    F 2, L, Q, S
22 on...Tombs] o'er their rotten
    Bones S *conj.*
29 Princes] Princesse F 1–2, L;
    Princes   Theobald *conj. in* S
49 *Camillo. So...Cabinet, and*
    Podrano.] *Cabinet.* | *Pod. So* F 1
49 *and* Podrano] *om.* F 1; *and*
    Podramo F 2+
50 is] *om.* L, Q
63 water.] ~ ? S+
75 *feeles*] *feel* F 2+
87 *eye*] *eyes* F 1
103.1 *Exeunt...Podrano*]   *Exit*

Lords F 1; *Ex. Lords* F 2, L, Q,
    S; *Exeunt...*Podramo C+
109 Thou] You F 2, L, S+; Your Q
110 the] their F 1
111 made] make F 2+
119 wilde] vild S *conj.*, C+
124 teeth] Meat S *conj.*
131 now,...drunkard!] ~ ?...~ ,
    F 1–2, L, Q, S
146 from] for S *conj.*
146–147 am,...things——] ~ ....
    ~ . F 1; ~ ,... ~ . F 2, L
147 Podrano] Podramo F 2+
160 there] they F 2, L, Q, S
164 As] And S
210.1 *Exeunt*] *Exit* F 2, L, Q, S

II.i

20 the] his Q
23 too] to L+
25 quarters] quartets F 1
28–33 What...Lion] *prose* F 1–2,
    L, Q; S *lines:* What...the |
    Like...Month | To...ake |

For it...most | Dismally...
    would | Chuse...Lion; C, W,
    D *line:* What...Tony, | If...
    chuse | A...sure | My...end,
    | I'd...gallows. | I...lion
45 worth] with Q

II.ii

9 his will] this with *or* this Will S
    conj.
46 minde.] ~—— S+

54 incitement] Inticement L, Q, S
56 the] that F 1+; the Seward *conj.*
    in S

57 earth] Earth's Seward *conj. in* S   60 vertue] vertues F 1, S, C, W
59 live] love F 1+; live D *conj.*   64 lazy] crazy C *conj.*

II.iii

10 she has you] 'tis you she has F 2   too, F 1–2, L, Q, S, C; diseases ∧
  +   . . . to, M *conj.*
32–33 diseases∧ . . . to,] diseases, . . .   37 month] mouth F 1

II.iv

4 doore] Doors S   'em∧ Seward *conj.* in S; set of
11 Sir,] ~ ? C   people call them∧ Heath *conj. in*
21 *3. Wife.*] 1. *W.* F 1+   D; set, people call them, De
25 too, . . . ye,] ~ , . . . ~ ? F 2, L,   50 Cassandra] Cassander F 2, L, Q,
  Q; ~ ? . . . ~ ; S+   S
31 Woman] *Women* F 1–2, L, S;   53–57 And . . . tayles] S, W, D *line:*
  Wom. C; 3 *Woman* W, D   And . . . Face, | Are . . . neatly
50 sect; people calls them∧] set∧   *and then as* F 1; C *lines:* And . . .
  people calls them∧ F 1; set∧   face, | Are . . . too, | Like . . .
  people call them∧ F 2, L, Q, S, C;   out: | They . . . tongues, | (For
  set, people call them∧ M *conj.*,   . . . hop'd, | New tails
  W, D; And yet People call   54 to] two S+
  them∧ S *conj.*; Yet People call   61 are] art F 2, L, S, C

II.v

29 Beside] Besides F 2+ (−D)   43 great] yet Seward *conj. in* S
29 soules old] Soul grows old S   43 unto] to F 1
  conj.   46 must∧] ~ , C+
37 thy] *om.* L, Q   50 Musick∧] ~ ; S+
39 hung] hang F 1+ (−D)   52.1 *Exeunt severally.*] 'Exit.' *after*
43 Our . . . soules:————] *followed by*   presently., *line* 51, *and* 'Exeunt.'
  a duplicate of line 47 F 1–2, L, Q,   *after line* 52 F 1+
  S

II.vi

0.1 *Knocking within.*] *after* Doores.,   be | Enter'd . . . now; S *lines:*
  II.v.52 F 1–2, L, Q, S   What a Noise | Do . . . Guard; |
1–3 What . . . now] *prose* Q; F 1–2,   You . . . enter'd; | He's . . . now;
  L *line:* What . . . fellowes | A . . .   C+ *line:* What . . . guard! |

You...enter'd; | He...now

4.1 *following*] *following, and Foole*
following F 1

16 gentlewoman] gent. F 1–2, L, Q,
S, C; gentlewoman M *conj.*

20–21 2. *Citizen*. ...3. *Citizen*.] *om.*
F 1–2, L, Q, S; 1 *Cit*. ...2 *Cit*.
C+

23 brusled] bruised M *conj.*

25.1–25.3 *Enter*...*them*] *The King,*
Queene, Valerio, Evanthe, La-
dies, Attendants, Camillo, Clean-
thes, Sorano, Menallo F 1+

(–D); *Enter* Frederick, Maria,
Valerio, Evanthe, Sorano, Ladies, *and* Attendants D

25.5 *A Curtaine drawne.*] *as line* 25.1
F 1+ (–D)

34 servants,] ~ ˌ F 1–2, L, Q, S

35.1 *The* Graces *sing.*] *om.* F 1–2,
L, Q; One of the *Graces* sings.
S, C

45.2 *Poverty,*] *om.* F 1–2, L, Q;
Poverty, Theobald *conj. in* S

48 Comeˌ] ~ , C+

49 a bed] i'bed F 2, L, Q, S, C

III.i

0.1 *Monkes*] Friars D

0.2–0.3 *discover*...*Chaire*] *om.*C+

III.ii

20 ruin'd] run'd L

27 of] for M *conj.*

66 all perish] perish; all S

110 deliver] delire [*i.e.*, make deli-
rious] S *conj.*

115 good...ye] may it do ye with
it F 1

119 Heaven...yet,] F 1, S *follow*
with And when you please, and
how allay my miseries [*cf. line*
127]. | *Enter Frederick.*; *om. the*

F 1 *line and direction* S *conj.*

120–127 Looke...miseries.] *om.* F 2,
L, Q

120–121 Looke...pitty, | To...
me,] *lines transposed* F 1, S, W;
om. F 2, L, Q

120–121 youthˌ...kneele;] ~ !...
~ , C, D

124 mine] my S, C

126 armes] aims M *conj.*, D

III.iii

0.1 *Enter*...*Sorano.*] *om.* F 1

38 minutes] minute's F 2+

70 upon] on S

89 up but prevention;] ~ : ~
~ —— F 2+

89 but] by M *conj.*

96.1 *Enter*...*Foole.*] *after line* 88
F 1–2, L, Q, S, C

103 goody] good F 2, L, Q, S

125 more,——] ~ , ˌ F 1–2, L, S;
~ . ˌ C, W

131 Woman] Women F 1–2, L, Q

138 I...counsell.] Wilt take my
Counsel? *continued to Tony* S
conj.

141 A] My W

141–142 happy;...Grace.] happy
follow it. | *Evan.* That shall be

my Care; these——[*i.e., length
and happiness must be left to the
gods*] | Goodness rest your
Grace.——That shall—— S
conj.
154 learne] learnt F1
166 ye] yea F1

177 mindes] mind F2, L, S
197 desire] desires F2, L, Q, S
202 tother] other L+
211 loves] Life's S *conj.*
225 stop] ope S *conj.*
243 honour] honour'd F1

IV.i

18 this] the Q
28 vertues] virtue's S+
36 heaven] Heav'ns L, Q, S, C
46–47 favours. . . .His] favours. |
Mar. He weeps agen, his F1+;
He weeps agen *as stage-direction*
D *conj.*

51 lyes] lie C, W
57 part] *om.* F1
62 Worshipt] Worship F2, L, Q, S
72 too] *om.* F2, L, Q, S, C
101 my honest] and honest Q
105 asse?] ~ , F1–2, L, Q; ~ ; S;
~ ! C+

IV.ii

0.1, 1 Podrano] *Podramo* L+
2 *Exit.*] *followed by ' Enter Cassandra.' and forty-five lines (see
Appendix, pp.* 481–2) F1;
*followed by forty-five lines and
'Enter* Cassandra.' *after line* [43]
F2+
3 *Frederick.*] *om.* F1
4–10 As. . .Lady.] S *lines:* As. . .
may | Do. . .Sir: | Sickly. . .
Majesty. | She's breeding then? |
She. . .Colour, | And. . .Sir, |
And her disgusts. | And. . .
Chamber? | Yes, Sir. | And. . .
Jellies. | I. . .Lady,; C *lines:*
As. . .case | That's. . .some-
times | And. . .majesty. | She's
breeding then? | She. . .qualms |
As. . .disgusts. | *then as* S; W

lines as C *except* She. . .colour, |
And. . .sir, | And her disgusts,
W
5 fond, an't] ~ ᴧ on't, F1+
(−D); fond, an't ᴧ S *conj.*
15 fann] face F1
30 thee] her F1
41 affliction] afflictions C, W
46–53 *Frederick.* You. . .Sir.] *om.*
F2+
50 lead] live F1 (first version)
52 Your] If F1 (second version)
86 Grace desire] desire Grace Q
114 excellence in] excellent F2, L, Q
120 Bawd ᴧ though,] ~ ᴧ ~ ᴧ F1;
~ , ~ ᴧ F2+ (−D)
127–128 ye. . .ye] you. . .you F2+
(−D)

IV.iii

9 not] *om.* F 1–2, L, Q
24–25 Doe. . .Ladies] C *lines:* Do
. . .favours | Are. . .please? |
There. . .ladies
29 whether he] whether be L
42 reverent] reverend F 2+ (−D)
47 e're] on F 1+
48–50 That. . .one] F 1–2, L, Q
line: That. . .blest, | That. . .
Chronicle, | A faithfull one; W
lines: That. . .blest, | That. . .
hands | To. . .one; D *lines:*
That. . .blest, | That. . .beget |
A. . .one
48 kept] keep S
59 pleasure] Pleaser Q
69 corruptnesse] Corruptress Q
102–103 cold;——. . .this;]~ ; ∧ . . .

~ ; F 1; ~ ; ∧ . . .~ . S+
105 growne proud] grown so proud
L, Q, S
117 dare] dares F 2, L, Q, S
132 that. . .him.] what. . .~ ? F 1
138 from] for F 1+
157 deaths] Death S
162 woman] Women S
182 do] dare C *conj.*
187 unconsiderate] inconsiderate F 2,
L, Q, S, C
190 offered∧ faire,] ~ ∧ ~ ∧ F 1–2;
~ , ~ ∧ M *conj.*, W, D
196 too,] ~ ∧ F 2+
213 Foole, unexampled∧] ~ , ~ ,
F 1; ~ ∧ ~ , F 2+ (−D)
213 shall] still Heath *conj. in* D

IV.iv

1 Curse] Curst F 1–2, L, Q
1 sights] light S *conj.*, C
4 cares] care F 1+; cares D *conj.*
7 him∧ Lord.] ~ —— ~ ! C+
19 *in a Couch*] in a Coach F 1; on a
Couch F 2+
20 blow, blow] blow, blow, blow
S

23 And, rivers,] ~ ∧ ~ ∧ F 1+
(−D)
24 fire, the] Fire, to the S
28 till] until S
45 their] the F 1–2, L, Q
50 Betwixt. . .and] 'Twixt the cold
bears, far from Seward *conj. in*
S (*preface*), C

IV.v

22 thou] thine F 1; thou art F 2–W
23 tell *Evanthe*] tell thee, *Evanthe*
F 2, L, Q
35 times] time F 2+
41 mine] my F 2, L, Q, S, C
48 unable,] ~ ∧ F 1–2, L, Q

52–53 me,. . .have∧. . .me;] ~ .
. . . ~ ;. . .~ ∧ Q
61 too,] ~ ∧ F 1–2, L, Q, S
117–118 *Evanthe.* Pray. . .sing.] *om.*
L

479

V.i

21 The] That the S
37 Heaven] Heav'n's S, C, W

39 Ever] Even S
63 uses] issues W

V.ii

0.1 Podrano] *Podramo* C+
5 with] *om.* F2, L, Q
21.1 *Suitors pass by.*] *om.* F1
28 a] *om.* S

29 *Post Teas*] *Post Kaes* F1–2, L, Q
31 A] And F1–2, L, Q, S, C; A   S
conj.
32 too] tho' S *conj.*

V.iii

7 their's] their S
12 i'th] into the F2, L, Q, C
41 *Enter...Castruchio.*] *after line*
40 F1–2, L,Q, S,C; *after line* 51
W, D
41 Evanthe,] *om.* W, D (*see notes on*
lines 61, 72)
41 Foole,] *om.* W (*see note on line*
72)
41 Castruchio] *om.* F2+ (*see note*
on line 61)
49 be yours, lovers] be your lovers
F1; be lovers F2, L, Q; be
lovers, Sir S, C, W
57 leere] jeere F1–2, L, Q, S
59–61 How...ye.] *marked as aside*
D
61 ye.] ye. *Re-enter* Castruchio *with*
Evanthe. D
62 *Exit* Castruchio.] *om.* F1–2, L,
Q, S, C
72 *Enter...Cutpurse.*] *after line* 64
F1–2, L, Q; *Enter Evanthe,*
Lawyer, Physician, Captain, and
Cut-purse. after line 61 S; *the*
same after line 64 C; *the same*
adding Tony, *after line* 62 W
73 to] unto S, C, W
101 outsides] outside F2, L, Q, S, C

108 Treasury] Treasure Q
139 And] To F1–2, L, Q, S, C;
And to W, D; And M *conj.*
143 Then farewell Madam] *continued*
to Physitian S *conj.*
146 be] me F2
159 thing. ...] thing. | *Enter*
Valerio disguis'd. | *Fred. Away*
with her, let her dye instantly. |
Evan. F1–2, L, Q; *as* F1, *with*
hiatus marked after instantly. S;
as present text but without hiatus
marked C, W, D
172 dispised, still laugh] *Fred. Des-*
pised still? | *Evan. Laugh* S *conj.*
173.1 *Enter...disguis'd.*] *after* thing.
line 159 F1–2, L, Q, S
179 A] *om.* L (*pulled type?*)
179 *Abidos*] *Abidig* F1
180 My...*Egla,*] *line repeated* F1
(*Agenor*ᴧ)
193–195 flew...He] fly...Till he S
conj.
197 Shranke] Shrunk F2+ (−D)
293 good] *om.* F2, L, Q
324 smell] swell F2
328 water,] ~ ; C, W, D
334 deere] dearest Q

APPENDIX

The following is Fletcher's first attempt at the interview between Frederick and Valerio in IV.ii, in F 1 occurring after line 2. As the Textual Introduction explains (pp. 362f), Fletcher recast the scene and rewrote this portion as lines 40–134 of the present edition, evidently intending to cancel his earlier effort. The lines are reprinted as they appear in F 1, a historical collation being provided in the footnotes. For the sigla, see p. 474.

    Fred. I know he wants no additions to his tortures,
He has enough for humane blood to carry,
Yet I must vex him further;
So many that I wonder his hot youth
And high-bred spirit breakes not into fury;
I must yet torture him a little further,
And make my selfe sport with his miseries,
My anger is too poore else. Here he comes,   *Valerio.*
Now my young married Lord, how do you feele your self?
You have the happinesse you ever aimed at,   [10]
The joy and pleasure.
    Val Would you had the like Sir.
    Fred. You tumble in delights with your sweet Lady,
And draw the minutes out in deare embraces,
You live a right Lords life.
    Val. Would you had tryed it,
That you might know the vertue but to suffer,
Your anger though it be unjust and insolent,
Sits hansomer upon you then your scorne,
To do a wilfull ill and glory in it,   [20]
Is to do it double, double to be damn'd too.
    Fred. Hast thou not found a loving and free Prince,
High in his favours too; that has confer'd
Such hearts ease, and such heapes of comfort on thee,
All thou coudest aske.
    Val. You are too growne a tyrant
Upon so suffering, and so still a subject;
You have put upon me such a punishment,

        [3] Yet...further;] *om.* C *conj.*, D
        [8] *Valerio.*] *Enter* Val. F 2+
        [9] young married] young-married C, W, D
        [26] too...tyrant] grown a tyrant too F 2, L, Q, S

481

That if your youth were honest it would blush at:
But you are a shame to nature, as to vertue.   [30]
Pull not my rage upon ye, 'tis so just,
It will give way to no respect; my life,
My innocent life, I dare maintaine it Sir,
Like a wanton prodigall you have flung away,
Had I a thousand more I would allow 'em,
And be as carelesse of 'em as your will is;
But to deny those rights the Law has given me,
The holy Law, and make her life the pennance,
Is such a studied and unheard of malice,
No heart that is not hyred from Hell dare think of;   [40]
To do it then too, when my hopes were high,
High as my blood, all my desires upon me,
My free affections ready to embrace her,
And she mine owne; do you smile at this, ist done well?
Is there not heaven above you that sees all?

[37] has] hath F2+ (−D)   [40] hyred] hot C conj.
[45] all?] all? Exit Val. F2+

RULE A WIFE AND HAVE A WIFE

edited by

GEORGE WALTON WILLIAMS

TEXTUAL INTRODUCTION

Rule a Wife and Have a Wife (Greg, *Bibliography*, no. 598) appears in Sir Henry Herbert's Office-book as licensed on 19 October 1624, and as performed at Court on 2 November and 26 December before the year was out.[1] It enjoyed considerable subsequent popularity on the seventeenth-century stage – Pepys saw it in 1661 and in 1662; and, in adaptations by David Garrick, James Love, W. Oxberry, and J. P. Kemble, it played regularly during the eighteenth and nineteenth centuries. A reviewer in *The Edinburgh Review of* February 1816 observed that the play was 'one of the very best comedies that ever was written; and holds, to this day, undisputed possession of the stage'.[2] This theatrical popularity had its parallel on the book-stands. The two Quarto editions of 1640 and 1697[3] introduced a steady stream of editions of the play in its original form or in adaptations, in single editions or in collections. From 1717, the date of the Third Quarto, until 1879, the British Library Catalogue of Printed Books lists thirty-two editions or issues. The play was also translated into German by C. G. Schmidt (1770) and

---

[1] Gerald Eades Bentley, *The Jacobean and Caroline Stage*, III (Oxford, 1956), 408.

[2] 'Schlegel on *the Drama*', *Edinburgh Review*, XXVI, no. 51 (February 1816), 105; quoted also in Benno Leonhardt, 'Die Text varianten von Beaumont und Fletchers [Werke]...V. Rule a Wife and Have a Wife', *Anglia*, XXIV (1901), 323. The reviewer was, presumably, Hazlitt.

[3] There were only two seventeenth-century Quarto editions. On the titlepage of the copy of Q2 (1697) at the Huntington Library (No. 152845), however, the last digit of the date has been changed in ink from '7' to '6', and '27. Octob.' has been added, perhaps indicating the date of purchase. The same correcting hand has added in the upper left-hand corner of the page '10ᵈ', presumably the price of purchase. It would seem that honest Sam. Briscoe, the publisher, had postdated his book by over two months. The copy is without question the 1697 Quarto, though its title-page has given rise to the theory that there was also a 1696 Quarto (see *National Union Catalogue*). Greg (*Bibliography*, II, 735) records an undated edition at the Library of Congress, 'Printed for R. Bulters' [sic], which he dates 'probably after 1700'. Since Morrison's *Index of Printers...[in] Wing's Short-Title Catalogue... 1641–1700* (Charlottesville, 1955) has no entry for 'Bulters', the edition in question must be that printed for R. Butters, now dated '[179–]' (*National Union Catalogue* (London, 1971), CLXXV, 221, 222).

485

by Karl Ludwig Kannegiesser (1808), both versions titled *Der beste Mann*, and into French by F. G. J. S. Andrieux as *L'école des épouseurs* (Paris, 1822).[1]

Sir Henry licensed the play as 'by John Fletcher', and though it has often been published under the joint authorship of Beaumont and Fletcher, no serious critic has challenged the original ascription of single authorship. Mr Hoy confirms the traditional view on the basis of the number of *ye* forms in the text (213) and the 'frequent occurrence of the contraction *'um* (for *'em*) [32 times]'.[2]

In writing *Rule a Wife*, as frequently, Fletcher turned to Spanish material. The source for the plot of Perez and Estifania is almost certainly Cervantes' *novela*, *El Casamiento Engañoso*, the eleventh tale in his *Novelas Ejemplares* (1613), perhaps more accessible to Fletcher in the French translation by the Sieur d'Audiguier, published in Paris in 1615.[3] The source of the plot of Leon and Margarita would appear to be Salas Barbadillo's *El Sagaz Estacio*, published in 1620, in which the situation of 'the complaisant husband' closely parallels Leon's before he attempts to rule his wife.[4] Since it is likely that the date of licensing (1624) represents the date of the completion of the play, *Rule a Wife* is one of the last plays that Fletcher wrote. Its performances later in the same year were introduced by a Prologue, presumably by Fletcher, making capital of the recent sensational success of Middleton's *A Game At Chess* played by the King's Men in August:[5]

---

[1] Leonhardt, 'Die Text varianten', pp. 233, 325. An adaptation in German, *Stille Wasser sind tief*, by F. L. Schröder, was printed in Berlin *c.* 1780 by H. A. Rottman (a copy in the Folger Shakespeare Library bears a manuscript notation of 1786).

[2] Cyrus Hoy, 'The Shares of Fletcher and his Collaborators in the Beaumont and Fletcher Canon (1)', *Studies in Bibliography*, VIII (1956), 129–46, esp. p. 142.

[3] Bentley, *Jacobean Stage*, III, 410; R. Warwick Bond (ed.), *Rule a Wife and Have a Wife* (*The Variorum Edition*), III (London, 1908), 361.

[4] Edward M. Wilson, '*Rule a Wife and Have a Wife* and *El Sagaz Estacio*', *Review of English Studies*, XXIV (1948), 189–94, argues that the indebtedness to this Spanish source is so close that Fletcher must have been able to read it in its Spanish original (no known French or English translation dates from Fletcher's lifetime); Bentley, disbelieving, suggests that Fletcher 'may well have heard the story of the Spanish novel, or he may have used a derivative which has not yet been cited' (p. 411).

[5] Bond (ed.), *Rule a Wife and Have a Wife*, pp. 361, 369.

doe not your looks let fall,
Nor to remembrance our late errors call,
Because this day w'are Spaniards *all againe.*
(Prologue, lines 3–5)

The first edition of the play was printed in Oxford by Leonard Lichfield, '*Printer to the University*', in 1640. On the bases of the treatment of the Fletcherian *ye* forms and of the presence of the spelling *hir* (for *her*), Mr Hoy argues that in company with *The Woman's Prize* and *A Wife for a Month* the Quarto text of *Rule a Wife* derives from a manuscript prepared by Edward Knight, book-keeper to the King's Men in 1624.[1] Such a manuscript could well have been 'a prompt-book or . . . directly descended from a prompt-book'; evidence for such an assertion is slight, but such directions as '*A letter.*' (I.i.69), '*Noise below.*' and '*Cacafogo makes a noise below.*' (V.v.15, 17, 26) would seem to suggest prompt authority.[2] More telling examples are the directions that at entrance supply a character with a prop that she must conceal until later in the scene: '*Enter . . . Estifania with a paper*' (C4, II.iv.0.1), '*Enter Estifania with a Casket*' (F3, IV.i.4.1), '*Enter . . . . Estifania with a Pistoll, and a Dagge.*' (H4, V.iv.0.1). These notices for props, theatrical in nature and of service to the actor and to the book-keeper, may very well point to prompt copy behind the Quarto. (The present edition emends these directions, in each instance mentioning the prop when it is melodramatically revealed later in the scene (respectively, at line 105, line 71, line 25).) These indications of theatrical origin offer some support to the idea that Lichfield secured his copy for the play from the players themselves while they were playing for the King at Oxford, and may explain in part why Lichfield should have ventured into the printing of a play at all.[3]

---

[1] Hoy, 'Fletcher and his Collaborators', p. 142.

[2] J. D. Jump (ed.), *Rollo Duke of Normandy* (Liverpool, 1948), p. xiii. The direction for '*Noise below*' at V.v.15 would seem particularly to be a prompter's warning direction (though only two lines ahead of the noise it requires), because the characters respond to all the other under-stage sounds in this scene (lines 17, 26, 98, and 38, 44, 99) – but not to this one.

[3] Jump has argued that the copy for *Rollo* was also from prompt (p. xiii). The Lichfield printing-shop, established by John Lichfield in 1617 and, after his death in 1635, continued by his son Leonard, confined its output to learned academic works,

The Quarto is printed with two-skeleton work. Though the text of the running titles is the same for verso and for recto – some form of '*Rule a Wife, and Have a Wife*' – there are no instances of titles swapped in the sequence of sheets after Sheet A. The titles follow this system:

Recto   I   B1,   C2–H2,   I1
    III   B2,   C1–H1,   I2   and A4
    v   B3,   C4–H4,   I3
    VII   B4,   C3–H3,   I4

Verso   II   B1^v,   C2^v–H2^v,   I1^v and A3^v (?)
    IV   B2^v,   C1^v–H1^v,   I2^v
    VI   B3^v,   C4^v–H4^v,   I3^v and A4^v
    VIII   B4^v,   C3^v–H3^v,   —

The skeletons are interchanged between Sheets B and C and again between Sheets H and I. Titles III, V, II, and IV use upper-case '*W*' for '*Wife*'; Titles I, VII, VI, and VIII use lower-case '*w*' for 'wife' (both times in each title). The compositors make no effort to be uniform in this detail (except that the title for page A3^v, which uses both upper- and lower-case forms, is discarded or reworked); however, the three titles that are first composed without the medial comma receive that comma at the time of composing C3^v, C4^v, and D2 (these changes towards uniformity are the work of one compositor), so that all titles have the comma by the close of printing. In view of the fact that neither the title nor the head-title has this medial comma, the fastidiousness of the compositor is surprising.

The composition of the Quarto is shared by two workmen, Compositor *P* and Compositor *Q*, their shares being most readily

sermons, and commendatory university poems, until Leonard undertook the innovation of plays. This new interest probably reflects the charter of privileges, granted 3 March 1636, that allowed printers to the University 'to print and publish any books of any kind which are not publicly condemned' (Falconer Madan, *Oxford Books* (Oxford, 1912), II, 129, and Appendix D (not B as there cited)). Leonard printed Thomas Randolph's *The Muses' Looking-Glass* and *Amyntas* (Greg, *Bibliography*, nos. 547 and 548) in a single Quarto volume in 1638 (2nd edition, 1640) and Jasper Mayne's *The City Match* (Greg, *Bibliography*, no. 568) in 1639. Interestingly enough, Mayne's play (though not produced) was scheduled for presentation before the King at Oxford in August of 1636. I am indebted to my student, Mrs Barbara Fitzpatrick for the account of the Lichfield shop.

distinguished by their treatment of spacing at medial commas: Compositor P usually inserts a space after a medial comma, Compositor Q usually does not.[1] An analysis of this single characteristic divides the stints:

P:　A3–4　　　　B3–4^{v}C1–2^v　　　　　D3–4^{v}E1–2^v　　F1–2^v
Q: A2　　A4^{v}B1–2^v　　　　C3–4^{v}D1–2^v　　　　E3–4^v

P:　　　G1–2^v　　　　H3–4^{v}I1–2^v
Q: F3–4^v　　G3–4^{v}H1–2^v　　　　I3–4^v

The scheme reveals that one compositor set four (consecutive) pages of a sheet while his fellow set the other four.[2] Across Sheets B and C, C and D, D and E, G and H, H and I, each compositor's stint consisted of eight consecutive pages – i.e., B3–4^{v}C1–2^v. Though the scheme does not require *seriatim* setting, it strongly suggests it, and the little evidence available from type-shortage supports that system in Sheet G ('P' and 'L' are inadequate in pages G4 and G4^v).[3] Other variant characteristics confirm this division: Compositor P prefers the speech-heading '*Duk.*', Compositor Q prefers '*Duke*' (evidence is conflicting on H3); Compositor P prefers the form 'wee'l', Compositor Q prefers 'weele'; Compositor P prefers the form 'Pre thee', Compositor Q prefers 'Preethee'.

As has been noted by others, Leonard Lichfield published the first Quarto of *Rule a Wife* in conjunction with the Second Quarto of *Rollo Duke of Normandy*; he thought them both the unaided work of John Fletcher. 'It may be inferred...[that he] regarded the printing of these two quartos almost as a single job': the two titlepages were printed – as far as possible – from the same setting of type; the same ornamental head- and tail-pieces and the same rules were used in both Quartos, and, 'possibly', some act headings

---

[1] Mrs Fitzpatrick has prepared the details of this analysis.

[2] It is no requirement that he should set the consecutive pages in consecutive order, but it is likely that he did. And when his stint crossed in consecutive order from one sheet to the next, it seems highly probable that he set his pages *seriatim*.

[3] The last sheet (I), always a special case, may have been set by formes, outer first – P setting 1 and 2^v, Q setting 3 and 4^v, then P setting 1^v and 2, Q setting 3^v and 4. As the shortage of 'P' is found on pages F2^v and F3, set respectively by P and Q, it is possible that the two compositors here used the same cases.

are common to both texts.[1] As an indication of that 'single job', we may note that Lichfield enlivened his two titlepages with a pair of matching ornaments. He might have used a single ornament, but loyal to his King even in the late days of 1640, Lichfield chose the lion and the unicorn for the Quartos, for *Rollo* the lion (dexter), rampant, guardant, and facing to its left – as it were, into what is to follow – for *Rule a Wife* the unicorn (sinister), rampant, and facing to its right – as it were, into what has preceded. Since we may be sure that these royal emblems were not chosen lightly, we may suppose also that their assignment to the two titlepages was designed deliberately to reproduce the position of the beasts as supporters of the royal arms and that, therefore, taking heraldic precedence, *Rollo* is the elder of the pair.[2] To decide which of a pair of twins issued first from the groaning bed of a press is, perhaps, a matter of small consequence, yet that the Quartos were twins of the same birth is clear from the fact that a copy of each Quarto – now both Bodleian copies 1 – was owned and signed by Robert Burton, who died on 25 January 1640.[3]

The rules and act headings are, indeed, common to both texts, but as the pattern of sharing is more readily observed in the act headings than in the rules, the following analysis addresses itself to the act headings only. There are two settings of type used for act headings in *Rollo*, the act number being changed for each act as the setting is re-used through the Quarto. The short heading

[1] Jump (ed.), *Rollo Duke of Normandy*, p. xiii.

[2] I am obliged to Mr James Day for the details of the heraldry. It is virtually certain that King Charles did actually receive this pair of books as a royal compliment, for a copy of *Rollo*, owned by him, survives in a collection of nine Fletcher plays that was bound for the King in a single volume about 1640 (Percy Simpson, 'King Charles the First as Dramatic Critic', *Bodleian Quarterly Record*, VII (1935–7), 257–62, and 320). Perhaps *Rule a Wife* was in another such volume.

[3] Greg records (*Bibliography*, II, 734) these details. It is conceivable, as he suggests, that the plays were actually printed in 1639; it is certain that they have a common birth. There is no indication that they were intended to be bound together (such a binding would preclude the possibility of their being placed side by side with the lion and the unicorn in their proper supporting roles), and Burton's copies were separates. Mrs Fitzpatrick has called to my attention a sales notice of a Hull bookseller in 1644 for *Rule a Wife* singly (*The Library*, 6th ser., 1 (1979), 128); she has noted also that the first five editions of Burton's *Anatomy* were printed by the Lichfield shop, the latest in 1638.

(44 mm), appears at the head of Acts 1, 3, and 4; the long heading (50 mm), with periods after the nouns, appears at the head of Act 5. The same act headings appear in *Rule a Wife*, the short heading before Acts 2, 3, and 4 and the long heading before Acts 1 and 5.

Rollo	Act	*Rule a Wife*
short (A2)	1	long (A3)
[*omit*] (B4^v)	2	short (B4^v)
short (D3)	3	short (D2)
short (F3)	4	short (F2^v)
long (H4)	5	long (H1)

The most economical explanation of this evidence is that when the compositors began the two plays, they undertook to provide separate act headings for each play (presumably to be re-used for each act).[1] As they progressed, having realized that they could manage with a single heading only, the compositor working on *Rule a Wife* put his long heading aside and borrowed the short heading devised for *Rollo* (the compositor on *Rollo* had forgotten to use the heading for his Act 2). The compositors used the same short heading for Act 3 and again for Act 4. We must suppose that at this point the short heading was pied, for both compositors retrieved the long heading originally devised for *Rule a Wife* and used it for Act 5 in both plays.

Such an analysis suggests strongly that the two Quartos were printed not one after the other but simultaneously and concurrently.

The compositorial patterns of the two Quartos confirm the theory of the concurrency of the printing. The same sort of alternation found in *Rule a Wife* occurs also in *Rollo*, and the stints of the two compositors are exactly complementary from Sheet B through Sheet G of both Quartos.[2]

---

[1] The fact that the running-titles used in *Rule a Wife* for A3^v(?), A4, A4^v reappear in Sheet B indicates that, for that play, printing began with Sheet A. The same is no doubt true for the companion piece.

[2] We depend here on the identification of the two compositors of *Rollo* prepared by Jump (*Rollo Duke of Normandy*, p. xi), and we believe that those compositors are the same as those at work also in *Rule a Wife*. We have, therefore, adopted Jump's designations (*P*, *Q*).

491

B	C	D	E	F	G
$B1-2^v3-4^v$	$C1-2^v3-4^v$	$D1-2^v3-4^v$	$E1-2^v3-4^v$	$F1-2^v3-4^v$	$G1-2^v3-4^v$

P: Rollo Rule Rule Rollo Rollo Rule Rule Rollo Rule Rollo Rule Rollo
Q: Rule Rollo Rollo Rule Rule Rollo Rollo Rule Rollo Rule Rollo Rule

In Sheet A, as Jump has noted, there is insufficient evidence to sustain a thesis of such intricacy, and in Sheets H through K though the alternating pattern of composition continues for each Quarto (see above for *Rule a Wife*), the evidence is conflicting rather than complementary.[1] The patterning as I have sketched it here for these sheets, however, is sufficient to demonstrate that the Quartos exhibit the signs of concurrent printing.

It would be gratifying to be able to say that the evidence from watermarks also supported the theory of concurrency, but all that can be said at the present time is that such evidence does not disprove the theory. If we suppose that each of the plays was assigned to one specific press for its entire printing, while the compositors shuttled back and forth from press to press (perhaps also shifting from one set of type-cases to another: see p. 489, n. 3), then it would presumably follow that a stack of paper might have been assigned to each press; there would be no *prima facie* reason that the two stacks of paper must have any watermarks in common. Still, inquiry reveals, tentatively, that a stock of paper marked with a bunch of grapes was used in *Rollo* (Sheets A and C) and in *Rule a Wife* (Sheets A–H) and that another stock marked with a trident crown was used in *Rollo* (Sheets B, D–I) and in *Rule a Wife* (Sheet I).[2]

Lichfield's Quarto of *Rule a Wife* is cleanly printed, though minor adjustments have been introduced in the present edition in order to clarify and standardize. The Quarto is characterized by a more limited use of distinguishing type than is usually found in prints of this period. Though such a practice may derive from university style (different from the commercial style of London), it may more likely reflect the habits of Edward Knight, the bookkeeper. In the display piece, the Prologue (perhaps not copied by

---

[1] For further conclusions on the concurrency of the two Quartos, see the Introduction to *Rollo* in the present series (forthcoming).

[2] I have examined exemplars at the British Library and at the Huntington Library.

Knight), Compositor *Q* set in distinguishing type: place-names twice ('Spaine'), persons named by a national adjective ('Spaniards'), and a word thought to have a technical or foreign connotation ('Vestalls'). In the text of the dialogue, however, his pattern is slightly different. He distinguished '*Spaine*' (II.iv.33), '*Goletta*' (IV.i.82), '*Europe*' (V.ii.51), but he did not distinguish 'Flanders' (I.i.121), 'Babell' (IV.i.22; V.ii.17), or the 'Indies' (IV.iii.199). He did not distinguish national adjectives; he did distinguish foreign words or phrases. Compositor *P* did not distinguish place-names ('Indies', 'Flanders', 'Spaine' (four times), 'England', 'Elisium'). He did not distinguish national adjectives; he did distinguish foreign words or phrases. Both compositors distinguished proper names of characters in the play and of others (e.g., '*Ovid*', '*Penelope*'). The conclusion from this evidence suggests (1) that the manuscript italicized proper names and foreign words and phrases only, and (2) that the compositors were reasonably faithful to their copy in this matter, though Compositor *Q*, careful in display, was less careful in dialogue.[1]

Another unusual feature of the Quarto, and presumably of the manuscript behind it, is its tendency to divide into two parts words usually regarded as single forms even in 1640. Though it is found twice in the stints of Compositor *Q* – 'Every where' (I.v.i), 'a foot' (III.v.41) – this feature is common in the work of Compositor *P*: 'May be' (II.ii.30), 'afore hand' (III.ii.60), 'a loofe' (III.iii.35), 'pre thee' (III.v.180; IV.i.168; V.iv.31), 'a way' (V.iii.29), 'a foot' (V.iii.31; V.iv.17). These have been accepted in the text as forms sufficiently normal in the period as not to require emendation; three other examples of the same feature (also in *P*'s share) seem to require correction as substantive changes, and so indeed thought the Second Folio: 'all most' (V.iii.29) and '*with in*' (V.v.12) and 'A bove' (I.vi.32).

The punctuation of the Quarto is unusually light. The standard

---

[1] The present text emends in accordance with those conclusions (see Emendations of Accidentals). Compositor *Q*'s three foreign place-names are normalized to roman type; Compositor *P*'s oversight, 'Basto' (II.ii.9), is italicized (though his 'portigues' (V.v.6) is not); both Compositors' oversights in proper names are italicized (Comp. *Q*: 'Margaretta' (I.ii.22), 'Mars' (II.iv.69), 'Palmerin' (IV.i.129), 'Neptune (V.v.175); Comp. *P*: 'Margarita' (V.v.7)).

493

marks are the comma and the period; semi-colons, colons, and question-marks are extremely rare, as are, of course, exclamation-points and parentheses. The pointing is, in fact, almost below the level of acceptability, and absence of marks leads often to hesitation or misinterpretation. The present edition has attempted to retain the lightness, adding few commas and semi-colons and fewer colons still, though the Folio punctuates with colons regularly. Question-marks, also common in the Folio, have been added as necessary to interpretation, but they have not been used for exclamations. The Quarto has two dashes – one for an interrupted speech, one for a change of direction within a speech – which the Folio copies and to which it adds seven more: two for interruption, five for change of direction or tone within a speech; the present edition adds many more to designate interrupted speeches and changes of tone or address. Some few parentheses are added to point up the presence of parenthetical expressions; these are also minimal, in keeping with the rarity (two only) of these forms in the Quarto.

The dialogue of the play is in verse throughout. Long lines, never indented, are turned over at the right margin. Few errors in lineation occur; none is serious. At III.i.14–15 and 25–6 the text presents the problem of apportioning three consecutive part-lines: the disposition made here agrees with Bond in the former, disagrees with Bond in the latter. Four speeches begin with short initial lines: Altea's at II.i.44–8, Margarita's at IV.iii.72–4, Margarita's at V.v.171–5, and – as a special case – Leon's at IV.iii.124–6.[1] On page 13ᵛ, Compositor Q, sensing a need to expand his copy so as to have text on all the pages of the last sheet in the volume, divided lines V.iii.166 and 168 (making four of two) in order to make his text run over to page 14. He managed further, dividing line 178, to turn his three lines of over-run into four; he then filled up the page with one word, 'FINIS'. He might have printed

---

[1] To these might be added Alonzo's speech at I.ii.42–4, as it is lined in the Quarto. The present text follows Professor Bowers' suggestion. Bond's solution to this vexation is to divide line 43 – 'I am a soldier, and too sound a body | Becomes me not. Farewell, Sanchio.' – but as this is probably the only example in the Quarto of this sort of lineation in which the long line – 'And too sound a body becomes me not,' – is printed without a medial break, Bond's version is probably unacceptable.

the Epilogue on 14 also, but he preferred to use every page of his sheet, and he printed it alone on 14ᵛ, dividing line 8 to make the Epilogue one line longer than it should be (perhaps thinking also that he was preserving a rhyme pattern).

The characters present few difficulties. The character of Michael Perez is regularly Michaell ('*Mich.*') in speech-prefixes in the first scene of the play, thereafter Perez, though he is addressed as '*Don Michaell*' throughout. There seems to be no special significance in the shift. The Ladies attending on Margarita have been consolidated in earlier editions; here they have separate status. The first group appears in this edition as 'Old Ladies' in I.iv (three persons) and in II.i (two persons); the second as 'Ladies' in II.iii and III.i. The first would seem to be old wise-women in the country; the second, ladies in waiting of the household (see further, Textual Note to I.iv.o.1). The character of Altea is sometimes designated with the prefix '4.' in II.i; II.iii; and III.i. The solution to this problem is obvious, but the cause of the problem has not been identified heretofore.

When Altea makes her first entrance, talking with the Old Ladies in I.iv, she is given the prefix '*Alt.*' for her four speeches (lines 9, 12, 18, 20). When she makes her second entrance, with Margarita and two of the Old Ladies in II.i, she is given the prefix '4.' for her nine speeches (lines 24, 26, 44, 49, 52, 53, 58, 60, 66). When she makes her third entrance with Margarita and two Ladies in II.iii, she is given the prefix '4.' for her six speeches (lines 1, 9, 12, 34, 60, 71). When she makes her fourth entrance, Altea is an attendant lady and mute (II.iv.86.1–137). When she makes her fifth entrance with Margarita and the Boy in III.i, she is given the prefix '*Altea.*', for her first speech and '4.' for her thirteen speeches in the rest of the scene. For her subsequent entrances at the end of the play in V.iii and V.v, Altea is given a prefix based on her name.

Addressing the problem of the '4.' in II.i, Weber offered the explanation that Altea received this prefix because she was the fourth person mentioned in the initial stage-direction; Dyce and Bond supported this explanation *faute de mieux*. Surely, better is available, and Weber's explanation will scarcely explain II.i. Though Altea is the fourth person mentioned in the direction for II.i, no

495

intelligent system would include Margarita as the first in a series of which the other members were servants. Altea is also the fourth person to speak in the scene, but her first speech, the twelfth speech of the scene, is here at line 24. The prefix '4.' seems hardly significant if it records only that her name appears fourth in the direction. But if we grant Weber's point for II.i, we must expect it to be valid also for II.iii and III.i. In II.iii, Altea is the second person mentioned in the entry-direction, and her first speech, the second speech of the scene, is at line 1. In III.i, Altea is the second person mentioned in the entry-direction. She is the first to speak in the scene, and for this speech her prefix is '*Altea.*'; all subsequent speeches have the prefix '4.'. Finally, in I.iv Altea is the fourth person to enter, the fourth servant in the scene, and the fourth person to speak; her prefix is '*Alt.*'. Clearly, the prefix '4.' has no numerical significance in any of these scenes.

Since the form '4.' cannot be defended as an acceptable prefix in terms of staging, we may examine the pattern of the compositors who set the play. If we assume *seriatim* setting, we can recognize that when Compositor Q met the name on B2 for the first time (I.iv), the full name appeared in the entry-direction with the prefix '*Alt.*' on the next line. With the full name in his mind, Compositor Q could recognize that the prefix was '*Alt.*' and so could continue correctly throughout the scene on B2ᵛ. When next he met the prefix, he was setting C3 (II.iii.34); he did not have the name as a guide, and he set the prefix as '4.' three times on C3–3ᵛ. When next he met the character (in III.i), he set the full name in the entry-direction and, again, as the first prefix in the scene on D2. Seven lines later, on D2ᵛ, he had forgotten the name and he reverted to '4.' for the entire sequence of six prefixes. When Compositor P met the full name on B4ᵛ for the first time (II.i.0.1), he set it without difficulty. He encountered the prefix on the next page – but in a new sheet (C1) – and with no immediate reference to the full name (perhaps after a night's delay) he set the prefix as '4.' nine times on C1–1ᵛ. On C2ᵛ, though the full name appears in the entry-direction (II.iii.0.1) and twice later in the dialogue of his stint, Compositor P was so well accustomed to the number prefix that he set '4.' three times more. In III.i, on D3ᵛ, D4, and D4ᵛ he continued to set '4.' seven times, in spite of the presence of the full name in dialogue. The compositors set the prefixes correctly thereafter (in V.iii; V.v) and had no difficulty anywhere with the prefixes for Alonzo (throughout '*Alon.*').

Since both compositors set the form '4.' and since neither had difficulty in spelling the full name (frequently in directions and dialogue), we may posit a manuscript formation for an abbreviation of the prefix, 'A' or 'At' that resembled the characters for '4' or '4th' and so misled both men. One exemplar of the Quarto (Wake Forest University, Winston-Salem, North Carolina), annotated in what appears to be ink of the seventeenth century, has attempted (without much success) to correct the erroneous designations. In II.i, the speeches given to '4.' are reassigned to the First and Second Old Ladies; in the first part of II.iii and III.i the prefix '4.' is corrected to '*Al.*' (II.iii.1; III.i.1–38); in the latter part of both scenes, the prefix '4.' is replaced by '1.', signifying perhaps one of the ladies in waiting in II.iii and in III.i the First Lady who has entered at III.i.45.1 and (in the Quarto) remains onstage for the rest of the scene.[1]

The compositors have a slight tendency to omit or to mislocate speech-headings. At four places, editors have felt the need to supply a new prefix and to begin a new speech. Three of these have survived critical scrutiny: '*Perez.*' (II.ii.30, Seward), '*Leon.*' (IV.iii.17, Colman), '*Leon.*' or '*Margarita.*' (V.v.158, Seward or Coleridge); the fourth is '*Alonzo.*' (IV.ii.13, the present editor). This prefix for Alonzo is inserted between two successive prefixes for Sanchio in one stretch of dialogue (p. 584). Three 'extra' prefixes follow entrances by one character that interrupt a single, continuing speech of another character: for Estifania at IV.i.124 after Cacafogo's entrance, for Leon at IV.iii.124,[2] after Perez' entrance, and for Leon

[1] Though these corrections may be thought to represent marks for a prompt-book, they seem scarcely more than corrections to a reading-text. In the same category: at IV.iii.17 the Quarto prefix '*Lor.*' is, with some justice, changed to '*Leon.*', and at II.iii.6 '*Exit Lady.*' is corrected to '*Exit Altea.*' Only in I.iv does there seem any theatrical function to these changes, for here the part of the Third Old Lady is cut and her two speeches reassigned, thus saving one actor.

[2] It is notable that this prefix, '*Leon.*', the first word of the page (G 4), is preceded by a catchword 'What' (G 3ᵛ). Of seventeen instances when a fresh speech heads a page in this Quarto, only two catchwords provide the first word of the speech and

at V.v.135[1] after Perez' and Estifania's entrance. Two prefixes, critics now agree, have been mistakenly printed as part of a dialogue line (III.v.152; V.v.162), and two others have been mistakenly printed one line too high, thus appropriating a part-line of the preceding speaker (III.v.81; IV.i.50).

Though the entry-directions normally are centred in the block of dialogue, eight such directions appear in the right margin (six of them on pages of Compositor Q). Minor adjustments in positioning many of the entry-directions have been made, but the discrepancies between the original and the edition are negligible and do not seem to exhibit any pattern. The act divisions in this edition follow those of the Quarto, which regularly mark the beginning of each act and provide also notice of 'SCENA. 1.' (see above), though they mark no other scenes. The act divisions seem to be acceptably correct, and the scene divisions present no problems; they have remained unquestioned in all editions since Weber numbered them. On two occasions, the text requires the exit and immediate re-entry of a character (or characters). Margarita and Altea leave the stage at the end of Act II and reappear immediately at the beginning of Act III; at the end of Act IV, Leon and Margarita probably leave the stage at the final '*Exeunt.*' and reappear immediately at the beginning of Act V.[2] Both these instances demonstrate that Fletcher shaped the play so as to utilize intervals in staging at the Blackfriars Theatre and at Court, probably with inter-act music.[3] There are no indications of any other musical

not the prefix. The other example is a special case (B2/B2ᵛ): the catchword is 'Shee'; the first line is '2. Shee'.

[1] These three prefixes all head short lines. Estifania's is the concluding line of her speech, and, as it does not occur immediately below the entry-direction, invites the speculation that a matching part-line is missing (perhaps something like: '*Cacafogo.* A beaten thing, but – *Estifania.* May I crave your leave sir?'). The two prefixes for Leon follow the entry-direction immediately (but see the preceding note). Leon's prefix in Act IV introduces a three-line speech with an initial short line; that in Act V concludes the speech.

[2] Though there is no exit-direction specifically for them, they could leave the stage on Leon's last line (IV.iii.214), four lines before the close of the scene.

[3] At III.v.193, Perez leaves the stage; four lines later he reappears at the beginning of IV.i. Though this is not strictly an 'immediate re-entry', it is a violation of the 'law of re-entry' in requiring so brief a time offstage; as such, it probably also indicates an act interval.

features in the play, though Dyce has argued that there should be a song at III.i.23 (see Textual Note on III.i.0.1).

The transmission of the text is not without interest. The first reprinting of the text of the 1640 Quarto appears in Kirkman's *The Wits, or Sport upon Sport* (1672). Here under the title '*An Equall Match*' are in prose the sections of the play treating the cozenings of Perez and Estifania (III.ii; III.iv; IV.i.1–101), with frequent omission of a line or two and rare change of a word'.[1] Three of those changes are of note: (1) at III.ii.30 for Q1 'basinesse' Kirkman reads 'laziness', anticipating Seward's later correct emendation; (2) at III.iv.8 for Q1 'The palsy and picklocks, fy' Kirkman reads 'the palsy and picklocks fit', so removing still further from the correct form; (3) at III.iv.51 for Q1 'wide' Kirkman reads 'wild', anticipating the same error in Langbaine. The First Quarto was the copy for the Second Folio (1679), which in its turn was the copy for the Second Quarto (1697) and for Langbaine's edition of the *Works* in 1711. (It is evident from errors at IV.iii.17 and V.ii.62 that F2, not Q2, was the copy for Langbaine.) One curiosity in the transmission of the text is the fact that George Saintsbury prepared his edition of the play for Charles Mills Gayley's *Representative English Comedies*, volume III, published in 1914, without reference to R. Warwick Bond's edition in A. H. Bullen's *Variorum*, volume III, published in 1908. Saintsbury's text seems often to depart from Dyce, reverting to Weber, 'of whose work', Saintsbury admits, 'I think, after careful examination, rather more highly than I once did'.[2] In consequence, of course, Saintsbury's text is less useful than one might have expected it to be.

The text of the present edition has been set up from a typescript of the exemplar of the First Quarto at the British Library; it has been verified against the exemplars at the Huntington Library and at Wake Forest University.[3] In preparing the edition I have consulted also the critical comments of J. Monck Mason, *Comments on the Plays of Beaumont and Fletcher* (London, 1798), John

[1] Bond (ed.), *Rule a Wife and Have a Wife*, p. 366.
[2] Saintsbury, in Charles Mill Gayley, *Representative English Comedies*, III, 212.
[3] I am much indebted to Mr Lowell Frey and Miss Elizabeth Deis and Mr John Morey who collaborated in the preparation of the typescript and produced a very correct document.

Mitford, *Cursory Notes on Various Passages in the Text of Beaumont and Fletcher* (London, 1856), Kenneth Deighton, *Conjectural Emendations: The Old Dramatists* (Westminster, 1896), and the extensive Introduction by R. Warwick Bond to his edition of the play in the Bullen *Variorum* (1908). The list of the 'Dramatis Personæ' (page 501) omits the names of the actors of the several parts given in the copy-text, Q2.

Dramatis Personæ.

Duke *Medina*,
Don Juan de Castro,
Michaell Perez, the Copper Captain,
Cacafogo, a Usurer,
Sanchio,
Alonzo,
[*Leon*]

       Women.
Donna Margarita, the Heiress,
Estifania, her Maid, Wife to the Copper Captain,
Donna Clara,
Altea,
[Three Old Ladies]
Two Ladies

[*Lorenzo*, Coachman, Old Woman,
Servants, Attendants,
Two Maids, Boy]

    [The Scene: Civill, and a Country House nearby.]

    Dramatis...Ladies] Q2; *om.* Q1, F2

10

Prologue.

Pleasure attend yee, and about yee sit
The springs of mirth fancy delight and wit
To stirre you up, doe not your looks let fall,
Nor to remembrance our late errors call,
Because this day w'are Spaniards *all againe,*
The story of our Play, and our Sceane Spaine:
The errors too, doe not for this cause hate,
Now we present their wit and not their state.
Nor Ladies be not angry if you see,
A young fresh beauty, wanton and too free,   10
Seeke to abuse her Husband, still tis Spaine,
No such grosse errors in your Kingdome raigne,
W'are Vestalls *all, and though we blow the fire,*
We seldome make it flame up to desire,
Take no example neither to beginne,
For some by president delight to sinne:
Nor blame the Poet if he slip aside,
Sometimes lasciviously if not too wide.
But hold your Fannes close, and then smile at ease,
A cruell Sceane did never Lady please.   20
Nor Gentlemen, pray be not you displeas'd,
Though we present some men fool'd, some diseas'd,
Some drunke, some madde: we meane not you, you'r free,
We taxe no farther then our Comedie,
You are our friends, sit noble then and see.

11 her] F2; your Q1   12 raigne] F2; raignes Q1
13 W'are] stet Q1

502

Rule a Wife and Have a Wife.

Enter Juan de Castro, *and* Michaell Perez.

Perez.   Are your companies full Coronell?
Juan.   No not yet sir:
   Nor will not be this month yet, as I reckon.
   How rises your commaund?
Perez.   We pick up still,
   And as our monies hold out, we have men come,
   About that time I thinke we shall be full too;
   Many young gallants goe.
Juan.   And unexperienced,
   The warres are dainty dreams to young hot spirits,
   Time and experience will allay those visions;
   We have strange things to fill our numbers,
   There's one *Don Leon*, a strong goodly fellow,   10
   Recommended to me from some noble Friends,
   For my *Alferes*, had you but seen his person,
   And what a Giants promise it protesteth.
Perez.   I have heard of him and that he hath serv'd before too.
Juan.   But no harm done, nor never meant, *Don Michael*,
   That came to my eares yet, aske him a question,
   He blushes like a girle, and answers litle,
   To the point lesse; he wears a sword a good one,
   And good cloaths too, he is whole skin'd, has no hurt yet,
   Good promising hopes, I never yet heard certainly   20
   Of any Gentleman that saw him angry.
Perez.   Preserve him, hee'l conclude a peace if need be;
   Many as strong as he will goe along with us,
   That sweare as valiantly as heart can wish,
   Their mouths charg'd with six oaths at once, and whole ons,

*10 strong] Colman (Theobald *conj.*); strange Qq, F2
25 mouths] F2; mouth Q1

503

That make the drunken Dutch creepe into mole-hils.

Juan.   Tis true, such we must looke for, but *Michaell Perez*,
    When heard you of *Donna Margaretta*, the great heiresse?

Perez.   I heare every hower of her, though I never saw her,
    She is the main discourse; noble *Don Juan de Castro*,   30
    How happy were that man cood catch this wench up,
    And live at ease, she is faire, and young, and wealthy,
    Infinite wealthy, and as gratious too
    In all her entertainements, as men report.

Juan.   But shee is proud sir, that I know for certaine,
    And that coms seldome without wantonnesse,
    He that shall marry her, must have a rare hand.

Perez.   Would I were married, I would find that wisdome,
    With a light reyne to rule my wife; if ever woman
    Of the most subtlest mould went beyond mee,   40
    I would give the boyes leave to whoote me out o'th parish.

Enter a Servant.

Servant.   Sir there be two gentlewomen attend to speak with yee.

Juan.   Wait on them in.

Perez.   Are they two handsome women?

Servant.   They seem so, very handsome, but they are vail'd sir.

Perez.   Thou put'st sugar in my mouth, how it melts with me,
    I love a sweet young wench.

Juan.   Wait on them in I say.

                              Exit Servant.

Perez.   *Don Juan.*

Juan.   How you itch *Michaell*, how you burnish!
    Will not this souldiers heat out of your bones yet,
    Doe your eyes glow now?

Perez.   There be two.

Juan.   Say honest,
    What shame have you then?

Perez.   I would faine see that,   50
    I have been in the Indies twice, and have seen strange things,
    But two honest women: one I read of once.

Juan.   Pre thee be modest.

Perez.   Ile be any thing.

Enter Servant, Donna Clara, *and* Estifania *vail'd.*

Juan.   You are welcome Ladies.   [*Exit* Servant.]
Perez [apart].   Both hooded, I like um well though,
  They come not for advice in law sure heather,
  May be they would learne to raise the picke, I am for 'um.
  They are very modest, tis a fine preludium.
Juan.   With mee or with this gentleman, would you speak Lady?
Clara.   With you sir as I guesse, *Juan de Castro.*
Perez [apart].   Her curtaine opens, she is a pretty gentlewoman.   60
Juan.   I am the man, and shall be bound to fortune,
  I may doe any service to your beauties.
Clara.   Captaine, I heare you are marching downe to Flanders,
  To serve the Catholick King.
Juan.   I am sweet Lady.
Clara.   I have a kinsman and a noble friend,
  Imploy'd in those warres, may be sir you know him,
  Don Campusano Captaine of *Carbines*,
  To whom I would request your Noblenesse,
  To give this poore remembrance.   [*Gives*] *A letter.*
Juan.   I shall doe it,
  I know the Gentleman a most worthy Captaine.   70
Clara.   Something in private.
Juan.   Step aside: Ile serve thee.
                                   Exeunt Juan *and* Clara.
Perez.   Prethee let me see thy face.
Estifania.   Sir you must pardon me,
  Women of our sort that maintaine faire memories,
  And keep suspect off from their chastities,
  Had neede weare thicker vailes.
Perez.   I am no blaster of a Ladies beauty,
  Nor bold intruder on her speciall favours,
  I know how tender reputation is,
  And with what guards it ought to be preserv'd Lady,
  You may to me.
Estifania.   You must excuse me Seignior,   80

I come not here to sell my selfe.

Perez.   As I am a Gentleman,
By the honour of a souldier.

Estifania.   I beleeve you.
I pray you be civill, I beleeve you would see me,
And when you have seen me, I beleeve you will like me,
But in a strange place, to a stranger too,
As if I came on purpose to betray you,
Indeed I will not.

Perez.   I shall love you dearely,
And tis a sinne to fling away affection,
I have no Mistresse, no desire to honour
Any but you, [*aside*] will not this oyster open?——   90
I know not, you have struck me with your modesty——
[*Aside*] She will draw sure;——so deep, and taken from me
All the desire I might bestow on others;
Quickly before they come.

Estifania.   Indeed I dare not.
But since I see you are so desirous Sir
To view a poore face that can merit nothing
But your repentance——

Perez.   It must needs be excellent.

Estifania.   And with what honesty you aske it of me,
When I am gone let your man follow me,
And view what house I enter, thither come,   100
For there I dare be bold to appeare open.
And as I like your vertuous carriage then,
I shall be able to give welcome to you;

Enter Juan, Clara *and Servants.*

Shee hath done her businesse, I must take my leave sir.

Perez.   Ile kisse your faire white hand, and thank ye Lady,
My man shall wait, and I shall be your servant.
Sirrah, come neare, hark.

Servant.   I shall doe it faithfully.   *Exit.*

Juan.   You will command me no more services?

*103.1 and Servants] a Servant Qq, F2

506

Clara.   To be carefull of your noble health, deare Sir,
That I may ever honour you.

Juan.   I thank you,   110
And kisse your hands,——wait on the Ladies down there.

> *Exeunt Ladies and Servants.*

Perez.   You had the honour to see the face that came to you?

Juan.   And 'twas a faire one, what was yours, *Don Michaell?*

Perez.   Mine was i'th 'clipse, and had a clowd drawn over it,
But I believe well, and I hope tis handsome,
Shee had a hand would stirre a holy Hermite.

Juan.   You know none of um?

Perez.   No.

Juan.   Then I doe Captaine,
But ile say nothing till I see the proofe on't,
Sit close *Don Perez*, or your worship's caught,
I feare a fly.

Perez.   Were those she brought love letters?   120

Juan.   A packet to a kinsman now in Flanders;
Yours was very modest me thought.

Perez.   Some young unmanag'd thing;
But I may live to see——

Juan.   Tis worth experience,
Let's walk abroad and view our companies.

> *Exeunt.*

Enter Sanchio *and* Alonzo.   [I. ii]

Sanchio.   What, are you for the wars *Alonzo?*

Alonzo.   It may be I,
It may be no, e'ne as the humour takes me;
If I finde peace amongst the female creatures,
And easie entertainment, ile stay at home,
I am not so far obliged yet to long marches,
And mouldy biskets to run mad for honour,
When you are all gone I have my choice before me.

Sanchio.   Of which hospitall thou wilt sweat in; wilt thou never
leave whoring?

Alonƶo.   There is lesse danger in't then gunning *Sanchio,*   10
   Though we be shot sometimes the shot's not mortall,
   Besides it breaks no limbs.
Sanchio.   But it disables um,
   Do'st thou see how thou pul'st thy legs after thee,
   As they hung by points?
Alonƶo.   Better to pull um thus then walke on wooden ones,
   Serve bravely for a billet to support me.
Sanchio.   Fy, fy, tis base.
Alonƶo.   Do'st thou count it base to suffer?
   Suffer abundantly? tis the crowne of honour;
   You think it nothing to lie twenty daies
   Under a surgeons hands that has no mercy.
Sanchio.   As thou hast done I am sure; but I perceive now   20
   Why you desire to stay, the orient heiresse,
   The *Margaretta* sir.
Alonƶo.   I would I had hir.
Sanchio.   They say she will marry.
Alonƶo.   Yes, I think she will.
Sanchio.   And marry suddenly as report goes too,
   She feares hir youth will not hold out *Alonƶo.*
Alonƶo.   I would I had the sheathing on't.
Sanchio.   They say too
   Shee has a greedy eye that must be fed
   With more than one mans meat.
Alonƶo.   Would she were mine,
   I would cater for her well enough: but *Sanchio,*
   There be too many great men that adore her,   30
   Princes, and Princes fellowes that claime priviledge.
Sanchio.   Yet those stand off ith' way of marriage,
   To be tied to a mans pleasure is a second labour.
Alonƶo.   Shee has bought a brave house here in towne.
Sanchio.   I have heard so.
Alonƶo.   If shee convert it now to pious uses,
   And bid poore Gentlemen welcome.
Sanchio.   When comes shee to it?
Alonƶo.   Within these two daies, she is in the countrey yet,
   And keeps the noblest house.

Sanchio.   Then there's some hope of her,
Wilt thou goe my way?
Alonzo.   No, no, I must leave you
And repaire to an old Gentlewoman that has credit with her,   40
That can speak a good word.
Sanchio.   Send thee good fortune,
But make thy body sound first.
Alonzo.   I am a souldier,
And too sound a body becomes me not,
Farewell *Sanchio.*

                                 Exeunt.

             Enter a Servant *of* Michael Perez.   [I. iii]

Servant.   Tis this, or that house, or I have lost mine ayme,
They are both faire buildings, she walked plaguy fast,
And hereabouts I lost her,

                Enter Estifania.

                stay, that's she,
Tis very she,——she makes me a low curt'sie,
Let me note the place, the street I well remember.
                           Exit [Estifania].
She is in againe, certaine some noble Lady,
How happy should I be if she love my Master:
A wondrous goodly house, here are brave lodgings,
And I shall sleep now like an Emperour,
And eat abundantly, I thank my fortune,   10
Ile back with speed, and bring him happy tidings.
                                Exit.

               Enter three Old Ladies.   [I. iv]

1. Old Lady.   What should it mean, that in such hast we are sent
   for?
2. Old Lady.   Belike the Lady *Margaret* has some businesse
Shee would break to us in private.

            *0.1 Old Ladies] *old Ladies* Qq, F2

3. Old Lady.   It should seeme so.
Tis a good Lady, and a wise young Lady.
2. Old Lady.   And vertuous enough too I warrant yee
For a yong woman of her yeares: tis pittie
To load her tender age with too much virtue.
3. Old Lady.   Tis more sometimes then we can well away with.

Enter Altea.

Altea.   Good morrow Ladies.
Old Ladies.   Morrow my good Madam.
1. Old Lady.   How does the sweet young beauty, Lady *Margaret?*   10
2. Old Lady.   Has she slept well after her walke last night?
1. Old Lady.   Are her dreames gentle to her minde?
Altea.   All's well,
Shee's very well, she sent for you thus suddenly
To give hir counsell in a businesse
That much concernes her.
2. Old Lady.   Shee does well and wisely,
To aske the counsell of the ancientst, Madame,
Our yeares have run through many things she knows not.
Altea.   Shee would faine marry.
1. Old Lady.   Tis a proper calling,
And well beseemes her yeares, who would she yoke with?
Altea.   Thats left to argue on, I pray come in   20
And break your fast, drink a good cup or two,
To strengthen your understandings, then sheele tell ye.
2. Old Lady.   And good wine breeds good counsell, wele yeeld
to ye.

                                        Exeunt.

Enter Juan de Castro, *and* Leon.   [I. v]

Juan.   Have you seen any service?
Leon.   Yes.
Juan.   Where?
Leon.   Every where.
Juan.   What office bore yee?

9 *Old Ladies.*] *All.* Qq, F2

Leon.   None, I was not worthy.

Juan.   What Captaines know you?

Leon.   None, they were above me.

Juan.   Were you never hurt?

Leon.   Not that I well remember,
But once I stole a Hen, and then they beat me;
Pray aske me no long questions, I have an ill memory.

Juan [*aside*].   This is an Asse,——did you never draw your sword
   yet?

Leon.   Not to doe any harme I thank heaven for't.

Juan.   Nor nere tane prisoner?

Leon.   No, I ran away,
For I had nere no mony to redeeme me.   10

Juan.   Can you endure a Drum?

Leon.   It makes my head ake.

Juan.   Are you not valiant when you are drunk?

Leon.   I think not,
But I am loving Sir.

Juan [*aside*].   What a lump is this man,——
Was your Father wise?

Leon.   Too wise for me I'me sure,
For he gave all he had to my younger brother.

Juan.   That was no foolish part ile beare you witnesse.
Canst thou lye with a woman?

Leon.   I think I could make shift sir,
But I am bashfull.

Juan.   In the night?

Leon.   I know not,
Darknesse indeed may doe some good upon me.

Juan.   Why art thou sent to me to be my officer,   20
I, and commended too, when thou darst not fight?

Leon.   There be more officers of my opinion,
Or I am cozend sir, men that talke more too.

Juan.   How wilt thou scape a bullet?

Leon.   Why by chance,
They aime at honourable men, alas I am none sir.

Juan [*aside*].   This fellow has some doubts in's talk, that strikes me
He cannot be all foole:

Enter Alonzo.

welcome *Alonzo.*

Alonzo. What have you got there, temperance into your company?
The spirit of peace? we shall have warres by th'ounce then.

Enter Cacafogo.

O here's another Pumpion, let him loos for luck sake,   30
The cram'd sonne of a starv'd Usurer, *Cacafogo;*
Both their brains butterd, cannot make two spoonefulls.
Cacafogo. My Fathers dead: I am a man of warre too,
Monyes, demeanes; I have ships at sea too, captaines.
Juan. Take heed o'th Hollanders, your ships may leake else.
Cacafogo. I scorne the Hollanders, they are my drunkards.
Alonzo. Put up your gold sir, ile borrow it else.
Cacafogo. I am satisfied, you shall not;——
Come out, I know thee, meet mine anger instantly.
Leon. I never wrong'd yee.
Cacafogo.   Thou hast wrong'd mine honor,   40
Thou look'dst upon my Mistris thrice lasciviously,
Ile make it good.
Juan.   Doe not heat your selfe, you will surfeit.
Cacafogo. Thou wan'st my mony too, with a pair of base bones,
In whom there was no truth, for which I beat thee,
I beat thee much, now I will hurt thee dangerously.
This shall provoke thee.   *He strikes.*
Alonzo.   You struck too low by a foot sir.
Juan. You must get a ladder when you would beat this fellow.
Leon. I cannot chuse but kick againe, pray pardon mee.
                    [*He kickes.*]
Cacafogo. Hadst thou not ask'd my pardon, I had killd thee,
I leave thee as a thing despis'd, *asso*   50
Les manus a vostra Siniare, a Maistre.   *Exit* Cacafogo.
Alonzo. You have scap'd by miracle, there is not in all Spaine,
A spirit of more fury then this fire drake.
Leon. I see he is hasty, and I would give him leave,
To beat me soundly if he would take my bond.

41 look'dst] F2; look'st Q1   *50–51 asso...Maistre.] stet Q1

Juan.   What shall I doe with this fellow?
Alonzo.   Turne him off,
  He will infect the campe with cowardice,
  If he goe with thee.
Juan.   About some week hence sir,
  If I can hit upon no abler officer,
  You shall hear from mee.
Leon.   I desire no better.   60

                                              Exeunt.

                Enter Estifania *and* Perez.   [I. vi]

Perez.   You have made mee now too bountifull amends, Lady,
  For your strict carriage when you saw me first,
  These beauties were not meant to be conceal'd,
  It was a wrong to hide so sweet an object,
  I coo'd now chide yee, but it shall be thus,
  No other anger ever touch your sweetnesse.
Estifania.   You appear to mee so honest, and so civill,
  Without a blush sir, I dare bid yee welcome.
Perez.   Now let mee aske your name.
Estifania.   Tis *Estifania*,
  The heire of this poore place.
Perez.   Poore doe you call it?   10
  There's nothing that I cast mine eyes upon,
  But shewes both rich and admirable, all the roomes
  Are hung as if a Princesse were to dwell here,
  The Gardens, Orchards, every thing so curious:
  Is all that plate your owne too?
Estifania.   Tis but litle,
  Only for present use, I have more and richer,
  When need shall call, or friends compell me use it,
  The sutes you see of all the upper chambers,
  Are those that commonly adorne the house;
  I think I have besides, as faire as Civill,   20
  Or any towne in Spaine can paralell.

        *20-21 Civill, | Or] civill, | Or Q1; civil, | As F2, Q2

                          513

Perez [*aside*].   Now if she be not married, I have some hopes,——
  Are you a maide?
Estifania.   You make me blush to answer,
  I ever was accounted so to this hower,
  And that's the reason that I live retir'd sir.
Perez.   Then would I counsell you to marry presently——
  If I can get her, I am made for ever,——
  For every yeare you loose, you loose a beauty,
  A husband now an honest carefull husband,
  Were such a comfort; will ye walke above staires?   30
Estifania.   This place will fit our talke, tis fitter farre sir,
  Above there are day-beds, and such temptations
  I dare not trust sir.
Perez [*aside*].   She is excellent wise withall too.
Estifania.   You nam'd a husband, I am not so strict sir,
  Nor ti'de unto a Virgins solitarinesse,
  But if an honest, and a noble one,
  Rich, and a souldier, for so I have vowed he shall be,
  Were offer'd mee, I think I should accept him,
  But above all he must love.
Perez.   He were base else;
  [*Aside*] There's comfort ministred in the word soldier,   40
  How sweetly should I live.
Estifania.   I am not so ignorant,
  But that I know well, how to be commanded,
  And how againe to make my selfe obeyd sir,
  I wast but little, I have gather'd much,
  My riall not the lesse worth, when tis spent,
  If spent by my direction, to please my husband;
  I hold it as indifferent in my duty,
  To be his maid i'th kitchin, or his Cook,
  As in the Hall to know my selfe the Mistris.
Perez [*aside*].   Sweet, Rich, and provident, now fortune stick to
    mee;——   50
  I am a souldier, and batchilour, Lady,
  And such a wife as you, I cood love infinitely,
  They that use many words, some are deceitfull,
  I long to be a husband, and a good one,

For tis most certaine I shall make a president
For all that follow me to love their Ladies.
I am young you see, able I would have you think too,
If't please you know, try me before you take mee:
'Tis true I shall not meet in equall wealth with ye,
But Jewels, Chaines, such as the warre has given mee,   60
A thousand duckets I dare presume on
In ready gold, now as your care may handle it,
As rich cloths too, as any he bears armes Lady.
Estifania.   You are a true gentleman, and faire, I see by yee,
And such a man I had rather take.
Perez.   Pray doe so,
Ile have a Priest o'th sudden.
Estifania.   And as suddenly
You will repent too.
Perez.   Ile be hang'd or drown'd first,
By this and this, and this kisse.
Estifania.   You are a Flatterer,
But I must say there was something when I saw you
First, in that most noble face, that stirr'd my fancy.   70
Perez.   Ile stirre it better ere you sleepe sweet Lady,
Ile send for all my trunks and give up all to yee,
Into your owne dispose, before I bed yee,
And then sweet wench——
Estifania.   You have the art to cozen mee.
                                    Exeunt.

            Enter Margarita, *and two* Old Ladies, *and* Altea.   II. i

Margarita.   Sit downe and give me your opinions seriously.
1. Old Lady.   You say you have a mind to marry Lady.
Margarita.   Tis true, I have for to preserve my credit,
Yet not so much for that as for my state Ladies,
Conceave me right, there lies the maine o'th question,
Credit I can redeeme, mony will imp it,
But when my monie's gone, when the law shall ceaze that,
And for incontinency strip me of all——

            0.1 Old] Dyce; *om.* Qq, F2

1. Old Lady.   Doe you finde your body so malitious that way?

Margarita.   I finde it as all bodies are that are young and lusty,   10
Lazy, and high fed, I desire my pleasure,
And pleasure I must have.

2. Old Lady.   'Tis fit you should have,
Your years require it, and 'tis necessary,
As necessary as meat to a young Lady,
Sleep cannot nourish more.

1. Old Lady.   But might not all this be, and keep ye single?
You take away variety in marriage,
The abundance of the pleasure you are bar'd then,
I'st not abundance that you aime at?

Margarita.   Yes;
Why was I made a woman?   20

2. Old Lady. And every day a new?

Margarita.   Why faire and young but to use it?

1. Old Lady.   You are still i'th right, why would you marry
then?

Altea.   Because a husband stops all doubts in this point,
And cleers all passages.

2. Old Lady.   What husband mean yee?

Altea.   A husband of an easy faith, a foole,
Made by her wealth, and moulded to her pleasure,
One though he see himselfe become a monster,
Shall hold the doore, and entertaine the maker.

2. Old Lady.   You grant there may be such a man?

1. Old Lady.   Yes marry,   30
But how to bring um to this rare perfection.

2. Old Lady.   They must be chosen so, things of no honour,
Nor outward honesty.

Margarita.   No 'tis no matter,
I care not what they are, so they be lusty.

2. Old Lady.   Me thinks now a rich Lawyer, some such fellow,
That carries credit, and a face of awe,
But lies with nothing but his clients businesse.

Margarita.   No ther's no trusting them, they are too subtill,
The Law has moulded 'um of naturall mischiefe.

516

1. Old Lady.   Then some grave governor,
Some man of honour, yet an easy man.   40
Margarita.   If he have honour I am undone, ile none such,
Ile have a lusty man, honour will cloy mee.
Altea.   Tis fit ye should Lady;
And to that end, with search and wit and labour,
I have found one out, a right one and a perfect,
He is made as strong as brasse, is of brave years too,
And doughty of complexion.
Margarita.   Is he a Gentleman?
Altea.   Yes and a Souldier, as gentle as you would wish him,
A good fellow, wears good cloaths.
Margarita.   Those ile allow him,
They are for my credit, does he understand   50
But litle?
Altea.   Very litle.
Margarita.   Tis the better,
Has not the warres bred him up to anger?
Altea.   No,
He will not quarrell with a dog that bites him,
Let him be drunke or sober, is one silence.
Margarita.   Has no capacity what honour is?
For that's the souldiers god.
Altea.   Honor's a thing too subtill for his wisdome,
If honour lye in eating, he is right honorable.
Margarita.   Is he so goodly a man doe you say?
Altea.   As you shall see Lady,
But to all this is but a trunke.   60
Margarita.   I would have him so,
I shall adde branches to him to adorne him,
Goe, finde me out this man, and let me see him,
If he be that motion that you tell me of,
And make no more noise, I shall entertaine him,
Let him be here.
Altea.   He shall attend your Ladiship.
                                                    Exeunt.

*48 doughty] F2; doubty Q1

517

Enter Juan, Alonzo, *and* Perez.   [II. ii]

Juan.   Why thou art not married indeed?
Perez.   No, no, pray think so,
  Alas I am a fellow of no reckoning,
  Not worth a Ladies eye.
Alonzo.   Woodst thou steale a fortune,
  And make none of all thy friends acquainted with it,
  Nor bid us to thy wedding?
Perez.   No indeed,
  There was no wisdome in't, to bid an Artist,
  An old seducer, to a femall banquet,
  I can cut up my pye without your instructions.
Juan.   Was it the wench i'th vaile?
Perez.   *Basta* 'twas she,
  The prettiest rogue that ere you look'd upon,   10
  The lovingst theefe.
Juan.   And is she rich withall too?
Perez.   A mine, a mine, there is no end of wealth Coronell.
  I am an asse, a bashfull foole, prethee Coronell,
  How doe thy companies fill now?
Juan.   You are merry sir,
  You intend a safer warre at home belike now.
Perez.   I doe not think I shall fight much this year Coronell,
  I finde my selfe given to my ease a litle,
  I care not if I sell my foolish company,
  They are things of hazard.
Alonzo [*aside*].   How it angers mee,
  This fellow at first sight should win a Lady,   20
  A rich young wench, and I that have consum'd
  My time and art in searching out their subtleties,
  Like a fool'd Alchimist blow up my hopes still.——
  When shall we come to thy house and be freely merry?
Perez.   When I have manag'd hir a litle more,
  I have a house to entertaine an army.
Alonzo.   If thy wife be faire, thou wilt have few lesse come to
  thee.

Perez. But whe're they'l get entertainment is the point Sinior,
I beat no drum.
Alonzo.   You need none but her taber.
Perez. May be ile march after a month or two,   30
To get mee a fresh stomack, I find Coronell
A wantonnesse in wealth, methinks I agree not with,
Tis such a trouble to be married too,
And have a thousand things of great importance,
Jewells and plate, and fooleries molest mee,
To have a mans brains whimsied with his wealth:
Before I walk'd contentedly.

Enter Servant.

Servant. My Mistris sir is sick, because you are absent,
She mournes and will not eate.
Perez.   Alas my Jewell,——
Come ile goe with thee;——gentlemen your faire leaves,   40
You see I am tide a litle to my yoke,
Pray pardon mee, would ye had both such loving wives.
                              Exit Perez [*with*] Servant.
Juan. I thank yee for your old bootes:——never be blank *Alonzo,*
Because this fellow has out stript thy fortune,
Tell me ten daies hence what he is, and how
The gratious state of matrimony stands with him;
Come, lets to dinner, when *Margarita* comes
Wee'l visit both, it may be then your fortune.
                                        Exeunt.

Enter Margarita, Altea, *the* Ladies [*in waiting*].   [II. iii]

Margarita. Is he come?
Altea.   Yes Madame, has been here this halfe houre,
I have question'd him of all that you can aske him,
And finde him as fit as you had made the man,

-----
28 whe're] (Bullen *conj.*,ᴀ *i.e.,* whether); where Qq, F 2
30 *Perez.*] Seward; *om.* Qq, F 2
*35 plate] Dyce (Mason *conj.*); plates Qq, F 2

519

He will make the goodliest shadow for iniquity.

Margarita.   Have ye searcht him Ladies?

Ladies.   Is a man at all points,
  A likely man.

Margarita.   Call him in *Altea*.   *Exit* Altea.

Enter Leon, Altea.

A man of a good presence,——pray ye come this way,——
  Of a lusty body,——is his mind so tame?

Altea.   Pray ye question him, and if you finde him not
  Fit for your purpose, shake him off, there's no harme done.   10

Margarita.   Can you love a young Lady?——How he blushes.

Altea.   Leave twirling of your hat, and hold your head up,
  And speak to'th Lady.

Leon.   Yes, I think I can,
  I must be taught, I know not what it meanes Madam.

Margarita.   You shall be taught, and can you when she pleases
  Goe ride abroad, and stay a week or two?
  You shall have men and horses to attend ye,
  And mony in your purse.

Leon.   Yes I love riding,
  And when I am from home I am so merry.

Margarita.   Be as merry as you will: can you as hansomely   20
  When you are sent for back, come with obedience,
  And doe your dutie to the Ladie loves you?

Leon.   Yes sure, I shall.

Margarita.   And when you see her friends here,
  Or noble kinsmen, can you entertaine
  Their servants in the Celler, and be busied,
  And hold your peace, what ere you see or heare of?

Leon.   Twere fit I were hang'd else.

Margarita.   Let me try your kisses,——
  How the foole shakes,——I will not eat ye sir,——
  Beshrew my heart he kisses wondrous manly,——
  Can ye doe any thing else?

5 *Ladies.*] *Omnes.* Qq, F 2
*6 *Exit* Altea.] Langbaine; *Exit Lady.* Qq, F 2

Leon.   Indeed I know not;
But if your Ladiship will please to instruct me,
Sure I shall learne.
Margarita.   You shall then be instructed;
If I should be this Lady that affects yee,
Nay, say I marry yee?
Altea.   Harke to the Lady.
Margarita.   What money have yee?
Leon.   None Madam, nor friends,
I wood doe any thing to serve your Ladiship.
Margarita.   You must not look to be my master Sir,
Nor talk ith house as though you wore the breeches,
No, nor command in any thing.
Leon.   I will not.
Alas I am not able, I have no wit Madam.
Margarita.   Nor doe not labour to arrive at any,
Twill spoile your head, I take ye upon charity,
And like a servant ye must be unto me,
As I behold your duty I shall love ye,
And as you observe me, I may chance lye with ye,
Can you mark these?
Leon.   Yes indeed forsooth.
Margarita.   There is one thing,
That if I take ye in I put ye from me,
Utterly from me, you must not be sawcy,
No, nor at any time familiar with me,
Scarce know me, when I call ye not.
Leon.   I will not,
Alas I never knew my selfe sufficiently.
Margarita.   Nor must not now.
Leon.   Ile be a dog to please ye.
Margarita.   Indeed you must fetch and carry as I appoint ye.
Leon.   I were too blame else.
Margarita.   Kisse me agen;——a strong fellow,
There is a vigor in his lips:——if you see me
Kisse any other, twenty in an houre sir,
You must not start, nor be offended.

Leon.   No,
  If you kisse a thousand I shall be contented,
  It will the better teach me how to please ye.
Altea.   I told ye Madam.
Margarita.   Tis the man I wisht for;——   60
  The lesse you speak——
Leon.   Ile never speak againe Madam,
  But when you charge me, then ile speak softly too.
Margarita.   Get me a Priest, ile wed him instantly,——
                               [Exit one of the Ladies.]
  But when you are married sir, you must wait upon me,
  And see you observe my lawes.
Leon.   Else you shall hang me.
Margarita.   Ile give ye better clothes when you deserve um,——
  Come in, and serve for witnesses.
Ladies.   We shall Madam.
Margarita.   And then away to'th citty presently,
  Ile to my new house and new company.   *[Exit with* Ladies].
Leon.   A thousand crownes are thine, and I am a made man.   70
Altea.   Doe not break out too soone.
Leon.   I know my time wench.
                                   Exeunt.

               Enter Clara *and* Estifania.   [II. iv]

Clara.   What, have you caught him?
Estifania.   Yes.
Clara.   And doe you finde him
  A man of those hopes that you aim'd at?
Estifania.   Yes too,
  And the most kinde man, and the ablest also
  To give a wife content, he is sound as old wine,
  And to his soundness rises on the pallat,
  And there's the man; I finde him rich too *Clara.*
Clara.   Hast thou married him?

     67 *Ladies.*] *Omnes.* Qq, F2
    0.1 Estifania.] Dyce; *Estifania with a paper.* Qq, F2

Estifania.   What, dost thou think I fish without a bait wench?
  I bob for fooles? he is mine own I have him,
  I told thee what would tickle him like a trout,   10
  And as I cast it so I caught him daintily,
  And all he has I have 'stow'd at my devotion.
Clara.   Does thy Lady know this? she is comming now to towne,
  Now to live here in this house.
Estifania.   Let her come,
  She shall be welcome, I am prepar'd for hir,
  She is mad sure if she be angry at my fortune,
  For what I have made bold.
Clara.   Dost thou not love him?
Estifania.   Yes, intirely well,
  As long as there he staies and looks no farther
  Into my ends, but when he doubts, I hate him,   20
  And that wise hate will teach me how to cozen him,
  [For he has studied well the rules men use,]
  How to decline their wives, and curb their manners,
  To put a sterne and strong reyne to their natures,
  And holds he is an Asse not worth acquaintance,
  That cannot mould a divell to obedience,
  I owe him a good turne for these opinions,
  And as I finde his temper I may pay him.

                        Enter Perez.

  O here he is, now you shall see a kinde man.
                              [Clara *walks apart.*]
Perez.   My *Estifania,* shall we to dinner lambe,
  I know thou staist for me.
Estifania.   I cannot eat else.   30
Perez.   I never enter but me thinks a Paradise
  Appeares about me.
Estifania.   You are welcome to it Sir.
Perez.   I think I have the sweetest seat in Spaine wench,
  Me thinks the richest too, weele eat ith garden
  In one o'th arbours, there tis coole and pleasant,

        *21.1 [For...use]] *stet* Q1

                    523

And have our wine cold in the running fountain.——
Who's that?

Estifania.   A friend of mine Sir.

Perez.   Of what breeding?

Estifania.   A Gentlewoman Sir.

Perez.   What businesse has she?
Is shee a learned woman i'th Mathematicks,
Can shee tell fortunes?

Estifania.   More then I know Sir.   40

Perez.   Or has she ere a letter from a kinswoman,
That must be delivered in my absence wife,
Or comes she from the Doctor to salute ye,
And learne your health? she looks not like a confessor.

Estifania.   What need all this, why are you troubled Sir?
What doe you suspect? she cannot cuckold ye,
Shee is a woman Sir, a very woman.

Perez.   Your very woman may doe very well Sir
Toward the matter, for though she cannot performe it
In her own person, she may doe it by Proxie,   50
Your rarest jugglers work still by conspiracy.

Estifania.   Cry ye mercy husband, you are jealous then,
And happily suspect me.

Perez.   No indeed wife.

Estifania.   Me thinks you should not till you have more cause
And cleerer too: I am sure you have heard say husband,
A woman forced will free her selfe through iron,
A happy, calme, and good wife discontented
May be taught tricks.

Perez.   No, no, I doe but jest with ye.

Estifania [*to* Clara].   To morrow friend ile see you.

Clara.   I shall leave ye
Till then, and pray all may goe sweetly with ye.   *Exit.* 60
                                                 Knock.

Estifania.   Why where's this girle, whose at the doore?

Perez.   Who knocks there?
Is't for the king ye come, you knock so boisterously?
Look to the doore.

Enter Maid.

Maid [*apart to* Estifania].   My Lady, as I live Mistris, my Ladie's
    come,
  Shee's at the doore, I peept through, and I saw her,
  And a stately company of Ladies with her.   [*Exit.*]
Estifania [*aside*].   This was a week too soon, but I must meet with
    her,
  And set a new wheele going, and a subtile one,
  Must blind this mighty *Mars*, or I am ruin'd.
Pere₂.   What are they at doore?
Estifania.   Such my *Michael*   70
  As you may blesse the day they enter'd here,
  Such for our good.
Pere₂.   Tis well.
Estifania.   Nay, 'twill be better
  If you will let me but dispose the businesse,
  And be a stranger to it, and not disturb me;
  What have I now to doe but to advance your fortune?
Pere₂.   Doe, I dare trust thee, I am asham'd I was angry,
  I finde thee a wise young wife.
Estifania [*aside*].   Ile wise your worship
  Before I leave ye,——pray ye walk by and say nothing,
  Only salute um, and leave the rest to me Sir,
  I was borne to make ye a man.   [*Exit.*]
Pere₂.   The rogue speaks heartily,   80
  Her good will colours in her cheeks, I am borne to love her,
  I must be gentler to these tender natures,
  A souldiers rude harsh words befit not Ladies,
  Nor must we talke to them as we talk to our Officers,
  Ile give her way, for tis for me she works now,
  I am husband, heire, and all she has.

Enter Margarita, Estifania, Leon, Altea, *and* Ladies.

Who are these, what flanting things?
A woman of rare presence, excellent faire,

76 was] Seward; am Qq, F2   79 um] him Q1; them F2, Q2

525

This is too big for a bawdy house, too open seated too.

Estifania.   My husband Lady.

Margarita.   You have gain'd a proper man.   90

Perez.   What ere I am, I am your servant Lady.

                    Kisses [Margarita *and walks apart with* Estifania].

Estifania.   Sir, be rul'd now, and I shall make ye rich,
    This is my cozen, that Gentleman dotes on her,
    Even to death, see how he observes her.

Perez.   She is a goodly woman.

Estifania.   She is a mirrour,
    But she is poore, she were for a Princes side else,
    This house she has brought him too as to hir own,
    And presuming upon me, and upon my curtesie;
    Conceive me short, he knowes not but she is wealthy,
    Or if he did know otherwise, 'twere all one,   100
    He is so far gone.

Perez.   Forward, she has a rare face.

Estifania.   This we must carry with discretion husband,
    And yeeld unto her for foure daies.

Perez.   Yeeld our house up,
    Our goods and wealth?

Estifania.   All this is but in seeming
    To milke the lover on, doe you see this writing?

                              [*Takes out a paper.*]

    Two hundred pound a yeare when they are married,
    Has she sealed too for our good; the time's unfit now,
    Ile shew it you to morrow.

Perez.   All the house?

Estifania.   All, all, and weele remove too, to confirme him.
    They'le into'th country suddenly agen   110
    After they are matcht, and then sheele open to him.

Perez.   The whole possession wife? look what you doe,
    A part o'th house.

Estifania.   No, no, they shall have all,
    And take their pleasure too, tis for our 'vantage;
    Why, whats foure daies? had you a sister sir,

          *91.1 *Kisses.*] stet Q1   100 he] F2; she Q1
          105.1 S.D.] om. Qq, F2 (*relocated from line 0.1*)

                              526

A Neece or Mistris that required this curtesie,
And should I make a scruple to doe you good?
Perez. If easily it would come back——
Estifania.   I sweare Sir,
As easily as it came on; ist not pitty
To let such a Gentlewoman for a little help?
You give away no house.   120
Perez.   Cleere but that question.
Estifania. Ile put the writings into your hand.
Perez.   Well then.
Estifania. And you shall keep them safe.
Perez.   I am satisfied;
[*Aside*] Wood I had the wench so too.
Estifania.   When she has married him,
So infinite his love is linckt unto hir,
You, I, or any one that helps at this pinch
May have heaven knowes what.
Perez.   Ile remove the goods streight,
And take some poore house by, tis but for foure daies.
Estifania. I have a poore old friend; there weele be.
Perez.   Tis well then.
Estifania. Goe handsome off, and leave the house cleere.
Perez.   Well.
Estifania. That little stuffe weele use shall follow after;   130
And a boy to guide ye, peace and we are made both.
                            Exit Perez.
Margarita. Come, let's goe in, are all the roomes kept sweet,
    wench.
Estifania. They are sweet and neat.
Margarita.   Why where's your husband?
Estifania.   Gone
    Madam.
When you come to your own he must give place Lady.
Margarita. Well, send you joy, you would not let me know't,
Yet I shall not forget ye.
Estifania.   Thank your Ladyship.
                            Exeunt.

120 help?] stet Q1

527

Enter Margarita, Altea, *and Boy.*   III. i

Altea.   Are you at ease now, is your heart at rest,
  Now you have got a shadow, an *umbrella*
  To keep the scorching worlds opinion
  From your faire credit?
Margarita.   I am at peace *Altea.*
  If he continue but the same he shewes,
  And be a master of that ignorance
  He outwardly professes, I am happy;
  The pleasure I shall live in and the freedome
  Without the squint-eye of the law upon me,
  Or prating liberty of tongues, that envy.   10
Altea.   You are a made woman.
Margarita.   But if he should prove now
  A crafty and dissembling kind of husband,
  One read in knavery, and brought up in the art
  Of villany conceal'd——
Altea.   My life, an Innocent.
Margarita.   That's it I ayme at,
  That's it I hope too, then I am sure I rule him,
  For Innocents are like obedient children
  Brought up under a hard mother in law, a cruel,
  Who being not us'd to break-fasts and collations,
  When they have course bread offerd um, are thankfull,   20
  And take it for a favour too; are the roomes made ready
  To entertaine my friends? I long to dance now
  And to be wanton; let me have a song.
                    [*Boy sings; then, exit Boy.*]
  Is the great couch up, the Duke *Medina* sent?
Altea.   Tis up and ready.
Margarita.   And day beds in all chambers?
Altea.   In all Lady,
  Your house is nothing now but various pleasures;
  The Gallants begin to gaze too.
Margarita.   Let um gaze on,

I was brought up a Courtier, high and happy,
And company is my delight, and courtship,   30
And hansome servants at my wil; where's my good husband,
Where does he wait?
Altea.   He knowes his distance Madam,
I warrant ye, he is busie in the celler
Amongst his fellow servants, or asleep,
Till your command awake him.
Margarita.   Tis well *Altea.*
It should be so, my ward I must preserve him.

     Enter Leon [*and* Servant *and talk apart*].

Who sent for him, how dare he come uncall'd for,
His bonnet on too?
Altea.   Sure he sees you not.
Margarita.   How scornefully he lookes.
Leon.   Are all the chambers
Deckt and adorn'd thus for my Ladies pleasure,   40
New hangings every houre for entertainment,
And new plate bought, new jewels to give lustre?
Servant.   They are, and yet there must be more and richer,
It is her will.
Leon.   Hum, is it so, tis excellent,
It is her will too, to have feasts and banquets,
Revells and masques?
Servant.   She ever lov'd um dearely,
And we shall have the bravest house kept now sir,
I must not call ye master she has warn'd mee,
Nor must not put my hat off to ye.
Leon.   Tis no fashion,
What though I be hir husband, I am your fellow,   50
I may cut first.
Servant.   That's as you shall deserve sir.
Leon.   And when I lye with her?
Servant.   May be ile light yee.
On the same point you may doe mee that service.   [*Exit.*]

      *50 husband...fellow] *stet* Q1

Enter 1. Lady.

1. *Lady.*   Madame, the Duke *Medina* with some captaines
    Will come to dinner, and have sent rare wine,
    And their best services.
Margarita.   They shall be welcome,
    See all be ready in the noblest fashion,
    The house perfum'd,   [*Exit* 1. Lady.]
                    now I shall take my pleasure,
    And not my neighbour Justice maunder at mee,
    [*To Leon*] Goe, get your best cloths on, but till I call yee,   60
    Be sure you be not seene, dine with the gentlewomen,
    And behave your selfe cleanly sir, tis for my credit.

Enter 2. Lady.

2. *Lady.*   Madame, the Lady *Julia*——
Leon [*aside*].   That's a bawde,
    A three pild bawde, bawde major to the army.
2. *Lady.*   Has brought her coach to wait upon your Ladiship,
    And to be inform'd if you will take the aire this morning.
Leon [*aside*].   The neat aire of hir nunnery.
Margarita.   Tell her no,
    I'th afternoone Ile call on hir.
2. *Lady.*   I will Madame.   *Exit.*
Margarita.   Why are not you gone to prepare your selfe,
    May be you shall be sewer to the first course,   70
    A portly presence——*Altea* he looks leane,
    Tis a wash knave, he will not keep his flesh well.
Altea.   A willing, madame, one that needs no spurring.
Leon.   Faith madame, in my little understanding,
    You had better entertaine your honest neighbours,
    Your friends about yee, that may speake well of yee,
    And give a worthy mention of your bounty.
Margarita.   How now what's this?
Leon.   Tis only to perswade yee,
    Courtiers are but tickle things to deale withall,
    A kind of march-pane men that will not last Madame,   80

530

An egge and pepper goes farther then their potions,
And in a well built body, a poore parsnip
Will play his prize, above their strong potabiles.
Margarita. The fellowes mad.
Leon [aside]. He that shall counsell Ladies,
That have both licorish and ambitious eyes,
Is either mad, or drunke, let him speake Gospell.
Altea [aside]. He breaks out modestly.
Leon. Pray ye be not angry,
My indiscretion has made bold to tell yee,
What youl find true.
Margarita. Thou darest not talke.
Leon. Not much Madame,
You have a tye upon your servants tongue,   90
He dares not be so bold as reason bids him,
'Twere fit there were a stronger on your temper,
Nere look so sterne upon me, I am your husband,
But what are husbands? read the new worlds wonders,
And you will scarce finde such deformities,
Such husbands as this monstrous world produces,
They are shadowes to conceale your veniall vertues,
Sailes to your mills, that grinde with all occasions,
Balls that lye by you, to wash out your staines,
And bills naild up with horne before your stories,   100
To rent out lust.
Margarita. Doe you hear him talke?
Leon. I have done Madame,
An oxe once spoke, as learned men deliver,
Shortly I shall be such, then Ile speak wonders,
Till when I tye my self to my obedience.   *Exit.*
Margarita. First ile untye my selfe, did you mark the Gentleman,
How boldly and how sawcily he talkd,
And how unlike the lumpe I took him for,
The peece of ignorant dowe? he stood up to me

95–96 And...produces,] Dyce (Mason *conj.*); Such...produces, | And...defor-
mities Qq, F2
101 lust] Seward; last Qq, F2

And mated my commands, this was your providence,
Your wisdome, to elect this gentleman, 110
Your excellent forecast in the man, your knowledge,
What think ye now?
Altea. I think him an asse still,
This boldnesse some of your people have blowne into him,
This wisdome too with strong wine, 'tis a Tirant,
And a Philosopher also, and findes out reasons.
Margarita. Ile have my celler lockt, no schoole kept there,
Nor no discovery, Ile turne my drunkards,
Such as are understanding in their draughts,
And dispute learnedly the whyes and wherefores,
To grasse immediatly, Ile keep all fooles, 120
Sober or drunk, still fooles, that shall know nothing,
Nothing belongs to mankind, but obedience,
And such a hand ile keep over this husband.
Altea. He will fall againe, my life he cryes by this time,
Keep him from drink, he has a hye constitution.

Enter Leon.

Leon. Shall I weare my new sute Madame?
Margarita. No your old clothes,
And get you into the country presently,
And see my hawkes well train'd, you shall have victualls,
Such as are fit for sawcy pallats sir,
And lodgings with the hindes it is to good too. 130
Altea. Good madame be not so rough, with repentance,
You see now he's come roun'd agen.
Margarita. I see not
What I expect to see.
Leon. You shall see Madame,
If it shall please your Ladyship.
Altea. Hee's humbled,
Forgive good Lady.
Margarita. Well goe get you handsome,
And let me heare no more.
Leon [*aside*]. Have ye yet no feeling,

532

Ile pinch ye to the bones then my proud Lady.   *Exit.*
Margarita.   See you preserve him thus upon my favour,
    You know his temper, tye him to the grindstone,
    The next rebellion Ile be rid of him,   140
    Ile have no needy rascalls I tye to me,
    Dispute my life, come in and see all handsome.   [*Exit.*]
Altea [*aside*].   I hope to see you so too, I have wrought ill else.
                                                                          Exit.

                        Enter Perez.   [III. ii]

Perez.   Shall I never returne to mine owne house againe?
    We are lodg'd here in the miserablest dog-hole,
    A conjurers circle gives content above it,
    A hawks mew is a princely pallace to it,
    We have a bed no bigger then a basket,
    And there we lye like butter clapt together,
    And sweat our selves to sawce immediatly;
    The fumes are Infinite inhabit here too,
    And to that so thick, they cut like marmalette,
    So various too, they'l pose a gold finder,   10
    Never returne to mine own paradise?
    Why wife I say, why *Estifania*.
Estifania (*within*).   I am going presently.
Perez.   Make hast good jewell,——
    I am like the people that live in the sweet Ilands:
    I dye I dye if I stay but one day more here,
    My lungs are rotten with the damps that rise,
    And I cough nothing now but stinks of all sorts,
    The inhabitants we have are two starv'd rats,
    For they are not able to maintain a cat here,
    And those appear as fearfull as two divells,   20
    They have eat a map of the whole world up already,
    And if we stay a night we are gone for company;
    Ther's an old woman that's now grown to marble,
    Dri'd in this brick hill, and she sits i'th chimnie,

        24 brick hill] *i.e.*, brick kiln

Which is but three tiles rais'd like a house of cards,
The true proportion of an old smok'd Sibill,
There is a young thing too that nature meant
For a maid servant, but tis now a monster,
She has a huske about hir like a chesnut
With lasinesse, and living under the line here,   30
And these two make a hollow sound together,
Like froggs or winds between two doores that murmur:
Mercy deliver mee;

Enter Estifania.

                o are you come wife,
Shall we be free agen?
Estifania.   I am now going,
And you shall presently to your own house sir,
The remembrance of this small vexation,
Will be argument of mirth for ever:
By that time you have said your orisons,
And broke your fast, I shall be back and ready,
To usher you to your old content, your freedome.   40
*Pere*z.   Break my neck rather, is there any thing here to eat
But one another, like a race of Canniballs?
A peece of butter'd wall you think is excellent,
Let's have our house agen immediatly,
And pray yee take heed unto the furniture,
None be imbesseld.
Estifania.   Not a pinne I warrant yee.
*Pere*z.   And let um instantly depart.
Estifania.   They shall both,
There's reason in all curtesies they must both,
For by this time I know she has acquainted him,
And has provided too she sent me word sir,   50
And will give over gratefully unto you.
*Pere*z.   Ile walke i'th Church-yard,
The dead cannot offend more then these living,
An houre hence Ile expect ye.

        30 lasinesse] Langbaine; basinesse Q1, F2; business Q2

Estifania.   Ile not faile sir.

Perez.   And doe you heare, let's have a handsome dinner,
  And see all things be decent as they have been,
  And let me have a strong bath to restore mee,
  I stink like a fish-stall shambles, or an oile shop.

Estifania.   You shall have all,——[*aside*] which some interpret
    nothing,——
  Ile send ye people for the trunks afore hand,   60
  And for the stuffe.

Perez.   Let um be known and honest,
  And doe my service to your neece.

Estifania.   I shall sir,
  But if I come not at my hower come thither,
  That they may give you thanks for your faire curtesy,
  And pray ye be brave for my sake.

Perez.   I observe ye.

                                                        Exeunt.

              Enter Juan de Castro, Sanchio, *and* Cacafogo.   [III. iii]

Sanchio.   Thou art very brave.

Cacafogo.   I have reason, I have mony.

Sanchio.   Is mony reason?

Cacafogo.   Yes and rime too Captaine,
  If ye have no mony y'ar an asse.

Sanchio.   I thank ye.

Cacafogo.   Ye have manners, ever thank him that has mony.

Sanchio.   Wilt thou lend mee any?

Cacafogo.   Not a farthing Captaine,
  Captaines are casuall things.

Sanchio.   Why so are all men,
  Thou shalt have my bond.

Cacafogo.   Nor bonds nor fetters Captaine,
  My mony is mine owne, I make no doubt on't.

Juan.   What dost thou doe with it?

                    *58 fish-stall] stall-fish Qq, F2
  2 rime] Q1(c), F2; ruine Q1(u)   4 manners] F2; meaner Q1

Cacafogo.   Put it to pious uses,   10
   Buy wine and wenches, and undoe young coxcombs,
   That would undoe mee.
Juan.   Are those hospitalls?
Cacafogo.   I first provide to fill my hospitalls,
   With creatures of mine owne that I know wretched,
   And then I build; those are more bound to pray for mee,
   Besides I keep th'inheritance in my name still.
Juan.   A provident charity, are you for the warres sir?
Cacafogo.   I am not poore enough to be a souldier,
   Nor have I faith enough to ward a bullet.
   This is no lineing for a trench I take it.
Juan.   Ye have said wisely.
Cacafogo.   Had you but my mony,   20
   You would sweare it Coronell, I had rather drill at home
   A hundred thousand crownes, and with more honour,
   Then exercise ten thousand fooles with nothing,
   A Wise man safely feeds, fooles cut their fingers.
Sanchio.   A right state-usurer, why dost thou not marry,
   And live a reverend Justice?
Cacafogo.   Is't not nobler
   To command a reverent Justice, then to be one?
   And for a wife, what need I marry Captaine,
   When every courteous foole, that owes me mony,
   Owes me his wife too, to appease my fury?   30
Juan.   Wilt thou goe to dinner with us?
Cacafogo.   I will goe,
   And view the pearle of Spaine, the orient faire one,
   The rich one too, and I will be respected,
   I beare my patent here, I will talke to her,
   And when your Captaineships shall stand a loofe,
   And pick your noses, I will pick the purse,
   Of hir affection.
Juan.   The Duke dines there to day too,
   The Duke *Medina.*
Cacafogo.   Let the King dine there,

35 Captaineships] Q 2; Captaines ships Q 1; Captain's Ships F 2
38 Duke] Seward; Duke of Qq, F 2

536

He owes me mony, and so farre's my creature,
And certainly I may make bold with mine own, Captain.   40
Sanchio.   Thou wilt eate monstrously.
Cacafogo.   Like a true borne Spaniard,
Eate as I were in England where the beefe growes,
And I will drink aboundantly and then,
Talke ye as wantonly as *Ovid* did,
To stirre the intellectualls of the Ladies;
I learnt it of my Fathers amorous Scrivener.
Juan.   If we should play now, you must supply mee.
Cacafogo.   You must pawne a horse troope,
And then have at ye Coronell.
Sanchio.   Come let's goe.
[*Apart to* Juan] This rascall will make rare sport, how the Ladies 50
Will laugh him leane agen.
Juan [*apart to* Sanchio].   If I light on him
Ile make his purse sweat too.
Cacafogo.   Will ye lead gentlemen?
                                                        Exeunt.

                Enter Perez, *an* Old Woman, *and* Maid.   [III. iv]

Perez.   Nay pray ye come out, and let me understand ye,
And tune your pipe a litle higher Lady,
Ile hold ye fast: rub, how came my trunks open,
And my goods gone, what picklock spirit?
Old Woman.   Ha what would ye have?
Perez.   My goods agen, how came my trunks all open?
Old Woman.   Are your trunks open?
Perez.   Yes and my cloths gone,
And chaines, and Jewels,——how she smels like hung beefe,
The palsy and pick locks, fy how she belches
The spirit of garlick.
Old Woman.   Where's your gentlewoman?
The young faire woman.

51 laugh him leane agen] Bond; laugh at him Q1(c), F2; laugh him, leave ager
Q1(u)
  6 my] Colman; *om.* Qq, F2   8 pick locks] Seward; picklocks Qq, F2

Perez.   What's that to my question?   10
  She is my wife: and gone about my businesse.
Maid.   Is she your wife sir?
Perez.   Yes sir, is that wonder;
  Is the name of wife unknown here?
Old Woman.   Is she truely,
  Truely your wife?
Perez.   I think so for I married her,
  It was no vision sure.
Maid.   She has the keyes sir.
Perez.   I know she has, but who has all my goods spirit?
Old Woman.   If you be married to that Gentlewoman,
  You are a wretched man, she has twenty husbands.
Maid.   She tells you true.
Old Woman.   And she has cozend all sir.
Perez.   The Divell she has, I had a faire house with her,   20
  That stands hard by, and furnisht roially.
Old Woman.   You are cozend too, tis none of hirs good gentleman,
  It is a Ladies; what's the Ladies name wench?
Maid.   The Lady *Margarita*, she was her servant
  And kept the house, but going from her sir,
  For some lewd tricks she plaid——
Perez.   Plague a the Divell,
  Am I i'th full Meridian of my wisdome
  Cheated by a stale queane,——what kinde of Lady
  Is that that owes the house?
Old Woman.   A young sweet Lady.
Perez.   Of a low stature?
Old Woman.   She is indeed but litle,   30
  But she is wondrous faire.
Perez.   I feele I am cozend.
  Now I am sensible I am undone,
  This is the very woman sure, that cozen
  She told me would entreat but for foure daies,
  To make the house hirs, I am intreated sweetly.
Maid.   When she went out this morning, that I saw Sir,
  Shee had two women at the doore attending,

And there she gave um things, and loaded um,
But what they were——I heard your trunks to open,
If they be yours.
Perez.   They were mine while they were laden,   40
But now they have cast their calves, they are not worth owning,
Was she hir Mistris say you?
Old Woman.   Her own Mistris,
Her very Mistris, Sir, and all you saw
About, and in that house was hirs.
Perez.   No plate,
No jewels, nor no hangings?
Maid.   Not a farthing,
Shee is poore, sir, a poore shifting thing.
Perez.   No money?
Old Woman. Abominable poore, as poore as we are,
Money as rare to her unlesse she steale it,
But for one civill gowne hir Lady gave hir,
Shee may goe bare good Gentlewoman.
Perez.   I am mad now,   50
I think I am as poore as she, I am wide else,
One civill sute I have left too, and that's all,
And if she steale that she must flea me for it,
Where does she use?
Old Woman.   You may finde truth as soone,
Alas a thousand conceal'd corners sir, shee lurks in,
And here she gets a fleece, and there another,
And lives in mists and smoakes where none can finde her.
Perez. Is shee a whore too?
Old Woman.   Litle better Gentleman,
I dare not say shee is so sir, because she is yours, sir,
But these five yeares she has firkt a pretty living,   60
Untill she came to serve; [*aside*] I feare he will knock my
Braines out for lying.
Perez.   She has serv'd me faithfully,
A whore, and theefe, two excellent morrall learnings
In one she Saint, I hope to see her legend.

40 were laden] F 2; are laden Q 1

Have I been fear'd for my discoveries,
And courted by all women to conceale um,
Have I so long studied the art of this sex,
And read the warnings to young Gentlemen:
Have I profest to tame the pride of Ladies,
And make um beare all tests, and am I trickt now,
Caught in myne own nooze? here's a royall left yet,   70
Theres for your lodging and your meat for this week.
A silk-worme lives at a more plentifull ordinary,
And sleeps in a sweeter box; farewell great grandmother,
If I doe finde you were an accessary,
Tis but the cutting off two smoakie minutes.
Ile hang ye presently.
Old Woman [*aside*].   And I deserve it,——
I tell but truth.
Perez.   Nor I, I am an asse mother.

                                          Exeunt.

              Enter the Duke Medina, Juan de Castro, Alonzo,   [III. v]
                    Sanchio, Cacafogo, *Attendants.*

Duke.   A goodly house.
Juan.   And richly furnisht too Sir.
Alonzo.   Hung wantonly, I like that preparation,
     It stirres the bloud unto a hopefull banquet,
     And intimates the Mistris free and joviall,
     I love a house where pleasure prepares welcome.
Duke.   Now *Cacafogo*, how like you this mansion?
     Twere a brave pawne.
Cacafogo.   I shall be master of it,
     Twas built for my bulk, the roomes are wide and spacious,
     Ayerie, and full of ease, and that I love well,
     Ile tell you when I tast the wine my Lord,   10
     And take the heighth of hir table with my stomack,
     How my affections stand to the young Lady.

76 two] Seward; too Q1, F2; wo Q2   *78 Nor] *stet* Q1
*0.1 Duke Medina] Colman; *Duke, Medina* Q1; *Duke of Medina* F2, Q2

Enter Margarita, Altea, *Ladies, and Servants.*

Margarita.   All welcome to your Grace, and to these souldiers,
   You honour my poore house with your faire presence,
   Those few slight pleasures that inhabit here sir,
   I doe beseech your Grace command, they are yours;
   Your servant but preserves um to delight ye.
Duke.   I thank ye Lady, I am bold to visit ye,
   Once more to blesse mine eyes with your sweet beauty,
   'Tas been a long night since you left the Court,   20
   For till I saw you now, no day broke to me.
Margarita.   Bring in the Dukes meat.   [*Exit Servant.*]
Sanchio [*apart to* Juan].   She is most excellent.
Juan [*apart to* Sanchio].   Most admirable faire as ere I looked on,
   I had rather command her then my regiment.
Cacafogo [*aside*].   Ile have a fling, tis but a thousand Duckets,
   Which I can cozen up agen in ten daies,
   And some few jewels to justifie my knavery,
   Say I should marry her, sheele get more mony
   Then all my usurie, put my knavery to it,
   Shee appears the most unfallible way of purchase,   30
   I cood wish her a size or two stronger, for the incounter,
   For I am like a Lyon where I lay hold,
   But these Lambs will endure a plaguie load,
   And never bleat neither, that sir, time has taught us.
   I am so vertuous now, I cannot speak to her,
   The arrant'st shamefac'd asse, I broile away too.

Enter Leon.

Margarita.   Why where's this dinner?
Leon.   Tis not ready Madam,
   Nor shall not be untill I know the guests too,
   Nor are they fairely welcome till I bid um.
Juan [*apart*].   Is not this my *Alferes*? he looks another thing,   40
   Are miracles a foot againe?
Margarita.   Why sirra,
   Why sirra you.

541

Leon.   I heare you saucy woman,
And as you are my wife command your absence,
And know your duty, tis the crowne of modesty.
Duke.   Your wife?
Leon.   Yes good my Lord, I am her husband,
And pray take notice that I claime that honour,
And will maintaine it.
Cacafogo.   If thou beest her husband,
I am determin'd thou shalt be my Cuckold,
Ile be thy faithfull friend.
Leon.   Peace durt and dunghill,
I will not loose my anger on a rascall,   50
Provoke me more, ile beat thy blowne body
Till thou reboundst agen like a Tennis ball.
Alonzo [apart to Sanchio].   This is miraculous.
Sanchio [apart to Alonzo].   Is this the fellow
That had the patience to become a foole,
A flurted foole, and on a sudden break,
As if he would shew a wonder to the world,
Both into bravery, and fortune too?
I much admire the man, I am astonisht.
Margarita.   Ile be divorced immediatly.
Leon.   You shall not.
You shall not have so much will to be wicked.   60
I am more tender of your honour Lady,
And of your age; you took me for a shadow,
You took me to glosse over your discredit,
To be your foole, you had thought you had found a coxcomb;
I am innocent of any foule dishonour I meane to ye,
Only I will be knowne to be your Lord now,
And be a faire one too, or I will fall for't.
Margarita.   I doe command ye from me thou poore fellow,
Thou cozen'd foole.
Leon.   Thou cozen'd foole, tis not so,
I will not be commanded: I am above ye: 70
You may divorce me from your favour Lady,

48 shalt] F2; shall Q1   *64 had thought] *stet* Q1

But from your state you never shall, ile hold that,
And hold it to my use, the law allowes it,
And then maintaine your wantonnesse Ile wink at it.
Margarita.   Am I braved thus in mine own house?
Leon.   Tis mine Madam,
You are deceav'd I am Lord of it, I rule it
And all that's in't, you have nothing to doe here Madam,
But as a servant to sweep clean the lodgings,
And at my farther will to doe me service,
And so ile keep it.
Margarita.   As you love mee give way.   80
It shall be better.
Leon.   I will give none Madame,
I stand upon the ground of mine own honour
And will maintaine it, you shall know me now,
To be an understanding feeling man,
And sensible of what a woman aimes at,
A young proude woman that has will to saile with,
An itching woman, that her blood provokes too,
I cast my cloude off and appeare my selfe,
The master of this little peece of mischiefe,
And I will put a spell about your feet Lady,   90
They shall not wander but where I give way now.
Duke.   Is this the fellow that the people pointed at,
For the meere signe of man, the walking image?
He speaks wondrous highly.
Leon.   As a husband ought sir,
In his owne house, and it becomes me well too,
I think your grace would grieve if you were put to it,
To have a wife or servant of your owne,
For wives are reckon'd in the ranke of servants,
Under your own roofe to command ye.
Juan.   Brave,
A strange convertion, thou shalt lead in chiefe now.   100
Duke.   Is there no difference betwixt hir and you sir?

*81 It...better. *Leon.* I will] Seward; *Leon.* It...better, I will Qq, F2

Leon.   Not now my Lord, my Fortune makes me even,
And as I am an honest man, I am nobler.
Margarita.   Get me my coach.
Leon.   Let me see who dare get it
Till I command, ile make him draw your coach,
And eat your Coach too, (which will be hard diet)
That executes your will; or take your coach Lady,
I give you liberty, and take your people
Which I turne off, and take your will abroad with ye,   110
Take all these freely, but take me no more,
And so farewell.
Duke.   Nay sir you shall not carry it   [*Draws.*]
So bravely off, you shall not wrong a Lady
In a high huffing straine, and think to beare it,
We stand not by as bawds to your brave fury,
To see a Lady weepe.
Leon.   They are teares of anger,
I beseech ye note um not worth pitty,
Wrung from her rage, because her will prevailes not,
She would sownd now if she could not cry,
Else they were excellent and I should grieve too,   120
But falling thus, they show nor sweet nor orient,
Put up my Lord, this is oppression,
And calls the sword of Justice to releeve mee,
The law to lend her hand, the king to right me,
All which shall understand how you provoke mee;
In mine own house to brave mee, is this princely?
Then to my guard,   [*Draws.*]
                and if I spare your Grace,
And doe not make this place your monument,
Too rich a tombe for such a rude behaviour,
I have a cause will kill a thousand of ye,
Mercy forsake me.   130
Juan.   Hold faire sir I beseech ye,
The Gentleman but pleads his own right nobly.

102 my Lord] Colman; Lord Qq, F2
*105–106 coach...Coach too] Seward; coach too...Coach Qq, F2

Leon.   He that dares strike against the husbands freedome,
The husbands curse stick to him, a tam'd cuckold,
His wife be faire and young, but most dishonest,
Most impudent, and have no feeling of it,
No conscience to reclaime her from a Monster,
Let her lye by him like a flattering ruine,
And at one instant kill both name and honour,
Let him be lost, no eye to weepe his end,
Nor finde no earth that's base enough to bury him;   140
Now sir fall on, I am ready to oppose ye.
Duke.   I have better thought, I pray sir use your wife well.
Leon.   Mine own humanity will teach me that sir,
                                                    [*Put up swords.*]
And now you are all welcome, all, and wee'l to dinner,
This is my wedding day.
Duke [*aside*].   Ile crosse your joy yet.
Juan.   I have seen a miracle, [*to* Leon] hold thine own souldier,
Sure they dare fight in fire that conquer women.
Sanchio.   Has beaten all my loose thoughts out of mee,
As if he had thresht um out o'th huske.

Enter Perez.

Perez.   Save ye,
Which is the Lady of the house?
Leon.   That's she sir,   150
That pretty Lady, if you would speak with her.
Juan.   Don Michael——
Leon [*aside*].   Another darer come?
Perez [*apart to* Juan].   Pray doe not know mee, I am full of
        businesse,
When I have more time ile be merry with ye,
[*Aside*] It is the woman,——good Madame tell me truly,
Had you a maid call'd *Estifania*?
Margarita.   Yes truly had I.
Perez.   Was she a maid doe you think?

*152 Don Michael——Leon. Another] Dyce (Heath conj.); Don Michael Leon,
another Q1; Don Michael, Leon, another F2, Q2

545

Margarita.   I dare not sweare for her,
For she had but a scant fame.
Perez.   Was she your kinse-woman?
Margarita.   Not that I ever knew; now I look better
I think you married her, give you much joy sir,   160
You may reclaime her, 'twas a wild young girle.
Perez.   Give me a halter; is not this house mine Madame,
Was not she owner of it? pray speak truly.
Margarita.   No, certainly, I am sure my mony paid for it,
And I nere remember yet I gave it you sir.
Perez.   The hangings and the plate too?
Margarita.   All are mine sir,
And every thing you see about the building,
She only kept my house when I was absent,
And so ill kept it, I was weary of her.
Sanchio [apart to Juan].   What a Divell ailes hee?
Juan [apart to Sanchio].   Is possest ile assure you.   170
Perez.   Where is your maide?
Margarita.   Doe not you know that have her?
She is yours now, why should I look after hir?
Since that first hower I came I never saw her.
Perez.   I saw her later [*aside*] would the Divell had had her,
It is all true I finde, a wild-fire take her.
Juan.   Is thy wife with child *Don Michaell?* thy excellent wife.
Art thou a man yet?
Alonzo.   When shall we come and visit thee?
Sanchio.   And eate some rare fruit, thou hast admirable Orchards,
You are so jealous now, pox a your jealousy,
How scurvily you look.
Perez.   Pre thee leave fooling,   180
I am in no humor now to foole and prattle,——
Did she nere play the wagge with you?
Margarita.   Yes many times,
So often that I was asham'd to keep her,
But I forgave her sir, in hope she would mend still,
And had not you o'th instant married her,
I had put her off.

Perez.   I thank ye [*aside*] I am blest still,
Which way so ere I turne I am a made man,
Miserably gull'd beyond recovery.
Juan.   Youl stay and dine.
Perez.   Certaine I cannot Captaine,
Hark in thine eare, I am the arrant'st puppy,   190
The miserablest Asse, but I must leave ye,
I am in hast, in hast,——blesse ye good madame,
And you prove as good as my wife.   *Exit.*
Leon.   Will you come neer sir, will your grace but honour me,
And tast our dinner, you are nobly welcome,
All angers past I hope, and I shall serve yee.
Juan.   Thou art the stock of men, and I admire thee.

                                        Exeunt.

                    Enter Perez.   IV. i

Perez.   Ile goe to a conjurer but ile find this pol-cat,
This pilfring whore, a plague of vayles I cry,
And covers for the impudence of women,
Their sanctity in show will deceive Divells,

                    Enter Estifania.

[*Aside*] It is my evill Angell let me blesse mee.
Estifania [*aside*].   Tis he, I am caught, I must stand to it stoutly,
And show no shake of feare, I see he is angry,
Vext at the uttermost.
Perez.   My worthy wife,
I have been looking of your modesty,
All the towne over.
Estifania.   My most noble husband,   10
I am glad I have found ye, for in truth I am weary,
Weary and lame with looking out your Lordship.
Perez.   I have been in bawdy howses——
Estifania.   I beleeve ye,
And very lately too.

Perez.   Pray ye pardon mee,
To seek your Ladiship; I have been in cellers,
In private cellers, where the thirsty bawds
Heare your confessions; I have been at plaies,
To look you out amongst the youthfull actors,
At Puppet shewes, you are Mistris of the motions;
At goshippings I hearkned after ye,   20
But amongst those confusions of lewd tongues
There's no distinguishing beyond a Babell.
I was amongst the Nuns because you sing well,
But they say yours are bawdy songs, they mourn for ye,
And last I went to Church to seek you out,
Tis so long since you were there, they have forgot ye.
Estifania.   You have had a pretty progresse, ile tell mine now:
To look you out, I went to twenty Taverns.
Perez.   And are you sober?
Estifania.   Yes, I reele not yet sir,
Where I saw twenty drunk, most of em souldiers,   30
There I had great hope to finde you disguisd too.
From hence to'th dicing house, there I found
Quarrels needlesse, and senselesse, swords, and pots, and candle-
     sticks,
Tables, and stooles, and all in one confusion,
And no man knew his friend, I left this Chaos,
And to the Chyrurgions went, he willd me stay,
For saies he learnedly, if he be tipled,
Twenty to one he whores, and then I heare of him.
If he be mad, he quarrels, then he comes too,
I sought ye where no safe thing would have ventred   40
Amongst diseases base, and vild, vild women,
For I remembred your old Roman axiom,
The more the danger, still the more the honour.
Last to your Confessor I came, who told me
You were too proud to pray, and here I have found ye.
Perez [*aside*].   She beares up bravely, and the rogue is witty,
But I shall dash it instantly to nothing,——
Here leave we off our wanton languages,

And now conclude we in a sharper tongue.
Why am I cozend?

Estifania.   Why am I abused?   50
Perez.   Thou most vild, base, abominable——
Estifania.   Captaine.
Perez.   Thou stinking overstewd, poore, pocky——
Estifania.   Captaine.
Perez.   Doe you Eccho me?
Estifania.   Yes Sir, and goe before ye,
And round about ye, why doe you rayle at me
For that, that was your own sin, your own knavery?
Perez.   And brave me too?
Estifania.   You had best now draw your sword Captaine,
Draw it upon a woman, doe brave Captaine,
Upon your wife, oh most renowned Captaine.
Perez.   A plague upon thee, answer me directly,
Why didst thou marry me?
Estifania.   To be my husband;   60
I had thought you had had infinite, but i'm cozend.
Perez.   Why didst thou flatter me, and shew me wonders,
A house, and riches, when they are but shadowes,
Shadowes to me?
Estifania.   Why did you work on me?
(It was but my part to requite you Sir)
With your strong souldiers wit, and swore you would bring me
So much in chaines, so much in jewels husband,
So much in right rich cloathes?
Perez.   Thou hast um rascall;
I gave um to thy hands, my trunks and all;
And thou hast opend um, and sold my treasure.   70
Estifania.   Sir, Theres your treasure, sell it to a tinker
                                        [*Shewes*] *a Casket.*
To mend old kettles, is this noble usage?

---

50 Why am I cozend? *Estifania.* Why] Colman; *Estif.* Why am I cozend, Why
Qq, F2
*61 had thought] *stet* Q1
71 *a Casket.*] *om.* Qq, F2 (*relocated from line* 4.1)

Let all the world view here the Captaines treasure,
A man would think now these were worthy matters:
Here's a shooing-horne chaine, gilt over, how it senteth
Worse then the mouldy durty heel it served for,
And heres another of a lesser value,
So little, I would shame to tye my dog in't,
These are my joynter, blush and save a labour,
Or these else will blush for ye.
Perez.   A fire subtle ye,   80
Are ye so crafty.
Estifania.   Heres a goodly jewell,
Did not you win this at Goletta Captaine,
Or took it in the field from some brave *Bashaw*,
How it sparkles like an old Ladies eyes,
And fills each roome with light like a close lanthorne,
This would doe rarely in an Abby window,
To cosen Pilgrims.
Perez.   Preethee leave prating.
Estifania.   And here's a chaine of whitings eyes for pearles,
A mussell-monger would have made a better.
Perez.   Nay, preethee wife, my cloathes, my cloathes.
Estifania.   Ile tell yee,   90
Your cloathes are paralells to these, all counterfet.
Put these and them on, you are a man of copper,
A kinde of candlestick, these you thought my husband,
To have cozend me withall, but I am quit with you.
Perez.   Is there no house then, nor no grounds about it?
No plate nor hangings?
Estifania.   There are none sweet husband,
Shadow for shadow is an equall justice,
Can you raile now, pray put your fury up sir,
And speak great words, you are a souldier, thunder.
Perez.   I will speak litle, I have plaid the foole,   100
And so I am rewarded.
Estifania.   You have spoke well sir,
And now I see you are so conformable,
Ile heighthen you againe, goe to your house,

They are packing to be gone, you must sup there,
Ile meet ye, and bring clothes, and cleane shirts after,
And all things shall be well; [*aside*] ile colt ye once more,
And teach ye to bring copper.
Perez.   Tell me one thing,
I doe beseech thee tell me, tell me truth wife,
However I forgive thee, art thou honest?
The Beldam swore——
Estifania.   I bid her tell you so sir,   110
It was my plot, alas my credulous husband,
The Lady told you too——
Perez.   Most strange things of thee.
Estifania.   Still twas my way, and all to try your sufferance,
And she denied the house?
Perez.   She knew me not;
No, nor no title that I had.
Estifania.   Twas well carried;
No more, I am right and straight.
Perez.   I would beleeve thee,
But heaven knowes how my heart is, will ye follow me?
Estifania.   Ile be there straight.
Perez [*aside*].   I am fooled, yet dare not finde it.
                                        Exit Perez.
Estifania.   Goe silly foole, thou maist be a good souldier
In open field, but for our private service   120
Thou art an asse, ile make thee so or misse else.

                    Enter Cacafogo.

Here comes another Trout that I must tickle,
And tickle daintily, I have lost my end else.
May I crave your leave sir?
Cacafogo.   Preethee be answered, thou shalt crave no leave,
I am in my meditations, doe not vex me,
[*Apart*] A beaten thing, but this houre a most brused thing,
That people had compassion on, it looked so,
The next Sir *Palmerin*; heres fine proportion,
An Asse, and then an Elephant, sweet justice,   130

Theres no way left to come at her now, no craving,
If mony could come neere, yet I would pay him;
I have a mind to make him a huge cuckold,
And mony may doe much, a thousand duckets,
Tis but the letting blood of a ranck heire.

Estifania.   Pray ye heare me.

Cacafogo.   I know thou hast some wedding ring to pawn now,
Of Silver and guilt with a blind posy in't,
(Love and a mill-horse should goe round togither),
Or thy childs whistle, or thy squirills chaine,   140
Ile none of um, [*apart*] I would she did but know me,
Or would this fellow had but use of mony,
That I might come in any way.

Estifania.   I am gone sir,
And I shall tell the beauty sent me to ye,
The Lady *Margarita*——

Cacafogo.   Stay I prethee,
What is thy will, I turne me wholly to ye,
And talk now till thy tongue ake, I will heare yee.

Estifania.   She would entreat ye sir——

Cacafogo.   She shall command sir,
Let it be so I beseech thee my sweet gentlewoman,
Doe not forget thy selfe.

Estifania.   She does command then,   150
This curtesy, because she knowes you are noble——

Cacafogo.   Your Mistris by the way.

Estifania.   My naturall Mistris——
Upon these Jewels sir, they are faire and rich,
And (view um) right——   [*He takes Casket.*]

Cacafogo.   To doubt um is an heresy.

Estifania.   A thousand duckets, 'tis upon necessity
Of present use, her husband sir is stubborne.

Cacafogo.   Long may he be so.

Estifania.   She desires withall,
A better knowledge of your parts and person,
And when you please to doe her so much honour——

*154 right] stet Q1

552

Cacafogo.   Come let's dispatch.

Estifania.   In troath I have heard hir say sir,   160
    Of a fat man she has not seen a sweeter,
    But in this businesse sir——

Cacafogo.   Let's doe it first,
    And then dispute, the Ladies use may long for't.

Estifania.   All secrecy she would desire, she told me
    How wise you are.

Cacafogo.   We are not wise to talke thus,
    Carry her the gold, ile look her out a jewell,
    Shall sparkle like her eyes, and thee another,
    Come pre thee come, I long to serve thy lady,
    Long monstrously, [*aside*] now valor I shall meet ye,
    You that dare Dukes.

Estifania [*aside*].   Green goose you are now in sippets.   170

                              Exeunt.

        Enter the Duke, Sanchio, Juan, Alonzo.   [IV. ii]

Duke.   He shall not have his will, I shall prevent him,
    I have a toy here that will turne the tide,
    And sodainly, and strangely; heere *Don Juan*,   [*Gives a paper.*]
    Doe you present it to him.

Juan.   I am commanded.   *Exit.*

Duke.   A fellow founded out of Charity,
    And moulded to the height contemne his maker,
    Curbe the free hand that fram'd him? This must not be.

Sanchio.   That such an oyster shell should hold a pearle,
    And of so rare a price, in prison, was she made
    To be the matter of her own undoing,   10
    To let a slovenly unwieldy fellow,
    Unruly and selfe will'd, dispose her beauties?

Alonzo.   We suffer all sir in this sad Eclipse,
    She should shine where she might show like her selfe,
    An absolute sweetnesse, to comfort those admire her,
    And shed her beames upon her friends.

       *10 matter] *stet* Q1   *13 *Alonzo.* We] Qq, F2

Sanchio.　　　　　　　　　　　We are gulld all,
　And all the world will grumble at your patience,
　If she be ravish't thus.
Duke.　　　　　　　　　Nere feare it *Sanchio*,
　Weel have her free againe, and move at Court,
　In her cleere orbe: but one sweet handsomenesse,　　　　20
　To blesse this part of Spaine, and have that slubberd?
Alonȝo.　Tis every good mans cause, and we must stir in it.
Duke.　Ile warrant he shall be glad to please us,
　And glad to share too, we shall heare anon
　A new song from him, let's attend a little.

　　　　　　　　　　　　　　　　　　　Exeunt

　　　　Enter Leon *with a commission, and* Juan.　　　　[IV. iii]

Leon.　Coronell, I am bound to you for this noblenesse,
　I should have been your officer, tis true sir,
　And a proud man I should have been to have serv'd you,
　'T as pleas'd the King out of his boundlesse favours,
　To make me your companion, this commission
　Gives me a troope of horse.
Juan.　　　　　　　　　I rejoyce at it,
　And am a glad man we shall gain your company;
　I am sure the King knows you are newly married,
　And out of that respect gives you more time sir.
Leon.　Within foure daies I am gone, so he commands me,　　10
　And tis not mannerly for me to argue it,
　The time growes shorter still, are your goods ready?
Juan.　They are aboard.
Leon.　　　　　　　　Who waits there?

　　　　　　　　　Enter Servant.

Servant.　　　　　　　　　　　Sir.
Leon.　　　　　　　　　　　Doe you heare ho,
　Goe carry this unto your Mistris sir,

　　0.1 Leon *with a commission, and* Juan.] Dyce; *Leon, and Iuan with a commission.*
Qq, F2

　　　　　　　　　　　554

And let her see how much the King has honour'd mee,
Bid hir be lusty, she must make a souldier.   *Exit* [Servant].
Lorenzo.

            Enter Lorenzo.

Lorenzo.   Sir.

Leon.   Goe take downe all the hangings,
And pack up all my cloths, my plate and Jewels,
And all the furniture that's portable,
Sir when we lye in garrison, 'tis necessary   20
We keep a handsome port, for the kings honour;
And doe you heare, let all your Ladies wardrobe
Be safely plac'd in trunks, they must along too.

Lorenzo.   Whether must they goe sir?

Leon.   To the warres *Lorenzo*
And you and all, I will not leave a turne-spit,
That has one dram of spleene against a Dutchman.

Lorenzo.   Why then Saint *Jaques* hey, you have made us all sir,
And if we leave ye——does my Lady goe too?

Leon.   The stuffe must goe to morrow towards the sea sir,
All all must goe.

Lorenzo.   Why *Pedro*, *Vasco*, *Dego*.   30
Come help me, come come boyes, soldadoes, comrades,
Wee'l fley these beere-bellied rogues, come away quickly. *Exit.*

Juan [*aside*].   Has taken a brave way to save his honour,
And crosse the Duke, now I shall love him dearely,
By the life of credit thou art a noble gentleman.

            Enter Margarita *led by two Ladies.*

Leon.   Why how now wife, what sick at my preferment?
This is not kindly done.

Margarita.   No sooner love ye,
Love ye intirely sir, brought to consider
The goodnesse of your mind and mine owne duty,
But loose you instantly, be divorc'd from ye,   40

---

*17 *Lorenzo. Enter* Lorenzo.] Seward (Sympson *conj.*); *Enter Lorenzo.* Qq, F 2
17 *Leon.*] Q 2; *om.* Q 1, F 2   27 sir] F 2; sit Q 1

This is a cruelty, ile to the King
And tell him 'tis unjust to part two soules,
Too minds so neerely mixt.

Leon.   By no means sweet heart.

Margarita.   If he were married but foure daies as I am——

Leon [*aside*].   He would hang himselfe the fift, or fly his Country.

Margarita.   He would make it treason for that tongue that durst
But talke of warre, or any thing to vexe him,
You shall not goe.

Leon.   Indeed I must sweet wife,
What shall I loose the King for a few kisses?
Wee'l have enough.

Margarita.   Ile to the Duke my cozen,   50
He shall to th' King.

Leon.   He did me this great office,
I thank his grace for't; should I pray him now
To undoe't againe, fye 'twere a base discredit.

Margarita.   Would I were able sir to bear you company,
How willing should I be then, and how merry,
I will not live alone.

Leon.   Be in peace you shall not.   *Knock within.*

Margarita.   What knockings this? oh heaven my head, why
rascals
I think the war's begun i'th house already.

Leon.   The preparation is, they are taking downe,
And packing up the hangings, plate and Jewels,   60
And all those furnitures that shall befit me
When I lye in garrison.

Enter Coachman.

Coachman.   Must the Coach goe too Sir?

Leon.   How will your Lady passe to'th sea else easily?
We shall finde shipping for't there to transport it.

Margarita.   I goe? alas.

Leon.   Ile have a maine care of ye,
I know ye are sickly, he shall drive the easier,

64 for't] F2; fort Q1

556

And all accommodation shall attend ye.

Margarita.   Would I were able.

Leon.   Come I warrant ye,
Am not I with ye sweet?——are her cloaths packt up,
And all her linnens?——give your maids direction,   70
You know my times but short, and I am commanded.

Margarita.   Let me have a nurse,
And all such necessary people with me,
And an easie bark.

Leon.   It shall not trot I warrant ye,
Curveat it may sometimes.

Margarita.   I am with child sir.

Leon.   At foure daies warning? this is something speedy,
Doe you conceave as our jennets doe with a west winde?
My heire will be an arrant fleet one Lady,
Ile sweare you were a maid when I first lay with ye.

Margarita.   Pray doe not sweare, I thought I was a maid too,   80
But we may both be cozend in that point Sir.

Leon.   In such a strait point sure I could not erre Madam.

Juan [aside].   This is another tendernesse to try him,
Fetch hir up now.

Margarita.   You must provide a cradle,
And what a troubles that.

Leon.   The sea shall rock it,
Tis the best nurse; twill roare and rock together,
A swinging storme will sing you such a lullaby.

Margarita.   Faith let me stay, I shall but shame ye Sir.

Leon.   And you were a thousand shames you shall along with me,
At home I am sure you'le prove a million,   90
Every man carries the bundle of his sinnes,
Upon his own back, you are mine, Ile sweat for ye.

Enter Duke, Alonzo, Sanchio.

Duke.   What Sir, preparing for your noble journey?
Tis well and full of care.
I saw your minde was wedded to the warre,
And knew you would prove some good man for your country,

Therefore faire Cozen with your gentle pardon,
I got this place, what mourne at his advancement?
You are too blame, he will come agen sweet cozen,
Meane time like sad *Penelope* and sage,   100
Amongst your maids at home, and huswifely——
Leon.   No sir, I dare not leave her to that solitarinesse,
She is young, and griefe or ill newes from those quarters
May dayly crosse her, she shall goe along Sir.
Duke.   By no meanes Captaine.
Leon.   By all meanes an't please ye?
Duke.   What take a young and tender bodied Lady,
And expose her to those dangers, and those tumults,
A sickly Lady too?
Leon.   Twill make hir well Sir,
Theres no such friend to health as wholsome travell.
Sanchio.   Away, it must not be.
Alonzo.   It ought not Sir,   110
Goe hurry her, it is not humane Captaine.
Duke.   I cannot blame her teares, fright her with tempests
With thunder of the warre? I dare sweare if she were able——
Leon.   Shee is most able.
And pray ye sweare not, she must goe theres no remedy,
Nor greatnesse, nor the trick you had to part us,
Which I smell too ranck, too open, too evident,
(And I must tell you Sir, tis most unnoble)
Shall hinder me: had she but ten houres life,
Nay lesse, but two houres, I would have her with me,   120
I would not leave her fame to so much ruine,
To such a desolation and discredit
As her weaknesse and your hot will wood worke her too.

Enter Perez.

What Masque is this now?
More tropes and figures, to abuse my sufferance,
What cozen's this?
Juan.   *Michael Van Owle,* how dost thou?
In what dark barne or tod of aged Ivy

Hast thou lyen hid?

Perez.   Things must both ebbe and flow Coronell,
And people must conceale, and shine agen.
You are welcome hither as your friend may say Gentlemen,   130
A pretty house yee see hansomely seated,
Sweet and convenient walkes, the waters cristall.

Alonzo.   He's certaine mad.

Juan.   As mad as a French Tayler,
That has nothing in's head but ends of fustians.

Perez.   I see you are packing now my gentle cozen,
And my wife told me I should finde it so,
Tis true I doe, you were merry when I was last here,
But twas your will to try my patience Madam.
I am sorry that my swift occasions
Can let you take your pleasure here no longer,   140
Yet I would have you think my honourd cozen,
This house and all I have are all your servants.

Leon.   What house, what pleasure sir, what doe you mean?

Perez.   You hold the jest so stiffe, twill prove discurtious,
This house I meane, the pleasures of this place.

Leon.   And what of them?

Perez.   They are mine Sir, and you know it,
My wives I meane, and so conferd upon me,
The hangings Sir I must entreat your servants,
That are so busie in their offices,
Againe to minister to their right uses;   150
I shall take view oth plate anon, and furnitures
That are of under place, you are merry still cozen,
And of a pleasant constitution,
Men of great fortunes make their mirths *ad placitum.*

Leon.   Preethee good stubborne wife, tell me directly,
Good evill wife leave fooling and tell me honestly,
Is this my kinsman?

Margarita.   I can tell yee nothing.

Leon.   I have many kinsmen, but so mad a one,
And so phantastick——all the house?

130 Gentlemen] Q 2; Gentlemā Q 1, F 2

559

Perez.   All mine,
And all within it, I will not bate ye an ace ont,   160
Can you not receave a noble curtesie,
And quietly and handsomely as ye ought Couze,
But you must ride oth top ont.
Leon.   Canst thou fight?
Perez.   Ile tell ye presently, I cood have done sir.
Leon.   For ye must law and claw before ye get it.
Juan.   Away, no quarrels.
Leon.   Now I am more temperate,
Ile have it proved if you were never yet in Bedlam,
Never in love for thats a lunacy,
No great state left ye that you never lookt for,
Nor cannot mannage, thats a ranke distemper,   170
That you were christend, and who answer'd for ye,
And then I yeeld.
Perez.   Has halfe perswaded me I was bred ith' moone,
I have nere a bush at my breech, are not we both mad,
And is not this a phantastick house we are in,
And all a dreame we doe? will ye walk out sir,
And if I doe not beat thee presently
Into a sound beliefe, as sense can give thee,
Brick me into that wall there for a chimney peece,
And say I was one oth *Caesars*, done by a seale-cutter.   180
Leon.   Ile talke no more,——come weele away immediatly.
Margarita.   Why then the house is his, and all thats in it,
[*Aside*] Ile give away my skin but Ile undoe yee,——
I gave it to his wife, you must restore Sir,
And make a new provision.
Perez.   Am I mad now
Or am I christend, you my pagan cozen,
My mighty Mahound kinsman, what quirk now;
You shall be welcome all, I hope to see sir
Your Grace here, and my coze, we are all souldiers,
And must doe naturally for one another.   190
Duke.   Are ye blank at this, then I must tell ye Sir,
Ye have no command, now ye may goe at pleasure

And ride your asse troope, twas a trick I us'd
To try your jealousie upon entreatie,
And saving of your wife.
Leon.   All this not moves me,
Nor stirs my gall, nor alters my affections,
You have more furniture, more houses Lady,
And rich ones too, I will make bold with those,
And you have Land ith Indies as I take it,
Thither weele goe, and view a while those clymats,   200
Visit your Factors there, that may betray ye,
Tis done, we must goe.
Margarita.   Now thou art a brave Gentleman,
And by this sacred light I love thee dearely,
[*To* Perez] The house is none of yours, I did but jest Sir,
Nor you are no coze of mine, I beseech yee vanish,
I tell you plaine, you have no more right then he has,
Thou senselesse thing, your wife has once more foold ye:
Goe ye and consider.
Leon.   Good morrow my sweet cozen,
I should be glad sir——
Perez.   By this hand she dies for't,
Or any man that speakes for her.   *Exit* Perez.
Juan.   These are fine toyes.   210
Margarita.   Let me request you stay but one poore month,
You shall have a Commission and ile goe too,
Give me but will so far.
Leon.   Well I will try ye,——
Good morrow to your Grace, we have private businesse.
Duke [*aside*].   If I misse thee agen, I am an arrant bungler. [*Exit.*]
Juan.   Thou shalt have my command, and ile march under thee,
Nay be thy boy before thou shalt be bafled,
Thou art so brave a fellow.
Alonzo.   I have seen visions.
                                        Exeunt.

193 us'd] F2; use Q1
*207 Thou] Bond (Mason *conj.*); that Qq, F2

Enter Leon *with a letter, and* Margarita.   V. i

Leon.   Come hether wife, doe you know this hand?
Margarita.   I doe Sir.
    Tis *Estifanias*, that was once my woman.
Leon.   She writes to me here, that one *Cacafogo*
    A usuring jewellers son (I know the rascall)
    Is mortally fallne in love with ye.
Margarita.   Is a monster,
    Deliver me from mountaines.
Leon [aside].   Doe you goe a birding for all sorts of people?——
    And this evening will come to ye and shew ye jewels,
    And offers any thing to get accesse to ye,
    If I can make or sport or profit on him,   10
    (For he is fit for both) she bids me use him,
    And so I will, be you conformable,
    And follow but my will.
Margarita.   I shall not faile sir.
Leon.   Will the Duke come againe doe you think?
Margarita.   No sure Sir,
    Has now no pollicie to bring him hither.
Leon [aside].   Nor bring you to him, if my wit hold faire, wife:——
    Lets in to dinner.
                                              Exeunt.

                    Enter Perez.   [V. ii]

Perez.   Had I but lungs enough to bawle sufficiently,
    That all the queanes in Christendome might heare me,
    That men might run away from the contagion,
    I had my wish; would it were most high treason,
    Most infinite high, for any man to marry,
    I meane for any man that would live hansomely,
    And like a Gentleman, in his wits and credit;
    What torments shall I put her to, *Phalaris* bull now?
    Pox they love bulling too well, though they smoak for't,

                3 the] Seward; *om.* Qq, F2

Cut her apeeces, every peece will live still,   10
And every morsell of her will doe mischiefe;
They have so many lives, there's no hanging of um,
They are too light to drowne, they are cork and feathers,
To burne too cold, they live like Salamanders;
Under huge heaps of stones to bury her,
And so depresse her as they did the Giants;
She will move under more then built old Babell,
I must destroy her.

Enter Cacafogo *with a Casket.*

Cacafogo. Be cozend by a thing of clouts, a she moth,
That every silkmans shop breeds; to be cheated,   20
And of a thousand duckets by a whim wham.
Perez. Who's that is cheated, speak againe thou vision,
But art thou cheated? minister some comfort,
Tell me directly art thou cheated bravely,
Come, preethee come, art though so pure a coxcomb
To be undone? doe not dissemble with me,
Tell me I conjure thee.
Cacafogo.   Then keep thy circle,
For I am a spirit wild that flies about thee,
And who ere thou art, if thou be'st humane,
Ile let thee plainly know, I am cheated damnably.   30
Perez. Ha, ha, ha.
Cacafogo. Dost thou laugh? damnably, I say most damnably.
Perez. By whom, good spirit? speak, speak ha, ha, ha.
Cacafogo.   I will utter,
Laugh till thy lungs crack, by a rascall woman,
A lewd, abominable, and plain woman?
Dost thou laugh still?
Perez.   I must laugh, preethee pardon me,
I shall laugh terribly.
Cacafogo.   I shall be angry,
Terrible angry, I have cause.
Perez.   Thats it,
And tis no reason but thou shouldst be angry,

Angry at heart, yet I must laugh still at thee,   40
By a woman cheated, art' sure it was a woman?
Cacafogo.   I shall break thy head, my vallour itches at thee.
Perez.   It is no matter, by a woman cozend,
   A reall woman?
Cacafogo.   A reall divell,
   Plague of her jewels and her copper chaines,
   How rank they smell.
Perez.   Sweet cozend sir let me see them,
   I have been cheated too, I would have you note that
   And lewdly cheated, by a woman also,
   A scurvie woman, I am undone sweet Sir,
   Therefore I must have leave to laugh.
Cacafogo.   Pray ye take it,   50
                              [*Gives Casket.*]

   You are the merriest undone man in Europe.
   What need we fiddles, bawdy songs and sack,
   When our own miseries can make us merry?
Perez.   Ha, ha, ha.
   I have seene these jewels, what a notable penniworth
   Have you had next your heart, you will not take Sir
   Some twenty Duckets?
Cacafogo.   Thou art deceiv'd I will take——
Perez.   To cleere your bargaine now.
Cacafogo.   Ile take some ten,
   Some any thing, some halfe ten, halfe a Ducket.
Perez.   An excellent lapidary set these stones sure,   60
   Doe you mark their waters?
Cacafogo.   Quick-sand choak their waters,
   And hirs that brought um too, but I shall finde hir.
Perez.   And so shall I, I hope, but doe not hurt her,
   You cannot finde in all this kingdome,
   If you had need of cozening, (as you may have,
   For such grosse natures will desire it often,
   Tis at some time too a fine variety,)
   A woman that can cozen ye so neatly;

                62 brought] Q2; bought Q1, F2

[*Aside*] She has taken halfe mine anger off with this trick. *Exit.*
Cacafogo.   If I were valiant now, I would kill this fellow,   70
I have mony enough lies by me at a pinch
To pay for twenty rascalls lives that wax me,
Ile to this Lady, there I shall be satisfied.

                                                                Exit.

                        Enter Leon *and* Margarita.   [V. iii]

Leon.   Come, weele away unto your country house,
And there weele learne to live contentedly,
This place is full of charge, and full of hurrey,
No part of sweetnesse dwels about these citties.
Margarita.   Whether you will, I wait upon your pleasure;
Live in a hollow tree Sir, Ile live with ye.
Leon.   I, now you strike a harmony a true one,
When your obedience waits upon your husband,
And your sick will aimes at the cure of honour,
Why now I dote upon ye, love ye dearely,   10
And my rough nature falls like roaring streames,
Cleerely and sweetly into your embraces;
O what a jewell is a woman excellent,
A wise a vertuous and a noble woman,
When wee meet such, we bear our stamps on both sides,
And through the world we hold our current virtues,
Alone we are single meadalls, only faces,
And weare our fortunes out in useless shadowes,
Command you now, and ease me of that trouble,
Ile be as humble to you as a servant,   20
Bid whom you please, invite your noble friends,
They shall be welcome all, visit acquaintance,
Goe at your pleasure, now experience
Has link't you fast unto the chain of goodnesse:
                Clashing swords. A cry within, Downe with their swords.
What noise is this, what dismall cry?

            *2 contentedly] Langbaine; contently Qq, F2
            *9 cure] Seward; care Qq, F2

                            565

Margarita.   Tis lowd too.
Sure ther's some mischiefe done i'th street, look out there.
Leon.   Look out and help.

Enter a Servant.

Servant.   Oh sir the Duke *Medina.*
Leon.   What of the Duke *Medina?*
Servant.   Oh sweet gentleman,
Is allmost slain.
Margarita.   A way a way and help him,
All the house help.   *Exit with* Servant.
Leon.   How slain? why *Margarita,*   30
Why wife,——sure some new device they have a foot againe,
Some trick upon my credit, I shall meet it,
I had rather guide a ship Imperiall
Alone, and in a storme, then rule one woman.

Enter Duke, Margarita, Sanchio, Alonzo, *Servant.*

Margarita.   How came ye hurt sir?
Duke.   I fell out with my friend the noble Coronell,
My cause was naught, for 'twas about your honour:
And he that wrongs the Innocent nere prospers,
And he has left me thus; for charity,
Lend me a bed to ease my tortur'd body,   40
That ere I perish I may show my penitence,
I feare I am slaine.
Leon.   Help gentlemen to carry him,
There shall be nothing in this house my Lord,
But as your owne.
Duke.   I thank ye noble sir.
Leon.   To bed with him, and wife give your attendance.

Enter Juan.

Juan.   Doctors and surgions.
Duke.   Doe not disquiet me,
But let me take my leave in peace.

29 allmost] F2 (almost): all most Q1   30 *with*] Colman; *om.* Qq, F2

566

Exeunt Duke, Sanchio, Alonzo, Margarita, *Servant.*
Leon.   Afore me,
  Tis rarely counterfeited.
Juan.   True, it is so sir,
  And take you heed, this last blow doe not spoile ye,
  He is not hurt, only we made a scuffle,   50
  As though we purpos'd anger; that same scratch
  On's hand he took, to colour all and draw compassion,
  That he might get into your house more cunningly,
  I must not stay, stand now, and y'are a brave fellow.
Leon.   I thank ye noble Coronell, and I honour ye.   *Exit* Juan.
  Never be quiet?

Enter Margarita

Margarita.   He's most desperate ill sir,
  I doe not think these ten months will recover him.
Leon.   Does he hire my house to play the foole in,
  Or does it stand on Fairy ground we are haunted?
  Are all men and their wives troubled with dreams thus?   60
Margarita.   What aile you sir?
Leon.   Nay what aile you sweet wife,
  To put these daily pastimes on my patience?
  What dost thou see in mee, that I should suffer thus?
  Have not I done my part like a true husband,
  And paid some desperate debts you never look'd for?
Margarita.   You have done handsomely I must confesse sir.
Leon.   Have I not kept thee waking like a hawke?
  And watcht thee with delights to satisfy thee?
  The very tithes of which had wonne a widow.
Margarita.   Alas I pitty ye.
Leon.   Thou wilt make me angry,   70
  Thou never saw'st me mad yet.
Margarita.   You are alwaies,
  You carry a kind of bedlam still about ye.
Leon.   If thou persuest me farther I run stark mad,
  If you have more hurt Dukes or Gentlemen,

47 *Servant*] F2; *Servants* Q1   *59 haunted?] Dyce; haunted, Qq, F2

To lye here on your cure, I shall be desperate,
I know the trick, and you shall feel I know it,
Are ye so hot that no hedge can containe ye?
Ile have thee let blood in all the veines about thee,
Ile have thy thoughts found too, and have them open'd,
Thy spirits purg'd, for those are they that fire ye,   80
Thy maid shall be thy Mistris thou the maid,
And all those servile labours that she reach'd at
Shalt goe through cherefully, or else sleep empty,
That maid shall lye by me to teach you duty,
You in a pallat by to humble ye,
And greeve for what you loose.
Margarita.   I have lost my selfe sir,
And all that was my base selfe, disobedience,   *Kneeles.*
My wantonnesse my stubbornenesse I have lost too,
And now by that pure faith good wives are crown'd with,
By your own noblenesse——
Leon.   I take ye up,   90
And weare ye next my heart, see you be worth it.

Enter Altea.

Now what with you?
Altea.   I come to tell my Lady,
There is a fulsome fellow would fain speak with her.
Leon.   Tis *Cacafogo*, goe and entertaine him,
And draw him on with hopes.
Margarita.   I shall observe ye.
Leon.   I have a rare designe upon that gentleman,
And you must work too.
Altea.   I shall sir most willingly.
Leon.   A way then both, and keep him close in some place
From the Dukes sight, and keep the Duke in too,
Make um beleeve both; Ile find time to cure um.   100

Exeunt.

*82–83 reach'd at | Shalt] Bond; reach at, | And Qq, F2

Enter Perez, *and* Estifania.   [V. iv]

Perez. Why now darst thou meet me againe thou rebell,
And knowst how thou hast used mee thrice, thou rascall,
Were there not waies enough to fly my vengeance,
No holes nor vaults to hide thee from my fury,
But thou must meet me face to face to kill thee?
I would not seek thee to destroy thee willingly,
But now thou comest to invite me, and comest upon mee;
How like a sheep-biting Rogue taken i'th manner,
And ready for the halter dost thou look now,
Thou hast a hanging look thou scurvy thing, hast nere a knife   10
Nor never a string to lead thee to Elisium?
Be there no pittifull Pothecaries in this towne,
That have compassion upon wretched women,
And dare administer a dramme of rats-bane,
But thou must fall to mee?
Estifania.   I know you have mercy.
Perez. If I had tunnes of mercy thou deserv'st none,
What new tricks is now a foot, and what new houses
Have you i'th aire, what orchards in apparition,
What canst thou say for thy life?
Estifania.   Litle or nothing,
I know you'l kill me, and I know tis uselesse   20
To beg for mercy, pray let me draw my book out,
And prey a litle.
Perez.   Doe a very litle,
For I have farther businesse then thy killing,
I have mony yet to borrow, speak when you are ready.
Estifania. Now now sir now,   *Shewes a Pistoll and a Dagge.*
                        come on, doe you start off from me,
Doe you sweat great Captaine, have you seen a spirit?
Perez. Doe you weare gunnes?
Estifania.   I am a souldiers wife sir,
And by that priviledge I may be arm'd,

*0.1 Estifania.] Seward; *Estifania with a Pistoll, and a Dagge.* Qq, F2
25 *and a Dagge.] om.* Qq, F2   26 sweat] Langbaine; swear Qq, F2

Now whats the newes, and let's discourse more friendly,
And talk of our affaires in peace.
Perez.   Let me see,   30
Pre thee let me see thy gun, 'tis a very pretty one.
Estifania.   No no sir you shall feele——
Perez.   ·   Hold ye villaine,
What thine own husband?
Estifania.   Let mine own husband then,
Be in's own wits, there, there's a thousand duckets,
                                        [*Shewes a purse.*]
Who must provide for you? and yet you'l kill me.
Perez.   I will not hurt thee for ten thousand millions.
Estifania.   When will you redeem your Jewels? I have pawn'd um,
You see for what, we must keep tooch.
Perez.   Ile kisse thee,
And get as many more, ile make thee famous,
Had we the house now.
Estifania.   Come along with mee,   40
If that be vanish't there be more to hyre sir.
Perez.   I see I am an asse when thou art neere me.
                                        [*Exeunt.*]

Enter Leon, Margarita, *and* Altea *with a Taper.*   [V. v]

Leon.   Is the foole come?
Altea.   Yes and i'th celler fast,
And there he staies his good houre till I call him,
He will make dainty musick among the sack-butts,
I have put him just sir, under the Dukes chamber.
Leon.   It is the better.
Altea.   Has given me roially,
And to my Lady a whole load of portigues.
Leon.   Better and better still, goe *Margarita,*
Now play your prize, you say you dare be honest,
Ile put ye to your best.
Margarita.   Secure your selfe sir,
Give me the candle, passe away in silence.   10

Exeunt Leon *and* Altea.
She knocks.

Duke [within].   Who's there? oh oh.
Margarita.   My Lord.
Duke (within).   Have ye brought me comfort?
Margarita.   I have my Lord,
  Come forth 'tis I, come gently out Ile help ye,
  Come softly too,

            Enter Duke *in a gowne.*

            how doe you?
Duke.   Are there none here?
  Let mee look round; we cannot be too wary,
  Oh let me blesse this houre, are you alone sweet friend?
Margarita.   Alone to comfort you.   Cacafogo *makes a noise below.*
Duke.   What's that you tumble?
  I have heard a noise this halfe houre under mee,
  A fearfull noise.
Margarita [aside].   The fat thing's mad i'th celler,
  And stumbles from one hogs-head to another,   20
  Two cups more, and he nere shall find the way out,——
  What doe you feare? come, sit downe by mee chearefully,
  My husband's safe, how doe your wounds?
Duke.   I have none Lady,
  My wounds I counterfeited cunningly,
  And fained the quarrell too, to injoy you sweet,
  Let's loose no time,   *Noise below.*
            heark the same noise againe.
Margarita.   What noise, why look ye pale? I heare no stirring;
  [*Aside*] This goblin in the vault will be so tipled,——
  You are not well I know by your flying fancy,
  Your body's ill at ease, your wounds——
Duke.   I have none,   30
  I am as lusty and as full of health,
  High in my blood——
Margarita.   Weak in your blood you would say,

    12 *within*] F 2; *with in* Q 1   15 wary,] wary, *Noise below.* Q 1 +

            571

How wretched is my case willing to please ye,
And find you so disable.
Duke.   Beleeve me Lady——
Margarita.   I know you will venter all you have to satisfy me,
Your life I know, but is it fit I spoile yee,
Is it my love doe you think?
Cacafogo (*below*).   Here's to the Duke.
Duke.   It named me certainly,
I heard it plainly sound.
Margarita.   You are hurt mortally,
And fitter for your prayers sir then pleasure,   40
What starts you make? I would not kisse you wantonly,
For the worlds wealth; have I secur'd my Husband,
And put all doubts aside to be deluded?
Cacafogo (*below*).   I come I come.
Duke.   Heaven blesse mee.
Margarita.   And blesse us both, for sure this is the Divell,
I plainly heard it now, he will come to fetch ye,
A very spirit, for he spoke under ground,
And spoke to you just as you would have snatcht me,
You are a wicked man, and sure this haunts ye,
Would you were out o'th house.
Duke.   I would I were,   50
A that condition I had leapt a window.
Margarita.   And that's the least leap if you mean to scape sir,
Why what a frantick man were you to come here,
What a weak man to counterfeit deep wounds,
To wound another deeper.
Duke.   Are you honest then?
Margarita.   Yes then and now, and ever, and excellent honest,
And exercise this pastime but to shew ye,
Great men are fooles sometimes as well as wretches,
Would you were well hurt with any hope of life,
Cut to the braines, or run clean through the body,   60
To get out quietly as you got in sir,
I wish it like a friend that loves ye dearely,
For if my husband take ye, and take ye thus

A counterfeit, one that would clip his credit,
Out of his honour he must kill ye presently,
There is no mercy nor an hower of pitty,
And for me to intreat in such an agony,
Would shew me litle better then one guilty;
Have you any mind to a Lady now?
Duke.   Would I were off faire,
If ever Lady caught me in a trap more——   70
Margarita.   If you be well and lusty, fy fy shake not,
You say you love me, come, come bravely now,
Dispise all danger, I am ready for ye.
Duke.   She mocks my misery, thou cruell Lady.
Margarita.   Thou cruell Lord, wouldst thou betray my honesty,
Betray it in mine own house, wrong my husband,
Like a night theefe, thou darst not name by day-light?
Duke.   I am most miserable.
Margarita.   You are indeed,
And like a foolish thing you have made your selfe so,
Could not your own discretion tell ye sir,   80
When I was married I was none of yours?
Your eyes were then commanded to look off me,
And I now stand in a circle and secure,
Your spells nor power can never reach my body,
Mark me but this, and then sir be most miserable,
Tis sacriledge to violate a wedlock,
You rob two Temples, make your selfe twice guilty,
You ruine hirs, and spot hir noble husbands.
Duke.   Let me be gone, Ile never more attempt ye.
Margarita.   You cannot goe, 'tis not in me to save ye,   90
Dare ye doe ill, and poorely then shrinke under it?
Were I the Duke *Medina,* I would fight now,
For you must fight and bravely, it concernes you,
You doe me double wrong if you sneak off sir,
And all the world would say I lov'd a coward,
And you must dye too, for you will be killd,
And leave your youth, your honour and your state,

*77 name] *stet* Q1   87 Temples] F2; Templers Q1

573

And all those deere delights you worship't heere.   *Noise below.*
Duke.   The noise againe.
Cacafogo (*below*).   Some small beere if you love me.
Margarita.   The Divell haunts you sure, your sinnes are mighty,   100
A drunken Divell too, to plague your villany.
Duke.   Preserve me but this once.
Margarita.   There's a deep well
In the next yard, if you dare venter drowning,
It is but death.
Duke.   I would not dye so wretchedly.
Margarita.   Out of a garrat window Ile let you downe then,
But say the rope be rotten, 'tis huge high too.
Duke.   Have you no mercy?
Margarita.   Now you are frighted thoroughly,
And find what tis to play the foole in folly,
And see with cleere eyes your detested sin,
Ile be your guard.
Duke.   And ile be your true servant,   110
Ever from this houre vertuously to love ye,
Chastly and modestly to look upon ye,
And here I seale it.   [*Kisses her.*]
Margarita.   I may kisse a stranger,
For you must now be so.

                Enter Leon, Juan, Alonzo, Sanchio.

Leon.   How doe you my Lord?
Me thinks you look but poorely on this matter.
Has my wife wounded ye? you were well before,
Pray sir be comforted, I have forgot all,
Truly forgiven too, wife you are a right one,
And now with unknowne nations I dare trust yee.
Juan.   No more fain'd fights my Lord, they never prosper.   120

            [*Enter* Altea, Cacafogo, *and Servant.*]

Leon.   Who's this? the Divell in the vault?
Altea.   Tis he sir,

    *98 heere] F2 (here); heare Q1   *108–109 folly...sin] folly...folly Qq, F2

And as lovingly drunk, as though he had studied it.

Cacafogo.   Give me a cup of Sack, and kisse me Lady,
Kisse my sweet face, and make thy husband cuckold,
An Ocean of sweet Sack, shall we speak treason?

Leon.   He is divilish drunk.

Duke.   I had thought he had beene a devill,
He made as many noyses and as horrible.

Leon.   Oh a true lover sir will lament lowdly,——
Which of the butts is your Mistris?

Cacafogo.   Butt in thy belly.

Leon.   Theres two in thine I am sure, 'tis growne so monstrous.   130

Cacafogo.   Butt in thy face!

Leon.   Goe carry him to sleepe,
A fooles love should be drunke, he has paid well for't too.
When he is sober let him out to raile,
Or hang himselfe, there will be no losse of him.

Exeunt Cacafogo *and Servant.*

Enter Perez, *and* Estifania.

Who's this? my Mauhound cozen?

Perez.   Good Sir, tis very good, would I had a house too,
For there is no talking in the open ayre,
My Tarmogant Couze, I would be bold to tell ye,
I durst be merry too, I tell you plainly,
You have a pretty seat, you have the luck on't,   140
A pretty Lady too, I have mist both,
My Carpenter built in a myst I thank him,
Doe me the curtesie to let me see it,
See it but once more, But I shall cry for anger.
Ile hire a Chandlers shop close under ye,
And for my foolerie, sell sope and whip-cord,
Nay if you doe not laugh now and laugh heartily
You are a foole couze.

Leon.   I must laugh a litle,
And now I have done couze thou shalt live with me
My merry couze, the world shall not divorce us,   150
Thou art a valiant man, and thou shalt never want,

Will this content thee?

Perez.   Ile crye, and then ile be thankfull,
Indeed I will, and ile be honest to ye.
I would live a swallow here I must confesse,
Wife I forgive thee all if thou be honest,
At thy perill, I beleeve thee excellent.

Estifania.   If I prove otherwaies, let me beg first.

Margarita.   Hold this is yours, some recompence for service,
Use it to nobler ends then he that gave it.

Duke.   And this is yours, your true commission, Sir,   160
Now you are a Captaine.

Leon.   You are a noble Prince Sir.
And now a souldier.

Gentlemen.   We all rejoyce in't.

Juan.   Sir, I shall wait upon you through all fortunes.

Alonzo.   And I.

Altea.   And I must needs attend my Mistris.

Leon.   Will you goe sister?

Altea.   Yes indeed good brother,
I have two ties, mine own bloud, and my Mistris.

Margarita.   Is she your sister?

Leon.   Yes indeed good wife,
And my best sister, for she prov'd so wench,
When she deceav'd you with a loving husband.

Altea.   I would not deale so truly for a stranger.   170

Margarita.   Well I could chide yee,
But it must be lovingly and like a sister,——
Ile bring you on your way, and feast yee nobly,
For now I have an honest heart to love yee,
And then deliver you to the blew *Neptune.*

Juan.   Your colours we must weare, and weare em proudly,
Weare em before the bullet, and in bloud too,
And all the world shall know we are vertues servants.

---

*158 *Margarita.*] Bond (Coleridge *conj.*); *om.* Qq, F2
*162 souldier. *Gentlemen.* We] Seward; souldier, Gentleman, we Qq, F2
166 two] F2; too Q1
176 we] Dyce (Mason *conj.*); you Qq, F2

Duke.   And all the world shall know, a noble minde
Makes women beautifull and envie blinde.   180

Exeunt.

FINIS.

EPILOGUE.

Good night our worthy friends, and may you part
Each with as merry and as free a hart
As you came hither; to those noble eyes
That daine to smile on our poore faculties,
And give a blessing to our labouring ends,
As we hope many, to such fortune sends
Their own desires, wives faire as light as chast;
To those that live by spight wives made in hast.

6 *sends* Q1(c), F2; *send* Q1(u)

577

TEXTUAL NOTES

Prologue

11 *her*]   The Quarto '*your*' is a compositor's anticipation of '*your*' in line 12.

13 *W'are*]   Sympson suggested '*You're*', adopted by Seward, Colman, Weber, and Dyce. Heath (manuscript Notes, quoted by Dyce), supporting the Quarto, argues: 'The sense is, We players pretty nearly resemble the ancient Vestals; we keep the fire of love alive and gently blow it'; but Dyce counters: 'To suppose that the poet would make "these harlottry players" call themselves "*vestals*" is surely ridiculous.' Saintsbury believes that calling themselves '*vestals*' might be ironic, 'as it certainly would be to apply the word to an Elizabethan audience'. Bond suggests that the irony might be shared equally: '*all* implies, "we, *no less than you*"'; but 'the allusion to the Vestals' task...is much more appropriate to the actors than to the audience'. The audience in this Prologue is addressed throughout in the second person (e.g., lines 1, 12, and 25); '*W'are...all*', therefore, must represent the players who, knowing full well that they are not virginal vestals, know also that though they titillate only, they can depend upon their auditors to make the flame grow up to desire, in spite of the warning against following '*president...to sinne*'.

I.i

10 strong]   Theobald suggested 'strong' for Q1 'strange', which is, indeed, an easy misreading, influenced by 'strange' immediately above in line 9. Mason's gloss, 'uncommonly', to justify 'strange' is certainly forced; Leon's person naturally (not unnaturally) promises the work of a giant – which it fulfills in Act V. Later, at line 23, Theobald suggested the reverse emendation, 'strange' for Q1 'strong', as a response to line 9, but 'strong' used ironically is not inappropriate there. See V.v.109.

103.1 *and Servants*.]   As the Quarto stipulates the plural at the exit, line 111.1, it is best to provide the plural here at the entry. The small liberty of bringing on several servants requires less than the large liberty of disregarding the Quarto plural at line 111.1 and inventing the awkward direction to call within.

I.iv

0.1 Old Ladies] These three ancient guardians of social protocol are evidently three countrywomen whom Margarita consults in matters of the heart. (Alonzo, it will be noted, similarly repairs to 'an old Gentlewoman' (I.ii.40).) Two of these three reappear (called 'two Ladies' in Q1) in II.i, but there is no reference to the third, who may have been deleted because Fletcher realized he had nothing for a third person to do (she speaks two lines in I.iv) or through the exigencies of staging or casting. In II.iii; II.iv; III.i; III.v; IV.iii, 'Ladies' appear, attendant on Margarita. Weber argued that these latter ladies are 'resident in the house, not to be identified with those of I.iv, II.i', and Bond supports him. They are probably correct, for though in II.i she accepts the advice of the Old Ladies to marry, Margarita rejects their ideas of the kind of man she should marry – 'a rich Lawyer' (line 35), 'some grave governor' (line 40) – preferring 'a foole' (line 26), the kind of man proposed by Altea; to him Margarita turns her attention in the remainder of the scene (II.i.44–66). This kind of man she submits to be 'searcht' (II.iii.5) by Ladies of an understanding more sophisticated than that of the rural Old Ladies. She takes these new Ladies with her to her new city house and to 'new company' (II.iii.69 and II.iv, etc.). (Dyce thought the Old Ladies appeared also in II.iii.) This edition separates the two groups by classifying the countrywomen as 'Old Ladies' – not as 'old Ladies' as in Qq and F2 – and by terming them so in the entry-direction of the present scene and, following Dyce, by emending the entry-direction of the later scene, II.i, from 'two Ladies' to 'two Old Ladies'. Prefixes in both scenes are standardized accordingly.

I.v

50–51 asso...Maistre.] Seward printed Theobald's attempt to put this into something like Spanish (baso las manos a vostra Seignoria), Weber corrected it (Beso las manos à vuestra sennoria), and Dyce corrected it again (...á...señoria). Dyce submitted the passage to 'a very acute Spaniard', but even he was unable to make sense of 'a Maistre'. Saintsbury thought that these words were a 'clumsy French gloss on..."señoria."' Professor Bruce Wardropper suggests the possibility that 'the real Spanish ought to be "asso [for asgo] las manos" (I seize, or grasp, the hands); this is only a possibility because for clasping hands Spanish uses a different verb'. I have accepted that suggestion, as I cannot explain how 'beso' could be misread as 'asso', even though Professor Wardropper prefers 'beso', 'which is more normal Spanish'. ('Basilus manus' occurs also in The Pilgrim (IV.iii.92) in F1, spoken by a Welshman.) 'Siniare' (i.e., 'Señoría') is the courtesy title extended to noblemen ('Es la cortesía que se da a los señores titulados', *s.v.* in Sebastián de Covarrubias, *Tesoro de la lengua castellana o española* (1611), ed. M. de Riquer (Barcelona, 1943)). '*Maistre*' is an ancient variant (in this spelling perhaps confused in Fletcher's mind with French 'maître') of the standard *maestro*. Professor Wardropper notes that though '*maestro* was the dominant form in the time of Beaumont and Fletcher, *maestre* was still very much alive in certain contexts', 'though indeed subordinate to *maestro*'. *Maestre* was a title of honour, taken from the Roman ('Es dignidad, y está tornada de aquella antigua de los romanos, *magister equitum*' (Covarrubias, *ibid.*). In the expression *maestre de campo* it denoted a high rank in the militia ('oficio grande en la milicia' (*ibid.*). 'The fact that Cacafogo is talking to two military men suggests. . . that he has in mind the *maestre de campo*, even though his knowledge of military ranks is a bit shaky.' 'The *a* here, though technically an ethical dative, is close to the so-called "personal *a*" which is used before all object nouns designating persons.' In context it is clear that Cacafogo, turning from Leon as a thing despised, takes a ceremonious departure from the other men: 'I grasp hands to Your Lordship (Don Juan, a colonel), [and] to you, Master (Alonzo, a captain).' (I am much indebted to Professor Wardropper's insights and assistance here.)

I.vi

20–21 Civill, Or] The misapprehension that the adjective was intended led the Folio compositor into his error: 'as fair, as civil, | As any town'. Had the Quarto used italics for place-names, the error would not have occurred. The same spelling for the city (Seville) is used also in *Love's Cure* (I.i.10) in F 1.

II.i

48 doughty] The *O.E.D.* describes the Q1 'doubty' as an erroneous spelling of 'doughty'; the Q1 spelling represents another word 'doubty', i.e., 'full of doubt', not the sense required here.

II.ii

35 plate] Though the Q1 'plates' is a possible reading (see *Antony and Cleopatra*, V.ii.92 TLN 3310), Mason's conjecture, adopted by Dyce and Bond, is surely correct. Perez speaks later of 'plate. . .jewels. . .hangings' (III.iv.44–5), and Leon describes the same *objets d'art* as 'hangings. . . plate. . .jewels' (III.i.41–2). The plural form here results evidently from contamination; the singular collective appears also at I.vi.14–15; III.v.166; IV.i.95–6; IV.iii.18, 60, 151.

II.iii

6 *Exit* Altea.]   Since Altea is required to enter in the direction immediately following, she must go off here. The '*Lady*' of the Quarto direction
cannot therefore be one of the Ladies who speak in lines 5 and 6. The
immediate re-entry after the exit-direction suggests, however, that Altea
does not actually leave the stage.

II.iv

0.1 Estifania.]   The Quarto adds '*with a paper*'. The paper is produced
at line 105. Since the paper has no purpose until that dramatic moment,
the direction for it here is a direction to the actor – not to the reader.
The direction for the reader appears at line 105. Bond observes: 'at present
Estifania has no need of it, not expecting Margarita for a week'. We must
suppose that Estifania always carries a bit of paper with her for use in
just such emergencies. See also Introduction (p. 487) and IV.i.4.1 and
V.iv.0.1 (and Textual Note on the latter), and *Cupid's Revenge*, V.iv.0.1–
73.1, for the same kind of early notice.

21+1]   All editors have agreed that at least one line is lost here. Seward
added 'A Lady-tamer He, and reads Men warnings', a conjecture serviceable
enough and one that has been accepted by all editors. In Lamb's copy of
F2, S. T. Coleridge has suggested 'The best on't tis [*sic*], he professes to
teach husbands'. Both of these conjectures derive from Perez' description
of himself:

> Have I so long studied the art of this sex,
> And read the warnings to young Gentlemen:
> Have I profest to tame the pride of Ladies...?
> (III.iv.67–9)

Objection to either of the guesses is profitless, but it might be noted that
'read the warnings' does not necessarily mean 'read warnings to men'
or 'teach husbands'. It is as likely that Perez' activities have been to study
and to read: the former so that he may know the arts of women, the latter
so that he may be acquainted with the warnings that have been prepared
for gentlemen like himself. It is certain that his attitude (in II.ii) to his
unmarried friends is not admonitory. After he discovers that he has been
duped, he then proposes to 'read men warnings': 'That men might run
away from the contagion' (V.ii.3). Another conjecture might hit the mark
more closely than its predecessors have: 'For he has studied well the rules
men use,'.

91.1 *Kisses*.]   Though the dialogue makes clear that Perez kisses Margarita,
the Q1 direction is only '*kisses*.' As the catchword, '*Estif.*' is immediately

below the direction, Saintsbury misread the lines as '*Kisses Estif.*', noting
a supposed Quarto error. Since Weber, editors have read '*Kisses her.*'
120 help?] The Folio adds a dash to Quarto 'help', reading 'help——',
one of few dashes added in that edition. The addition is erroneous; it
supposes an interrupted speech, and that supposition is based on the notion
that 'let' means 'allow'; it means 'hinder' or 'impede', as Colman saw.

III.i

0.1 *and Boy*] Dyce is certainly correct in supposing that 'the Boy is
introduced...merely for the purpose of singing a song'. Bond, concurring,
adds the direction at line 24; the present edition provides also for the Boy's
exit. The text of the song would presumably accommodate itself to
Margarita's wish to be wanton and so provoke her question about the
couch.
24 Duke] See textual note at III.v.0.1.
50 husband...fellow] Professor Bowers provides the following interpretation of this speech of Leon's:

'Leon is agreeing with the Servant that the Servant's hat need not be removed
since it is not necessarily a fashion to do so. He then continues in the same vein.
Even though I am her husband I am still regarded as your fellow, and hence it is
[acceptable] not to remove your hat or do other ceremonies. However, do I
not have some privileges, such as cutting first?'

Professor Bowers suggests that 'cut first' may have reference to dividing
a pack of cards, and Weber glossed it as 'to carve first at the servants'
table'; there is certainly a sexual meaning also (as at II.ii.8).
   If an argument could be sustained that the compositor had interchanged
the two offices and that the line should read 'though I be your fellow, I
am hir husband, I may cut first' the last words would be a statement of
privilege.

III.ii

58 fish-stall] The Q1 'stall-fish' has caused considerable editorial pain;
Bond surveys the tradition:

'Seward read *stale-fish shambles* in text and *stale fish-shambles* in his note, adding:
"A stall for fish and a fish-shambles seems to differ but as a part from the whole."
Colman *stall-fish*, *shambles*, inserting comma and explaining as two objects, "fish-
stall" and "butcher's shambles." Weber kept his comma, but explained *stall-fish*
(more reasonably) as a fish that has lain long on the stall and not in fresh water.
Dyce read *stale fish-shambles* without further comment. We retain the Q, F
reading, believing that one object is meant: "A place where stall-fish (in Weber's
sense) are destroyed."'

On the assumption that the compositor was confused by the repetition of *st* and *sh* forms in 'strong...restore...stink...fish-stall shambles... shop' and so by transposition produced the Quarto reading, the present edition reverses the elements in the hyphenated compound, providing thereby a clear reading requiring no gloss. A shambles is usually a place pertaining to meat and butchers, but Fletcher here uses the word in its rare association with fish. (The *O.E.D.* gives an example of such use in 1554.)

III.iv

78 Nor] F2 reads 'Not', but neither word is easily explained. The present edition preserves the Quarto text of this speech and of the preceding (in spite of the suggestions of earlier editors), but it divides the Old Woman's speech: the first half, aside, admits that the Old Woman has been lying (line 62); the second half, aloud, professes her honesty – another lie, of course.

III.v

0.1 Duke Medina] Though this form seemed curious to the compositors of both Q1 and F2 – the former inserting a comma to indicate two persons, the latter intruding 'of' – it is present in the dialogue (III.i.54; V.iii.27, 28; V.v.92), and by emendation in this edition (III.i.24; III.iii.38), where the omission of 'of' regularizes the metre.

64 had thought]   See textual note at IV.i.61.

81 It...better. *Leon.* I will]   The emendation of Seward, here adopted, which gives 'It shall be better,' to Margarita rather than to Leon, has been supported by Mason ('no doubt') and Bond; Colman, Coleridge, Dyce, and Saintsbury give the line to Leon. Weber, though he does not follow Seward's emendation, argues that it is 'very plausible' because 'the words "I will give none Madame," begin a new line, which renders it very probable that the speaker's name [*Leon.*] was accidentally placed a line higher than intended'. The Quarto lines:

> And so ile keep it.
> *Marg.* As you love mee give way.
> *Leon.* It shall be better,
> I will give none Madame,

It seems on balance likelier that the location of the prefix is wrong and the division of the line is right than that the location of the prefix is right and the division of the line is wrong. Some support for the emendation may derive from the near parallel in the conversation between Perez and Estifania in which she says: 'Nay, 'twill be better | If you will let me but dispose the businesse' (II.iv.72–3).

105–106 coach...Coach too]   Bond recognized that the Quarto 'draw your coach too, | And eat your Coach' would seem to be a 'mistake of the transcriber or printer', but like all earlier editors, he declined to follow Seward's emendation, printed in the present text. It is clear that the placing of 'too' after the first 'coach' and not the second is a compositorial anticipation. The emendation improves the metre of both lines.

152 *Juan. Don Michael—— Leon.* Another] The present text follows Dyce and Bond in dividing the line (printed in the Quarto as a single speech) between two speakers; Saintsbury thought their emendations 'ingenious' but very doubtful. It seems unlikely that '*Leon*', here a prefix, could ever have been intended as direct address, since the character is never addressed by his name in the entire play (he is referred to mockingly as '*Don Leon*' at I.i.10). Leon supposes that Perez, whom he scarcely knows (I.i.12; II.iv.86.1–132), is a darer as the Duke has been (III.v.132). There is, perhaps, an irony as well: in the parallel plots Leon and Perez are both darers, though Leon does not know it. The scansion of the line requires that '*Michael*' should be trisyllabic as it is at II.iv.70. See also IV.i.170.

197 *Juan.*] It is noteworthy that though Leon's invitation is extended to the Duke ('your grace'), the Duke, whose anger is not past (see IV.ii), does not reply. Juan, the good soldier, 'covers' the Duke's discourtesy.

IV.i

61 had thought] This passage and an earlier one, III.v.64, both suggest an error of compositorial anticipation, and as both are set by the same compositor (E4^v, F3^v), one is tempted to find him twice making the same error. However, as the contexts are identical, the anagnorises of the two plots – 'you had thought you had found a coxcomb' (Leon to Margarita); 'I had thought you had had infinite' (Estifania to Perez) – it is preferable to regard the form as characteristic of Fletcher. A third, minor, example occurs at V.v.126 – 'I had thought he had beene a devill' (Duke to Leon).

154 right] 'Right' is an adjective, parallel to 'fair and rich', as in 'wife you are a right one' (V.v.118). See also IV.i.116.

IV.ii

10 matter] Seward proposed 'maker', as in line 6; query: 'master'?

13 *Alonzo.* We] It is clear that Q1 is in error by providing a prefix for Sanchio at line 8 and another, presumably while he still is talking, at line 16. The simple solution, that of F2, is to drop the second prefix; the other solution, adopted in the present edition, is to provide a prefix for another speaker between the two. The addition of the prefix for Alonzo here is based on the assumption that it is likelier that the compositor overlooked a prefix at line 13 than that he invented one in the middle of line 16 and divided that line on two lines of type. At IV.i.124, there is a similar duplicated prefix. I have conjectured there that a speech has been lost; here I

believe we have the speech (lines 13–16). It seems awkward that Sanchio should say both 'We suffer all' (line 13) and 'We are gulld all' (line 16). See Textual Introduction (pp. 497–8 for comment on this and other duplicated prefixes.

IV.iii

17 *Lorenzo*.] Since something is required to occasion the entrance of Lorenzo, Sympson's conjecture, scanning easily, has been adopted by all editors. But Leon's phrase – 'Doe you heare ho' at line 13 – seems more a call to a servant off-stage than a remark to a servant standing by.

207 Thou] Editors for 200 years have struggled with this crux, but none of them has presented a solution acceptable to the majority of them; the present editor is in the same tradition. The seventeenth-century texts read:

> you have no more right than he
> Has, that senseless thing, your wife has once more fool'd ye.

Seward dropped the 'he', reading: 'no more right than has | That senseless thing'. He glossed 'thing' as 'a Chair, Table, or anything near her'. All subsequent editors have rejected that sort of inanimate reference, yet Colman, Weber, Dyce, retaining the 'he', let it refer to 'any indifferent person in [the] company', and so repeat the essence of Seward's error. Saintsbury, following Darley's text (which here seems to have misprinted Weber's), has imagined that 'your wife' is in apposition to 'That senseless thing', a reading untenable since Margarita would not call Estifania 'senseless' (in fact, we know her to be shrewd and ingenious). Bond adopts Mason's conjecture (in the present text), which does not answer two objections: 'that' is an unlikely misreading of 'thou'; and who is 'he'? Bond rejects the antecedent Leon after what seems the sincerity of lines 202–3 and suggests the Duke, who is her cousin (as Perez is not) and may well be thought by the audience to have some familial rights to the house. Such a reference to the Duke would, furthermore, seem a discourtesy to the Duke. Perhaps we must accept Bond's guess that 'he' is a misprinting for 'she'. (At II.iv.100 'she' is misprinted for 'he'.) But the change of pronoun does not relieve the problem of 'that'.

V.iii

2 contentedly] Though the Quarto reading is certainly intelligible, its metrical deficiency rings unpleasantly in these set speeches (lines 1–24) in which Fletcher has been at some pains to produce regularity. Of these lines, five are pentameters, one has an eleventh stressed syllable (line 15), one is hypermetrical with two unstressed final syllables, and seventeen are hypermetrical with one unstressed final syllable. This passage well exemplifies Bond's observation: 'The verse exhibits the most marked degree of

[Fletcher's]...special characteristics – a double or triple ending to almost every line, rarely a line run-on, and no prose at all' (p. 361). In this passage, crafted with particular care to be perfect Fletcher, a deficient line is not acceptable. The *O.E.D.* lists this passage as the sole entry for this 'rare' word, 'probably, as the metre suggests, merely an error for *contentedly*'. When Perez, the other 'wife-ruler', describes in a comparable context his sense of the quiet life, he uses the same word, 'contentedly' (II.ii.37).

9 cure]   The Quarto form results from an easy *u/a* misreading. One would scarcely expect a will that was sick to accomplish anything by aiming at the care of honour. Better that it should aim at the cure that honour provides. Colman thought the will, 'sick of its former pursuits', would aim at caring for her honour; Dyce thought Seward's emendation 'most unnecessary'.

59 haunted?]   Dyce and Bond have probably caught the sense of this difficult line: 'is it because it stands on fairy ground that we are haunted?'

82–83 reach'd at | Shalt]   I follow this reconstruction of Bond, having nothing preferable to offer. Though the 'And' of line 83 is not impossibly a compositor's duplication, 'Shalt' is no necessary replacement for it; 'reach', or even 'reache', is not a particularly easy misreading of 'reach'd'. Deighton conjectured 'reached at Shall'; Dyce was sure that a line was lost: 'not the smallest doubt'.

V.iv

0.1 Estifania].   As at II.iv and IV.i the Quarto presents a direction that is not appropriate before a later action in the scene. At line 25 the Quarto prints '*shewes a Pistoll*' (to which this edition adds from line 0.1 '*and a Dagge*'), and it is evident from Perez' reaction that he has seen neither weapon before. Perez speaks of 'gunnes' at line 27 and of 'thy gun' at line 31; still, as both are mentioned, both must be shown. (Weber, Dyce, and Bond provide a direction for Perez to draw his sword at line 1.)

V.v

77 name]   Why is there reluctance to name in the daylight? Should we read 'nimm' (i.e., 'steal')? Not a difficult minim error.

98 heere]   Q1 'heare' may reflect a variant spelling of 'heere' in the manuscript; it appears nowhere else in the Quarto. But I prefer to regard it as erroneous, influenced by the compositor's awareness of the under-stage sound-effects. This compositor's preference is 'here', but he sets 'heere' at IV.ii.3. ('deere', 'beere', lines 98, 99). An argument could be advanced that the line should read:

And all those deere delights you worship't. [*Noise below.*] Heare!

108–109 folly...sin]   The Quarto reads:

And find what tis to play the foole in folly
And see with cleere eyes your detested folly,

in which the repetition of 'folly' is a compositor's duplication. Colman and Saintsbury change the first 'folly' to 'vice' and Dyce and Bond change it to 'sin'; Seward and Weber change the second 'folly' to 'crime' and 'vice' (respectively). In the assumption that in a duplication of this sort it is at least as likely that the compositor repeated the first word in the second position as that he anticipated the second word in the first position, the present edition emends the second 'folly'. Though 'play the foole in folly' is somewhat tautological ('a poor expression at any rate' – Weber), Seward thought the phrase 'not unjustifiable'. I would suggest that as the earnestness of Margarita is here at its firmest, with the stronger adjective, 'detested', we need the stronger noun – i.e., 'crime', 'vice', 'sin' – and with the weaker phrase 'play the foole' the less reprehensible word, 'folly'. Someone indulging in an action detestable is not playing the fool, he is being criminal, vicious, or sinful, and his action must, therefore, be detested; it may not be regarded as foolish. It is perhaps likely also that the emendation should be a monosyllable; of those suggested, the word 'sin' in line 109 will copy the alliterative pattern of line 108, though Seward's conjectured 'crime' might be suitable. The same sort of compositorial duplication occurs at I.i.9–10 and perhaps at III.iii.11–12, all set by the same compositor.

158 *Margarita.*] It is clear that a prefix has been omitted here: Estifania, herself in service, does not reward someone else for service. Seward printed '*Leon.*', not unreasonably, but Coleridge's emendation, '*Margarita.*', is preferable; she it is, as Bond points out, who has received the money from Cacafogo (who gave it for ignoble ends; see V.v.6), and she it is to whom Estifania has been in service. It is, furthermore, dramatically effective to have Margarita give Estifania something after Leon has given Perez something – the two couples thus balance.

162 souldier.| *Gentlemen.* We]   From Seward's time the Quarto 'Gentleman,' has been admitted by all editors to be an error for 'Gentlemen', perhaps a simple misprint (as at IV.iii.130). The present edition follows Seward and Dyce in supposing the word to be a prefix; Colman, Weber, Saintsbury, and Bond retain the word as dialogue (as in the Quarto) and supply an additional prefix for 'We all rejoyce in't.' The resolution of these differences must arise from the acceptance of the hypothesis that the error derives not from the compositor's failure to include a prefix, but from his failure to recognize one when he saw it in the middle of the line of dialogue (as at III.v.152). No additional prefix is appropriate. Bond supposes that the word 'Gentlemen' (as dialogue in the line of text) 'led to the omission of "Gentlemen." (the prefix)', but the insertion of 'Gentlemen' in the text produces a metrical irregularity quite out of keeping with the regularity of the concluding lines of the play. It is more economical to suppose that the manuscript form in the line was 'Gent', abbreviated as for a prefix, and that the compositor mistook it for dialogue and expanded it, producing the erroneous singular 'Gentleman' in the process.

PRESS-VARIANTS IN Q1 (1640)

[Copies collated: BL (British Library 644.b.30), TCC (Trinity College, Cambridge), CSmH (Henry E. Huntington Library C11073/59779), DFo (Folger Shakespeare Library), NcWiW (Wake Forest University, Winston-Salem, North Carolina 151664), NjP (Princeton University), PU (University of Pennsylvania, Furness Collection)]

SHEET A (*outer forme*)

Uncorrected DFo

Sig. A1
line 8   Gent.] Gent:

SHEET B (*outer forme*)

First State PU

Sig. B2ᵛ
I.v.0.1   *Le n] Leon*

SHEET E (*inner forme*)

Uncorrected BL, DFo, NcWiW

Sig. E1ᵛ
III.iii.2 rime] ruine
Sig. E2
III.iii.51 laugh at him.] laugh him, leave ager.

SHEET I (*outer forme*)

Uncorrected NcWiW

Sig. I4ᵛ
Epi. 6 ſends] ſend

EMENDATIONS OF ACCIDENTALS

Dramatis Personæ

2 *Medina*] of *Modena* Q2
5 *Cacafogo*] *Cacofogo* Q2
7 *Alonzo*] *Alonso* Q2

12 *Donna*] *om.* Q2
15 Two Ladies] First Lady, | Second
Lady, Q2 (*after line* 12)

Prologue

22 *fool'd,*] F2; ~ ∧ Q1

25 *friends,*] F2; ~ ∧ Q1

I.i

I.i] ACTUS. 1. SCENA. 1 Q1; *Actus*
Primus. Scena Prima. F2; ACT
1. SCENE 1. Q2
1 (*et seq. this scene*) *Perez.*] *Mich.*
Qq, F2
3–6 We...goe.] Qq, F2 *line:* We
...out, | We have...thinke |
We shall...goe.
5 too;] ~ , Qq, F2
8 visions;] Q2; ~ , Q1, F2
15 *Michael,*] F2; ~ ∧ Q1
18 lesse;] Q2; ~ , Q1, F2
22 be;] Q2; ~ , Q1, F2
28 heiresse?] F2; ~ . Q1
30 discourse;] ~ , Q1; ~ : F2, Q2
39 wife;] ~ , Q1; ~ : F2, Q2
42 Sir...yee.] Qq, F2 *line:* Sir...
speak | With yee.
45 put'st] F2; putst' Q1
49–50 Say...then?] *one line in* Qq,
F2
50 then?] F2; ~ . Q1
53.1 Donna∧] F2; *Donna,* Q1
56–57 May...preludium.] Qq, F2
line: May...picke, | I am...
preludium.

58 With...Lady?] Qq, F2 *line:*
With...gentleman, | would...
Lady?
71.1 Juan∧] *Iuan.* Q1; ~ , F2,
Q2
80–81 You must...selfe.] Qq, F2
line: You must...come | Not
...selfe.
81–82 As...souldier.] *one line in*
Qq, F2
90 open?——] ~ ? ∧ Qq, F2
91 modesty——] ~ , Q1; ~ ; F2,
Q2
92 sure;——] ~ ; ∧ Qq, F2
92 me∧] F2; ~ ? Q1
97 repentance——] ~ . Qq, F2
103 you;] F2; ~ , Q1
103.1 *beside lines* 102–103 *in* Q1; *on*
line 102.1 *in* F2, Q2
106 servant.] ~ , Q1; ~ ; F2, Q2
111 hands,——] ~ , ∧ Qq, F2
112 you?] F2; ~ . Q1
113 *Don*] F2; *don* Q1
114 it,] ~ ∧ Q1; ~ . F2, Q2
124.1 *Exeunt*] F2; *Exit* Q1

I.ii

1 What,] F 2; ~ ∧ Q 1
2 me;] ~ , Q 1; ~ . F 2, Q 2
8 Of...whoring?] Qq, F 2 *line:*
   Of...thou | Never...whoring?
12 Do'st] D'ost Q 1; Dost F 2, Q 2
12–13 Do'st...points?] Qq, F 2
   line: Do'st...they | Hung...
   points.

13 points?] ~ . Qq, F 2
17 abundantly?] F 2; ~ , Q 1
22 *Margaretta*] F 2; Margaretta Q 1
40–42 And...first] Qq, F 2 *line:*
   And...Gentlewoman | That
   ...word. | Send...first.
44.1 *Exeunt*] F 2; *Exit* Q 1

I.iii

0.1 Servant] F 2; *servant* Q 1
3 s.d. *beside lines* 2–3 *in* Q 1; *on*
   line 2.1 *in* F 2, Q 2

10 abundantly,...fortune.] ~ ....
   ~ , Q 1; ~ : ...~, F 2, Q 2

I.iv

Prefixes for the Old Ladies *are simple*
numerals in Q 1; F 2, Q 2 *add* '*Lady*'
0.1 Old Ladies] *old Ladies* Qq, F 2
1 What...for?] Qq, F 2 *line:*

What...hast | We...for?
17 ancientst,] F 2; ~ ∧ Q 1
23 And...ye.] Qq, F 2 *line:* And
   ...counsell, | Wele...ye.

I.v

0.1 Leon] F 2; Le n Q 1
7 Asse,——] ~ , ∧ Qq, F 2
12–13 I think...Sir.] *one line in* Qq,
   F 2
13 man,——] ~ , ∧ Q 1, F 2; ~ . ∧
   Q 2
26 strikes] striks Q 1; strike F 2, Q 2
26 me∧] ~ , Qq, F 2
27 s.d. *on line* 26.1 *in* Q1q, F 2
28 there,] F 2; ~ ∧ Q 1
29–32 The spirit...spoonefulls.]
   Qq, F 2 *line:* The spirit...
   warres | By...Pumpion, | Let
   ...sonne | Of...butterd, |
   Cannot...spoonefulls.

29 then.] F 2; ~ , Q 1
29.1 *beside* warres (*line* 29) *in* Q 1;
   on line below wars *in* F 2, Q 2
31 *Cacafogo*;] ~ , Qq, F 2
34 Monyes...captaines.] Qq, F 2
   line: Monyes...too, | Captaines.
38 not;——] ~ , ∧ Qq, F 2
47 You...fellow.] Qq, F 2 *line:*
   You...beat | This fellow.
50–51 I leave...*Maistre*.] *prose in*
   Qq, F 2
50–51 *asso* | *Les*] *assoles* Qq, F 2
51 *Siniare*,] *siniare*∧ Qq, F 2
60.1 *Exeunt*] *Exit* Qq, F 2

I.vi

1 Lady,] Q2; ~ ∧ Q1, F2
9–10 Tis...place.] *one line in* Qq, F2
9 *Estifania*] Q2; *Estifanie* Q1, F2
10 it?] F2; ~ , Q1
19 house;] ~ , Qq, F2
22 hopes,——] ~ , ∧ Qq, F2
26 presently——] ~ , Qq, F2
27 ever,——] ~ , ∧ Qq, F2
30 comfort;] F2; ~ , Q1
30 staires?] F2; ~ . Q1
39 else;] ~ , Qq, F2
41–42 I am...commanded,] Qq, F2 *line:* I am...well, | How... commanded,

46 husband;] ~ , Qq, F2
50–51 Sweet...Lady,] Qq, F2 *line:* Sweet...stick | To...Lady,
56 Ladies.] Q2; ~ , Q1, F2
58 mee:] ~ , Q1; ~ . F2, Q2
59–63 Qq, F2 *line:* 'Tis...wealth | With...warre | Has...dare | Presume...your | Care...as | Any...Lady.
65–66 Pray...sudden.] *one line in* Qq, F2
66–67 And...too.] *one line in* Qq, F2
74 wench——] ~ . Qq, F2

II.i

Prefixes for the two Old Ladies *are numerals in* Q1; F2, Q2 *add* '*Lady*'.

II.i.] ACTUS 2. SCENA 1. Q1; *Actus Secundus. Scena Prima.* F2; ACT II. SCENE 1. Q2
0.1 Margarita] F2; *Margaretta* Q1
7–8 But...all——] Qq, F2 *line:* But...shall | Ceaze...me | Of all——
8 all——] ~ . Qq, F2
9 way?] F2; ~ . Q1
16 single?] ~ . Qq, F2
19 at?] F2; ~ . Q1
19–20 Yes...woman?] *one line in* Qq, F2

19 Yes;] ~ ∧ Qq, F2
20 woman?] F2; ~ . Q1
22 it?] F2; ~ . Q1
23 then?] F2; ~ , Q1; ~ ∧ Q2
24 (*et seq. this scene*) *Altea.*] F2 (*some form of the name*); 4. Q1
25 yee?] F2; ~ . Q
26 faith,] F2; ~ ∧ Q
30 man?] ~ . Qq, F2
30–31 Yes...perfection.] Qq, F2 *line:* Yes...rare | Perfection.
51 understand∧] F2; ~ , Q1
53–54 No...him,] *one line in* Qq, F2

II.ii

1 indeed?] F2; ~ . Q1
5 wedding?] F2; ~ . Q1
7 seducer,] ~ ∧ Qq, F2
9 vaile?] F2; ~ . Q1
9 *Basta*] Basto Qq, F2
11 too?] F2; ~ . Q1

14 now?] F2; ~ . Q1
23 still.——] ~ , ∧ Q1; ~ ? ∧ F2, Q2
24 merry?] F2; ~ . Q1
27 If...thee.] Qq, F2 *line:* If... lesse | Come to thee.

39 Jewell,——] ~ , ∧ Qq, F 2
40 thee;——] ~ , ∧ Qq, F 2
43 I...*Alonzo*,] Qq, F 2 *line:* I...

yee | For...*Alonzo*,
43 bootes:——] ~ , ∧ Qq, F 2
46 him;] ~ , Qq, F 2

II.iii

1 (*et seq. this scene*) *Altea*.] F 2
(*some form of the name*); 4. Q 1
5–6 Is...likely man.] *one line in*
Qq, F 2
7 ——pray...way,——] ∧ ~ ...
~ , ∧ Qq, F 2
8 body,——] ~ , ∧ Qq, F 2
8 tame?] F 2; ~ . Q 1
10 Fit...done.] Qq, F 2 *line:* Fit
...harme | Done.
11 Lady?——] ~ ? ∧ Qq, F 2
26 of?] F 2; ~ . Q 1
27 kisses,——] ~ , ∧ Qq, F 2
28 ——I...sir,——] ∧ ~ ... ~ ,
∧ Qq, F 2
29 manly,——] ~ , ∧ Qq, F 2
34 Nay,] ~ ∧ Qq, F 2

37 master] Q 2 (Master); M^r. Q 1, F 2
42 head,] F 2; ~ ∧ Q 1
46 these?] F 2; ~ . Q 1
50–51 I will...sufficiently.] *one
line in* Qq, F 2
54–55 ——a strong...lips:——]
∧ ~ ... ~ : ∧ Qq, F 2
57–58 No...contented,] *one line in*
Qq, F 2
60–61 Tis...speak] *one line in* Qq,
F 2
60–61 ——The...speak∧——] ∧
~ ... ~ . ∧ Qq, F 2
63 instantly,——] ~ , ∧ Qq, F 2
64–65 But...lawes.] Qq, F 2 *line:*
But...wait, | Upon...lawes.
66 um,——] ~ , ∧ Qq, F 2

II.iv

1 What,] F 2; ~ ∧ Q 1
7 him?] F 2; ~ . Q 1
8 What,] ~ ∧ Qq, F 2
33 Spaine] *Spaine* Qq, F 2
36 fountain.——] ~ ∧ ∧ Q 1; ~ . ∧
F 2, Q 2
44 health?] F 2; ~ , Q 1
45 Sir?] F 2; ~ . Q 1; ~ , Q 2
46 suspect?] ~ , Qq, F 2
60.1 *on line* 61 *in* Qq, F 2
61 doore?] F 2; ~ . Q 1
69 *Mars*] F 2; Mars Q 1
74 me;] ~ , Qq, F 2
75 fortune?] F 2; ~ . Q 1
78 leave ye,——] ~ , ∧ Qq, F 2
84–86 Nor...has.] Qq, F 2 *line:*
Nor...to | Our...she | Works
...has.

87–89 Who...too.] Qq, F 2 *line:*
Who...woman | Of...big |
For...too.
87 things]? ~, Qq, F 2
92–94 Sir...her.] Qq, F 2 *line:* Sir
...now, | And...cozen, | That
...her.
98 curtesie;] Q 2; ~ , Q 1; ~ . F 2
103–104 Yeeld...wealth?] *one line in*
Qq, F 2
104 wealth?] F 2; ~ . Q 1
105 writing?] ~ , Qq, F 2
106 Two hundred pound] 200^l Qq,
F 2
108 house?] F 2; ~ . Q
112 wife?] F 2; ~ , Q 1
114 'vantage;] ~ , Q 1; ~ . F 2, Q 2
115 daies?] F 2; ~ . Q 1

118 *Perez̦.*] *not indented in* Q 1
118 back——] ~ . Qq, F 2
119 on;] ~ , Qq, F 2
120 help?] ~ , Q 1; ~ —— F 2, Q 2

123–124 I am...too.] *one line in* Qq,
    F 2
132.1 *beside* neat. *in line* 134 *in* Qq, F 2
133 sweet,] ~ ₐ Qq, F 2

III.i

III.i] ACTUS 3. SCENA I Q 1; *Actus*
    Tertius. Scena Prima. F 2; ACT
    III. SCENE I. Q 2
4 credit?] ~ . Qq, F 2
7 happy;] ~ , Qq, F 2
11 (*et seq. in this scene*) *Altea.*] F 2
    (*some form of the name*); 4. Q 1
14 conceal'd——] ~ . Qq, F 2
21–24 And...sent?] Qq, F 2 *line:*
    And...roomes | Made...now |
    And...up, | The...sent?
21 too;] ~ , Q 1; ~ . F 2, Q 2
22 friends?] F 2; ~ , Q 1
23 song.] ~ , Qq, F 2
27 pleasures;] ~ ₐ Q 1; ~ , F 2, Q 2
31 wil;] ~ , Q 1; ~ : F 2, Q 2
36 him.] F 2; ~ , Q 1; ~ : Q 2
36.1 *beside 'Altea.' on line* 35 *in* Q 1;
    on line below him. *in line* 35 *in*
    F 2, Q 2
38 too?] F 2; ~ . Q 1
42 lustre?] F 2; ~ . Q 1
47 masques?] ~ . Qq, F 2

52 her?] ~ . Qq, F 2
63, 65, 68 2. *Lady*] F 2 (2 *Lady*); 2.
    Q 1
63 *Julia*——] ~ . Qq, F 2
67–68 Tell...her.] *one line in* Qq,
    F 2
71 presence——] ~ , Q 1, F 2; ~ :
    Q 2
93 me,] F 2; ~ ₐ Q 1
94 husbands?] F 2; ~ , Q 1
108 dowe?] ~ , Q 1, F 2 (dow), Q 2
    (dough)
112 now?] F 2; ~ . Q 1
113–115 This...reasons.] Qq, F 2
    line: This...blowne | Into...
    wine, | 'Tis...findes | Out
    reasons.
132–133 I see...to see.] *one line in*
    Qq, F 2
133–134 You...Ladyship.] *one line*
    in Qq, F 2
141 rascalls ₐ] F 2; ~ , Q 1

III.ii

1 againe?] F 2; ~ , Q 1
7–8 immediatly;...too,] ~ , ...
    ~ ; Q 1, F 2; ~ ;...~ ; Q 2
13 jewell,——] ~ , Qq, F 2
22 company;] ~ , Q 1; ~ . F 2, Q 2
33 mee;] ~ , Q 1; ~ . F 2, Q 2

33 s.d. *on line below line* 32 *in* Qq,
    F 2
34 agen?] F 2; ~ . Q 1
42 Cannibals?] F 2; ~ . Q 1
59 ——which...nothing,——] ₐ
    ~ ...~ , ₐ Qq, F 2

III.iii

0.1 Sanchio] *Sancho* Qq, F 2
2 reason?] F 2; ~ . Q 1; ~ , Q 2
6–7 Why...bond.] *one line in* Qq,
    F 2
14 build;] ~ , Q 1; ~ : F 2, Q 2

21 home ₐ] F 2; ~ , Q 1
22 gentleman] gentle- | man Q 1
26 Justice?] F 2; ~ . Q 1
26–27 Is't...one ?] *one line in* Qq,
    F 2

27 one?] F 2; ~ , Q 1
30 fury?] F 2; ~ . Q 1
31 us?] F 2; ~ . Q 1
31–33 I...respected,] Q 2, F 2 *line:*
  I...orient | Faire...respected,
37–38 The Duke dines... *Medina.*]
  one line in Q 2, F 2

40 own,] F 2; ~ ∧ Q 1
45 Ladies;] F 2; ~ , Q 1
51 laugh him.] laugh him, Q 1; *var.*
  F 2, Q 2
51–52 If...too.] *one line in* Q 1, F 2
52 gentlemen?] F 2; ~ . Q 1

III.iv

4 spirit?] F 2; ~ . Q 1
5 open?] F 2; ~ . Q 1
7 Jewels,——] ~ , ∧ Q 1; ~ : ∧
  F 2, Q 2
8 belches∧] ~ , Qq, F 2
10 question?] F 2; ~ , Q 1
12 sir?] F 2; ~ , Q 1
13 here?] F 2; ~ . Q 1
13–14 Is she...wife?] *one line in*
  Qq, F 2
14 wife?] F 2; ~ , Q 1
16 spirit?] F 2; ~ . Q 1
23 Ladies;] ~ , Q; *om.* F 2 Q 2
23 wench?] ~ . Q; *om.* F 2, Q 2
26 plaid——] ~ . Qq, F 2
28 queane,——] ~ , ∧ Q; ~ ! ∧
  F 2, Q 2
30–31 She...faire.] *one line in* Qq,
  F 2

39 were——] F 2; ~ , Q 1
41–42 But...you?] Qq, F 2 *line:*
  But...worth | Owning...
  you?
42–43 Her...saw] *one line in* Qq,
  F 2
44–45 No plate...hangings?] *one
  line in* Qq, F 2
45–46 Not...thing.] *one line in* Qq,
  F 2
58–60 Litle...living,] Qq, F 2 *line:*
  Litle...because | She is...
  firkt | A pretty living,
71 nooze?] F 2; ~ , Q 1
74 box;] ~ , Q 1; ~ : F 2, Q 2
77–78 And...truth.] *one line in*
  Qq, F 2
77 it,——] ~ , ∧ Qq, F 2

III.v

0.2 Sanchio] F 2; *Sancho* Q 1
6 mansion?] F 2; ~ , Q 1
18 ye,] F 2; ~ . Q 1
20 'Tas] Tas Q 1; 'T has F 2, Q 2
40 *Alferes?*] F 2; *Alferes:* Q 1
41–42 Why...you.] *one line in* Qq,
  F 2
57 too?] F 2; ~ , Q 1
62 age;] F 2; ~ , Q 1
62 shadow,] ~ . Q 1; ~ ; F 2, Q 2
75 house?] F 2; ~ . Q 1
76–77 You...Madam,] Qq, F 2
  line: You...in't, | You...
  Madam,

93 image?] F 2; ~ , Q 1
99–100 Brave...now.] Qq, F 2
  line: Brave...lead | In chiefe
  now.
101 sir?] F 2; ~ . Q 1
115–116 They...pitty,] *one line in*
  Qq, F 2
124 mee;] ~ , Qq, F 2
125 princely?] F 2; ~ , Q 1
129–130 I...me.] *one line in* Qq, F 2
140 him;] ~ , Q 1; . F 2; ~ : Q 2
149–151 Save...her.] Qq, F 2 *line:*
  Save...house. | That's...
  Lady, | If...her.

150 house?] F 2; ~ . Q 1
152 Michael——] ~ ∧ Qq, F 2
155 woman,——] ~ , ∧ Q; ~ : ∧
    F 2, Q 2
159 knew;] ~ , Qq, F 2
161 her,] F 2; ~ ∧ Q 1
162 halter;] ~ , Q 1; ~ : F 2, Q 2
163 it?] ~ , Qq, F 2

172 hir?] F 2; ~ . Q 1
177 yet?] F 2; ~ . Q 1
181 prattle,——] ~ , ∧ Qq, F 2
182 you?] F 2 ~ . Q 1
182–183 Yes. . .her,] one line in Qq,
    F 2
192 hast,——] ~ , ∧ Qq, F 2

IV.i

IV.i] ACTUS 4. SCENA I. Q 1; Actus
    Quartus. Scena Prima. F 2; ACT
    IV. SCENE I. Q 2
4.1 s.d. on line below 5 in Qq, F 2
13 howses——] ~ . Qq, F 2
13–14 I beleeve. . .too.] one line in
    Q, F 2
15 Ladiship;] ~ , Qq, F 2
27 now:] F 2; ~ ∧ Q 1
30 drunk,] F 2; ~ ∧ Q 1
41 diseases∧ base,] ~ , ~ , Q 1; ~ ,
    ~ ∧ F 2, Q 2
47 nothing,——] ~ , ∧ Q; ~ . ∧
    F 2, Q 2
50 cozend?] F 2; ~ , Q 1
50 abused?] F 2; ~ . Q 1
51 abominable——] F 2; ~ , Q 1
52 pocky——] F 2; ~ . Q 1
55 knavery?] F 2; ~ . Q 1
56 too?] F 2; ~ . Q 1
64 to me?] F 2; ~ . Q 1
65 (It. . .Sir)] F 2; ∧ ~ . . .~ , Q 1
68 cloathes?] F 2; ~ . Q 1
72 usage?] F 2; ~ , Q 1

80–81 A. . .crafty.] one line in Qq,
    F 2
82 Goletta] Goletta Qq, F 2
109 honest?] F 2; ~ , Q 1
110 swore——] ~ . Qq, F 2
112 too——] ~ . Qq, F 2
114 house?] ~ . Qq, F 2
117 me?] F 2; ~ . Q
124 May] F 2; Estif. May Q 1
128 so,] F 2; ~ . Q
129 Palmerin;] Palmerin, Q 1, F 2;
    Palmerin, Q 2
139 (Love. . .togither),] ∧ ~ . . .
    ~ ∧, Qq, F 2
145 Margarita——] ~ , Qq, F 2
148 sir——] ~ . Qq; ~ , F 2
151–152 noble——. . .Mistris——]
    ~ . . . .~ , Qq, F 2
154 (view um)] ∧. . .∧ Qq, F 2
154 right——] ~ . Qq, F 2
157–158 She. . .person,] one line in
    Qq, F 2
159 honour——] ~ . Qq, F 2
162 sir——] ~ . Q, F 2

IV.ii

3 strangely;] ~ , Qq, F 2
9–10 And. . .undoing,] Qq, F 2
    line: And. . .prison, | Was. . .
    undoing,

9 price,] ~ ∧ Qq, F 2
12 beauties?] F 2; ~ , Q 1
20 orbe:] F 2; ~ , Q 2
21 slubberd?] F 2; ~ . Q 1

IV.iii

7 company;] ~ , Qq, F 2
12 ready?] F 2; ~ . Q 1
13–14 Doe...sir,] *one line in* Qq,
F 2
24 sir?] F 2; ~ . Q 1
27 Saint *Jaques*] St Jaques Q 1; S^t
Jaques F 2; St. *Jaques* Q 2
28 ye——...too?] ~ ₐ...~ . Qq,
F 2
30 *Vasco*] F 2; *vasco* Q
36 preferment?] F 2; ~ , Q 1
44 am——] ~ . Qq, F 2
49 kisses?] F 2; ~ , Q
50–51 Ile...King.] *one line in* Qq,
F 2
52 for't;...now ₐ] ~ ,...~ , Qq,
F 2
56 *Knock*] *knock* Q 1, F 2; *knocks* Q 2
57 this?] F 2; ~ , Q 1
65 goe?] F 2; ~ ₐ Q 1
69 sweet?] F 2; ~ , Q 1
69–70 ——are...linnens?——] ₐ
~ ...~ ? ₐ Qq, F 2
76 warning?] F 2; ~ , Q 1
77 winde?] F 2; ~ , Q 1
84–85 You...that.] *one line in* Qq,
F 2
101 huswifely——] ~ . Qq, F 2

108 too?] F 2; ~ . Q 1
110 Away,] ~ ₐ Qq, F 2
113 With...were able——] Qq, F 2
line: With...warre? | I...were
able——
113 warre?] ~ . Qq, F 2
113 able——] ~ . Qq, F 2
124 What] F 2; *Leon.* What Q 1
126 *Owle*] *owle* Qq, F 2
148 entreat ₐ] ~ , Qq, F 2
150 uses;] ~ , Qq, F 2
159 phantastick——] F 2; ~ , Q 1
159 house?] F 2; ~ . Q 1
170 distemper,] ~ ₐ Q 1; ~ ; F 2;
~ ? Q 2
176 doe?] F 2; ~ , Q 1
181 more,——] ~ , ₐ Qq, F 2
183 yee,——] ~ , ₐ Qq, F 2
185–186 Am...cozen,] *one line in*
Qq, F 2
186 cozen,] F 2; ~ ₐ Q 1
206–207 I tell...ye:] Qq, F 2 *line:*
I tell...he | Has...ye:
208–209 Good...sir——] *one line*
in Qq, F 2
209 sir——] ~ . Qq, F 2
213 ye,——] ~ , ₐ Qq, F 2

V.i

V.i.] ACTUS. 5. SCENA. 1. Q 1; *Actus*
Quintus. Scena Prima. F 2; ACT
V. SCENE I. Q 2
5–6 Is a...mountaines.] *one line in*
Qq, F 2
7 people?——] ~ , ₐ Q; ~ ? ₐ
F 2, Q 2

12–13 And so...my will.] *one line*
in Qq, F 2
14 think?] F 2; ~ . Q 1
16 faire, wife:——] ~ ₐ ~ : ₐ Qq,
F 2

V.ii

7 credit;] ~ , Q 1; ~ . F 2,
  Q 2
8 now?] F 2; ~ , Q 1
12 um,] 'em, F 2; um ₍ Q 1
26 undone?] F 2; ~ , Q 1
32 laugh?] F 2; ~ ₍ Q 1
33 spirit?] ~ ₍ Qq, F 2
33–34 I . . . woman,] one line in Qq,
  F 2
36 still?] F 2; ~ . Q 1
37–38 I shall be . . . cause.] one line
  in Qq, F 2

38–39 Thats . . . angry,] one line in
  Qq, F 2
44 woman?] F 2; ~ . Q 1
51 Europe] Europe Qq, F 2
53 merry?] F 2; ~ . Q 1
57 Duckets?] F 2; ~ . Q 1
57 take——] ~ ₍ Qq, F 2
58–59 Ile . . . Ducket.] Qq, F 2 line:
  Ile . . . halfe ten, | Halfe a Ducket.
65–67 (as . . . variety,)] F 2; ₍ ~ . . .
  ~ , ₍ Q 1
68 neatly;] ~ , Qq, F 2

V.iii

12 embraces;] ~ , Q 1; ~ . F 2, Q 2
24.1 Downe] downe Q 1, F 2
25.1 beside lines 23–25 in Qq, F 2
25 cry?] F 2; ~ . Q 1
26 street,] F 2; ~ ₍ Q 1
28 Medina?] F 2; ~ . Q 1
28–29 Oh . . . slain.] one line in Qq,
  F 2
29–30 A way . . . house help.] one
  line in Qq, F 2
31 wife,——] ~ , ₍ Qq, F 2
39 thus;] ~ ₍ Qq, F 2
47 Exeunt] Exit Q 1; Ex. F 2, Q 2
51 anger;] F 2; ~ , Q 1
55 honour ye.] F 2; ~ ~ , Q 1

56 quiet?] F 2; ~ . Q 1
60 thus?] F 2; ~ . Q 1
62 patience?] F 2; ~ , Q 1
63 thus?] ~ , Qq, F 2
65 for?] F 2; ~ . Q 1
77 containe ye?] F 2; ~ , Q 1
87 Kneeles] kneeles Qq, F 2
90 noblenesse——] ~ . Qq, F 2
90–92 I . . . you?] Qq, F 2 line: I . . .
  heart, | See . . . you?
91.1 on line below noblenesse——
  in line 90 Qq, F 2
94 Cacafogo,] F 2; ~ ₍ Q 1
100 both;] ~ , Qq, F 2

V.iv

7 But . . . mee;] Qq, F 2 line: But
  . . . me, | And . . . mee,
7 mee;] ~ , Qq, F 2
8 sheep-biting] F 2; sheep biting
  Q 1
25 Shewes] shewes Qq, F 2
26 spirit?] F 2; ~ . Q 1

27 gunnes?] F 2; ~ . Q 1
32 feele——] ~ . Qq, F 2
32–33 Hold . . . husband?] one line
  in Qq, F 2
35 you?] ~ , Qq, F 2
37 Jewels?] ~ , Qq, F 2

V.v

1 come?] F 2; ~ . Q 1
7 *Margarita*] F 2; Margarita Q 1
9–10 Secure. . .silence.] Qq, F 2
line: Secure. . .candle, | Passe
. . .silence.
10 *Exeunt*] *Exit* Q; *Ex.* F 2, Q 2
11 there?] ~ , Qq, F 2
12 comfort?] F 2; ~ . Q 1
14 s.d. *beside* my Lord *in line* 12 *in*
Q; *on line below line* 13 *in* F 2, Q 2
14 you?] F 2; ~ . Q 1
14 here?] F 2; ~ , Q 1
15 *Noise*] *noise* Qq, F 2
16 friend?] F 2; ~ . Q 1
17 tumble?] F 2; ~ , Q 1
20 hogs-head] F 2; hogs head Q 1
21 out,——] ~ , ∧ Q 1; ~ . ∧ F 2,
Q 2
22 feare?] F 2; ~ , Q 1
23 wounds?] F 2; ~ . Q 1
26 s.d. *beside* cunningly, *in line* 24
in Qq, F 2
27 pale?] F 2; ~ , Q 1
27 stirring;] ~ , Qq, F 2
28 tipled,——] ~ , ∧ Q 1; ~ . ∧ F 2,
Q 2
30 wounds——] ~ . Qq, F 2
30–31 I have. . .health,] *one line in*
Qq, F 2
32 blood——] ~ . Qq, F 2
34 Lady——] ~ . Qq, F 2
37 think?] F 2; ~ . Q 1
41 make?] F 2; ~ , Q 1
43 deluded?] F 2; ~ , Q 1
55 then?] F 2; ~ . Q 1
63–65 For. . .presently,] Qq, F 2

line: For. . .counterfeit, | One
. . .honour | He. . .presently,
64 credit,] ~ ∧ Qq, F 2
65 honour∧] ~ , Qq, F 2
68 guilty;] ~ , Qq, F 2
69 now?] F 2; ~ . Q 1
70 more——] ~ ∧ Qq, F 2
77 light?] F 2; ~ . Q 1
81 yours?] F 2; ~ , Q 1
107 Have] F 2; have Q 1
107 mercy?] F 2; ~ . Q 1
113–114 I may. . .so.] *one line in* Qq,
F 2
114 Lord?] ~ , Qq, F 2
116 ye?] ~ , Qq, F 2
121–122 Tis. . .it.] *one line in* Qq,
F 2
126 devill,] Q 2; ~ . Q 1, F 2
128 lowdly,——] ~ , ∧ Qq, F 2
129 Mistris?] F 2; ~ . Q 1
131 face !] ~ ? Q 1; ~ . F 2, Q 2
132 drunke,] F 2; ~ ∧ Q 1
134.1 *Exeunt*] *Exit.* Q 1; *Exit* F 2,
Q 2
135 Who's] *Leon.* Who's Qq, F 2
161 Sir.] ~ , Qq, F 2
166 I. . .Mistris.] Qq, F 2 line: I. . .
bloud, | And. . .Mistris.
168 And. . .wench,] Qq, F 2 *line:*
And. . .sister, | For. . .wench,
172 sister,——] ~ , ∧ Qq, F 2
175 *Neptune*] F 2; Neptune Q 1
178 And. . .servants.] Qq, F 2 *line:*
And. . .know | We. . .servants.
179–180 And. . .blinde.] *italic in* Qq,
F 2

Epilogue

8 *To*. . .*hast.*] lined as in F 2, Q 2; Q 1 lines: *To*. . .*spight* | *Wives*. . .*hast.*

HISTORICAL COLLATION

[This collation against the present text includes the three seventeenth-century
editions (Q1, 1640; F2, 1679; Q2, 1697), and the editions of Langbaine
(L, 1717), Theobald, Seward and Sympson (S, 1750), Colman (C, 1778),
Weber (W, 1812), Dyce (D, 1843), Bond (*Variorum*) (V, 1908), and Saintsbury (in Gayley, *Representative English Comedies*) (G, 1914). Omission of a
siglum indicates that the text concerned agrees with the reading of the lemma.]

Prologue

11 *her*] *your* Q1
12 *raigne*] *raignes* Q1

13 *W'are*] *You're* S, C, W
17 *slip*] slipt W, G

I.i

2 not] *om.* Q2
9 numbers] numbers up S
10 strong] strange Q1+(−C)
23 strong] stout S
25 mouths] mouth Q1
32 and wealthy] ad wealthy Q2
40 subtlest] subtle F2−C
42 yee] you F2+(−V)
43 them] 'em F2+
52 But] But for S
55 heather] hither F2+
56 to raise] *om.* L

56 picke] Pike F2+
83 you be] be S
103.1 *and Servants*] *a Servant* Qq,
    F2, V; *and Servant* L, S, C, W,
    G; *om.* D
104 hath] has Q2
105 ye] you F2+(−V)
111.1 *and Servants*] *and Servant* L, S,
    C, W, G; *To Servants within* D,
    V
114 i'th'clipse] i'th'eclipse C−G

I.ii

3 amongst] among L−W, G
6 biskets] Bisket Q2
12 thou see] see S
13 As] As if S

16 Do'st thou] Dost S
23 Yes] *om.* F2, Q2 L
44 Farewell] so, farewell S

I.iii

1 mine] my F2+(−V)

5 well] will Q2, G

I.iv

0.1 Old Ladies] *old Ladies* Q 1+
2 Belike] Be like L, S
5 I] that I   S

6 pittie] a pity Q 2
9 *Old Ladies.] All.* Q 1+

I.v

1 Every where] Everywhere G
9 ran] run C, W
26 strikes] striks Q 1; strike F 2+
(−V)
30 him] *om.* S
31 starv'd] stav'd F 2, Q 2, L
41 look'dst] look'st Q 1

43 wan'st] want'st L; won'st C;W,
wann'st D, V
50–51 *asso Les] assoles* Qq, F 2, L;
baso las S, C; *Beso las* W, D, V, G
51 *manus] manos* S+
51 *Siniare] Seignoria* S+
51 *a Maistre] om.* S+

I.vi

18 chambers] chamber F 2, L, S
20–21 Civill, | Or] civil, | As F 2,
Q 2, L; *Sevil,* | *Or* S+
32 Above] A bove Q 1

59 in] an W
61 I] too I   S
63 cloths] cloaths Q 2, L+

II.i

0.1 Old Ladies] *Ladies* Q 1+(−D)
13 Your] You Q 2
23 would] should C, W
24 (*et seq. this scene*) *Altea.*] 4.
Q 1
48 doughty] doubty Q 1
49 as gentle] but as gentle S

53 Has] Have F 2+(−V)
54 will not] won't S
55 is] he's S, C, W, D, G
56 Has] H'as F 2–S, D, V; H'has C;
He has W, G
61 is] he's S, C, W, D, G

II.ii

14 companies] companions C
24 thy house] th'House S
28 But] *om.* S
28 whe're] where Q 1+

28 they'l] they'd Q 2
30 *Perez.] om.* Q 1–L
35 plate] plates Q 1–W, G
42 Pray] 'ray W

II.iii

1 (et seq. this scene) Altea.] 4.   Q 1
1 has] ha's F 2–S, D, V; h'has C;
  he has W, G
5 Ladies] Omnes Q 1–C, G; All W
6 Exit Altea.] Exit Lady. Qq, F 2
9 ye] om. S, C
12 your head] you head G

64 upon] on S
67 witnesses] witness F 2–S
67 Ladies] Omnes Q 1–C, G; All
  W; Altea and Ladies D, V
70 and] om. S; an D
71 too] so L

II.iv

0.1 Estifania.] Estifania with a
  paper. Q 1+(−D)
6 I] om. F 2, Q 2, L
13 thy] th' S
36 cold] cool'd L–G (−V)
45 need] needs Q 2
65 I saw] saw W
71 here] there F 2, Q 2 L
76 was] am Qq, F 2, L, W, V, G

77 Ile] Ill C
79 um] him Q 1; them F 2+
86.1 Estifania] om. L, S
87 what] that L
89 big] big sure S
98 and upon] and on S
100 he] she Q 1
119 pitty] a pity Q 2
136 you joy] your joy Q 2

III.i

11 (et seq. in this scene) Altea.] 4.
  Q 1
24 Duke] Duke of Q 1+(−S)
39 scornefully] scornful Q 2
70 first] fire F 2, Q 2, L
79 but] om. S
79 tickle] fickle Q 2
81 farther] further C, W
82 in] om. Q 2
95–96 And...deformities, | Such
  ...produces,] Such...produ-

ces, | And...deformities Q 1+
  (−D, V)
100 horne] horns L, S, C, W, D, G
101 lust] last Qq, F 2, L
125 he has] he's S; h'has C
131–132 Altea. Good...repentance,
  | You...agen] Leon. Good... |
  repentance | Alt. You...agen.
  S
134 shall] om. S

III.ii

8 inhabit] inhabited L
24 brick hill] Brick-kiln L+
30 lasinesse] basinesse Qq, F 2
37 be] be an S
58 fish-stall shambles] stall-fish

shambles Qq, F 2, L, V, G;
stall-fish, shambles, C, W;
stale-fish Shambles S: stale fish-
shambles D

III.iii

2 rime] Q1(c)+; ruine Q1(u)
4 manners] meaner Q1
8 owne] *om.* F2, Q2, L
35 Captaineships] Captaines ships Q1; Captain's Ships F2

38 Duke] Duke of Q1+(−S)
51 him leane agen.] him, leave ager. Q1(u); at him. Q1(c), F2, Q2, L, S, C; at him! Leave anger! W, D, G

III.iv

6 my cloths] cloths Qq, F2, L, S, G
8 pick locks] picklocks Q1, F2, L, G; Pick-locks Q2; pick looks C
22 gentleman] Gentlewoman S
23 It...wench?] *om.* F2, Q2, L
33 cozen] Cousin F2+
40 were laden] are laden Q1

45 jewels] Jewel L, S
51 wide] wild L
60 But] *om.* F2, Q2, L, S
62 for lying] *om.* S
76 two] wo Q2; too Q1, F2, L
77 And I] And I'd W, V; An I D
78 Nor] Not F2, Q2, L

III.v

0.1 Duke Medina] *Duke, Medina* Q1; *Duke of* Medina F2, Q2, L, S, D, V
23 on] upon F2, Q2, L
30 unfallible] infallible F2+
48 shalt] shall Q1
50 loose] lose F2+
51 blowne] blown-up S
57 into] in F2, Q2, L
64 had thought] thought S
73 And...allowes it,] *om.* F2, Q2, L
75 mine own] my own Q2
79 farther] further C, W
81 It...*Leon.* I will] *Leon.* It...I will Qq, F2, L, C, W, D, G
102 my Lord] Lord Qq, F2, L, S
105–106 coach,...Coach too,] coach too,...Coach, Q1+(−S)
116 I] I do S
118 would] would e'en S

118 sownd] swound F2, Q2, L, D, G; swoon S, C, W
120 they] thy S
128–130 behaviour, I...ye, Mercy forsake me] behaviour, Mercy forsake me. I...ye S
135 have] h'have S
148 Has] H'as F2, Q2, L, D, V; H'has C; Ha's S; He has W, G
152 *Juan. Don Michael—— Leon.* Another] *Iu. Don. Michael Leon,* another Q1; *Iuan. Don Michael, Leon,* another F2, Q2, L, S, C, W, G
170 Is] He's F2+(−V)
170 ile] I S
176 thy wife] th'Wife S
188 Miserably] Miserable L
193 And you] And may you S, C, W; An you D, V

IV.i

4.1 Estifania.] *Estifania with a Casket.* Q1+
13 ye] you F2+(−V)
23 you] they L
45 I have] I   C
50 Why am I cozend? *Estifania.* Why] *Estif.* Why am I cozened, Why Qq, F2, L, S
54 round] around G
54 you rayle] ye rail Q2
61 had thought] thought S, C, W

75 shooing-horne] Shooting-horn L
84 How] See how S
87 Pilgrims] Pilgrims with S
89 mussell-monger] Muscle-monger F2+(−G)
94 quit] quick L
97 an] as F2, Q2, L, S
98 your fury up] up your fury F2, Q2, L
116 straight] strait Q2
138 and] *om.* S

IV.ii

3 heere] hear F2, Q2, L
7 This] 'T   S
13 *Alonʒo.* We] We Q1+

16 *Sanchio.* We] We F2+
23 he] ye he S

IV.iii

0.1 Leon *with a commission, and* Juan.] *Leon, and Iuan with a commission* Q1–W, G
4 'T as] 'T has F2+(−Q2 'Thas)
6 I] I do F2, Q2, L, S
17 *Lorenʒo. Enter* Lorenzo.] *Enter Lorenʒo.* Qq, F2, L
17 *Lorenʒo.* Sir [*name as prefix*]] *Lorenʒo,* Sir [*as address*] F2, L
17 *Leon.* Goe] Goe Q1, F2, L, S
23 must] must go G
24 Whether] Whither F2+(−S; Whe'er)
27 sir] sit Q1
30 *Dego*] *Diego* C+
64 for't] fort Q1
67 accommodation] accommodations S, C

70 linnens] linnen F2–S
74 And an] An S
82 strait] straight C, W
111 humane] human L
117 smell] smell out S
126 cozen's] cousin's F2+
128 lyen] lain Q2, C+
130 Gentlemen] Gentlemā Q1, F2
147 wives] wifes F2+
161 Can you not] Can't you S
165 ye get] we get Q2
167 if you] you S
172 I] I'll G
193 us'd] use Q1
194 your] you Q2
206 he has] has S
207 Thou] that Qq, F2, L; That, C, W, D

603

V.i

2 *Estifanias*] *Estifania* F 2, Q 2, L
4 A] An F 2+

5 Is a] He's a S, D; He is C, W
8 will] he'll S

V.ii

3 the] *om.* Qq, F 2, L, G
12 of] *om.* W
29 who ere] whosoe'er S
29 humane] human L+

46 let me] let's S
62 brought] bought Q 1, F 2, L
67 at some time] sometimes S

V.iii

2 contentedly] contently Qq, F 2, D
9 cure] care Q 1+(–S)
15 bear] bare Q 2
29 allmost] almost F 2+; all most Q 1
30 *with*] *om.* Qq, F 2, L, S
47 *Servant*] *Servants* Q 1
59 ground...haunted?]ground... haunted, Qq, F 2; Ground?... haunted: L, S, C, W, G (±)
61 Nay] *om.* S
63 thus] this S

73 farther] further F 2+
81 Thy] The L; Th' S
81–82 maid, | And] maid∧ | To W, G
82 those] her S
82–83 that she reach'd at | Shalt goe] that she reach at, | And goe Qq, F 2, F, G; thou shalt reach at, | And go S, C; that she reaches at, | And go W; that she reach'd at, | [*line omitted*] | And go D
97 you] yon Q 2

V.iv

0.1 Estifania.] *Estifania with a Pistoll, and a Dagge.* Q 1, F 2, V; *Estifania with a Pistoll, and a Dagge.* Q 2, L, G
7 and] *om.* S
17 tricks is] trick is F 2, Q 2, L, D;

Trick's S, C, W, G
23 farther] further C, W, G
25 *and a Dagge*] *om.* Q 1+
26 sweat] swear Qq, F 2
32 Hold] Hold, hold S, C, W

604

V.v

5 Has] H'as S, V; He has C, W, D, G
9 best] test S, C
12 *within*] *with in* Q 1
15 wary,] wary, *Noise below.* Q 1 +
17 you tumble] Rumble S
53 were you] you were G
87 Temples] Templers Q 1
98 heere] heare Q 1
108–109 folly...sin] folly...folly Qq, F 2, L, S; vice...folly C, G; sin...folly D, V; folly ... vice W
114 Sanchio.] Sanchio, Cacafogo, *and* Altea. L, S, C

126 had thought] thought S
156 At] And at S
157 otherwaies] otherwise G
158 *Margarita.* Hold] Hold Qq, F 2, L; *Leon.* Hold S, C, W, D, G
162 souldier.   *Gentlemen.*   We] souldier, Gentleman, we Qq, F 2, L; souldier, gentlemen. *Omnes.* We C, W, G; soldier, gentlemen. *Gentlemen.* We V
166 two] too Q 1
166 mine] my C, W, G
176 we] you Q 1+(−D, V)

Epilogue

5 *ends*] end D
6 *sends*] Q 1(c), F 2, L, S, V, G; *send* Q 1(u), C, W, D